Oracle Press

D1633359

Oracle9*i* DBA Handbook

ORACLE® *Oracle Press*™

Oracle9*i* DBA Handbook

Kevin Loney
Marlene Theriault
and the experts at TUSC

McGraw-Hill/Osborne

New York   Chicago   San Francisco
Lisbon   London   Madrid   Mexico City   Milan
New Delhi   San Juan   Seoul   Singapore   Sydney   Toronto

McGraw-Hill/Osborne
2100 Powell Street, 10th Floor
Emeryville, California 94608
U.S.A.

To arrange bulk purchase discounts for sales promotions, premiums, or fund-raisers, please contact McGraw-Hill/Osborne at the above address. For information on translations or book distributors outside the U.S.A., please see the International Contact Information page immediately following the index of this book.

Oracle9i DBA Handbook

4567890 DOC DOC 019876543

ISBN 0-07-219374-3

Publisher
Brandon A. Nordin

Vice President & Associate Publisher
Scott Rogers

Acquisitions Editor
Lisa McClain

Project Editors
Judith Brown
Jody McKenzie

Acquisitions Coordinator
Athena Honore

Technical Editor
Scott Gossett

Copy Editor
Judith Brown

Proofreader
Marian Selig

Indexer
Claire Splan

Computer Designers
George Toma Charbak, Tara A. Davis,
Mickey Galicia, Lauren McCarthy

Illustrators
Michael Mueller, Lyssa Wald

Series Design
Jani Beckwith

Cover Series Design
Damore Johann Design, Inc.

This book was composed with Corel VENTURA™ Publisher.

To Sue, Emily, Rachel, and Jane
for their love and support.

—K. L.

To Nelson, Marc, and Jean
who help make my world a
happier place in which to live.

—M. T.

About the Authors

Kevin Loney, a senior technical management consultant with TUSC, is an internationally recognized expert in the design, development, administration, and tuning of Oracle databases. An Oracle developer and DBA since 1987, he has implemented both transaction processing systems and data warehouses. He provides expert assistance to companies for the implementation and tuning of their business-critical Oracle applications.

The author of numerous technical articles, he is the lead author or coauthor for best-selling books including *Oracle8i: The Complete Reference, Instant Oracle PL/SQL Scripts*, and *Oracle8 Advanced Tuning and Administration*. He regularly presents at Oracle user conferences in North America and Europe.

Marlene Therialt has more than 19 years experience as an Oracle database administrator. She is lead author or coauthor of the *Oracle Security Handbook, Oracle8i Networking 101, Oracle DBA 101, Oracle8i DBA Handbook*, and *Oracle Security*. She has presented technical papers and tutorials at Oracle conferences all over the world. Marlene is noted for her ability to make difficult concepts easily understandable. She and her husband, Nelson, are avid recreational walkers. She can be reached at mtheriault@mindspring.com.

Contents at a Glance

PART III
Networked Oracle

Contents

PART I
Database Architecture

PART II

Database Management

PART III
Networked Oracle

Acknowledgments

This book is the product of two authors, many contributors, and more editors than you can imagine. Special thanks to Scott Gossett for his timely, thorough, and accurate technical review of the manuscript.

Thanks to the contributors and editors from TUSC, including Kamila Bajaria, Brad Brown, Judy Corley, Kevin Gilpin, Mark Greenhalgh, Matt Malcheski, Rich Niemiec, Allen Peterson, Sabina Schoenke, Randy Swanson, Joe Trezzo, Jake Van der Vort, and Bob Yingst. Thanks to TUSC for its support during the writing process.

Thanks to the team at McGraw-Hill/Osborne, including Athena Honore and Lisa McClain. Special thanks to Judith Brown and Scott Rogers for their late-innings help.

Thanks to those readers who suggested topics, changes, or corrections. Thanks to Eyal Aronoff and Rachel Carmichael, among others, for their advice, comments, corrections, and friendship.

If you have comments regarding the book or are looking for additional DBA materials, please see http://www.kevinloney.com. The scripts from this book, as well as additional technical material, will be posted on that site.

Introduction

hether you're an experienced DBA, a new DBA, or an application developer, you need to understand how Oracle9i's new features can help you to best meet your customers' needs. In this book, you will find coverage of the newest features as well as ways of merging those features into the management of an Oracle database. The emphasis throughout is on managing the database's capabilities in an effective, efficient manner to deliver a quality product. The end result will be a database that is dependable, robust, secure, and extensible.

Several components are critical to this goal, and you'll see all of them covered here in depth. A well-designed logical and physical database architecture will improve performance and ease administration by properly distributing database objects. You'll see appropriate monitoring, security, and tuning strategies for stand-alone and networked databases. Backup and recovery strategies are provided to help ensure the database's recoverability. Each section focuses on both the features and the proper planning and management techniques for each area.

Networking issues and the management of distributed and client/server databases are thoroughly covered. Oracle Net, networking configurations, materialized views, location transparency, and everything else you need to successfully implement a distributed or client/server database are described in detail in Part III of this book. You'll also find real-world examples for every major configuration.

In addition to the commands needed to perform DBA activities, you will also see the Oracle Enterprise Manager screens from which you can perform similar functions. "Solutions" sections throughout the book offer common solutions to the most frequently encountered problems.

By following the techniques in this book, your systems can be designed and implemented so well that tuning efforts will be minimal. Administering the database will become easier as the users get a better product, while the database works—and works well.

PART
I

Database
Architecture

CHAPTER
1

Getting Started with the
Oracle Architecture

ith every release, Oracle adds new features or changes existing features. With the release of Oracle9i, many new exciting features and functionality changes have been added. At the same time, Oracle has added new tools to simplify database administration tasks. In Part I of this book, you will see an overview of the Oracle architecture and its implementation. You will see the architecture through the steps required to create an Oracle database, both manually and using the Oracle9i Database Configuration Assistant.

In Part II of this book, you will see specific guidelines for managing aspects of an Oracle database, such as managing rollback or undo segments and establishing passwords. Part III of the book deals with using Oracle in a networked environment. At the end of the book, you will find an appendix containing the command syntax for the most-used SQL commands.

In this chapter, you'll see examples of the components of an Oracle database and the basic implementation concepts that guide their usage. Administering an Oracle database requires knowing how these different components interact, where they fit in the big picture, and how to best customize the system to meet your needs. In many ways, this chapter is a road map to the detailed discussions of database administration in the rest of the book.

Overview of Databases and Instances

Two basic concepts have to be understood in order to make any sense out of the Oracle architecture: databases and instances. In the following two major sections, you will see descriptions of both of these concepts and their implementation in Oracle.

Databases

A *database* is a set of data. Oracle provides the ability to store and access data in a manner consistent with a defined model known as the relational model. Because of this, Oracle is referred to as a relational database management system (RDBMS). Most references to a "database" refer not only to the physical data but also to the combination of physical, memory, and process objects described in this chapter.

Data in a database is stored in tables. Relational tables are defined by their *columns*, and are given a name. Data is then stored as *rows* in the table. Tables can be related to each other, and the database can be used to enforce these relationships. A sample table structure is shown in Figure 1-1.

In addition to storing data in relational format, Oracle (as of Oracle8) supports object-oriented (OO) structures such as abstract datatypes and methods. Objects can be related to other objects, and objects can contain other objects. As you will see in Chapter 5, you can use object views to enable OO interfaces to your data without making any modifications to your tables.

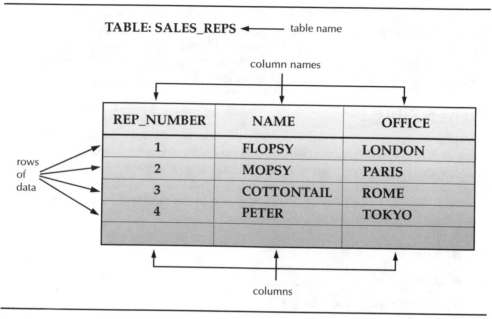

FIGURE 1-1.   *Sample table structure*

Whether you use relational structures or OO structures, an Oracle database stores its data in files. Internally, there are database structures that provide a logical mapping of data to files, allowing different types of data to be stored separately. These logical divisions are called tablespaces. The next subsections describe tablespaces and files.

Tablespaces

A *tablespace* is a logical division of a database. Each database has at least one tablespace (called the *SYSTEM* tablespace). You can use additional tablespaces to group users or applications together for ease of maintenance and for performance benefits. Examples of such tablespaces would be USERS for general use and UNDO for undo segments (which will be described later in this section). A tablespace can belong to only one database.

Datafiles

Each tablespace is made up of one or more files, called *datafiles,* on a disk. A datafile can belong to one and only one tablespace. Datafiles can be resized after their creation. Creating new tablespaces requires creating new datafiles. Once a datafile has been added to a tablespace, the datafile cannot be removed from the tablespace, and it cannot be associated with any other tablespace.

If you store database objects in multiple tablespaces, then you can separate them at the physical level by placing their respective datafiles on separate disks. This separation of data is an important tool in planning and tuning the way in which the database handles the I/O requests made against it. The relationship among databases, tablespaces, and datafiles is illustrated in Figure 1-2.

Other Files

The database's datafiles, as just described, provide the physical storage for the database's data. Thus, they are both internal structures, since they are tied directly to tablespaces, and external, since they are physical files. The planning process for their distribution across devices is described in Chapter 4.

The following types of files, although related to the database, are separate from the datafiles. These files include the following:

- Redo logs
- Control files
- Trace files and the alert log

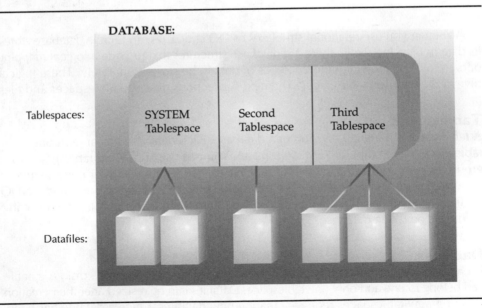

FIGURE 1-2. *Relationship among databases, tablespaces, and datafiles*

Redo Logs

Oracle maintains logs of all transactions against the database. These transactions are recorded in files called *online redo log files*. Redo log files are used to recover the database's transactions in their proper order in the event of a database crash. The redo log information is stored external to the database's datafiles.

Redo log files also let Oracle streamline the manner in which it writes data to disk. When a transaction occurs in the database, it is entered in the redo log buffers, while the data blocks affected by the transaction are not immediately written to disk.

Each Oracle database will have three or more online redo log files. Oracle writes to online redo log files in a cyclical fashion: after the first log file is filled, it writes to the second log file, until that one is filled. When all of the online redo log files have been filled, it returns to the first log file and begins overwriting its contents with new transaction data. If the database is running in ARCHIVELOG mode, the database will make a copy of the online redo log files before overwriting them. These archived redo log files can then be used to recover any part of the database to any point in time (see Chapter 11).

Redo log files may be mirrored (replicated) by the database. Mirroring the online redo log files allows you to mirror the redo log files without relying on the operating system or hardware capabilities of the operating environment. See Chapter 2 for details on this mirroring capability.

Control Files

A database's overall physical architecture is maintained by its *control files*. Control files record control information about all of the files within the database. Control files maintain internal consistency and guide recovery operations.

Since the control files are critical to the database, multiple copies are stored online. These files are typically stored on separate disks to minimize the potential damage due to disk failures. The database will create and maintain the control files specified at database creation.

The names of the database's control files are specified via the CONTROL_FILES initialization parameter. If you need to add a new control file to a database, you can shut down the instance, copy one of the existing control files to the new location, add the new location to the CONTROL_FILES parameter setting, and restart the instance.

Trace Files and the Alert Log

Each of the background processes running in an instance has a trace file associated with it. The *trace file* will contain information about significant events encountered by the background process. In addition to the trace files, Oracle maintains a file called the *alert log*. The alert log records the commands and command results of major events in the life of the database. For example, tablespace creations, redo log switches, recovery operations, and database startups are recorded in the alert log. The alert log is a vital source of information for day-to-day management of a database; trace files are most useful when attempting to discover the cause of a major failure.

You should monitor your alert log daily. The entries in the alert log will inform you of any problems encountered during database operations, including any ORA-0600 internal errors that occur. To make the alert log easier to use, you may wish to automatically rename it each day. For example, if the alert log is named alert_orcl.log, you could rename it so its filename includes the current date. The next time Oracle tries to write to the alert log, no file with the name alert_orcl.log will be found, so the database will create a new one. You will then have the current alert log (alert_orcl.log) as well as the previous alert log. Separating alert log entries in this fashion may make analyzing the alert log entries a more efficient process.

Oracle Managed Files

In versions of Oracle prior to Oracle9i, when you remove a tablespace from the database, the underlying datafiles used to support the tablespace are not automatically removed. Likewise, when you remove a redo log file or control file, the physical files are left behind. In Oracle9i, you can enable Oracle Managed Files (OMF) to help relieve the burden of file management. OMF also includes a feature to enable Oracle to automatically create and remove files from the operating system as necessary to support database activity.

There have been times in the past when a DBA removed a tablespace from the database and forgot to delete the file from the operating system as well. The forgotten underlying file would not only take up physical disk space but could cause confusion when someone else was performing disk maintenance procedures, especially if the DBA who dropped the tablespace was no longer around to say that the underlying file could be safely removed. Many orphan files remain on disks in many companies.

When you enable OMF, Oracle uses file system directories rather than filenames for creating supporting files like control files, redo log files, and datafiles, and creates appropriate names for the files automatically. When files are deleted, the underlying operating system files are automatically removed. Thus, with OMF, there are no obsolete files left behind to cause confusion and waste space.

The databases most suited in which to use OMF in its initial form are very low-end databases with a small number of users. OMF is also suited for databases that use a logical volume manager or large, extensible files. Oracle Managed Files are discussed in more detail in Chapter 4.

Instances

In order to access the data in the database, Oracle uses a set of background processes that are shared by all users. In addition, there are memory structures (collectively known as the System Global Area, or SGA) that store the most recently queried data from the database. The largest of the SGA sections, the data block buffer cache, the Shared SQL Pool, the Large Pool, and the Java Pool typically constitute over 95 percent of the memory allocated to the SGA. These memory areas help to improve database performance by decreasing the amount of I/O performed against the datafiles.

A database *instance* (also known as a *server*) is a set of memory structures and background processes that access a set of database files. It is possible for a single database to be accessed by multiple instances (known as the Real Application Clusters option). The relationship between instances and databases is illustrated in Figure 1-3.

The parameters that determine the size and composition of an instance are either stored in an initialization file called init.ora or housed within the database in a server parameter file referred to as the SPFILE and stored in spfile.ora.

The initialization parameter file is read during instance startup and may be modified by the DBA. Any modifications made to the initialization file will not take effect until the next startup. The name of an instance's initialization file usually includes

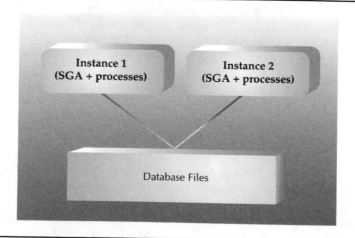

FIGURE I-3.   *Instances and datafiles in Oracle*

the name of the instance; if the instance is named ORCL, the file will usually be named initorcl.ora. Oracle has been making more and more parameters within the database dynamically tunable. The parameter changes may remain in effect even after shutdowns and startups, regardless of the contents of the initialization parameter file. In Oracle9i, the DBA can use the SPFILE instead of the init.ora file and make initialization parameter changes either temporary or permanent. The SPFILE will be discussed later in this chapter.

About Software Installation

When you receive your new software disks from Oracle Corporation, your inclination may be to immediately find a machine and install the new version. In earlier versions of Oracle, that approach wasn't much of a problem because the space and memory requirements were pretty low compared to today's software. However, in today's more resource-intensive versions, you must take the time to carefully plan your Oracle software deployment.

Today's Oracle software code can sometimes be challenging to install correctly the first time. For example, the Oracle9iAS Portal product requires many preinstallation steps before you actually run the installation disks. To successfully install the Oracle product set(s) that your company has purchased, you must first examine the installation instructions included with the software CD-ROM set. Each platform can have different installation instructions and requirements, especially in the area of operating system levels and patches. For example, Oracle9i on a Windows NT platform requires that the operating system be Windows NT version 4.0 with service pack 6.0a installed, while Windows 2000 requires Release 2. Therefore, be sure to verify what level of the operating system and which patches are required before you begin installation. Some versions of Oracle will not build and link successfully without the correct operating system libraries available.

If you have a current CSI (customer support identification) number, you can establish an account or log onto an existing account on Oracle's technical support Web site, MetaLink (http://metalink.oracle.com), and check for installation information and any known problems cited in the bug database documentation. You can also establish a free account with the Oracle Technology Network (http://technet.oracle.com) to check on the latest software releases and installation information.

Since each installation of the Oracle software varies with each platform, a detailed examination of the installation process is outside the scope of this book. However, the installation guide included with your Oracle installation CD-ROM set will detail the amount of memory and disk space required to successfully install the Oracle software. Ensuring that you have enough real memory and disk space is mandatory for a successful Oracle product installation. You should find help with the installation process in the Oracle-supplied installation documentation and by checking the MetaLink and Technology Network Web sites.

Oracle Installation Options and Components

Regardless of the operating system version, there are three different levels of Oracle software available for you to install based on what your company has purchased. The available types are

- **Enterprise Edition**   Includes the installation of the following: a preconfigured seed database; networking services; licensable Oracle Options; database environment tools; the Oracle Enterprise Manager framework of management tools, including Console, Management Server, and Intelligent Agent; Oracle utilities; and online documentation. Products most commonly used for data warehousing and transaction processing are also included.

- **Standard Edition**   Includes the installation of the following: a preconfigured seed database, networking services, Oracle Enterprise Manager Console, and Oracle utilities.

- **Personal Edition**   Includes the installation of the following: a preconfigured seed database that supports a single-user development and deployment environment that requires full compatibility with Oracle9i Enterprise Edition and Oracle9i Standard Edition.

You can use the Custom option to install or reinstall individual products.

There is also a front-end database application available to support Oracle networking and client interaction with a database located on a separate server. Oracle networking features are covered in Chapter 13. The Client installation types available are as follows:

- **Administrator**   Includes the installation of the following: the Oracle Enterprise Manager Console, including enterprise management tools, networking services, utilities, basic client software, and online documentation.

- **Runtime**   Includes the installation of the following: networking services and support files.

You can use the Custom option to install or reinstall individual components available in the Administrator and Runtime options.

There are three management installation types available as follows:

- **Oracle Management Server**   Consists of the following: the Oracle Management Server, which processes all system management tasks and administers the distribution of these tasks to Intelligent Agents on managed nodes across the enterprise, as well as basic client software and online documentation.

■ **Oracle Internet Directory**   Consists of the following: a Lightweight Directory Access Protocol (LDAP)–enabled Oracle Internet Directory Server, LDAP-enabled client tools, and the Oracle Internet Directory database schema.

■ **Oracle Integration Server**   Consists of the following: XML-enabled components, including Oracle9i JVM, a workflow engine, and advanced queuing.

Again, you can use the Custom option to install or reinstall individual products. Although the management software can be installed during the regular Enterprise Edition software installation, you should install the database product set with the preconfigured database first and then rerun the installation disks to install the management products. During the Enterprise Edition installation, the framework for the management server software is installed. The management software requires a database for its support, and you can use the preconfigured database created during the initial Enterprise Edition installation as the location rather then letting the management software installation create an additional database for each of the management options.

Separately Licensed Options
Along with the products delivered on the Oracle9i distribution disks, other software options are available at additional cost. The current list of added-cost options includes the following:

■ Oracle Advanced Security

■ Oracle Change Management Pack

■ Oracle Data Mining

■ Oracle Diagnostics Pack

■ Oracle Label Security

■ Oracle Management Pack for SAP

■ Oracle Management Pack for Oracle Applications

■ Oracle OLAP

■ Oracle Partitioning

■ Oracle Real Application Cluster (formerly Oracle Parallel Server)

■ Oracle Spatial

■ Oracle Tuning Pack

NOTE
Some of these products may be installed on your system during software installation. If you have not paid an additional amount for these products, verify with your Oracle salesperson that you have been licensed to run them.

Creating a Database

Based on the Oracle software installation type you have selected, you are given the opportunity to create a preconfigured database. We strongly urge you to allow Oracle to create a preconfigured database for several reasons. With a preconfigured database, you will be able to

- Verify that the software installed correctly enough to be able to create a database

- Examine the new Oracle features in a pristine environment

- See what is different in the new version's database, if you have existing Oracle databases in earlier versions

After the Oracle software has been installed, the Oracle Database Configuration Assistant is run to gather the necessary information to create a database. Because you can run the Oracle Database Configuration Assistant after the software has been installed, the database creation steps shown here will reflect the postinstallation database creation steps and descriptions.

Using the Oracle Database Configuration Assistant

When the Oracle Database Configuration Assistant is started, a welcome screen is presented first, followed by a screen that prompts for the operation you want to perform. Your choices are as follows:

- Create a Database—create a new database.

- Configure Database Options in a Database—change the configuration from a dedicated server to a shared server or to add options that were not previously included in your database creation, such as the added-cost options listed earlier in this chapter.

- Delete a Database—delete the database and all of its associated operating system files.

■ Manage Templates—modify existing database templates or create new ones. The advantage of having database creation templates is that you can quickly and easily create duplicate databases without having to specify the necessary parameters more than once. Within the template management option, you can create a template from an existing one, create a template based on an existing local or remote database structure, or create a template from an existing database including the data within the database. The last option is wonderful for creating a new database that mirrors a production one as an application development environment or as the basis for a standby database (discussed in Chapter 11).

Choosing a Database Template

When you opt to create a new database, the next screen displays the Oracle-supplied database templates based on a projected pattern of user interaction within the new database, including

■ General Purpose—a variety of database tasks are performed, including simple transactions as well as complex queries.

■ Online Transaction Processing (OLTP)—each transaction, either reading, writing, or deleting data from the database, is a relatively simple operation that processes a small amount of information, but there are many users performing a large number of concurrent transactions.

■ Data Warehousing or Decision Support System (DSS)—numerous complex queries are performed processing large quantities of data requiring high availability, excellent response time, and accuracy. In a DSS environment, the queries range from simple queries returning a small number of records to complex queries that sort many thousands of records over several tables.

■ Customized—this option enables you to create a database customized for your users' processing environment.

■ Software Only—this option requires you to provide extensive information on which to base the database creation.

NOTE
Oracle recommends that you create at least one seed database to serve as a template for future database creations.

Figure 1-4 shows the Oracle Database Configuration Assistant, Database Templates screen with the General Purpose database option selected. There is a button at the bottom of the screen that enables you to show the details of the database configuration. You can examine the proposed options but cannot, at this point in the database preparations, modify any of the values. The options shown are common options, including some unlicensed product installations, initialization parameters, datafile, control file, and redo log file locations.

Declaring the Database Name and Registering the Database

You will be prompted to supply both a global database name and an instance (SID) name for the new database. The standard global database extension is .world, and you can supply this value unless you have an established domain name to use. Check

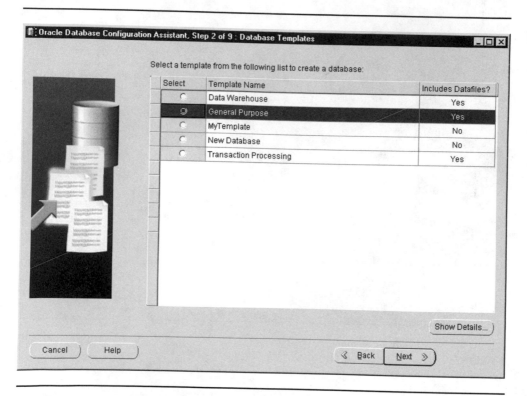

FIGURE 1-4. *Database Templates screen*

with your system administrator to verify whether there is a specific domain name you must use instead of the .world extension. When you type in the global database name, the same value up to the "." will be automatically placed in the SID field. For example, if you enter the global database name MYDB.world in the Global Database name field, the value MYDB will automatically be written in the SID field. Figure 1-5 shows the Database Identification screen with the value MYDB.world entered.

The next option deals with network configuration for the new database and lets you register the database within a directory service. If you have already configured a directory server such as Oracle Internet Directory or Microsoft Access, you can

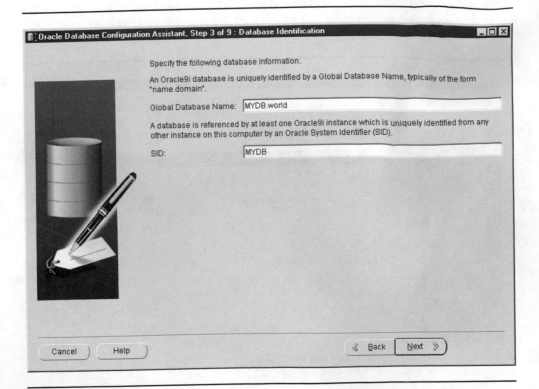

FIGURE 1-5. *Database Identification screen*

opt to register the new database within that server. The default value, as shown in Figure 1-6, is not to register the database.

Dedicated Versus Shared Server Option

The Database Connection Options screen, as shown in Figure 1-7, enables you to specify the way each client will connect to the database. If your new database is going to support a low number of clients or the clients are going to remain connected to the database for long periods of time, select the Dedicated Server Mode. Figure 1-7 shows the Dedicated Server Mode selected.

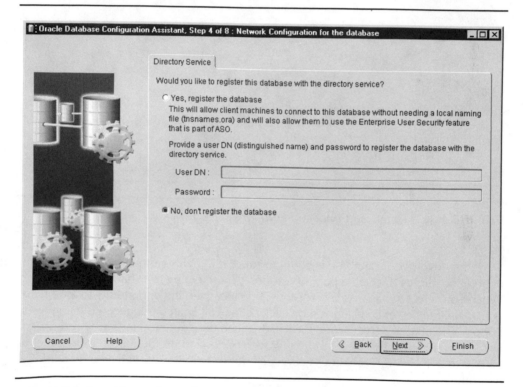

FIGURE 1-6.   *Network Configuration for the Database screen*

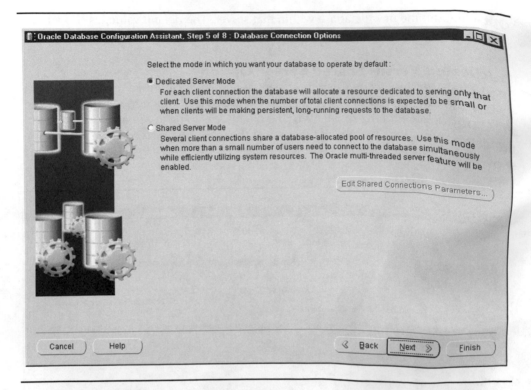

FIGURE 1-7. *Database Connection Options screen*

If, however, your database is going to support a high volume of clients, you can enable the clients to share a pool of resources by selecting the Shared Server Mode. When you select the Shared Server Mode, you are given the opportunity to modify the default Shared Server configuration by clicking the Edit Shared Connections Parameters button. The Shared Server Mode Basic/Advanced configuration tabs are presented, as shown in Figure 1-8. You can modify the connection protocol from its default of TCP to SPX, NMP, TCPS (the secure TCP option), or IPC, as well as modifying the following:

■ Number of Dispatchers—used as messengers to pass the queries to the database and return the responses to the clients. The default is 1 dispatcher.

■ Maximum Number of Connections per Dispatcher—the maximum number of network connections to allow for each dispatcher.

■ Maximum Number of Dispatchers—a static value. You must reboot the database to modify the value once it is set. The value defaults to whichever is higher: 5 or the value you set.

■ Number of Server Processes—a dynamic parameter that defines how many server processes will be created when an instance is started. The value varies between the number designated and the maximum number of server processes declared. The value will never go below the number of server processes defined for this variable.

■ Maximum Number of Server Processes—a static parameter that defaults to whichever is greater: 20 or two times the value of MAX_SERVERS.

The Advanced Shared Server Mode tab includes the options shown in Figure 1-9. The advanced options include the ability to enable multiplexing of shared server connections. Multiplexing allows the Oracle Connection Manager Connection Concentration feature in which multiple client network sessions are funneled through a single transport protocol connection. You can define the mode in which you want the connection concentration to be enabled. The options are

■ Off—disables the feature for both incoming and outgoing connections

■ On—enables the feature for all connections

■ Incoming Connections—enables the feature for incoming connections only

■ Outgoing Connections—enables the feature for outgoing connections only

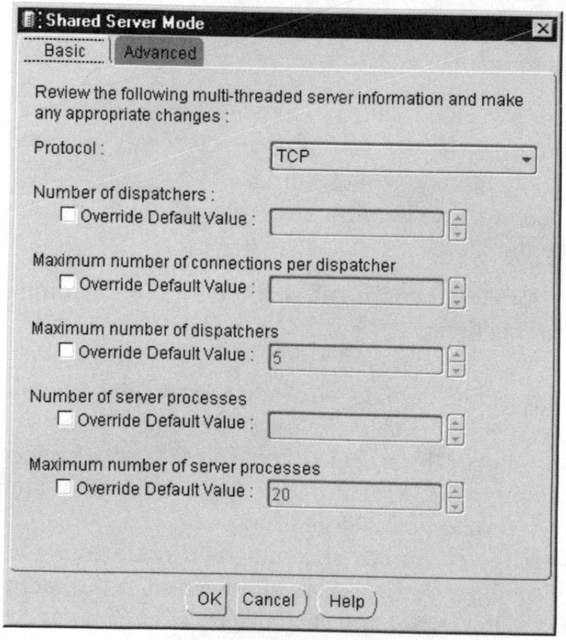

FIGURE 1-8.   *Shared Server Mode, Basic tab*

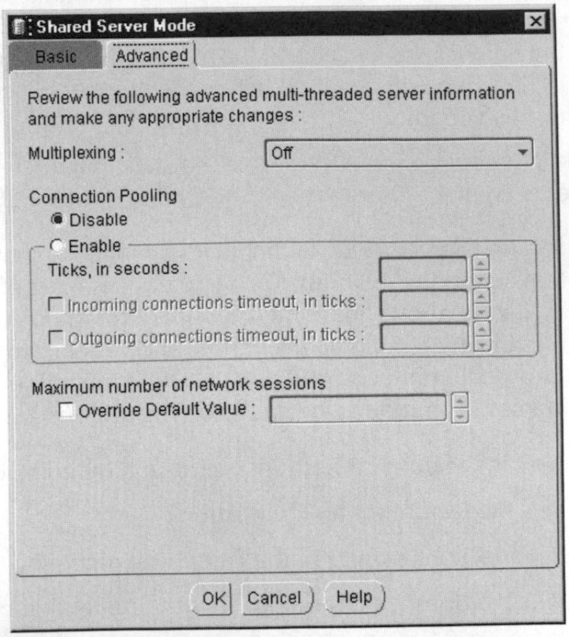

FIGURE 1-9. *Shared Server Mode, Advanced tab*

Using Connection Pooling, you can maximize the number of physical network connections to a shared server. You have the choice of specifying the following options:

- Disable—Connection Pooling is disabled for both incoming and outgoing network connections.

- Enable—Connection Pooling is enabled for both incoming and outgoing network connections.

If you enable Connection Pooling, you must specify the size of the network measure known as a *tick*. You specify the value for the size of a tick in seconds. After establishing the size of a tick, you specify the amount of time, in ticks, that an incoming connection should wait before timing out. You also specify the amount of time, in ticks, that an outgoing connection should wait before timing out.

The final value in the Advanced Shared Server Mode configuration tab is the maximum number of network sessions to allow for each dispatcher. You can find more information on Oracle Net and shared servers in Chapter 13.

Initialization Parameter Configuration: Memory

Oracle uses shared memory areas to manage its memory and file structures. Before examining the parameters you can modify using the Initialization Parameters screen, here is detailed information about the basic memory structures that Oracle uses and how they are used. The following structures are explained:

- System Global Area (SGA)—the size of the SGA will depend on the sizes of the other memory structure parameter values.

- Data block buffer cache

- Dictionary cache

- Redo log buffer

- Shared SQL Pool

- The Large Pool

- The Java Pool

- Multiple buffer pools

- Context areas

- Program Global Area (PGA)

System Global Area (SGA)

If you were to read a chapter of this book, what would be the quickest way of passing that information on to someone else? You could have the other person read that chapter as well, but it would be quickest if you could hold all of the information in memory and then pass that information from your memory to the second person.

The *System Global Area (SGA)* in an Oracle database serves the same purpose—it facilitates the transfer of information between users. The SGA also holds the most commonly requested structural information about the database.

Buffer Caches

Historically, the SGA has been a static allocation of memory shared across all Oracle processes. The memory size is calculated based on the values of parameters in the init.ora file, and once allocated, the memory area cannot grow or shrink. To change the size of any of the values on which the SGA is based, you must first shut down the database, change the value of the parameter in the init.ora file, and then restart the database. Shutting down a 24x7x365 database to change a parameter can impact production systems.

To solve this problem, Oracle has introduced a dynamic SGA area in Oracle9i. The SGA configuration can now be changed while the database is running, so you can modify the buffer cache and Shared Pool on the fly without shutting down the database. You can also impose limits at database startup on how much physical memory is used for the SGA. In this way, you can underallocate memory for the buffer cache, Shared Pool, and Large Pool at startup, and then they can grow and shrink as they need to based on their workloads. You establish a maximum overall size for the SGA, and Oracle allocates areas of the memory to the various memory components.

To perform the memory allocation management, Oracle has provided a new unit of allocation for the SGA called a *granule* that represents an amount of contiguous virtual memory and is based on the size of the parameter SGA_MAX_SIZE. To determine a granule's size, you can look at the total size of the SGA. If the SGA total size is less than 128MB, each granule will be 4MB in size. If the SGA is larger than 128MB, the granule size defaults to 16MB.

You can determine the allocated granules for the components of the buffer cache that owns granules. The buffer cache can grow and shrink based on the granule boundaries. Initially, the minimum amount of granules to be allocated is three: one for the fixed SGA (including redo buffers), one for the buffer cache, and one for the Shared Pool. The Shared Pool has to be at least 8MB in size so the minimum is four granules when each granule is 4KB.

Oracle9i supports different database block sizes within one database, and each block size must have an associated memory cache. More details about the buffer caches and memory allocations are available in Chapter 8.

Dictionary Cache

Information about database objects is stored in the data dictionary tables. For example, data dictionary information includes user account data, datafile names, segment names, extent locations, table descriptions, and privileges. When this information is needed by the database (for example, to check a user's authorization to query a table), the data dictionary tables are read and the data that is returned is stored in the SGA in the *dictionary cache.*

The data dictionary cache is managed via an LRU (least recently used) algorithm. The size of the dictionary cache is managed internally by the database; it is part of the Shared SQL Pool, whose size is set via the SHARED_POOL_SIZE parameter in the database's initialization parameter file.

If the dictionary cache is too small, the database will have to repeatedly query the data dictionary tables for information needed by the database. These queries are called *recursive calls*, and are slower to resolve than are queries that can be handled solely by the dictionary cache in memory. For information on monitoring the usage of the dictionary cache, see Chapters 8 and 9.

Redo Log Buffer

Redo log files are described in the section "Redo Logs" earlier in this chapter. Redo entries describe the changes that are made to the database. Redo entries are written to the online redo log files so that they can be used in roll-forward operations during database recoveries. Before being written to the online redo log files, however, transactions are first recorded in the SGA in an area called the *redo log buffer*. The database then periodically writes batches of redo entries to the online redo log files, thus optimizing this operation.

The size (in bytes) of the redo log buffers is set via the LOG_BUFFER parameter in the initialization parameter file.

Shared Pool Area

The Shared Pool area stores the data dictionary cache and the *library cache*—information about statements that are run against the database. While the buffer pool and dictionary cache enable sharing of structural and data information among users in the database, the library cache allows the sharing of commonly used SQL statements.

The shared SQL area contains the execution plan and parse tree for SQL statements run against the database. The second time that an identical SQL statement is run (by any user), it is able to take advantage of the parse information available in the Shared SQL Pool to expedite its execution. For information on monitoring the usage of the Shared SQL Pool, see the STATSPACK reports, described in Chapter 9.

The Shared Pool area is managed via an LRU algorithm. As the shared SQL area fills, less recently used execution paths and parse trees will be removed from the library cache to make room for new entries. If your Shared SQL Pool is too small, statements will be continually reloaded into the library cache, affecting performance. You can dynamically modify the size of the Shared Pool by revising the SHARED_ POOL_SIZE parameter (in bytes). The initial SHARED_POOL_SIZE is established in the initialization parameter file. The value you set must be an integer multiple of the granule size.

The Shared Pool area includes the library cache, the data dictionary cache, and the shared SQL area. You can validate this by looking at the V$SQLSTAT view. Unless you set the initialization parameter SGA_MAX_SIZE to a size larger than all of the memory required by the initialization parameters, you cannot resize anything. Alternatively, you can reduce the size of the Shared Pool; in this way, you can give memory to the buffer cache or reduce the size of the buffer cache and give that memory to the Shared Pool. If you set the SGA_MAX_SIZE quite large, you have the flexibility to change either or both.

The Large Pool

The Large Pool is an optional memory area. If you use the Shared Server option or frequently perform backup/restore operations, those operations may be more efficient if you create a Large Pool. The third area that the Large Pool is used for is message buffers for parallel query. The size of the Large Pool, in bytes, is set initially via the LARGE_POOL_SIZE initialization parameter.

NOTE
The Large Pool is not dynamic in the current versions.

The Java Pool

The Java Pool, as its name suggests, services the parsing requirements for Java commands. The Java Pool's size is set, in bytes, via the JAVA_POOL_SIZE initialization parameter introduced in Oracle8i. The JAVA_POOL_SIZE initialization parameter must be set to a minimum size based on your database granule size. For example, the default size should be 24MB on UNIX if you have a 4MB granule size, and 32MB if you have a 16MB granule size.

Multiple Buffer Caches

You can create multiple buffer cache areas within your SGA to support multiple database block sizes. You can use multiple buffer caches to separate large data sets from the rest of your application, reducing the likelihood they will contend for the same resources within the buffer cache. For each buffer cache you create, you need to specify its size.

When creating buffer caches, you establish their size in the initialization parameter file. The following example shows entries for a 4KB and a 16KB block size cache. In this example, the default database block size is 8KB.

```
DB_CACHE_SIZE = 128M
DB_4K_CACHE_SIZE = 64M
DB_16K_CACHE_SIZE = 128M
DB_BLOCK_SIZE = 8K
```

In this example, the memory allocated to support 4KB blocks is 64MB, while the allocation to support 16KB blocks is set at 128MB. The values you establish must not exceed the stated SGA_MAX_SIZE limit for all components. If your set of values exceeds the SGA limit you've set, your database will not open. You can have up to five different block sizes within your Oracle9i database.

Database Configuration Assistant Initialization Parameter Screens

Figure 1-10 shows the Database Configuration Assistant, Initialization Parameters Memory tab with default values filled in. You can view all of the initialization parameters by clicking on the All Initialization Parameters button at the bottom of the screen. If you have limited memory resources, you can scale back the Shared

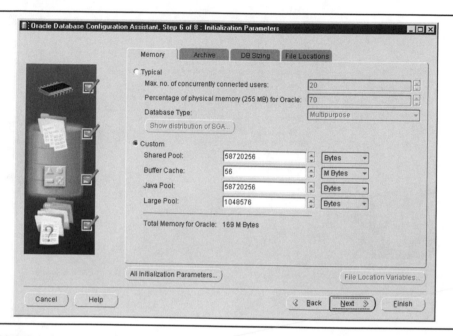

FIGURE I-10.   *Initialization Parameters, Memory tab*

Pool and Java Pool values, but you cannot scale the Java Pool value below a factor of the granule size, and you must ensure a large enough value for Shared Pool to support your memory structure requirements. If you do not have a lot of Java code, 20MB should be enough.

The second tab within the Initialization Parameters screen is the Archive tab shown in Figure 1-11. A later section in the chapter discusses the various background processes associated with a database. Because database creation involves running many scripts that load large amounts of data to the database structures, we recommend that you not activate archive logging while Oracle is building the new database. You can enable archive logging after the database has been created and the database structures have been populated.

The third tab of the Initialization Parameter screen enables you to specify the sort area size and character set for the new database. Figure 1-12 shows the DB Sizing tab. The Sort Area Size can be changed either dynamically or in the initialization parameter file after the database is built.

Once you have declared a character set value for the database, you can only alter the value if you have chosen a superset character set from the available character set list. You can establish both a database character set and an international character set for your new database. The character set defines how Oracle will translate and present character values when data is returned for a query. When data is inserted into the

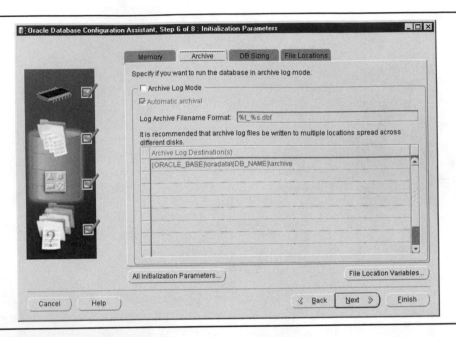

FIGURE 1-11. *Initialization Parameters, Archive tab*

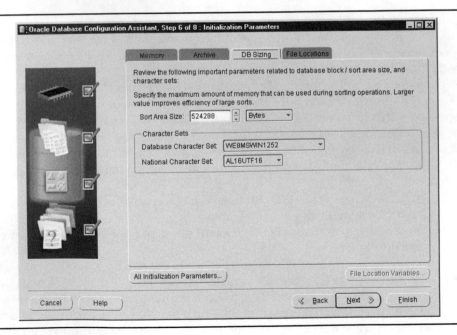

FIGURE 1-12. *Initialization Parameters, DB Sizing tab*

database, Oracle uses a *pass-through* approach and does not evaluate the incoming characters to ensure that they will be recognized when they are returned. You can find more information about character sets in the *Oracle9i Globalization Support Guide*. The values shown in Figure 1-12 are the default values for a Windows environment and are a good choice for this platform.

With the final Initialization Parameters tab, shown in Figure 1-13, you can alter the location of the init.ora parameter file, enable the use of a persistent stored parameter file (SPFILE), and modify the location of trace files.

Notice the use of global parameter values in the various filenames. You can see the translation of the values by clicking on the File Location Variables button at the bottom of the screen. Figure 1-14 shows the values for this example. You cannot change the values presented in this screen unless you are creating a database using the New Database template option. With any other template option, you will be given the opportunity to change the values in the next Database Configuration Assistant screen.

To modify the locations of the control files, datafiles, and redo log groups, you can use the Database Storage option shown in Figure 1-15.

On the left side of the screen is a navigation tree, and on the right is an explanation. You still cannot change the default file variables as shown in Figure 1-14, but you can interactively alter the file locations and sizing options for each of the files. Unfortunately, modifying all of the datafile locations can be a tedious process.

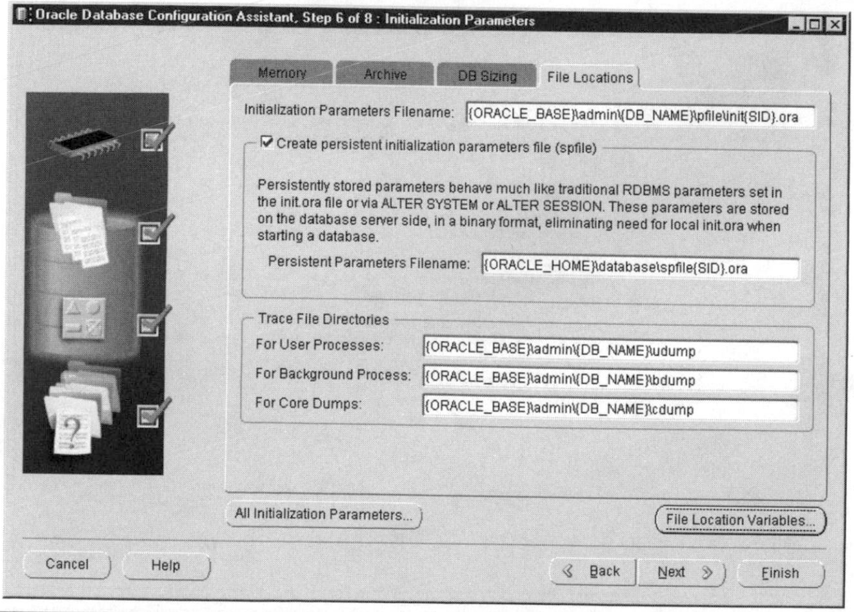

FIGURE 1-13.   *Initialization Parameters, File Locations tab*

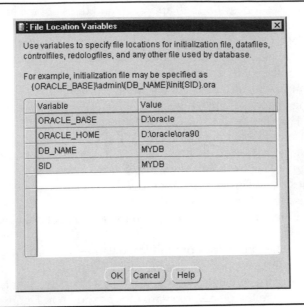

FIGURE 1-14. *File Location Variables screen*

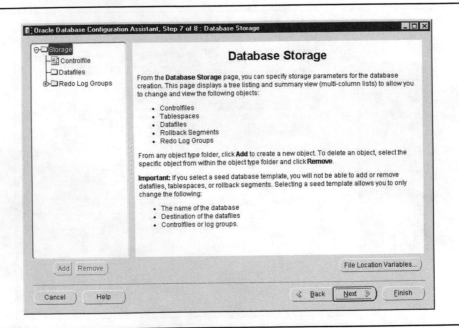

FIGURE 1-15. *Database Storage screen*

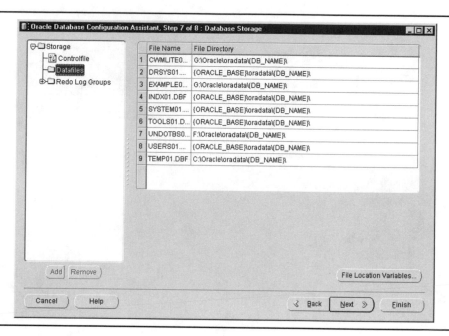

FIGURE 1-16.   *Database Storage, Datafiles screen*

Figure 1-16 shows the Datafiles option with some of the datafile locations altered to reflect different file locations. Chapter 4 covers datafile location considerations.

The next step in the database configuration process is to instruct Oracle either to create the database, store the database template, or both. Figure 1-17 shows the Creation Options screen with both options selected and a name and comment for the new database creation template, explaining that it is to be used for development database creations.

When you opt to save your template, a summary of the template is presented for your review, and you can continue or cancel the operation.

If you choose to have the database created and you do not have enough disk space to support the database creation, you will receive a warning. You are prompted to either continue or cancel the operation. The illustration shows a sample warning:

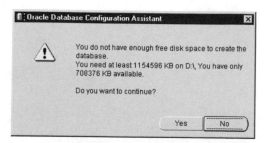

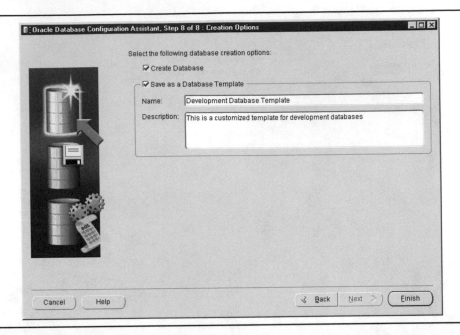

FIGURE 1-17. *Creation Options screen*

Examining the New Database

One of the first things you'll notice when you allow Oracle to create a database is that the default database users are predominantly created with their accounts locked and their very well known passwords preexpired. Oracle is making a solid effort to ensure better security for your database from the point of creation on.

In a future release of Oracle9*i*, all accounts that are created in the database by default will be locked, and passwords will be expired except for SYS and SYSTEM. You will be prompted to supply passwords for these accounts during database creation. In the current release, when you allow Oracle to create a database, you are given the opportunity immediately after database creation to modify the passwords for the default accounts that are created unlocked with their standard passwords. There were five initial accounts left unlocked with their known password on Windows NT Oracle9*i*, version 9.0.1.0.0. The accounts that were immediately available in an Oracle9*i* database were

- SYS
- SYSTEM

- DBSNMP
- AURORAJISUTILITY$
- AURORAORBUNAUTHENTICATED
- OUTLN
- SCOTT
- OSE$HTTP$ADMIN

When a new database was manually created using a **create database** script, the default users, all with ACCOUNT_STATUS=OPEN, were

- SYS
- SYSTEM
- DBSNMP
- OUTLN

Manually Creating a Database

There are several steps involved in creating a database manually. Some of the steps are operating-system dependent. For example, in a Windows environment, you must first run oradim, an executable program used to create a database service, before you can create a database.

The steps you follow to create a database manually are as follows:

1. Write a database creation script. A sample database creation script is shown is step 6.

2. Create the directory structure to house the new database. Follow the optimal flexible architecture guidelines described in Chapter 4.

3. Modify an existing or Oracle-supplied sample init.ora file to reflect the parameters for the new database.

4. Declare the Oracle SID name. On a Windows platform you type the following command at the operating system prompt:

```
set ORACLE_SID = mydb
```

In UNIX:

```
export ORACLE_SID=mydb
```

5. Connect to the database via SQL*Plus as either **SYSTEM/MANAGER as sysdba** or **/ as sysdba**, and issue the command to start up the database in nomount mode as follows:

```
startup nomount pfile="D:\oracle\admin\mydb\scripts\initMYDB.ora";
```

Substitute your initialization parameter for the **pfile** parameter value shown here.

6. Once the database has been started, use the database creation script that you have written. Here is a sample database creation script:

```
create database MYNEW
maxinstances 1
maxloghistory 1
maxlogfiles 5
maxlogmembers 5
maxdatafiles 100
datafile 'D:\oracle\oradata\mydb\system01.dbf'
   size 325M reuse autoextend on next 10240K maxsize unlimited
character set WE8MSWIN1252
national character set AL16UTF16
logfile group 1 ('d:\oracle\oradata\mydb\redo01.log') size 100M,
        group 2 ('d:\oracle\oradata\mydb\redo02.log') size 100M,
        group 3 ('d:\oracle\oradata\mydb\redo03.log') size 100M
default temporary tablespace TEMP
tempfile 'd:\oracle\oradata\mydb\temp01.dbf'
   extent management local uniform size 1M
undo tablespace UNDO_TS datafile
'd:\oracle\oradata\mydb\temp01.dbf'
   size 150M reuse autoextend on next 10240K maxsize unlimited
;
```

7. Once the database is created, run the following scripts: catalog.sql, catproc.sql, catexp.sql, and any other scripts that are needed to support your installed products. The scripts are located in the $ORACLE_HOME/rdbms/admin directory on a UNIX system and ORACLE_HOME\rdbms\admin in a Windows environment. Review the scripts before running them, as many of the catalog scripts call other catalog scripts.

8. To ensure tighter security, at a minimum modify the SYSTEM and SYS passwords to something other than the default MANAGER and CHANGE_ON_INSTALL, respectively.

In the script example shown in step 6, the UNDO tablespace is created. The initialization parameters to support this feature are as follows:

```
undo_management=AUTO
undo_tablespace=UNDOTBS
```

The only parameter that you cannot change after database creation is the database block size that you declare in the init.ora file before database creation. The parameter DB_BLOCK_SIZE is used to establish this value. For example, the following line establishes a default database block size of 8KB.

```
DB_BLOCK_SIZE=8k
```

To see the parameters in effect in your database, query the V$PARAMETER dynamic view:

```
select Name, Value, IsDefault
    from V$PARAMETER;
```

Background Processes

The relationships between the database's physical and memory structures are maintained and enforced by *background processes*. These are the database's own background processes, which may vary in number depending on your database's configuration. These processes are managed by the database and require little administrative work.

Trace files are only created when there is a problem. The naming convention and location for the background process trace files differ across operating systems and database versions. In general, the trace filenames will contain either the background process name or the operating system process ID for the background process. You can set the BACKGROUND_DUMP_DEST initialization parameter to specify a location for the background process trace files. The trace files become most important when you are debugging problems with the database. Serious problems that affect the background processes usually are logged in the database's alert log.

The alert log is usually located in the BACKGROUND_DUMP_DEST directory. Typically, that directory is the /admin/*INSTANCE_NAME*/bdump directory under the ORACLE_BASE directory.

NOTE
You can use V$BGPROCESS to see a complete list of the available background processes in your database.

SMON

When you start the database, the *SMON* (System Monitor) process performs instance recovery as needed (using the online redo log files). It also cleans up the database, eliminating transactional objects that are no longer needed by the system.

SMON serves an additional purpose: it coalesces contiguous free extents into larger free extents. The free space fragmentation process is conceptually described in Chapter 4. For some tablespaces, DBAs must manually perform the free space coalescence; instructions for performing this task are given in Chapter 8. SMON only coalesces free space in tablespaces whose default **pctincrease** storage value is nonzero.

PMON

The *PMON* (Process Monitor) background process cleans up failed user processes. PMON frees up the resources that the user was using. Its effects can be seen when a process holding a lock is killed; PMON is responsible for releasing the lock and making it available to other users. Like SMON, PMON wakes up periodically to check if it is needed.

DBWR

The *DBWR* (Database Writer) background process is responsible for managing the contents of the data block buffer cache and the dictionary cache. DBWR performs batch writes of changed blocks from the SGA to the datafiles.

Although there is only one SMON and one PMON process running per database instance, you can have multiple DBWR processes running at the same time, depending on the platform and operating system. Using multiple DBWR processes helps to minimize contention within DBWR during large operations that span datafiles. The number of DBWR processes running is set via the DB_WRITER_PROCESSES parameter in the database's initialization parameter file. If your system does not support asynchronous I/O, you can create a single DBWR process with multiple DBWR I/O slaves; the number of DBWR I/O slaves is set via the DBWR_IO_SLAVES initialization parameter. With asynchronous I/O you can have multiple DBWn processes, and without asynchronous I/O you use DBWR I/O slaves.

If you create multiple DBWR processes, the processes will not be named DBWR; instead, they will have a numeric component. For example, if you create five DBWR processes, the operating system names of the processes may be DBW0, DBW1, DBW2, DBW3, and DBW4.

LGWR

The *LGWR* (Log Writer) background process manages the writing of the contents of the redo log buffer to the online redo log files. LGWR writes log entries to the online redo log files in batches. The redo log buffer entries always contain the most up-to-date status of the database, since the DBWR process may wait before writing changed blocks from the data block buffers to the datafiles.

LGWR is the only process that writes to the online redo log files and the only one that directly reads the redo log buffers during normal database operation. The online redo log files are written to in sequential fashion, as opposed to the fairly random accesses that DBWR performs against the datafiles. If the online redo log files are mirrored, LGWR writes to the mirrored sets of logs simultaneously. See Chapter 2 for details on this mirroring capability.

CKPT

Checkpoints help to reduce the amount of time needed to perform instance recovery. Checkpoints cause DBWR to write all of the blocks that have been modified since the last checkpoint to the datafiles. The CKPT process updates the datafile headers and control files to record the checkpoint. Checkpoints occur automatically when an online redo log file fills; the LOG_CHECKPOINT_INTERVAL and LOG_CHECKPOINT_TIMEOUT parameters in the database instance's initialization file may be used to set a more frequent checkpoint.

The CKPT background process separates the two functions of LGWR in earlier database versions (signaling checkpoints and copying redo entries) between two background processes.

ARCH

The LGWR background process writes to the online redo log files in a cyclical fashion; after filling the first log file, it begins writing the second, until that one fills, and then begins writing to the third. Once the last online redo log file is filled, LGWR begins to overwrite the contents of the first redo log file.

When Oracle is run in ARCHIVELOG mode, the database makes a copy of each redo log file after it fills. These archived redo log files are usually written to a disk device. The archiving function is performed by the *ARCH* background process. Databases using this option may encounter contention problems on their redo log disk during heavy data transaction times, since LGWR will be trying to write to one redo log file while ARCH is trying to read another. They may also encounter database lockups if the archive log destination disk fills. At that point, ARCH freezes, which prevents LGWR from writing, which in turn prevents any further transactions from occurring in the database until space is cleared for the archived redo log files.

You can establish multiple archived redo log destination areas, and can specify the number of areas that must be successful for the instance to continue.

For details on the management of the archiving and database backup processes, see Chapter 11.

RECO

The *RECO* background process resolves failures in distributed databases. RECO attempts to access databases involved in in-doubt distributed transactions and resolve those transactions. This process is only created if the Distributed option is supported on the platform and the DISTRIBUTED_TRANSACTIONS parameter in the initialization file is set to a value greater than zero.

NOTE
The default init.ora file will be created with a nonzero value for DISTRIBUTED_TRANSACTIONS.

CJQ*n*

Oracle's job queue management relies on background processes for the execution of data refreshes and other scheduled jobs. The coordinator process, named CJQ0, selects the jobs to be executed and spawns job queue processes (J000 to J999) where the maximum number is specified by the initialization parameter JOB_QUEUE_PROCESSES to execute them. The maximum number of job processes created for an instance is set via the JOB_QUEUE_PROCESSES parameter in the database's initialization file.

LMS*n*

Multiple *LMS* processes, named LCK0 through LCK9, are used for interinstance locking when the Oracle Real Application Clusters option is used.

D*nnn*

Dispatcher processes are part of the shared server architecture; they help to minimize resource needs by handling multiple connections. At least one dispatcher process must be created for each protocol that is being supported on the database server. Dispatcher processes are created at database startup, based on the initialization parameter DISPATCHERS, and can be created or removed while the database is open.

Server: S*nnn*

Server processes are created to manage connections to the database that require a dedicated server. Server processes may perform I/O against the datafiles. The maximum number of server processes is specified by the initialization parameter SHARED_SERVERS.

Parallel Query Server Processes: P*nnn*

If you enable the Parallel Query option within your database, a single query's resource requirements may be distributed among multiple processors. The number of parallel query server processes started when the instance starts is determined by the PARALLEL_MIN_SERVERS parameter. Each of those processes will be present at the operating system level; as more processes are needed to parallelize operations, more parallel query server processes will be started. Each of the parallel query server processes will have a name, such as P000, P001, and P002, at the operating system level. The maximum number of parallel query server processes is set via the PARALLEL_MAX_SERVERS initialization parameter.

Parallel query server processes do not generate trace files unless an error occurs.

Internal Database Structures

Once the database is created, you can create internal structures to support applications. The elements that are internal to the database include the following:

- Tables, columns, constraints, and datatypes (including abstract datatypes)
- Partitions and subpartitions
- Users and schemas
- Indexes, clusters, and hash clusters
- Views
- Sequences
- Procedures, functions, packages, and triggers
- Synonyms
- Privileges and roles
- Database links
- Segments, extents, and blocks
- Rollback segments
- Snapshots and materialized views

Tables, Columns, and Datatypes

Tables are the storage mechanism for data within an Oracle database. As shown previously in Figure 1-1, tables contain a fixed set of columns. The columns of a table describe the attributes of the entity being tracked by the table. Each column has a name and specific characteristics.

A column has a *datatype* and a *length*. For columns using the NUMBER datatype, you can specify their additional characteristics of precision and scale. *Precision* determines the number of significant digits in a numeric value. *Scale* determines the placement of the decimal point. A specification of NUMBER (9,2) for a column has a total of nine digits, two of which are to the right of the decimal point. The default precision is 38 digits, which is also the maximum precision. The available datatypes are listed in Table 1-1.

In addition to the datatypes listed in Table 1-1, Oracle provides alternatives for ANSI standard datatypes. For ANSI datatypes CHARACTER and CHAR, use Oracle's CHAR datatype. For the ANSI datatypes CHARACTER VARYING and CHAR VARYING, use Oracle's VARCHAR2 datatype. For the ANSI NUMERIC, DECIMAL, DEC, INTEGER, INT, and SMALLINT datatypes, use Oracle's NUMBER datatype. For the ANSI standard FLOAT, REAL, and DOUBLE PRECISION datatypes, Oracle supports a FLOAT datatype within PL/SQL.

Datatype	Description
CHAR	A fixed-length character field, up to 2000 bytes in length.
NCHAR	A fixed-length field for multibyte character sets. Maximum size is 2000 characters or 2000 bytes per row, depending on the character set, with the default at 1 byte.
VARCHAR2	A variable-length character field, up to 4000 characters in length.
NVARCHAR2	A variable-length field for multibyte character sets. Maximum size is 4000 characters or 4000 bytes per row, depending on the character set, with a default of 1 byte.
DATE	A fixed-length, 7-byte field used to store all dates. The time is stored as part of the date. When queried, the date will be in the format DD-MON-YY, as in 22-APR-01 for April 22, 2001, unless you override the date format by setting the initialization parameter NLS_DATE_FORMAT.
INTERVAL DAY TO SECOND	A period of time, fixed at 11 bytes, represented as days, hours, minutes, and seconds. The precision values specify the number of digits in the DAY and the fractional SECOND fields of the date. The precision defaults to 2 for days and 6 for seconds but can be from 0 to 9.
INTERVAL YEAR TO MONTH	A period of time, fixed at 5 bytes, represented as years and months. The precision value specifies the number of digits in the YEAR field of the date. The precision defaults to 2 for years but can be from 0 to 9.

TABLE 1-1. *Oracle Datatypes*

Datatype	Description
TIMESTAMP	A value that can vary from 7 to 11 bytes, representing a date and time, including fractional seconds, based on the operating system clock value. The precision value specifies the number of digits in the fractional second part of the SECOND date field. The precision defaults to 6 but can be from 0 to 9.
TIMESTAMP WITH TIME ZONE	A value, fixed at 13 bytes, representing a date and time, plus an associated time zone setting. The time zone can be an offset from UTC, such as '-5:0' or a region name, such as 'US/Pacific'.
TIMESTAMP WITH LOCAL TIME	Varying from 7 to 11 bytes, this datatype is similar to TIMESTAMP WITH TIME ZONE except that the data is normalized to the database time zone when stored, and adjusted to match the client's time zone when retrieved.
NUMBER	A variable-length number column. Allowed values are zero and positive and negative numbers. The internal storage required for a NUMBER value is approximately half of the number of significant digits in the value. You take the overall length, say 9, divide it by 2, round to a whole number, and add 1 for a positive number. Therefore, a nine-digit number takes 6 bytes to store.
LONG	A variable-length field, up to 2GB in length.
RAW	A variable-length field used for binary data up to 2000 bytes in length.
LONG RAW	A variable-length field used for binary data up to 2GB in length.
BLOB	Binary large object, up to 4GB in length.
CLOB	Character large object, up to 4GB in length.
NCLOB	CLOB datatype for multibyte character sets, up to 4GB in length.
BFILE	External binary file; size is limited by the operating system.
ROWID	Binary data representing a RowID. All RowIDs are 6 bytes for normal indexes on nonpartitioned tables, local indexes on partitioned tables, and for row pointers used for chained or migrated rows. The RowID is 10 bytes only for global indexes on partitioned tables.
UROWID	Binary data used for data addressing, up to 4000 bytes in length that can support both logical and physical RowID values as well as foreign tables accessed through a gateway.

TABLE 1-1. *Oracle Datatypes* (continued)

You can create your own abstract datatypes beginning with Oracle8 when you install the Object option. You can also use special REF datatypes that reference row objects elsewhere in the database when you create object tables (see Chapter 5).

The tables owned by the user SYS are called the *data dictionary tables*. The data dictionary tables provide a system catalog that the database uses to manage itself. The data dictionary is created by a set of catalog scripts provided by Oracle. Each time you install or upgrade a database, you will need to run scripts that either create or modify the data dictionary tables. When you install a new option in your database, you may need to run additional catalog scripts. The user SYSTEM owns views into the data dictionary tables.

Tables are related to each other via the columns they have in common. You can require the database to enforce these relationships via *referential integrity*. If you use Oracle's object-oriented features, rows may be related to each other via internal references called object IDs (see Chapter 5). Referential integrity is enforced at the database level via constraints.

Temporary Tables

Like a regular table, a temporary table is a storage mechanism for data within an Oracle database. A temporary table consists of columns that have datatypes and lengths. Unlike a regular table, a temporary table's definition persists but the data inserted into the table remains for either the duration of a session or the duration of a transaction. Creating the temporary table as a *global* temporary table ensures that all sessions connecting to the database can see and use the table. Multiple sessions can insert rows of data into the temporary table. However, each data row within the table is only visible to the session that inserts that row into the table.

The data contained within a temporary table is either session specific or transaction specific based on the keywords you use within the **on commit** clause associated with the temporary table. You can specify either **on commit delete rows** or **on commit preserve rows**. The complete **create global temporary table** syntax can be found in Appendix A.

Temporary tables became available in Oracle8i and provide a vehicle for buffering results or a result set when your applications must run multiple DML statements during a transaction or session. You'll find a complete description of temporary tables in Chapter 5.

Constraints

You can create *constraints* on the columns of a table; when a constraint is applied to a table, every row in the table must satisfy the conditions specified in the constraint definition. In the following **create table** command, an EMPLOYEE table is created with several constraints:

```
create table EMPLOYEE
 (EmpNo              NUMBER(10)     PRIMARY KEY,
  Name               VARCHAR2(40)   NOT NULL,
  DeptNo             NUMBER(2)      DEFAULT 10,
  Salary             NUMBER(7,2)    CHECK (salary<1000000),
  Birth_Date         DATE,
  Soc_Sec_Num        CHAR(9)        UNIQUE,
  foreign key (DeptNo) references DEPT(DeptNo))
tablespace USERS;
```

First, note that the table is given a name (EMPLOYEE). Each of its columns is named (EmpNo, Name, etc.). Each column has a specified datatype and length. The EmpNo column is defined as a NUMBER datatype, with no scale—this is the equivalent of an integer. The Name column is defined as a VARCHAR2(40); this will be a variable-length column up to 40 characters in length.

The *primary key* of the table is the column or set of columns that makes every row in that table unique. A primary key column will be defined within the database as being NOT NULL. This means that every row that is stored in that table must have a value for that column; it cannot be left NULL. The NOT NULL constraint can be applied to the columns in the table, as shown for the Name column in the above example.

A column can have a DEFAULT constraint, which will generate a value for a column when a row is **insert**ed in a table but no value is specified for a column.

The CHECK constraint ensures that values in a specified column meet a certain criterion (in this case, that the Salary column's value is less than 1,000,000). A CHECK constraint cannot reference a separate table. A NOT NULL constraint is treated by the database as a CHECK constraint.

Another constraint, UNIQUE, guarantees uniqueness for columns that should be unique but are not part of the primary key. In this example, the Soc_Sec_Num column has a UNIQUE constraint, so every record in this table must have a unique value for this column.

A *foreign key* constraint specifies the nature of the relationship between tables. A foreign key from one table references a primary key that has been previously defined elsewhere in the database. For example, if a table called DEPT had a primary key of DeptNo, then the records in DEPT would list all of the valid DeptNo values. The DeptNo column in the EMPLOYEE table shown in the preceding listing *references* that DEPT.DeptNo column. By specifying EMPLOYEE.DeptNo as a foreign key to DEPT.DeptNo, you guarantee that no DeptNo values can be entered into the EMPLOYEE table unless those values already exist in the DEPT table.

The constraints in the database help to ensure the referential integrity of the data. Referential integrity provides assurance that all of the references within the database are valid and all constraints have been met.

Abstract Datatypes

As of Oracle8, you can define your own datatypes when you install the Object option in the database. For example, you may create a datatype that contains the multiple parts of a person's name—first name, last name, middle initial, and suffix—as a single datatype. In the following listing, the NAME_TY datatype is created:

```
create type NAME_TY as object
(First_Name      VARCHAR2(25),
 Middle_Initial  CHAR(1),
 Last_Name       VARCHAR2(30),
 Suffix          VARCHAR2(5));
/
```

You can use your user-defined datatypes to standardize the usage of data within your applications. For example, you can use the NAME_TY datatype anywhere you would use any other datatype. In the following example, the EMPLOYEE table is created again; this time, the NAME_TY datatype is the datatype for the EMPLOYEE.Name column:

```
create table EMPLOYEE
(EmpNo            NUMBER(10)      PRIMARY KEY,
 Name             NAME_TY,
 DeptNo           NUMBER(2)       DEFAULT 10,
 Salary           NUMBER(7,2)     CHECK (salary<1000000),
 Birth_Date       DATE,
 Soc_Sec_Num      CHAR(9)         UNIQUE,
 foreign key (DeptNo) references DEPT(DeptNo))
tablespace USERS;
```

The Name column of the EMPLOYEE table contains four attributes, as shown in the NAME_TY creation statement. If you define *methods*—programs that act on the attributes of datatypes—on the NAME_TY datatype, then you can apply those methods to the values of the Name column in the EMPLOYEE table. See Chapter 5 for examples of the use and management of abstract datatypes and other object-oriented structures.

Constructor Methods

When you create an abstract datatype, Oracle automatically creates a constructor to support DML for the column that uses the datatype. For the NAME_TY datatype, the constructor method is named NAME_TY, and the parameters for the method are the attributes of the datatype. See Chapter 5 for examples of the use of constructor methods.

Object Tables

An object table is a table whose rows are all objects—they all have object identifier (OID) values. You can create an object table via the **create table** command. For example, you can use the **create table** command in the following listing to create a NAME table based on the NAME_TY datatype:

```
create table NAME of NAME_TY;
```

You will then be able to create references from other tables to the row objects in the NAME object table. If you create references to the NAME row objects, you will be able to select NAME rows via the references—without directly querying the NAME table. See Chapter 5 for examples of the use of row objects and the simulation of row objects via object views.

Nested Tables and Varying Arrays

A nested table is a column (or columns) within a table that contains multiple values for a single row in the table. For example, if you have multiple addresses for a person, then you may create a row in a table that contains multiple values for an Address column, but only one value for the rest of the columns. Nested tables can contain multiple columns and an unlimited number of rows. A second type of collector, called a varying array, is limited in the number of rows it can contain.

An in-depth discussion of the use of nested tables and varying arrays is beyond the scope of this book; see *Oracle8i: The Complete Reference*, by Kevin Loney (Osborne/McGraw-Hill-Oracle Press, 2000) for detailed examples of these structures and their related syntax. In general, nested tables give you more flexibility in data management than varying arrays. Both nested tables and varying arrays require you to modify the SQL syntax you use to access your data. In general, you can simulate the data relationships of nested tables via related relational tables.

Partitions and Subpartitions

As your tables grow larger, their maintenance grows more difficult. In very large databases, you may greatly simplify your database administration activities by splitting a large table's data across multiple smaller tables. For example, you may split a table into separate smaller tables based on the time, department, or product values in the table.

NOTE
Partitions are only available to companies that have purchased and installed the Partitioning option.

You can specify value ranges for the database to use when splitting a larger table into smaller tables. These smaller tables, called *partitions*, are generally simpler to manage than larger tables. For example, you can **truncate** the data in a single partition without truncating the data in any other partition. Oracle will treat the partitioned table as a single large table, but you can manage the partitions as separate objects.

Partitions may also improve the performance of an application. Since the optimizer will know the range values used as the basis for the partitions, the optimizer may be able to direct queries to use only specific partitions during table accesses. Because less data may be read during the query processing, the performance of the query should improve.

You can partition indexes as well as tables. The ranges of values for the partitions of a partitioned index may match the ranges used for the indexed table—in which case the index is called a *local index*. If the index partitions do not match the value ranges used for the table partitions, the index is called a *global index*.

As of Oracle8*i*, you can partition partitions, creating *subpartitions*. For example, you can partition a table on one set of values and then partition the partitions based on a second partition method. As of Oracle9*i*, you can create *list partitions* in addition to range and hash partitions. See Chapter 15 for a description of the management issues for partitions, subpartitions, local indexes, and global indexes.

Users

A *user* account is not a physical structure in the database, but it does have important relationships to the objects in the database: users own the database's objects. The user SYS owns the data dictionary tables; these store information about the rest of the structures in the database. The user SYSTEM owns views that access these data dictionary tables for use by the rest of the users in the database.

When you create objects in the database, the objects are created under user accounts. You can customize each user account to use a specific tablespace as its default tablespace.

You can tie database accounts to operating system accounts, allowing users to access the database from the operating system without having to enter passwords for both the operating system and the database. Users can then access the objects they own or to which they have been granted access.

Schemas

The set of objects owned by a user account is called the user's *schema*. You can create users who do not have the ability to log into the database. Such user accounts provide a schema that can be used to hold a set of database objects separate from other users' schemas.

Indexes

For Oracle to find data, each row in each table is labeled with a *RowID*. This RowID tells the database exactly where the row is located (by file, block within that file, and row within that block).

NOTE
An index-organized table does not have traditional Oracle RowIDs. Instead, its primary key acts as a logical RowID.

An index is a database structure used by the server to quickly find a row in a table. There are three primary types of indexes: cluster indexes, table indexes, and bitmap indexes. Cluster indexes store the cluster key values in clusters (see the next section for further details on the use of clusters). A table index stores the values of a table's rows along with the physical location where the row is located (its RowID). A bitmap index is a special type of table index designed to support queries of large tables with columns that have few distinct values.

Each index entry consists of a key value and a RowID. You can index a single column or a set of columns. Oracle stores index entries using a B*tree mechanism, guaranteeing a short access path to the key value. When a query accesses the index, it finds the index entries that match the query criteria. The entry's matching RowID value provides Oracle the physical location for the associated row, reducing the I/O burden required to locate the data.

Indexes both improve performance and (optionally) ensure uniqueness of a column. Oracle automatically creates an index when a UNIQUE or PRIMARY KEY constraint clause is specified in a **create table** command. You can manually create your own indexes via the **create index** command. See Appendix A for the full syntax and options of the **create index** command.

You can create indexes on one or more columns of a table. In the example of the EMPLOYEE table given earlier, Oracle will automatically create unique indexes on the EmpNo and Soc_Sec_Num columns since they have been specified as PRIMARY KEY and UNIQUE, respectively. Dropping an index will not affect the data within the previously indexed table.

As of Oracle7.3, you can create *bitmap indexes*. Bitmap indexes are useful when the data is not very selective—there are very few distinct values in the column. Bitmap indexes speed searches in which such nonselective columns are used as limiting conditions in queries. Bitmap indexes are most effective for very static data.

As of Oracle8, you can create indexes that *reverse* the order of the data prior to storing it. That is, an entry whose data value is 1002 will be indexed as 2001. The reversing of the data order prior to indexing helps keep the data better distributed within the index. Because they reverse the data values, reverse order indexes are only useful if you will be performing equivalence operations in your queries, such as

```
where key_col_value = 1002
```

If you are performing range searches, such as

```
where key_col_value > 1000
```

then reverse order indexes will not effectively meet your needs since consecutive values will not be stored near each other. Because consecutive rows will be stored apart from each other in the index, range queries cannot use reverse key indexes.

As of Oracle8, you can create an index-organized table. In an index-organized table (specified via the **organization index** clause of the **create table** command), the entire table is stored within an index structure, with its data sorted by the table's primary key. To create an index-organized table, you must specify a primary key constraint for the table. The index-organized table will not have RowIDs for its rows; Oracle will use the primary key value as a logical RowID value. As of Oracle8*i*, you can create secondary indexes on an index-organized table.

You can create function-based indexes based on Oracle functions or on user-defined functions. For example, you can create an index on **UPPER**(Name) instead of just the Name column if you know that the queries' **where** clauses will always use the **UPPER** function.

Clusters

Tables that are frequently accessed together may be physically stored together. To store them together, you can create a *cluster* to hold the tables. The data in the tables is then stored together in the cluster to minimize the number of I/Os that must be performed, and thus performance is improved.

The related columns of the tables are called the *cluster key*. The cluster key is indexed using a *cluster index*, and its value is only stored once for the multiple tables in the cluster. You must create a cluster index prior to **insert**ing any rows into the tables in the cluster.

Clusters may be beneficial for tables that are very frequently queried together. Within the cluster, rows from separate tables are stored in the same blocks, so queries joining those tables may perform fewer I/Os than if the tables were stored apart. However, the performance of **insert**s, **update**s, and **delete**s for clustered tables may be significantly worse than the same operations against nonclustered tables. Before clustering tables, evaluate the frequency with which they are queried together. If the tables are always queried together, you should consider merging them into a single table rather than clustering two tables.

Hash Clusters

A second type of cluster, a *hash cluster*, uses *hashing functions* on the row's cluster key to determine the physical location where the row should be stored. Hash clusters will yield the greatest performance benefit for equivalence queries, such as the one shown in the following listing:

```
select Name
  from EMPLOYEE
 where EmpNo = 123;
```

In this example, the EMPLOYEE table is queried for an exact match of the EmpNo column. If EMPLOYEE is part of a hash cluster, and EmpNo is part of the cluster key, then the database can use the hashing function to quickly determine where the data is physically located. The same performance gains would not be expected if the **where** clause had specified a range of values, as in the following listing:

```
select Name
  from EMPLOYEE
 where EmpNo > 123;
```

Finding a row in a standard indexed table may require multiple I/Os—one or more to find the key value in the index and another to read the row from the table. Using a hash algorithm reduces the number of I/Os required to return the row for equivalence queries.

Views

A *view* appears to be a table containing columns and is queried in the same manner that a table is queried. However, a view contains no data. Conceptually, a view can be thought of as a mask overlaying one or more tables, such that the columns in the view are found in one or more underlying tables. Thus, views do not use physical storage to store data. The definition of a view (which includes the query it is based on, its column layout, and privileges granted) is stored in the data dictionary.

When you query a view, the view queries the tables that it is based on and returns the values in the format and order specified by the view definition. Since there is no physical data directly associated with them, views cannot be indexed.

Views are frequently used to enforce row-level and column-level security on data. For example, you could grant a user access to a view that shows only that user's rows from a table, while not granting the user access to all of the rows in the table. Similarly, you could limit the columns the user can see via the view.

As of Oracle8, you can use *object views* to create an object-oriented layer above your tables. You can use object views to simulate abstract datatypes, object identifiers, and references.

Object Views

If you use abstract datatypes, you may encounter consistency issues during their implementation. Accessing the attributes of abstract datatypes requires you to use syntax that is not used for access of regular columns. As a result, you may need to change your enterprise SQL coding standards in order to support abstract datatypes. You will also need to remember which tables use abstract datatypes when performing transactions and queries against the tables.

Object views provide an important bridge on the path to abstract datatypes. You can use object views to give an object-relational presentation to your relational data. The underlying tables are unchanged, but the views support the abstract datatype definitions. From a DBA's perspective, little changes—you manage the tables as you would manage any other tables in the database. From a developer's perspective, object views provide object-relational access to the tables' data.

Sequences

Sequence definitions are stored in the data dictionary. Sequences are used to simplify programming efforts by providing a sequential list of unique numbers.

The first time a sequence is called by a query, it returns a predetermined value. Each subsequent query against the sequence will yield a value that is increased by its specified increment. Sequences can cycle, or may continue increasing until a specified maximum value is reached.

When you use a sequence, there is no guarantee that you will generate an unbroken string of values. For example, if you query the next value from a sequence for use in an **insert**, then yours is the only session that can use that sequence value. If you fail to commit your transaction, then your sequence value is not inserted into the table, and later **insert**s will use succeeding values from the sequence.

Procedures

A *procedure* is a block of PL/SQL statements that is stored in the data dictionary and is called by applications. You can use procedures to store frequently used application logic within the database. When the procedure is executed, its statements are executed as a unit. Procedures do not return any value to the calling program.

You can use stored procedures to help enforce data security. Rather than grant users access directly to the tables within an application, you can grant them the ability to execute a procedure that accesses the tables. When the procedure is executed, it will execute with the privileges of the procedure's owner. The users will be unable to access the tables except via the procedure.

Functions

Functions, like procedures, are blocks of code that are stored in the database. Unlike procedures, though, functions are capable of returning values to the calling program.

You can create your own functions and call them within SQL statements just as you execute the functions that Oracle provides.

For example, Oracle provides a function called **SUBSTR** that performs "substring" functions on strings. If you create a function called **MY_SUBSTR** that performs custom substring operations, you could call it within a SQL command:

```
select MY_SUBSTR('text') from DUAL;
```

If you do not own the **MY_SUBSTR** function, then you must have been granted EXECUTE permission on the function. You can only use a user-defined function within a SQL statement if the function does not modify any database rows.

Packages

You can use *packages* to arrange procedures and functions into logical groupings. The specifications and bodies are stored in the data dictionary. Packages are very useful in the administrative tasks required for the management of procedures and functions.

Different elements within the package can be defined as being "public" or "private." Public elements are accessible to the user of the package, while private elements are hidden from the user. Private elements may include procedures that are called by other procedures within the package.

The source code for functions, packages, and procedures is stored in the data dictionary tables. If your applications use packages heavily, you may need to greatly increase the size of your SYSTEM tablespace to accommodate the increase in data dictionary size.

The number and complexity of packages in use directly impacts the size of the Shared SQL Pool portion of the SGA.

Triggers

Triggers are procedures that are executed when a specified database event takes place. You may use them to augment referential integrity, enforce additional security, or enhance the available auditing options.

There are two types of triggers:

Statement triggers	Fire once for each triggering statement
Row triggers	Fire once for each row in a table affected by the statements

For example, a statement-level trigger fires once for a **delete** command that deletes 10,000 rows. A row-level trigger would fire 10,000 times for the same transaction.

For each trigger type, you can create a BEFORE trigger and AFTER trigger for each type of triggering event. Triggering events include **insert**s, **update**s, and **delete**s.

Statement triggers are useful if the code in the trigger action does not rely on the data affected. For example, you may create a BEFORE INSERT statement trigger on a table to prevent **insert**s into a table except during specific time periods.

Row triggers are useful if the trigger action relies on the data being affected by the transaction. For example, you may create an AFTER INSERT row trigger to **insert** new rows into an audit table as well as the trigger's base table.

As of Oracle8, you can create INSTEAD OF triggers. An INSTEAD OF trigger executes instead of the action that caused it to start. That is, if you create an INSTEAD OF INSERT trigger on an object view, the trigger's code executes and the **insert** that caused the trigger to be executed never occurs. If your view joins multiple tables in its query, an INSTEAD OF trigger can direct Oracle's actions if a user attempts to **update** rows via the view.

As of Oracle8i, you can create triggers on system-level events. You can trigger code to be executed when **create**, **alter**, or **delete** commands are issued. You can also use system events such as logons, logoffs, and database shutdowns and startups as triggering events. See the entry for **create trigger** in Appendix A for the command syntax.

A new trigger called the **on logon** trigger enables you to have environment values established and associated with a user from the point in time that the user connects to the database. This feature is particularly useful with the Virtual Private Database described in Chapter 10.

Synonyms

To completely identify a database object (such as a table or view) in a distributed database, you must specify the host machine name, the instance name, the object's owner, and the object's name. Depending on the location of the object, between one and four of these parameters will be needed. To screen this process from the user, developers can create synonyms that point to the proper object; thus, the user only needs to know the synonym name. Public synonyms are shared by all users of a given database. Private synonyms are owned by individual database account owners.

For example, the EMPLOYEE table that was previously described must be owned by an account—let's say that the owner is HR. From a different user account in the same database, that table could be referenced as HR.EMPLOYEE. However, this syntax requires that the second account know that the HR account is the owner of the EMPLOYEE table. To avoid this requirement, you can create a public synonym called EMPLOYEE to point to HR.EMPLOYEE. Anytime the EMPLOYEE synonym is referenced, it will point to the proper table. The following SQL statement creates the EMPLOYEE synonym:

```
create public synonym EMPLOYEE for HR.EMPLOYEE;
```

Synonyms provide pointers for tables, views, procedures, functions, packages, and sequences. They can point to objects within the local database or in remote databases. Pointing to remote databases requires the use of database links, as described shortly.

You cannot create synonyms for abstract datatypes. Furthermore, Oracle does not check the validity of a synonym when you create it. You should test your synonyms after you create them to ensure they are valid.

Privileges and Roles

In order to access an object owned by another account, the *privilege* to access that object must first have been granted. Typically, nonowners are granted the privilege to **insert**, **select**, **update**, or **delete** rows from a table or view. You can grant users privileges to **select** values from sequences and **execute** procedures, functions, packages, and abstract datatypes. No privileges are granted on indexes or triggers, since they are accessed by the database during table activity. You can grant **read** on directories (for BFILE datatypes and external tables) and **execute** on libraries (for external programs called by your application code). You can grant privileges to individual users or to PUBLIC, which gives the privilege to all users in the database.

You can create *roles*—groups of privileges—to simplify the privilege management process. You can grant privileges to a role, and grant the role in turn to multiple users. Adding new users to applications then becomes a much easier process to manage since it is simply a matter of granting or revoking roles for the user.

The relationship between privileges and roles is shown in Figure 1-18. In Figure 1-18*a*, the privileges required to grant **select** access on two tables to four users are shown as lines. In Figure 1-18*b*, the role capability is used to simplify the administration of the privileges. The privileges are granted to a single role, and that role is granted to the four users. Roles may be dynamically enabled and disabled within an application.

You can also use roles to grant system-level privileges, such as **create table**. System-level roles will be discussed in detail in Chapter 10.

Database Links

Oracle databases can reference data that is stored outside of the local database. When referencing such data, you must specify the fully qualified name of the remote object. In the synonym example given earlier, only two parts of the fully qualified name— the owner and the table name—were specified. What if the table is in a remote database?

To specify an access path to an object in a remote database, you will need to create a *database link*. Database links can either be public (available to all accounts in that database) or private (created by a user for only that account's use). When you

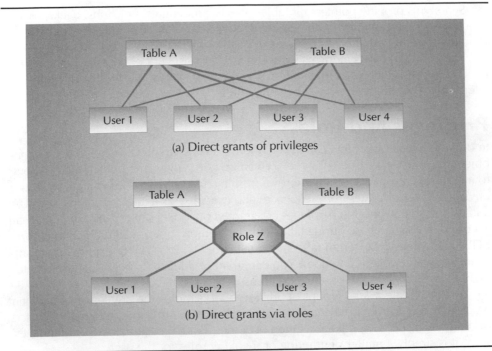

FIGURE 1-18. *Relationship between privileges and roles*

create a database link, you specify the name of the account to connect to, the password for the account, and the service name associated with the remote database. If you do not specify an account name to connect to, Oracle will use your local account name and password for the connection to the remote database. The following example creates a public link named MY_LINK:

```
create public database link MY_LINK
connect to HR identified by PUFFINSTUFF
using 'DB1';
```

In this example, the link specifies that when it is used, it will open up a session in the database identified by the service named DB1. When it opens the session in the DB1 instance, it will log in as the user account HR, with the password PUFFINSTUFF. The service names for instances are stored in configuration files used by Oracle Net. The configuration file for service names is called tnsnames.ora, and it specifies the host, port, and instance associated with each service name.

To use this link for a table, the link must be specified in the **from** clause, as in the following example:

```
select * from EMPLOYEE@MY_LINK;
```

The preceding query will access the EMPLOYEE table via the MY_LINK database link. You can create a synonym for this table, as shown in the following SQL command:

```
create synonym EMPLOYEE for EMPLOYEE@MYLINK;
```

Note that the fully qualified designation for the database object has been defined—its host and instance via its service name, its owner (HR) via the database link, and its name (EMPLOYEE).

The location of the EMPLOYEE table is thus completely transparent to the end user. You can move the EMPLOYEE table to a different schema or a different database; changing the database link's definition will redirect the synonym to the new location.

> **NOTE**
> *If a stored procedure, package, or trigger contains references to a database link, the link must exist for the PL/SQL to compile.*

Segments, Extents, and Blocks

Segments are the physical counterparts to logical database objects. Segments store data. Index segments, for example, store the data associated with indexes. The effective management of segments requires that the DBA know the objects that an application will use, how data will be entered into those objects, and the ways in which data will be retrieved.

Because a segment is a physical entity, it must be assigned to a tablespace in the database (and will thus be placed in one of the datafiles of that tablespace). A segment is made up of sections called *extents*—contiguous sets of Oracle blocks. Once the existing extents in a segment can no longer hold new data, the segment will obtain another extent. The extension process will continue as needed until no more free space is available in the tablespace's datafiles or until an internal maximum number of extents per segment is reached.

Each segment can have a limit to the maximum number of extents it can acquire. Although the theoretical limit to extents in a segment is in the billions, most database maintenance operations perform best if the number of extents per table is limited to less than 4000. You can specify the maximum number of extents per segment at the segment level, or you can use the default for the segment's tablespace.

When you drop a segment, its used extents become free extents. Oracle may reuse those free extents for new segments or for extensions of existing segments. Information about the management of specific types of segments is provided in Chapter 4 and Chapter 6.

Undo Segments and Rollback Segments

In order to maintain read consistency among multiple users in the database and to be able to roll back transactions, Oracle must have a mechanism for reconstructing a "before" image of data for uncommitted transactions. From version 6 through Oracle9*i*, Oracle has used *rollback segments* within the database to provide a before image of data. As of Oracle9*i*, you have the additional option of storing a before image of the data in an Oracle-managed undo tablespace in *undo segments*.

Transactions use rollback or undo segments to record the prior image of data that is changed. For example, a large **delete** operation requires a large undo or rollback segment to hold the records to be deleted. If the **delete** transaction is rolled back, Oracle will use the undo or rollback segment to reconstruct the data.

NOTE
Updates only store the before image of columns being updated and not the complete row.

Queries also use undo/rollback segments. Oracle performs read-consistent queries, so the database must be able to reconstruct data as it existed when a query started. If a transaction completes after a query starts, Oracle will continue to use that transaction's undo/rollback segment entries to reconstruct changed rows. In general, you should avoid scheduling long-running queries concurrently with transactions.

Undo segments or rollback segments will grow to be as large as the transactions they support. The effective management of undo segments and rollback segments is described in Chapter 7.

Materialized Views

You can use *materialized views* to provide local copies of remote data to your users, or to store replicated data within the same database. A materialized view is based on a query that may use a database link to select data from a remote database. Users can then query the materialized view, or the optimizer may dynamically redirect queries to use the materialized view instead of the source table. This feature is called *query rewrite* and can be enabled through an initialization parameter. You can implement materialized views to be either read-only or updatable. To improve performance, you can index the underlying table used by the materialized view.

Depending on the complexity of the materialized view's base query, you may be able to use a *materialized view log* to improve the performance of your replication operations. Replication operations may be performed automatically, based on a schedule you specify for each materialized view. See Chapter 16 of this book for details on the creation and maintenance of materialized views and materialized view logs.

Context Areas

Within the shared SQL area, there are both public and private areas. Every SQL statement issued by a user requires a private SQL area, which continues to exist until the cursor corresponding to that statement is closed. As of Oracle8, a private object cache is also used when object-relational features are used.

Program Global Area (PGA)

The *Program Global Area* (*PGA*) is an area in memory that is used by a single Oracle user process. The memory in the PGA is not sharable.

With Oracle9i, Oracle offers a new approach to SQL memory management: the Automated SQL Execution Memory Management feature. With this feature, the SQL memory area can be tuned without shutting the database down, and tuning is done automatically.

To accomplish PGA automatic tuning, the memory is differentiated between tunable and untunable memory. Tunable memory is the memory consumed by the SQL work area, while untunable is what's left. The DBA must enable this automatic tuning and must determine and allocate the amount of the PGA memory target. The equation Oracle uses to determine how much memory it has available for tuning is

```
UNTUNABLE_MEMORY_SIZE + TUNABLE_MEMORY_SIZE <= PGA_AGGREGATE_TARGET
```

When automated PGA tuning is enabled, the system can only control the tunable portion; so if the tunable portion is too small, Oracle will never be able to enforce the equation. In reality, the tunable area is generally very small (<1% of the PGA) for OLTP systems, and automatic SQL tuning lends itself much more to decision-support (data warehouse) workloads (>90% of the PGA), making data warehouse environments much more suited for using this feature.

To take advantage of this option, you must enable two parameters: PGA_AGGREGATE_TARGET and WORKAREA_SIZE_POLICY. The PGA_AGGREGATE_TARGET parameter is set in the initialization parameter file, while WORKAREA_SIZE_POLICY is a dynamic session- and system-level parameter that can be set using the commands **alter system** or **alter session**. The WORKAREA_SIZE_POLICY parameter has either one of two values: MANUAL, where tuning is performed using the parameter *_AREA_SIZE (such as SORT_AREA_SIZE), and AUTO, where tuning is performed dynamically/automatically.

The PGA_AGGREGATE_TARGET is a value between 10MB and 400GB that you can set in the initialization parameter file and alter dynamically to provide more optimal performance if it proves to be too big or too small. You can use bytes, kilobytes (K), megabytes (M), or gigabytes (G) to set its value. If PGA_AGGREGATE_TARGET is not set, the WORKAREA_SIZE_POLICY has a default value of MANUAL in which case the *_AREA_SIZE parameters will be used. When enabled, the automatic tuning goals are to ensure that the overall PGA memory should never exceed the PGA_AGGREGATE_TARGET. The tunable memory area is regulated so a process never runs out of memory; by regulating work areas, throughput and response time should be optimized.

If you are using the Shared Server, part of the UGA (User Global Area) may be stored in the SGA. The Shared Server architecture allows multiple user processes to use the same server process, thus reducing the database's memory requirements. If the Shared Server is used, the user session information is stored in the SGA rather than in the PGA. If you use Shared Server, you should increase the size of the Shared SQL Pool to accommodate the additional shared memory requirements. The UGA is part of the Large Pool if it is defined.

Backup/Recovery Capabilities

The Oracle database features a number of backup and recovery options. Each of these will be described in detail in Chapter 11. The available options are described in the following sections.

Export/Import

The Export utility queries the database and stores its output in a binary file. You can select the portions of the database that are exported. You may export the entire database, a user's or a set of users' schema(s), or a specific set of tables.

Full system exports read the full data dictionary tables as well as the application data. You can use a full export to completely re-create a database, since the data dictionary tracks users, datafiles, and database objects.

The Export utility performs a logical read of the database. To read information out of the binary dump file created by the export, you must use the Import utility. Import can selectively choose objects or users from the dump file to import. The Import utility will then attempt to insert that data into the database (rather than overwriting existing records).

Export and Import are part of most backup and recovery plans for small or development databases. Since Export reads the data at a point in time, you can only use exported data to recover the data as it was at that point in time. Exports are therefore most effective for backups of data that is not very volatile. For transaction-intensive environments, exports are rarely the best primary backup method; online backups are generally preferred.

Offline Backups

In addition to making logical backups of the database, you can make physical backups of its files. To make a physical backup of the database, you can use *online backups* and *offline backups.* Offline backups are performed by first shutting down the database; the files that constitute the database can then be backed up to a storage device (via disk-to-disk copies or tape writes). Once the backup is complete, you may reopen the database.

Even if offline backups are not the main backup and recovery option being implemented, it is still a good idea to make an offline backup of the database periodically (such as when the host it resides on undergoes routine maintenance).

Online Backups

Online backups are available for those databases that are being run in ARCHIVELOG mode (described in the "ARCH" process section earlier in the chapter). You can use online backups to make physical database backups while the database is open. During an online backup, you place tablespaces temporarily into a backup state, then restore them to their normal state when their files have been backed up. See Chapter 11 for details on implementing the online and offline backup options.

Recovery Manager (RMAN)

As of Oracle8, you can use the Recovery Manager (RMAN) utility to perform physical backups of your database. Rather than backing up an entire datafile, RMAN can perform incremental physical backups of your datafiles. During a full (*level 0*) datafile backup, all of the blocks ever used in the datafile are backed up. During a cumulative (*level 1*) datafile backup, all of the blocks used since the last full datafile backup are backed up. An incremental (*level 2*) datafile backup backs up only those blocks that have changed since the most recent cumulative or full backup. You can define the levels used for incremental backups.

The Recovery Manager keeps track of your backups either through a recovery catalog or by placing the required information into the control file for the database being backed up. The number of days' worth of RMAN records stored in a control file is set via the CONTROL_FILE_RECORD_KEEP_TIME initialization parameter.

The ability to perform incremental and cumulative backups of datafiles may greatly improve the performance of your backups if you have very large databases with isolated areas of transaction activity. See Chapter 12 for details of the implementation of RMAN and other backup methods.

Security Capabilities

The full security-related capabilities within Oracle will be described in detail in Chapter 10. In this section, you will see an overview of these capabilities within Oracle.

Account Security

You may protect database accounts via passwords. You can also enable an autologin capability, allowing users who have accessed a host account to access a related database account without entering a database password. Having an account or privileges in one database does not give a user an account or privileges in any other database.

System-Level Privileges

You can create system-level roles from the full set of system-level privileges (such as CREATE TABLE, CREATE INDEX, SELECT ANY TABLE) to extend the basic set of system-level roles. CONNECT, RESOURCE, and DBA are provided as standard roles for application users, developers, and DBAs, respectively.

Object Security

Users who have created objects may grant privileges on those objects to other users via the **grant** command. They can also **grant** a user access to tables **with grant option**, in which case that user (the grantee) can **grant** access to the tables to additional users.

Auditing

You can audit user activities that involve database objects via the **audit** command. **Audit**ed actions may include table accesses, login attempts, and DBA-privileged activities. The results of these **audit**s are stored in an audit table within the database. In addition to the provided **audit**ing capabilities, you can create database triggers to record changes in data values.

Fine-Grained Auditing

One failing of object auditing is that although you can see that the object was accessed and see who accessed it, you cannot see what values were changed and what the old values were. Oracle9i provides a PL/SQL package to enable fine-grained object auditing to help you track accessed information in your database and how the information has been modified. Fine-grained auditing is discussed in detail in Chapter 10.

Virtual Private Database

Oracle8i, Release 3, introduced the Virtual Private Database (VPD) to provide fine-grained access control coupled with a secure application context. With VPD you establish policies in the form of predicates (**where** clauses) that are attached to every query that users present to the database. An organization using VPD only needs to build a security structure once in the data server. Since the security policies are attached to the data instead of the application, security rules are enforced at all times and from any access approach. Thus, the data presented from a query is identical regardless of the connection mode: from an application, SQL*Plus, or an ODBC driver. VPD relies on several mechanisms to ensure data privacy for each user. To accomplish data separation, ensure that your tables are designed to enable restricting data access according to the values in one or more columns. Chapter 10 discusses VPD in detail.

Using OEM

Since Oracle7.3, the Oracle Enterprise Manager (OEM), a graphical user interface (GUI) tool, has been supplied to enable DBAs to manage their databases from a personal computer. With the release of Oracle9i, the OEM toolset provides a much more robust interface for remote database administration. With the release of OEM version 2 in Oracle8i, all DBAs can use the same central repository to perform their work. In addition to those changes, OEM version 2 includes task scheduling and assignment features to enable around-the-clock database coverage.

With all versions of OEM, you must make several key decisions prior to installing and configuring the tool. You will need to decide where the OEM repository is to be created and how and when you are going to perform backups to protect this repository. Since you can use OEM as an interface to the Oracle Recovery Manager (RMAN), recovery information can be stored in the OEM repository. Although there is nothing to stop you from creating the OEM repository in a production database, if you should lose this database, where will you get the recovery information? You may want to create a small, separate database in which to store the OEM repository. You should ensure that this repository is being backed up frequently so that recovery of the repository is assured. Also, once you declare a database as the repository database, it will no longer be available from the OEM Server Manager tool, although you will be able to start and stop the database if you launch the OEM console in stand-alone mode.

If you are the only DBA working with the OEM toolset, you will not have to consider who will handle administration of specific databases in your environment. If, however, there are several DBAs at the site, you will need to determine task definitions, database responsibilities, and schedules. With OEM, you can grant levels of access and privilege to each DBA in the group on a task-by-task basis. You can configure OEM to enable you to send email requests and assignments to other DBAs or take control of a problem to speed resolution.

If you have a previous version of OEM on your system, migrate the repository to the newest version to take advantage of the new features. If you have more than one repository on your system, you will need to take precautions to ensure that you migrate each version of the repository without damaging currently stored information.

With the Oracle9*i* release of OEM, you can examine the contents of the redo log files using the log miner feature described in Chapter 11.

Oracle supports SNMP (Simple Network Management Protocol). By supporting SNMP, Oracle products can be easily integrated into monitoring tools for systems and networks. Its SNMP support enables Oracle to be monitored by existing tools on enterprise networks. Key benefits of SNMP include the following:

- Easy integration into enterprise networks managed via SNMP tools

- Central monitoring of all services required for database access

- Support for automatic alerts for critical situations

- Support for automatic reactions to alert conditions

Although you do not have to use OEM to manage your databases, it provides a common interface to your databases. As your enterprise grows in size (and in number of databases and number of DBAs), the consistency of the DBA interface will support consistent implementation of your change control and production control processes.

CHAPTER
2

Hardware
Configurations and
Considerations

lthough each Oracle database will be built from the same basic components, the options available to you depend on your hardware platform and operating system. In this chapter, you will see the standard architectures available—the ways that the components are usually put together in the most common environments.

Regardless of the configuration you use, you must be able to guarantee your database's availability, recoverability, and security. As you add components to your environment, you add potential failure points. Your backup and recovery plans (see Chapter 11), security plans (see Chapter 10), monitoring plans (see Chapter 6), and tuning plans (see Chapter 8) must take all components of your hardware configuration into account.

Architecture Overview

An Oracle database consists of physical files, memory areas, and processes. The distribution of these components varies depending on the database architecture chosen.

The data in the database is stored in physical files (called *datafiles*) on a disk. As it is used, that data is stored in memory. Oracle uses memory areas to improve performance and to manage the sharing of data between users. The main memory area in a database is called the *System Global Area* (*SGA*). To read and write data between the SGA and the datafiles, Oracle uses a set of background processes shared by all users.

A database *server* (also known as an *instance*) is a set of memory structures and background processes that accesses a set of database files. The relationship between servers and databases is illustrated in Figure 2-1.

The characteristics of the database server—such as the size of the SGA and the number of background processes—are specified during startup. These parameters are stored in a file called init.ora. The init.ora file for a database usually contains the instance name in the filename; a database named ORA1 will typically have an init.ora file named initora1.ora.

The init.ora file may, in turn, call a corresponding config.ora file. If a config.ora file is used, it usually only stores the parameter values for unchanging information, such as database block size and database name. The initialization files are only read during startup; modifications to them will not take effect until the next startup. As of Oracle9i, you can use *server parameter files* in place of traditional init.ora parameter files. A server parameter file is a binary file that Oracle creates at the operating system level to store the database parameter settings. The **create spfile** command creates a server parameter file based on the database's current parameter settings; the file is automatically updated when you use the **alter system** command to change parameter settings. When you start the database, Oracle first checks for a system parameter file

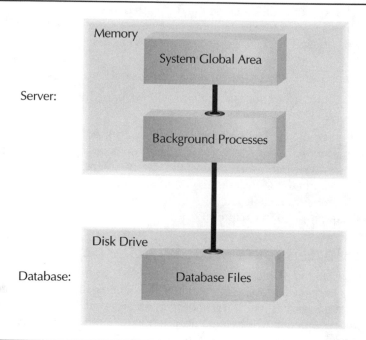

FIGURE 2-1. *Single server on a stand-alone host*

called spfile*instance_name*.ora, then a system parameter file called spfile.ora in the $ORACLE_HOME/dbs directory on a UNIX system; if neither exists, then it looks for the traditional init.ora file. You can use the **pfile** clause during **startup** commands to force the use of an init.ora file in place of an existing system parameter file. To create an init.ora file from an existing system parameter file, use the **create pfile** command.

Stand-Alone Hosts

The simplest conceptual configuration for a database is a single server accessing a single database on a stand-alone, single-disk host. In this configuration, shown in Figure 2-1, all of the files are stored on the server's sole device, and there are only one SGA and one set of Oracle background processes on the server.

The architecture shown in Figure 2-1 represents the minimum configuration. All other database configurations are modifications to this base structure.

The files stored on the disk include the database datafiles, online logfiles, control files, and the host's parameter file. As shown in Figure 2-1, there are two main interface points in the database:

■ Between the database files and the background processes

■ Between the background processes and the SGA

Tuning efforts mostly consist of improving the performance of these interface points. If the memory area dedicated to the database is large enough, then fewer repetitive reads will be performed against the database files. Since the files are all stored on the sole available disk device in this configuration, you should try to minimize the number of datafile accesses performed. File tuning topics are covered in detail in Chapter 4 and in Chapter 8.

Stand-Alone Hosts with Disk Arrays

If multiple disks are available, then the database files can be physically separated. Separating files improves database performance by reducing the amount of contention between the database files. During database operation, information from multiple files is commonly needed to service a transaction or query. If the files are not distributed across multiple disks, then the system will need to read from multiple files on the same disk concurrently. The separation of files across multiple disks is shown in Figure 2-2.

The database uses several types of files. These file types, and guidelines for their optimal distribution across multiple disks, are described in Chapter 4.

Control File Mirroring

The parameter file for the server that accesses the database is stored in the Oracle software directories, usually in a directory under the Oracle software base directory. In the default directory configuration, an init.ora file is stored in a directory named (for UNIX) /orasw/app/oracle/admin/instance_name/pfile. For NT systems, the init.ora file is stored in the \admin*instance name*\pfile directory under your Oracle software home directory. If you are using an init.ora file in place of a server parameter file and the instance name is ORA1, the init.ora file will be named initora1.ora and will be stored in /orasw/app/oracle/admin/ORA1/pfile. The init.ora file does not list the names of the datafiles or online redo log files for the database; these are stored within the control file and the data dictionary. However, the init.ora file does list the names of the control files for the database. On a multiple-disk host, the control files should be stored on separate disks on separate controllers. The database will keep them in sync. By storing mirrored control files on multiple disks, you greatly reduce the risk of database problems caused by media failures.

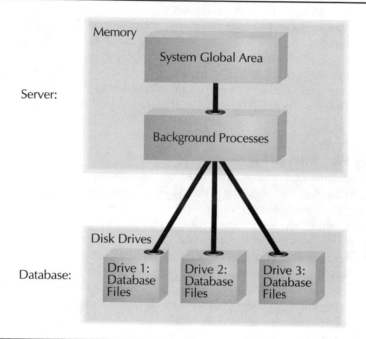

FIGURE 2-2.   *Single server on a stand-alone host with multiple disks*

The following listing shows the entry for the CONTROL_FILES parameter in the initialization parameter file:

```
control_files            = (/db01/oracle/ORA1/ctrl1ora1.ctl,
                            /db02/oracle/ORA1/ctrl2ora1.ctl,
                            /db03/oracle/ORA1/ctrl3ora1.ctl)
```

The preceding listing names the three control files. If the preceding entry is used during the database creation, then the database will automatically create the three control files listed here. If you want to add additional control files to an existing database, follow this procedure:

1. Shut down the database.

2. Copy one of the current control files to the new location.

3. Edit the init.ora file, adding the new control file's name to the CONTROL_FILES entry.

4. Restart the database.

The new control file will then be activated.

A single init.ora file can call multiple initialization files via the IFILE parameter. You can also nest initialization files. For example, init.ora may have an IFILE entry to include a file called tuning.ora. The tuning.ora file, in turn, may have an IFILE entry for a file called disktuning.ora containing tuning parameters related to disk I/O. You can use the support for multiple initialization files to group related parameters; however, you must be careful not to supersede a parameter setting by using it in more than one of the included files.

Redo Log File Mirroring

As noted in the previous section, the database will automatically mirror control files. The database can also mirror online redo log files. To mirror online redo log files, use *redo log groups.* If you use redo log groups, the database will mirror the files.

When mirroring redo log groups, the LGWR (Log Writer) background process simultaneously writes to all of the members of the current online redo log group. Thus, rather than cycling through the redo log files, it instead cycles through *groups* of redo log files. Since the members of a group are usually placed on separate disk drives, there is no disk contention between the files, and LGWR thus experiences little change in performance. See Chapter 4 for further information on the placement of redo log files.

You can create redo log groups via the **create database** command. You can also add redo log groups to the database after it has been created, via the **alter database** command. The following listing shows an example of the addition of a redo log group to an existing database. The group is referred to in this example as GROUP 4. Using group numbers eases their administration; number them sequentially, starting with 1.

```
alter database
add logfile group 4
('/db01/oracle/CC1/log_1c.dbf',
 '/db02/oracle/CC1/log_2c.dbf') size 5M;
```

To add a new redo log file to an existing group, use the **alter database** command shown in the following listing. The following example adds a third member to the GROUP 4 redo log group.

```
alter database
add logfile member '/db03/oracle/CC1/log_3c.dbf'
 to group 4;
```

When you use the **add logfile member** option of the **alter database** command, no file sizing information is specified. All members of the group must have the same size. Since the group already exists, the database already knows how large to make the new file.

Archived Redo Log File Mirroring

You can instruct the database to write multiple copies of each archived redo log file (starting with Oracle 8.0) as it is written. In init.ora, the LOG_ARCHIVE_DEST parameter sets the primary storage location for the archived redo log files. In Oracle8.0, you can use the LOG_ARCHIVE_DUPLEX_DEST parameter to specify a second location for your archived redo logs. While writing the archived redo log files, Oracle will write to both locations. The write to the primary location must always succeed; otherwise, the database will be unavailable when the LGWR process tries to write to that redo log file. Database activity will continue when that write succeeds.

The write to the second archive log destination area, as specified by LOG_ARCHIVE_DUPLEX_DEST, may be optional. If you set LOG_ARCHIVE_MIN_SUCCEED_DEST to 1, then the write to only one location (the first one, specified by LOG_ARCHIVE_DEST) must be successful. If the write to the secondary location fails, the database availability will not be interrupted.

The init.ora parameters for archive log destination areas change as of Oracle8i. In Oracle8i and above, the LOG_ARCHIVE_DEST parameter is obsolete, replaced by LOG_ARCHIVE_DEST_n. You can specify up to five archive log destination areas in Oracle8i and up to ten destination areas in Oracle9i, replacing n with the number of the destination. For example, you can specify two separate archived redo log destination areas via the LOG_ARCHIVE_DEST_1 and LOG_ARCHIVE_DEST_2 parameters, as shown in the following listing:

```
log_archive_dest_1 = '/db00/arch'
log_archive_dest_2 = '/db01/arch'
```

The Oracle8.0 LOG_ARCHIVE_MIN_SUCCEED_DEST parameter is obsolete in Oracle8i and above. In place of that parameter, you can use the LOG_ARCHIVE_DEST_STATE_n parameter to enable or disable archive log destinations. For example, to disable the second archive log destination, set LOG_ARCHIVE_DEST_STATE_2 to DEFER. By default, the state values are set to ENABLE.

If you do not use Oracle8's internal ability to mirror the archived redo log files, then you should mirror them at the operating system level. You can use RAID techniques (see Chapter 4) as part of the hardware mirroring approach. In general, you should favor the hardware system's mirroring solution over Oracle's, provided the hardware system can support mirroring without significant performance impact. Mirroring solutions that use Oracle's methods or the operating system methods are more portable across platforms but may impact your CPU usage.

Operating system mirroring solutions do not protect you from all potential problems. If there is a bad write to the logfile, operating system mirroring will copy the error to the mirror. Using Oracle mirroring, each file is written to separately, so if one of the writes to a redo log file fails, the database continues to run. In addition, the archiving process can archive faster if there are multiple redo log files in a group to read from while archiving.

Stand-Alone Hosts with Disk Shadowing

Many operating systems give you the ability to maintain duplicate, synchronized copies of files via a process known as *disk shadowing, volume shadowing,* or *mirroring.*

There are two benefits to shadowing your disks. First, the shadow set of disks serves as a backup in the event of a disk failure. In most operating systems, a disk failure will cause the corresponding disk from the shadow set to automatically take the place of the failed disk. Second, most operating systems that support volume shadowing can direct file I/O requests to use the shadow set of files instead of the main set of files. The redirection reduces the I/O load on the main set of disks and results in better performance for file I/Os. The use of disk shadowing is shown in Figure 2-3.

NOTE
Operating system–level disk shadowing may impact write performance if the operating system does not support asynchronous writes.

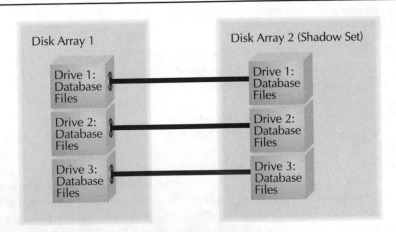

FIGURE 2-3.　*Disk shadowing*

The type of shadowing shown in Figure 2-3 is called RAID-1 (redundant array of independent disks) shadowing. In this type of shadowing, each disk in the main set of disks is paired, one-to-one, with a disk in the shadow set. Depending on your operating system, other shadowing options may be available. In RAID-3 and RAID-5 shadowing, for example, a set of disks is treated as a single logical unit, and each file is automatically "striped" across each disk. In RAID-3 and RAID-5, a parity-check system provides a means of recovering a damaged or failed member of the set of disks.

The method of shadowing that is used will affect how the files are distributed across devices. For example, datafiles that store tables are usually stored on a different disk than the datafiles that store those tables' indexes. However, if RAID-3 or RAID-5 is used, then the distinction between disks is blurred. Accessing a datafile when using those options will almost always require that all of the disks in the set be accessed, so contention between the disks is more likely. The magnitude of the potential contention should not be severe. In RAID-5, for example, the first block of data is stored on the first disk of a set, and the second block is stored on the next disk. In that configuration, the database only has to read a single block off a disk before moving on to the next disk. Any contention that results from multiple accesses of the same disk should therefore last only as long as it takes to perform a single block read.

The more significant tuning issue with RAID environments concerns their write performance. During a write operation, a RAID-5 system must read the original block, read the parity block, calculate the new parity data, and write the changed block and parity block to disk. The high volume of disk activity associated with writes in a RAID-5 system makes RAID-5 much more effective for write-once read-many applications (such as data warehouses) than for OLTP applications.

Very large databases tend to use more advanced forms of RAID, such as the RAID-S system used to manage EMC devices. In those environments, the data is striped across a large number of disk devices, reducing the opportunity for contention. Work with the system administrators to understand the way the data will be striped across the disks; the capacity and striping technology frequently resolve most I/O problems that may occur. Even in such self-managed environments, you should still use an OFA approach to separating your objects across tablespaces to simplify maintenance.

Stand-Alone Hosts with Multiple Databases

You can create multiple databases on a single host. Each database will have a separate set of files and will be accessed by a different server. Guidelines for appropriate directory structures are provided in Chapter 4.

Figure 2-4 shows a single host supporting two databases. Since each database requires an SGA and background processes, the host must be able to support the memory and process requirements that this configuration will place upon it.

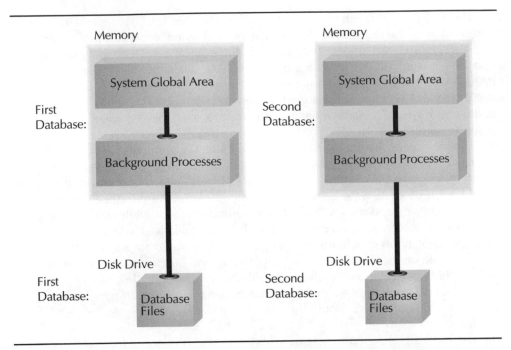

FIGURE 2-4. *Stand-alone host with multiple databases*

As noted earlier, these configurations are modifications to the base database architecture. In this case, you simply create a second database that mimics the structure of the first. Note that although the two databases are on the same host, they do not (in this case) communicate with each other. The background processes and user processes from the first database cannot access the database files from the second database.

Multiple databases on the same server typically share the same Oracle source code directories. The parameter files for the two databases in Figure 2-4 are stored in separate directories, since the instance name is part of the directory structure. For example, if the two server names were ORA1 and ORA2, then the associated init.ora files would be named initora1.ora and initora2.ora, respectively. The first would be stored in /orasw/app/oracle/admin/ORA1/pfile, and the second would be stored in /orasw/app/oracle/admin/ORA2/pfile. Their server parameters, like their datafiles, are completely independent of each other.

Although the databases may share the same source code directories, their datafiles should be stored in separate directories—and, if available, on separate disks. Sample directory structures for datafiles are provided in Chapter 4. If multiple databases have datafiles stored on the same device, then neither database's I/O statistics will accurately reflect the I/O load on that device. Instead, you will need to sum the I/O attributed to each disk by each database.

Simplifying the Upgrade Process

If your operating system can support multiple versions of the Oracle software, then the process for upgrading your Oracle database version may be greatly simplified. You may be able to upgrade from one incremental release to the next with minimal administrative effort. Oracle provides scripts to upgrade the data dictionary between releases or to downgrade the data dictionary to a prior release. See the README.doc file (in the /rdbms/doc subdirectory under your Oracle software home directory) for the names of the catalog upgrade scripts to use.

Networked Hosts

When hosts supporting Oracle databases are connected via a network, those databases can communicate via Oracle Net (formerly called SQL*Net and Net8). As shown in Figure 2-5, the Oracle Net drivers rely on the local networking protocol to achieve connectivity between two servers. The Oracle Net portion then supports communications between the application layers on the two servers. Oracle Net is described in Part III of the book.

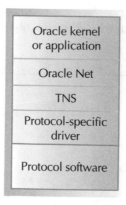

FIGURE 2-5. *Oracle Net architecture*

The database configuration options available in a networked environment depend on the network's configurations and options. The following sections describe the main architectures listed here:

- Networks of databases, used for remote queries

- Distributed databases, used for remote transactions

- Real Application Clusters, in which multiple servers access the same database

- Parallel query operations, in which multiple CPUs serve a single operation

- Client/server databases

- Three-tier architectures

- Web-accessible databases

- Oracle Enterprise Transparent Gateway access

- Standby databases

- Replicated databases

- External file access

- External table access

Networks of Databases

Oracle Net allows databases to communicate with other databases that are accessible via a network. Each of the servers involved must be running Oracle Net, as illustrated in Figure 2-6.

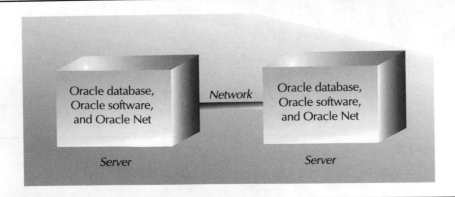

FIGURE 2-6.   *Networked hosts with databases*

In Figure 2-6, two hosts are shown. Each host can operate a database in stand-alone fashion, as was previously shown in Figure 2-1 and Figure 2-2. Each host in this example maintains a copy of the Oracle software and one or more Oracle databases.

For the databases to be able to communicate, their respective servers must be able to communicate with each other. As shown in Figure 2-6, the database layers of communication rely on the networking software and hardware to establish the communications link between the servers. Once that communications link is created, the database software can use it to transport data packets between remote databases.

The Oracle software used to transfer data between databases is called Oracle Net. In its simplest configuration, Oracle Net consists of a host process that waits for connections via a specific connection path. When those connections are detected, it follows the instructions passed via the connection and returns the requested data. A full description of Oracle Net is found in Part III.

For Oracle Net to receive and process communications, the host must run a process called a *listener*. The listener process must be running on each host that will be involved in the database communications. Each server must be configured to assign this process to a specific communications port (see Part III for an example).

Examples of the use of database connections are shown in the following sections. Networked database applications include queries against remote databases and transactions against multiple remote databases.

Remote Queries

Queries against remote Oracle databases use *database links* to identify the path that the query should take to find the data. A database link specifies, either directly or indirectly, the host, database, and account that should be used to access a specified object. The database link identifies the host and database to access by referring to the *service name* for that database. When a database link is referenced by a SQL statement, Oracle opens a session in the specified database and executes the SQL statement there. The data is then returned, and the remote session may stay open (it stays open by default) in case it is needed again. Database links can be created as public links (by DBAs, making the link available to all users in the local database) or as private links available only to the user creating the database link.

The following example creates a public database link called HR_LINK:

```
create public database link HR_LINK
connect to HR identified by PUFFINSTUFF
using 'hq';
```

The **create database link** command, as shown in this example, has several parameters:

■   The optional keyword **public**, which allows DBAs to create links for all users in a database

■ The name of the link (HR_LINK, in this example)

■ The account to connect to (if none is specified, then the local username and password will be used in the remote database)

■ The service name (hq), which is defined in the tnsnames.ora file

To use this link, simply add it as a suffix to table names in commands. The following example queries a remote table by using the HR_LINK database link:

```
select * from EMPLOYEE@HR_LINK
 where  Office='ANNAPOLIS';
```

Database links allow for queries to access remote databases. They also allow the information regarding the physical location of the data—its host, database, and schema—to be made transparent to the user. For example, if a user in the local database created a view based on a database link, any access of the local view would automatically query the remote database. The user performing the query would not have to know where the data resides.

The following listing illustrates location transparency. A view is created using the HR_LINK database link defined earlier in this section. Access to this view can then be granted to users in the local database, as shown here:

```
create view LOCAL_EMP
    as select * from EMPLOYEE@HR_LINK
 where Office='ANNAPOLIS';

grant select on LOCAL_EMP to PUBLIC;
```

When a user queries the LOCAL_EMP view, Oracle will use the HR_LINK database link to open a session using the connection information specified for the HR_LINK database link. The query will be executed and the remote data will be returned to the local user. The local user of LOCAL_EMP will not be informed that the data came from a remote database.

Remote Updates: The Advanced Replication Option

In addition to querying data from remote databases, you can **update** databases that are located on remote hosts. The **update**s against these remote databases can be combined with **update**s against the local database into a single logical unit of work: either they all get **commit**ted or they all get rolled back.

A sample set of transactions is shown in Figure 2-7. One of the transactions goes against a database on a remote host and one against the local host. In this example, a local table named EMPLOYEE is **update**d; a remote table named EMPLOYEE, in a

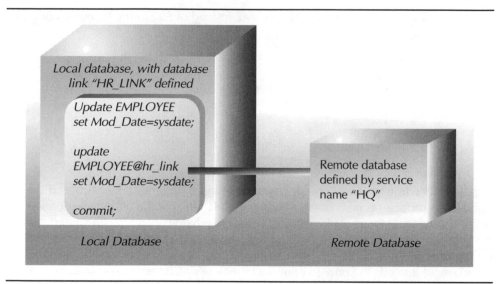

FIGURE 2-7.   *Sample distributed transaction*

database defined by the HR_LINK database link, is also **update**d as part of the same transaction. If either **update** fails, then both of the transactions will be rolled back. Coordination of remote transactions relies on Two-Phase Commit, described in greater detail in Part III.

All hosts involved in replication or distributed transactions must be running Oracle Net, be configured to support Oracle replication, and be configured to allow host-host communications. After Oracle Net is configured for each host, any files associated with it must be properly configured. These configuration files allow the database to interpret the service names shown in the **create database link** command earlier in this chapter.

Each host that runs Oracle Net may maintain a file called tnsnames.ora. The tnsnames.ora file defines the connect descriptors for the service names that are accessible from that host. For example, the following listing shows the tnsnames.ora file entry for the HQ service name used in the HR_LINK example:

```
HQ =(DESCRIPTION=
     (ADDRESS=
          (PROTOCOL=TCP)
          (HOST=HQ)
          (PORT=1521))
     (CONNECT DATA=
          (SID=loc)))
```

Oracle8*i* and above use SERVICE_NAME instead of SID in the tnsnames.ora file:

```
S817.us.oracle.com =
  (DESCRIPTION =
    (ADDRESS_LIST =
      (ADDRESS = (PROTOCOL = TCP)(HOST = sdg-lap)(PORT = 1521))
    )
    (CONNECT_DATA =
      (SERVICE_NAME = S817.us.oracle.com)
    )
  )
```

The preceding listing example shows a number of different aspects of the connection process (its parameters are specific to TCP/IP, but the underlying connection needs are the same for all platforms). First, there is the hardware addressing information—the protocol, the host name, and the communications port to use. The second section defines the instance name—in this case, loc. Since the tnsnames.ora file tells the database all it needs to know to connect to remote databases, you should keep the contents of this file consistent across hosts. See Part III for information on this and other aspects affecting the management of location transparency.

The logical unit of work for distributed transactions is processed via Oracle's implementation of Two-Phase Commit (2PC). If there is a network or server failure that prevents the unit of work from successfully completing, then it is possible that the data in the databases affected by the transactions will be out of sync. A background process, RECO, automatically checks for incomplete transactions and resolves them as soon as all of the resources it needs become available.

The maximum number of concurrent distributed transactions for a database is set via the DISTRIBUTED_TRANSACTIONS parameter of its init.ora file. If this parameter is set to 0, then no distributed transactions will be allowed and the recovery background process will not be started when the instance starts.

Two data dictionary views are helpful when diagnosing uncompleted distributed transactions. The DBA_2PC_NEIGHBORS view contains information about incoming and outgoing connections for pending transactions. DBA_2PC_PENDING contains information about distributed transactions awaiting recovery. If your distributed transaction encounters errors, check DBA_2PC_NEIGHBORS and DBA_2PC_PENDING for details.

Real Application Clusters

The configurations discussed previously in this chapter have featured databases that are accessed by a single server. However, depending on your hardware configurations, it may be possible to use multiple servers to access a single database. This configuration, previously called the *Oracle Parallel Server* (OPS) and now called *Real Application Clusters* (RAC), is illustrated in Figure 2-8.

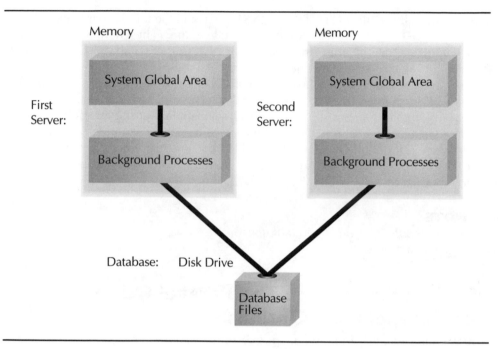

FIGURE 2-8. *Real Application Clusters (RAC)*

As shown in Figure 2-8, two separate servers share the same set of datafiles. Usually, these servers are located on separate hosts of a hardware cluster. A cluster is usually a group of individual hosts that have been connected with a high-bandwidth, low-latency interconnect fiber cable via which they pass messages to one another, allowing them to operate as a single entity. Using a clustered configuration provides the following benefits:

- More memory resources are available, since two machines are being used.

- If one of the hosts goes down, the other can still access the datafiles, thus providing a means of recovering from disasters.

- Users can be separated by the type of processing they perform, and high-CPU users will be kept on a separate host from regular online processing transactions.

When setting up a set of servers to use RAC, a number of database structures and parameters specific to RAC must be specified. First, to enable RAC, the parameter CLUSTER_DATABASE (formerly PARALLEL_SERVER) must be set to TRUE. You must also establish a value for CLUSTER_DATABASE_INSTANCES (previously called PARALLEL_SERVER_INSTANCES) in the init.ora parameter file. Set the CLUSTER_DATABASE_INSTANCES value to the highest number of databases you want to start at one time for a Real Application Cluster database, although you can set the value to 10 and then just start five databases.

The central database must be configured to handle separate servers, with a set of rollback segments that each database instance can use. To best manage these rollback segments, create a separate rollback segment tablespace for each server, using the instance name as part of the tablespace name. For example, if the instance names were ORA1 and ORA2, then the rollback segment tablespace names should be RBS_ORA1 and RBS_ORA2. For further information on rollback segments and undo tablespaces, see Chapter 7.

NOTE
You can only have one undo tablespace active at a time.

Multiple Processors: The Parallel Query and Parallel Load Options

You can take advantage of multiple processors to perform transactions and queries. The work performed to resolve a single database request can be performed by multiple, coordinated processors. Distributing the workload across multiple processors may improve the performance of transactions and queries.

The Parallel Query Option (PQO) architecture of Oracle allows almost all database operations to be parallelized. Operations that can take advantage of the PQO include **create table as select**, **create index**, full table scans, index scans, sorts, **insert**s, **update**s, **delete**s, and most queries.

NOTE
Parallel update and parallel delete are only available when the partition option is installed.

The extent to which parallelism is employed by the database depends on the **degree** and **instances** parameters of the **parallel** keyword used with these commands (see Appendix A). The **degree** parameter specifies the degree of parallelism—the number of query servers used on each instance—for the given operation. The **instances** parameter specifies how the operation is to be split among the instances of a RAC installation. You can specify your instance's parallelism rules—such as the minimum number of query servers—in the instance's parameter file. The maximum number of concurrently available parallel query server processes is set by the PARALLEL_MAX_SERVERS parameter in init.ora; the minimum number is set by the PARALLEL_MIN_SERVERS parameter. The number of disks on which a table's data is stored and the number of processors available on the server are used to generate the default parallelism for a query.

You can use the PARALLEL_AUTOMATIC_TUNING init.ora parameter to automatically set many of the available parallel query–related init.ora parameters. One of the automatically set parameters, PARALLEL_ADAPTIVE_MULTI_USER, will reduce the parallelism of your operations if there are multiple active users performing parallel operations in the database. Since there is a limit to the number of parallel query server processes available, reducing parallelism for an operation prevents it from using all of the available resources. You can also use the Database Resource Manager to limit parallelism, as described in Chapter 5.

In addition to parallelizing queries, you can parallelize data loads if you use the SQL*Loader Direct Path loader. See Chapter 8 for tips related to tuning bulk data inserts.

Client/Server Database Applications

In a host-host configuration, as described earlier in this chapter, an Oracle database exists on each host, and the databases communicate via Oracle Net. However, a host without a database can access a remote database, typically by having application programs on one host access a database on a second host. In that configuration, the host running the application is called a *client* and the other is called the *server*. This configuration is illustrated in Figure 2-9.

As shown in Figure 2-9, the client must have the ability to communicate across the network to the server. The application programs may be run on the client side, with the database used mainly for I/O. The CPU costs for running the application

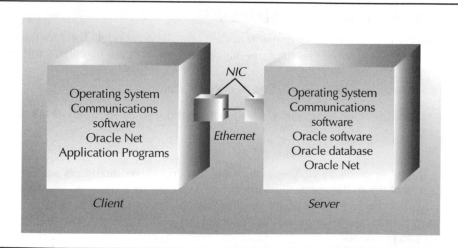

FIGURE 2-9.   *Client/server configuration*

programs are thus charged to the client PC rather than to the server. For this configuration to work, the client must be running Oracle Net. When the client's application program prompts the user for database connection information, the service name should be specified. The application will then open a session in the remote database.

Using a client/server configuration reduces the amount of work performed by the server. However, shifting an application to a client/server configuration will not automatically improve the system's performance, for two reasons:

- CPU resources may not have been a problem before. Usually, CPU resources are used often during the day and infrequently during off-hours. You may wish to alter the schedule of CPU usage by running batch processes or large programs at off-hours rather than introducing a client/server configuration as a solution for a CPU-bound system.

- The application may not have been redesigned. Designing for a client/server environment requires you to take into account the data volumes that are sent across the network for every database access. In server-based applications, this is not a problem. In client/server applications, the network traffic must be considered during planning and tuning.

There are many different ways to implement the client/server configuration, depending on the hardware that is available. The implementation shown in Figure 2-9 is fairly common; it would be used by an ad hoc query tool running on a PC to access an Oracle database running on a server.

Three-Tier Architectures

A three-tier architecture is an extension of the client/server model. The function of each tier is dependent on your implementation, but the tiers are usually as follows:

- A client, used for presentation of the application

- An application server, used for the application's business logic processing

- The database server, used for storage and retrieval of data

In a three-tier architecture, the application's processing requirements are moved from the client tier to the application server tier. Typically, the application server is more powerful than the client, so the application's performance may benefit. Performance may also be improved by reducing the amount of traffic between the database server and the client. Less data may be sent to the client, since more of the interaction may be performed between the application server and the database server.

The longer-term benefits of a three-tier configuration are derived from the simplified maintenance of the client. Since the application resides on the application server, most of the upgrades will be focused on upgrading the application server. If you do not have extensive configuration control on your client machines, a three-tier architecture may reduce your application maintenance costs.

However, migrating from a client/server architecture to a three-tier architecture is not always simple, straightforward, or beneficial. If you have a well-configured network, controlled client machines, and a well-tuned application, moving to a three-tier architecture may result in no benefits—and potential costs. For example, you will need to redesign your application to reduce network traffic between the clients and the application server; failing to do so may impact the performance of your application. Furthermore, the process for upgrading an application changes—instead of upgrading clients, you will be upgrading an application server used by many clients. Since the application server usage is centralized, you will encounter more difficulty in testing application changes without affecting all application users. However, when changing an application, you will only need to change the application on one server one time.

Figure 2-10 shows a generic three-tier configuration for an Oracle application. The application server and the database server communicate via Oracle Net. The protocol for communications between the clients and the application server depends on your environment; it may use Oracle Net, or it may use an Internet protocol such as HTTP.

In any configuration, your application should avoid unnecessary traffic between the client and the database. In a three-tier application, you should be particularly mindful of the traffic between the database and the client, since there are more components between them. The additional components between the client and the database may adversely impact the performance of every database query performed.

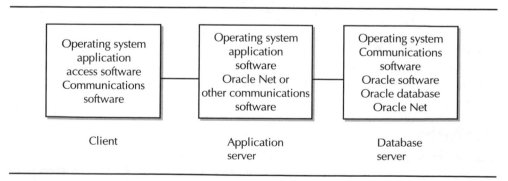

FIGURE 2-10. *Three-tier configuration*

In many three-tier applications, little data validation is performed at the client side, reducing the number of database lookups required during transaction processing. The lack of data validation queries may be offset via the use of drop-down list boxes of values or multiple-choice check boxes within the application.

Web-Accessible Databases
You can configure your databases to be accessible via the World Wide Web. External clients will communicate with your application software (middle tier) and then through your firewall router, which in turn will pass data requests to the database server. Web-accessible databases, in architecture, are based on the three-tier model shown in Figure 2-10. For example, the client tier may be your personal computer, running a Web browser. Your browser communicates with the middle-tier application software via HTTP. The middle tier communicates with the firewall router, which passes the requests to the database server via Oracle Net or via Internet Inter-ORB Protocol (IIOP) if Java is used within the database. The ideal architecture for secure Web accessibility is to field your Web application (middle tier) software behind one firewall and your database server behind a second firewall. Web configurations commonly use Oracle9iAS, Oracle's application server middle tier. See Part III of this book for a description of 9iAS and its administration.

Oracle Enterprise Gateway Access
You can create a database link to a service that is not an Oracle database. You can then query data via the database link, and the data will be queried as if the source data is an Oracle database.

To access non-Oracle data, you will need to use the Oracle Enterprise Gateway product (formerly called Oracle Transparent Gateway). A separate gateway is required for each type of database engine accessed. The gateway is run on the source host for the data being accessed. For example, if the source data is stored in an AS/400 database, then the Oracle Enterprise Gateway software for AS/400 is installed on the AS/400 server. When executed, the gateway software creates a listener on the source server that acts like an Oracle Net listener. You can then access specific data objects within the AS/400 database, provided you have a username and password for that database.

Oracle Enterprise Gateway is an extension of the server/server configuration shown in Figure 2-6; the difference is that one host's database and database software are non-Oracle.

Standby Databases
You can configure a second database as a standby copy of a primary database. A *standby* database is a special case of a server/server configuration. Each server has a full copy of the Oracle software, and the database file structures are usually

identical (if they are not, you will need to build a separate control file for the standby database). You must always create a separate control file for a standby database using the **alter database create standby controlfile as '*filename*'** command and then copy it to the standby database. The two hosts should use the same operating system versions and database software versions.

In the event of a disaster in the production database, you can open the standby database with little data lost—you will usually lose the contents of your online redo log files. As archived redo log files are generated by the production instance, they must be copied to the standby system either manually or by the ARCH process. The standby database remains in recovery mode until it is needed, although you can open it in a read-only fashion starting with Oracle8i and then return it to recovery mode. Once the standby database is opened in a read-write mode, it becomes the primary database and cannot be easily reconfigured as the standby database. In Oracle9i, a DBA can use the graceful failover methodology to fail over from the primary to the standby and later back to the primary as necessary very easily without re-creating either database.

To automate the transfer of archived redo log files to the standby database, use the LOG_ARCHIVE_DEST_*n* parameters. In place of a directory name, specify a service name as listed in the local tnsnames.ora file as the destination for the standby database's copy of the archived redo log files.

For example, the production database's parameter file may contain the following entries:

```
log_archive_dest_1 = '/db00/arch'
log_archive_dest_state_1 = enable
```

The first archive log destination area is the primary destination for new archived redo log files. The second set of parameters tells the database to write copies of the archived redo log files to the standby database's destination area. For this example, the standby database has a service name of STBY:

```
log_archive_dest_2 = "service=stby.world mandatory reopen=60"
log_archive_dest_state_2 = enable
```

The LOG_ARCHIVE_DEST_2 setting specifies the service name of the standby database. The STBY instance must be accessible via Oracle Net. If there is a connectivity problem, the ARCH process will attempt to reopen the connection 60 seconds later.

In Oracle8i, Release 3, a script-based implementation called the *Oracle8i Data Guard* was introduced to enable easier standby database management. Tasks such as managing the production database, the physical standby database, associated applications, and the log transport services are performed through a command-line interface. Oracle9i Data Guard is used to automate many of the tasks handled by the Oracle8i version using both a GUI interface and the DGMGRL command-line interface.

Each tool is used for different tasks. You use the GUI tool, the Data Guard Manager, for configuration, setup, and operational tasks and the command-line interface, DGMGRL, for basic monitoring using some of the V$ views; to issue role changes to fail over from one machine to another; and to establish the Data Guard environment. See the *Oracle Server Administrator's Guide* for further directions on setting up and maintaining standby databases and using Oracle9i Data Guard.

Replicated Databases

You can use Oracle's replication features to copy and propagate changes in data between databases. You can select the tables, columns, and rows to be replicated from the source database to its replica. In its architecture, a replicated environment is a server/server configuration, as shown in Figure 2-6.

Replicated databases are typically used for the following reasons:

- To support multiple sites for OLTP access. Large data-entry requirements at remote locations can benefit from replication, since multiple sites around the world can perform data entry concurrently. Transactions can be sent between databases so that the contents of all of the related databases are relatively up-to-date.

- To create read-only or reporting databases and data warehouses. You can use replication to separate your OLTP database from the database used to support your reporting requirements.

The first option in the preceding list is *multimaster replication*: multiple databases can make changes to the data, and those changes must be propagated to the other databases in the network. Multimaster database systems must account for the resolution of conflicts that may arise during transaction processing.

The second option in the preceding list is *read-only replication*, in which data is only replicated in one direction: from one source to one or more target databases. In general, read-only replication is much simpler to administer and configure than multimaster replication. You can use the read-only copy of the database for reporting, as the basis for a data warehouse, or as a test database. Since the replica is a separate database, you can create different indexing schemes, tables, and processes in the replica database.

For details on the configuration and administration of a replicated database, see Part III of this book.

External File Access

Oracle provides numerous methods for interacting with external files. You can use external files as data sources, as script sources, or as output files. The most common external file uses are as follows:

- As source code for scripts, written in SQL*Plus, SQL, or PL/SQL.

- As output from a SQL*Plus script, generated via the **spool** command.

- As input or output from a PL/SQL program, accessed via the UTL_FILE package.

- As output from a PL/SQL script, generated via use of the DBMS_OUTPUT package.

- As external data referenced within the database via the BFILE datatype. The BFILE datatype stores a pointer to an external binary file. You must first use the **create directory** command to create a directory pointer within Oracle to the directory in which the file is stored.

- As an external program accessed via DBMS_PIPE. The program must be written in a 3GL supported by Oracle, such as C, Ada, or COBOL.

Any time your application uses external files, you should be concerned about security. The security considerations include the following:

- Are passwords hardcoded in any of the files? Scripts that execute repeatedly must have some way of logging into the database.

- Are the files secure? Can another user read the files?

- If you use UTL_FILE, is the directory it uses (identified via the UTL_FILE_DIR parameter) secure? Users will be able to see all of the files in the directory.

- If you use BFILE datatypes, is the associated directory secure? Are the files protected against modification?

If your application relies on external files, you must be sure those files are backed up using the same schedule as the database backups. If the database is lost due to a disaster, the database backups may be used during the recovery—but if the associated external files have not been backed up, the application may not be usable.

External Table Access

As of Oracle9i, you can map external file structures as if they were read-only tables. Your DDL commands for the external data will specify the column definitions for the data and tell Oracle how to map those columns to the file data. You cannot perform DML operations on the external tables, and you cannot create indexes on them. See Chapter 15 for an example of the use of external tables.

CHAPTER
3

Planning and Managing
Tablespaces

he logical configuration of a database has a dramatic effect on its performance and its ease of administration. This chapter provides guidelines for choosing the proper tablespace layout for any Oracle database.

The effective distribution of the database's logical objects is part of the *Optimal Flexible Architecture* (OFA), a configuration guideline designed to simplify database administration and optimize flexibility. Depending on the installation option you choose, the standard OFA tablespace layout may be automatically created when you install Oracle. In this chapter, you will see explanations of that layout as well as explanations of different types and states of tablespaces. Even if you cannot guarantee the physical placement of files on large RAID systems, creating OFA-compliant tablespaces will simplify administration.

The End Product

The objective of the database design described here is to configure the database so that its objects are separated by object type and activity type. This configuration will greatly reduce the amount of administrative work that must be done on the database, while decreasing the monitoring needs as well. Problems in one area will not affect the rest of the database.

The logical objects within the database must be classified based on how they are to be used and how their physical structures impact the database. The classification process includes separating tables from their indexes and separating high-activity tables from low-activity tables. Although the volume of activity against objects can only be determined during production usage, a core set of highly used tables can usually be isolated. Additional considerations include read-only data, transportable data, and the type of management desired.

The Optimal Flexible Architecture (OFA)

In the following sections, you will see the object categories as defined by OFA. Following those descriptions, you will see how to use advanced options such as read-only tablespaces.

The Starting Point: The SYSTEM Tablespace

It is possible, though not advisable, to store all of the database's objects in a single tablespace; this is analogous to storing all your files in your root directory. The SYSTEM tablespace, which is the Oracle equivalent of a root directory, stores the data dictionary tables (owned by SYS). The SYSTEM tablespace is also the location of the SYSTEM rollback segment, and during database creation the SYSTEM tablespace is temporarily used to store a second rollback segment (which is then deactivated or dropped).

There is no reason for anything other than the data dictionary tables and the SYSTEM rollback segment to be stored in the SYSTEM tablespace. Storing other segment types in SYSTEM increases the likelihood of space management problems there, which may require the tablespace to be rebuilt. Since the only way to rebuild the SYSTEM tablespace is to re-create the database, anything that can be moved out of SYSTEM should be moved.

The *data dictionary tables* store all of the information about all of the objects in the database. *Data dictionary segments*, the physical storage for the data dictionary tables, are stored in the SYSTEM tablespace and are fairly static unless large structural changes are made to the applications within the database. Data dictionary segments are created during the database creation process and are generally fairly small.

NOTE
The SYSTEM tablespace will require over 300MB for an Oracle9i database.

The more procedural objects (such as triggers and procedures) you create and the more abstract datatypes and object-oriented features you use, the larger the data dictionary segments will be. Procedural objects such as triggers store PL/SQL code in the database, and their definitions are stored in the data dictionary tables.

By default, any new user created in your database will have a default tablespace of SYSTEM. To prevent users from creating objects in the SYSTEM tablespace, any quotas on SYSTEM (which gives them the ability to create objects there) must be revoked:

```
alter user USER quota 0 on SYSTEM;
```

When you create a user (via the **create user** command) you can specify a default tablespace:

```
create user USERNAME identified by PASSWORD
default tablespace TABLESPACE_NAME;
```

Once a user has been created, you can use the

```
alter user USERNAME default tablespace TABLESPACE_NAME;
```

command to reassign the default tablespace for a user. Specifying a default tablespace for users and developers will direct objects created without a **tablespace** clause to be stored outside of the SYSTEM tablespace.

NOTE
If a user is granted the UNLIMITED TABLESPACE system privilege or the RESOURCE role, that grant will override any quota set for the user.

The following sections describe each type of database object, its usage, and why it should be stored apart from the rest of the database. By developing a consistent logical architecture, you can simplify the development of a consistent physical architecture for your databases. The more consistent your physical database architecture is, the simpler your database administration activities become.

Separating Application Data Segments: DATA

Data segments are the physical areas in which the data associated with tables and clusters is stored. Data segments tend to be very actively accessed by the database, experiencing a high number of data manipulation transactions. Managing the access requests against the data segments is often the main goal of a production database.

A typical DATA tablespace contains all of the major tables associated with an application. The high I/O volumes against these tables make them ideal candidates for isolation in their own tablespace. If you isolate the application tables to a DATA tablespace, you can separate that tablespace's datafiles from the other datafiles in the database. The separation of datafiles across disk drives may improve performance (through reduced contention for I/O resources) and simplify file management.

Segments in a DATA tablespace are likely to be fragmented. If your data segments are fragmented, they were not properly sized when created. Managing fragmentation (see Chapter 4) also drives the need to separate DATA from other tablespaces in order to isolate and resolve fragmentation problems.

Within DATA, you may have multiple types of tables. Small, static tables have different storage characteristics and management requirements than large, active tables. See the DATA_2 tablespace later in this chapter for details on managing different table types.

Locally Managed Tablespaces

Non-SYSTEM tablespaces may be dictionary managed or locally managed beginning in Oracle8i. In a dictionary managed tablespace, Oracle maintains in the data dictionary several tables recording the space usage with the tablespace. In a locally managed tablespace, the space information is maintained in a bitmap segment in the first 64KB of the tablespace's first datafile by default. Additional bitmap segments may be required and will be added as necessary.

In versions prior to Oracle9i, tablespaces were created as dictionary managed tablespaces by default. As of Oracle9i, the default is for new tablespaces to be created as locally managed tablespaces. Locally managed tablespaces tend to require fewer reorganizations and are ideal for operations such as moving tablespaces among databases. The physical storage specifications for locally managed tablespaces are described in Chapter 4.

Separating Low-Usage Data Segments: DATA_2

When reviewing your list of data tables, you can very likely combine them into two or more groups based on their characteristics: some will contain very dynamic data, others very static data; the latter type of table may contain a list of countries, for example. The static data tables tend to experience less I/O than the active data tables; when queried, the access against a static data table is usually concurrent with an access against a dynamic data table.

Concurrent I/O can be split among multiple files (and thus among multiple disks, to reduce I/O contention) by placing all static data tables in a dedicated tablespace. Administrative functions performed against the DATA tablespace, such as defragmentation, now only occur against those tables most likely to require administrative intervention. Meanwhile, the tablespace for static data tables, DATA_2, should remain static and simple to maintain.

Depending on the size of your database and the features you use, you may have multiple types of DATA tablespaces. In addition to having a DATA_2 tablespace for your static tables, you may also have multiple types of DATA tablespaces for the following categories. Best practices suggest that you should have a separate tablespace for each functional area (accounting, sales, etc.) or for each application.

- **Aggregations (materialized views)** If you have a data warehouse, you will most likely store aggregations in separate tables. Since these tables are based on derived data and may be frequently dropped and re-created, you should isolate them from your primary transaction tables.

- **Replicated data (materialized views)** Like aggregations, replication uses materialized views and other objects to distribute data. Replicated rows are based on derived data, and may be dropped and re-created on a more frequent basis than your application's transaction tables.

- **Temporary work tables** If you frequently load data from other systems into your database, you may load that data into temporary tables before moving it into your transaction tables. Such temporary work tables, sometimes referred to as staging tables, should be separated from the rest of your database tables.

■ **Partitions** If you use partitioning extensively, you should separate your partitions across tablespaces (and, therefore, across datafiles). Separating your partitions across tablespaces will enable you to separate current data in the table from archival data in the table. If you need to transport a partitioned table into a new database, you will need to transport all of the table and index partition tablespaces.

How can you tell if a table is a static table? If you are not familiar with the application, then you may need to audit the accesses to tables in order to determine which tables are most actively used. Auditing (see Chapter 10) can record every time a table is accessed as well as the type of access performed (**insert, select,** etc.). Auditing of accesses for many tables will generate a large number of audit records, so perform the audits during a single week (or representative days) and then disable the audits. A single day of standard usage of the application should be sufficient to determine the usage pattern. When analyzing the audit results, you will be looking for the tables that are most frequently accessed as well as the most common types of access against each table. If the table has no **insert**s, **update**s, or **delete**s against it during normal usage, then it should be considered for migration out of the DATA tablespace into a more appropriate tablespace.

Separating Application Index Segments: INDEXES

The indexes associated with tables are subject to the same I/O and growth/ fragmentation considerations that encouraged the movement of data segments out of the SYSTEM tablespace. Index segments should not be stored in the same tablespace as their associated data tables, since they have a great deal of concurrent I/O during both data manipulation and queries. If the data is not inserted into the table ordered by its indexed columns, the I/O for the index segments may exceed the I/O to the table.

Index segments are subject to fragmentation due to improper sizing or unpredicted table growth. Isolating the application indexes to a separate tablespace greatly reduces the administrative efforts involved in defragmenting either the DATA or the INDEXES tablespace.

You can separate existing indexes from their tables via the **rebuild** option of the **alter index** command. If an index has been created in the same tablespace as the table it indexes, you can move it with a single command. In the following example, the EMPLOYEE$DEPT_NO index is moved to the INDEXES tablespace, and new **storage** values are assigned for it:

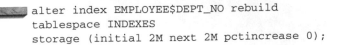

```
alter index EMPLOYEE$DEPT_NO rebuild
tablespace INDEXES
storage (initial 2M next 2M pctincrease 0);
```

If you use partitions, then you should separate the partition indexes from the table partitions. For example, you may create a table with ten partitions. If you create local partition indexes, then there will be ten local partition indexes—one for each of the table's partitions. You should store those partition indexes apart from the table partitions they index. If you create a global index on a partitioned table, then the entries in that index may be related to any of the table's partitions. If you use a global index, then you should separate that index from all of the table partitions for the table.

For example, if the SALES table is partitioned, then you can create local indexes on the SALES table's partitions. Each of those local index partitions should be stored apart from their respective table partitions. You can **truncate** individual partitions, and the related local index will be **truncate**d as well. If you create a global index that spans the entire SALES table, then that index should be stored apart from all of the SALES table's partitions.

When you create a table, the database will dynamically create an index for any PRIMARY KEY or UNIQUE constraint you specify (unless you first create the table without constraints, then create the indexes, then create the constraints). If you do not specify **tablespace** and **storage** parameters for those constraints during table creation, the database will automatically create those indexes in the same tablespace as the table, using the default storage parameters for that tablespace. To avoid this problem, use the **using index** clause of the **create table** command to separate your constraint indexes from the table, as shown in the following listing:

```
create table JOB
(Job_Code     NUMBER,
Description   VARCHAR2(35),
constraint JOB_PK primary key (Job_Code)
using index tablespace INDEXES
storage (initial 2M next 2M pctincrease 0))
tablespace DATA
storage (initial 5M next 5M pctincrease 0);
```

The JOB table will be created in the DATA tablespace, but its primary key index, JOB_PK, will be created in the INDEXES tablespace. Note that the JOB table and its primary key index have separate **storage** and **tablespace** clauses.

Separating Low-Usage Index Segments: INDEXES_2

The indexes for low-usage, static data tables also tend to be low usage and static. To simplify the administrative actions for the INDEXES tablespace, move the static tables' indexes to a separate INDEXES_2 tablespace. Separation also helps to improve performance tuning options, since concurrent I/O among indexes can now be split across disk drives.

If the low-usage indexes have already been created in the INDEXES tablespace, then they must be dropped and re-created in INDEXES_2. The index rebuild is usually done during the moving of low-usage tables to DATA_2.

The following listing shows a sample tablespace specification for an automatically created index. The following example creates a UNIQUE constraint on the Description column in a static table called EMPLOYEE_TYPE. The UNIQUE index that the database will create for the constraint is directed to be stored in the INDEXES_2 tablespaces.

```
alter table EMPLOYEE_TYPE
   add constraint UNIQ_DESCR  unique(DESCRIPTION)
using index tablespace INDEXES_2;
```

If the index already exists, you can use the **rebuild** clause of the **alter index** command to move the index from its current tablespace to a new tablespace. See the "Separating Application Index Segments: INDEXES" section earlier in this chapter.

If you create additional DATA tablespaces for materialized views, replicated tables, temporary work tables, and partitions, then you should create additional INDEX tablespaces to support the indexes for those tables.

Separating Tools Segments: TOOLS

Despite the previous sections' warnings about not storing data segments in the SYSTEM tablespace, many tools do. They do so not because they specifically call for their objects to be stored in the SYSTEM tablespace, but rather because they store them under the SYSTEM database account, which normally has the SYSTEM tablespace as its default area for storing objects. To avoid this problem, change the SYSTEM account's default tablespace to the TOOLS tablespace.

Many Oracle and third-party tools create tables owned by SYSTEM. If the tables have already been created in the database, their objects can be moved via the **move** option of the **alter table** command. See Chapter 5 for additional methods for moving existing objects.

The following listing shows part of this process, granting **quota** on the TOOLS tablespace to the APP_OWNER user:

```
alter user APP_OWNER quota 50M on TOOLS;
```

Separating Tools Indexes: TOOLS_I

If your database shows a lot of activity against the TOOLS tablespace, then the indexes for those TOOLS tables may be moved to a separate tablespace. You can use the

rebuild clause of the **alter index** command to move an existing index to a different tablespace while rebuilding it. In the following example, the TOOLTAB_PK index is moved to the TOOLS_I tablespace, and new **storage** values are assigned for it:

```
alter index TOOLTAB_PK rebuild
tablespace TOOLS_I
storage (initial 2M next 2M pctincrease 0);
```

Separating Rollback Segments: RBS

Rollback segments maintain both statement-level and transaction-level read consistency within the database. To isolate rollback segments (which incur I/O for transactions in the database) from the data dictionary, create a rollback segment tablespace that contains nothing but rollback segments. Isolating rollback segments also greatly simplifies their management (see Chapter 7 for details on rollback segments and undo tablespaces).

Once the RBS tablespace has been created, and a rollback segment has been activated within it, the second rollback segment in the SYSTEM tablespace can be dropped. You may find it useful to keep the second rollback segment in SYSTEM inactive but still available in the event of a problem with the RBS tablespace.

Rollback segments dynamically expand to the size of the largest transaction and shrink to a specified optimal size you define (see Chapter 7). I/O against rollback segments is usually concurrent with I/O against the DATA and INDEXES tablespaces. Separating rollback segments from data segments helps avoid I/O contention while making them easier to administer.

Separating Specialty Rollback Segments: RBS_2

If you are not using an undo tablespace, the rollback segments in the RBS tablespace should be of the proper size and number to support production usage of the application (see Chapter 7). There will almost always be a transaction (usually a batch transaction) whose size is unsupported by the production rollback segment configuration. When you execute that transaction, one of the production rollback segments will be taken over and extended greatly as the transaction uses up a large quantity of free space until it either succeeds or fails.

The production rollback segments should be dedicated for use by production users. Handle special transactional requirements (such as large data loads, aggregations, or **delete**s) by using a separate rollback segment. To specify a particular rollback segment, the application code must use the

```
set transaction use rollback segment SEGMENT_NAME
```

command prior to executing the transaction. The need for detailed settings of this sort within application code may call for greater involvement of DBAs within application teams (see Chapter 5). However, the **set transaction** command solves only part of the problem since the chosen rollback segment is still using space in the production RBS tablespace.

Create a separate rollback segment tablespace that will exist solely to support large transactions. Once this rollback segment is placed online for use, it can and will be used by all active transactions. The **set transaction use rollback segment** does not reserve the specified rollback segment for use by that transaction. When the transaction completes, the rollback segment may be taken offline until it is needed again.

Using an Undo Tablespace

As of Oracle9*i*, you can use an *undo tablespace* to place all undo data in a single tablespace. When you create an undo tablespace, Oracle manages the storage, retention, and space utilization for your rollback data via system-managed undo (SMU). No permanent objects are stored within the undo tablespace. See Chapter 7 for details on undo tablespaces.

Separating Temporary Segments: TEMP

Temporary segments are dynamically created objects within the database that store data during large sorting operations (such as **select distinct**, **union**, and **create index**). Due to their dynamic nature, temporary segments should not be stored with any other types of segments.

You can designate a tablespace as a "temporary" tablespace via the **create tablespace** and **alter tablespace** commands. If you designate a tablespace as a temporary tablespace, then you will not be able to create permanent segments such as tables and indexes within that tablespace. Furthermore, the temporary segment in that tablespace will not be dropped when its related command completes, reducing the amount of space management performed for that tablespace.

Unless you designate a tablespace as a temporary tablespace, temporary segments are dropped once the command they support completes. If you create a temporary tablespace, it creates a *sort segment*, which expands as necessary to accommodate all sorting taking place. The sort segment exists until the database is shut down and restarted. Separating temporary segments from SYSTEM removes a potential problem from the data dictionary area and creates a tablespace that is simple to administer.

You can specify a tablespace as a temporary tablespace at creation time, in which case no permanent objects can be created within it. You can query the contents of a tablespace ('PERMANENT' or 'TEMPORARY') from the DBA_TABLESPACES dictionary view. An existing permanent tablespace can be converted to a temporary tablespace via the **alter tablespace** *tablespace_name* **temporary** command.

You can use the **create user** command to specify a non-SYSTEM temporary tablespace, as shown in the following listing:

```
create user USERNAME identified by PASSWORD
default tablespace DATA
temporary tablespace TEMP;
```

If the account already exists, you can use the

```
alter user USERNAME temporary tablespace TEMP;
```

command to reassign the temporary tablespace. The **alter user** command will cause all future temporary segments created for that user's account to be created in TEMP.

NOTE
It is usually appropriate to alter the SYSTEM and SYS users' temporary tablespace setting to a non-SYSTEM tablespace.

Beginning in Oracle9i, you should define a non-SYSTEM default temporary tablespace when creating the database via the **default temporary tablespace** clause of the **create database** command. If you don't, Oracle will use the SYSTEM tablespace as the default temporary tablespace for all users and will write a warning to the alert log saying that a default temporary tablespace is recommended.

If you are using Oracle9i and have already created your database, you can use the **alter database** *database_name* **default temporary tablespace** *tablespace_name* command to change the default temporary tablespace.

Separating User-Specific Temporary Segments: TEMP_*USER*

Certain users, such as GL (the General Ledger schema) in an Oracle Applications database, may require much larger temporary segments than the rest of the application's users. In such a case, separate those temporary segments from the standard TEMP tablespace. This separation eases administration, since you can now design for the common usage of the system while handling the exceptions via TEMP_*USER*. In practice, name the tablespace after the name of the user, as in TEMP_GL or TEMP_SCOTT.

You can use the **create user** command to specify a temporary tablespace for a user:

```
create user USERNAME identified by PASSWORD
default tablespace TABLESPACE_NAME
temporary tablespace TEMP_USER;
```

If the user has already been created, the following command can be used to change the temporary tablespace setting:

```
alter user USERNAME temporary tablespace TEMP_USER;
```

The **alter user** command will cause all future temporary segments created for that user's account to be created in the user's custom TEMP_*USER* tablespace.

If your applications use a single database logon for all users, then your options are more limited; a change to the temporary tablespace assignment or sizing affects all users. In that configuration, you have two primary choices:

- Size the TEMP temporary tablespace to support extremely large transactions in addition to the smaller transactions. Don't create a second temporary tablespace.

- Create a TEMP_*USER* tablespace in addition to TEMP. Schedule the large transactions to run at off-hours. Prior to executing the large transactions, change the user's temporary tablespace setting to point to TEMP_*USER*.

Separating Users: USERS

Although they typically do not have object creation privileges in production databases, users may have such privileges in development databases. User objects as opposed to objects owned by functional areas such as accounting are generally transient in nature, and their sizing efforts are usually not thorough. As a result, user objects should be separated from the rest of the database to minimize the impact of user experimentation on the functioning of the database.

To separate the users' objects, change their default tablespace settings to the USERS tablespace and only grant quota there. You can use the **create user** command to specify an alternate default tablespace, as shown here:

```
create user USERNAME identified by PASSWORD
default tablespace USERS
temporary tablespace TEMP;
```

After a user's account has been created, you can use the

```
alter user USERNAME default tablespace USERS;
alter user USERNAME quota nnnn on USERS;
```

commands to reassign the default tablespace. Reassigning the default tablespace will direct objects created without a **tablespace** clause to be stored in USERS but will not move any objects created within the user's prior tablespace to the newly assigned one.

Additional Tablespace Types

Depending on your application, you may have additional types of objects in your database. Each distinct type of object should be stored in its own tablespace to minimize the impact that objects have on each other. The types are listed in the following table.

MVIEWS	For materialized views (either aggregations, joins, or replication). Materialized views' underlying tables and indexes are managed differently than most other objects in the database.
MVIEWS_I	For the indexes on your materialized views.
PARTITION*n*	For partitions (see Chapter 15). If you have the partitioning option installed, you can use partitions to distribute the I/O load and improve the ease of management for very large tables. You should identify the most commonly used partitions and manage them as if they were separate tables.
PARTITION*n*_I	For the local and global indexes associated with your partitions.
TEMP_WORK	For use during large data loads (see Chapter 15). Temporary work segments are characterized by large batch loads of data followed by deletion of the data or truncation of the table. You may also need a separate tablespace for the indexes for your temporary work tables.

If you do not use replication, materialized views, partitions, or temporary work tables for data loads, then you will not need any of these extra tablespaces. If you use partitions, you can move the partitions to different tablespaces once they exist (see Chapter 15 and the **alter table** command in Appendix A). If you use local partition indexes (see Chapter 15), you should separate the local indexes from their respective table partitions.

Advanced Tablespace Types

In addition to the common tablespace types, you can create tablespaces for more advanced tasks, as described in the following sections.

Global Temporary Table Tablespaces

You can use the **create temporary tablespace** command statement to create a temporary tablespace for schema objects that exist for the duration of a session. When issuing the command, specify the name and size of the tablespace's files via the **tempfile** clause. Beginning in Oracle9i, if you omit the **tempfile** clause and have set the DB_CREATE_FILE_DEST init.ora parameter to the name of a directory, Oracle will create a 100MB Oracle-managed tempfile in the default file destination specified in the parameter. You can modify the DB_CREATE_FILE_DEST parameter's setting via the **alter system** command.

Tempfile information is displayed in DBA_TEMP_FILES and V$TEMPFILE, while all other datafiles are in DBA_DATA_FILES and V$DATAFILE.

Read-Only Tablespaces

Tablespaces can be in either read-write or read-only mode. If the tablespace contains data that will not change, it may be placed in read-only mode. Tablespaces that are being transported from one database to another must be in read-only mode at the time of the transport. See Chapter 15 for details on transportable tablespaces. The following listing shows the command to make the TEMP_WORK tablespace read only:

```
alter tablespace TEMP_WORK read only;
```

Varying Block Size Tablespaces

As of Oracle9i, you can specify the database block size at the tablespace level. To select a block size, use the **blocksize** option of the **create tablespace** command. To specify a block size, you must have set values for the init.ora parameters DB_CACHE_SIZE and DB_*n*K_CACHE_SIZE. Your setting must correspond with the setting of one DB_*n*K_CACHE_SIZE parameter setting. You can have up to five different block sizes within your database. The SYSTEM tablespace block size, the undo tablespace, and the temporary tablespace must match the default database block size specified by the parameter DB_BLOCK_SIZE.

Undo Tablespaces

As of Oracle9i, you can use an undo tablespace in place of rollback segments. You can allocate undo space in an undo tablespace and let Oracle manage block contention, read consistency, and space management. See Chapter 7 for details on undo tablespaces.

Offline and Nologging Tablespaces

Most types of tablespaces can be taken offline (during maintenance operations) via the **offline** clause of the **alter tablespace** command. When created, a tablespace is brought online. A tablespace that is created with the **nologging** option will not generate redo entries for block-level transactions (such as **insert**s that use the APPEND hint) but will for normal **insert**, **update**, and **delete** statements.

Commonsense Logical Layouts

The resulting logical design of the database should meet the following criteria:

- Segment types that are used in the same way should be stored together.

- The system should be designed for its most common usage (transaction sizes, number of users, number of transactions, etc.).

- Separate areas should exist for exceptional transaction sizes, number of users, and number of transactions.

- Contention among tablespaces should be minimized.

- The data dictionary should be isolated.

Note that meeting these criteria requires the DBA to know the application being implemented: which tools it will use, which tables will be most active, when data loads will occur, which users will have exceptional resource requirements, and how standard transactions behave. Gaining this knowledge requires a very high level of DBA involvement in the application development process (see Chapter 5). Applications provided by a third-party vendor may require additional DBA attention.

Meeting these criteria results in a database whose varied segment types do not interfere with each other's resource requirements. Effective separation makes it much simpler to manage the database, and to isolate and resolve performance problems. When fragmentation of segments or free space does occur (see Chapter 4 and Chapter 8), it is much simpler to resolve when the database is laid out in this manner.

In this configuration, the only potential non-SYSTEM tablespace in which multiple types of segments may exist is the USERS tablespace. If the development environment is also used as a testing environment, then it may be a good idea to separate users' indexes into a USERS_I tablespace.

The combination of a sensible logical database layout with a well-designed physical database layout (see Chapter 4) results in systems that require very little tuning after the first postproduction check. The up-front planning efforts pay off immediately in both the flexibility and the performance of the database. The cost of implementing an OFA design from the start is minimal; it can be built into all of your database creation scripts automatically, and is a part of the database creation scripts automatically generated by the Oracle software installation process. The final overall design of the system should be an appropriate combination of the logical divisions shown in Table 3-1.

Once you establish your standard configuration, apply it whenever you create a new database. Applying a standard configuration will simplify administration, since each database will follow the same set of tablespace usage rules. Those rules, which separate segments by type and characteristics, isolate most problems and simplify their resolution.

Tablespace	Use
SYSTEM	Data dictionary
DATA	Standard-operation tables
DATA_2	Static tables used during standard operations
INDEXES	Indexes for the standard-operation tables
INDEXES_2	Indexes for the static tables
RBS	Standard-operation rollback segments
RBS_2	Specialty rollback segments used for data loads
TEMP	Standard-operation temporary segments
TEMP_*USER*	Temporary segments created by a specific user
TOOLS	RDBMS tools tables
TOOLS_I	Indexes for heavily used RDBMS tools tables
USERS	User objects, in development databases
USERS_I	User indexes, in testing databases
MVIEWS	Materialized views
MVIEWS_I	Indexes on the materialized views
PARTITION*n*	Partitions of table or index segments; create multiple tablespaces for them
PARTITION*n*_I	Local and global indexes on partitions
TEMP_WORK	Temporary tables used during data load processing

TABLE 3-1. *Logical Distribution of Tablespaces*

Solutions

You can use the suggested tablespace types in Table 3-1 to design a configuration that best meets your needs. In Table 3-2, you will see the configurations most commonly found in database applications.

Database Type	Tablespaces
Small development database	SYSTEM DATA INDEXES RBS TEMP USERS TOOLS
Production OLTP database	SYSTEM DATA DATA_2 INDEXES INDEXES_2 RBS RBS_2 TEMP TEMP_USER TOOLS
Production OLTP with historical data	SYSTEM DATA DATA_2 DATA_ARCHIVE INDEXES INDEXES_2 INDEXES_ARCHIVE RBS RBS_2 TEMP TEMP_USER TOOLS

TABLE 3-2.   *Common Tablespace Layouts*

Database Type	Tablespaces
Data warehouse	SYSTEM
	DATA
	DATA_2
	INDEXES
	INDEXES_2
	RBS
	RBS_2
	TEMP
	TEMP_USER
	TOOLS
	PARTITION*n*
	PARTITION*n*_I
	MVIEWS
	MVIEWS_I
	TEMP_WORK
	TEMP_WORK_I

TABLE 3-2. *Common Tablespace Layouts* (continued)

CHAPTER
4

Physical Database
Layouts

In this chapter, you will see how Oracle manages physical data storage, along with proposed physical database layouts for various application types and environments. These layouts will be the result of understanding the ways in which various database files operate and interact. Too often, the physical layout of the database is not planned; it is only considered when the database is experiencing performance problems. Just as the logical layout of the database should be planned (see Chapter 3), the physical layout of the database's files must be designed and implemented to meet the database's goals. Failure to plan the layouts before creating the database will result in a recurring cycle of layout-related problems and performance tuning efforts.

In this chapter, you will see where to place database-related files relative to each other to ensure optimal recoverability and performance as well as a method for verifying the planned layout. You will also see the suggested directory structure for the system's disks and an overview of database space usage.

Database File Layout

By establishing the clear goals of the file distribution design, and by understanding the nature of the database (transaction oriented versus read intensive), you can determine the proper distribution of database files across any number of devices. In this chapter you will see designs for the most common configurations as well as guidelines for applying them to any situations not directly covered.

The design process requires you to understand

1. Sources of I/O contention among datafiles

2. I/O bottlenecks among all database files

3. Concurrent I/O among background processes

4. The security and performance goals for the database

5. The available system hardware and mirroring architecture

6. The other applications using the same resources

In many cases, only the datafile contention, hardware mirroring, and disk acquisition tasks (tasks 1, 5, and 6) are performed before creating databases, thus designing contention into the system. If you complete all of the steps listed here, the end product will be a physical database layout that has your needs designed into it.

I/O Contention among Datafiles

When designing your logical database layout, follow the design procedures given in Chapter 3. Doing so should result in a database that contains some combination of the tablespaces shown in Table 4-1.

Tablespace	Use
SYSTEM	Data dictionary
DATA	Standard-operation tables
DATA_2	Static tables used during standard operations
INDEXES	Indexes for the standard-operation tables
INDEXES_2	Indexes for the static tables
RBS or undo	Standard-operation rollback segments or system-managed undo
RBS_2	Specialty rollback segments used for data loads
TEMP	Standard-operation temporary segments
TEMP_*USER*	Temporary segments created by a specific user
TOOLS	RDBMS tools tables
TOOLS_I	Indexes for heavily used RDBMS tools tables
USERS	User objects, in development databases
USERS_I	User indexes, in testing databases
MVIEWS	Materialized views
MVIEWS_I	Indexes on the materialized views
PARTITION*n*	Partitions of table or index segments; create multiple tablespaces for them
PARTITION*n*_I	Local and global indexes on partitions
TEMP_WORK	Temporary tables used during data load processing

TABLE 4-1. *Logical Distribution of Tablespaces*

Each of these tablespaces requires a separate datafile. You can monitor database I/O among datafiles after the database has been created; this capability is only useful during the planning stages if a similar database is available for reference. If no such database is available, then the DBA must estimate the I/O load for each datafile.

Start the physical layout planning process by estimating the relative I/O activity among the datafiles. In general, the datafiles for the tablespaces containing application tables will be very active, along with the index tablespaces, SYSTEM tablespace, and, for transaction-intensive applications, the undo tablespace. In transaction processing (OLTP) applications with many users generating small transactions, the application tables and indexes may be separated or partitioned among many tablespaces to reduce the I/O against any single datafile. In OLTP databases, the SYSTEM tablespace commonly has about half as much I/O as the data tablespaces. For data warehousing applications (featuring fewer, longer transactions and queries), the SYSTEM tablespace commonly accounts for about one-third of the I/O of the data tablespaces. The I/O against the undo tablespace or rollback segments depends on the volume of transactions in the database.

The I/O against the index tablespaces can vary widely, and often exceeds the I/O against the data tablespaces. Queries that are resolved without table accesses generate I/O only against the index tablespaces and the SYSTEM tablespace (when the user permissions are checked, etc.). During transactions, heavily indexed tables commonly report more I/O against their indexes than against the base tables, particularly if the indexes have a B-level value of 2 or more (see Chapter 8).

The TOOLS and USERS tablespaces should experience very little I/O in a production environment. TEMP and TEMP_WORK, in production, will only be used by large sorts; these sorts should mostly be performed via off-hours batch processes. The I/O against the MVIEWS tablespaces will be intense during the creation and refreshes of the materialized views, but will otherwise be limited to the queries the materialized views support.

In production databases, 90 percent or more of the I/O in the database may be concentrated in the combination of the SYSTEM, DATA, INDEX, and RBS/undo tablespaces. At a minimum, you should have a separate disk for each of those tablespaces. If the application tables and indexes are partitioned, you will need additional disks to distribute the partitions. As you distribute the datafiles across your disks, avoid adding additional tablespaces to the devices already serving those four tablespaces.

In most enterprise production systems, RAID technologies are used to distribute file I/O across multiple disks. For example, RAID-5 disks distribute both the files they support and the parity blocks used to recover them. In such environments, you will need to monitor the I/O at the RAID array level to make sure the array does not show an I/O backlog. For the UNIX environment, you can monitor the I/O to a device via the **sar -d** command. For example, the following partial output from a **sar -d** command shows the device name, percent busy, and average queue for nonzero I/O rates on different devices used for datafiles on a production system:

device	%busy	avque
ssd1	99	16.6
ssd2	74	4.9
ssd7	1	0.0
ssd8	63	1.1
sd35	30	0.3

The preceding output shows that four devices are each running at 30 percent or more of their I/O capacity, while one is barely used. Each of the four most-used devices has a queue of jobs waiting to use its I/O resources. As the percent busy increases, the average queue increases.

From a tuning perspective, there is nothing wrong with output that looks like:

device	%busy	avque
ssd1	99	0.0
ssd2	74	0.0
ssd7	1	0.0
ssd8	63	0.0
sd35	30	0.0

In this modified output, there are no waits occurring for I/O device access. The system is able to support the application's requests for data, even though it means one disk is busy 99 percent of the time. Although this is not a short-term problem, it is a long-term problem since it is likely that the I/O against all tablespaces will grow as the database grows in size, and the I/O requests will exceed the disks' capacity. In general, as long as the average queue is less than the number of disks in the RAID array, the system should be able to support the I/O requests without significant waits. If the disk is 99 or 100 percent used and the number of waits increases over time, you should either alter the system configuration or alter the distribution of data among your datafiles.

NOTE
Strategically, you should try to keep the I/O below 75 percent on each disk to support sudden and unexpected increases in I/O activity.

I/O Bottlenecks among All Database Files

Once you have estimated the I/O activity of the datafiles, you can plan the location of the datafiles relative to each other. In your design, you should also consider the other database file types available, as described in the following sections.

Online Redo Log Files

Online redo log files store the records of each transaction in the database except for block-level **nologging** transactions. Each database should have at least three online redo log files available to it. Oracle will write to one log file in a sequential fashion until it is filled, then it will start writing to the second redo log file. When the last online redo log file is filled, the database will begin overwriting the contents of the first redo log file with new transactions.

DBAs need to make sure that the online redo log files are mirrored by some means. You can use *redo log groups* to enable the database to dynamically maintain multiple sets of the online redo log files. Redo log groups use the database to mirror the online redo log files, thus minimizing the recovery problems caused by a single disk failure. You can also rely on the operating system to mirror the redo log files. Oracle mirroring is preferable because two or more different commands are sent to two or more devices. With operating system mirroring, if the write is bad to the original device, the operating system will copy the bad data to the mirror.

In OLTP databases, you should place online redo log files apart from datafiles because of potential I/O conflicts. Every transaction not executed with the **nologging** parameter in effect is recorded in the redo log files. Transaction entries are written to the online redo log files by the *LGWR (Log Writer)* background process. The data in the transactions is concurrently written to several tablespaces (such as the RBS rollback segments tablespace and the DATA tablespace). The writes to the tablespaces are done via the *DBWR (Database Writer)* background processes. Thus, even though the datafile I/O may be properly distributed, contention between the DBWR and LGWR background processes may occur if a datafile is stored on the same disk as a redo log file.

NOTE
The contention among background processes is only significant if it leads to I/O wait queues, as illustrated in the previous section.

If you must store a datafile on the same disk as redo log files, then it should not belong to the SYSTEM tablespace, the RBS tablespace, or a very active DATA or INDEX tablespace. All of these tablespaces may have direct conflicts with the redo log files and will increase the likelihood of the log writes being affected by the database reads.

Control Files

Control files are mirrored by Oracle; you can specify the number and name of the control files via the CONTROL_FILES parameter in the database's parameter file. If the control filenames are specified via this parameter during database creation, then they will be automatically created during the database creation process. The database will thereafter maintain the control files as identical copies of each other.

Each database should have a minimum of three copies of its control files, located across three separate physical devices to mitigate the impact of media failures. Although there is not a lot of data written starting with Oracle8, the CKPT process writes checkpoint progress records to the control file every three seconds.

Archived Redo Log Files

When Oracle is run in ARCHIVELOG mode, the database makes a copy of each online redo log file after it has filled. These archived redo log files are usually written to a disk device. They may also be written directly to a tape device, but this tends to be operator intensive.

The ARCH background process performs the archiving function. Databases using the ARCHIVELOG option will encounter contention problems on their online redo log disk during heavy data transaction times, since LGWR will be trying to write to one redo log file while ARCH is trying to read another. To avoid this contention, distribute the online redo log files across multiple disks. If you are running in ARCHIVELOG mode on a very transaction-oriented database, avoid LGWR-ARCH contention by splitting up your online redo log files across devices.

To further enhance the performance of the archiving process, create online redo log file groups with multiple members. The archiving process can archive faster if there are multiple redo log files in a group to read from while archiving. If you have enabled multiple archived redo log file destinations, you must account for the I/O being written to each of those target devices.

Each archived redo log file device, by its nature, will have the same amount of I/O as the online redo logs device. Archived redo log files should not be stored on the same devices as the SYSTEM, RBS, DATA, or INDEXES tablespaces, and they should not be stored on the same device as any of the online redo log files.

Oracle Software

The Oracle software files that are accessed during normal database operation vary according to the packages that are licensed for the host on which the server resides. The I/O against these files is not recorded within the database but is visible via utilities such as **sar** on the UNIX platform.

NOTE
If you encounter many data-related errors during application usage, you may see a significant increase in the activity against the help message file.

To minimize contention between the database files and the database code, avoid placing database files on the same disk device as the code files. If datafiles must be placed on that disk device, then the least frequently used datafiles should be placed there.

Concurrent I/O among Background Processes

When evaluating contention among various processes, you should identify the type of I/O being performed and its timing. Files contend with each other if I/O from one file interferes with I/O for the second file, so two randomly accessed files that are never accessed at the same time can be placed on the same device.

In RAID environments in which a single file may be distributed across multiple disks, there is much less likelihood of concurrent I/O requests against a single disk. With RAID environments, focus on isolating the arrays (as data arrays or index arrays) rather than attempting to isolate individual disks within arrays.

The background processes that read and write data to datafiles usually operate in a random manner. There are usually "hot spots" of concentrated activity, but it is difficult to predict where those spots will be and where they will next occur. The background processes that deal with the log files, LGWR and ARCH, perform sequential reads and writes.

LGWR will write to all members of the same redo log group at the same time, and the ARCH process can write to multiple destinations at the same time. DBWR may also be attempting to write to multiple files at once. There is thus the potential for DBWR to cause contention with itself as it writes out modified blocks of multiple tables. To combat this problem, most operating systems support the creation of multiple DBWR processes for each instance. The number of DBWRs is set via the initialization parameter DBWR_PROCESSES; you can also start multiple I/O slaves for a single DBWR process via the DBWR_IO_SLAVES parameter. Oracle recommends setting DBWR_IO_SLAVES to a value between n and $2n$, where n is the number of disks. In 8.0, but not in 8.1 or later releases, you can also start multiple LGWR I/O slaves (via the LGWR_IO_SLAVES parameter) and multiple ARCH I/O slaves (via ARCH_IO_SLAVES). As of 8.1, Oracle uses the DBWR_IO_SLAVES setting to determine how many LGWR and ARCH I/O slaves to start; setting DBWR_IO_SLAVES to a value greater than 0 sets the corresponding LGWR_IO_SLAVES and ARCH_IO_SLAVES settings each to 4. If you cannot enable multiple DBWR processes, you may be able to use asynchronous I/O to reduce internal DBWR contention. With asynchronous I/O, only one DBWR process is started since the I/O processing is performed asynchronously.

NOTE
Monitor V$WAITSTAT for data block waits. Significant numbers of data block waits may indicate the need for more DBWR processes. STATSPACK (see Chapter 9) dedicates several sections of its output report to database waits and background wait events.

The nature of the contention that will occur between the background processes is a function of the backup scheme used (ARCH), the transaction load on the system (LGWR), and the host operating system (DBWR). Designing a scheme that will minimize contention between files and processes requires a clear understanding of the ways in which those files and processes will interact in the production system.

Defining the Recoverability and Performance Goals for the System

Before designing the database's disk layout, the recoverability and performance goals for the layout must be clearly defined. The recoverability goals must take into account all processes that impact disks, including the storage area for archived redo log files and the storage area for backups (if disk-to-disk backups are performed). As part of defining your recoverability requirements, you should establish service level agreements with the business users defining the allowable downtime and data loss in the event of system failures and major disasters.

Recoverability of a database should always be a primary concern. The architecture put in place for recoverability may complement the performance tuning architecture. If the performance tuning design conflicts with the recoverability design, then the recoverability design must prevail.

NOTE
Since heterogeneous systems may feature some disks that are faster than others, the design must take into account the relative access speeds of the disks available.

In terms of performance goals, you should define the goals for your batch processes, administrative processes, query response time, and data loading operations. In each case, define both your primary goal and your stretch goal. During your application performance testing, strive to achieve the stretch goal without incurring I/O waits on the disks.

Defining the System Hardware and Mirroring Architecture

Since a separate systems management group typically allocates and manages the server's disk farm, DBAs must work with that team to design the system's hardware and mirroring architecture. The system architecture includes specifying

■   The number of disks required

- The models of disks required (for performance or size)

- The appropriate mirroring strategy for disk arrays

The number of disk arrays required will be driven by the size of the database and the volume of database I/O activity. Wherever possible, those disks should be dedicated to Oracle files to avoid contention with non-Oracle files. If the disk farm is heterogeneous, then the size and speed of the drives available should be taken into consideration when determining which are to be dedicated to Oracle files.

Disk mirroring provides fault tolerance with regard to media failures. Mirroring is performed either by maintaining a duplicate of each disk online (known as RAID-1 or *volume shadowing*) or by using a *parity-check* system among a group of disks (usually RAID-3 or RAID-5). The parity-check systems implicitly perform file striping across disks. In RAID-5, for example, each file is striped on a block-by-block basis across the disks in the mirroring group. A parity check is then written on another disk in the set so that if one disk is removed, its contents can be regenerated based on knowing the parity check and the contents of the rest of the mirrored set.

The system mirroring architecture impacts the distribution of database files across those disks. Disks that are mirrored on a one-to-one basis (RAID-1) can be treated as stand-alone disks. Disks that are part of a parity-check system (such as RAID-3 or RAID-5) must be considered as a set, and can take advantage of the implicit striping.

NOTE
In general, favor striping over a large number of small disks rather than over a small number of large disks.

Identifying Disks That Can Be Dedicated to the Database

Whatever mirroring architecture is used, the disks chosen must be dedicated to the database. Otherwise, the nondatabase load on those disks will impact the database, and that impact is usually impossible to forecast correctly. User directory areas, for example, may experience sudden increases in size—and wipe out the space that was intended for the archived redo log files, bringing the database to a halt. Other files may have severe I/O requirements that were not factored into the database I/O weights estimated earlier.

Supporting External Files

As of Oracle9*i*, you can reference external tables via SQL statements. If the data is stored in a consistent format, you can execute a **create table** command combined with SQL*Loader-like commands to allow Oracle to select from the external data.

You cannot perform DML commands on the external table, and you cannot create an Oracle index on it.

External tables must be stored in a physical directory previously identified via the **create directory** command. The directories created via your **create directory** commands must be treated as part of the database, and should be on isolated disk devices.

NOTE
Your backup and recovery procedures must also account for the external table data.

Choosing the Right Layout

For a disk layout to be acceptable:

- The database must be recoverable.

- The online redo log files must be mirrored via the system or the database.

- The database file I/O must not exceed the individual disk I/O throughput capacity.

- Contention between database background processes must be minimized.

- The disk performance must not hinder the achievement of the database performance goals.

- The system hardware and mirroring options must meet the recoverability and performance requirements.

- The database disks must be dedicated to database files.

With those goals in mind, you must also account for the future—how will the I/O rates to different files change over time? As new tables, indexes, and materialized views are added to the database, will they be stored in the existing tablespaces or new tablespaces? In existing datafiles or new datafiles? How active will these new objects be, and where should their files be placed?

Since the database structure is highly likely to change over time, you should choose a design that allows for growth, both in terms of space and I/O throughput. In the following sections, you will see guidance on making the compromises.

Minimizing the I/O Impact of Static Tables

Before making decisions on file placement, you should try to eliminate as many variables as possible. If the main data tablespaces, index tablespaces, undo tablespaces and SYSTEM account for 90 percent of the I/O in the database, then first make sure that the other 10 percent of the activity is controlled. For the small static tables (see the DATA_2 and INDEXES_2 descriptions in Chapter 3), set up a separate area in the data block buffer cache. The KEEP area of the data block buffer cache is separate from the main data block buffer cache. The initialization parameter to establish the KEEP cache size is DB_KEEP_CACHE_SIZE, as shown in the following listing:

```
DB_KEEP_CACHE_SIZE=16M
```

Assign the static tables and indexes to the KEEP cache. Consider a static table named COUNTRY:

```
alter table COUNTRY cache storage (buffer_pool KEEP);
```

> **NOTE**
> *See Appendix A for the full syntax of the* **storage** *clause.*

The COUNTRY table will be cached when it is read, and will be stored in the keep pool, apart from the main application tables. As a result, accesses of the COUNTRY table should not significantly impact the I/O burden on the disks. You can focus on balancing the four primary areas (DATA, INDEX, RBS/undo, and SYSTEM) without worrying about other tables, until new objects are added to the database.

Minimizing the I/O Impact of Administrative Processes

The I/O from backup processes and administrative actions (such as gathering statistics) cannot be easily altered. For backups, you should consider using incremental backup methods such as those available via RMAN (see Chapter 12). For administrative operations, consider using partitions (see Chapter 15) to isolate the data on which you are acting. Whenever possible, schedule your administrative operations to occur at times of very low user activity to minimize your impact on the I/O performance of the system.

Any batch operations that perform significant data movement (such as replication) or queries (such as periodic reports) should be scheduled to occur at times of low system usage. If the business requires the batch operations to be performed more frequently, you will need to factor the batch user's I/O needs into your estimates of overall system load and contention.

Making Compromises

Unless you have an infinite number of disks and controllers, your physical design for an enterprise production system will involve making compromises. It may not be possible to keep tables and indexes separate, or to separate online redo log files and undo tablespaces. Developing an effective design is an iterative process, based on a set of rules:

- Never compromise the recoverability of the database. Given a choice between 10 mirrored disks full of data or 20 unmirrored half-full disks, choose the mirrored solution. Operating systems and disk controllers for mirrored systems should distribute I/O requests across the mirrors, so the performance impact of the 10-disk option will not be as significant as you may think.

- Separate the most active DATA, INDEX, SYSTEM, and RBS/undo tablespace datafiles.

- Separate the most active tables from the largely inactive tables. Beyond simply separating the active tables from static codes tables, you should examine the application to determine which tables will store the bulk of the data. Often, less than 10 percent of an application's tables account for 80 percent of the I/O. Isolate those most active tables to give yourself more performance tuning options as the database grows in size and use.

- Partition the most active tables. Within each table, there are usually areas that are more active than others. In OLTP systems, most queries commonly go against the most recently entered data. In a large enterprise test system, half of the queries were against data from the most recent seven days. If you can partition the table to isolate the most actively accessed data, you can improve your ability to support the I/O performance requirements as the table grows. In a partitioned solution, the location of the I/O burden moves, but you maintain control over where that problem occurs and how it is solved.

- Allow room for growth, both in terms of I/O throughput and space.

- Monitor the I/O, both at the operating system level and within the database.

- Repeat the physical design process at regularly scheduled intervals and during the planning of major application changes. Revalidate the decisions made earlier based on the monitoring data available.

In the next section, you will see guidance on monitoring the I/O activity of existing systems. You should factor the monitoring data from your existing systems into your designs for new systems since at a minimum it should provide you with rough estimates of how the I/O activity is handled by your servers and how I/O is distributed in your databases. Once your application has gone through performance testing, you will be able to further refine your estimates and make judgments on your disk compromises.

Verification of I/O Estimates

The statistics tables within the data dictionary record the I/O for each datafile.
You can query the internal statistics tables to verify the assumptions used in the
design process.

The V$FILESTAT view records all I/O against the database since it was last
started. The following query reports the I/O by datafile, summed by disk device.

NOTE
*The script assumes that the devices are consistently
named and that the device name is five characters
long (see the SUBSTR of the DF.Name column). If
your device names are longer than that, you will
need to alter the script to meet your specifications.*

```
clear breaks
clear computes
break on Drive skip 1 on report
compute sum of Blocks_Read on Drive
compute sum of Blocks_Written on Drive
compute sum of Total_IOs on Drive
compute sum of Blocks_Read on Report
compute sum of Blocks_Written on Report
compute sum of Total_IOs on Report
ttitle skip center "Database File I/O by Drive" skip 2

select substr(DF.Name,1,5) Drive,
       DF.Name File_Name,
       FS.Phyblkrd+FS.Phyblkwrt Total_IOs,
       FS.Phyblkrd Blocks_Read,
       FS.Phyblkwrt Blocks_Written
  from V$FILESTAT FS, V$DATAFILE DF
 where DF.File#=FS.File#
 order by Drive, File_Name desc;
```

Sample output for this query is shown in the following listing.

NOTE
*The summation of the I/O totals by disk may not be
useful information if you are using RAID arrays.
Check with your system administrator regarding the
disk configuration in use.*

```
DRIVE  FILE_NAME                    TOTAL_IOS BLOCKS_READ BLOCKS_WRITTEN
-----  --------------------------   --------- ----------- --------------
/db01  /db01/oracle/CC1/sys.dbf        29551       27708           1843
       /db01/oracle/CC1/temp.dbf        4389           4           4385
*****                                --------- ----------- --------------
sum                                     33940       27712           6228

/db02  /db02/oracle/CC1/rbs01.dbf       1134           3           1131
       /db02/oracle/CC1/rbs02.dbf        349                        349
       /db02/oracle/CC1/rbs03.dbf        415           7            408
*****                                --------- ----------- --------------
sum                                      1898          10           1888

/db03  /db03/oracle/CC1/cc.dbf         57217       56820            397
*****                                --------- ----------- --------------
sum                                     57217       56820            397

/db04  /db04/oracle/CC1/ccindx.dbf     15759       14728           1031
       /db04/oracle/CC1/tests1.dbf
*****                                --------- ----------- --------------
sum                                     15759       14728           1031

*****                                --------- ----------- --------------
sum                                    108814       99270           9544
```

The data in the preceding listing shows the format of the queries' output. The output shows that the device called /db03 is the most heavily used device during database usage. There is only one datafile from this database on the /db03 device. The report output also shows that accesses against the file on /db03 are read intensive by an overwhelming margin.

The second most active device is /db01, which has two database files on it. Most of the activity on that disk is against the SYSTEM tablespace file, with the TEMP tablespace demanding much less I/O.

The sample data shown in the preceding listing should be compared to the data generated via the operating system monitoring commands such as the **sar** listings shown earlier in this chapter. If the database I/O is not causing waits to occur, and leaves room for growth in the application, the design is satisfactory. If the operating system shows waits occurring, you can use the query of V$FILESTAT to determine which files are most frequently accessed.

Which tables are most frequently accessed? The simplest way to determine this is to query V$SQL to see the queries being executed. Examine the queries with the highest values for executions, disk reads, and buffer gets to determine the tables most likely causing the I/O activity reported.

```
select Buffer_Gets,
       Disk_Reads,
       Executions,
```

```
        Buffer_Gets/Executions B_E,
        SQL_Text
   from V$SQL
order by Disk_Reads desc;
```

To determine the file I/O statistics during specific time periods, you can use the STATSPACK utility, as described in Chapter 9. The standard STATSPACK report lists the most I/O-intensive SQL during the time period. In Oracle9i, the report on expensive SQL reports the buffer gets, number of executions, buffer gets per execution, and time for each SQL statement listed. The output also shows the percentage of all buffer gets in the database attributed to each SQL statement. You can use the STATSPACK report data to quickly target queries generating substantial I/O loads within your database.

The STATSPACK report also shows the I/O by tablespace during the monitoring period. The data is presented ordered by tablespace activity and ordered by tablespace and file. You can use this portion of the report to monitor the file I/O during batch executions, administrative actions, or other scheduled activities.

Solutions

You can use the guidelines in this chapter to design a physical configuration for the logical configuration you designed in Chapter 3. The "Solutions" section of Chapter 3 presented four common logical configurations: small development database, production OLTP database, production OLTP database with historical data, and a data warehouse. In this section, you will see common physical layouts for those four database types.

NOTE
None of the solutions in this section considers the space requirements for the application software, Oracle software, or backups.

Small Development Database Layout

For a small database, you will typically have the following tablespaces: SYSTEM, DATA, INDEXES, RBS, TEMP, USERS, and TOOLS (see Table 3-2). To store them all on separate devices (and if the DATA tablespace is small enough), you only need seven disks. If you have fewer than seven disks, follow the guidelines in the "Making Compromises" section earlier in this chapter. Isolate the DATA, INDEXES, SYSTEM, and RBS/undo datafiles from the other files to the greatest extent possible. For example, on a five-disk system you may choose to place all datafiles other than DATA, INDEXES, SYSTEM, and RBS on one disk. You should still distribute the control files across multiple disks in the interest of recoverability.

If the system uses a RAID technology such as RAID-5, small development databases may have all of their files placed on the same RAID array. The database will be available unless there are simultaneous failures of multiple disks within the array.

Production OLTP Database Layout

A production OLTP database supports many small transactions. An OLTP database typically contains the following tablespaces: SYSTEM, DATA, DATA_2, INDEXES, INDEXES_2, RBS (or an undo tablespace), TEMP (and potentially additional temporary tablespaces), and TOOLS (see Table 3-2).

In a production OLTP database, the DATA and INDEXES tablespaces tend to grow rapidly, commonly exceeding one disk each. The rest of the tablespaces tend to grow at a much slower pace. The application tables and indexes are commonly partitioned to ease management of the tablespaces as the data volume grows. If the partitions are not frequently accessed concurrently, then there is no contention introduced by storing the DATA partitions on the same device or RAID array.

In a production OLTP system, the configuration is designed to optimize the performance of small transactions and small queries. The TEMP and TOOLS tablespaces should be seldom used. The design should place emphasis on supporting the spots of most intense activity in the DATA and INDEXES tablespaces, with partitions used to isolate the most active portions of the most active tables. The SYSTEM tablespace should also be isolated, since each database user and command will generate queries of the data dictionary. The RBS/undo tablespace activity is usually lighter than SYSTEM's. If you use rollback segments in lieu of an undo tablespace, create enough rollback segments to avoid rollback segment header contention (as reported in V$WAITSTAT and via the STATSPACK report).

If you do not have enough disks to support each major type of tablespace, you can store smaller tablespaces together. If you cache the small static tables, you may even store DATA_2 and INDEXES_2 together (see "Minimizing the I/O Impact of Static Tables" earlier in this chapter).

If you are using RAID arrays, try to isolate the DATA and INDEXES tablespaces on separate arrays. For a three-array system, you should put the DATA tablespaces on one array, the INDEXES on the second, and all other tablespaces on the third. Be sure to distribute the control files across arrays.

Production OLTP Database with Historical Data Layout

In addition to your current production data, you may be required to maintain historical data. Since the historical data will have different growth and access patterns than the current transactional data, you should store the historical data apart from the current DATA tablespace. As shown in Table 3-2, a production OLTP database with historical data will have the same tablespaces as a production OLTP database, plus two new tablespaces: DATA_ARCHIVE and INDEXES_ARCHIVE.

The archive areas may be seen as separate partitions of the DATA and INDEXES tablespaces, in which case you can follow the design advice provided in the previous section.

When you add historical data to the configuration, you have to know how the historical data will be used. If the old data is constantly referenced, you will need to separate it from the current DATA and INDEXES tablespaces. If both the current and historical DATA tablespaces are actively used, then you will encounter I/O contention if you store them on the same physical device.

If the historical data is not actively used, then you can store the historical data on the same devices as the current data without causing I/O contention. For example, if the historical data is only used by rarely executed reports or batch processes, there will be little I/O against the historical data and little I/O contention between the current and historical DATA tablespaces.

Data Warehouse Layout

The volume of data in a data warehouse may be significantly greater than that of any of your OLTP databases. As shown in Table 3-2, a data warehouse will likely contain each type of segment used by Oracle: data dictionary tables (SYSTEM tablespace), tables (DATA and DATA_2), indexes (INDEXES and INDEXES_2), small and large rollback segments (RBS and RBS_2 or an undo tablespace), temporary segments (TEMP and TEMP_USER), and tools tables (TOOLS). In addition to those segments, a data warehouse will usually also include partitions (PARTITIONS and PARTITIONS_I tablespaces), aggregate data (AGG_DATA and AGG_DATA_I), materialized views (MVIEWS and MVIEWS_I), and work tables used only during batch processing (TEMP_WORK and TEMP_WORK_I). When designing a physical layout for all those tablespaces, you need to consider the two entirely separate ways in which the data warehouse will be used: data loading and data retrieval.

In an OLTP database, the data loading process is performed by many users executing small **insert** and **update** transactions. In a data warehouse, the data loading process is usually a set of large batch operations that may take days or weeks to complete during each data load cycle. You therefore need to tune your database to optimize the batch data loading process. At the same time, you need to consider how users are retrieving the data once it has been loaded.

NOTE
Rather than loading the data into your warehouse, you may be able to use transportable tablespaces or external tables. See Chapter 15 for details.

As in an OLTP database, data warehouse users perform many small queries against a large number of tables. Although the base tables of a data warehouse are large, the end users should not be directly querying them; instead, they should be querying the heavily indexed aggregation tables. The data in the data warehouse should be denormalized so that it best supports the access paths most commonly followed by the end users.

When designing the data warehouse's physical layout, consider the batch loading and data retrieval uses separately. For a batch loading process that is not able to use transportable tablespaces or external tables, the primary tablespaces involved will be as follows:

SYSTEM	Data dictionary tables
TEMP_WORK	Temporary tables used during the data load process
TEMP_WORK_I	Indexes for the temporary work tables
TEMP_USER	Large temporary segments to support batch sorts
RBS_2/undo	Large rollback segments or system-managed undo to support the batch transactions
DATA	Tables
INDEXES	Indexes for the tables in the DATA tablespace
PARTITIONS	Table partitions
PARTITIONS_I	Indexes for the table partitions
MVIEWS	Materialized views
MVIEWS_I	Indexes for the materialized views
AGG_DATA	Aggregate tables and materialized views
AGG_DATA_I	Indexes for the aggregate tables and materialized views

Following the guidelines presented earlier in this chapter, you should separate the SYSTEM and RBS/undo tablespaces from all of the other tablespaces. You can optimize the remainder of the configuration by planning out your batch loading process. For example, many data warehouse systems load data from outside sources into temporary work tables. If your data comes into the database via flat files, then the normal data loading steps are as follows:

1. Load data from flat files into the TEMP_WORK tables for data cleaning operations.

2. Index the TEMP_WORK tables to improve the performance of data cleaning and movement operations; write indexes to TEMP_WORK_I.

3. Perform database transactions to move data from TEMP_WORK tables to DATA and PARTITIONS tables, using the RBS_2 tablespace for rollback

segments. As an alternative, you may be able to use DDL operations, moving tables and exchanging partitions to eliminate DML commands.

4. Index the tables in DATA and PARTITIONS, writing the indexes to INDEXES and PARTITIONS_I; use the TEMP tablespace for the associated temporary segments during the index creation.

5. If your data warehouse uses data from other databases, create local materialized views of the remote data in the MVIEWS tablespace using the RBS or undo tablespace. Index the materialized views in MVIEWS_I and use the TEMP tablespace for the associated temporary segments during the index creation.

6. Create aggregate tables in AGG_DATA, and index those tables in AGG_DATA_I using the RBS_2 tablespace for rollback segments; use the TEMP tablespace for the associated temporary segments during the index creation.

Before co-locating tablespaces on the same physical device, you need to consider the end-user data access requirements. Rather than just querying DATA and INDEXES during queries, users may also be accessing AGG_DATA, AGG_DATA_I, PARTITIONS, PARTITIONS_I, MVIEWS, and MVIEWS_I. If the I/O requests exceed the device capacities, you may need to separate all of those tablespaces.

As detailed in the preceding discussion, supporting a data warehouse requires you to support many types of tablespaces. However, these tablespaces are not all used concurrently. The TEMP_WORK and TEMP_WORK_I tablespaces, for example, are only used during the data loading process. Therefore, you may be able to co-locate them with other tablespaces (such as the MVIEWS and MVIEWS_I tablespaces) to reduce the number of disks used. Furthermore, you may choose to partition all of your nonstatic tables, effectively eliminating the need for the DATA and INDEXES tablespaces. Your final layout should reflect the file usage characteristics of your application. In an ideal data warehouse, the most commonly used tablespaces during queries are AGG_DATA_I, MVIEWS_I, and PARTITIONS_I, with very little access to the associated tables. If you are able to index your data warehouse tables so effectively that the tables are rarely accessed, you may be able to co-locate the AGG_DATA and PARTITIONS tablespaces without causing I/O contention.

File Location

In order to simplify database management, the files associated with a database should be stored in directories created specifically for each database. Database files from different databases should not be stored together.

Furthermore, the database's datafiles should be separated from the software used to access the database (despite the fact that this is the default for some of the installation programs). Active versions of all Oracle software should not be allowed to cause contention with the datafiles.

Storing the datafiles at the same level in a directory hierarchy will simplify the management procedures. It also allows you to avoid putting the instance identifier in the filename, using it instead as part of the directory path. This separation allows wildcards or search lists to be used when referencing them (if the disks are named in a consistent fashion). For example, in UNIX environments, all of the files belonging to a specific instance could be copied to a tape device with a single command, as in the following example:

```
> tar /dev/rmt/1hc /db0[1-8]/oracle/CASE
```

In this example, the system will write out to a tape device (/dev/rmt/1hc) the contents of the /oracle/CASE subdirectory on the devices named /db01 through /db08.

Database Space Usage Overview

In order to understand how space should be allocated within the database, you first have to know how the space is used within the database. In this section, you will see an overview of the Oracle database space usage functions.

When a database is created, it is divided into multiple logical sections called *tablespaces*. The SYSTEM tablespace is the first tablespace created. Additional tablespaces are then created to hold different types of data, as described in Chapter 3.

When a tablespace is created, *datafiles* are created to hold its data. These files immediately allocate the space specified during their creation. There is thus a one-to-many relationship between databases and tablespaces, and a one-to-many relationship between tablespaces and datafiles. You can add datafiles to a tablespace, and existing datafiles may be extended.

Each database will have multiple users, each of whom has a *schema*. Each user's schema is a collection of logical database objects such as tables and indexes. These objects refer to physical data structures (the physical tables and indexes) that are stored in tablespaces. Objects from a user's schema may be stored in multiple tablespaces, and a single tablespace can contain objects from multiple schemas.

When a database object (such as a table or index) is created, it is assigned to a tablespace via user defaults or specific instructions. A *segment* is created in that tablespace to hold the data associated with that object. The space that is allocated to the segment is never released until the segment is dropped, manually shrunk, or **truncate**d. See the "How to Deallocate Space from Segments" section later in this chapter for details on manually shrinking the space allocated to tables, indexes, and clusters.

A segment is made up of sections called *extents*—contiguous sets of Oracle blocks. Once the existing extents can no longer hold new data, the segment will obtain another extent to support additional **insert**s of data into the object. The extension process will continue until no more free space is available in the tablespace's datafiles or until an internal maximum number of extents per segment is reached. When a datafile fills, it can extend based on the storage rules defined for it.

The segment types available in Oracle include the following:

TABLE
INDEX
ROLLBACK
TEMPORARY
PARTITION
CLUSTER

Managing the space used by each is one of the basic functions of the DBA. Chapters 6, 7, 8, and 15 contain detailed information on the monitoring and tuning of these segments. The intent of the following overview sections is to aid in the planning of the segments' physical storage.

Implications of the storage Clause

The amount of space used by a segment is determined by its storage parameters. These parameters are specified when a segment is created, and may be altered later. If no specific storage parameters are given in the **create table**, **create index**, **create cluster**, or **create rollback segment** command, the database will use the default storage parameters for the tablespace in which it is to be stored. The storage parameters specify the **initial** extent size, the **next** extent size, the **pctincrease** (a factor by which each successive extent will geometrically grow), the **maxextents** (maximum number of extents), and **minextents** (minimum number of extents). After the segment has been created, the **initial** and **minextents** values cannot be altered. The default values for the storage parameters for each tablespace may be queried from the DBA_TABLESPACES views.

NOTE
To simplify your space management, use locally managed tablespaces, as described in the next section.

When a segment is created, it will acquire at least one extent. The initial extent will store data until it no longer has any free space available. You can use the **pctfree** clause to reserve, within each block in each extent, a percentage of space that will remain available for **update**s of existing rows in the block. When additional data is added to the segment, the segment will extend by obtaining a second extent of the size specified by the **next** parameter.

The **pctincrease** parameter is designed to minimize the number of extents in growing tables. A nonzero value for this parameter will cause the size of each successive extent to increase geometrically by the **pctincrease** factor specified. When first introduced, **pctincrease** helped to reduce the number of extents per segment; with an unlimited number of extents per segment supported there is no real need to use a **pctincrease** value other than 0 unless the table's data volume is far different from what its design called for.

NOTE
pctincrease cannot be used with locally managed tablespaces.

Locally Managed Tablespaces

You can use two different methods to track free and used space in a tablespace. The first method, which has been available since the advent of tablespaces, is to handle extent management via the data dictionary (dictionary managed tablespaces). In a dictionary managed tablespace, each time an extent is allocated or freed for reuse in a tablespace, the appropriate entry is **update**d in the data dictionary table.

The second method, available as of Oracle8i, handles extent management within the tablespaces themselves (locally managed tablespaces). In locally managed tablespaces, the tablespace manages its own space by maintaining a bitmap in each datafile of the free and used blocks or sets of blocks in the datafile. Each time an extent is allocated or freed for reuse, Oracle **update**s the bitmap to show the new status. Within a locally managed tablespace, all extents can have the same size or the system can automatically determine the size of extents.

To create a locally managed tablespace, specify the **local** option for the **extent management** clause in the **create tablespace** command. An example of the **create tablespace** command declaring a locally managed tablespace is shown here:

```
create tablespace CODES_TABLES
datafile '/u01/oracle/VLDB/codes_tables.dbf'
size 10M
extent management local uniform size 256K;
```

Assuming that the block size for the database in which this tablespace is created is 4KB, in this example, the tablespace is created with the extent management declared as **local** and with a uniform size of 256KB. Each bit in the bitmap describes 64 blocks (256/4). If the **uniform size** clause is omitted, the default is **autoallocate**. The default **size** for **uniform** is 1MB.

NOTE
*If you specify **local** in a **create tablespace**
command, you cannot specify a **default storage**
clause, **minextents**, or **temporary**. If you use
the **create temporary tablespace** command to
create the tablespace, you can specify **extent
management local**.*

Locally managed tablespaces can take over some of the space management
tasks performed by DBAs in dictionary managed tablespaces. Because of their
architecture, they are less likely to be fragmented, and their objects are less likely
to have space-related problems.

NOTE
*You cannot create the SYSTEM tablespace as locally
managed in Oracle8i or in Oracle9i when you
create the database, and it cannot be converted at
a later time.*

You can create a set of locally managed tablespaces with a small number of
storage parameters and resolve most of the space requests in your database. For
example, you could create three DATA tablespaces as shown here:

```
create tablespace DATA_SMALL
datafile '/u01/oracle/VLDB/data_small.dbf'
size 10M
extent management local uniform size 1M;

create tablespace DATA_MEDIUM
datafile '/u01/oracle/VLDB/data_medium.dbf'
size 100M
extent management local uniform size 4M;

create tablespace DATA_LARGE
datafile '/u01/oracle/VLDB/data_large.dbf'
size 1000M
extent management local uniform size 16M;
```

In this example, the DATA_SMALL tablespace creates objects with extent sizes
that are each 1MB; DATA_MEDIUM uses 4MB extent sizes, and DATA_LARGE uses
16MB extent sizes. If you have a small table, simply place it in the DATA_SMALL
tablespace. If it grows significantly in size, you can move it to the DATA_MEDIUM
or DATA_LARGE tablespace.

Within each of these example tablespaces, all objects will have the same storage parameters, simplifying any future maintenance you perform. Using consistent extent sizes also improves the reuse of space once an object has been dropped from the tablespace or moved.

The following sections describe space management of each major object type. Note that if you use locally managed tablespaces, many of the **storage** clause issues do not apply; you rely on the tablespace to manage the space based on the parameters defined at the tablespace level. Although this may result in some overallocation of space, it will greatly simplify the space management operations in your database.

Table Segments

Table segments, also called *data segments*, store the rows of data associated with tables or clusters. Each data segment contains a header block that serves as a space directory for the segment.

Once a data segment acquires an extent, it keeps that extent until the segment is either dropped or **truncate**d. Deleting rows from a table via the **delete** command has no impact on the amount of space that has been allocated to that table. The number of extents will increase until either (1) the **maxextents** value is reached (if one is set), (2) the user's quota in the tablespace is reached, or (3) the tablespace runs out of space (if the datafiles cannot autoextend). You can enable a datafile to extend automatically; see the "Automating Datafile Extensions" section later in this chapter.

To minimize the amount of wasted space in a data segment, tune the **pctfree** parameter. The **pctfree** parameter specifies the amount of space that will be kept free within each data block. The free space can then be used when **NULL**-valued columns are updated to have values, or when updates to other values in the row force the row to lengthen. The proper setting of **pctfree** is application specific since it is dependent on the nature of the updates that are being performed. For information on setting this and other storage parameters for tables and indexes, see Chapter 5.

You can use the **alter table** command to alter most storage parameters for an existing table. You can use the **move** option of the **alter table** command to change the tablespace assignment for a table.

Index Segments

Like table segments, *index segments* hold the space that has been allocated to them until they are dropped; however, they can also be indirectly dropped if the table or cluster they index is dropped. To minimize contention, indexes should be stored in a tablespace that is separated from their associated tables.

Indexes segments in dictionary managed tablespaces have **storage** clauses that specify their **initial**, **next**, **minextents**, **maxextents**, and **pctincrease** values, and they are as likely to be fragmented as their tables are.

You can use the **rebuild** option of the **alter index** command to alter the **storage** and **tablespace** settings for an index. For example, if you create an index with an overly large **initial** extent, you can reclaim the space from that extent by rebuilding the index and specifying a new value for **initial**, as shown in the following example. In the following listing, the JOB_PK index is rebuilt with an **initial** extent of 10MB.

```
alter index JOB_PK rebuild
tablespace INDEXES
storage (initial 10M next 10M pctincrease 0);
```

During the index **rebuild** process, both the old and the new indexes will exist in the database. Therefore, you must have enough space available to store both indexes prior to executing the **alter index rebuild** command.

While the index is being built, the optimizer can gather statistics about the index's contents. Use the **compute statistics** clause of the **create index** and **alter index rebuild** commands to generate the statistics while the index is built; the combined operation will be faster than separate creation and statistics-gathering commands.

Rollback Segments

Rollback segment functionality is discussed in detail in Chapter 7. The principles of sound design for tables also apply to rollback segments. Rollback segments will have multiple evenly sized extents that add up to their **optimal** total size (they will have a minimum of two extents when created).

Rollback segments can dynamically shrink to a specified size, or they can be manually shrunk to a size of your choosing. The **optimal** clause, which allows rollback segments to shrink to an **optimal** size after extending, helps to provide interim support to systems that have not been properly implemented for the way they are being used. Frequent shrinks (see Chapters 7, 8, and 9) indicate the need for the rollback segments to be redesigned.

For system-managed undo, Oracle automatically allocates and deallocates undo segments as processing requires. See Chapter 7 for a description of undo tablespaces and their associated undo retention parameters.

Temporary Segments

Temporary segments store temporary data during sorting operations (such as large queries, index creations, and **union**s). Each user has a temporary tablespace specified when the account is created via **create user**, or altered via **alter user**. The user's temporary tablespace must be a tablespace that has been designated as a temporary tablespace; as of Oracle9*i*, permanent tablespaces cannot be used for this purpose.

When you create a database, you can specify a default temporary tablespace for all users. For an existing database, you can change the default tablespace via the **alter database** command, as shown in the following listing:

```
alter database default temporary tablespace TEMP;
```

When you alter the database's default temporary tablespace assignment, users who had been pointed to the old default temporary tablespace will be redirected to the new default temporary tablespace. To see the current default temporary tablespace, execute the following query:

```
select Property_Value
   from DATABASE_PROPERTIES
  where Property_Name = 'DEFAULT_TEMP_TABLESPACE';
```

You can specify a tablespace as a "temporary" tablespace via the **create temporary tablespace** command. A temporary tablespace cannot be used to hold any permanent segments, only temporary segments created during operations. The first sort to use the temporary tablespace allocates a temporary segment within the temporary tablespace; when the query completes, the space used by the temporary segment is not dropped. Instead, the space used by the temporary segment is available for use by other queries, allowing the sorting operation to avoid the costs of allocating and releasing space for temporary segments. If your application frequently uses temporary segments for sorting operations, the sorting process should perform better if a dedicated temporary tablespace is used.

To dedicate an existing tablespace for temporary segments, specify the **temporary** clause of the **create tablespace** or **alter tablespace** command, as shown in the following listing:

```
alter tablespace TEMP temporary;
```

NOTE
If there are any permanent segments (tables or indexes, for example) stored in TEMP, the command shown in the preceding listing will fail.

To enable the TEMP tablespace to store permanent (nontemporary) objects, use the **permanent** clause of the **create tablespace** or **alter tablespace** command, as shown in the following listing:

```
alter tablespace TEMP permanent;
```

The Content column in the DBA_TABLESPACES data dictionary view displays the status of the tablespace as either "TEMPORARY" or "PERMANENT."

Free Space

A *free extent* in a tablespace is a collection of contiguous free blocks in the tablespace. A tablespace may contain multiple data extents and free extents (see Figure 4-1a). When a segment is dropped, its extents are deallocated and marked as free. In dictionary managed tablespaces, these free extents are not always recombined with neighboring free extents; the barriers between these free extents may be maintained (see Figure 4-1b). The SMON background process periodically coalesces neighboring free extents (see Figure 4-1c), provided the default **pctincrease** for the tablespace is nonzero.

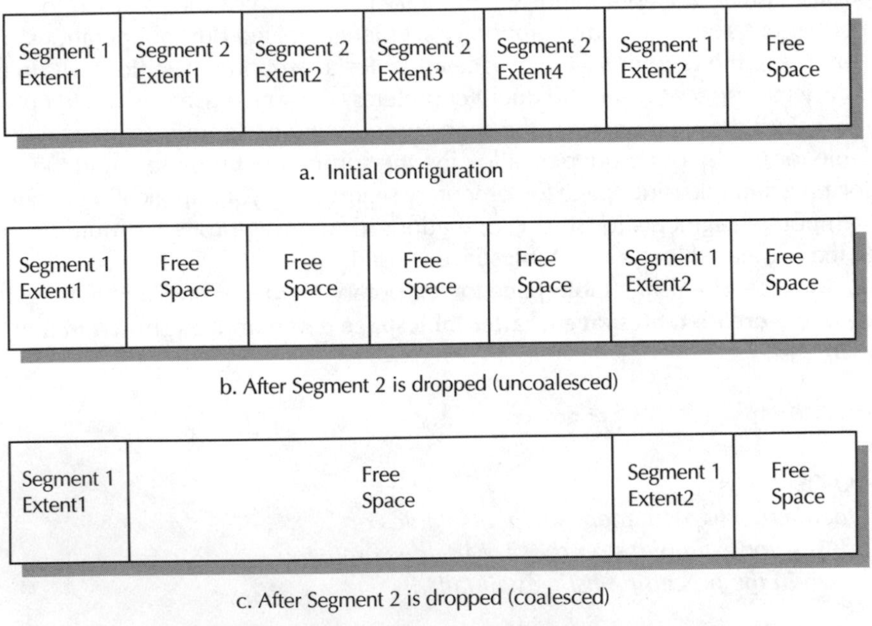

Segment 1 Extent1	Segment 2 Extent1	Segment 2 Extent2	Segment 2 Extent3	Segment 2 Extent4	Segment 1 Extent2	Free Space

a. Initial configuration

Segment 1 Extent1	Free Space	Free Space	Free Space	Free Space	Segment 1 Extent2	Free Space

b. After Segment 2 is dropped (uncoalesced)

Segment 1 Extent1	Free Space	Segment 1 Extent2	Free Space

c. After Segment 2 is dropped (coalesced)

FIGURE 4-1. *Free extent management in directory managed tablespaces*

NOTE
*The SMON background process only coalesces tablespaces whose default **pctincrease** value is nonzero. A **pctincrease** of 1 will force SMON to coalesce the adjacent free space in a tablespace but will only coalesce eight areas of adjoining extents at a time. Each of the eight coalesces will join two or more extents together to create one larger extent. For best space management, use locally managed tablespaces so that you never have to worry about coalescing. If you must use dictionary managed tablespaces, maintain a **pctincrease** of 0 and periodically coalesce any dropped extents manually.*

To force the tablespace to coalesce its free space, use the **coalesce** clause of the **alter tablespace** clause, as shown in the following listing:

```
alter tablespace DATA coalesce;
```

The preceding command will force the neighboring free extents in the DATA tablespace to be coalesced into larger free extents. The command will coalesce up to eight separate areas, just like SMON.

NOTE
*The **alter tablespace** command will not coalesce free extents that are separated by data extents.*

Locally managed tablespaces do not require the same degree of free space management. Since locally managed tablespaces can be configured to have consistent extent sizes for all segments, dropped extents are easily reused.

When allocating a new extent, Oracle will not merge contiguous free extents unless there is no alternative. In dictionary managed tables, this can result in the large free extent at the rear of the tablespace being used while the smaller free extents toward the front of the tablespace are relatively unused. The small free extents become "speed bumps" in the tablespace because they are not, by themselves, of adequate size to be of use. As this usage pattern progresses, the amount of space wasted in the tablespace increases.

In an ideal database, all objects are created at their appropriate size, and all free space is always stored together, a resource pool waiting to be used. If you can avoid dynamic space allocation during application usage, you remove both a performance impact and a source of potential application failure.

Resizing Datafiles

Existing datafiles can be resized via the **alter database** and **alter tablespace** commands. You can specify values for storage extension parameters for each datafile in a database; Oracle will use those values when automatically extending the datafile. Datafiles can also be extended manually, and can be resized down (to a smaller size) manually as well.

To manually extend a datafile, use the **alter database** command, as shown in the following example:

```
alter database
datafile '/db05/oracle/CC1/data01.dbf' resize 200M;
```

After the **alter database** command shown in the preceding example is executed, the specified file will be resized to 200MB in size. If the file was already more than 200MB in size, it will decrease in size to 200MB if possible. When the database shrinks the file, it shrinks it from the end. Therefore, if there is any segment stored at the physical end of the file, the database will not be able to shrink the file. If there are any extents stored past the point you specify (in this example, 200MB), then the **alter database** command in the preceding listing will fail. See Chapter 8 for a script that maps out your data storage locations within files.

Automating Datafile Extensions

When creating datafiles, you can specify parameters that will allow Oracle to automatically extend your datafiles. The datafiles could then be automatically extended whenever their current allocated length is exceeded. You can specify three sizing parameters for each datafile:

autoextend	A flag, set to ON or OFF to indicate if the file should be allowed to automatically extend. If set to OFF, the other sizing parameters will be set to zero.
next *size*	The size, in bytes, of the area of disk space to allocate to the datafile when more space is required. You can qualify the *size* value with "K" and "M," for kilobytes and megabytes, respectively.
maxsize *size*	The maximum size, in bytes, to which the datafile is allowed to extend. Set to **unlimited** if you do not want to limit the datafile size within Oracle. You can qualify the *size* value with "K" and "M," for kilobytes and megabytes, respectively.

If **maxsize unlimited** is specified, the maximum size of the datafile will be limited by the available space on the file's disk and the maximum file size supported by the operating system. The file size may also be limited by a file size quota set at the operating system level against the "oracle" userid.

The **autoextend**, **next**, and **maxsize** parameters can be specified for a datafile via the **create database**, **create tablespace**, **alter database**, and **alter tablespace** commands. In the following example, the **create tablespace** command creates a datafile that will automatically extend as needed:

```
create tablespace DATA
datafile '/db05/oracle/CC1/data01.dbf' size 200M
autoextend ON
next 10M
maxsize 250M;
```

The tablespace created in this example will have a single datafile with an initial size of 200MB. When that datafile fills, and the objects within it require additional space, the datafile will extend itself by 10MB. The extension process will continue as needed until the file has reached 250MB in size, at which point the file will have reached its maximum size.

You can add a new datafile, via the **alter tablespace** or **alter database** command, to enable **autoextend** capabilities for a tablespace. The command in the following listing adds a new datafile to the DATA tablespace, specifying **autoextend on** and **maxsize** 300MB:

```
alter tablespace DATA
add datafile '/db05/oracle/CC1/data02.dbf'
size 50M
autoextend ON
maxsize 300M;
```

How to Move Database Files

Once a file has been created in a database, you may need to move it to better manage its size or I/O requirements. In the following sections you'll see the procedures for moving datafiles, online redo log files, and control files. In all of the procedures, operating system commands are used to move the files; the Oracle commands serve primarily to reset the pointers to these files.

Moving Datafiles

There are two methods for moving datafiles: via the **alter database** command and via the **alter tablespace** command. The **alter tablespace** method only applies to datafiles whose tablespaces do not include SYSTEM, rollback segments, or temporary segments. The **alter database** method will work for all datafiles.

The alter database Method

When using the **alter database** method to move datafiles, the datafile is moved after the instance has been shut down. The steps involved are as follows:

1. Shut down the instance.

2. Use operating system commands to move the datafile.

3. Mount the database (but do not open it) and use **alter database** to rename the file within the database.

4. Start the instance.

5. Following verification of the change, perform a file system backup of the database.

For example, after shutting down the database, you may have moved a datafile to a new disk:

```
> mv /db01/oracle/CC1/data01.dbf /db02/oracle/CC1
```

For the database to recognize the new file location, you must mount the database (in this example, named CC1) and point it to the new location. The **alter database** command shown in the following listing does not rename the file; the file must have already been renamed or moved.

```
SQL> connect / as sysdba;
SQL> startup mount CC1;
SQL> alter database rename file
  2> '/db01/oracle/CC1/data01.dbf' to
  3> '/db02/oracle/CC1/data01.dbf';
```

At this point, you can open the database, verify that the action completed successfully, and then perform a file system backup of the database.

NOTE
*When the **alter database** command is executed, Oracle will check to see if the name you are naming the file to exists. If this step fails, check the accuracy of the destination filename.*

The alter tablespace Method

When using the **alter tablespace** method to move datafiles, the datafile is moved while the instance is still running. The steps involved, detailed in the following sections, are as follows:

1. Take the tablespace offline.

2. Use operating system commands to move the file.

3. Use the **alter tablespace** command to rename the file within the database.

4. Bring the tablespace back online.

NOTE
This method can only be used for non-SYSTEM tablespaces. It cannot be used for tablespaces that contain active rollback segments or temporary segments.

Step 1. Take the Tablespace Offline.　Use the **alter tablespace** command within SQL*Plus or OEM to put the tablespace into **offline** state, as shown in the following example. This command is executed while the instance is open.

```
SQL> alter tablespace DATA offline;
```

Step 2. Use Operating System Commands to Move the File.　In UNIX, the **mv** command moves files to new locations. The following example shows the data01.dbf file being moved from the device named /db01 to one named /db02:

```
> mv /db01/oracle/CC1/data01.dbf /db02/oracle/CC1
```

The filename must fully specify a filename using the conventions of your operating system.

Step 3. Rename the File Within the Database.　In the following example, the data01.dbf datafile moved in step 2 is renamed within the database. The database will then be able to access that file. The **alter tablespace** command shown here does not rename the file; the file must have already been renamed or moved.

```
SQL> alter tablespace DATA rename datafile
  2> '/db01/oracle/CC1/data01.dbf' to
  3> '/db02/oracle/CC1/data01.dbf';
```

Do not disconnect after this step is complete; stay logged into the database and proceed to step 4.

NOTE
*When the **alter tablespace** command is executed,
Oracle will check to see if the name you are naming
the file to exists. If this step fails, check the accuracy
of the destination filename.*

Step 4. Bring the Tablespace Back Online.   Use the **alter tablespace**
command to bring the tablespace back online.

```
SQL> alter tablespace DATA online;
```

The DATA tablespace will then be brought back online, using the new location
for the datafile.

Moving a Datafile with Oracle Enterprise Manager

Although there are two methods that can be used to move a datafile interactively
from the system level, there is only one way to perform the same task from the
Oracle Enterprise Manager (OEM). In the following section, you will see the steps to
follow within OEM to move a datafile from one directory location to another. In the
figures in this section, the datafile for the EXAMPLE tablespace will be moved from
the D:\Oracle\Ora90\oradata\mydb9\ to the G:\Oracle\oradata\mydb9\ directory.

Steps Required to Move a Datafile Using OEM
To move a datafile from one directory to another using OEM, follow the same steps
as described in the prior "The **alter tablespace** Method" section. In the following
example, the OEM toolset is used in place of SQL*Plus, and the actions can be
accomplished from a remote console.

The alter tablespace Method from OEM
When using the **alter tablespace** method to move datafiles, the datafile is moved
while the instance is still running. The steps involved, detailed in the following
sections, are as follows:

1. Take the tablespace offline.

2. From the Microsoft Explorer tool on Windows NT, move the datafile from
   the old folder to the new folder.

3. Use the datafile detail screen to modify the datafile name.

4. Bring the tablespace back online.

NOTE
*This method can only be used for non-SYSTEM
tablespaces. It cannot be used for tablespaces that
contain active rollback segments or temporary
segments.*

Step 1. Take the Tablespace Offline.   From the Oracle Storage Manager option
of the OEM, select the tablespace whose datafile is going to be moved. After selecting
the tablespace, use the pull-down menu, or right-click and select the option Take
Offline | Normal to put the tablespace into **offline** state, as shown in Figure 4-2.

The tablespace is changed to **offline** state (while the instance is still running) and
the Size and Used column values set to zero. After selecting the option to take the
tablespace offline, a confirmation screen will be displayed with the question, "Are
you sure you want to take this Tablespace Offline?"

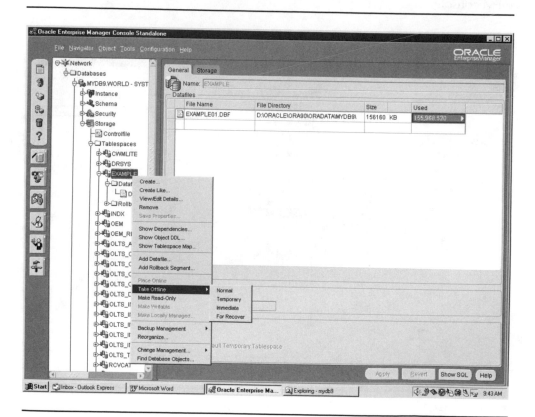

FIGURE 4-2.   *Right-click menu, Take Offline option*

Step 2. Use Microsoft Explorer to Move the File.   On Windows NT, use the
Microsoft Explorer tool to move the datafile. In UNIX, the **mv** command moves files
to new locations.

In Figure 4-3, the datafile is shown in the D:\Oracle\Ora90\oradata\mydb9\
directory. The cursor is used to click on the datafile, and with the left mouse button
depressed, the file is dragged from the current directory to the new directory
G:\Oracle\oradata\mydb9\. In Figure 4-4, the datafile is now shown located in
the G:\Oracle\oradata\mydb9\directory.

Step 3. Use the Datafile Detail Screen to Modify the Datafile Name.   In our
example, the Example01.dbf datafile moved in step 2 is renamed within the database;
the database will then be able to access that file. Renaming the directory name of the
datafile as shown here does not rename the file; the file must have already been
renamed or moved. Figures 4-5, 4-6, 4-7, and 4-8 show the progression of steps
that are taken to modify the datafile location and see the modification from the
OEM console.

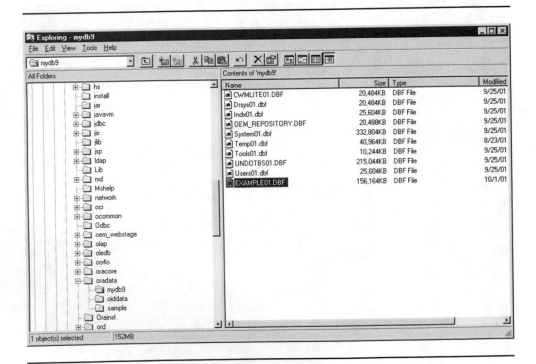

FIGURE 4-3.   *Original Windows NT file location*

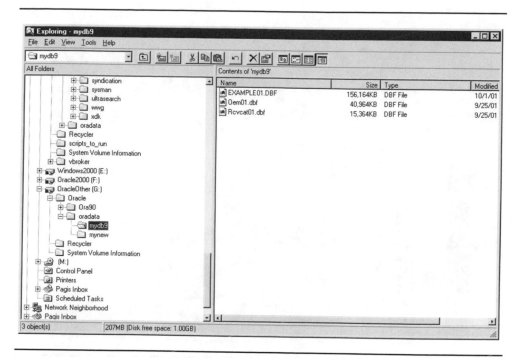

FIGURE 4-4.   *New Windows NT file location*

Figure 4-5 shows the original appearance of the screen prior to the datafile directory location being changed. The Object pull-down menu with the View/Edit Details option highlighted is shown as well.

Figure 4-6 shows the datafile detail with the directory change from the D: to the G: location. Notice that the Apply button at the bottom of the datafile detail screen is active. To make the change take effect, click on the Apply button. When you click on the Apply button, Oracle will check to see if the name you are naming the file to exists. If this step fails, check the accuracy of the destination filename.

To update the left screen of OEM and display the change, use the Refresh option (under the Navigator option on the OEM menu).

In Figure 4-7, the screen has been refreshed, and both the left screen and datafile detail screen now display the correct information. If the OEM tool had been exited and reentered, the change would also have been visible.

Do not disconnect from OEM after this step is complete; stay in this tool and proceed to step 4.

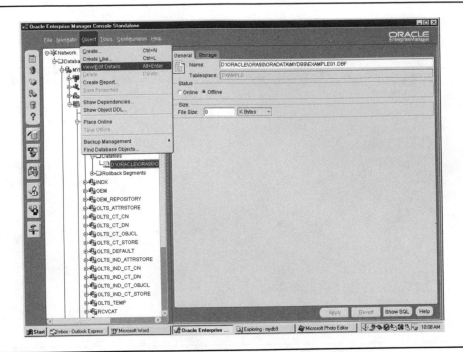

FIGURE 4-5. *OEM Management Console with Object | View/Edit Details option*

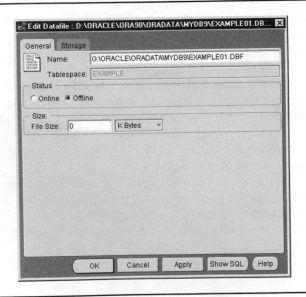

FIGURE 4-6. *View/Edit Datafile, General tab*

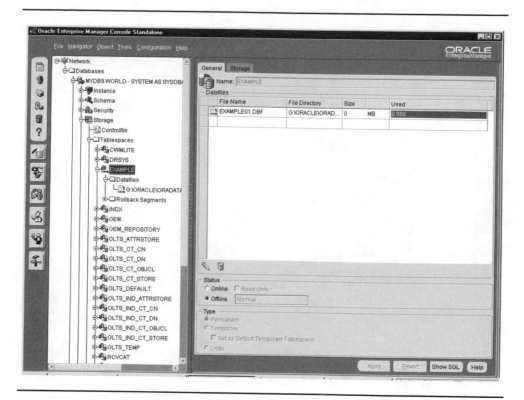

FIGURE 4-7.   *OEM Console screen with datafile modification completed*

Step 4. Bring the Tablespace Back Online.   Use either the pull-down menu, or right-click to bring the tablespace back online from within the Oracle Storage option of OEM. Select the option Place Online to place the tablespace into the **online** state, as shown in Figure 4-8.

After selecting the option to bring the tablespace online, a Confirmation screen will be displayed with the question, "Are you sure you want to bring this Tablespace Online?" Confirm your selection by clicking on the Yes option, or cancel the operation by selecting No. When you click on Yes, the EXAMPLE tablespace will be brought back online, using the new location for the datafile.

Moving Online Redo Log Files

Online redo log files can be moved while the database is shut down, and renamed within the database via the **alter database** command. The procedures for moving

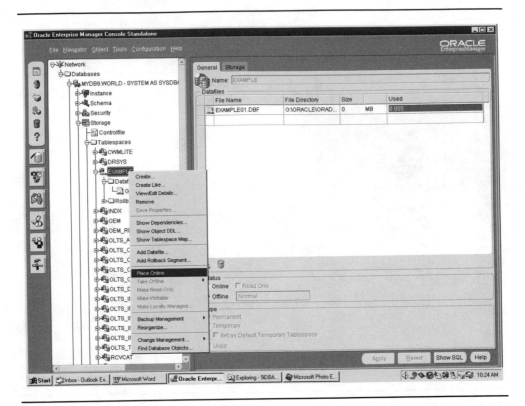

FIGURE 4-8. *Right-click menu, Place Online option*

online redo log files are very similar to those used to move datafiles via the **alter database** command.

First, the database is shut down and the online redo log file is moved. The database is then mounted and the **alter database** command is used to tell the database the new location of the online redo log file. The instance can then be opened, using the online redo log file in its new location.

The following example shows the UNIX **mv** command used to move the redo01CC1.dbf file while the database is shut down. In this example, the file is being moved from the device named /db05 to one named /db02:

```
> mv /db05/oracle/CC1/redo01CC1.dbf /db02/oracle/CC1
```

The filename must fully specify a filename using the conventions of your operating system.

For the database to recognize the new file location, you must mount the database (in this example, named CC1) and point it to the new location. The **alter**

database command shown in the following listing does not rename the file; the file must have already been renamed or moved.

```
SQL> connect / as sysdba;
SQL> startup mount CC1;
SQL> alter database rename file
  2> '/db05/oracle/CC1/redo01CC1.dbf' to
  3> '/db02/oracle/CC1/redo01CC1.dbf';
```

NOTE
*When the **alter database** command is executed, Oracle will check to see if the name you are naming the file to exists. If this step fails, check the accuracy of the destination filename.*

You can now open the database via the **alter database open** command. After verifying that the file was moved properly, perform a file system backup of the database.

Moving Control Files

The location of control files is specified in the initialization parameter file for the instance. To move a control file, you must shut down the instance, move the file, edit the initialization file, and then restart the instance.

The following listing shows the use of the UNIX **mv** command to move a control file to a new location. The following example shows the ctrl1CC1.ctl file being moved from the device named /db05 to one named /db02.

```
> mv /db05/oracle/CC1/ctrl1CC1.ctl /db02/oracle/CC1
```

The filename must fully specify a filename using the conventions of your operating system.

In your database parameter file, edit the entry for the *control_files* parameter:

```
control_files     = (/db01/oracle/CC1/ctrl1CC1.ctl,
                      /db03/oracle/CC1/ctrl1CC1.ctl,
                      /db05/oracle/CC1/ctrl1CC1.ctl)
```

Edit this entry to reflect the change to the file location:

```
control_files     = (/db01/oracle/CC1/ctrl1CC1.ctl,
                      /db03/oracle/CC1/ctrl1CC1.ctl,
                      /db02/oracle/CC1/ctrl1CC1.ctl)
```

You can now start the instance using the new control file location.

How to Deallocate Space from Segments

As of Oracle7.2, you can reclaim unused space from existing datafiles. As of Oracle7.3, you can reclaim space from tables, indexes, and clusters. In the following sections, you'll see examples of datafiles, tables, and indexes that are "shrunk" to reclaim previously allocated space.

Shrinking Datafiles

You can use the **alter database** command to reclaim unused space from datafiles. You cannot resize a datafile if the space you are trying to reclaim is currently allocated to a database object.

For example, if the datafile is 100MB in size, and 70MB of the datafile is currently in use, you will need to leave at least 70MB in the datafile. You can use the **resize** clause of the **alter database** command to reclaim the space, as shown in the following example:

```
alter database datafile '/db05/oracle/CC1/data01.dbf'
resize 80M;
```

As shown in the listing, you specify the name of the file to be shrunk and its new size. If there are no database objects beyond the first 80MB of the specified datafile, the datafile will be shrunk to 80MB.

If space is used within the datafile beyond the first 80MB, then an error will be returned. As shown in the following listing, the error will show the amount of space that is used within the datafile beyond the specified **resize** value:

```
alter database datafile '/db05/oracle/CC1/data01.dbf'
resize 80M;
*
ERROR at line 1:
ORA-03297: file contains 507 blocks of data beyond
requested RESIZE value
```

If the database block size is 4KB, then 507 database blocks is equivalent to 1.98MB. If you increase the **resize** value specified to 82MB, then the datafile can be resized.

To minimize the chances of encountering an error during free space reclamation from datafiles, you can "map" the free space within a datafile. Chapter 8 includes a script that maps the free and used space within a tablespace and datafile. If your free space is fragmented, Oracle may not be able to reclaim it all during a datafile resize operation.

Shrinking Tables, Clusters, and Indexes

When Oracle writes data to a segment, it updates the *high-water mark* for the segment. Internally, the high-water mark advances as blocks are put on the free list, normally five blocks at a time. The high-water mark points to the block immediately following the last block on the free list. If you **insert** thousands of rows in the table, the high-water mark will be incremented; if you **delete** the records, the high-water mark will *not* decrease. Aside from dropping and re-creating the table, the high-water mark for a segment is only reset when you issue a **truncate** command or the segment is dropped and re-created.

As of Oracle7.3, unused space above the high-water mark in a segment can be reclaimed. If you have overestimated the storage requirements for an object, you may wish to reclaim space that was allocated unnecessarily. You can reclaim the space from the segment without dropping and re-creating it—with the limitation that you can only reclaim the space above the high-water mark for the table.

Before you can reclaim space from a table, you should therefore determine the high-water mark for the table. In the following listing, the UNUSED_SPACE procedure within the DBMS_SPACE package is used to determine the space usage of the table named SPACES owned by the user OPS$CC1:

```
declare
        VAR1 number;
        VAR2 number;
        VAR3 number;
        VAR4 number;
        VAR5 number;
        VAR6 number;
        VAR7 number;
begin
    dbms_space.unused_space('OPS$CC1','SPACES','TABLE',
                        VAR1,VAR2,VAR3,VAR4,VAR5,VAR6,VAR7);
    dbms_output.put_line('OBJECT_NAME        = SPACES');
    dbms_output.put_line('---------------------------');
    dbms_output.put_line('TOTAL_BLOCKS       = '||VAR1);
    dbms_output.put_line('TOTAL_BYTES        = '||VAR2);
    dbms_output.put_line('UNUSED_BLOCKS      = '||VAR3);
    dbms_output.put_line('UNUSED_BYTES       = '||VAR4);
    dbms_output.put_line('LAST_USED_EXTENT_FILE_ID  = '||VAR5);
    dbms_output.put_line('LAST_USED_EXTENT_BLOCK_ID = '||VAR6);
    dbms_output.put_line('LAST_USED_BLOCK    = '||VAR7);
end;
/
```

Sample output of the preceding script for a 2MB SPACES table is shown in the following listing:

```
OBJECT_NAME     = SPACES
--------------------------
TOTAL_BLOCKS    = 500
TOTAL_BYTES     = 2048000
UNUSED_BLOCKS   = 200
UNUSED_BYTES    = 819200
```

The high-water mark of the table (in bytes) is the difference between the TOTAL_BYTES value and the UNUSED_BYTES value returned by this procedure call. The UNUSED_BLOCKS value represents the number of blocks above the high-water mark; the TOTAL_BLOCKS value reflects the total number of blocks allocated to the table.

If you want to reclaim space from the table, and its UNUSED_BLOCKS value is nonzero, you can use the **alter table** command to reclaim the space above the high-water mark. In the preceding example, the TOTAL_BLOCKS value is 500 and the UNUSED_BLOCKS value is 200, with a database block size of 4KB. You can reclaim the 200 unused blocks (800 KB).

If you want to leave 20 blocks within the table as unused space above the high-water mark, you can alter the table, specifying that the database keep 20 blocks—80KB.

To reclaim space from a table, use the **alter table** command, as shown in the following listing. The **keep** parameter specifies the amount of free space to keep.

```
alter table SPACES deallocate unused keep 80K;
```

If you had not specified the **keep** clause, the **minextents** and **initial** storage values for the table would have been preserved. If **keep** is used, you can eliminate free space from any extent—even from the **initial** extent if there is no data in any other extent!

NOTE
For locally managed tablespaces with segment space management specified as AUTO, use the SPACE_USAGE procedure of the DBMS_SPACE package instead of the UNUSED_SPACE procedure shown in the example.

You can deallocate space from clusters via the **deallocate unused** clause of the **alter cluster** command. After deallocating space from a segment, you should execute the DBMS_SPACE package's procedures again to see the new values for the total and unused blocks allocated to the segment.

You can deallocate space from indexes via the **deallocate unused** clause of the **alter index** command. However, there is another option for indexes that allows you even greater flexibility when manipulating index space usage—**alter index rebuild**, as described in the next section.

How to Rebuild Indexes

As of Oracle7.3, you can use the **alter index rebuild** command to rapidly change the **storage** and **tablespace** parameters for an existing index—without having to drop the original index.

When you use the **alter index rebuild** command, the existing index is used as the data source for the new index (instead of using the table as the data source), improving performance of index creation. During the index re-creation, you can change the index's **storage** and **tablespace** parameters.

In the following example, the IU_SPACES$DB_TS_CD index is rebuilt via the **alter index rebuild** command. Its **storage** parameters are changed to use an **initial** extent size of 16MB and a **next** extent size of 16MB in the INDX_1 tablespace.

```
alter index IU_SPACES$DB_TS_CD rebuild
storage (initial 16M next 16M pctincrease 0)
tablespace INDX_1;
```

While the new IU_SPACES$DB_TS_CD index is being built, it will exist simultaneously with the old index in the database. There must be enough space available to store both the old index and the new index in the database in order to use **alter index rebuild**. After the command has completed and the new index is available, the old index will be dropped automatically and the space will be reclaimed—but the space has to be available during the command execution or the new index creation will fail.

You can use the **alter index rebuild** command to quickly rebuild indexes while moving them to different tablespaces. Index rebuilds allow you to set up a simple maintenance schedule for the most used indexes in your database. If the records in a table are frequently **delete**d and **insert**ed, the space used by the indexes on the table will continue to grow, even if the overall number of records remains unchanged.

To reclaim the unusable space in an index, you can use the **alter index rebuild** command. Schedule a batch job to run periodically to rebuild the indexes on your most active tables. Run the batch job at off-hours to avoid scheduling conflicts with users. If you adhere to a maintenance schedule for your indexes, you will be able to reclaim the unusable space quickly. During each **alter index rebuild** command, specify both the **tablespace** and **storage** parameters for your index.

NOTE
*For information on rebuilding index partitions, see
Chapter 15.*

Online Index Rebuilds

You can rebuild indexes online while DML operations are performed against the
table or partition. The **alter index rebuild online** command does not support parallel
DML operations, bitmap indexes, cluster indexes, or indexes used to enforce referential
integrity constraints. For all other index types, the **rebuild online** command is a
powerful tool for high availability databases.

The following command rebuilds the EMP$DEPT_NO index online:

```
alter index EMP$DEPT_NO rebuild online
storage (initial 16M next 16M pctincrease 0)
tablespace INDX_1;
```

You must have enough space to store both the old index and the new index online
concurrently. While the rebuild is occurring, user transactions against the EMP table
will be supported.

Using Oracle Managed Files (OMFs)

As of Oracle9*i*, you can use Oracle Managed Files (OMFs) to simplify the
administration of database files. When you use OMFs, Oracle uses its file system
interfaces to create and delete datafiles, control files, and online redo log files as
required by your DDL commands. When you drop a tablespace using OMFs, for
example, Oracle will delete the datafiles associated with the tablespace rather than
leaving them on the file system.

Configuring the Environment

To enable the use of OMFs, you must set values for the following database
initialization parameters:

Parameter	Description
DB_CREATE_ FILE_DEST	The default directory for all datafiles and tempfiles when no file specification is given. Also used for online redo log files and control files if DB_CREATE_ONLINE_LOG_DEST_*n* is not specified.
DB_CREATE_ ONLINE_LOG _DEST_*n*	The default directory for online redo log files and control files when no file specification is given. *N* can be a number from 1 to 5, for each of the multiplexed online redo log and control files.

The DB_CREATE_FILE_DEST parameter tells Oracle where to create and find datafiles; the directory must already exist. When creating datafiles using OMFs, you can specify a directory or use the DB_CREATE_FILE_DEST parameter value by default.

NOTE
*You can change the values of DB_CREATE_FILE_DEST and DB_CREATE_ONLINE_LOG_DEST_n dynamically via the **alter system** and **alter session** commands.*

When you create an OMF, the filename is written to the alert log for future reference. Be sure to record the filenames in the event you need to perform recoveries or other file maintenance. The filename will include a unique string generated by Oracle to avoid overwriting existing files on the operating system.

Creating Oracle Managed Files

If you have configured the environment parameters to support OMFs, Oracle will manage files when you leave out the **datafile** or **logfile** clauses while creating datafiles and log files. For example, you may specify parameter values as

```
DB_CREATE_FILE_DEST='/u01/oracle/CC1'
DB_CREATE_ONLINE_LOG_DEST_1='/u02/oracle/CC1'
DB_CREATE_ONLINE_LOG_DEST_2='/u03/oracle/CC1'
```

If you now issue a **create database** command, Oracle will create OMFs as required. The following command creates the CC1 database:

```
create database cc1;
```

If you are using OMFs, this command will generate a 100MB autoextensible SYSTEM tablespace datafile in /u01/oracle/CC1, and two online log groups in each of the log destination areas.

NOTE
By default, the log files will be 100MB each.

Oracle will also automatically create an undo tablespace (see Chapter 7) with a 10MB autoextensible datafile in /u01/oracle/CC1. If you have not also set a value for the CONTROL_FILES initialization parameter, Oracle will create control files in the redo log destination areas.

In an existing database, you can create an OMF while creating a tablespace, provided the DB_CREATE_FILE_DEST initialization parameter is set. The following command will create an OMF for a new USERS_2 tablespace:

```
create tablespace USERS_2;
```

You can also specify storage and other parameters for the tablespaces. For example, you can create two OMFs for a tablespace with a single command:

```
create tablespace USERS_3
datafile size 500M, size 500M;
```

In this example, two 500MB datafiles will be created for the USERS_3 tablespace. Each of the files will be 500MB in size, and each will be autoextensible unless you also specify **autoextend off**.

To add an OMF datafile to an existing tablespace, use the **alter tablespace** command, as shown in the following listing:

```
alter tablespace USERS_3
add datafile size 300M;
```

To add online redo log files, use the **alter database** command:

```
alter database add logfile;
```

The preceding command will create a new log file with a member in each of the DB_CREATE_ONLINE_LOG_DEST_*n* locations.

Maintenance of Oracle Managed Files

You can manage OMFs the same as you manage user-managed files. For example, if Oracle creates an OMF named ORA_USERS_3_ERJ42201.dbf for your USERS_3 tablespace, you can move that file via the **alter tablespace** or **alter database** command, as shown earlier in this chapter. The following command will redirect Oracle's internal pointer to the /u04/oracle/CC1 directory for this file:

```
alter database rename file '/u01/oracle/CC1/ora_users_3_erj42201.dbf'
to 'u04/oracle/CC1/ora_users_3_erj42201.dbf';
```

You can rename the file to remove the eight-character uniqueness key if you wish.

NOTE
Using OMFs will not impact your ability to back up and recover the database via exports, file system backups, or RMAN.

When you drop a datafile that uses OMFs, Oracle will automatically drop the datafiles. The following command will drop the USERS_3 tablespace and delete its files at the operating system level:

```
drop tablespace USERS_3;
```

If you are using user-managed files, the USERS_3 tablespace's datafiles will remain on the operating system, even after the tablespace has been dropped.

Physically Fit

In your databases, the file allocation must be planned (using I/O estimates), and the allocation must be verified once the system goes into production. The file layout can be modified postproduction to better balance the I/O requirements of the files. The result will be a database that achieves its performance goals without sacrificing recoverability, and its recoverability goals without sacrificing performance.

Each facet of the database—tables, indexes, rollback segments/undo tablespaces, and temporary segments—must be sized correctly as well. Correct sizing requires knowing the way in which the data is to be entered, how it is to be stored, and the processes that will be performed on it once it gets there. The costs of planning the storage parameters are minimal when compared to the costs of manipulating the system once it has been released to production. Postproduction tuning should be a final, minor step in the physical design planning process.

PART
II

Database
Management

CHAPTER
5

Managing the
Development Process

anaging application development can be a difficult process. From a DBA's perspective, the best way to manage development is to become an integral part of teams involved in the process. In this chapter, you will see the activities involved in migrating applications into databases and the technical details needed for implementation, including the sizing of database objects.

This chapter focuses on controlling the activities that create objects in the database at various stages. These activities should follow the database planning activities that were described in Chapter 3 and Chapter 4. Chapters 6, 8, and 9 address the monitoring and tuning activities that follow the database creation.

Implementing an application in a database by merely running a series of **create table** commands fails to integrate the creation process with the other major areas (planning, monitoring, and tuning). The DBA must be involved in the application development process in order to correctly design the database that will support the end product. The methods described in this chapter will also provide important information for structuring the database monitoring and tuning efforts.

Three Critical Elements of Success

The life cycle of a database is defined by the four actions referred to previously: planning, creating, monitoring, and tuning. The elements of a successful implementation of this cycle can be identified as belonging to three key categories: *cultural processes, management processes,* and *technology.*

Managing the implementation efforts of database developers requires action in all three categories:

- **Cultural**   The corporate culture and the development team must support the DBA's involvement in the development process.

- **Management**   The developers' adherence to a life cycle methodology must be enforceable.

- **Technology**   The developers and DBAs must define mechanisms for making sure the appropriate level of involvement and attention to detail is taking place.

NOTE
Attempting to implement a development life cycle methodology without corporate buy-in or without technology that allows for the tracking of deliverables will yield little long-term benefit.

Cultural Processes

DBAs and developers working as part of the same development team can add substantial value to the development process. A joint DBA/developer team adds value by

- Building applications that are easier to maintain

- Building applications that are properly sized and configured, and thus require less downtime for maintenance

- Creating appropriate indexes to maximize query performance

- Identifying the tables and indexes that will be most frequently used by the application

- Identifying and correcting poorly constructed SQL to avoid performance impacts

- Identifying static query-only tables within the application

- Building into each application an understanding of the interface needs of outside applications

- Identifying technical problems earlier in the development process

- Identifying resource scheduling conflicts between online users and long-running batch processes

- Allowing the DBA, who will eventually provide much of the application's support, to accept partial ownership of the application during its development

The value the DBA adds to these efforts is greatly enhanced when the DBA understands the application and the business needs it serves. If you understand the business needs, you can better understand the developers' goals in their application development process. As another benefit, understanding the application and the business will greatly improve your ability to communicate effectively with the application developers and users. Working with the application development team from the beginning will improve your ability to properly size and tune the database used by the application.

Difficult to maintain, fragmented, slow, and isolated database applications cost the organization in terms of downtime, tuning time, and user frustration. These costs can be avoided by entering into team relationships between developers and DBAs early in the application development process. The methodology must clearly define the roles and responsibilities within these relationships and must be accepted by all levels within the personnel groups responsible for applications development.

Management Processes

To properly manage development efforts, the methodology must define the relationships between the different functional areas and the deliverables required in each phase of application development. For example, when does an application move out of development and into test, or from test to production? Who decides? The methodology dictates the answer. If the deliverables for the development section are completed, reviewed, and approved, then the application can be moved into the test environment, under whose constraints the developers must then work.

Defining the Environment

Most application environments are divided into two to five areas. They are *development, system test, stress test, acceptance test,* and *production.* For the purposes of this discussion, the three test areas will be combined. The exact number of areas maintained is methodology specific and may include additional areas for staging, quality assurance, or other business needs.

NOTE
Although it is not discussed in depth here, stress testing should be an integral part of the development process. In practice, stress testing is most effective when it is performed before acceptance testing; problems related to the usage load should be resolved prior to any acceptance testing.

Consider each of the areas. The methodology needs to specify what the finished product will be from each area, and what completing that section will provide to subsequent areas. Once the deliverables have been defined, the database needs for the different areas can be deduced.

In development, for instance, users may have free reign to make table changes, test new ideas, and create new objects. An integrated CASE (computer-aided systems engineering) tool should be used to maintain a synchronized logical model. The CASE repository should be used to generate the first set of database objects in each environment; the developers should be responsible for maintaining the CASE dictionary thereafter.

Once the system enters the test phase, its final configuration should be largely complete. At this point, the table volumes, user accounts, and performance needs should be identified. These requirements will allow the DBA to create a proper database for the application and to establish acceptable control limits for monitoring.

In production, developers are locked out. From the database's perspective, developers are just another set of users. All changes to database objects in the production database should have first passed through the test environment via a defined change control process.

In order to maintain the proper level of user system-level privileges, developer accounts must be configured differently for each area. The next section will describe the proper system role definitions for developers given the development, test, and production areas previously described.

Role Definitions

Of the system-level roles provided by Oracle, three roles (CONNECT, RESOURCE, and DBA) apply to the development environment (the others are related to the administration of the database, and are described in Chapter 10). You can create your own system-level roles to define system privileges beyond CONNECT, RESOURCE, and DBA, but these may be more difficult to use and maintain than the system-provided roles. You can grant roles to the users and developers depending on the system privileges they need in their environment.

CONNECT

The CONNECT role gives users privileges beyond just creating sessions in the database. In addition to the CREATE SESSION system privilege, the CONNECT role gives users the following system privileges: ALTER SESSION, CREATE CLUSTER, CREATE DATABASE LINK, CREATE SEQUENCE, CREATE SYNONYM, CREATE TABLE, and CREATE VIEW. That's far more than just connecting to the database. However, users with the CONNECT role do not have the ability to create tables or clusters (objects that use space in the database) unless you grant them a quota on a tablespace, or unless they have been granted the RESOURCE role (discussed next). See Chapter 10 for details on the granting of space quotas.

For most developers working in development and test databases, the CONNECT role should be granted along with the RESOURCE role. If you wish to limit the system privileges of your application users, you can create your own role—APPLICATION_USER—which has just the CREATE SESSION privilege:

```
create role APPLICATION_USER;
grant CREATE SESSION to APPLICATION_USER;
grant APPLICATION_USER to username;
```

RESOURCE

The RESOURCE role has the following system privileges: CREATE CLUSTER, CREATE INDEXTYPE, CREATE OPERATOR, CREATE PROCEDURE, CREATE SEQUENCE, CREATE TABLE, CREATE TRIGGER, and CREATE TYPE. Users who have the RESOURCE role are also granted the UNLIMITED TABLESPACE privilege, so they can override the quotas defined for them. You should grant the RESOURCE role to developers who will be creating PL/SQL objects such as procedures and triggers. If your developers use the Objects option, the RESOURCE role gives them the CREATE TYPE privilege, which enables them to create types and methods.

If you wish to restrict developers' privileges, then you can create your own role and grant system-level privileges to it. For example, you may want to restrict developers' ability to create tables and clusters, while permitting them to create indexes and procedural objects. If that is the case, then you could create a system-level role and grant it all of the system privileges that constitute RESOURCE except for the privileges you wish to exclude. In general, you should only grant developers the RESOURCE role in development; in test and production, the CONNECT role should be sufficient. If you give developers RESOURCE access to your production database, you will be giving away control of your database and severely impacting your ability to enforce a change control process.

DBA

The DBA role has all system privileges **with admin option** so the DBA can grant the system privileges to any other user. You should not grant the DBA role to application developers or users in any development, test, or production database. If you grant developers the DBA role in development, they may code their application with the assumption that they will have the same system privileges when the application is released into the production environment. If you cannot restrict access to DBA-privileged accounts, then you cannot guarantee the security of the data in your database, and that is one of the key job functions of the DBA.

By forcing the developers to identify and track the minimum privileges necessary for their application to function properly, you can bring a fully functional application to production with the fewest privileges required.

In Test and Production

The appropriate role designations for the test environment depend on how that environment is to be used. If it is to be used as a true acceptance test region, mirroring the eventual production database, then its roles should be assigned to mirror the production roles. If, however, developers will be allowed to make modifications to the test database, then they will require access to an account that has the same privileges that they have in the development environment.

The tables and other database objects used by the application are typically owned by a small number of accounts in test and production. If the change must be performed within the account that owns the application schema (for example, the creation of a database link), then the DBA can temporarily log into that account and perform the change. In general, developers should not have the RESOURCE role in a test environment. If a change is to be made to the system, the change should be made first in development and then migrated to test via a documented change control process.

NOTE
*You can use the **account lock** option of the **alter user** command to prevent logins to existing accounts. You can temporarily unlock accounts during maintenance periods.*

Deliverables

How do you know if the methodology is being followed? Doing so requires establishing a list of items called *deliverables* that must be completed during the application development. The methodology must clearly define, both in format and in level of detail, the required deliverables for each stage of the life cycle. These should include specifications for each of the following items:

- Entity relationship diagram

- Physical database diagram

- Space requirements

- Tuning goals for queries and transaction processing

- Security requirements

- Data requirements

- Query execution plans

- Acceptance test procedures

In the following sections, you will see descriptions of each of these items.

Entity Relationship Diagram
The *entity relationship (E-R) diagram* illustrates the relationships that have been identified among the entities that make up the application. E-R diagrams are critical for providing an understanding of the goals of the system. They also help to identify interface points with other applications, and to ensure consistency in definitions across the enterprise.

Physical Database Diagram
A *physical database diagram* shows the physical tables generated from the entities and the columns generated from the defined attributes in the logical model. A physical database diagramming tool is usually capable of generating the DDL necessary to create the application's objects.

You can use the physical database diagram to identify tables that are most likely to be involved in transactions. You should also be able to identify which tables are commonly used together during a data entry or query operation. You can use this information to effectively plan the distribution of these tables (and their indexes) across the available physical devices to reduce the amount of I/O contention encountered (see Chapters 3 and 4).

In data warehousing applications, the physical database diagram should show the aggregations and materialized views accessed by user queries. Although they contain derived data, they are critical components of the data access path and must be documented.

Space Requirements

The space requirements deliverable should show the initial space requirements for each database table and index. The recommendations for the proper size for tables, clusters, and indexes are shown in the "Sizing Database Objects" section later in this chapter.

Tuning Goals for Queries and Transaction Processing

Changes to the application design may have significant impact on the application's performance. Application design choices may also directly affect your ability to tune the application. Because application design has such a great effect on the DBA's ability to tune its performance, the DBA must be involved in the design process.

You must identify the performance goals of a system *before* it goes into production. The role of expectation in perception cannot be overemphasized. If the users have an expectation that the system will be at least as fast as an existing system, then anything less will be unacceptable. The estimated response time for each of the most-used components of the application must be defined and approved.

It is important during this process to establish two sets of goals: reasonable goals and stretch goals. *Stretch goals* represent the results of concentrated efforts to go beyond the hardware and software constraints that limit the system's performance. Maintaining two sets of performance goals helps to focus efforts on those goals that are truly mission critical versus those that are beyond the scope of the core system deliverables. In terms of the goals, you should establish control boundaries for query and transaction performance—the application performance will be judged to be "out of control" if the control boundaries are crossed.

Security Requirements

The development team must specify the account structure the application will use, including the ownership of all objects in the application and the manner in which privileges will be granted. All roles and privileges must be clearly defined. The deliverables from this section will be used to generate the account and privilege structure of the production application (see Chapter 10 for a full review of Oracle's security capabilities).

Depending on the application, you may need to specify the account usage for batch accounts separately from that of online accounts. For example, the batch accounts may use the database's autologin features, while the online users have to manually sign in. Your security plans for the application must support both types of users.

Like the space requirements deliverable, security planning is an area in which the DBA's involvement is critical. The DBA should be able to design an implementation that meets the application's needs while fitting in with the enterprise database security plan.

Data Requirements

The methods for data entry and retrieval must be clearly defined. Data entry methods must be tested and verified while the application is in the test environment. Any special data archiving requirements of the application must also be documented, since they will be application specific.

You must also describe the backup and recovery requirements for the application. These requirements can then be compared to the enterprise database backup plans (see Chapter 11 for guidelines). Any database recovery requirements that go beyond the site's standard will require modifying the site's backup standard or adding a module to accommodate the application's needs.

Execution Plans

Execution plans are the steps that the database will go through while executing queries. They are generated via the **explain plan** or **set autotrace** commands, as described in Chapter 8. Recording the execution plans for the most important queries against the database will aid in planning the index usage and tuning goals for the application. Generating them prior to production implementation will simplify tuning efforts and identify potential performance problems before the application is released. Generating the explain plans for your most important queries will also facilitate the process of performing code reviews of the application.

If you are implementing a third-party application, you may not have visibility to all of the SQL commands the application is generating. As described in Chapter 9, you can use the STATSPACK utility to monitor the most resource-intensive queries performed between two points in time. You can take STATSPACK "snapshots" before and after a test period and then evaluate the execution paths for the most common or most resource-intensive queries during a test period. See Chapter 9 for details on STATSPACK implementation.

Acceptance Test Procedures

The developers and users should very clearly define what functionality and performance goals must be achieved before the application can be migrated to production. These goals will form the foundation of the test procedures that will be executed against the application while it is in the test environment.

The procedures should also describe how to deal with unmet goals. The procedures should very clearly list the functional goals that must be met before the system can move forward. A second list of noncritical functional goals should also be provided. This separation of functional capabilities will aid in both resolving scheduling conflicts and structuring appropriate tests.

> **NOTE**
> As part of acceptance testing, all interfaces to the application should be tested and their input and output verified.

Resource Management and Stored Outlines

As of Oracle8i, developers and DBAs can use *stored outlines* to migrate execution paths between instances and the Database Resource Manager to control the allocation of system resources among database users. Stored outlines and resource management are important components in a managed development environment. The Database Resource Manager gives DBAs more control over the allocation of system resources than is possible with operating system controls alone.

Implementing the Database Resource Manager

You can use the Database Resource Manager to allocate percentages of system resources to classes of users and jobs. For example, you could allocate 75 percent of the available CPU resources to your online users, leaving 25 percent to your batch users. To use the Database Resource Manager, you will need to create *resource plans*, *resource consumer groups*, and *resource plan directives*.

Prior to using the Database Resource Manager commands, you must create a "pending area" for your work. To create a pending area, use the CREATE_ PENDING_ AREA procedure of the DBMS_RESOURCE_MANAGER procedure. When you have completed your changes, use the VALIDATE_PENDING_AREA procedure to check the validity of the new set of plans, subplans, and directives. You can then either submit the changes (via SUBMIT_PENDING_AREA) or clear the changes (via CLEAR_ PENDING_AREA). The procedures that manage the pending area do not have any input variables, so a sample creation of a pending area uses the following syntax:

```
execute DBMS_RESOURCE_MANAGER.CREATE_PENDING_AREA();
```

If the pending area is not created, you will receive an error message when you try to create a resource plan.

To create a resource plan, use the CREATE_PLAN procedure of the DBMS_RESOURCE_MANAGER package. The syntax for the CREATE_PLAN procedure is shown in the following listing:

```
CREATE_PLAN
(plan                        IN VARCHAR2,
 comment                     IN VARCHAR2,
 cpu_mth                     IN VARCHAR2 DEFAULT 'EMPHASIS',
 active_sess_target_mth      IN VARCHAR2 DEFAULT      'ACTIVE_SESS_ABSOLUTE',
 parallel_degree_limit_mth   IN VARCHAR2 DEFAULT      'PARALLEL_DEGREE_LIMIT_ABSOLUTE',
 queueing_mth                IN VARCHAR2 DEFAULT      'FIFO_TIMEOUT')
```

When you create a plan, give the plan a name (in the *plan* variable) and a comment. By default, the CPU allocation method will use the "emphasis" method, allocating CPU based on percentage. The following example shows the creation of a plan called DEVELOPERS:

```
execute DBMS_RESOURCE_MANAGER.CREATE_PLAN -
 (Plan => 'DEVELOPERS', -
  Comment => 'Developers, in Development database');
```

NOTE
The hyphen (-) character is a continuation character in SQL*Plus, allowing a single command to span multiple lines.

In order to create and manage resource plans and resource consumer groups, you must have the ADMINISTER_RESOURCE_MANAGER system privilege enabled for your session. DBAs have this privilege with the **with admin option**. To grant this privilege to non-DBAs, you must execute the GRANT_SYSTEM_PRIVILEGE procedure of the DBMS_RESOURCE_MANAGER_PRIVS package. The example in the following listing grants the user MARTHA the ability to manage the Database Resource Manager:

```
execute DBMS_RESOURCE_MANAGER_PRIVS.GRANT_SYSTEM_PRIVILEGE -
 (grantee_name => 'Martha',  -
  admin_option => TRUE);
```

You can revoke MARTHA's privileges via the REVOKE_SYSTEM_PRIVILEGE procedure of the DBMS_RESOURCE_MANAGER package.

With the ADMINISTER_RESOURCE_MANAGER privilege enabled, you can create a resource consumer group using the CREATE_CONSUMER_GROUP procedure within DBMS_RESOURCE_MANAGER. The syntax for the CREATE_CONSUMER_GROUP procedure is shown in the following listing:

```
CREATE_CONSUMER_GROUP
      (consumer_group IN VARCHAR2,
       comment         IN VARCHAR2,
       cpu_mth         IN VARCHAR2 DEFAULT 'ROUND-ROBIN')
```

You will be assigning users to resource consumer groups, so give the groups names that are based on the logical divisions of your users. The following example creates two groups—one for online developers and a second for batch developers:

```
execute DBMS_RESOURCE_MANAGER.CREATE_CONSUMER_GROUP -
  (Consumer_Group => 'Online_developers', -
   Comment => 'Online developers');

execute DBMS_RESOURCE_MANAGER.CREATE_CONSUMER_GROUP -
  (Consumer_Group => 'Batch_developers', -
   Comment => 'Batch developers');
```

Once the plan and resource consumer groups are established, you need to create resource plan directives and assign users to the resource consumer groups. To assign directives to a plan, use the CREATE_PLAN_DIRECTIVE procedure of the DBMS_RESOURCE_MANAGER package. The syntax for the CREATE_PLAN_DIRECTIVE procedure is shown in the following listing:

```
CREATE_PLAN_DIRECTIVE
      (plan                     IN VARCHAR2,
       group_or_subplan         IN VARCHAR2,
       comment                  IN VARCHAR2,
       cpu_p1                   IN NUMBER   DEFAULT NULL,
       cpu_p2                   IN NUMBER   DEFAULT NULL,
       cpu_p3                   IN NUMBER   DEFAULT NULL,
       cpu_p4                   IN NUMBER   DEFAULT NULL,
       cpu_p5                   IN NUMBER   DEFAULT NULL,
       cpu_p6                   IN NUMBER   DEFAULT NULL,
       cpu_p7                   IN NUMBER   DEFAULT NULL,
       cpu_p8                   IN NUMBER   DEFAULT NULL,
       active_sess_pool_p1      IN NUMBER   DEFAULT UNLIMITED,
       queueing_p1              IN NUMBER   DEFAULT UNLIMITED,
       parallel_degree_limit_p1 IN NUMBER   DEFAULT NULL,
       switch_group             IN VARCHAR2 DEFAULT NULL,
       switch_time              IN NUMBER   DEFAULT UNLIMITED,
```

```
switch_estimate          IN BOOLEAN   DEFAULT FALSE,
max_est_exec_time        IN NUMBER    DEFAULT UNLIMITED,
undo_pool                IN NUMBER    DEFAULT UNLIMITED,
parallel_degree_limit_p1 IN NUMBER    DEFAULT NULL);
```

The multiple CPU variables in the CREATE_PLAN_DIRECTIVE procedure support the creation of multiple levels of CPU allocation. For example, you could allocate 75 percent of all of your CPU resources (level 1) to your online users. Of the remaining CPU resources (level 2), you could allocate 50 percent to a second set of users. You could split the remaining 50 percent of resources available at level 2 to multiple groups at a third level. The CREATE_PLAN_DIRECTIVE procedure supports up to eight levels of CPU allocations.

The following example shows the creation of the plan directives for the Online_ developers and Batch_developers resource consumer groups within the DEVELOPERS resource plan:

```
execute DBMS_RESOURCE_MANAGER.CREATE_PLAN_DIRECTIVE -
  (Plan => 'DEVELOPERS', -
   Group_or_subplan => 'Online_developers', -
   Comment => 'online developers', -
   Cpu_p1 => 75, -
   Cpu_p2=> 0, -
   Parallel_degree_limit_p1 => 12);

execute DBMS_RESOURCE_MANAGER.CREATE_PLAN_DIRECTIVE -
  (Plan => 'DEVELOPERS', -
   Group_or_subplan => 'Batch_developers', -
   Comment => 'Batch developers', -
   Cpu_p1 => 25, -
   Cpu_p2 => 0, -
   Parallel_degree_limit_p1 => 6);
```

In addition to allocating CPU resources, the plan directives restrict the parallelism of operations performed by members of the resource consumer group. In the preceding example, batch developers are limited to a degree of parallelism of 6, reducing their ability to consume system resources. Online developers are limited to a degree of parallelism of 12.

To assign a user to a resource consumer group, use the SET_INITIAL_CONSUMER_ GROUP procedure of the DBMS_RESOURCE_MANAGER package. The syntax for the SET_INITIAL_CONSUMER_GROUP procedure is shown in the following listing:

```
SET_INITIAL_CONSUMER_GROUP
    (user           IN VARCHAR2,
     consumer_group IN VARCHAR2)
```

If a user has never had an initial consumer group set via the SET_INITIAL_ CONSUMER_GROUP procedure, then the user is automatically enrolled in the resource consumer group named DEFAULT_CONSUMER_GROUP.

To enable the Resource Manager within your database, set the RESOURCE_ MANAGER_PLAN database initialization parameter to the name of the resource plan for the instance. Resource plans can have subplans, so you can create tiers of resource allocations within the instance. If you do not set a value for the RESOURCE_ MANAGER_ PLAN parameter, then resource management is not performed in the instance.

You can dynamically alter the instance to use a different resource allocation plan via the **set initial_consumer_group** clause of the **alter system** command. For example, you could create a resource plan for your daytime users (DAYTIME_ USERS) and a second for your batch users (BATCH_USERS). You could create a job that each day executes this command at 6:00 A.M.:

```
alter system set initial_consumer_group = 'DAYTIME_USERS';
```

At a set time in the evening, change consumer groups to benefit the batch users:

```
alter system set initial_consumer_group = 'BATCH_USERS';
```

The resource allocation plan for the instance will thus be altered without needing to shut down and restart the instance.

When using multiple resource allocation plans in this fashion, you need to make sure you don't accidentally use the wrong plan at the wrong time. For example, if the database is down during a scheduled plan change, your job that changes the plan allocation may not execute. How will that affect your users? If you use multiple resource allocation plans, you need to consider the impact of using the wrong plan at the wrong time. To avoid such problems, you should try to minimize the number of resource allocation plans in use.

In addition to the examples and commands shown in this section, you can update existing resource plans (via the UPDATE_PLAN procedure), delete resource plans (via DELETE_PLAN), and cascade the deletion of a resource plan plus all of its subplans and related resource consumer groups (DELETE_PLAN_CASCADE). You can update and delete resource consumer groups via the UPDATE_ CONSUMER_ GROUP and DELETE_CONSUMER_GROUP procedures, respectively. Resource plan directives may be updated via UPDATE_PLAN_DIRECTIVE and deleted via DELETE_PLAN_DIRECTIVE.

When you are modifying resource plans, resource consumer groups, and resource plan directives, you should test the changes prior to implementing them. To test your changes, create a pending area for your work. To create a pending area, use the CREATE_PENDING_AREA procedure of the DBMS_RESOURCE_ MANAGER package. When you have completed your changes, use the VALIDATE_ PENDING_ AREA procedure to check the validity of the new set of plans, subplans, and directives.

You can then either submit the changes (via SUBMIT_PENDING_AREA) or clear the changes (via CLEAR_PENDING_AREA). The procedures that manage the pending area do not have any input variables, so a sample validation and submission of a pending area uses the following syntax:

```
execute DBMS_RESOURCE_MANAGER.VALIDATE_PENDING_AREA();
execute DBMS_RESOURCE_MANAGER.SUBMIT_PENDING_AREA();
```

Implementing Stored Outlines

As you migrate from one database to another, the execution paths for your queries may change. Your execution paths may change for several reasons:

- You may be using different optimizers in different databases (cost-based in one, rule-based in another).

- You may have enabled different optimizer features in the different databases.

- The statistics for the queried tables may differ in the databases.

- The frequency with which statistics are gathered may differ among the databases.

- The databases may be running different versions of the Oracle kernel.

The effects of these differences on your execution paths can be dramatic, and can have a negative impact on your query performance as you migrate or upgrade your application. To minimize the impact of these differences on your query performance, Oracle introduced a feature called a *stored outline* in Oracle8i.

A stored outline stores a set of hints for a query. Those hints will be used every time the query is executed. Using the stored hints will increase the likelihood that the query will use the same execution path each time. Hints do not mandate an execution path (they're hints, not commands), but decrease the impact of database moves on your query performance. You can view the outlines and related hints via the USER_ OUTLINES and USER_OUTLINE_HINTS views, based on the SYS tables named OL$ and OL$HINTS.

To start creating hints for all queries, set the CREATE_STORED_OUTLINES init.ora parameter to TRUE. If you set CREATE_STORED_OUTLINES to TRUE, then all of the outlines will be saved under the DEFAULT category. As an alternative, you can create custom categories of outlines and use the category name as a value in the database initialization file, as shown in the following listing:

```
CREATE_STORED_OUTLINES = development
```

In the preceding example, stored outlines will be stored for queries within the DEVELOPMENT category.

You must have the CREATE ANY OUTLINE system privilege in order to create an outline. Use the **create outline** command to create an outline for a query, as shown in the following listing:

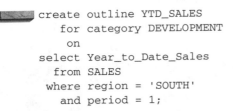

```
create outline YTD_SALES
    for category DEVELOPMENT
     on
select Year_to_Date_Sales
  from SALES
 where region = 'SOUTH'
   and period = 1;
```

NOTE
If you do not specify a name for your outline, the outline will be given a system-generated name.

If you have set CREATE_STORED_OUTLINES to TRUE in your initialization file, Oracle will create stored outlines for your queries; using the **create outline** command gives you more control over the outlines that are created.

NOTE
You can create outlines for DML commands and for **create table as select** *commands.*

Once an outline has been created, you can alter it. For example, you may need to alter the outline to reflect significant changes in data volumes and distribution. You can use the **rebuild** clause of the **alter outline** command to regenerate the hints used during query execution, as shown below:

```
alter outline YTD_SALES rebuild;
```

You can also rename an outline via the **rename** clause of the **alter outline** command, as shown here:

```
alter outline YTD_SALES rename to YTD_SALES_REGION;
```

You can change the category of an outline via the **change category** clause, as shown in the following example:

```
alter outline YTD_SALES_REGION change category to DEFAULT;
```

For the stored outlines to be used by the optimizer, set the USE_ STORED_ OUTLINES initialization parameter to TRUE or to a category name (such as DEVELOPMENT in the earlier examples). If the stored outline use is enabled, any query with a stored outline will use the hints generated when the outline was created. You can also enable USE_ STORED_OUTLINES at the session level via the **alter session** command.

NOTE
If the outline is being used, the V$SQL.Outline_Category column will display the name of the outline category for the SQL statement.

To manage stored outlines, use the OUTLN_PKG package, which gives you three capabilities:

- Drop outlines that have never been used.

- Drop outlines within a specific category.

- Move outlines from one category to another.

Each of these three capabilities has a corresponding procedure within OUTLN_ PKG. To drop outlines that have never been used, execute the DROP_UNUSED procedure, as shown in the following listing:

```
execute OUTLN_PKG.DROP_UNUSED;
```

To drop all of the outlines within a category, execute the DROP_BY_CAT procedure. The DROP_BY_CAT procedure has the name of the category as its only input parameter. The following example drops all of the outlines within the DEVELOPMENT category:

```
execute OUTLN_PKG.DROP_BY_CAT -
   (category_name => 'DEVELOPMENT');
```

To reassign outlines from an old category to a new category, use the UPDATE_ BY_CAT procedure, as shown in the following example:

```
execute OUTLN_PKG.UPDATE_BY_CAT -
  (old_category_name => 'DEVELOPMENT', -
  new_category_name => 'TEST');
```

To drop a specific outline, use the **drop outline** command.

Sizing Database Objects

Choosing the proper space allocation for database objects is critical. Developers should begin estimating space requirements before the first database objects are created. Afterwards, the space requirements can be refined based on the actual usage statistics. In the following sections, you will see the space estimation methods for tables, indexes, and clusters. You'll also see methods for determining the proper setting for **pctfree** and **pctused**.

Why Size Objects?

You should size your database objects for three reasons:

- To preallocate space in the database, thereby minimizing the amount of future work required to manage objects' space requirements

- To reduce the amount of space wasted due to overallocation of space

- To improve the likelihood of a dropped free extent being reused by another segment

You can accomplish all of these goals by following the sizing methodology shown in the following sections. This methodology is based on Oracle's internal methods for allocating space to database objects. Rather than rely on detailed calculations, the methodology relies on approximations that will dramatically simplify the sizing process while simplifying the long-term maintainability of the database.

The Golden Rule for Space Calculations

Keep your space calculations simple, generic, and consistent across databases. There are far more productive ways to spend your work time than performing extremely detailed space calculations that Oracle may ignore anyway. Even if you follow the most rigorous sizing calculations, you cannot be sure how Oracle will load the data into the table or index.

Consider an index on a table with 100,000 rows. During tests, loading the data into the table in sorted order required 920 blocks for the index. The table and index were then truncated and the data was reloaded in a nonsorted order; the index now required 1370 blocks. The 49 percent increase in space required by the index was due to Oracle's internal index management processes, discussed in Chapter 8. If you can't reliably be within 49 percent of the correct answer, why spend a lot of time on sizing exercises?

In the following section, you'll see how to simplify the space estimation process, freeing you to perform much more useful DBA functions. These processes should be followed whether you are generating the **default storage** values for a dictionary managed tablespace or the extent sizes for locally managed tablespaces.

The Ground Rules for Space Calculations

Oracle follows a set of internal rules when allocating space:

- Oracle only allocates whole blocks, not parts of blocks.

- Oracle allocates sets of blocks, usually in multiples of five blocks.

- Oracle may allocate larger or smaller sets of blocks depending on the available free space in the tablespace.

The first two rules can serve as the basis for fairly exact space estimates, but the third overrides the first two. Even if you try to allocate exactly 20 blocks for a table, Oracle may find a free extent that is 22 blocks and use it rather than leave a 2-block free extent.

Your goal should be to work with Oracle's space allocation methods instead of against them. If you use consistent extent sizes, you can largely delegate the space allocation to Oracle.

The Impact of Extent Size on Performance

There is no direct performance benefit gained by reducing the number of extents in a table. In some situations (such as in parallel query environments), having multiple extents in a table can significantly reduce I/O contention and enhance your performance. Regardless of the number of extents in your tables, the extents need to be properly sized.

Oracle reads data from tables in two ways: by RowID (usually immediately following an index access) and via full table scans. If the data is read via RowID, then the number of extents in the table is not a factor in the read performance. Oracle will read each row from its physical location (as specified in the RowID) and retrieve the data.

If the data is read via a full table scan, then the size of your extents can impact performance to a very small degree. When reading data via a full table scan, Oracle will read multiple blocks at a time. The number of blocks read at a time is set via the DB_FILE_ MULTIBLOCK_READ_COUNT database initialization parameter, and is limited by the operating system's I/O buffer size. For example, if your database block size is 4KB and your operating system's I/O buffer size is 64KB, then you can read up to 16 blocks per read during a full table scan. In that case, setting DB_FILE_ MULTIBLOCK_ READ_COUNT to a value higher than 16 will not change the performance of the full table scans.

Your extent sizes should take advantage of Oracle's ability to perform multiblock reads during full table scans. Thus, if your operating system's I/O buffer is 64KB, then your extent sizes should be a multiple of 64KB.

Consider a table that has ten extents, each of which is 64KB in size. For this example, the operating system's I/O buffer size is 64KB. To perform a full table scan, Oracle must perform ten reads (since 64KB is the operating system I/O buffer size). If the data is compressed into a single 640KB extent, Oracle still must perform ten reads to scan the table. Compressing the extents results in no gain in performance.

If the table's extent size is not a multiple of the I/O buffer size, then the number of reads required may increase. For the same 640KB table, you could create eight extents that are 80KB each. To read the first extent, Oracle will perform two reads: one for the first 64KB of the extent, and a second read for the last 16KB of the extent (reads cannot span extents). To read the whole table, Oracle must therefore perform two reads per extent, or 16 reads. Reducing the number of extents from ten to eight increased the number of reads by 60 percent.

To avoid paying a performance penalty for your extent sizes, you must therefore choose between one of the following strategies:

1. Create extents that are significantly larger than your I/O size. If the extents are very large, then very few additional reads will be necessary even if the extent size is not a multiple of the I/O buffer size.

2. Set DB_FILE_MULTIBLOCK_READ_COUNT to take full advantage of the I/O buffer size for your operating system. Note that setting it too high may make the optimizer think that full table scans are more efficient than they actually are, resulting in changes to existing execution plans.

3. If you must create small extents, choose extent sizes that are a multiple of the I/O buffer size for your operating system.

If the I/O buffer size for your operating system is 64KB, then your pool of extent sizes to choose is 64KB, 128KB, 256KB, 512KB, 1MB, and so on. In the next section, you will see how to further reduce the pool of extent sizes from which to choose.

To maximize the reuse of dropped free extents in dictionary managed tablespaces, use a pool of extent sizes that meets the following criterion: *every extent size will hold an integral multiple of every smaller extent size*. The simplest implementation of this rule is to create extent sizes that increase by doubling: 1MB, 2MB, 4MB, 16MB, 32MB. To reduce the number of extent sizes to manage, you can quadruple the values instead of doubling: 1MB, 4MB, 16MB, and so on. Using those values for extent sizes will eliminate I/O problems and will enhance the likelihood that dropped extents will be reused.

Sizing the Objects

To effectively manage your space, all you need to do is select a set of space values that meet the criteria described in the preceding sections. Once the space allocations are finalized, separate them by tablespace. For example:

```
create tablespace DATA_1M
datafile '/u01/oracle/VLDB/data_1m.dbf'
```

```
size 100M
extent management local uniform size 1M;

create tablespace DATA_MEDIUM
datafile '/u01/oracle/VLDB/data_4m.dbf'
size 400M
extent management local uniform size 4M;

create tablespace DATA_LARGE
datafile '/u01/oracle/VLDB/data_16m.dbf'
size 16000M
extent management local uniform size 16M;
```

In this example, three separate DATA tablespaces are created, with extent sizes of 1MB, 4MB, and 16MB. If you need to create a table 3MB in size, you can either create it with three 1MB extents in DATA_1M or with one 4MB extent in DATA_4M. A table that will grow to 10MB can be placed in DATA_4M.

As your tables grow in size, your default storage clauses will grow in a consistent fashion, following the space rules and your standards for extent sizes. DATA_64M would be next, followed by DATA_256M and DATA_1G. Use the same extent sizes across your databases to ease space management of your entire database environment.

As the extent sizes grow, the distribution of extent sizes across tablespaces will usually result in a separation of table types—small static tables will be isolated in the tablespaces with small extent sizes. Large transaction processing tables (or their partitions) will be segregated to the large extent size tables, simplifying later management and tuning activities.

In the following sections you will see guidelines for estimations of the space usage for your objects. Since the target sizes (1MB, 4MB, 16MB, etc.) are not close together, the following estimations do not include highly detailed calculations.

NOTE
As of Oracle9i, the database block size may change at the tablespace level. Be sure the extent sizes you choose account for the largest block size in use in the database. Limiting the usage of nonstandard block sizes in the database will simplify cross-database maintenance and your sizing procedures.

Estimating Space Requirements for Nonclustered Tables

To estimate the space required by a table, you only need to know four values:

- The database block size

- The **pctfree** value for the table

- The average length of a row
- The expected number of rows in the table

To calculate the exact space requirements for a table, you will need additional information (such as the number of columns). To perform a quick estimate, these four pieces of information are all you need.

Each database block has an area used for overhead within the block. Estimate the block overhead for tables to use 90 bytes. Therefore, the available space in a block is as follows:

Database Block Size	Available Space (in bytes)	Percent Available
2KB	1958	96%
4KB	4006	98%
8KB	8102	99%
16KB	16294	99%

Even for small block sizes, the impact of the block header on the available free space is very small. A portion of that available space will be kept free, available for updates of rows previously inserted into the block. The **pctfree** setting for the table sets the size of the free space that is unused during **insert**s. Multiply the available space by the **pctfree** value to determine how much space is reserved. Subtract that value from the available space in the block to determine how much space is available to hold newly **insert**ed rows.

For example, for a 4KB block size and a table with a **pctfree** setting of 10, the available space is

```
4006 bytes - (0.1*4006 bytes) = 3605.4 bytes, rounded down to 3605 bytes.
```

In every database block in this example, there are 3605 bytes available for new records. To arrive at almost that exact answer a little quicker, you could take the space not allocated to **pctfree** (90 percent) times the percent of the block available (98 percent, as shown in the previous table):

```
0.90 * 0.98 = 0.882
```

So roughly 88 percent of each block (3604 bytes) is available.

NOTE
*It is rare for a block to be filled exactly to its **pctfree** setting. Most blocks will be taken off the free list before that limit is reached, so these calculations generate the upper limit in terms of storage efficiency.*

To estimate the space used by a table's rows, you should generate sample data and analyze its storage. Analyzing an accurate sample of 10,000 rows should tell you how large an average row is. If you do not have a representative sample data set to use, you can calculate the expected space usage.

To calculate the space usage, estimate your average row length. Estimate the length of a DATE value to be 8 bytes, and estimate the length of a NUMBER value to be 4 bytes. For VARCHAR2 columns, estimate the actual length of the values stored in the columns. If you have sample data available, you can use the **VSIZE** function to calculate the space used by column values. If the sample data has been recently analyzed, you can query the table's Avg_Row_Len column value from DBA_TABLES.

NOTE
These estimates incorporate additional column overhead. In reality, a DATE value stores 7 bytes, while a NUMBER value's stored length depends on its number of significant digits. Internal storage for NUMBER values varies from 2 bytes (1 or 2 significant digits) to 20 bytes (38 significant digits).

For example, you may have a table with 10 columns and an estimated average row length of 60 bytes. You expect to have 25,000 rows in the table. The data in the table will need

```
60 bytes/row * 25,000 rows = 1,500,000 bytes = 1464 KB
```

The data will require 1464KB, but only 88 percent of each block is available. Therefore, the table will need

```
1464 KB / 0.882 = 1660 KB
```

The sizing estimation exercise is complete. You can place this table in your DATA_1M tablespace, in which case it will acquire two extents and have 340 blocks left for growth. You could place it in your DATA_256K tablespace, in which case it would acquire 7 extents (1792KB) with 132KB left for growth. If space is available, place it in the DATA_1M tablespace.

In the next section, you will see how to estimate space for indexes.

Estimating Space Requirements for Indexes
The estimation process for indexes parallels the estimation process for tables. The estimation process described in this section does not generate exact space allocation requirements; rather, it enables you to quickly estimate the space requirements and

match them to a set of standard extent sizes. To estimate the space required by an index, you only need to know four values:

- The database block size
- The **pctfree** value for the index
- The average length of an index entry
- The expected number of entries in the index

Each database block has an area used for overhead within the block. Estimate the block overhead for an index to be 161 bytes. Therefore, the available space in a block is as follows:

Database Block Size	Available Space (in bytes)	Percent Available
2KB	1887	92%
4KB	3935	96%
8KB	8031	98%
16KB	16221	99%

A portion of that available space will be kept free, based on the **pctfree** setting for the index. However, index values should not be frequently updated. For indexes, **pctfree** is commonly set to a value below 5. To estimate how much space is available for index entries, multiply the space not dedicated to **pctfree** by the percent of space available per block (shown in the prior table).

For example, for a 4KB block size and an index with a **pctfree** setting of 2, the available space is

```
0.98 * 0.96 = 94 % free, or 3654 bytes
```

In every database block in this example, there are 3854 bytes available for new index entries.

Next, estimate the average row length of an index entry. If the index is a concatenated index, estimate the length of each column's values and add them together to arrive at the total entry length. If you have sample data available, you can use the **VSIZE** function to calculate the space used by column values. Estimate the length of a DATE value to be 8 bytes, and estimate the length of a NUMBER value to be 4 bytes. For VARCHAR2 columns, estimate the actual length of the values stored in the columns.

NOTE
These estimates incorporate additional column overhead. In reality, a DATE value stores 7 bytes, while a NUMBER value's stored length depends on its number of significant digits. Internal storage for NUMBER values varies from 2 bytes (1 or 2 significant digits) to 20 bytes (38 significant digits).

For example, you may have an index with three columns and an estimated average row length of 17 bytes. If you expect to have 25,000 entries in the index, the space it requires is

```
17 bytes/entry * 25,000 entries = 425,000 bytes = 415 KB
```

From our prior calculation, we know that 94 percent of each block is available for index inserts, so the space required by the index entries is

```
415 KB / 0.94 = 442 KB
```

The sizing estimate is now complete. You can store this index in your INDEXES_ 256K tablespace, in which case it will acquire two extents and have 70 blocks left for expansion. Since the order of rows inserted impacts the space requirements for indexes, you should always overallocate the space required. Even if the actual space usage exceeds this estimate by 50 percent, placing the index in INDEXES_256K will support the index easily.

To see the detailed space calculations for tables and indexes, refer to the *Oracle9i Server Administrator's Guide.*

Estimating the Proper pctfree

The **pctfree** value represents the percentage of *each data block* that is reserved as free space. This space is used when a row that has already been stored in that data block grows in length, either by updates of previously **NULL** fields or by updates of existing values to longer values.

There is no single value for **pctfree** that will be adequate for all tables in all databases. To simplify space management, choose a consistent set of **pctfree** values:

■   For indexes whose key values are rarely changed: 2

■   For tables whose rows never change: 2

■   For tables whose rows seldom change: 5

■   For tables whose rows frequently change: 10 to 30

Why maintain free space in a table or index even if the rows do not change? Oracle needs space within blocks to perform block maintenance functions. If there is not enough free space available (for example, to support a large number of transaction headers during concurrent inserts), Oracle will temporarily allocate part of the block's **pctfree** area, then deallocate it when complete. You should choose a **pctfree** value that supports this allocation of space. To reserve space for transaction headers in **insert**-intensive tables, set the **initrans** and **maxtrans** parameters to nondefault values. In general, your **pctfree** area should be large enough to hold several rows of data.

Since **pctfree** is tied to the way in which updates occur in an application, determining the adequacy of its setting is a straightforward process. The **pctfree** setting controls the number of records that are stored in a block in a table. To see if **pctfree** has been set correctly, first determine the number of rows in a block. As described in Chapter 8, you can use the DBMS_STATS package to gather statistics. If the **pctfree** setting is too low, the number of chained rows will steadily increase.

NOTE
*When rows are moved due to inadequate space in the **pctfree** area, the move is called a row migration. Row migration will impact the performance of your transactions.*

Determining the Proper pctused

The **pctused** value determines when a used block is re-added to the list of blocks into which rows can be inserted. For example, consider a table that has a **pctfree** value of 20 and a **pctused** value of 50. When rows are inserted into the table, Oracle will keep 20 percent of each block free (for use by later **update**s of the **insert**ed records). If you now begin to **delete** records from the block, Oracle will not automatically reuse the freed space inside the blocks. New rows will not be **insert**ed into the block until the block's used space falls below its **pctused** percentage—50 percent.

The **pctused** value, by default, is set to 40. If your application features frequent deletions, and you use the default value for **pctused**, then you may have many blocks in your table that are only 40 percent used.

For most systems, you can set **pctused** so that **pctused** plus **pctfree** equals 80. If your **pctfree** setting is 20 percent, then set your **pctused** value to 60 percent. That way, at least 60 percent of each block will be used, saving 20 percent of the block for **update**s and row extensions.

Calculating Sizes for Clustered Tables

Clusters are used to store data from different tables in the same physical data blocks. They are appropriate to use if the records from those tables are frequently queried together. By storing them in the same data blocks, the number of database block reads needed to fulfill such queries decreases, thereby improving performance. They may have a negative performance impact on data manipulation transactions and on queries that only reference one of the tables in the cluster.

Because of their unique structure, clustered tables have different storage requirements than nonclustered tables. Each cluster stores the tables' data and maintains a *cluster index* that it uses to sort the data.

The columns within the cluster index are called the *cluster key*—the set of columns that the tables in the cluster have in common. Since the cluster key columns determine the physical placement of rows within the cluster, they should not be subject to frequent **update**s. The cluster key is usually the foreign key of one table that references the primary key of another table in the cluster.

After the cluster has been created, the cluster index is created on the cluster key columns. After the cluster key index has been created, data can then be entered into the tables stored in the cluster. As rows are **insert**ed, the database will store a cluster key and its associated rows in each of the cluster's blocks.

NOTE
Because of their complex structure, the sizing of clusters is more complex than that of either indexes or tables, even when using this simplified method.

Sizing a cluster thus involves elements of table sizing and index sizing. For this example, consider a simple table: a three-column table, each column of which has a datatype and length of VARCHAR2(10). If this table is very frequently joined to another table, then it may be appropriate to cluster the two tables together. For the purposes of this example, assume that the second table has two columns: a VARCHAR2(10) column and a VARCHAR2(5) column, the former of which is used to join the tables together.

Since the two tables are joined using the VARCHAR2(10) column that they have in common, that column will be the cluster key.

First, estimate the amount of space used by the block header; this is space that Oracle will use to manage the data within the block. The size of the cluster block header is approximately 110 bytes. The percentage of space available, by block size, is

Database Block Size	Available Space (in bytes)	Percent Available
2KB	1938	94%
4KB	3986	97%
8KB	8082	98%
16KB	16274	99%

Next, factor in the cluster's **pctfree** setting and multiply that by the percent available to determine how much space will be kept free for row **update**s. If you use a **pctfree** of 10, the percentage of each space available for rows in a 4KB block size database will be

```
0.90 * 0.97 = 87 %
```

Clusters require additional space for table header areas: 4 times the number of tables, plus 4 bytes. Unless you have a large number of tables in the cluster, this will not be a significant factor. In a two-table cluster, the 8 bytes per block does not change the percent of space available.

Next, calculate the space required for a single row in each of the tables, excluding the length due to the column(s) in the cluster key. If the sample data is available, use the **VSIZE** function to determine the actual space used by the data.

For this example, assume the average row length for TABLE1's nonclustered columns will be 20, and the average row length for TABLE2's nonclustered column is 3.

```
Average row length = 23 bytes
```

Each row in the cluster has *row header* information stored with it. The total row space requirements, including the header space requirements, are calculated via the following formula. In the formula, a "long" column is one in which the data value is more than 250 characters long. This distinction is necessary because of the number of length bytes that the database must store for the values.

```
Row header space = 4 bytes
                   + number of columns
                   + number of long columns
```

Combining the average row length with the row header space yields

```
Space used per row = average row length + row header space
    = 23 + 4 + number of columns + number of long columns
    = 23 + 4 + 3 + 0
    = 30 bytes
```

Thus, each cluster entry will require 30 bytes. The row header space is only significant if the nonclustered columns are very short, as in this example.

The next step in the cluster sizing process is to determine the value of the **size** parameter, which is unique to clusters. The **size** parameter is the estimated number of bytes required by a cluster key and its associated rows.

The **size** parameter is dependent on the distribution of the data. That is, how many rows are there in a table for each distinct value in the cluster key? To determine these values, query the clustered tables and divide the number of records in the table by the number of distinct cluster key values.

```
select
    COUNT(DISTINCT(column name))/    /* Num of records in table*/
    COUNT(*)  rows_per_key           /* Num of cluster key values*/
from tablename;
```

For this example, assume that in TABLE1 there are 30 rows per cluster key value. In TABLE2, there is one row per cluster key value for this example.

The **size** parameter also needs to know the average length of the cluster key value. Query the clustered tables using the **VSIZE** query shown previously.

```
select
    AVG(NVL(VSIZE(cluster key column),0)) Avg_Key_Length
from TABLE1;
```

For this example, assume that the average key column value is 5 bytes. You can now calculate the value for **size**:

```
SIZE=
    (Rows per cluster key in Table1*Average row size for Table1)+
    (Rows per cluster key in Table2*Average row size for Table2)+
    cluster key header+
    column length of the cluster key+
    average length of cluster key+
    2*(Rows per cluster key in Table1+Rows per cluster key in
    Table2+ Rows per cluster key for any other tables in the cluster)
```

The "cluster key header" is 19 bytes in length. Thus, for the example data:

```
SIZE    = (30 rows per key in Table1*20 bytes per row)+
    (1 row per key in Table2*3 bytes per row)+
    19  bytes for the cluster key header+
    10  bytes for the column length of the cluster key+
    5   bytes for the average length of the cluster key+
    2*(30 rows+1 row)
    = (30*20)+(1*3)+19+10+5+(2*31)
    = 600+3+19+10+5+62
    = 699 bytes
```

Each cluster key will require 699 bytes, rounded up to 700 bytes. The cluster key will be placed in the available space in the database block. From the earlier calculation, 87 percent of each 4KB block (3563 bytes) is available, so five cluster keys will fit in each block. The number of blocks required is therefore equal to one-fifth of the number of cluster keys. Based on the expected number of cluster key values, determine which of your standard extent size tablespaces is best suited for the cluster.

Sizing Functional Indexes

As of Oracle8i, you can create *functional indexes*. For example, you can create an index on **UPPER**(Name) instead of just Name. Functional indexes significantly enhance your query tuning capabilities. When sizing a functional index, follow the same method used to size a standard index, as shown in the prior sections of this chapter. The internal storage space for NAME and **UPPER**(Name) is identical for your calculations.

Reverse Key Indexes

As of Oracle8i, you can create *reverse key indexes*. In a reverse key index, the values are stored backwards—for example, a value of 2201 is stored as 1022. If you use a standard index, then consecutive values are stored near each other. In a reverse key index, consecutive values are not stored near each other. If your queries do not commonly perform range scans, and you are concerned about I/O contention in your indexes, reverse key indexes may be a tuning solution to consider. When sizing a reverse key index, follow the same method used to size a standard index, as shown in the prior sections of this chapter.

Sizing Bitmap Indexes

If you create a bitmap index, then Oracle will dynamically compress the bitmaps generated. The compression of the bitmap may result in substantial storage savings. To estimate the size of a bitmap index, estimate the size of a standard (B*-tree) index on the same columns using the formulas provided in the preceding sections of this chapter. After calculating the space requirements for the B*-tree index, divide that size by 10 to determine the most likely maximum size of a bitmap index for those columns. In general, bitmap indexes will be between 2 and 10 percent of the size of a comparable B*-tree index.

Sizing Index-Organized Tables

An index-organized table is stored sorted by its primary key. The space requirements of an index-organized table closely mirror those of an index on all of the table's columns. The difference in space estimation comes in calculating the space used per row, since an index-organized table does not have RowIDs.

For an index-organized table, length of the index entry header is 2 bytes, as opposed to 8 bytes in a B*-tree index. For tables with many columns or long strings, this change will not have a significant impact. The following listing gives the calculation for the space requirement per row for an index-organized table. Note that this storage estimate is for the entire row, including its out-of-line storage.

```
Space used per row = Avg_Row_Length
                   + Number of columns
                   + Number of long columns
                   + 2 header bytes
```

Sizing Tables That Contain Large Objects (LOBs)

LOB data (in BLOB or CLOB datatypes) is usually stored apart from the main table. You can use the **lob** clause of the **create table** command to specify the storage for the LOB data. In the main table, Oracle stores a **lob** locator value that points to the LOB data. Estimate a length of 24 bytes for the **lob** locator value.

Oracle does not always store the LOB data apart from the main table. In general, the LOB data is not stored apart from the main table until the LOB data exceeds 4KB in length. Therefore, if you will be storing short LOB values, you need to consider its impact on the storage of your main table. If your LOB values are less than 4000 characters, you may be able to use VARCHAR2 datatypes instead of LOB datatypes for the data storage.

Sizing Partitions

You can create multiple *partitions* of a table. In a partitioned table, multiple separate physical partitions constitute the table. For example, a SALES table may have four partitions: SALES_NORTH, SALES_SOUTH, SALES_EAST, and SALES_WEST. You should size each of those partitions using the table sizing methods described earlier in this chapter. You should size the partition indexes using the index sizing methods shown earlier in this chapter. See Chapter 15 for further details on partition management.

Sizing Temporary Tables

As of Oracle8i, you can create *temporary tables* to hold temporary data during your application processing. The table's data can be specific to a transaction or maintained throughout a user's session. When the transaction or session completes, the data is truncated from the table.

To create a temporary table, use the **create global temporary table** option of the **create table** command. To delete the rows at the end of the transaction, specify **on commit delete rows**, as shown here:

```
create global temporary table MY_TEMP_TABLE
(Name      VARCHAR2(25),
 Street    VARCHAR2(25),
 City      VARCHAR2(25))
on commit delete rows;
```

You can then **insert** rows into MY_TEMP_TABLE during your application processing. When you **commit**, Oracle will **truncate** MY_TEMP_TABLE. To keep the rows for the duration of your session, specify **on commit preserve rows** instead.

From the DBA perspective, you need to know if your application developers are using this feature. If they are, you need to account for the space required by their temporary tables during their processing. Temporary tables are commonly used to improve processing speeds of complex transactions, so you may need to balance the performance benefit against the space costs. You can create indexes on temporary tables to further improve processing performance, again at the cost of increased space usage.

NOTE
*Temporary tables and their indexes do not acquire any space until the first **insert** into them occurs. When they are no longer in use, their space is deallocated.*

You cannot partition or cluster temporary tables, nor can you create foreign keys on them. No parallel DML is supported against temporary tables.

Sizing Tables Based on Abstract Datatypes

Oracle introduced object-relational structures into the database in Oracle8. Of these new structures, the two most critical features are *abstract datatypes* and *constructor methods*. Abstract datatypes define the structure of data—for example, an ADDRESS_TY datatype may contain attributes for address data, along with methods for manipulating that data. When you create the ADDRESS_TY datatype, Oracle will automatically create a constructor method called ADDRESS_TY. The ADDRESS_TY constructor method contains parameters that match the datatype's attributes, facilitating **insert**s of new values into the datatype's format. In the following sections, you will see how to create tables that use abstract datatypes, along with information on the sizing and security issues associated with that implementation.

As of Oracle8, you can create tables that use abstract datatypes for their column definitions. For example, you could create an abstract datatype for addresses, as shown here:

```
create type ADDRESS_TY as object
(Street    VARCHAR2(50),
 City      VARCHAR2(25),
 State     CHAR(2),
 Zip       NUMBER);
/
```

NOTE
You must have installed the Objects option in order to be able to create abstract datatypes.

Once the ADDRESS_TY datatype has been created, you can use it as a datatype when creating your tables, as shown in the following listing:

```
create table CUSTOMER
(Name      VARCHAR2(25),
 Address   ADDRESS_TY);
```

When you create an abstract datatype, Oracle creates a *constructor method* for use during **insert**s. The constructor method has the same name as the datatype, and its parameters are the attributes of the datatype. When you **insert** records into the CUSTOMER table, you need to use the ADDRESS_TY datatype's constructor method to **insert** Address values.

```
insert into CUSTOMER values
('Joe',ADDRESS_TY('My Street', 'Some City', 'ST', 10001));
```

In this example, the **insert** command calls the ADDRESS_TY constructor method in order to insert values into the attributes of the ADDRESS_TY datatype.

The use of abstract datatypes increases the space requirements of your tables by 8 bytes for each datatype used. If a datatype contains another datatype, then you should add 8 bytes for each of the datatypes.

Using Object Views

The use of abstract datatypes may increase the complexity of your development environment. When you query the attributes of an abstract datatype, you must use a syntax that is not used against tables that do not contain abstract datatypes. If you do not implement abstract datatypes in all of your tables, you will need to use one syntax for some of your tables and a separate syntax for other tables—and you will need to know ahead of time which queries use abstract datatypes.

For example, the CUSTOMER table uses the ADDRESS_TY datatype described in the previous section.

```
create table CUSTOMER
(Name      VARCHAR2(25),
 Address   ADDRESS_TY);
```

The ADDRESS_TY datatype, in turn, has four attributes: Street, City, State, and Zip. If you want to select the Street attribute value from the Address column of the CUSTOMER table, you may write the following query:

```
select Address.Street from CUSTOMER;
```

However, that query *will not work*. When you query the attributes of abstract datatypes, you must use correlation variables for the table names. Otherwise, there may be an ambiguity regarding the object being selected. To query the Street attribute, use a correlation variable (in this case, "C") for the CUSTOMER table, as shown in the following listing:

```
select C.Address.Street from CUSTOMERC;
```

As shown in this example, you need to use correlation variables for queries of abstract datatype attributes *even if the query only accesses one table*. There are therefore two features of queries against abstract datatype attributes: the notation used to access the attributes and the correlation variables requirement. In order to implement abstract datatypes consistently, you may need to alter your SQL standards to support 100 percent usage of correlation variables. Even if you use correlation variables consistently, the notation required to access attribute values may cause problems as well, since you cannot use a similar notation on tables that do not use abstract datatypes.

Object views provide an effective compromise solution to this inconsistency. The CUSTOMER table created in the previous examples assumed that an ADDRESS_ TY datatype already existed. But what if your tables already exist? What if you had previously created a relational database application and are trying to implement object-relational concepts in your application without rebuilding and re-creating the entire application? What you would need is the ability to overlay object-oriented (OO) structures such as abstract datatypes on existing relational tables. Oracle provides *object views* as a means for defining objects used by existing relational tables.

If the CUSTOMER table already existed, you could create the ADDRESS_TY datatype and use object views to relate it to the CUSTOMER table. In the following listing, the CUSTOMER table is created as a relational table, using only the normally provided datatypes:

```
create table CUSTOMER
(Name        VARCHAR2(25) primary key,
 Street      VARCHAR2(50),
 City        VARCHAR2(25),
 State       CHAR(2),
 Zip         NUMBER);
```

If you want to create another table or application that stores information about people and addresses, you may choose to create the ADDRESS_TY datatype. However, for consistency, that datatype should be applied to the CUSTOMER table as well. The following examples will use the ADDRESS_TY datatype created in the previous section.

You can create an object view based on the CUSTOMER table, using any datatype you have defined. To create an object view, use the **create view** command. Within the **create view** command, specify the query that will form the basis of the view. The code for creating the CUSTOMER_OV object view is shown in the following listing:

```
create view CUSTOMER_OV (Name, Address) as
select Name,
       ADDRESS_TY(Street, City, State, Zip)
  from CUSTOMER;
```

The CUSTOMER_OV view will have two columns: the Name and the Address columns (the latter is defined by the ADDRESS_TY datatype). Note that you cannot specify **object** as an option within the **create view** command.

There are several important syntax issues presented in this example. When a table is built upon existing abstract datatypes, you select column values from the table by referring to the names of the columns (such as Name) instead of their constructor methods. When creating the object view, however, you refer to the names of the constructor methods (such as ADDRESS_TY) instead. Also, you can use **where** clauses in the query that forms the basis of the object view. You can therefore limit the rows that are accessible via the object view.

If you use object views, then you as the DBA will administer relational tables the same way as you did before. You will still need to manage the privileges for the datatypes (see the upcoming section of this chapter for information on security management of abstract datatypes), but the table and index structures will be the same as they were before the creation of the abstract datatypes. Using the relational structures will simplify your administration tasks while allowing developers to access objects via the object views of the tables.

You can also use object views to simulate the references used by row objects. Row objects are rows within an object table. To create an object view that supports row objects, you need to first create a datatype that has the same structure as the table.

```
create or replace type CUSTOMER_TY as object
(Name         VARCHAR2(25),
 Street       VARCHAR2(50),
 City         VARCHAR2(25),
 State        CHAR(2),
 Zip          NUMBER);
/
```

Next, create an object view based on the CUSTOMER_TY type, while assigning OID (object identifier) values to the records in CUSTOMER.

```
create view CUSTOMER_OV of CUSTOMER_TY
  with object identifier (Name) as
select Name, Street, City, State, Zip
  from CUSTOMER;
```

The first part of this **create view** command gives the view its name (CUSTOMER_OV) and tells Oracle that the view's structure is based on the CUSTOMER_TY datatype. An object identifier, also known as an OID, identifies the row object. In this object view, the Name column will be used as the OID. In Oracle8.0 and Oracle8i, use **with object OID** in place of **with object identifier** in this **create view** example. The **with object OID** syntax is still supported in Oracle9i but is being deprecated.

If you have a second table that references CUSTOMER via a foreign key/primary key relationship, then you can set up an object view that contains references to CUSTOMER_OV. For example, the CUSTOMER_CALL table contains a foreign key to the CUSTOMER table, as shown here:

```
create table CUSTOMER_CALL
(Name             VARCHAR2(25),
 Call_Number      NUMBER,
 Call_Date        DATE,
 constraint CUSTOMER_CALL_PK
    primary key (Name, Call_Number),
 constraint CUSTOMER_CALL_FK foreign key (Name)
    references CUSTOMER(Name));
```

The Name column of CUSTOMER_CALL references the same column in the CUSTOMER table. Since you have simulated OIDs (called pkOIDs) based on the primary key of CUSTOMER, you need to create references to those OIDs. Oracle provides an operator called **MAKE_REF** that creates the references (called pkREFs). In the following listing, the **MAKE_REF** operator is used to create references from the object view of CUSTOMER_CALL to the object view of CUSTOMER:

```
create view CUSTOMER_CALL_OV as
select MAKE_REF(CUSTOMER_OV, Name) Name,
       Call_Number,
       Call_Date
  from CUSTOMER_CALL;
```

Within the CUSTOMER_CALL_OV view, you tell Oracle the name of the view to reference and the columns that constitute the pkREF. You could now query CUSTOMER_OV data from within CUSTOMER_CALL_OV by using the DEREF operator on the Customer_ID column.

```
select DEREF(CCOV.Name)
   from CUSTOMER_CALL_OV CCOV
 where Call_Date = TRUNC(SysDate);
```

You can thus return CUSTOMER data from your query without directly querying the CUSTOMER table. In this example, the Call_Date column is used as a limiting condition for the rows returned by the query.

Whether you use row objects or column objects, you can use object views to shield your tables from the object relationships. The tables are not modified; you administer them the way you always did. The difference is that the users can now access the rows of CUSTOMER as if they are row objects.

Sizing Object Tables and REFs

When you create an object table, Oracle generates an OID value for each of the rows in the table. An OID (Object ID) value adds 16 bytes to the average row length. When you create a table that has a reference to an object table, that table will contain a column with a REF datatype. When estimating the space requirements for a table, estimate the length of the REF datatype column to be 16 bytes.

Security for Abstract Datatypes

The examples in the previous sections assumed that the same user owned the ADDRESS_TY datatype and the CUSTOMER table. What if the owner of the datatype is not the table owner? What if another user wants to create a datatype based on a datatype you have created? In the development environment, you should establish guidelines for the ownership and use of abstract datatypes.

For example, what if the account named DORA owns the ADDRESS_TY datatype, and the user of the account named GEORGE tries to create a PERSON_TY datatype? GEORGE executes the following command:

```
create type PERSON_TY as object
(Name      VARCHAR2(25),
 Address   ADDRESS_TY);
/
```

If GEORGE does not own the ADDRESS_TY abstract datatype, then Oracle will respond to this **create type** command with the following message:

```
Warning: Type created with compilation errors.
```

The compilation errors are caused by problems creating the constructor method when the datatype is created. Oracle cannot resolve the reference to the ADDRESS_TY datatype since GEORGE does not own a datatype with that name.

GEORGE will not be able to create the PERSON_TY datatype (which includes the ADDRESS_TY datatype) unless DORA first **grant**s him EXECUTE privilege on her type. The following listing shows this **grant**:

```
grant EXECUTE on ADDRESS_TY to George;
```

Now that the proper **grant**s are in place, GEORGE can create a datatype that is based on DORA's ADDRESS_TY datatype.

```
create or replace type PERSON_TY as object
(Name      VARCHAR2(25),
 Address   Dora.ADDRESS_TY);
/
```

GEORGE's PERSON_TY datatype will now be successfully created. However, using datatypes based on another user's datatypes is not trivial. For example, during **insert** operations, you must fully specify the name of the owner of each type. GEORGE can create a table based on his PERSON_TY datatype (which includes DORA's ADDRESS_ TY datatype), as shown in the following listing:

```
create table GEORGE_CUSTOMERS
(Customer_ID   NUMBER,
 Person        PERSON_TY);
```

If GEORGE owned PERSON_TY and ADDRESS_TY datatypes, then an **insert** into CUSTOMER would use the format:

```
insert into GEORGE_CUSTOMERS values
(1,PERSON_TY('SomeName',
   ADDRESS_TY('StreetValue','CityValue','ST',11111)));
```

This command will not work. During the **insert**, the ADDRESS_TY constructor method is used, and DORA owns it. Therefore, the **insert** command must be modified to specify DORA as the owner of ADDRESS_TY. The following example shows the corrected **insert** statement, with the reference to DORA shown in bold:

```
insert into GEORGE_CUSTOMERS values
(1,PERSON_TY('SomeName',
   Dora.ADDRESS_TY('StreetValue','CityValue','ST',11111)));
```

You cannot use a synonym for another user's datatype. You will need to refer to the datatype's owner during each **insert** command. Whenever possible, limit the ability to create abstract datatypes to those users who will own the rest of the application schema objects.

NOTE
*When you create a synonym, Oracle does not check the validity of the object for which you are creating a synonym. If you **create synonym x for y**, Oracle does not check to make sure that "y" is a valid object name or valid object type. The validation of that object's accessibility via synonyms is only checked when the object is accessed via the synonym.*

In a relational-only implementation of Oracle, you grant the EXECUTE privilege on procedural objects, such as procedures and packages. Within the object-relational implementation of Oracle, the EXECUTE privilege is extended to cover abstract datatypes as well. The EXECUTE privilege is used because abstract datatypes can include *methods*—PL/SQL functions and procedures that operate on the datatype. If you grant someone the privilege to use your datatype, you are granting the user the privilege to execute the methods you have defined on the datatype. Although DORA did not yet define any methods on the ADDRESS_TY datatype, Oracle automatically creates constructor methods that are used to access the data. Any object (such as PERSON_TY) that uses the ADDRESS_TY datatype uses the constructor method associated with ADDRESS_TY.

You cannot create public types, and you cannot create public synonyms for your types. Therefore, you will either need to reference the owner of the type or create the type under each account that can create tables in your database. Neither of these is a simple solution to the problem of datatype management.

Indexing Abstract Datatype Attributes

In the preceding example, the GEORGE_CUSTOMERS table was created based on a PERSON_TY datatype and an ADDRESS_TY datatype. As shown in the following listing, the GEORGE_CUSTOMERS table contains a normal column— Customer_ ID—and a Person column that is defined by the PERSON_TY abstract datatype:

```
create table GEORGE_CUSTOMERS
(Customer_ID     NUMBER,
 Person          PERSON_TY);
```

From the datatype definitions shown in the previous section of this chapter, you can see that PERSON_TY has one column—Name—followed by an Address column defined by the ADDRESS_TY datatype.

When referencing columns within the abstract datatypes during queries, **update**s, and **delete**s, specify the full path to the datatype attributes. For example, the following query returns the Customer_ID column along with the Name column. The Name column is an attribute of the datatype that defines the Person column, so you refer to the attribute as Person.Name.

```
select C.Customer_ID, C.Person.Name
   from GEORGE_CUSTOMERS C;
```

You can refer to attributes within the ADDRESS_TY datatype by specifying the full path through the related columns. For example, the Street column is referred to as Person.Address.Street, which fully describes its location within the structure of the table. In the following example, the City column is referenced twice—once in the list of columns to select and once within the **where** clause.

```
select C.Person.Name,
       C.Person.Address.City
  from GEORGE_CUSTOMERS C
 where C.Person.Address.City like 'C%';
```

Because the City column is used with a range search in the **where** clause, the optimizer may be able to use an index when resolving the query. If an index is available on the City column, Oracle can quickly find all of the rows that have City values starting with the letter "C" as requested by the query.

To create an index on a column that is part of an abstract datatype, you need to specify the full path to the column as part of the **create index** command. To create an index on the City column (which is part of the Address column), you can execute the following command:

```
create index I_GEORGE_CUSTOMERS$CITY
on GEORGE_CUSTOMERS(Person.Address.City);
```

This command will create an index named I_GEORGE_CUSTOMER$CITY on the Person.Address.City column. Whenever the City column is accessed, the optimizer will evaluate the SQL used to access the data and determine if the new index can be useful to improve the performance of the access.

When creating tables based on abstract datatypes, you should consider how the columns within the abstract datatypes will be accessed. If, like the City column in the previous example, certain columns will commonly be used as part of limiting conditions in queries, then they should be indexed. In this regard, the representation of multiple columns in a single abstract datatype may hinder your application performance, since it may obscure the need to index specific columns within the datatype.

When you use abstract datatypes, you become accustomed to treating a group of columns as a single entity, such as the Address columns or the Person columns. It is important to remember that the optimizer, when evaluating query access paths, will consider the columns individually. You therefore need to address the indexing requirements for the columns even when you are using abstract datatypes. In addition, remember that indexing the City column in one table that uses the ADDRESS_TY datatype does not affect the City column in a second table that uses the ADDRESS_TY datatype. If there is a second table named BRANCH that uses the ADDRESS_TY datatype, then *its* City column will not be indexed unless you create an index for it.

Quiescing and Suspending the Database

As of Oracle9i, you can temporarily quiesce or suspend the database during your maintenance operations. Using these options allows you to keep the database open during maintenance, avoiding the time or availability impact associated with database shutdowns.

While the database is quiesced, no new transactions will be permitted by any accounts other than SYS and SYSTEM. New queries or attempted logins will appear to be hung until you unquiesce the database. The quiesce feature is useful when performing table maintenance or complicated data maintenance. To use the quiesce feature, you must first enable the Database Resource Manager, as described earlier in this chapter.

While logged in as SYS or SYSTEM (other SYSDBA-privileged accounts cannot execute these commands), quiesce the database:

```
alter system quiesce restricted;
```

Any non-DBA sessions logged into the database will continue until their current command completes, at which point they will become inactive. In Real Application Cluster configurations, all instances will be quiesced.

Do not use the quiesce option as part of your file system backups for the database. For online backups of a quiesced database, you will still need to alter the tablespaces into **begin backup** and **end backup** modes. See Chapter 11 for further details on backup strategies.

To see if the database is in quiesced state, log in as SYS or SYSTEM and execute the following query:

```
select Active_State from V$INSTANCE;
```

The Active_State column value will be either NORMAL (unquiesced), QUIESCING (active non-DBA sessions are still running), or QUIESCED.

To unquiesce the database:

```
alter system unquiesce;
```

Instead of quiescing the database, you can suspend it. A suspended database performs no I/O to its datafiles and control files, allowing the database to be backed up without I/O interference. To suspend the database:

```
alter system suspend;
```

Although the **alter system suspend** command can be executed from any SYSDBA privileged account, you can only resume normal database operations from the SYS and SYSTEM accounts. Use SYS and SYSTEM to avoid potential errors while resuming the database operations. In Real Application Cluster configurations, all instances will be suspended. To see the current status:

```
select Database_Status from V$INSTANCE;
```

The database will be either SUSPENDED or ACTIVE. To resume the database, log in as SYS or SYSTEM and execute the following command:

```
alter system resume;
```

Iterative Development

Iterative development methodologies typically consist of a series of rapidly developed prototypes. These prototypes are used to define the system requirements as the system is being developed. These methodologies are attractive because of their ability to show the customers something tangible as development is taking place. However, there are a few common pitfalls that occur during iterative development that undermine its effectiveness.

First, effective *versioning* is not always used. Creating multiple versions of an application allows certain features to be "frozen" while others are changed. It also allows different sections of the application to be in development while others are in test. Too often, one version of the application is used for every iteration of every feature, resulting in an end product that is not adequately flexible to handle changing needs (which was the alleged purpose of the iterative development).

Second, the prototypes are not thrown away. Prototypes are developed to give the customer an idea of what the final product will look like; they should not be intended as the foundation of a finished product. Using them as a foundation will not yield the most stable and flexible system possible. When performing iterative development, treat the prototypes as temporary legacy systems.

Third, the development/test/production divisions are clouded. The methodology for iterative development must very clearly define the conditions that have to be met before an application version can be moved to the next stage. It may be best to keep the prototype development completely separate from the development of the full application.

Finally, unrealistic time lines are often set. The same deliverables that applied to the structured methodology apply to the iterative methodology. The fact that the application is being developed at an accelerated pace does not imply that the deliverables will be any quicker to generate.

Iterative Column Definitions

During the development process, your column definitions may change frequently. As of Oracle8i, you can drop columns from existing tables. You can drop a column immediately, or you can mark it as "unused," to be dropped at a later time. If the column is dropped immediately, the action may impact performance. If the column is marked as unused, there will be no impact on performance. The column can actually be dropped at a later time when the database is less heavily used.

To drop a column, use either the **set unused** clause or the **drop** clause of the **alter table** command. You cannot drop a pseudocolumn, a column of a nested table, or a partition key column. See Appendix A for the full syntax and restrictions for the **alter table** command.

In the following example, column Col2 is dropped from a table named TABLE1:

 `alter table TABLE1 drop column Col2;`

You can mark a column as unused:

 `alter table TABLE1 set unused column Col3;`

Marking a column as unused does not release the space previously used by the column. You can drop the unused columns:

 `alter table TABLE1 drop unused columns;`

You can query USER_UNUSED_COL_TABS, DBA_UNUSED_COL, and ALL_UNUSED_COL_TABS to see all tables with columns marked as unused.

NOTE
Once you have marked a column as unused, you cannot access that column. If you export the table after designating a column as unused, the column will not be exported.

You can drop multiple columns in a single command, as shown in the following listing:

 `alter table TABLE1 drop (Col4, Col5);`

NOTE
*When dropping multiple columns, the **column** keyword of the **alter table** command should not be used; it causes a syntax error. The multiple column names must be enclosed in parentheses, as shown in the preceding listing.*

If the dropped columns are part of primary keys or unique constraints, then you will also need to use the **cascade constraints** clause as part of your **alter table** command. If you drop a column that belongs to a primary key, Oracle will drop both the column and the primary key index.

If you cannot arrange for a maintenance period during which you can drop the columns, mark them as unused. The next time the database is quiesced, you can complete the maintenance from the SYS or SYSTEM account.

Moving Tables Online

As of Oracle9i, you can perform table maintenance online. In Oracle8i, your online table maintenance was limited to moving tables from one tablespace to another, or adding columns and constraints to existing tables. In Oracle9i, you can change a table's definition while it is accessible by the application users. For example, you can partition a previously nonpartitioned table while it is being used—a significant capability for high-availability OLTP applications.

> **NOTE**
> *You cannot perform online reorganizations for tables with no primary keys, for tables that have materialized views and materialized view logs defined on them, for materialized view container tables, for advanced queueing tables, or for IOT overflow tables.*

The following example shows the steps involved in redefining a table online. First, verify that the table can be redefined. For this example the CUSTOMER table will be created in the SCOTT schema and then redefined:

```
create table CUSTOMER
(Name        VARCHAR2(25) primary key,
 Street      VARCHAR2(50),
 City        VARCHAR2(25),
 State       CHAR(2),
 Zip         NUMBER);
```

Verify that the table can be redefined by executing the CAN_REDEF_TABLE procedure of the DBMS_REDEFINITION package. Its input parameters are the username and the table name.

```
execute DBMS_REDEFINITION.CAN_REDEF_TABLE('SCOTT','CUSTOMER');
```

The table is a candidate for online redefinition if the procedure returns the message

```
PL/SQL procedure successfully completed.
```

If it returns an error, the table cannot be redefined online, and the error message will give the reason.

Next, create an interim table, in the same schema, with the desired attributes of the redefined table. For example, we can partition the CUSTOMER table. To simplify this example, the **tablespace** and **storage** clauses for the partitions are not shown here.

```
create table CUSTOMER_INTERIM
 (Name          VARCHAR2(25) primary key,
  Street        VARCHAR2(50),
  City          VARCHAR2(25),
  State         CHAR(2),
  Zip           NUMBER)
 partition by range (Name)
  (partition PART1    values less than ('L'),
   partition PART2    values less than (MAXVALUE))
 ;
```

You can now execute the START_REDEF_TABLE procedure of the DBMS_REDEFINITION package to start the redefinition process. Its input variables are the schema owner, the table to be redefined, the interim table name, and the column mapping (similar to the list of column names in a select query). If no column mapping is supplied, then all of the column names and definitions in the original table and the interim table must be the same.

```
execute DBMS_REDEFINITION.START_REDEF_TABLE -
   ('SCOTT','CUSTOMER','CUSTOMER_INTERIM');
```

Next, create any triggers, indexes, grants, or constraints required on the interim table. In this example, the primary key has already been defined on CUSTOMER_INTERIM; you could add the foreign keys, secondary indexes, and grants at this point in the redefinition process. Create the foreign keys disabled until the redefinition process is complete.

When the redefinition process completes, the indexes, triggers, constraints, and grants on the interim table will replace those on the original table. The disabled referential constraints on the interim table will be enabled at that point.

To finish the redefinition, execute the FINISH_REDEF_TABLE procedure of the DBMS_REDEFINITION package. Its input parameters are the schema name, original table name, and interim table name:

```
execute DBMS_REDEFINITION.FINISH_REDEF_TABLE -
   ('SCOTT','CUSTOMER','CUSTOMER_INTERIM');
```

You can verify the redefinition by querying the data dictionary:

```
select Table_Name, High_Value
   from DBA_TAB_PARTITIONS
  where owner = 'SCOTT';


TABLE_NAME                 HIGH_VALUE
---------------------- ------------------------
CUSTOMER                   MAXVALUE
CUSTOMER                   'L'
```

To abort the process after executing the START_REDEF_TABLE procedure, execute the ABORT_REDEF_TABLE procedure (input parameters are the schema, original table name, and interim table name).

Forcing Cursor Sharing

Ideally, application developers should use bind variables in their programs to maximize the reuse of their previously parsed commands in the Shared SQL Pool. If bind variables are not in use, you may see many very similar statements in the library cache—queries that differ only in the literal value in the **where** clause.

Statements that are identical except for their literal value components are called *similar* statements. Similar statements can reuse previously parsed commands in the Shared SQL Pool if the CURSOR_SHARING initialization parameter is set to SIMILAR or FORCE. In general, you should favor using SIMILAR (new with Oracle9i) over FORCE, since SIMILAR will allow for a new execution plan to be generated reflecting any histogram data known about the literal value.

Setting CURSOR_SHARING to EXACT reuses previously parsed commands only when the literal values are identical.

To use stored outlines with CURSOR_SHARING set to FORCE or SIMILAR, the outlines must have been generated with that CURSOR_SHARING setting in effect.

Technology

The in-process deliverables must be made available while development is under way. Since most development teams include multiple developers (and now, at least one DBA), a means of communication must be established. The communication channels will help maintain consistency in planning and execution.

Four technological solutions are needed in order to make the methodology work: CASE tools, shared directories, project management databases, and discussion databases.

CASE Tools

You can use a CASE tool to generate the entity relationship diagram and the physical database diagram. CASE tools can create the entity relationship diagram and usually have an integrated data dictionary. CASE tools may allow for entities to be shared across applications and can store information about table volumes and row sizes. This functionality will help to resolve several of the deliverables that have been defined in this chapter. CASE tools should allow different versions of a data model to be maintained or frozen, supporting versioning and prototyping.

The SQL commands that create the database objects for the application should be generated directly from the CASE tool. You may also use the CASE tool to create generic versions of applications based on the defined database objects.

Shared Directories

Several of the deliverables, such as the backup requirements, have no specific tool in which they must be created. These deliverables should be created in whatever tools are most appropriate and available at your site. The resulting files should be stored in shared project directories so that all involved team members can access them. The formats and naming conventions for these files must be specified early in the development process.

Project Management Databases

In order to communicate the status of the application and its deliverables to people outside the development team, a project management database should be maintained. The project management database should provide an outsider with a view of the project and its current milestones. This information will allow those people who are not directly involved in the project (such as systems management personnel) to anticipate future requirements. The project management database also allows for the impact of scheduling changes or delays on the critical-path milestones to be analyzed, possibly resulting in modifications to the resource levels assigned to the tasks in the project.

Discussion Databases

Most of the information in these three shared areas—the CASE tools, the shared deliverables directories, and the project management databases—represents a consensus of opinion. For example, several team members may have opinions about the backup strategy, and the system management and DBA staffs must have input as well. To facilitate this communication, a set of discussion databases (usually using a groupware product on a local area network) can be created. Drafts can be posted to these areas before the final resolution is placed in the shared deliverables directory.

Managing Package Development

Imagine a development environment with the following characteristics:

- None of your standards are enforced.

- Objects are created under the SYS or SYSTEM accounts.

- Proper distribution and sizing of tables and indexes is only lightly considered.

- Every application is designed as if it were the only application you intend to run in your database.

As contrary as these conditions are, they are occasionally encountered during the implementation of purchased packaged applications.

Properly managing the implementation of packages involves many of the same issues that were described for the application development processes in the previous sections. This section will provide an overview of how packages should be treated so they will best fit with your development environment.

Generating Diagrams

Most CASE tools have the ability to *reverse engineer* packages into a physical database diagram. Reverse engineering consists of analyzing the table structures and generating a physical database diagram that is consistent with those structures, usually by analyzing column names, constraints, and indexes to identify key columns. However, normally there is no one-to-one correlation between the physical database diagram and the entity relationship diagram. Entity relationship diagrams for packages can usually be obtained from the package vendor; they are helpful in planning interfaces to the package database.

Space Requirements

Most Oracle-based packages provide fairly accurate estimates of their database resource usage during production usage. However, they usually fail to take into account their usage requirements during data loads and software upgrades. You should carefully monitor the package's undo requirements during large data loads. A spare DATA tablespace may be needed as well if the package creates copies of all of its tables during upgrade operations.

Tuning Goals

Just as custom applications have tuning goals, packages must be held to tuning goals as well. Establishing and tracking these control values will help to identify areas of the package in need of tuning (see Chapters 8 and 9).

Security Requirements

Unfortunately, many packages that use Oracle databases fall into one of two categories: either they were migrated to Oracle from another database system, or they assume they will have full DBA privileges for their object owner accounts.

If the packages were first created on a different database system, then their Oracle port very likely does not take full advantage of Oracle's functional capabilities such as sequences, triggers, and methods. Tuning such a package to meet your needs may require modifying the source code.

If the package assumes that it has full DBA authority, then it must not be stored in the same database as any other critical database application. Most packages that require DBA authority do so in order to add new users to the database. You should determine exactly which system-level privileges the package administrator account actually requires (usually just CREATE SESSION and CREATE USER). You can create a specialized system-level role to provide this limited set of system privileges to the package administrator.

Packages that were first developed on non-Oracle databases may require the use of the same account as another Oracle-ported package. For example, ownership of a database account called SYSADM may be required by multiple applications. The only way to resolve this conflict with full confidence is to create the two packages in separate databases.

Data Requirements

Any processing requirements that the packages have, particularly on the data entry side, must be clearly defined. These requirements are usually well documented in package documentation.

Version Requirements

Applications you support may have dependencies on specific versions and features of Oracle. For example, a packaged application may be certified on versions 8.1.6.1 and 9.0.1.0 but not on version 8.1.7. If you use packaged applications, you will need to base your kernel version upgrade plans on the vendor's support for the different Oracle versions. Furthermore, the vendor may switch the optimizer it supports—for example, rule based in one version but cost based in the next. Your database environment will need to be as flexible as possible in order to support these changes.

Because of these restrictions outside of your control, you should attempt to isolate the application to its own instance. If you frequently query data across applications, the isolation of the application to its own instance will increase your reliance on database links. You need to evaluate the maintenance costs of supporting multiple instances against the maintenance costs of supporting multiple applications in a single instance.

Execution Plans

Generating execution plans requires accessing the SQL statements that are run against the database. The shared SQL area in the SGA (see Chapter 1 and Chapter 8) maintains the SQL statements that are executed against the database. Matching the SQL statements against specific parts of the application is a time-consuming process. It is best to identify specific areas whose functionality and performance are critical to the application's success, and work with the package's support team to resolve performance issues. You can use the STATSPACK utility (see Chapter 9) to gather all of the commands generated during testing periods, and then determine the explain plans for the most resource-intensive queries in that set. If the commands are still accessible via the V$SQL view, you can tell Oracle9i to display the execution path along with the query. See Chapter 8 for details on automating the display of explain plans.

Acceptance Test Procedures

Purchased packages should be held to the same functional requirements that custom applications must meet. The acceptance test procedures should be developed before the package has been selected; they can be generated from the package selection criteria. By testing in this manner, you will be testing for the functionality that you need, rather than what the package developers thought you wanted.

Be sure to specify what your options are in the event the package fails its acceptance test for functional or performance reasons. Critical success factors for the application should not be overlooked just because it is a purchased application.

The Testing Environment

When establishing a test environment, follow these guidelines:

- It must be larger than your production environment. You need to be able to forecast future performance.

- It must contain known data sets, explain plans, performance results, and data result sets.

- It must be used for each release of the database and tools, as well as for new features.

- It must support the generation of multiple test conditions to enable the evaluation of the features' business costs. You do not want to have to rely on point analysis of results; ideally, you can determine the cost/benefit curves of a feature as the database grows in size.

- It must be flexible enough to allow you to evaluate different licensing cost options.

- It must be actively used as a part of your technology implementation methodology.

When testing transaction performance, be sure to track the incremental load rate over time. In general, the indexes on a table will slow the performance of loads when they reach a second internal level. See Chapter 8 for details on indexes and load performance.

When testing, your sample queries should represent each of the following groups:

- Queries that perform joins, including merge joins, nested loops, outer joins, and hash joins

- Queries that use database links

- DML that uses database links

- Each type of DML statement (**insert**s, **update**s, and **delete**s)

- Each major type of DDL statement, including table creations, index rebuilds, and grants

- Queries that use Parallel Query Option, if that option is in use in your environment

The sample set should not be fabricated; it should represent your operations, and it must be repeatable. Generating the sample set should involve reviewing your major groups of operations as well as the OLTP operations executed by your users. The result will not reflect every action within the database, but will allow you to be aware of the implications of upgrades and thus allow you to mitigate your risk and make better decisions about implementing new options.

The Managed Environment

The result of implementing the three critical elements—cultural processes, management processes, and technology—will be a development environment that has quality control built into it, allowing improvements to be made in the development process. The production applications will benefit from this in the form of improved performance, better integration with other enterprise applications, and simpler maintenance. To the greatest extent possible, work with the development teams directly to understand the business needs, simplify the implementation, and structure the change control process.

CHAPTER
6

Monitoring
Space Usage

atabase administrators need to monitor critical factors related to the effective running of their Oracle databases. Types of monitoring include performance monitoring, security checks, transaction monitoring, and space monitoring. Performance, security, and transaction monitoring are described in Chapters 7, 8, 9, and 10. In this chapter, you will see how to effectively monitor space problems that can cause database availability or manageability issues.

To avoid continuously managing space, you need

- An understanding of how the database will be used by its applications

- A well-structured database

- A set of metrics that gauge the database's health

- A systematic method for making those measurements and determining trends

The first two points, on database design, have been covered in Chapters 3–5. This chapter addresses the third and fourth points, providing measurement guides and a method for monitoring them. This chapter will concentrate on measuring physical elements of the database via a "Command Center" database. Chapters 7 through 10 will expand on the monitoring of transactions, memory areas, and security issues.

Common Problem Areas

There are several potential problem areas in almost all Oracle databases. These include the following:

- Running out of free space in a tablespace

- Insufficient space for temporary segments

- Rollback segments that have reached their maximum extension

- Fragmentation of data segments and free space

- Improperly sized SGA areas

An effective database monitoring system should be able to detect unacceptable values for each of these areas. In the following sections, you will see a synopsis of the problem areas to be tracked, followed by details for creating a system tailored for their monitoring. The system is not as comprehensive as the monitoring tools sold by third-party vendors, but it does provide a solid basis for monitoring the most critical success factors for databases.

Running Out of Free Space in a Tablespace

Each tablespace in the database has one or more datafiles assigned to it. If you are not using autoextendable datafiles, then the total space in all of the datafiles in a tablespace serves as the upper limit of the space that can be allocated in the tablespace.

When a segment is created in a tablespace, space is allocated for the initial extent of the segment from the available free space in the tablespace. When the initial extent fills with data, the segment acquires another extent. This process of extension continues either until the segment reaches a maximum number of extents or until the free space in the tablespace is less than the space needed by the next extent.

The free space in a tablespace therefore provides a cushion of unallocated space that can be used either by new segments or by the extensions of existing segments. If the available free space falls to a value that does not allow new segments or extents to be created, additional space will have to be added to the tablespace (by adding new datafiles or resizing existing datafiles).

Therefore, you should monitor not only the current available free space in tablespaces, but also the trend in the available free space—is there more or less available today than there was a week ago? You must be able to determine the effectiveness of the current space allocation and predict what it will look like in the near future.

Insufficient Space for Temporary Segments

Temporary segments store temporary data during sorting operations (such as large queries, index creations, and **union**s) and when temporary tables are created. Each user has a temporary tablespace specified when the account is created via the create user or **alter user** command. In Oracle9i, you can create a default temporary tablespace, and all users who are not specifically assigned a temporary tablespace will be assigned to the default temporary tablespace. The temporary tablespace should be pointed to someplace other than the SYSTEM tablespace.

When a temporary segment is created, it uses the default storage parameters for that tablespace. You cannot alter the storage parameters of an existing temporary segment. You can alter the storage parameters for a temporary segment, but the changes will not take effect until the next time you start the database. The temporary segment extends itself as necessary to support the transactions using it. If the tablespace is not designated as a temporary tablespace, the temporary segment will be deallocated by SMON when the operation completes or encounters an error. If the tablespace is designated as a temporary tablespace, the temporary segment will not be deallocated after the transaction completes; its space will be reused by later transactions.

If the temporary tablespace runs out of free space during the execution of a sorting operation, the datafile will grow to accommodate the space needed if the **autoextend** parameter is set for the datafiles or the tempfiles; if not, the operation will fail. Since it is difficult to accurately size such segments, it is important to monitor whether the temporary tablespace created to hold them is large enough. As with data tablespaces, both the current value and the trend will be monitored via the scripts provided in this chapter.

Rollback Segments That Have Reached Their Maximum Extension

If you do not use an undo tablespace available starting with Oracle9i (see Chapter 7), rollback segments will be involved in every transaction that occurs within the database, allowing the database to maintain read consistency across transactions. During database creation, the DBA specifies the number and size of rollback segments available, but the values can be modified later.

Since rollback segments are created within the database, they must be created within a tablespace. The first rollback segment, called *SYSTEM*, is stored in the SYSTEM tablespace. Further rollback segments are usually created in at least one other separate tablespace. Because rollback segments are created in tablespaces, their maximum size is limited to the amount of space in the tablespaces' datafiles.

Since rollback segments allocate new space in the same manner as data segments, they are subject to two potential problems: running out of available free space in the tablespace and reaching the maximum allowable number of extents. When either situation is encountered, the transaction that is forcing the rollback segment to extend will fail. A single transaction cannot span multiple rollback segments. Since a single rollback segment can support multiple concurrent transactions, multiple transactions may be competing for the empty blocks available in the rollback segment. Thus, in addition to tracking the free space (current and trends) for tablespaces that contain rollback segments, the number of extents in each segment must also be monitored. The limitation on maximum number of extents is minimized starting in Oracle8i since the number of extents is no longer limited by the block size by default as it was in Oracle8 and lower. The default number of extents for rollback segments in Oracle8i is 4096 and in Oracle9i, 32,765; the DBA can specify UNLIMITED EXTENTS when creating the rollback segments.

The **optimal** storage parameter is available only for rollback segments. The **optimal** parameter sets the optimal size of a rollback segment; when it extends beyond this size, it will later dynamically eliminate unused extents to shrink itself. You can use the dynamic performance table V$ROLLSTAT to track the number of times each rollback segment extends and shrinks. The monitoring system provided here monitors both space usage by rollback segments and the number of times they extend and shrink.

Fragmentation of Data Segments

Oracle manages space in segments by allowing a segment to acquire multiple extents. While allocating extents allows for flexibility when sizing tables, it can also cause performance degradation. Oracle's official statement is that tables with 4096 or fewer extents will not encounter performance problems because of the number of extents. Ideally, a segment's data will be stored in a manageable number of extents. All of the data does not have to be in a single extent, but the number of extents should not be so great as to adversely affect your ability to manage the segment.

NOTE
In general, you will not see a significant impact on the time required to perform DDL operations until a segment exceeds several thousand extents. The monitoring system shown in this chapter uses a lower threshold value to serve as an early warning system for incorrectly sized segments. You can alter the threshold values to suit your needs.

Each segment in the database has a maximum allowable number of extents. You can specify **unlimited** or a numeric value for a segment's maximum number of extents. The default number of extents is 4096 in Oracle8i and is **unlimited** in Oracle9i. Any transaction that causes a segment to attempt to exceed its maximum number of extents will fail; such failures are unlikely if you are using the default storage parameters. The monitoring utility provided in this chapter will track the current extension and the extension trends for segments in the database.

Fragmented Free Space

Just as data segments can become fragmented, the available free space in a tablespace can become fragmented. This problem is most prevalent in dictionary-managed tablespaces whose default **pctincrease** storage value is *not* set to 0. To minimize the impact of **pctincrease 0**, you can run a script to coalesce the tablespace's free space on a nightly basis.

When a segment is dropped, its extents are deallocated and are marked as being "free." However, these free extents are not always recombined with neighboring free extents. The barriers between these free extents may be maintained, affecting the free space available to a new data extent.

If the default **pctincrease** for a dictionary-managed tablespace is nonzero, Oracle automatically combines neighboring free extents into single, large extents. However, it is possible that free extents may be physically separated from each other by data extents, blocking their combination with other free extents.

To detect these potential problems, the utility provided in this chapter tracks the number and size of the available free extents in each tablespace. To avoid this problem in Oracle8i and above, use locally managed tablespaces.

Improperly Sized SGA Areas

The size of the System Global Area (SGA) used to store shared memory objects for a database is set via the database's init.ora parameters. In Oracle9i, you can set the database initialization parameter SGA_MAX_SIZE to allow dynamic changes to several areas within the SGA. The scripts and utilities detailed in Chapters 8 and 9 describe the monitoring of the database's memory areas.

Target Selection

Based on the common problem areas described, the following statistics will be targeted by the monitoring scripts:

- Current free space in all tablespaces
- Rate of change in free space for all tablespaces
- Total current space usage by temporary segments
- Size and number of extents for rollback segments
- Number of extents for all segments

This target list is a minimum acceptable starting point that you customize for each database under your control. The target list should be expanded to include those statistics that, combined, determine the success or failure of the system. For each statistic, you should define upper and lower control limits. Once the acceptable ranges have been defined, you can implement the monitoring system. Note that the ranges may be related to either the physical measurements (such as free space in a tablespace) or to the rate at which they change.

The following sections focus on the creation of a system that monitors the database for the targeted statistics. Additional statistics reports are provided following the standard memory and space monitoring scripts.

The End Product

Before describing the configuration and implementation of the monitoring system, decide what the output should provide. In this section, you will see sample listings from the system that will be described in this chapter. If further detail or different information is needed, you can easily modify the system.

The first report, shown in Figure 6-1, is a trend report of free space by tablespace for all databases. This report shows the current percentage of unallocated (free) space in each tablespace (the TS column) of each database (the DB_NM column). The current free space percentage is shown in the Today column of the sample

```
                    Percent Free Trends for Tablespaces

                         4Wks   3Wks   2Wks   1Wk
DB_NM         TS         Ago    Ago    Ago    Ago    Today  Change
----------    ----------  ----   ----   ----   ----   -----  ------
CASE          CASE         56     56     55     40     40     -16
              USERS        86     64     75     77     76     -10
              SYSTEM       22     22     22     21     21     -1
              TOOLS        25     25     25     25     25
              RBS          32     32     32     32     32
              TEMP        100    100    100    100    100


CC1           CC           94     94     93     92     92     -2
              TESTS        71     70     70     70     70     -1
              SYSTEM       24     24     24     24     24
              RBS          32     32     32     32     32
              CCINDX       51     51     51     51     51
              TEMP        100    100    100    100    100
```

FIGURE 6-1.   *Free space trends of Tablespaces trend report*

report. The other columns show the free space percentage for each tablespace for the last four weeks. The change between today's free space percentage and its value as of four weeks ago is shown in the Change column. The tablespaces experiencing the greatest negative changes in free space percentage are listed first.

The report shown in Figure 6-1 shows the current values, the previous values, and the trend for the percentage of free space in each tablespace. This report is part of the output from the monitoring scripts you will see in this chapter.

The SQL scripts used to generate this report include a variable that can be set to restrict the output to only those tablespaces whose free space percentages have changed more than a given threshold value. The script may also be restricted to show specific databases or tablespaces. Note that these threshold limits, which are used to define whether the system is "in control" or "out of control," can also be hardcoded into the reports, allowing you to use the report as an exception report for your databases.

You can view extent allocation among segments in the report shown in Figure 6-2. This report, also generated from the monitoring scripts shown in this chapter, shows the trends in extent allocation for all segments that presently have more than ten extents. It shows all rollback segments regardless of their extent procurement.

The report shown in Figure 6-2 shows the current number of extents (the Today column) for each of the segments listed. The segment's database (DB_NM),

Extent Trends for Segments with 1000 or more Extents

DB_NM	TS	Owner	Name	Type	Blocks	4Wks Ago	3Wks Ago	2Wks Ago	1Wk Ago	Today	Change
CASE	CASE	CASEMGR	TEMP_TBL	TABLE	10000				2000	2000	2000
			TEMP_IDX	INDEX	8000				1600	1600	1600
	RBS	SYSTEM	ROLL1	ROLLBACK	3800	19	19	19	19	19	
			ROLL2	ROLLBACK	3800	19	19	19	19	19	
	USERS	AL1	TEST1	TABLE	12000		1200	1200	1200	1200	1200
			TEST2	TABLE	14000		1400	1400	1400	1400	1400
CC1	RBS	SYSTEM	ROLL1	ROLLBACK	3800	19	19	19	19	19	
			ROLL2	ROLLBACK	3800	19	19	19	19	19	

FIGURE 6-2. *Extent trends for Segments sample report*

tablespace (TS), owner (Owner), name (Name), and type (Type) are listed to fully identify it. The segment's current size in Oracle blocks (the Blocks column) is also shown. The current and previous number of extents are shown, as well as the change in the number of extents from four weeks ago to today (the Change column).

NOTE
There is no need to worry about rollback segments when system-managed undo segments are used to replace rollback segments in Oracle9i.

The report shown in Figure 6-2 shows the current values, the previous values, and the trend for the number of extents for fragmented segments. The report also shows these statistics for all rollback segments. This report is part of the output from the monitoring application provided in this chapter.

This report can also be customized to show only those values that have changed. However, it is more informative when all of the alert (>999 extents) records are shown. The report output can then be compared with the free space trends report to reach conclusions about the database. Given these two example reports, you could conclude that

- All rollback segments appear to be appropriately sized. None of them have increased in size despite the creation of new tables in the databases. (Note: This assumes that the **optimal** sizes of the rollback segment have not yet been reached.)

■ The AL1 user in the CASE database has created several tables in the USERS tablespace. Although they have contributed to the decline in the free space in that tablespace, they cannot by themselves account for the dip down to 64 percent three weeks ago. That dip appears to have been caused by transient tables (since the space has since been reclaimed).

■ The CASE_MGR account has impacted a production tablespace by creating a temporary table and index in the CASE tablespace. These segments should be moved unless they are part of the production application.

These two reports, which are generated from the application described in the rest of this chapter, are sufficient to measure all of the variables listed as targets earlier in this section—free space, rollback segments status, extent allocation, and trends for these. More importantly, they provide information about the appropriateness of the database design, given the application's behavior. The sample reports show that the rollback segments were sized correctly, but that the CASE_MGR account has created developmental tables in a production database—a lack of control in the production system that may eventually cause a production failure. Even if the sample report shows that the current sizes of the tables that CASE_MGR created are small, the lack of process control should be a concern regardless of the object size.

Since it is helpful to see a summary of each database, the final sample report summarizes the CC1 database. The summary report lists all files and tablespaces, and the space details for each. The CC1 database shown in the report is the Command Center database, which will be defined in the next section of this chapter.

The sample output shown in Figure 6-3 is divided into two sections. In the first section, each of the datafiles in the databases is listed (the File nm column), along with the tablespace it is assigned to (the Tablespace column). The number of Oracle blocks (Orablocks) and bytes (Bytes) in each datafile are also displayed in this section.

In the second half of the report, the free space statistics for the tablespaces are displayed. For each tablespace, the number of free extents is displayed (NumFrExts). This column shows how many fragments the available free space in a tablespace is broken into. The largest single free extent, in Oracle blocks, is shown in the MaxFrExt column, as well as the sum of all free space in the tablespace (SumFrBl). The percentage of the tablespace that is unallocated is shown in the PercentFr column.

The MaxFrPct column displays the ratio of the largest single free extent to the total free space available. A high value for this column indicates that most of the free space available is located in a single extent. The last two columns display the free space available in bytes (DiskFrBy) out of the total available disk bytes (SumFileBy) for each tablespace.

The report shown in Figure 6-3 provides an overview of the space usage in the database. The first section shows where the free space is coming from—the datafiles assigned to the tablespaces—and the second section shows how that free space is

```
                    Oracle Tablespaces in CC1
                    Check Date = 27-MAY-01

Tablespace   File nm                       Orablocks        Bytes
----------   ---------------------------   ---------   -------------
CC           /db03/oracle/CC1/cc.dbf          30,720      62,914,560
CCINDX       /db04/oracle/CC1/ccindx.dbf      20,480      41,943,040
RBS          /db02/oracle/CC1/rbs01.dbf        5,120      10,485,760
             /db02/oracle/CC1/rbs02.dbf        5,120      10,485,760
             /db02/oracle/CC1/rbs03.dbf        5,120      10,485,760
SYSTEM       /db01/oracle/CC1/sys01.dbf      102,400     209,715,200
TEMP         /db01/oracle/CC1/temp01.dbf      15,360      31,457,280
TESTS        /db04/oracle/CC1/tests01.dbf     30,720      62,914,560


                 Oracle Free Space Statistics for CC1
                  (Extent Sizes in Oracle blocks)
                     Check Date = 27-MAY-01

Tablespace   NumFrExts MaxFrExt  SumFrBl PercentFr MaxFrPct  DiskFrBy   SumFileBy
----------   --------- --------  ------- --------- -------- ---------- ----------
CC                   1    21504    21504     70.00      100   44040192   62914560
CCINDX               1    15360    15360     75.00      100   31457280   41943040
RBS                  3     2019     2057     13.39       98    4212736   31457280
SYSTEM               1    67580    67580     66.00      100  138403840  209715200
TEMP                 6    12800    15360    100.00       83   31457280   31457280
TESTS                1    21504    21504     70.00      100   44040192   62914560
```

FIGURE 6-3.   *Sample space summary report*

currently being used. This report is part of the output of the monitoring application provided in this chapter.

The combination of the reports shown in Figures 6-1, 6-2, and 6-3 is sufficient to measure all of the targets listed earlier. They were all generated based on queries against a single Command Center database. The database design is given in the next section, followed by instructions for data acquisition and a set of standard queries to provide a baseline for your reporting needs.

Creating the Command Center Database

Establishing a separate database that is used solely for monitoring other systems resolves three problems with traditional Oracle database monitoring capabilities:

■ Monitoring activities can be coordinated across multiple databases.

■ The monitoring activities will not affect the space usage in the system they are monitoring.

■ Trends can be detected for the parameters being monitored.

In this section, you will see the scripts needed for the creation, structure, and implementation of a stand-alone monitoring database.

The system described here is a *reactive monitor*. It is not designed to perform proactive, real-time monitoring of systems. The monitoring system should ideally be called from a system or network monitor, and this entire monitoring function can then be given to the systems management team.

The monitoring database in this example is given the instance name CC1 to designate it as the first Command Center database in the system. Based on your system architecture, you may wish to have multiple databases to perform this function. The database architecture is shown in the following table; the architecture assumes you are using rollback segments instead of an undo tablespace.

SYSTEM tablespace	300MB; for an Oracle8i database, 150MB should be sufficient.
RBS tablespace	30MB; two 10MB rollback segments, 10MB free
CC tablespace	30MB
CCINDX tablespace	20MB
TESTS tablespace	30MB
TEMP tablespace	15MB
Redo logs	Three 10MB redo logs

The design of the application that will store the monitoring results is fairly simple. For each instance, the system will store descriptive information about its location and usage as well as information about each file in each database. The CC1 database will also record each tablespace's free space statistics, and every segment will be checked for excessive extents. Figure 6-4 shows the physical database diagram for the monitoring tables.

A view of the FILES table, called FILES_TS_VIEW, is created by grouping the FILES table by instance ID, tablespace (TS), and check date (Check_Date). Here, instance ID is needed because the monitoring database will be used to monitor several databases. FILES_TS_VIEW is needed when comparing data in the FILES table (allocated space) with data in the SPACES table (used and free space).

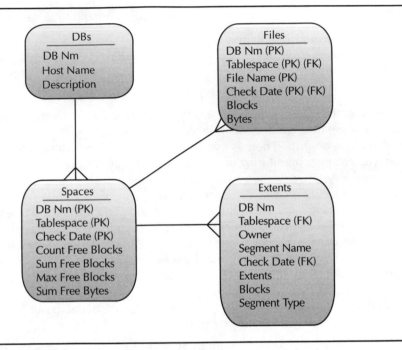

FIGURE 6-4. *Physical database diagram for the Command Center database*

The DDL for creating these objects is given in the following listing. The objects are described in Table 6-1.

```
drop table dbs;

rem * This table will store information about instances*/

create table DBS
(Db_Nm          VARCHAR2(8),      /*instance name*/
 Host_Nm        VARCHAR2(8),      /*host (server) name*/
 Description    VARCHAR2(80))     /*instance description*/
tablespace CC
storage (initial 64K next 64K pctincrease 0);

drop table FILES;
```

```
rem /*This table will store information about datafiles*/

create table FILES
(Db_Nm         VARCHAR2(8),     /*instance name*/
TS             VARCHAR2(30),    /*tablespace name*/
Check_Date     DATE,            /*date entry was made */
File_Nm        VARCHAR2(80),    /*file name*/
Blocks         NUMBER,          /*size of the file*/
Bytes          NUMBER,          /*size of the file in bytes*/
primary key(Db_Nm, TS, Check_Date, File_Nm))
tablespace CC
storage (initial 128K next 128K pctincrease 0);


drop view FILES_TS_VIEW;


rem /*This view groups the file sizes by tablespace*/

create view FILES_TS_VIEW as
select
    Db_Nm,                         /*instance name*/
    TS,                            /*tablespace name*/
    Check_Date,                    /*date entry was made */
    SUM(Blocks) Sum_File_Blocks,   /*blocks allocated for ts*/
    SUM(Bytes)  Sum_File_Bytes     /*bytes allocated for ts*/
from FILES
group by
    Db_Nm,
    TS,
    Check_Date;


drop table SPACES;


rem /*This table will store information about free space*/

create table SPACES
(Db_Nm         VARCHAR2(8),     /*instance name*/
TS             VARCHAR2(30),    /*tablespace name*/
Check_Date     DATE,            /*date entry was made */
Count_Free_Blocks NUMBER,       /*number of free extents*/
Sum_Free_Blocks   NUMBER,       /*free space, in Ora blocks*/
Max_Free_Blocks   NUMBER,       /*largest free extent */
Sum_Free_Bytes    NUMBER,       /*free space, in bytes*/
primary key (Db_Nm, Ts, Check_Date))
tablespace CC
storage (initial 128K next 128K pctincrease 0);
```

```
drop table EXTENTS;

rem /*This table will store information about extents */

create table EXTENTS
(Db_Nm      VARCHAR2(8),    /*instance name*/
TS          VARCHAR2(30),   /*tablespace name*/
Seg_Owner   VARCHAR2(30),   /*segment owner*/
Seg_Name    VARCHAR2(32),   /*segment name*/
Seg_Type    VARCHAR2(17),   /*segment type*/
Extents     NUMBER,         /*number of extents allocated*/
Blocks      NUMBER,         /*number of blocks allocated*/
Check_Date DATE             /*date entry was made */
) tablespace CC
storage (initial 128K next 128K pctincrease 0);

create index I_EXTENTS$KEYS
on EXTENTS(Db_Nm, TS, Seg_Owner, Seg_Name, Check_Date)
tablespace CCINDX
storage (initial 128K next 128K pctincrease 0);
```

These database structures allow the DBA to track all of the targets listed previously, across all databases. There is no table for rollback segments. Rollback segments will be tracked via the EXTENTS table if their extent count exceeds the specified limit. There is no need to track this information when using system-managed undo segments in Oracle9i (see Chapter 7).

Object	Description
DBS	Table for storing descriptive information about instances
FILES	Table for storing information about files
FILES_TS_VIEW	View of the FILES table, grouped by tablespace
SPACES	Table for storing information about free space
EXTENTS	Table for storing information about used extents

TABLE 6-1. *Tables and Views in the Command Center Database*

NOTE
Alter the storage parameters and tablespace designations to match your standards, as established in Chapter 5.

Getting the Data

The first object listed in Table 6-1, DBS, is provided as a reference for sites where there are multiple DBAs. You can use the DBS table to enter descriptive information about instances; DBS is the only table of this application that requires manual data entry. All other data will be automatically loaded into the tables. All of the standard data reports will also be automated, with ad hoc capabilities available as well.

The data that is needed to populate these tables is accessible via the SYSTEM account of each database. (A secondary DBA account may also be used for this purpose; this account requires access to DBA-privileged tables, so a specialized system role or the SELECT_CATALOG_ROLE may be used for this purpose.)

Within the CC1 database, you can create an account that will own the monitoring application; this account does not require the DBA role. Within the owner account, create private database links to a DBA-privileged account in each remote database. The database link's name should be the same as the name of the instance that it links to. For example:

```
create database link CASE
connect to system identified by m99yhvasd44e
using 'case';
```

The CASE link shown in this listing accesses the SYSTEM account in the database identified by the service name 'case'. When used, it will log into that database as the user system.

Note that the **connect to** line is not necessary if the username and password will be the same on the remote system as they are on the local system. See Chapter 9 for details on the **connect to current user** clause for database links.

NOTE
Anyone who is able to gain unauthorized access to your monitoring database may be able to access your production databases via the database links you establish. Be sure to carefully secure the monitoring database.

The outline of the data acquisition process is shown in Figure 6-5. In the data acquisition process, a batch scheduler will be used to call a command script that will start the process. The job should be scheduled to run daily, at off-peak hours.

As shown in Figure 6-5, the monitoring application will perform the following steps:

1. The command script (called ins_cc1) calls a SQL*Plus script (named inserts.sql) that lists all of the databases to monitor.

2. Each of those databases is checked via a SQL*Plus script (named ins_all.sql).

3. The results of those queries are stored in tables in the Command Center database by ins_all.sql.

4. The command script then generates alert reports based on the latest values in the Command Center database.

To start the system, construct a command file that is run using the operating system's batch scheduler. A sample shell file for UNIX, to be called via **cron**, is shown in the following listing. For NT, you can use the **at** command. The following script first sets up its environment variables to point to the CC1 database, which is either an Oracle8*i* or Oracle9*i* database since SQL*Plus is used to start the database.

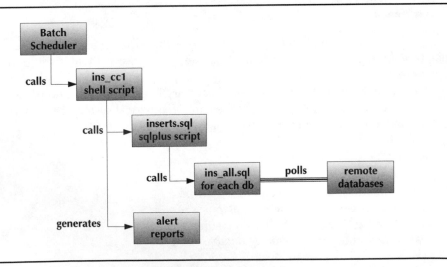

FIGURE 6-5. *Process flow for database monitoring*

Once the database is opened, a command is executed to start the inserts.sql script. After the data processing completes, the CC1 database is again shut down.

```
# file: ins_cc1
#
# This script is run once daily to insert records into the
# CC1 database recording the space usage of the databases
# listed in inserts.sql file called by this file. New
# databases need to have new links created in CC1 and have
# to have entries in the inserts.sql script.
#
ORACLE_SID=cc1; export ORACLE_SID
ORAENV_ASK=NO; export ORAENV_ASK
. oraenv
cd /orasw/dba/CC1
sqlplus <<EOF
connect system/manager as SYSDBA;
start inserts
shutdown
EOF
```

The ins_cc1 script assumes that the database is closed when this monitoring is not taking place. Keeping the database closed allows the memory normally used by CC1's SGA and background processes to be freed during regular working hours. Monitoring is assumed to be taking place once a day, at a fixed time when the system is lightly loaded.

The shell script shown in the previous listing calls a file named inserts.sql, located in the /orasw/dba/CC1 directory. A sample inserts.sql file is shown below. The inserts.sql script calls the ins_all.sql script for each database that is to be monitored. Once each database's statistics have been gathered, two alert reports, named space_watcher.sql and extent_watcher.sql, are executed.

```
rem
rem   file:  inserts.sql
rem   location:  /orasw/dba/CC1
rem   Called from ins_cc1 shell script.
rem   New entries must be made here every time a new database
rem   is added to the system.
rem
set verify off
@ins_all CASE
@ins_all CC1
analyze table FILES compute statistics;
analyze table SPACES compute statistics;
analyze table EXTENTS compute statistics;
@space_watcher
@extent_watcher
```

The inserts.sql file lists all of the databases for which monitoring statistics will be gathered. When new databases are added to the system, an additional line should be added for each. The inserts.sql file thus provides a layer of process management that allows easy changes without altering the submitted batch program or the SQL statements that access the remote databases.

After executing the ins_all.sql script for two databases (CASE and CC1), the inserts.sql script analyzes the tables that store the monitoring data. The analysis of the tables is necessary to guarantee the performance of the reports against the monitoring tables. Since the data in the monitoring tables changes frequently, these tables should be frequently analyzed.

The last two lines in this script call a pair of SQL scripts named space_watcher.sql and extent_watcher.sql. These scripts will generate versions of the "Percent Free Trends for Tablespaces" and "Extent Trends for Segments with 1000 or More Extents" reports shown earlier in Figures 6-1 and 6-2, respectively. Because they will be used for alerting purposes, only rows with changes exceeding defined limits will be shown in the next listing.

NOTE
You can alter the threshold for the number of extents at which a monitoring record is generated via the ins_all.sql script shown in the next listing.

Continuing down the process path depicted in Figure 6-5, the next step is to run a script (ins_all.sql) that inserts records into all applicable monitoring tables based on queries against remote databases. These queries use the database links created earlier to search each instance in turn and record the statistics returned. A sample ins_all.sql SQL*Plus script for **insert**s into the FILES, SPACES, and EXTENTS tables is shown in the next listing.

The first part of the ins_all.sql script **insert**s records into the FILES table. It queries each database for information about all of its datafiles, the tablespaces to which they are assigned, and their sizes.

The second part of the script queries the free space statistics of each database. It stores the output in the SPACES table, recording the number of free extents in each tablespace, the total free space available, and the size of the largest single free extent.

The third part of the script checks the space usage by segments and stores its results in the EXTENTS table. It records the information needed to identify the segment (such as its owner and name), as well as its current size and number of extents. To limit the number of records returned by this query, only rollback segments and segments with greater than nine extents are selected.

```
rem
rem   file:  ins_all.sql
rem   location:  /orasw/dba/CC1
rem   Used to perform all inserts into CC1 monitoring
rem   tables. This script is called from inserts.sql for
rem   each instance.
rem   For best results, name the database links after the
rem   instances they access.
rem
insert into FILES
    (Db_Nm,
    TS,
    Check_Date,
    File_Nm,
    Blocks,
    Bytes)
select
    UPPER('&&1'),        /*insert database link,instance name*/
    Tablespace_Name,     /*tablespace name*/
    TRUNC(SysDate),      /*date query is being performed*/
    File_Name,           /*full name of database file*/
    Blocks,              /*number of database blocks in file*/
    Bytes                /*number of bytes in the file*/
from sys.DBA_DATA_FILES@&&1
/
commit;
rem
insert into SPACES
    (Db_Nm,
    Check_Date,
    TS,
    Count_Free_Blocks,
    Sum_Free_Blocks,
    Max_Free_Blocks,
    Sum_Free_Bytes)
select
    UPPER('&&1'),        /*insert database link,instance name*/
    TRUNC(SysDate),      /*date query is being performed*/
    Tablespace_Name,     /*tablespace name*/
    COUNT(Blocks),       /*num. of free space entries */
    SUM(Blocks),         /*total free space in the tablespace*/
    MAX(Blocks),          /*largest free extent in the ts*/
    SUM(Bytes)           /*total free bytes in the tablespace*/
from sys.DBA_FREE_SPACE@&&1
```

```
group by Tablespace_Name
/
commit;
rem
insert into EXTENTS
    (Db_Nm,
    TS,
    Seg_Owner,
    Seg_Name,
    Seg_Type,
    Extents,
    Blocks,
    Check_Date)
select
    UPPER('&&1'),      /*insert database link,instance name*/
    Tablespace_Name,  /*tablespace name*/
    Owner,            /*owner of the segment*/
    Segment_Name,     /*name of the segment*/
    Segment_Type,     /*type of segment (ex. TABLE, INDEX)*/
    Extents,          /*number of extents in the segment*/
    Blocks,           /*number of database blocks in segment*/
    TRUNC(SysDate)    /*date the query is being performed*/
from sys.DBA_SEGMENTS@&&1
where Extents>999          /*only record extended segments*/
or Segment_Type = 'ROLLBACK'   /*or rollback segments*/
/
commit;
rem
undefine 1
```

Since these two **where** clauses establish the threshold for the extent alert report, change the extent limit to best suit your needs.

> **NOTE**
> *For segments in locally managed tablespaces, the space usage data is available via the standard dictionary views, so no modifications to these scripts are necessary for locally managed tablespaces.*

The preceding series of scripts will perform all of the data acquisition functions necessary to generate the reports shown earlier in this chapter. If you plan to monitor this data more frequently than daily, the primary keys of the tables will need to be modified to include both Check_Date and Check_Hour (for hourly reporting).

Now that the data has been inserted into the CC1 monitoring tables, you can use Oracle to automatically generate alert reports. The alert reports are created via the space_watcher.sql and extent_watcher.sql files called from the inserts.sql file shown earlier.

Generating Alert Reports

The alert reports are modifications to the generic free space and extent trends reports shown in Figures 6-1 and 6-2. The alert reports feature **where** and **group by** clauses to eliminate those entries that have not exceeded some threshold value. The setting of the threshold values should be customized for each site—they are based on the control limits defined during the target variable selection process.

Since the alert reports are called automatically following the insertion of records into the Command Center database, you may wish to have their output automatically mailed, printed, or posted to an internal Web page so they will be seen each morning before the production users begin to access the databases.

The following script generates the space trend report for tablespaces whose percentage of free space has changed by at least 5 percent in the last four weeks:

```
rem
rem   file:   space_watcher.sql
rem   location:   /orasw/dba/CC1
rem   Called from inserts.sql
rem
column Db_Nm format A8
column TS format A20
column Week4 format 999 heading "1Wk|Ago"
column Week3 format 999 heading "2Wks|Ago"
column Week2 format 999 heading "3Wks|Ago"
column Week1 format 999 heading "4Wks|Ago"
column Today format 999
column Change format 999

set pagesize 60
break on Db_Nm skip 2
ttitle center 'Tablespaces whose PercentFree values have -
decreased 5 pct this month' skip 2

select
   SPACES.Db_Nm,
   SPACES.TS,
   MAX(DECODE(SPACES.Check_Date, TRUNC(SysDate-28),
      ROUND(100*Sum_Free_Blocks/Sum_File_Blocks),0)) Week1,
   MAX(DECODE(SPACES.Check_Date, TRUNC(SysDate-21),
      ROUND(100*Sum_Free_Blocks/Sum_File_Blocks),0)) Week2,
   MAX(DECODE(SPACES.Check_Date, TRUNC(SysDate-14),
      ROUND(100*Sum_Free_Blocks/Sum_File_Blocks),0)) Week3,
   MAX(DECODE(SPACES.Check_Date, TRUNC(SysDate-7),
```

```
        ROUND(100*Sum_Free_Blocks/Sum_File_Blocks),0)) Week4,
    MAX(DECODE(SPACES.Check_Date, TRUNC(SysDate),
        ROUND(100*Sum_Free_Blocks/Sum_File_Blocks),0)) Today,
    MAX(DECODE(SPACES.Check_Date, TRUNC(SysDate),
        ROUND(100*Sum_Free_Blocks/Sum_File_Blocks),0)) -
    MAX(DECODE(SPACES.Check_Date, TRUNC(SysDate-28),
        ROUND(100*Sum_Free_Blocks/Sum_File_Blocks),0)) Change
from SPACES, FILES_TS_VIEW FTV
where SPACES.Db_Nm = FTV.Db_Nm          /*same DB name*/
and SPACES.TS = FTV.TS                   /*same TS name*/
and SPACES.Check_Date = ftv.Check_Date   /*same check date*/
and exists                               /*does ts exist?*/
    (select 'x' from SPACES x
    where x.Db_Nm = SPACES.Db_Nm
    and x.TS = SPACES.TS
    and x.Check_Date = TRUNC(SysDate))
group by
    SPACES.Db_Nm,
    SPACES.TS
having                  /*has percentfree dropped 5 pct?*/
(  MAX(DECODE(SPACES.Check_Date, TRUNC(SysDate),
        ROUND(100*Sum_Free_Blocks/Sum_File_Blocks),0)) -
    MAX(DECODE(SPACES.Check_Date, TRUNC(SysDate-28),
        ROUND(100*Sum_Free_Blocks/Sum_File_Blocks),0))
>5    )
or                      /*is percentfree less than 10?*/
(  MAX(DECODE(SPACES.Check_Date, TRUNC(SysDate),
        ROUND(100*Sum_Free_Blocks/Sum_File_Blocks),0)) <10)
order by SPACES.Db_Nm,
    DECODE(MAX(DECODE(SPACES.Check_Date,TRUNC(SysDate),
        ROUND(100*Sum_Free_Blocks/Sum_File_Blocks),0)) -
    MAX(DECODE(SPACES.Check_Date, TRUNC(SysDate-28),
        ROUND(100*Sum_Free_Blocks/Sum_File_Blocks),0)),0,9999,
    MAX(DECODE(SPACES.Check_Date,TRUNC(SysDate),
        ROUND(100*Sum_Free_Blocks/Sum_File_Blocks),0)) -
    MAX(DECODE(SPACES.Check_Date, TRUNC(SysDate-28),
        ROUND(100*Sum_Free_Blocks/Sum_File_Blocks),0))),
    MAX(DECODE(SPACES.Check_Date,TRUNC(SysDate),
        ROUND(100*Sum_Free_Blocks/Sum_File_Blocks),0))

spool space_watcher.lst
/
spool off
```

If the **exists** section is left out of the above query, then all tablespaces will be shown, even after they have been dropped from the database. The two limiting conditions within the **having** clauses define the threshold for the alert report. In this

```
              Tablespaces whose Percent Free values have
                  decreased 5 pct this month

                  4Wks   3Wks   2Wks   1Wk
DB_NM       TS     Ago    Ago    Ago    Ago    Today   Change
---------   ----------   ----   ----   ----   ----   -----   ------
CASE        CASE          56     56     55     40      40      -16
            USERS         86     64     75     77      76      -10
```

FIGURE 6-6. *Sample alert report for tablespace percent free trends*

example, only those tablespaces whose percent free values have decreased by more than 5 percent in the past 28 days will pass the first **having** condition. The second **having** condition identifies those tablespaces whose current percent free value is less than 10 percent, regardless of its trends.

If incremental changes in specific databases are critical to their success, then you may wish to add a **having** clause to this report that lists those specific databases regardless of their trends.

Sample output (based on the percent free trend report in Figure 6-1) is shown in Figure 6-6.

The space_watcher alert report does not show fluctuations that have since been resolved (for example, a four-week percent free trend of 70-70-20-70-70 would not be shown). The space_watcher alert report should be run and viewed on a daily basis. If a tablespace's space problems have been resolved, that tablespace will no longer be shown in the report's output.

The second report is the extent watcher (extent_watcher.sql). Like the space watcher report, this SQL*Plus query uses the **group by** clause to transpose multiple rows into multiple columns for a single row. This report provides a subset of the data listed in the generic extent trends report that was shown in Figure 6-2.

```
rem
rem   file:   ext_watcher.sql
rem   location:   /orasw/dba/CC1
rem   Called from inserts.sql
rem
column Db_Nm format A8
column TS format A18
column Seg_Owner format a14
column Seg_Name format a32
column Seg_Type format a8
```

```
column Blocks format 99999999
column Week4 format 9999 heading "1Wk|Ago"
column Week3 format 9999 heading "2Wks|Ago"
column Week2 format 9999 heading "3Wks|Ago"
column Week1 format 9999 heading "4Wks|Ago"
column Today format 9999
column Change format 9999

set pagesize 60 linesize 132
break on Db_Nm skip 2 on TS skip 1 on Seg_Owner
ttitle center 'Segments whose extent count is over 1000' -
skip 2

select
    EXTENTS.Db_Nm,
    EXTENTS.TS,
    EXTENTS.Seg_Owner,
    EXTENTS.Seg_Name,
    EXTENTS.Seg_Type,
    MAX(DECODE(EXTENTS.Check_Date, TRUNC(SysDate),
           Blocks,0)) Blocks,
    MAX(DECODE(EXTENTS.Check_Date, TRUNC(SysDate-28),
           Extents,0)) Week1,
    MAX(DECODE(EXTENTS.Check_Date, TRUNC(SysDate-21),
           Extents,0)) Week2,
    MAX(DECODE(EXTENTS.Check_Date, TRUNC(SysDate-14),
           Extents,0)) Week3,
    MAX(DECODE(EXTENTS.Check_Date, TRUNC(SysDate-7),
           Extents,0)) Week4,
    MAX(DECODE(EXTENTS.Check_Date, TRUNC(SysDate),
           Extents,0)) Today,
    MAX(DECODE(EXTENTS.Check_Date, TRUNC(SysDate),
           Extents,0)) -
    MAX(DECODE(EXTENTS.Check_Date, TRUNC(SysDate-28),
           Extents,0)) Change
from EXTENTS
where exists  /*did this segment show up today?*/
    (select 'x' from EXTENTS x
    where x.Db_Nm = EXTENTS.Db_Nm
    and x.TS = EXTENTS.TS
    and x.Seg_Owner = EXTENTS.Seg_Owner
    and x.Seg_Name = EXTENTS.Seg_Name
    and x.Seg_Type = EXTENTS.Seg_Type
    and x.Check_Date = TRUNC(SysDate))
group by
    EXTENTS.Db_Nm,
    EXTENTS.TS,
    EXTENTS.Seg_Owner,
```

```
    EXTENTS.Seg_Name,
    EXTENTS.Seg_Type
order by EXTENTS.Db_Nm, EXTENTS.TS,
    DECODE(MAX(DECODE(EXTENTS.Check_Date,TRUNC(SysDate),
        Extents,0)) -
    MAX(DECODE(EXTENTS.Check_Date, TRUNC(SysDate-28),
        Extents,0)),0,-9999,
    MAX(DECODE(EXTENTS.Check_Date,TRUNC(SysDate),
        Extents,0)) -
    MAX(DECODE(EXTENTS.Check_Date, TRUNC(SysDate-28),
        Extents,0))) desc,
    MAX(DECODE(EXTENTS.Check_Date,TRUNC(SysDate),
        Extents,0)) desc

spool extent_watcher.lst
/
spool off
```

The only portion of this query that limits the records to be shown is the **exists** clause that queries to see if the segment was returned from the current day's query. The report assumes that the threshold values for the "number of extents" variable was enforced during the **insert** into the EXTENTS table (see ins_all.sql, shown in the "Getting the Data" section of this chapter). The EXTENTS table is the only table that has the threshold enforced during **insert**s rather than during querying, since there may be thousands of segments in a database.

Sample output from the extent_watcher.sql report is shown in Figure 6-7. No restrictions beyond those enforced during the **insert** were needed to produce the alert report.

The Space Summary Report

Since every day's statistics are being stored in the CC1 Command Center database, a summary report can be generated for any database, for any specified date. The summary report should be generated on a weekly basis via the batch scheduler and should be available online to the DBA. Having the report available online will shorten the time delay in getting the report, since the CC1 database is usually kept closed after its daily batch run is completed (as specified in the ins_cc1 shell script).

The space summary report should be run once for each database. The report generates an output file whose name includes the name of the database link that was used in the query. The script takes two parameters:

- The database link name. (Since this will be stored in the output file's name, it should have the same name as the instance it accesses.)

- The check date (since this report can be run for any date).

```
              Extent Trends for Segments with 1000 or more Extents

                                                    4Wks 3Wks 2Wks  1Wk
   DB_NM TS     Owner    Name    Type    Blocks   Ago  Ago  Ago  Ago Today Change
   ----- ------ -------- ------- -------- ------  ---- ---- ---- ---- ----- ------
   CASE  CASE   CASEMGR  TEMP_TBL TABLE   10000                   2000 2000  2000
                         TEMP_IDX INDEX    8000                   1600 1600  1600

         RBS    SYSTEM   ROLL1   ROLLBACK  3800    19   19   19   19   19
                         ROLL2   ROLLBACK  3800    19   19   19   19   19

         USERS  AL1      TEST1   TABLE    12000         1200 1200 1200 1200  1200
                         TEST2   TABLE    14000         1400 1400 1400 1400  1400

   CC1   RBS    SYSTEM   ROLL1   ROLLBACK  3800    19   19   19   19   19
                         ROLL2   ROLLBACK  3800    19   19   19   19   19
```

FIGURE 6-7. *Sample alert report for extent usage trends*

The report is divided into two sections. The first part queries the FILES table to determine the current filenames and sizes for the database. The second part of the report compares the values in the SPACES table (free space sizes) to those in the FILES table (via the FILES_TS_VIEW view). Because these tables contain information about the space allocated to a tablespace, and the amount of it that has yet to be allocated, the percentage of free space remaining in each tablespace can be measured.

```
rem
rem space_summary.sql
rem  parameter 1: database link name
rem  parameter 2: check date
rem
rem  to call this report from within sqlplus:
rem  @space_summary link_name Check_Date
rem
rem  Example:
rem  @space_summary CASE 27-MAY-01
rem
set pagesize 60 linesize 132 verify off feedback off
set newpage 0
column TS heading 'Tablespace' format A18
column File_Nm heading 'File nm' format A40
column Blocks heading 'Orablocks'
column Percentfree format 999.99
column Diskblocks format 99999999
```

```
column Cfb format 9999999 heading 'NumFrExts'
column Mfb format 9999999 heading 'MaxFrExt'
column Sfb format 9999999 heading 'SumFrBl'
column Dfrb format 9999999 heading 'DiskFrBy'
column SumFileBy format 9999999 heading 'SumFileBy'
column Bytes heading 'Bytes'
column Maxfrpct heading 'MaxFrPct' format 9999999


break on TS
ttitle center 'Oracle Tablespaces in ' &&1 skip center -
'Check Date = ' &&2 skip 2 center
spool &&1._space_summary.lst
select
    Ts,                      /*tablespace name*/
    File_Nm,                 /*file name*/
    Blocks,                  /*Oracle blocks in the file*/
    Bytes                    /*bytes in the file*/
  from FILES
 where Check_Date = '&&2'
   and Db_Nm = UPPER('&&1')
 order by TS, File_Nm
/
ttitle center 'Oracle Free Space Statistics for ' &&1 -
skip center '(Extent Sizes in Oracle blocks)' skip center -
'Check Date = ' &&2 skip 2
select
    SPACES.TS,                       /*tablespace name*/
    SPACES.Count_Free_Blocks Cfb,    /*number of free extents*/
    SPACES.Max_Free_Blocks Mfb,      /*lgst free extent*/
    SPACES.Sum_Free_Blocks Sfb,      /*sum of free space*/
    ROUND(100*Sum_Free_Blocks/Sum_File_Blocks,2)
        Percentfree,                 /*percent free in TS*/
    ROUND(100*Max_Free_Blocks/Sum_Free_Blocks,2)
     Maxfrpct,                       /*ratio of largest extent to sum*/
    SPACES.Sum_Free_Bytes Dfrb,      /*disk bytes free*/
    Sum_File_Bytes SumFileBy         /*disk bytes allocated*/
 from SPACES, FILES_TS_VIEW FTV
where SPACES.Db_Nm = FTV.Db_Nm
  and SPACES.TS = FTV.TS
  and SPACES.Check_Date = FTV.Check_Date
  and SPACES.Db_Nm = UPPER('&&1')
  and SPACES.Check_Date = '&&2'
/
spool off
undefine 1
undefine 2
undefine 3
```

A sample output report is shown in Figure 6-8. Based on the **spool** command listed in the query, the output file will be called CC1_space_summary.lst. This is based on using the period (**.**) as the concatenation character in SQL*Plus.

Figure 6-8 is identical to Figure 6-3 earlier in this chapter. The sample output shown in Figure 6-8 is divided into two sections. In the first section, each of the datafiles in the databases is listed (the File nm column), along with the tablespace it is assigned to (the Tablespace column). The number of Oracle blocks (Orablocks) and bytes (Bytes) in each datafile is also displayed in this section.

In the second half of the report, the free space statistics for the tablespaces are displayed. For each tablespace, the number of free extents is displayed (NumFrExts). This column shows how many fragments the available free space in a tablespace is broken into. The largest single free extent, in Oracle blocks, is shown in the MaxFrExt column, as well as the sum of all free space in the tablespace (SumFrBl). The percentage of the tablespace that is unallocated is shown in the PercentFr column.

```
                   Oracle Tablespaces in CC1
                    Check Date = 27-MAY-01

Tablespace     File nm                    Orablocks         Bytes
-------------- --------------------------- ---------     -------------
CC             /db03/oracle/CC1/cc.dbf       30,720        62,914,560
CCINDX         /db04/oracle/CC1/ccindx.dbf   20,480        41,943,040
RBS            /db02/oracle/CC1/rbs01.dbf     5,120        10,485,760
               /db02/oracle/CC1/rbs02.dbf     5,120        10,485,760
               /db02/oracle/CC1/rbs03.dbf     5,120        10,485,760
SYSTEM         /db01/oracle/CC1/sys01.dbf   102,400       209,715,200
TEMP           /db01/oracle/CC1/temp01.dbf   15,360        31,457,280
TESTS          /db04/oracle/CC1/tests01.dbf  30,720        62,914,560

              Oracle Free Space Statistics for CC1
                 (Extent Sizes in Oracle blocks)
                    Check Date = 27-MAY-01

Tablespace    NumFrExts MaxFrExt  SumFrBl PercentFr MaxFrPct  DiskFrBy  SumFileBy
------------- --------- --------  ------- --------- --------  --------- ----------
CC               1       21504    21504    70.00     100     44040192   62914560
CCINDX           1       15360    15360    75.00     100     31457280   41943040
RBS              3        2019     2057    13.39      98      4212736   31457280
SYSTEM           1       67580    67580    66.00     100    138403840  209715200
TEMP             6       12800    15360   100.00      83     31457280   31457280
TESTS            1       21504    21504    70.00     100     44040192   62914560
```

FIGURE 6-8. *Sample space summary report*

The MaxFrPct column displays the ratio of the largest single free extent to the total free space available. A high value for this column indicates that most of the free space available is located in a single extent. The last two columns display the free bytes available (DiskFrBy) out of the total available bytes (SumFileBy) for each tablespace.

Purging Data

Left unchecked, the tables described in the previous sections will grow until they use all of the free space in the available tablespaces. To prevent problems with data volume, you should periodically **delete** records from the EXTENTS, SPACES, and FILES tables.

The amount of data to retain depends on your needs. If you never need data more than 60 days old from these tables, then you can automate the data purges as part of the data **insert** process. For example, at the end of the ins_all.sql script that performs the **insert**s, you could add the following commands:

```
delete from FILES
 where Check_Date < sysdate-60;
commit;

delete from SPACES
 where Check_Date < sysdate-60;
commit;

delete from EXTENTS
 where Check_Date < sysdate-60;
commit;
```

If you execute this command each day, then the size of the **delete** transactions should be small enough to be supported by the rollback segments.

If the tables become large, you can improve the performance of the **delete**s by creating indexes on the Check_Date columns of the FILES, SPACES, and EXTENTS tables.

Periodic purges of this nature can cause your space usage within indexes to become inefficient. Following a purge, rebuild the primary key indexes on the tables as well as any other indexes you create on the Command Center tables.

Monitoring Memory Objects

In addition to monitoring space usage, you can monitor the activity in the SGA. Oracle continuously updates a set of internal statistics related to SGA usage in dynamic performance views called the V$ views.

To facilitate monitoring of SGA statistics in Oracle 8.1.6 and above, Oracle provides a set of scripts called STATSPACK. Chapter 9 provides an overview of the use of STATSPACK and its output. STATSPACK replaces the UTLBSTAT/UTLESTAT utilities provided with earlier versions of Oracle.

Additional Alerts and Warnings

In the following sections, you will see scripts that highlight additional potential problems within a database. The alert conditions include poorly distributed I/O and segments that cannot extend.

Monitoring File I/O Distribution

The following SQL*Plus scripts generate a listing of all database files, by disk, and total the I/O activities against each disk. The scripts' output helps to illustrate how well the file I/O is currently being distributed across the available devices.

> **NOTE**
> *Both queries assume that the drive names are five characters long (such as /db01). If your drive names are other than five characters long, you will need to modify the **SUBSTR** functions in the queries and the formatting commands for the Drive column.*

```
clear columns
clear breaks
column Drive format A5
column File_Name format A30
column Blocks_Read format 99999999
column Blocks_Written format 99999999
column Total_IOs format 99999999
set linesize 80 pagesize 60 newpage 0 feedback off
ttitle skip center "Database File I/O Information" skip 2
break on report
compute sum of Blocks_Read on report
compute sum of Blocks_Written on report
compute sum of Total_IOs on report

select substr(DF.Name,1,5) Drive,
       SUM(FS.Phyblkrd+FS.Phyblkwrt) Total_IOs,
       SUM(FS.Phyblkrd) Blocks_Read,
       SUM(FS.Phyblkwrt) Blocks_Written
  from V$FILESTAT FS, V$DATAFILE DF
 where DF.File#=FS.File#
 group by substr(DF.Name,1,5)
 order by Total_IOs desc;
```

Sample output is shown in the following listing:

```
DRIVE  TOTAL_IOS  BLOCKS_READ  BLOCKS_WRITTEN
-----  ---------  -----------  --------------
/db03      57217        56820             397
/db01      39940        27712            6228
/db04      15759        14728            1031
/db02       1898           10            1888
           ---------  -----------  --------------
sum       108814        99270            9544
```

The second file I/O query shows the I/O attributed to each datafile, by disk:

```
clear breaks
clear computes
break on Drive skip 1 on report
compute sum of Blocks_Read on Drive
compute sum of Blocks_Written on Drive
compute sum of Total_IOs on Drive
compute sum of Blocks_Read on Report
compute sum of Blocks_Written on Report
compute sum of Total_IOs on Report
ttitle skip center "Database File I/O by Drive" skip 2

select substr(DF.Name,1,5) Drive,
       DF.Name File_Name,
       FS.Phyblkrd+FS.Phyblkwrt Total_IOs,
       FS.Phyblkrd Blocks_Read,
       FS.Phyblkwrt Blocks_Written
  from V$FILESTAT FS, V$DATAFILE DF
 where DF.File#=FS.File#
 order by Drive, File_Name desc;
```

Sample output for this query is shown in the following listing:

```
DRIVE  FILE_NAME                      TOTAL_IOS  BLOCKS_READ  BLOCKS_WRITTEN
-----  -----------------------------  ---------  -----------  --------------
/db01  /db01/oracle/CC1/sys.dbf           29551        27708            1843
       /db01/oracle/CC1/temp.dbf           4389            4            4385
*****                                 ---------  -----------  --------------
sum                                       33940        27712            6228

/db02  /db02/oracle/CC1/rbs01.dbf          1134            3            1131
       /db02/oracle/CC1/rbs02.dbf           349                          349
       /db02/oracle/CC1/rbs03.dbf           415            7             408
*****                                 ---------  -----------  --------------
sum                                        1898           10            1888
```

```
/db03  /db03/oracle/CC1/cc.dbf              57217         56820            397
*****                                     ---------   -----------   --------------
sum                                         57217         56820            397

/db04  /db04/oracle/CC1/ccindx.dbf          15759         14728           1031
       /db04/oracle/CC1/tests01.dbf
*****                                     ---------   -----------   --------------
sum                                         15759         14728           1031

*****                                     ---------   -----------   --------------
sum                                        108814         99270           9544
```

The data in the preceding listing shows the format of the queries' output. The first part of the report shows a drive-by-drive comparison of the database I/O against datafiles. The output shows that the device called /db03 is the most heavily used device during database usage. The second report shows that the I/O on device /db03 is due to one file, since no other database files exist on that drive for the CC1 database. The report output also shows that accesses against the file on /db03 are read-intensive by an overwhelming margin.

The second most active device is /db01, which has two database files on it. Most of the activity on that disk is against the SYSTEM tablespace file, with the TEMP tablespace demanding much less I/O. The SYSTEM tablespace's readings will be high during these queries because you are not looking at I/O for a specific interval, but for the entire time that the database has been opened.

The preceding reports are excellent for detecting possible conflicts among file I/O loads. Given these reports and the I/O capacity of your devices, you can correctly distribute your database files to minimize I/O contention and maximize throughput. See Chapter 4 for further information on minimizing I/O contention.

Segments at Maximum Extension

The alert reports in this chapter use control limit criteria that are established at the system level (for example, 1000 extents per segment). However, you should compare the current extent usage of segments against the limits defined specifically for that segment via the segment's **maxextents** storage parameter.

The following SQL*Plus report detects any segment that is within a specified factor of its maximum extension. The report is written to access databases via a database link, and the link name is used as part of the output file's name. The multiplier value should always be greater than 1—it is the value by which the actual extent count will be multiplied when it is compared with the maximum extent count. To determine which segments are within 20 percent of their maximum extension, set the multiplier value to 1.2.

The following query checks four different types of segments: clusters, tables, indexes, and rollback segments. For each one, it determines whether the current number of extents is approaching the maximum number of extents that segment can have (as set via the **maxextents** storage parameter). The "multiplier" variable is used to determine how close to its maximum extension a segment must be before it is returned via this query. If the segment is approaching its maximum extension, then its owner, name, and current space usage information will be returned.

NOTE
*As of Oracle7.3, you can specify a **maxextents** value of **unlimited**. When you specify a **maxextents** value of **unlimited** for a segment, ORACLE assigns the segment a **maxextents** value of 2,147,483,645. Therefore, a segment with a **maxextents** value of **unlimited** could theoretically reach its maximum extension, although that is highly unlikely.*

```
rem
rem  file:  over_extended.sql
rem  parameters:  database link name (instance name), multiplier
rem
rem  The "multiplier" value should always be greater than 1.
rem  Example:  To see segments that are within 20 percent of
rem  their maximum extension, set the multiplier to 1.2.
rem
rem  Example call:
rem  @over_extended CASE 1.2
rem

select
    Owner,                    /*owner of segment*/
    Segment_Name,             /*name of segment*/
    Segment_Type,             /*type of segment*/
    Extents,                  /*number of extents already acquired*/
    Blocks                    /*number of blocks already acquired*/
from DBA_SEGMENTS@&&1 s
where                         /*for cluster segments*/
(S.Segment_Type = 'CLUSTER' and exists
(select 'x' from DBA_CLUSTERS@&&1 c
where C.Owner = S.Owner
and C.Cluster_Name = S.Segment_Name
and C.Max_Extents < S.Extents*&&2))
or                            /*for table segments*/
(s.segment_type = 'TABLE' and exists
(select 'x' from DBA_TABLES@&&1 t
where T.Owner = S.Owner
and T.Table_Name = S.Segment_Name
and T.Max_Extents < S.Extents*&&2))
```

```
or                              /*for index segments*/
(S.Segment_Type = 'INDEX' and exists
(select 'x' from DBA_INDEXES@&&1 i
where I.Owner = S.Owner
and I.Index_Name = S.Segment_Name
and I.Max_Extents < S.Extents*&&2))
or                              /*for rollback segments*/
(S.Segment_Type = 'ROLLBACK' and exists
(select 'x' from DBA_ROLLBACK_SEGS@&&1 r
where R.Owner = S.Owner
and R.Segment_Name = S.Segment_Name
and R.Max_Extents < S.Extents*&&2))
order by 1,2

spool &&1._over_extended.lst
/
spool off
undefine 1
undefine 2
```

The output file for this report will contain the database link name in its title. The output file's name uses the period (.) as the concatenation character in SQL*Plus.

Segments That Cannot Extend into the Available Free Space

In addition to monitoring the segments that are near their extent limits, you should regularly query the database to determine whether any of the segments cannot extend into the available free space in the tablespace. The following query is an alert report, and the records returned by the query should be addressed immediately.

There are two separate queries for this report. The first query, shown in the following listing, determines whether there is enough space in the tablespace for a segment's next extent:

```
select Owner, Segment_Name, Segment_Type
  from DBA_SEGMENTS
 where Next_Extent >
(select SUM(Bytes) from DBA_FREE_SPACE
  where Tablespace_Name = DBA_SEGMENTS.Tablespace_Name);
```

The preceding query may report segments that are not problems. For example, the tablespace's datafiles may be set to **autoextend**, in which case the tablespace's available free space is limited by the maximum datafile size.

If a table name is returned by the preceding query, there is not enough free space in the tablespace to store the next extent of the table, even if all the space in the tablespace were coalesced. This is an alert condition; you can create a separate query that may identify the table as a problem before it reaches the alert stage. The following query returns the name of any segment whose next extent will not fit in the single largest free extent in the tablespace:

```
select Owner, Segment_Name, Segment_Type
   from DBA_SEGMENTS
 where Next_Extent>
(select MAX(Bytes) from DBA_FREE_SPACE
   where Tablespace_Name = DBA_SEGMENTS.Tablespace_Name);
```

Coalescing free space may resolve some of the space issues. However, if the tablespace's free space is divided among datafiles or separated by data segments, you may not be able to increase the maximum available free extent size.

If you cannot support another extent for an actively used segment, you may either need to add space to the tablespace or change the storage parameters for your segments.

Rate of Space Allocation Within an Object

As described in Chapters 4 and 5, you can simplify your database space administration activities by properly sizing your database objects. However, a properly sized object may not be reported by the Command Center database and similar alert reports, even if it has the potential to cause problems.

For example, you may create a SALES table that is estimated to need 1GB per year. If you allocate a 1GB extent for the table, it should not acquire a new extent for many months, and thus it will not show up in the Command Center reports. If the table does not acquire any new extents, the free space in the tablespace may be unchanged, so the space watcher report will not list that tablespace. However, the space usage within the table may present a problem.

If the space in the table is being used at a greater rate than expected, the table will need to extend sooner than anticipated. For a large transaction table, an unexpected extension may have a significant impact on the space available. Using the scripts provided in the preceding section, you should be able to anticipate segment extensions that will encounter space problems. You can use the following query to determine which segments are likely to extend.

The following query uses the statistics columns of the data dictionary views, so it is only valid for objects that have been analyzed. Furthermore, the value of the query's output is directly related to the frequency with which the objects are analyzed. Since the query relies on the overall space usage statistics, you can use the **estimate statistics** option when analyzing the tables. The query will report any object whose block usage is within 10 percent of its current allocated usage.

The first part of the **union** query, shown in the following listing, selects the data for the database's tables. The **column** commands format the data so it will fit in an 80-column screen width.

```
column Owner format A12
column Table_Name format A20
column Empty format 99999
column Pctusd format 999.99

select T.Owner,
       T.Table_Name,
       S.Segment_Type,
       T.Blocks Used,
       T.Empty_Blocks Empty,
       S.Blocks Allocated,
       T.Blocks/S.Blocks Pctusd
  from DBA_TABLES T, DBA_SEGMENTS S
 where T.Owner = S.Owner
   and T.Table_Name = S.Segment_Name
   and S.Segment_Type = 'TABLE'
   and T.Blocks/S.Blocks > 0.95
 order by 7  desc
```

Sample data for the preceding query is shown in the following listing:

OWNER	TABLE_NAME	SEGMENT	USED	EMPTY	ALLOCATED	PCTUSD
APPOWN	REGION	TABLE	46	0	47	.98
APPOWN	MANUFACTURER	TABLE	210	4	215	.98
APPOWN	VOUCHER_HEADER	TABLE	251	5	257	.98
APPOWN	PO_HEADER	TABLE	459	10	470	.98
APPOWN	VOUCHER_LINE	TABLE	869	5	890	.98
APPOWN	PO_LINE	TABLE	491	0	505	.97

As shown in the output, several of the tables in the database have used over 95 percent of the blocks they have allocated. The tables with the highest percentage of space usage, if they are active transaction tables, are likely to extend. You should evaluate the tables to determine whether the tables are likely to extend. For example, the first table in the output listing, REGION, may be unlikely to extend unless you are frequently adding new regions. The VOUCHER_HEADER and VOUCHER_LINE tables, however, are transaction tables and are likely to extend.

The full query, shown in the following listing, reports the tables and indexes approaching their current space allocation:

```
column Owner format A12
column Table_Name format A20
column Empty format 99999
column Pctusd format 999.99

select T.Owner,
       T.Table_Name,
       S.Segment_Type,
       T.Blocks Used,
       T.Empty_Blocks Empty,
       S.Blocks Allocated,
       T.Blocks/S.Blocks Pctusd
  from DBA_TABLES T, DBA_SEGMENTS S
 where T.Owner = S.Owner
   and T.Table_Name = S.Segment_Name
   and S.Segment_Type = 'TABLE'
   and T.Blocks/S.Blocks > 0.95
union all
select I.Owner,
       I.Index_Name,
       S.Segment_Type,
       I.Leaf_Blocks Used,
       S.Blocks-1-I.Leaf_Blocks Empty,
       S.Blocks Allocated,
       I.Leaf_Blocks/S.Blocks Pctusd
  from DBA_INDEXES I, DBA_SEGMENTS S
 where I.Owner = S.Owner
   and I.Index_Name = S.Segment_Name
   and S.Segment_Type = 'INDEX'
   and I.Leaf_Blocks/S.Blocks > 0.95
order by 7 desc, 2, 1
```

The preceding query will display the data for tables and indexes in the same report. The data will be ordered by the percentage of allocated space used, with the highest percentages listed first.

You can extend this report by building a history table and storing the allocated percentage used over time. However, such a history may not be very valuable. For example, the allocated percentage will be reduced when a segment acquires a new extent, so the allocated percentage used will fluctuate over time, even for active tables. This report is most useful either as an alert for all of your segments or for tracking the space usage of specific segments.

The Well-Managed Database

The effective management of any system requires strategic planning, quality control, and action to resolve out-of-control parts of the system. The database management systems described in this chapter provide a broad foundation for the monitoring of all of your databases. Individual databases may require additional monitoring to be performed, or may have specific thresholds. These can be easily added to the samples shown here.

Establishing a Command Center database allows the other databases in the system to be monitored without impacting the measures being checked. The Command Center database also allows for easy addition of new databases to the monitoring system and trend analysis of all statistics. The Command Center database should be tied in to your existing operating system monitoring programs in order to coordinate the distribution and resolution of alert messages.

Like any system, the Command Center database must be planned. The examples in this chapter were designed to handle the most commonly monitored objects in the database, and threshold values were established for each. Do not create the CC1 database until you have fully defined what you are going to monitor and what the threshold values are. Once that has been done, create the database—and in a great example of recursion, use the monitoring database to monitor itself.

CHAPTER
7

Managing Transactions

hen users **insert**, **delete**, or **update** data, Oracle preserves before images of the data as it existed before the change. Any query that starts before the change is committed will see the old version of the data, while the session making the changes will see the new version. To provide this read consistency, Oracle9i offers two solutions. The first solution, rollback segments, has been available since Oracle6. Oracle9i adds automatic undo management as a new option for read consistency within your databases. You may use either rollback segments or undo tablespaces in your Oracle9i databases but not both at the same time.

To choose an undo method, use the UNDO_MANAGEMENT initialization parameter in your system parameter file or init.ora file. If UNDO_MANAGEMENT is set to MANUAL (its default in 9i's initial release), rollback segments will provide undo management. If UNDO_MANAGEMENT is set to AUTO, then an undo tablespace (also known as system-managed undo) will provide undo management. If you use system-managed undo (SMU), then you must specify an undo tablespace via the UNDO_TABLESPACE initialization parameter.

The following sections of this chapter describe both rollback segments and undo tablespaces. Although undo tablespaces serve the same purpose as rollback segments (read consistency), they also add a new capability, undo retention, which can enhance your database administration effectiveness.

Rollback Segments Overview

This section will cover the key managerial tasks that DBAs need to perform for rollback segments. You will see

- The basic functional aspects of rollback segments
- The unique way in which they use available space
- How to monitor their usage
- How to select the correct number and size of rollback segments for your database

NOTE
In this section, all examples and remarks assume you are using rollback segments as your undo management technique.

The SQL command **rollback** allows users to undo transactions that have been made against a database. The **rollback** command is available for any **update**, **insert**, or **delete** transaction; it is not available for changes to database objects (such as **alter table** commands). When you **select** data that another user is changing, Oracle uses the rollback segments to show you the data as it existed before the changes began.

How the Database Uses Rollback Segments

Rollback segments are involved in every transaction that occurs within the database. The number and size of rollback segments available are specified by the DBA during database creation.

Since rollback segments are created within the database, they must be created within a tablespace. The first rollback segment, called *SYSTEM*, is stored in the SYSTEM tablespace. Further rollback segments are usually created in at least one other tablespace. Because rollback segments are created in tablespaces, their maximum size is limited to the amount of space in the tablespaces' datafiles. Appropriate sizing of rollback segments is therefore a critical task. Figure 7-1 depicts the storage of rollback segments in tablespaces.

A *rollback segment entry* called a *change vector* contains the before image of the columns being changed for one row. Several change vectors can be created for each transaction. Each transaction must be completely contained within one rollback segment. A single rollback segment can support multiple transactions at the same time. The number of rollback segments available may become a critical factor for the database's performance as multiple concurrent transactions contend for access to the rollback segments. Figure 7-2 illustrates the relationship between rollback segments and rollback segment entries.

The database assigns transactions to rollback segments in a least recently used/ round-robin fashion, resulting in a fairly even distribution of the number of transactions across the pool of rollback segments. Although you can specify which rollback segment

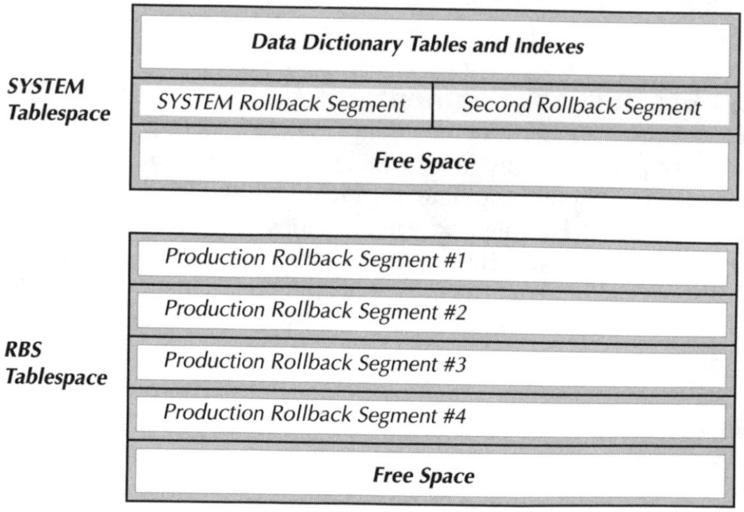

FIGURE 7-1. *Storage of rollback segments in tablespaces*

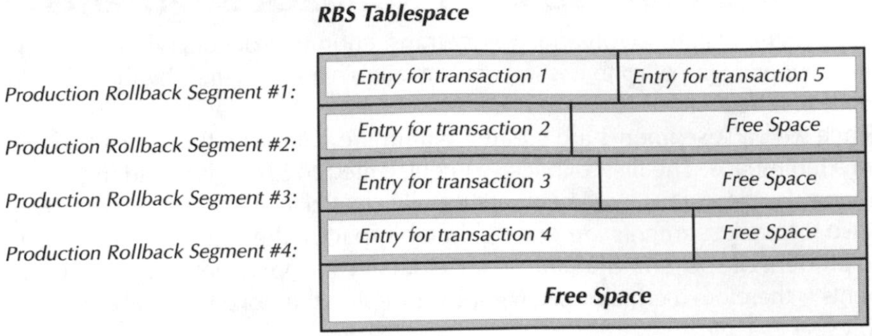

RBS Tablespace

Production Rollback Segment #1:

Production Rollback Segment #2:

Production Rollback Segment #3:

Production Rollback Segment #4:

Entry for transaction 1	Entry for transaction 5
Entry for transaction 2	Free Space
Entry for transaction 3	Free Space
Entry for transaction 4	Free Space
Free Space	

FIGURE 7-2. *Storage of rollback segment entries in rollback segments*

a transaction should use (see "Specifying a Rollback Segment for a Transaction," later in this chapter), most transactions use the default. Because of the round-robin assignment method used, it is usually not advantageous to have rollback segments of varied sizes.

You can create rollback segments that are designated as *private* or *public*, making the rollback segment available to a single instance or to multiple instances that access that database. Private rollback segments are explicitly acquired when an instance opens a database (as shown in the "Activating Rollback Segments" section of this chapter). If a second instance accesses the same database, then it may not use the same private rollback segment that the first instance has already acquired. Instead, it can either use its own private rollback segments, or it can draw from a pool of public rollback segments.

The SYSTEM Rollback Segment

The SYSTEM rollback segment is created automatically during database creation. Its name and storage parameters are not specified in the **create database** command. The SYSTEM rollback segment is automatically created in the SYSTEM tablespace.

The usage of the SYSTEM rollback segment varies depending on your configuration. If your database has multiple tablespaces (as almost all databases do), then you will have to create a second rollback segment to support them. If other rollback segments are available, then the SYSTEM rollback segment is used only to drop rollback segments or when all available slots are used in all other rollback segments. The normal rollback segments are used for all other activity. You can verify this by dumping the system rollback segment with the following command both before and after creating a table for example.

```
alter system dump undo header SYSTEM;
```

Each time you issue the preceding command, Oracle will create a trace file located in the user dump file destination area (usually the /udump subdirectory below the ORACLE_BASE/admin/*instance_name* directory). By comparing the trace files before and after your commands, you can see the transaction table entries in the rollback segment headers.

Each rollback segment header will contain an extent map, a sample of which is shown in the following listing:

```
*****************************************************************************
Undo Segment:  SYSTEM (0)
*****************************************************************************
   Extent Control Header
   -----------------------------------------------------------------
   Extent Header:: spare1: 0      spare2: 0       #extents: 5      #blocks: 49
                  last map  0x00000000  #maps: 0      offset: 4128
      Highwater::  0x00400010  ext#: 1      blk#: 4      ext size: 10
   #blocks in seg. hdr's freelists: 0
   #blocks below: 0
   mapblk  0x00000000  offset: 1
                  Unlocked
     Map Header:: next  0x00000000  #extents: 5    obj#: 0      flag: 0x40000000
   Extent Map
   -----------------------------------------------------------------
    0x00400003  length: 9
    0x0040000c  length: 10
    0x00400095  length: 10
    0x0040009f  length: 10
    0x004000a9  length: 10
```

When you execute DDL commands, you may see changes in the transaction table portions of the SYSTEM rollback segment's trace file. If the rollback segment has to extend to support the changes, the extension will be reflected in the rollback segment header information written during the **alter system dump undo header SYSTEM** command.

The Second Rollback Segment

If your database will have multiple tablespaces, then you will have to create a second rollback segment. You cannot write to any objects in a non-SYSTEM tablespace unless there is at least one rollback segment available. During database creation, the rollback segment will be created in the SYSTEM tablespace automatically by Oracle. Postcreation, however, the second rollback segment should not be made available for production transactions; doing so would put the SYSTEM tablespace's free space in jeopardy during large transactions. The system rollback segment should be used only during database creation and for rollback segment maintenance. As soon as a tablespace for rollback segments has been created, create rollback segments in it and deactivate or drop the second rollback segment in the SYSTEM tablespace.

With regard to rollback segments, your database creation procedures should do the following:

- Create a database, which automatically creates a SYSTEM rollback segment in the SYSTEM tablespace.

- Create a dictionary-managed tablespace called RBS for further rollback segments.

- Create additional rollback segments in the RBS tablespace.

- Deactivate the second rollback segment (r0) in the SYSTEM tablespace and activate the new rollback segments in RBS.

NOTE
By default, a tablespace is created as locally managed. Rollback segments can be created in either a locally managed or a dictionary managed tablespace. If the tablespace is locally managed, it must use the autoallocate method of extent management in Oracle9i and the uniform size method of extent management in Oracle8i. Reference the ALLOCATION_TYPE column in DBA_TABLESPACES where "autoallocate" shows up as "system" and "uniform" shows up as "uniform."

Although it is no longer needed after database creation, you may want to keep the second rollback segment available but inactive. To do this, deactivate the rollback segment (see "Activating Rollback Segments" later in this chapter), but do not drop it. This rollback segment can then be quickly reactivated during emergency situations that affect the RBS tablespace.

The Production Rollback Segments

Non-SYSTEM *production rollback segments* store the rollback segment entries generated by transactions running against the database. They support the use of the **rollback** command to restore the previous image of the modified records. They are also used to roll back transactions that are aborted prior to completion, either because of a problem with the rollback segment or because of user cancellation of the transaction. During queries, change vectors stored in rollback segments are used to construct a consistent before image of the data that was changed—but not committed—prior to the execution of the query. Planning a database's number and sizes for rollback segments is addressed in the "Choosing the Number and Size" section later in this chapter.

Activating Rollback Segments

Activating a rollback segment makes it available to the database users. A rollback segment may be deactivated without being dropped. A deactivated rollback segment will maintain the space already allocated to it, and can be reactivated at a later date. The following examples provide the full set of rollback segment activation commands.

An active rollback segment can be deactivated via the **alter rollback segment** command.

```
alter rollback segment SEGMENT_NAME offline;
```

To drop a rollback segment, use the **drop rollback segment** command.

```
drop rollback segment SEGMENT_NAME;
```

To create a rollback segment, use the **create rollback segment** command, as shown in the following listing:

```
create rollback segment SEGMENT_NAME
tablespace RBS;
```

Note that the example **create rollback segment** command creates a private rollback segment (since the **public** keyword was not used) in a non-SYSTEM tablespace called RBS. Since no storage parameters are specified, the rollback segment will use the default storage parameters for that tablespace. (You will see the space management details for rollback segments later in this chapter.)

Although the rollback segment has been created, it is not yet in use by the database. To activate the new rollback segment, bring it online using the following command:

```
alter rollback segment SEGMENT_NAME online;
```

Once a rollback segment has been created, you should list it in the database's initialization parameter file. A sample initialization entry for rollback segments is shown in the following listing:

```
rollback_segments    = (r0,r1,r2)
```

NOTE
The SYSTEM rollback segment should never be listed in the init.ora file. The SYSTEM rollback segment can never be dropped; it is always acquired along with any other rollback segments that the instance may acquire.

In the preceding example, the rollback segments named r0, r1, and r2 are online. If you take a rollback segment offline, remove its entry from the parameter file. When you take a rollback segment offline, it will remain online until its current active transactions complete. You can view the PENDING OFFLINE status of a rollback segment via the V$ROLLSTAT view, as described later in this chapter.

Specifying a Rollback Segment for a Transaction

You can use the **set transaction** command to specify which rollback segment a transaction should use. You should execute the **set transaction** command before large transactions to ensure that they use rollback segments that are created specifically for them.

The settings that are specified via the **set transaction** command will be used only for the current transaction. The following example shows a series of transactions. The first transaction is directed to use the ROLL_BATCH rollback segment. The second transaction (following the second **commit**) will be randomly assigned to a production rollback segment.

```
commit;

set transaction use rollback segment ROLL_BATCH;
insert into TABLE_NAME
select * from DATA_LOAD_TABLE;

commit;

REM*  The commit command clears the rollback segment assignment.
REM*  Implicit commits, like those caused by DDL commands, will
REM*  also clear the rollback segment designation.

insert into TABLE_NAME select * from SOME_OTHER_TABLE;
```

Space Usage Within Rollback Segments

When a transaction begins, Oracle starts writing a rollback segment entry in a rollback segment. The entry cannot expand into any other rollback segments, nor can it dynamically switch to use a different rollback segment. The entry begins writing to the next available block within the current extent of the rollback segment that the transaction is assigned to. Each block within that extent must contain information for only one active transaction. When a user **commit**s, Oracle checks to see if there is at least 400 bytes of free space available within the block. If so, the block is put in the free pool in the rollback segment.

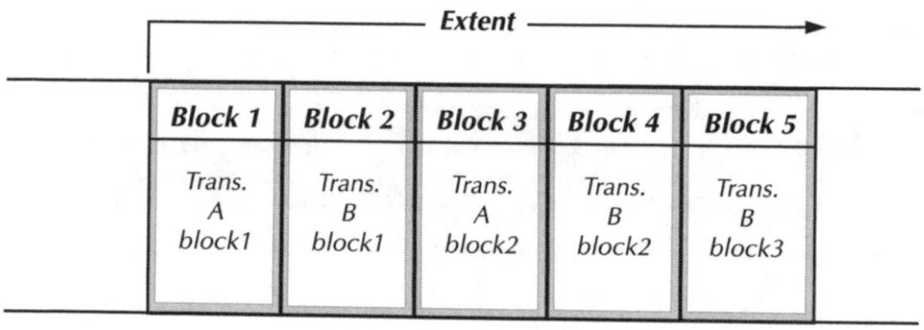

Block 1	Block 2	Block 3	Block 4	Block 5
Trans. A block1	Trans. B block1	Trans. A block2	Trans. B block2	Trans. B block3

FIGURE 7-3. *Two transactions in a single rollback segment extent*

To see the free block pool of a rollback segment, use the **alter system dump undo header** *segment_name* command. The free block pool will be written to the trace file created by this command, under the section titled "FREE BLOCK POOL."

When a user needs a block, Oracle will always try to use one available in the free pool before using the next block in the current extent after the high-water mark. Different transactions assigned to a particular rollback segment will use blocks from the same extent (termed the *current* extent) until all available blocks are used (see Figure 7-3).

Figure 7-3 shows the first five blocks of an extent of a rollback segment. Two separate transactions are storing active rollback information in that rollback extent. When a transaction can no longer acquire space within the current extent, the rollback segment looks at the next extent in sequence to see if it can continue writing the rollback segment entry there.

If the current extent is the last extent within the rollback segment, then the database will attempt to extend the entry into its first extent.

However, the next extent may already be in use. If it is, then the rollback segment will be forced to acquire a new extent. The entry will then be continued in this new extent. This process of selective extension is illustrated in Figure 7-4.

As shown in Figure 7-4a, a transaction (referred to here as "transaction A") presently has its entry data stored in four extents of rollback segment r1. Since it started in extent #3 of this rollback segment, we know that extent #3 was the current extent for that rollback segment. At this point, it has acquired four extents and is in search of a fifth.

Since it already occupies the last extent (extent #6) of the rollback segment, the database checks to see if the first extent of that rollback segment contains any active transaction data. If it does not, then that extent is used as the fifth extent of transaction A's entry (see Figure 7-4b). If, however, that extent is actively being used by a transaction, then the rollback segment will dynamically extend itself and extent #7 will then be used as the fifth extent of transaction A (see Figure 7-4c).

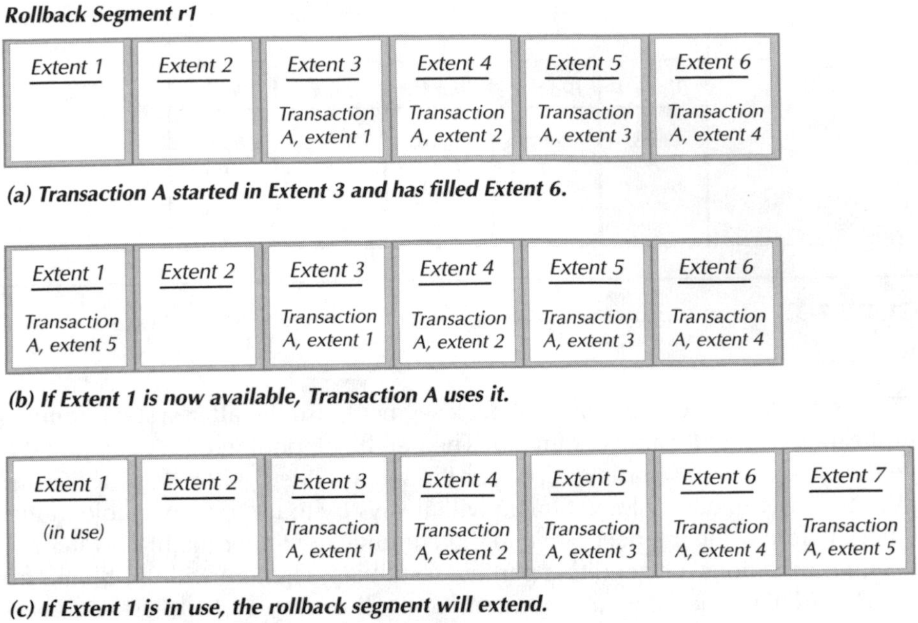

Rollback Segment r1

Extent 1	Extent 2	Extent 3	Extent 4	Extent 5	Extent 6
		Transaction A, extent 1	Transaction A, extent 2	Transaction A, extent 3	Transaction A, extent 4

(a) Transaction A started in Extent 3 and has filled Extent 6.

Extent 1	Extent 2	Extent 3	Extent 4	Extent 5	Extent 6
Transaction A, extent 5		Transaction A, extent 1	Transaction A, extent 2	Transaction A, extent 3	Transaction A, extent 4

(b) If Extent 1 is now available, Transaction A uses it.

Extent 1	Extent 2	Extent 3	Extent 4	Extent 5	Extent 6	Extent 7
(in use)		Transaction A, extent 1	Transaction A, extent 2	Transaction A, extent 3	Transaction A, extent 4	Transaction A, extent 5

(c) If Extent 1 is in use, the rollback segment will extend.

FIGURE 7-4. *Selective extension of rollback segments*

NOTE
Figure 7-4 has been edited for simplicity. Multiple transactions may be active in each extent.

Once a transaction is complete, its data is not deleted from the rollback segment. The old rollback data remains in the rollback segment to service the queries and transactions that began executing before the transaction was committed. This may cause a problem with long queries; namely, they may get the following error message:

```
ORA-1555:  snapshot too old (rollback segment too small)
```

This error arises from the definition of "active" data. Consider the large transaction referred to as transaction A in Figure 7-4. If a long-running query accesses the same table as transaction A, then it will need to use the change vectors stored by transaction A's rollback segment entry to create read-consistent images of the data block as they were before the changes were made. However, once transaction A has completed, the extents used by transaction A will be inactive if all users using those extents also either **commit**ted or rolled back their transaction. Those extents may then be overwritten by other transactions, even though the separate long-running query against those blocks has not completed. The query, upon attempting to re-create the read-consistent data blocks using the change vectors that were stored in the overwritten extents, will fail. This situation is depicted in Figure 7-5.

As shown in Figure 7-5, a transaction can span multiple extents. In Figure 7-5*a*, transaction A uses five extents of a rollback segment and then completes. Other users may be using that data even after the transaction completes. For example, if other users were querying the data before transaction A completed, they would need the change vectors stored in the rollback segment blocks in order to reconstruct the table's data for their queries. The rollback entry data for transaction A is inactive, but it is in use. When transaction B begins (Figure 7-5*b*), it starts in the current extent of the rollback segment. When it extends beyond the second extent, the rollback segment entry data from transaction A is overwritten (since it is inactive) and any process using that rollback segment entry data will fail (since it is in use).

There are two problems that are the true cause of the query's failure. First, a long-running query is being executed at the same time as data manipulation transactions. Batch processing and online transaction processing are being performed simultaneously

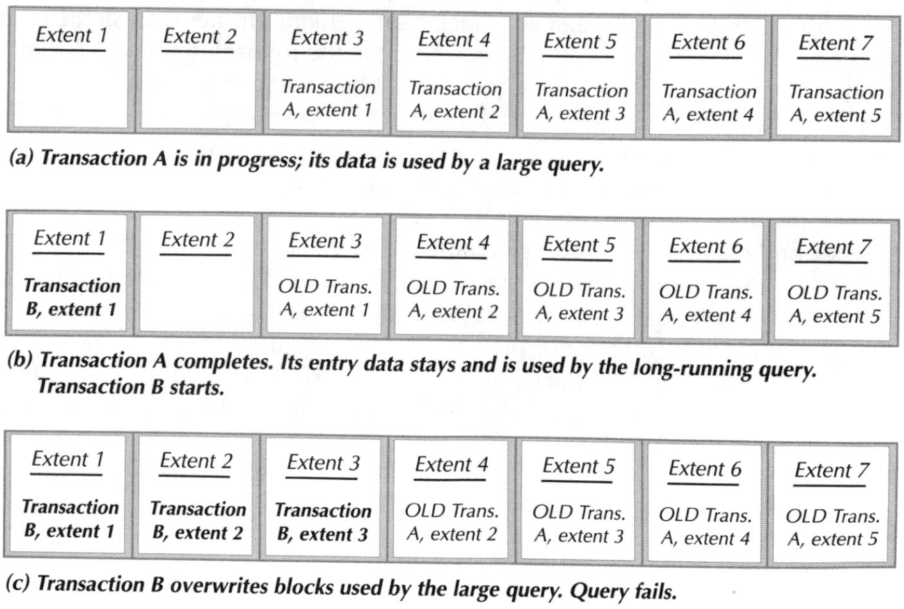

Extent 1	Extent 2	Extent 3	Extent 4	Extent 5	Extent 6	Extent 7
		Transaction A, extent 1	Transaction A, extent 2	Transaction A, extent 3	Transaction A, extent 4	Transaction A, extent 5

(a) Transaction A is in progress; its data is used by a large query.

Extent 1	Extent 2	Extent 3	Extent 4	Extent 5	Extent 6	Extent 7
Transaction B, extent 1		OLD Trans. A, extent 1	OLD Trans. A, extent 2	OLD Trans. A, extent 3	OLD Trans. A, extent 4	OLD Trans. A, extent 5

(b) Transaction A completes. Its entry data stays and is used by the long-running query. Transaction B starts.

Extent 1	Extent 2	Extent 3	Extent 4	Extent 5	Extent 6	Extent 7
Transaction B, extent 1	**Transaction B, extent 2**	**Transaction B, extent 3**	OLD Trans. A, extent 2	OLD Trans. A, extent 3	OLD Trans. A, extent 4	OLD Trans. A, extent 5

(c) Transaction B overwrites blocks used by the large query. Query fails.

FIGURE 7-5. *Query failure due to "snapshot too old" error*

in the database. From the earlier discussions of rollback segment functionality, the problems with this strategy should be clear: the long-running query must not only access all of the tables and indexes it needs to complete, but must also access data stored in the rollback segments to return a consistent version of the data.

Since it must continue to access the rollback segments until it completes, the long-running query requires that the rollback segment entries it is using not be overwritten. But once those entries have completed, there is no guarantee that this will be the case. The advice given in the error message ("rollback segment too small") solves the problem by resolving the second, related problem: to avoid overwriting existing entries in the rollback segment, add more space to it so it will take longer to wrap around back to the first extent.

Adding more space to the rollback segment is not a true solution. It is only a delaying tactic, since the rollback segment may eventually overwrite all of its data blocks. The proper solution is to schedule long-running queries at times when online transaction processing is at a minimum.

The optimal storage Clause

As shown previously in Figure 7-4, rollback segments dynamically extend to handle large transaction entry loads. Once the transaction that forced the extension completes, the rollback segment *keeps* the space that it acquired during the extension. This can be a major cause of rollback segment space management problems. A single large transaction may use all of the available free space in the rollback segment tablespace, preventing the other rollback segments in that tablespace from extending.

The potential space management problem is solved via two changes in the **storage** clause used for rollback segments. First, the **pctincrease** parameter is not supported for rollback segments, forcing rollback segments to grow at an even pace rather than at a geometrically increasing rate.

The second change in the **storage** clause for rollback segments is the addition of a parameter called **optimal**. The **optimal** parameter allows DBAs to specify an optimal length of the rollback segment (in bytes). When the rollback segment extends beyond this length, it later dynamically *shrinks* itself by eliminating its oldest extent. The following example shows a rollback segment creation statement with a **storage** clause in which the initial and next values are set to 1MB each and the **optimal** parameter is used:

```
create rollback segment SEGMENT_NAME
storage (initial 1M next 1M optimal 20M)
tablespace RBS;
```

At first glance, the **optimal** parameter seems like a terrific option—it prevents a single rollback segment from using all of the free space in a tablespace. However, note that the database is

- Dynamically extending the rollback segment, causing performance degradation

- Dynamically choosing and eliminating old extents, causing performance degradation

- Eliminating inactive data earlier than it would have under the old method

The last point causes databases with **optimal** sizes set too low to experience a greater incidence of the "snapshot too old" scenario depicted in Figure 7-5. The increased incidence of this scenario is due to the fact that old transaction data may now be eliminated in two ways: by being overwritten and by being discarded during shrinks.

When a transaction completes, the rollback segment checks its **optimal** size value. If it is beyond its **optimal** size, it will eliminate its oldest extent used for storing change vectors. Extent numbers always start with extent zero for any kind of segment, including rollback segments. Extent zero includes the header block for the segment as the first block of the segment. For rollback segments, the transaction table is in the segment header, so, extent zero can never be dropped. Dropping the oldest extent used for storing change vectors keeps the rollback segment to the **optimal** size while servicing queries. Shrinking the rollback segment has the side effect of reducing the amount of inactive rollback data available to current transactions.

What would have happened if there had been no inactive extents in the rollback segment when it exceeded its **optimal** size? The rollback segment would have continued to extend to support the transaction.When a transaction needs another rollback segment block and there are none available in the current extent, the transaction checks to see if the next extent is available. If no transactions are active, the next extent becomes the "current" extent for the rollback segment. Oracle next checks to see if **optimal** has been set for the rollback segment, and if so, it checks to see if the rollback segment is larger than **optimal**. If the rollback segment is larger than **optimal**, Oracle tests to see if the next extent is available, and if so, it is dropped. Oracle continues to check the next extent to see if it is available, and if it is and the rollback segment is larger than **optimal**, the extent is dropped until either the **optimal** setting is reached, the minimum number of extents is reached, or the next extent is not available.

Monitoring Rollback Segment Usage

The monitoring requirements for rollback segments are similar to those for data segments (see Chapter 6). To see the current space allocation for a database's rollback segments, query the DBA_SEGMENTS dictionary view, where the Segment_Type column equals 'ROLLBACK':

```
select * from DBA_SEGMENTS
 where Segment_Type = 'ROLLBACK';
```

Table 7-1 lists the major columns of interest that will be returned from this query.

The value for the **optimal** parameter is not stored in DBA_SEGMENTS. Rather, it is stored in the OptSize column of the dynamic performance table named V$ROLLSTAT. To retrieve this value, query V$ROLLSTAT, joining it to V$ROLLNAME to get the rollback segment's name.

```
select N.Name,          /* rollback segment name */
       S.OptSize        /* rollback segment OPTIMAL size */
from V$ROLLNAME N, V$ROLLSTAT S
where N.USN=S.USN;
```

If no **optimal** size was specified for the rollback segment, then the OptSize value returned by this query will be **NULL**.

Since rollback segments are physical segments in the database, they are included in the space monitoring scripts given in Chapter 6. The tablespace space monitoring programs will report any change in the free space available in the RBS or SYSTEM tablespaces. The extent monitoring scripts store records for all of the rollback segments regardless of their number of extents. By doing this, all changes in the rollback segment space allocations can be detected immediately. The queries for the space monitoring scripts in Chapter 6 query the DBA_SEGMENTS view, the main columns of which are listed in Table 7-1.

Shrinking Rollback Segments

You can use the **shrink** clause of the **alter rollback segment** command to shrink rollback segments to any size you want. If you do not specify a size that the rollback segment should shrink to, then it will shrink to its **optimal** size. You cannot shrink a rollback segment to fewer than two extents.

In the following listing, the r1 rollback segment is altered twice. The first command shrinks R1 to 15MB. The second command shrinks the R1 rollback segment to its **optimal** size.

```
alter rollback segment R1 shrink to 15M;

alter rollback segment R1 shrink;
```

Column Name	Description
Segment_Name	Name of the rollback segment
Tablespace_Name	Tablespace in which the rollback segment is stored
Header_File	File in which the first extent of the rollback segment is stored
Bytes	Actual allocated size of the rollback segment, in bytes
Blocks	Actual allocated size of the rollback segment, in Oracle blocks
Extents	Number of extents in the rollback segment
Initial_Extent	Size, in Oracle blocks, of the initial extent
Next_Extent	Size, in Oracle blocks, of the next extent
Min_Extents	Minimum number of extents for the rollback segment
Max_Extents	Maximum number of extents for the rollback segment

TABLE 7-1. *Rollback Segment–Related Columns in DBA_SEGMENTS*

Monitoring Current Status

You can query the DBA_ROLLBACK_SEGS view for information about the rollback segments' status. This view contains the storage parameters (including Tablespace_Name, Initial_Extent, Next_Extent, Min_Extents, Max_Extents, and Relative_FNo) provided in DBA_SEGMENTS. It includes two additional columns, which are listed in Table 7-2.

The status of a rollback segment will be one of the values listed in Table 7-3. You can only bring a rollback segment online if its current status is either OFFLINE or PARTLY AVAILABLE. A rollback segment will have a status value of PARTLY AVAILABLE if it contains data used by an in-doubt or recovered transaction that spans databases (see Part III for information on distributed transactions).

Column Name	Description
Status	Status of the rollback segment.
Instance_Num	Instance the rollback segment belongs to. For a single-instance system, this value is **NULL**.

TABLE 7-2. *Additional Columns in DBA_ROLLBACK_SEGS*

Status	Description
IN USE	The rollback segment is online.
AVAILABLE	The rollback segment has been created, but has not been brought online.
OFFLINE	The rollback segment is offline.
PENDING OFFLINE	The rollback segment is in the process of going offline.
INVALID	The rollback segment has been dropped. Dropped rollback segments remain listed in the data dictionary with this status.
NEEDS RECOVERY	The rollback segment contains data that cannot be rolled back, or is corrupted.
PARTLY AVAILABLE	The rollback segment contains data from an unresolved transaction involving a distributed database.

TABLE 7-3.   *Rollback Segment Status Values in DBA_ROLLBACK_SEGS*

Monitoring Dynamic Extensions

Rollback segments can extend and shrink. In addition, rollback segment entries *wrap* from one extent to another within a rollback segment each time they move beyond the current extent. All three of these actions require the database to perform additional work to handle transactions, potentially degrading transaction performance. Extending and shrinking are expensive and should be avoided. Wrapping to the next extent without extending or shrinking is not expensive but does indicate that the extent sizes may be too small.

Consider the case of a large transaction that extends beyond its **optimal** value when an entry wraps and causes the rollback segment to expand into another extent. The sequence of events to handle this looks like this:

1. The transaction begins.

2. An entry is made in the rollback segment header for the new transaction entry.

3. The transaction entry acquires a block in the current extent of the rollback segment.

4. The entry continues in the current extent along with all other transactions assigned to that rollback segment until all available blocks have been used, and the entry must then wrap into the next extent. If the next extent is not available, the rollback segment must extend.

5. The rollback segment extends.

6. The data dictionary tables for space management are updated.

7. The transaction completes.

8. The next transaction that causes the rollback segment to wrap to the next extent will check to see if the rollback segment is larger than **optimal** and will cause it to shrink as defined above. If the rollback segment is currently using extent 12, it checks to see if 13 is available. If so, it becomes the current extent and Oracle checks to see if the rollback segment is larger than **optimal**. If so, extent 14 is checked to see if it is available. If so, it will be dropped. Oracle continues to check the next extent to see if it is available, and if it is and the rollback segment is larger than **optimal**, the extent is dropped until either the **optimal** setting is reached, the minimum number of extents is reached, or the next extent is not available.

If the rollback segment had been sized so that the entry fit in the space already allocated by the rollback segment, the sequence of events would instead look like this:

1. The transaction begins.

2. An entry is made in the rollback segment header for the new transaction entry.

3. The transaction entry acquires blocks in an extent of the rollback segment.

4. The transaction completes.

The savings in the amount of overhead needed for space management are clear. Note that wraps that occur without extends are not costly.

You can use the V$ROLLSTAT dynamic performance table to monitor the incidence of shrinks, wraps, and extensions. The columns available in V$ROLLSTAT are shown in Table 7-4. When querying V$ROLLSTAT, you will also want to query V$ROLLNAME. The V$ROLLNAME table maps the rollback segment number to its name (for example, 'SYSTEM','R0'). The goal for sizing rollback segments is to have them extend or shrink only rarely. If they frequently extend and shrink, the size specified for **optimal** is incorrectly set.

Column Name	Description
Usn	Rollback segment number.
Extents	Number of extents in the rollback segment.
RsSize	The size of the rollback segment, in bytes.
Writes	The number of bytes of entries written to the rollback segment.
Xacts	The number of active transactions.
Gets	The number of rollback segment header requests.
Waits	The number of rollback segment header requests that resulted in waits.
Optsize	The value of the **optimal** parameter for the rollback segment.
Hwmsize	The highest value (high-water mark), in bytes, of RsSize reached during usage.
Shrinks	The number of shrinks that the rollback segment has had to perform in order to stay at the **optimal** size.
Wraps	The number of times a rollback segment entry has wrapped from one extent into another.
Extends	The number of times that the rollback segment had to acquire a new extent.
Aveshrink	The average number of bytes freed during a shrink.
Aveactive	The average size of active extents.
Status	Status of the rollback segment; similar to the status values listed earlier. Values are ONLINE (same as 'IN USE') and PENDING OFFLINE (same as 'PARTLY AVAILABLE').
Curext	Current extent.
Curblk	Current block.

TABLE 7-4. *Columns Available in V$ROLLSTAT*

There is a one-to-one relationship between V$ROLLNAME and V$ROLLSTAT. They both have a primary key called USN (Undo Segment Number). When querying the tables in an ad hoc fashion, join them on this key, as shown in the following example:

```
select
    N.Name,                      /* rollback segment name */
    S.RsSize                     /* rollback segment size */
from V$ROLLNAME N, V$ROLLSTAT S
where N.USN=S.USN;
```

FromV$ROLLSTAT, you can determine the number of times a rollback segment has wrapped since the last database startup (the Wraps column), the number of times it has extended (the Extends column), the number of times it has shrunk (the Shrinks column), and the average amount by which it has shrunk (AveShrink). Rollback segments that frequently extend and shrink should be increased in size; use the AveShrink value to estimate a more appropriate **optimal** setting for the rollback segment.

Transactions per Rollback Segment

Determining the users who own active entries in each rollback segment effectively answers two questions: how are the rollback segments currently distributed, and who is where?

Transactions acquire locks within the rollback segment header. The V$LOCK table can thus be joined to V$ROLLNAME. Since locks are owned by processes, you can join the V$LOCK to V$PROCESS to see a mapping of user processes in V$PROCESS to rollback segment names in V$ROLLNAME.

```
REM   Users in rollback segments
REM
column rr heading 'RB Segment' format a18
column us heading 'Username' format a15
column os heading 'OS User' format a10
column te heading 'Terminal' format a10
select R.Name rr,
       nvl(S.Username,'no transaction') us,
       S.Osuser os,
       S.Terminal te
```

```
  from V$LOCK L, V$SESSION S, V$ROLLNAME R
 where L.Sid = S.Sid(+)
   and trunc(L.Id1/65536) = R.USN
   and L.Type = 'TX'
   and L.Lmode = 6
order by R.Name
/
```

Sample output for the preceding query is shown in the following listing:

```
RB Segment          Username          OS User     Terminal
------------------  ----------------  ----------  ----------
R01                 APPL1_BAT         georgehj    ttypc
R02                 APPL1_BAT         detmerst    ttypb
```

The output shows that only two users are actively writing to the rollback segments
(two different sessions of the APPL1_BAT Oracle user, by two different operating
system users). Each user is writing to a rollback segment that no one else is using.
Rollback segments R01 and R02 are the only rollback segments presently used by
active transactions. If there were more than one user using a rollback segment, there
would be multiple records for that rollback segment.

Data Volumes in Rollback Segments

You can query V$ROLLSTAT to determine the number of bytes written to a rollback
segment. V$ROLLSTAT contains a column called Writes that records the number
of bytes that have been written to each rollback segment since the database was
last started.

To determine the amount of activity in a rollback segment for a specific time
interval, select the Writes value at the start of the test period. When the testing
completes, query that value for the then-current value. The difference will be the
number of bytes written to the rollback segment during that time interval. Since
shutting down the database resets the statistics in the V$ROLLSTAT table, it is
important that the database remain open during the testing interval.

Select the Writes value from the V$ROLLSTAT table using the following query:

```
select
    N.Name,                      /* rollback segment name */
    S.Writes                     /* bytes written to date */
from V$ROLLNAME N, V$ROLLSTAT S
where N.USN=S.USN;
```

Detecting the size of the rollback segment entry created by a single transaction requires combining these queries with a command given earlier in this chapter. First, isolate the transaction by executing it in a database in which it is the only process. Direct the transaction to a specific rollback segment via the

```
set transaction use rollback segment SEGMENT_NAME
```

command. Then, query the Writes column of the V$ROLLSTAT table for that rollback segment. When the transaction completes, requery V$ROLLSTAT. The exact size of the transaction's rollback segment entry will be the difference between the two Writes values.

Using Oracle Enterprise Manager to Manage Rollback Segments

You can use Oracle Enterprise Manager (OEM) to perform many rollback segment management functions. You can use OEM to create rollback segments, make them available by placing them online and offline, shrink them, or remove them. You can also create a new rollback segment with the same characteristics as an existing one; this option is called **create like**. In this section, you will see the steps required to manage your rollback segments via OEM.

Creating a Rollback Segment from OEM

To create a rollback segment from within the OEM Console, follow these steps:

1. Either from the Object pull-down menu or by clicking the green cube icon at the left-hand side of the screen, select the Create option.

2. From the Create selection list, highlight the Rollback Segment option and click the Create button at the bottom of the selection panel.

3. Fill in the appropriate information in the Create Rollback Segment screen. OEM will confirm the creation of the new rollback segment.

The following illustration shows the Create selection screen with the Rollback Segment option selected.

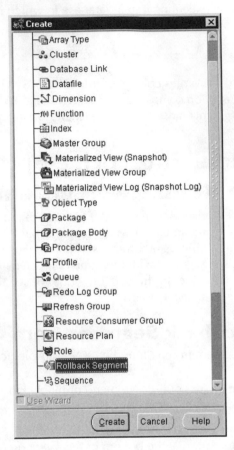

Once you have clicked the Create button, OEM will display the Create Rollback Segment dialog box with two available tabs: General and Storage. On the General tab, enter the following information about the new rollback segment:

■ The new rollback segment's name

■ The rollback segment tablespace name

■ Whether it is to be placed online or offline

■ Whether it is to be public

The following illustration shows the Create Rollback Segment dialog box with the appropriate information filled in for the General tab. The default tablespace that is selected for the new rollback segment is the first tablespace in the tablespace list. The other default value is Online. You must be careful to select the correct tablespace for the rollback segment.

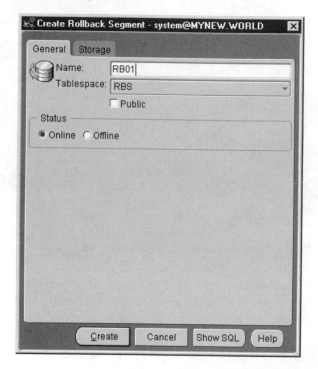

The Storage tab enables you to specify the storage options for the new rollback segment, as shown in the next illustration. The Show SQL option has been selected to show the rollback segment creation script that will be used.

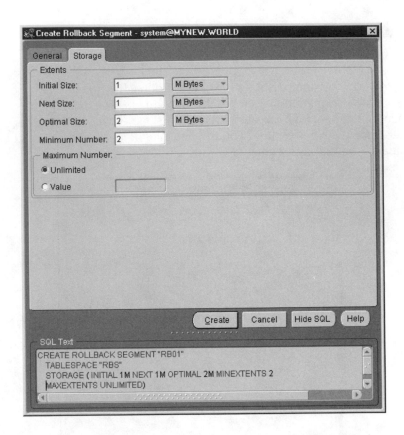

Once the new rollback segment has been created, an informational screen will be displayed to show you that the rollback segment has been created. Click Okay to confirm the creation of the new rollback segment.

Creating a Rollback Segment Like an Existing Rollback Segment

OEM gives you the ability to create a rollback segment whose structure is an exact duplicate of a current rollback segment. To create a new rollback segment based on the structure of an existing rollback segment, follow these steps:

1. Select the rollback segment to be duplicated.

2. From the main menu, using the right mouse button, or by selecting the double-cube icon on the left side of the OEM Console screen, select the Create Like option.

3. Fill in the appropriate information in the Create Rollback Segment dialog box. OEM will confirm the creation of the new rollback segment.

Once you have selected the rollback segment to duplicate, OEM will display the Create Rollback Segment dialog box as described previously. If you want to create the new rollback segment exactly like the current segment, you need only enter a name for the new rollback segment and click the Create button.

NOTE
*Although you can modify any of the presented values, we recommend that you create the rollback segments with different names but identical storage and **optimal** values.*

Once the new rollback segment has been created, an informational screen will be displayed to show you that the rollback segment has been created. Confirm the creation of the new rollback segment by clicking the Okay prompt, and the new rollback segment will be available.

Placing a Rollback Segment Online

To place a rollback segment online and make it available, follow these steps:

1. Select the rollback segment that is currently offline.

2. From the Object pull-down menu, or using the right mouse button, select the Place Online option.

3. Confirm the selection.

Once the selection has been made, the action confirmation window will be displayed to confirm that the action selected is the correct one. OEM will prompt you with the question "Are you sure you want to bring the Rollback Segment Online?" Choose Yes to bring the rollback segment online.

Placing a Rollback Segment Offline

The steps that are used to place a rollback segment offline and make it unavailable are as follows:

1. Select the rollback segment that is currently online.

2. From the Object pull-down menu, or using the right mouse button, select the Place Offline option.

3. Confirm the selection.

Once the selection has been made, the action confirmation window will be displayed to confirm that the action selected is the correct one.

Removing a Rollback Segment

To remove a rollback segment, follow these steps:

1. Select the rollback segment to be removed.

2. From the Object pull-down menu, or using the right mouse button, select the Remove option.

3. Confirm the selection.

Once the selection has been made, the action confirmation window will be displayed to confirm that the action selected is the correct one. When OEM displays the prompt "Are you sure you want to remove rollback segment <rollback_name>?" choose Yes to confirm the removal of the rollback segment, or No to cancel the operation.

Choosing the Number and Size

You can use the descriptions of rollback segment entries given in this chapter to properly design the appropriate rollback segment layout for your database. Note that the final design will be different for each database, unless your databases are functionally identical with respect to their transactions.

The design process involves determining the transaction volume and estimating the number and type of transactions. In the following sections you will see this process illustrated for a sample application. You can derive the proper number, size, and structure of the rollback segments from this transaction data.

Transaction Entry Volume

The first step in the design process is to determine the total amount of rollback segment entry data that will be active or in use at any instant. Note that there are two distinct types of entries being considered here:

- *Active* entries, which have not yet been committed or rolled back

- *Inactive, in-use* (IIU) entries, which have been committed or rolled back, but whose data is in use by separate processes (such as long-running queries)

Rollback segment entries that are inactive, and are not in use by separate processes, are unimportant in these calculations.

The key to managing rollback segments effectively is to minimize the amount of inactive, in-use (IIU) entry data. As a DBA, you have no way of detecting the amount of rollback segment space being used by IIU entries. Their existence only becomes evident when users begin reporting the ORA-1555 "snapshot too old" error described previously in this chapter (see Figure 7-5).

Minimizing the amount of IIU data in rollback segments involves knowing when long-running queries are being executed. If they are occurring concurrently with multiple transactions, there will be a steady accumulation of IIU rollback segment entries. No matter how large the rollback segments are, poor transaction distribution will ultimately cause queries to fail.

To solve this problem, isolate all large queries so that they run at times when very little transaction activity is occurring. This isolation minimizes the amount of IIU rollback segment entry data while also helping to prevent potential concurrent I/O contention between the queries and the transactions.

To determine the amount of rollback segment entry data being written to the rollback segments, use the queries given in the "Data Volumes in Rollback Segments" section shown previously. Each large transaction should be sized via the methods described there (in a test environment). Sizing of transactions should be a standard part of the database sizing process during application development.

NOTE
If you are not forcing large transactions into specific rollback segments, each rollback segment must be large enough to support the largest anticipated transaction.

Care should also be taken to minimize the amount of inactive, in-use rollback data that is shared between transactions. Large amounts of IIU data would result from concurrent transactions in which one transaction referenced a table that the other was manipulating. If this is minimized, the result will be a system whose rollback segment data needs are distributed and measurable.

There is overhead associated with each transaction. However, this header information is counted in the statistics queries given in the previous sections of this chapter. Thus, those queries give a very accurate report of the amount of rollback segment space that is needed.

Number of Transactions

Once the total amount of rollback segment entry data is known, the number of transactions must be considered. In general, create one rollback segment for every four concurrent transactions. During testing of the application, monitor the V$WAITSTAT view; if the number of waits for "undo segment header" blocks steadily increases, add rollback segments to your database.

When possible, group transactions according to their size. You can verify your estimates of the number of active transactions in your rollback segments via the Xacts column of V$ROLLSTAT. It is common to underestimate both the number of concurrent transactions and the size of the largest transactions. The estimation difficulty generally arises from not having a testing environment that mimics the number of concurrent production users and the growth of your database over time. If you use undo tablespaces in place of rollback segments, Oracle gathers statistics that can help you better estimate the number of transactions executed.

Determining the optimal Size

The **optimal** size of a rollback segment must accommodate the transaction volume and the overhead needed to manage the transactions. The design should allow most of the transactions to be handled within a single extent.

In addition to the rollback entry space, you need to allocate space for the rollback segment header (the first block of the rollback segment) and for the IIU data. You can use the following statement to dump the rollback segment header:

```
alter system dump undo header ROLLBACK_SEGMENT_NAME;
```

The more concurrent users there are, the more potential IIU data exists. If long-running queries are executing concurrently with online transactions that use the same data, the space allocation for IIU data value will have to be set high. The amount of IIU data may exceed the currently used transaction volume. If the transactions have been distributed correctly, then no long-running queries will be run concurrently with data manipulation transactions. Even so, there may be some overlap between the transactions. This overlap results in IIU space, and usually requires at least 10 percent of the rollback segment's transaction volume.

The final overhead factor is the free space within the rollback segment. The free space must accommodate the worst-case scenario of transaction allocations—the largest transaction plus an average allocation of smaller transactions. In general, 10 percent to 30 percent of your rollback segments may be kept as free space.

The **optimal** size should be the sum of the rollback header space, the transaction space, and the IIU space. The free space should be above the **optimal** setting, allowing the rollback segment to extend as needed. You can monitor its extensions and usage via the V$ROLLSTAT view. Rollback segments are commonly created with 20 or more extents.

Creating the Rollback Segments

In general, rollback segments supporting your production users should all be created with identical storage parameters. You can use the default storage settings for your rollback segment tablespace to enforce the desired storage values for the rollback segments. The following listing shows an example of the **alter tablespace** command:

```
alter tablespace RBS
default storage
(initial 1M next 1M minextents 100)
```

When creating rollback segments in the RBS tablespace, you now only have to specify the tablespace and the **optimal** value, as shown in the following set of commands:

```
create rollback segment R4 tablespace RBS
    storage (optimal 100M);
alter rollback segment R4 online;
```

The RBS tablespace will have to contain at least enough space to hold all of the rollback segments you create in it, and will need adequate free space to support the concurrent extensions of multiple rollback segments. Figure 7-6 shows a potential layout for the RBS tablespace.

In the layout shown in the figure, six equally sized rollback segments are shown. An additional area of free space of the same size is added at the bottom. That free space will be available for adding a seventh segment (if rollback segment header contention is a problem) or for temporary extensions of the rollback segments.

Figure 7-6 also shows that these rollback segments may be separated into their own files. In such files, a small amount of space will be reserved for overhead. The figure shows seven 120MB files; you could also have stored all of the rollback segments in a single datafile. Using multiple files may improve your options during database tuning efforts, since these files could be placed on different disks to distribute the transaction I/O load.

Production Versus Data Load Rollback Segments

Data load transactions are used to manipulate large volumes of data in an application. These transactions may include initial data loads or the creation of large summary tables from detail tables. Data loading transactions involve data volumes that are orders of magnitude greater than those generated by most production users.

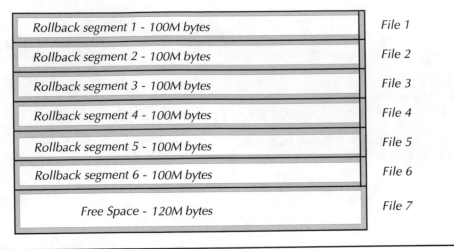

FIGURE 7-6. *Potential layout for the sample RBS tablespace*

Data loads deal with large volumes of data, and the transactions within those loads tend to be large. The transaction size—and the required rollback segment size—is driven by the frequency with which **commit**s are executed within the data loading procedure.

Data load transactions must be assigned to specific rollback segments. You can use the

```
set transaction use rollback segment SEGMENT_NAME
```

command, or you can deactivate all but one production rollback segment (during off-peak hours). The size of the data load transactions should be measured using the V$ROLLSTAT queries shown previously in this chapter.

Once the data load transactions have been isolated to specific rollback segments, those rollback segments should be isolated in a separate tablespace such as RBS_2. The RBS_2 tablespace, as described in Chapter 3, is used solely for rollback segments that have extraordinary space requirements. Placing them in RBS_2 allows their extensions into the RBS_2 free space to be performed without impacting the free space available to the production rollback segments (in the RBS tablespace). See Chapter 15 for a discussion of the support of large batch transactions.

The result will be production rollback segments that are properly sized and preallocated. Their extents are designed to be large enough to handle an entire transaction. Space is allocated to handle those transactions that are not properly distributed. The worst-case scenario is covered, and the best-case scenario is achieved: the time machine works.

Solutions

In the preceding sections, you saw the process for configuring the rollback segment layout for a sample application. In this section, you will see common rollback segment configurations for two types of applications: OLTP applications and data warehouses.

OLTP Applications

An OLTP (online transaction processing) application supports many users executing small transactions. To support many small transactions, you should have many rollback segments, each of which has many extents. To begin configuring your rollback segments for an OLTP database, you must first determine the number of concurrent users in your database. If you have an active database, you can query the Sessions_Highwater column of the V$LICENSE view to see the highest number of concurrent users reached since the database was last started.

```
select Sessions_Highwater from V$LICENSE;
```

The Sessions_Highwater value is the maximum number of rollback segments required for the database. If the number of rollback segments equals the Sessions_ Highwater value, then each transaction may have its own rollback segment. Since your database is not always at its maximum usage (and users in OLTP applications are not constantly entering new transactions), divide the Sessions_Highwater value by 4 to determine your starting value for the number of rollback segments. If your Sessions_Highwater value is 100, then you should create 25 rollback segments to support your users.

NOTE
Unless all users are forced to use specific rollback segments, you cannot control the number of transactions in any single rollback segment. Within a single extent, Oracle may create change vectors for multiple users.

You will need to monitor your rollback segments postproduction to determine if there are extends, and shrinks occurring.

Data Warehouses/Batch Applications

Data warehouses support two distinct types of transactions: small transactions executed by users and very large transactions executed during the loading of data into the database. To support the small transactions, determine the maximum number of concurrent users by querying V$LICENSE.

```
select Sessions_Highwater from V$LICENSE;
```

Since data warehouse users typically perform a small number of large transactions, divide the Sessions_Highwater value by 10 to establish a starting value for the number of rollback segments. If you have 100 concurrent users, create ten rollback segments to support them. Create those ten rollback segments with 20 extents each, and size the extents to support the transaction sizes your users are executing.

Batch processing should use the same rollback segments as defined above so all users can make use of all available rollback segments. If there are specific batch processes you can control, you may force the batch transactions to use very large rollback segments instead of the randomly assigned rollback segments. In many data warehouses, the data loading process is serialized—only one table load or aggregation is occurring at a time. If your data warehouse data loading process is serialized, then you only need to have one rollback segment to support the data load. If you have multiple large transactions concurrently active in the data loading process, then you will need to have multiple large rollback segments available. The data loading rollback segments should have a small number of large extents.

Although you can set the datafiles for a rollback segment tablespace to **autoextend**, doing so prevents you from having control over the space usage in your database. If you set a limit to the maximum number of extents in the rollback segment, and the tablespace's datafiles cannot extend, then the maximum size of any batch transaction is limited. Any transaction that attempts to acquire more rollback segment space than the defined maximum will fail, and will force you to reevaluate your space estimates. If you use the **autoextend** option for your datafiles and do not limit the maximum size of your rollback segments, then a single large transaction can use all of the available space on your disks. If possible, limit the size of your transactions during your batch data loads.

In a data warehouse, your batch loading processes typically do not occur at times when online warehouse users are accessing the database. Therefore, you should be able to place all but the batch load rollback segments in OFFLINE state. If the small rollback segments for the users are online, then your batch loading transactions may accidentally use them, causing problems with your ability to manage the rollback segment space allocation in the rest of the database. If you isolate your batch data loading rollback segments from your users' rollback segments, you will be able to effectively manage the space requirements of those very different types of transactions.

Using Undo Tablespaces

As of Oracle9i, you can use automatic *undo management* to place all undo data in a single tablespace. When you create an undo tablespace, Oracle manages the storage, retention, and space utilization for your rollback data via system-managed undo (SMU).

To start using SMU, you must first create an undo tablespace using the following command:

```
create undo tablespace undo_stuff datafile 'filespec' size 20m;
```

Next, set the UNDO_MANAGEMENT initialization parameter in your system parameter file or init.ora file to AUTO. Specify your undo tablespace via the UNDO_TABLESPACE initialization parameter. You will not need to create or manage any rollback segments within the undo tablespace. Shut down the database and use the updated init.ora or spfile.ora to start up the database.

You can use OEM to create your SMU tablespace by selecting the Create option and choosing the Tablespace entry from the object selection list. Once you have selected the Tablespace entry and clicked the Create button at the bottom of the panel, the Create Tablespace dialog box is presented, as shown in the illustration.

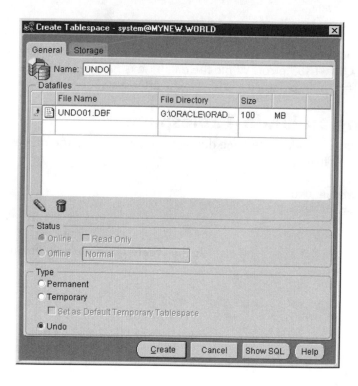

Although a Storage tab is visible within the Create Tablespace dialog box, when you select the Undo option, the storage parameters become unavailable. Once the tablespace has been created, a message box appears telling you that the tablespace has been created. Click OK to acknowledge the message.

To prevent runaway transactions from using all available undo resources for both rollback segments and undo segments, you can use the UNDO_POOL option of the Resource Manager (see Chapter 5). The UNDO_POOL option sets the maximum undo space available to the resource consumer group as a whole; when the quota is reached, no further transactions are permitted until group members **commit** or stop their transactions.

Setting Undo Retention

You can explicitly manage how long Oracle retains undo data in the undo tablespace via the UNDO_RETENTION initialization parameter. Retaining undo serves two purposes: it supports the retention of inactive, in-use (IIU) data for long-running queries, and it supports queries that show the prior state of current data.

For example, if you set

```
UNDO_RETENTION=600
```

then Oracle will make a best effort to retain all committed undo data in the database for 600 seconds. With that setting, any query taking less than 10 minutes should not result in an ORA-1555 error. While the database is running, you can change the UNDO_RETENTION parameter value via the **alter system** command.

Creating an Undo Tablespace

You can create an undo tablespace during the database creation process, as shown in the following listing:

```
create database UNDODB
undo tablespace UNDO_TBS
...
```

In an existing database, you can use the **create tablespace** command to create an undo tablespace:

```
create undo tablespace UNDO_TBS
datafile '/u01/oracle/undodb/undo_tbs_1.dbf'
size 100m;
```

See Appendix A for the full syntax of the **create tablespace** command.

Once you have created an undo tablespace, you can manage it via the **alter tablespace** command. For example, you can add datafiles to the undo tablespace or rename existing datafiles the same as you would for any other tablespace. To stop using a tablespace as your undo tablespace, use the **alter system** command to set a new value for the UNDO_TABLESPACE initialization parameter, or change that parameter during a database shutdown/startup.

NOTE
You cannot have more than one active undo tablespace within a database at any given time.

Monitoring an Undo Tablespace

The primary view for gathering statistics on the undo tablespace usage is V$UNDOSTAT. The V$UNDOSTAT view provides a histogram of the retained data usage. In ten-minute intervals, Oracle records the total number of undo blocks consumed in the UndoBlks column of V$UNDOSTAT, and the number of transactions supported in the TxnCount column. You can use the data from V$UNDOSTAT to determine if the undo tablespace is properly sized for the transaction volume of the application. Oracle maintains 144 rows in V$UNDOSTAT, reflecting the past day's statistics.

Other columns of interest in V$UNDOSTAT include MaxQuerylen, which records the duration in seconds of the longest query executed; the undo retention must be greater than this value. If the NoSpaceErrCnt column of V$UNDOSTAT has a nonzero value, you should add space to the undo tablespace to avoid future space-related errors.

System-Managed Undo Solutions

When using system-managed undo, you need to follow the same basic guidance provided for rollback segment management: isolate the largest transactions and avoid executing long-running queries during times when many small transactions will be executed. If you implement those guidelines, you will simplify your undo tablespace management. For OLTP systems with small transaction sizes, you will commonly need a small amount of undo retention; you will be focusing more on supporting a large number of small transactions.

For batch transactions, the undo tablespace must be larger than the largest transaction's undo requirements. You may need to add datafiles to the undo tablespace to support extremely large transactions. When implementing a mixed environment in which batch transactions run concurrently with OLTP transactions, you should limit the undo quota for your users to make sure you do not exceed the space available in the undo tablespace. If the V$UNDOSTAT view shows that space-related errors have been occurring, increase the available space, better segregate the transactions, and lower the retention time.

CHAPTER
8

Database Tuning

erformance tuning is a part of the life of every database application, and the earlier performance is addressed, the more likely it will be successfully resolved. As noted in previous chapters, most performance problems are not isolated symptoms, but rather the result of the system design. Tuning efforts should therefore focus on identifying and fixing the underlying flaws that yield the unacceptable performance.

Tuning is the final step in a four-step process: planning (Chapters 3 and 4), implementing (Chapter 5), and monitoring (Chapter 6) must precede it. If you tune only for the sake of tuning, then you are failing to address the full cycle of activity, and will likely never resolve the underlying flaws that caused the performance problem.

Most of the database objects that can be tuned are discussed elsewhere in this book—for example, rollback segments and undo tablespaces are covered thoroughly in Chapter 7. This chapter will only discuss the tuning-related activities for such objects, while separate chapters cover planning and monitoring activities.

In the following sections, you will see tuning activities for the following areas:

- Application design
- SQL
- Memory usage
- Data storage
- Data manipulation
- Physical storage
- Logical storage
- Network traffic

Tuning Application Design

Why should a DBA tuning guide include a section on application design? And why should this section come first? Because nothing you can do as a DBA will have as great an impact on the system performance as the design of the application. The requirements for making the DBA's involvement in application development a reality are described in Chapter 5. In designing an application, you can take several steps to make effective and proper use of the available technology, as described in the following sections.

Effective Table Design

"No major application will run in Third Normal Form."

George Koch—*Oracle8i: The Complete Reference*

No matter how well designed your database is, poor table design will lead to poor performance. Not only that, but overly rigid adherence to relational table designs will lead to poor performance. That is due to the fact that while fully relational table designs (said to be in the *third normal form*) are logically desirable, they are physically undesirable.

The problem with such designs is that although they accurately reflect the ways in which an application's data is related to other data, they do not reflect the normal access paths that users will employ to access that data. Once the user's access requirements are evaluated, the fully relational table design will become unworkable for many large queries. Typically, the first problems will occur with queries that return a large number of columns. These columns are usually scattered among several tables, forcing the tables to be joined together during the query. If one of the joined tables is large, then the performance of the whole query may suffer.

In designing the tables for an application, developers should therefore consider denormalizing data—for example, creating small summary tables from large, static tables. Can that data be dynamically derived from the large, static tables on demand? Of course. But if the users frequently request it, and the data is largely unchanging, then it makes sense to periodically store that data *in the format in which the users will ask for it.*

For example, some applications store historical data and current data in the same table. Each record may have a timestamp column, so the current record in a set is the one with the most recent timestamp. Every time a user queries the table for a current record, the user will need to perform a subquery (such as **where timestamp_col = (select max(timestamp_col) from table where emp_name='*some name*'**). If two such tables are joined, there will be two subqueries. In a small database, this may not present a performance problem, but as the number of tables and rows increases, performance problems will follow. Partitioning the historical data away from the current data or storing the historical data in a separate table will involve more work for the DBAs and developers but should improve the long-term performance of the application.

User-centered table design, rather than theory-centered table design, will yield a system that better meets the users' requirements. Design options include separating a single table into multiple tables, and the reverse—combining multiple tables into one. The emphasis should be on providing the users the most direct path possible to the data they want in the format they want.

Distribution of CPU Requirements

The limiting factor to your database's performance may be the availability of CPU resources. Short of purchasing additional CPU power for the available servers, you have several options for managing the CPU resources:

- The CPU load should be scheduled: time long-running batch queries or update programs to run at off-peak hours. Rather than run them at lower operating system priority while online users are performing transactions, run them at normal operating system priority at an appropriate time. Maintaining their normal priority level while scheduling the jobs appropriately will minimize potential locking, rollback, and CPU conflicts.

- Take advantage of the opportunity to physically shift CPU requirements from one server to another. Wherever possible, isolate the database server from the application's CPU requirements. The data distribution techniques described in Part III of this book will result in data being stored in its most appropriate place, and the CPU requirements of the application may be separated from the I/O requirements against the database.

- Consider using Oracle's Real Application Cluster (RAC) technology (formerly known as Oracle Parallel Server) to spread the database access requirements for a single database across multiple instances.

- Use the database resource management features introduced in Oracle8*i*. You can use the Database Resource Manager to establish resource allocation plans and resource consumer groups. You can use Oracle's capabilities to change the resource allocations available to the consumer groups. See Chapter 5 for details on creating and implementing resource consumer groups and resource plans via the Database Resource Manager.

- Use the Parallel Query Option (PQO) to distribute the processing requirements of SQL statements among multiple CPUs. Parallelism can be used by almost every SQL command, including the **select**, **create table as select**, **create index**, **recover**, and SQL*Loader Direct Path loading options.

The degree to which a transaction is parallelized depends on the defined degree of parallelism for the transaction. Each table can have a defined degree of parallelism (see the **create table** and **alter table** commands in Appendix A), and a query can override the default degree of parallelism by using the PARALLEL hint. Oracle evaluates the number of CPUs available on the server and the number of disks on which the table's data is stored in order to determine the default degree of parallelism.

The maximum available parallelism is set at the instance level. The PARALLEL_ MAX_SERVERS initialization parameter sets the maximum number of parallel query server processes that can be used at any one time by all the processes in the database. For example, if you set PARALLEL_MAX_SERVERS to 32 for your instance, and you run a query that uses 30 parallel query server processes for its query and sorting operations, then only two parallel query server processes are available for all of the rest of the users in the database. Therefore, you need to carefully manage the parallelism you allow for your queries and batch operations. You can use the PARALLEL_ADAPTIVE_MULTI_USER initialization parameter to limit the parallelism of operations in a multiuser environment. The PARALLEL_ADAPTIVE_MULTI_USER feature is automatically turned on if you set the PARALLEL_AUTOMATIC_TUNING initialization parameter value to TRUE. As of Oracle8i, you can limit the parallelism available to the resource consumer groups defined within your database. See Chapter 5 for details on implementing the Database Resource Manager and resource plans.

For each table, you can set a default degree of parallelism via the **parallel** clause of the **create table** and **alter table** commands. The *degree of parallelism* tells Oracle how many parallel query server processes to attempt to use for each part of the operation. For example, if a query that performed both table scanning and data sorting operations had a degree of parallelism of 5, then there could be 11 parallel query server processes used—5 for scanning, 5 for sorting, and 1 for coordinating the other 10 processes. You can also specify a degree of parallelism for an index when it is created, via the **parallel** clause of the **create index** command.

The minimum number of parallel query server processes started is set via the PARALLEL_MIN_SERVERS initialization parameter. In general, you should set this parameter to a very low number (less than 5). Setting this parameter to a low value will force Oracle to repeatedly start new query server processes, but it will greatly decrease the amount of memory held by idle parallel query server processes. If you set a high value for PARALLEL_MIN_SERVERS, then you may frequently have idle parallel query server processes on your server, holding onto the memory they had previously acquired but not performing any functions. You can use this feature to speed up parallel queries that you expect to finish in just a few seconds. You can set an idle time parameter (hidden in Oracle9i) that tells Oracle how many minutes a parallel query server process can be idle before it is terminated by the database. Parallelizing operations distributes their processing requirements across multiple CPUs; however, you should use these features carefully. If you use a degree of parallelism of 5 for a large query, then you will have five separate processes accessing the data. If you have that many processes accessing the data, then you may create contention for the disks on which the data is stored, hurting performance. When using the PQO, you should selectively apply it to those tables whose data is well distributed over many physical devices. Also, you should avoid using it for all tables; as noted earlier, a single query may use all of the available parallel query server processes, eliminating the parallelism for all of the rest of the transactions in your database.

If the table is partitioned, then parallel DML will be limited in versions prior to Oracle9i. In Oracle8.0 and Oracle8i, a partitioned table can only use one parallel query server process per partition when performing parallel DML. Oracle9i offers intrapartition parallelism, allowing your queries to be served by multiple parallel query server processes per partition.

Effective Application Design

In addition to the application design topics described later in this chapter, there are several general guidelines for Oracle applications.

First, applications should minimize the number of times they request data from the database. Options include the use of sequences, PL/SQL blocks, and denormalization of tables. You can use distributed database objects such as snapshots and (as of Oracle8i) materialized views to help reduce the number of times a database is queried.

NOTE
Even mildly inefficient SQL can impact your database's performance if it is executed frequently enough.

Second, different users of the same application should query the database in a very similar fashion. Consistent access paths increase the likelihood that requests may be resolved by information that is already available in the SGA. The sharing of data includes not only the tables and rows retrieved but also the queries that are used. If the queries are identical, then the parsed version of a query may already exist in the shared SQL area (see V$SGASTAT), reducing the amount of time needed to process the query. As of Oracle9i, new cursor sharing enhancements in the optimizer increase the likelihood of statement reuse within the shared pool, but the application needs to be designed with statement reuse in mind.

Third, you should restrict the use of dynamic SQL. Dynamic SQL, which uses the DBMS_SQL package, is always reparsed even if an identical query exists in the Shared Pool. Dynamic SQL is a useful feature, but it should not be used for the majority of an application's database accesses.

Stored procedures are available for use in application development. When they are used, the same code may be executed multiple times, thus taking advantage of the Shared Pool. You can also manually compile procedures, functions, and packages to avoid run-time compilation. When you create a procedure, Oracle automatically compiles it. If the procedure later becomes invalid, the database must recompile it before executing it. To avoid incurring this compilation cost at run time, use the **alter procedure** command shown in the following listing:

```
alter procedure MY_RAISE compile;
```

You can view the SQL text for all procedures in a database via the Text column in the DBA_SOURCE view. The USER_SOURCE view will display the procedures owned by the user performing the query. Text for packages, functions, and package bodies is also accessible via the DBA_SOURCE and USER_SOURCE views, which in turn reference a table named SYS.SOURCE$. Since SOURCE$ is part of the data dictionary, the procedural code is stored in the SYSTEM tablespace. Therefore, if you use stored procedures and packages, you must be sure to allocate more space to the SYSTEM tablespace—possibly increasing its size to more than double its original size.

The first two design guidelines discussed—limiting the number of user accesses and coordinating their requests—require the application developer to know as much as possible about how the data is to be used and the access paths involved. For this reason, it is critical that users be as involved in the application design as they are in the table design. If the users spend long hours drawing pictures of tables with the data modelers and little time with the application developers discussing the access paths, the application will most likely not meet the users' needs.

Tuning SQL

As with application design, the tuning of SQL statements seems far removed from a DBA's duties. However, DBAs should be involved in reviewing the SQL that is written as part of the application. A well-designed application may still experience performance problems if the SQL it uses is poorly tuned. Application design and SQL problems cause most of the performance problems in properly designed databases.

The key to tuning SQL is to minimize the search path that the database uses to find the data. In most Oracle tables, each row has a RowID associated with it. The RowID contains information about the physical location of the row—its file, the block within that file, and the row within the database block.

When a query without a **where** clause is executed, the database will usually perform a *full table scan*, reading every block from the table. During a full table scan, the database locates the first block of the table and then reads sequentially through all other blocks in the table. For large tables, full table scans can be very time consuming. Running the query in parallel reduces that time.

When specific rows are queried, the database may use an index to help speed the retrieval of the desired rows. An index maps logical values in a table to their RowIDs, which in turn map them to a specific physical location. Indexes may either be unique—in which case there is no more than one occurrence for each value—or nonunique. Indexes only store RowIDs for column values in the indexed columns. Nothing is stored in the index if the column is null for a particular row.

You may index several columns together. This is called a *concatenated* index, and it will be used if its leading column is used in the query's **where** clause. As of Oracle9i, the optimizer can also use a *skip-scan* approach in which a concatenated index is used even if its leading column is not in the query's **where** clause. Skip-scan approaches are not as efficient as those that use the leading column of the index.

Indexes must be tailored to the access path needed. Consider the case of a three-column, concatenated index. As shown in the following listing, it is created on the City, State, and Zip columns of the EMPLOYEE table:

```
create index CITY_ST_ZIP_NDX
on EMPLOYEE(City, State, Zip)
tablespace INDEXES;
```

If a query of the form

```
select * from EMPLOYEE
 where State='NJ';
```

is executed, then the index will *not* be used in Oracle8i, because its *leading* column (City) is not used in the **where** clause. In Oracle9i, the skip-scan feature of the optimizer allows the CITY_ST_ZIP_NDX to be used to satisfy this query. If users will frequently run this type of query, then the index's columns should be reordered with State first in order to reflect the actual usage pattern.

It is critical that the table's data be as ordered as possible. If users are frequently executing *range* queries—selecting those values that are within a specified range—then having the data ordered may require fewer data blocks to be read while resolving the query, thus improving performance. The ordered entries in the index will point to a set of neighboring blocks in the table rather than blocks that are scattered throughout the datafile(s).

For example, a range query of the type shown in this listing:

```
select *
   from EMPLOYEE
 where Empno between 1 and 100;
```

will require fewer data blocks to be read if the physical records in the EMPLOYEE table are ordered by the Empno column. This should improve the performance of the query. To guarantee that the rows are properly ordered in the table, extract the records to a flat file, sort the records in the file, and then **delete** the old records and reload them from the sorted file.

As an alternative to extracting data to a flat file, you can use Oracle's internal sorting procedures to sort your data. Ideally, you could reorder rows for a table by creating a second table, via the **create table as select** command. Prior to Oracle9i, the **create table as select** and **insert as select** commands do not allow you to specify an **order by** clause.

To circumvent this limitation in versions prior to Oracle8i, create a view on the base table. Views now support the **order by** clause, so you can create a view and select from it to populate an ordered table.

```
create or replace view EMPLOYEE_VIEW as
select *  from COMPANY
 order by Empno;
```

You can now create a table selecting from EMPLOYEE_VIEW; the effect will be that a duplicate copy of EMPLOYEE will be created, with the rows properly sorted.

```
create table EMPLOYEE_ORDERED
    as select * from EMPLOYEE_VIEW;
```

In the preceding example, the data was ordered by the Empno value. Often, you may need to order the data by an attribute column instead, such as the Name column. If the data is ordered to support the most-used range queries, and is densely stored within each block, then you can minimize the number of blocks read during each query and thereby improve the performance of your queries.

Impact of Order on Load Rates

Indexes impact the performance of both queries and data loads. During **insert**s, the impact of the rows' order has a significant impact on load performance. Even in heavily indexed environments, properly ordering the rows prior to **insert** may improve load performance by 50 percent.

As an index grows, Oracle allocates new blocks. If a new index entry is added beyond the last entry, the new entry will be added to the last block in the index. If the new entry causes Oracle to exceed the space available in that block, the entry will be moved to a new block, leaving all of the original entries intact. There is very little performance impact from this block allocation.

If the inserted rows are not ordered, then new index entries will be written to existing index node blocks. If there is no more room in the node where the new value is added, the node will split in two. Fifty percent of the index entries will be left in the original node and 50 percent will be moved to a new node. As a result, the performance suffers during loads (because of the additional space management activity) and during queries (since the index contains more unused space, requiring more blocks to be read).

In benchmark tests, an index was created on the Name column of the EMPLOYEE table. When the rows were **insert**ed with the Name values highly unordered, the number of blocks used by the index increased by 50 percent and the load rate decreased by over 50 percent. If you have multiple indexes on your table, order the rows during **insert**s by the index that is most frequently used during range queries if you want to tune the query operations; to tune the **insert** operations, order by the most complex index.

> **NOTE**
> *There is a significant drop in load performance when an index increases its number of internal levels. The point at which the increase occurs is dependent on the database block size and the length of the index key values. To see the number of levels, analyze an index and then select its Blevel column value from DBA_INDEXES. For best load performance, keep the Blevel values as low as possible.*

Because of the way Oracle manages its indexes internally, load rates will be affected each time a new index is added (since it is unlikely that rows will be inserted with the data sorted correctly for multiple columns). Strictly from a load rate perspective, favor fewer multicolumn indexes over multiple single-column indexes.

Additional Indexing Options

If the data is not very selective, then you may consider using bitmap indexes. As described in Chapter 15, bitmap indexes are most effective for queries against large, static data sets with few distinct values. You can create both bitmap indexes and normal (B*-tree) indexes on the same table, and Oracle will perform any necessary index conversions dynamically during query processing. You cannot have both a normal and bitmapped index on the same column within a table. See Chapter 15 for details on using bitmap indexes.

If two tables are frequently queried together, then clusters may be effective in improving performance. Clusters store rows from multiple tables in the same physical data blocks, based on their logical values (the cluster key). See Chapter 5 for more information on clusters.

Queries in which a column's value is compared to an exact value (rather than a range of values) are called *equivalence* queries. A *hash cluster* stores a row in a specific location based on its value in the cluster key column. Every time a row is inserted, its cluster key value is used to determine which block it should be stored in; this same logic can be used during queries to quickly find data blocks that are needed for retrieval. Hash clusters are designed to improve the performance of equivalence queries; they will not be as helpful in improving the performance of the range queries discussed earlier.

Reverse indexes provide another tuning solution for equivalence queries. In a reverse index, the bytes of the index are stored in reverse order. In a traditional index, two consecutive values are stored next to each other. In a reverse index, consecutive values are not stored next to each other. For example, values 2004 and 2005 are stored as 4002 and 5002, respectively, in a reverse index. While not appropriate for range scans, reverse indexes may reduce contention for index blocks if many equivalence queries are performed.

NOTE
You cannot reverse a bitmap index.

As of Oracle8i, you can create *functional indexes*. Prior to Oracle8i, any query that performed a function on a column could not use that column's index. Thus, this query could not use an index on the Name column:

```
select * from EMPLOYEE
  where UPPER(Name) = 'JONES';
```

but this query could:

```
select * from EMPLOYEE
  where Name = 'JONES';
```

because the second query does not perform a function on the Name column. As of Oracle8i, you can create indexes that allow function-based accesses to be supported by index accesses. Instead of creating an index on the column Name, you can create an index on the column expression UPPER(Name), as shown in the following listing:

```
create index EMP_UPPER_NAME on
EMPLOYEE(UPPER(Name));
```

Although functional indexes can be useful, be sure to consider the following points when creating them:

- Can you restrict the functions that will be used on the column? If so, can you restrict all functions from being performed on the column?

- Do you have adequate storage space for the additional indexes?

- When you drop the table, you will be dropping more indexes (and therefore more extents) than before. How will that impact the time required to drop the table?

Function-based indexes are useful, but you should implement them sparingly. The more indexes you create on a table, the longer all **insert**s, **update**s, and **delete**s will take. To create a function-based index, you must have the QUERY REWRITE system privilege, and the following parameters must be set in the initialization parameter file:

```
QUERY_REWRITE_ENABLED=TRUE
```

Generating Explain Plans

How can you determine which access path the database will use to perform a query? This information can be viewed via the **explain plan** command. This command will evaluate the execution path for a query and will place its output into a table (named PLAN_TABLE) in the database. A sample **explain plan** command is shown in the following listing:

```
explain plan
set Statement_Id = 'TEST'
for
select * from EMPLOYEE
where City > 'Y%';
```

The first line of this command tells the database to explain its execution plan for the query without actually executing the query. The second line labels this query's records in the PLAN_TABLE with a Statement_Id equal to TEST. Following the keyword **for**, the query to be analyzed is listed.

The account that is running this command must have a PLAN_TABLE in its schema. Oracle provides the **create table** commands needed for this table. The file, named utlxplan.sql, is usually located in the /rdbms/admin subdirectory under the Oracle software home directory. Users may run this script to create the table in their schemas.

NOTE
You should drop and re-create the plan table following each Oracle upgrade, since new columns may be added by the upgrade scripts.

Query the plan table using the query in the following listing. Records in that table are related to each other, so the **connect by** clause of the **select** statement can be used to evaluate the hierarchy.

```
select ID ID_plus_exp,
Parent_ID parent_id_plus_exp,
LPAD(' ',2*(level-1))|| /* Indent for the level */
Operation|| /* The operation */
```

```
DECODE(other_tag,null,'','*')|| /* will display an '*' if parallel */
DECODE(options,null,'',' ('||options||')')|| /* display the options */
DECODE(object_name,null,'',' of '''||object_name||'''')||
DECODE(object_type,null,'',' '||object_type||')')||
DECODE(id,0,decode(optimizer,null,'',' optimizer='||optimizer))||
DECODE(cost,null,'',' (cost='||cost|| /* display cost info. */
DECODE(cardinality,null,'',' card='||cardinality)|| /* cardinality */
DECODE(bytes,null,'',' bytes='||bytes)||')') plan_plus_exp,
object_node object_node_plus_exp /* parallel and remote info */
from PLAN_TABLE
start with ID=0 and Statement_ID='TEST'
connect by prior ID=Parent_ID and Statement_ID='TEST'
order by ID,Position;
```

This query will report on the types of operations the database must perform to resolve the query. The first three columns of the sample output are shown in the following listing:

```
   i     p  PLAN_PLUS_EXP
---- ----  -----------------------------------------------------------
   0         SELECT STATEMENT optimizer=CHOOSE
   1     0   TABLE ACCESS (BY INDEX ROWID) of 'EMPLOYEE'
   2     1     INDEX (RANGE SCAN) of 'CITY_ST_ZIP_NDX' NON-UNIQUE)
```

To read the explain plan, read the order of operations from inside out of the hierarchy until you come to a set of operations at the same level of indentation; then read from top to bottom. In this example, there are no operations at the same level of indentation; therefore, you read the order of operations from inside out. The first operation is the index range scan, followed by the table access; the SELECT STATEMENT operation displays the output to the user. Each operation has an ID value (the first column) and a parent ID value. In more complex explain plans, you may need to use the parent ID values to determine the order of operations.

This plan shows that the data that is returned to the user comes via a Table Access by RowID. The RowIDs are supplied by an index range scan, using the CITY_ST_ZIP_NDX index described earlier.

NOTE
As of Oracle8i, you can use stored outlines to save the execution path for a query. See Chapter 5 for details on the implementation of stored outlines.

You can use the **set autotrace on** command in SQL*Plus to automatically generate the **explain plan** output and trace information for every query you run. The autotrace-generated output will not be displayed until after the query has completed, while the **explain plan** output is generated without running the command. To enable autotrace-generated output, a PLAN_TABLE must either be created in the schema in which the autotrace utility will be used, or it must be created in the SYSTEM schema and access granted to the schema that will use the autotrace utility. The script plustrce.sql creates the PLUSTRACE role. Located in the sqlplus/admin directory under the Oracle software home directory, the script is automatically run as part of the database creation scripts for Oracle9i. Users must have the PLUSTRACE role enabled prior to executing **set autotrace on**.

When evaluating the output of the **explain plan** command, you should make sure that the most selective indexes (that is, the most nearly unique indexes) are used by the query. If a nonselective index is used, you may be forcing the database to perform unnecessary reads to resolve the query. A full discussion of SQL tuning is beyond the scope of this book, but you should focus your tuning efforts on making sure that the most resource-intensive SQL statements are using the most selective indexes possible.

If the tables and indexes are analyzed, both the **set autotrace on** command and the **explain plan** query shown in the previous listing will report a "cost" for each step. The cost is related to the number of I/Os and internal processes Oracle must execute to complete the step. The reported costs are cumulative, so the cost for one step includes that step's cost plus the costs of all of its child steps. The costs cannot be compared across dissimilar queries, and the lowest-cost version of the query may not be the best query for your users.

As of Oracle9i, you can use a V$ view, V$SQL_PLAN, to see the execution plan for all statements presently in the library cache. The following listing provides a brief version of the execution plan for each statement found:

```
select SQL_Text,
LPAD(' ',2*(Level-1))||Operation||' '||Options||' '
||Object_Name||' '
||DECODE(Object_Node,'','','['||Object_Node||'] ')
||DECODE(Optimizer,'','','['||Optimizer||'] ')
||DECODE(id,0,'Cost = '||Position) Query
from V$SQLAREA, V$SQL_PLAN
where V$SQLAREA.Address = V$SQL_PLAN.Address
and V$SQLAREA.Hash_Value = V$SQL_PLAN.Hash_Value
connect by prior ID = Parent_ID
and prior V$SQL_PLAN.Address = V$SQL_PLAN.Address
and prior V$SQLAREA.Hash_Value = V$SQL_PLAN.Hash_Value
start with ID = 0
and V$SQLAREA.Address = V$SQL_PLAN.Address
and V$SQLAREA.Hash_Value = V$SQL_PLAN.Hash_Value
order by V$SQLAREA.Address
```

In general, transaction-oriented applications (such as multiuser systems used for data entry) judge performance based on the time it takes to return the first row of a result set.

For transaction-oriented applications, you should focus your tuning efforts on using indexes to reduce the time required to return the first row of the result set.

If the application is batch oriented (with large transactions and reports), you should focus on improving the time it takes to complete the overall transaction instead of the time it takes to return the first row from the transaction. Improving the overall throughput of the transaction may require using full table scans in place of index accesses—and may improve the overall performance of the application.

If the application is distributed across multiple databases, focus on reducing the number of times database links are used in queries. If a remote database is frequently accessed during a query, then the cost of accessing that remote database is paid each time the remote data is accessed. Even if the cost of accessing the remote data is low, accessing it thousands of times will eventually place a performance burden on your application. See the "Reducing Network Traffic" section later in this chapter for additional tuning suggestions for distributed databases.

Tuning Memory Usage

In Chapter 9, you will see how to use Oracle's STATSPACK toolset to summarize the changes in database statistics for a given period. You can use the STATSPACK utilities and queries of the data dictionary tables to identify problem areas in the database's memory allocation.

The data block buffer cache and the Shared Pool are managed via a *least recently used (LRU)* algorithm. A preset area is set aside to hold values; when it fills, the least recently used data is eliminated from memory and written back to disk. An adequately sized memory area keeps the most frequently accessed data in memory; accessing less frequently used data requires physical reads.

The *hit ratio* is a measure of how well the data buffer cache is handling requests for data. In its general form, it is calculated as

```
Hit Ratio = (Logical Reads - Physical Reads)/Logical Reads
```

Thus, a perfect hit ratio would have a value of 1.00. In that instance, all requests for database blocks (logical reads) would be fulfilled without requesting any data from datafiles (physical reads); all requests would be handled by the data that is already in memory. See Chapter 9 for details on using the STATSPACK utility to calculate hit ratios during different time periods.

The overall hit ratio for an application will be lowered by its batch activity. Note that the hit ratio in a database is cumulative, reflecting all of the processing performed since the last time the database was started. A single poorly written query or long-running batch job will adversely affect your hit ratio long after it completes. To avoid this impact, you can measure the hit ratio during specific time intervals.

You can see the queries performing the logical and physical reads in the database via the V$SQL view. V$SQL reports the cumulative number of logical and physical reads performed for each query currently in the Shared Pool, as well as the number of times each query was executed. The script in the following listing will show the SQL text for the queries in the Shared Pool, with the most I/O-intensive queries listed first. The query also displays the number of logical reads (buffer gets) per execution.

```
select Buffer_Gets,
       Disk_Reads,
       Executions,
       Buffer_Gets/Executions B_E,
       SQL_Text
  from V$SQL
 order by Disk_Reads desc;
```

If the Shared Pool has been flushed, queries executed prior to the flush will no longer be accessible via V$SQL. However, the impact of those queries can still be seen, provided the users are still logged in. The V$SESS_IO view records the cumulative logical reads and physical reads performed for each user's session. You can query V$SESS_IO for each session's hit ratio, as shown in the following listing:

```
select SESS.Username,
       SESS_IO.Block_Gets,
       SESS_IO.Consistent_Gets,
       SESS_IO.Physical_Reads,
       round(100*(SESS_IO.Consistent_Gets
          +SESS_IO.Block_Gets-SESS_IO.Physical_Reads)/
         (decode(SESS_IO.Consistent_Gets,0,1,
             SESS_IO.Consistent_Gets+SESS_IO.Block_Gets)),2)
               session_hit_ratio
  from V$SESS_IO sess_io, V$SESSION sess
 where SESS.Sid = SESS_IO.Sid
   and SESS.Username is not null
 order by Username;
```

You can manipulate the actions of the LRU algorithm in the data block buffer cache via the **cache** option. Normally, when a full table scan is executed, the table's blocks are placed on the least recently used end of the LRU list so that they will be overwritten first. When the **cache** option is used, Oracle will place these blocks at the most recently used end of the LRU list. That table's data will still be subject to the LRU algorithms that manage the SGA caches, but it will stay in the SGA longer than if it had been treated normally. The **cache** option can be specified at a table level via the **create table** and **alter table** commands, and can also be specified via query hints. The **cache** option is most useful for frequently accessed tables that change infrequently. You can then run queries that will reload the most-used tables into the SGA caches each time the database is restarted.

To see the objects whose blocks are currently in the data block buffer cache, query the X$BH table in SYS's schema, as shown in the following query. In the following listing, the SYS and SYSTEM objects are excluded from the output so the DBA can focus on the application tables and indexes present in the SGA:

```
select Object_Name,
       Object_Type ,
       count(*) Num_Buff
  from SYS.X$BH a, SYS.DBA_OBJECTS b
 where A.Obj = B.Object_Id
   and Owner not in ('SYS','SYSTEM')
 group by Object_Name, Object_Type;
```

With all of the areas of the SGA—the data block buffers, the dictionary cache, and the Shared Pool—the emphasis should be on sharing data among users. Each of these areas should be large enough to hold the most commonly requested data from the database. In the case of the Shared Pool, it should be large enough to hold the parsed versions of the most commonly used queries. When they are adequately sized, the memory areas in the SGA can dramatically improve the performance of individual queries and of the database as a whole.

You can create a *Large Pool* within the SGA to be used when Oracle requests large contiguous areas of memory within the Shared Pool (such as during use of the multithreaded server). To create the Large Pool, set a value (in bytes) for the LARGE_POOL_SIZE initialization parameter. By default, the Large Pool is not created. Setting some parameters like PARALLEL_AUTOMATIC_TUNING = TRUE will also set the LARGE_POOL_SIZE parameter to a nonzero value.

You can reserve an area within the Shared Pool for large objects via the SHARED_POOL_RESERVED_SIZE initialization parameter. The "reserved size" is set aside for the Shared Pool entries of large objects (such as large packages).

Rather than reserving space in the Shared Pool, you may wish to selectively *pin* packages in memory. Pinning packages immediately after starting the database will increase the likelihood that a large enough section of contiguous free space is available in memory. The KEEP procedure of the DBMS_SHARED_POOL package designates the packages to pin in the Shared Pool. As shown in the following listing, you must first reference the object to be pinned:

```
alter procedure APPOWNER.ADD_CLIENT compile;
execute DBMS_SHARED_POOL.KEEP('APPOWNER.ADD_CLIENT','P');
```

Pinning of packages is more closely related to application management than application tuning, but it can have a performance impact. If you can avoid dynamic management of fragmented memory areas, you minimize the work Oracle has to do when managing the Shared Pool.

As noted in Chapter 5, Oracle reads multiple blocks at a time during a full table scan. The number of blocks read during each physical read is determined by the setting of the DB_FILE_MULTIBLOCK_READ_COUNT initialization parameter. The number of blocks read at a time is limited by the I/O buffer size of your operating system. If your operating system buffer size is 128KB, and your database block size is 4KB, then you should set DB_FILE_MULTIBLOCK_READ_COUNT to a value of 32 (128KB divided by the 4KB block size). If you set it to a lower value, the performance of your full table scans will be adversely affected.

You can determine the maximum multiblock setting in your environment via the following steps:

1. Create a new tablespace with a single datafile.

2. Create a single unindexed table in that tablespace.

3. Query V$FILESTAT to verify the starting statistics for the test.

4. Perform a full table scan on the table.

5. Query V$FILESTAT to determine the ending statistics for the test, and subtract the starting statistics from them. Divide the PhyBlkRds value by PhyRds to determine the effective multiblock read count.

6. Drop the tablespace.

The following listing illustrates these steps:

```
create tablespace tester
datafile 'E:\Oracle\Oradata\orcl\tester.dbf' size 10M reuse
default storage (initial 1M next 1M pctincrease 0);

Tablespace created.

rem  The next step creates a table based on an existing table
rem  in this database.

create table TESTING
tablespace tester
as select * from perftest.emp
where rownum < 50000;

select relative_fno from dba_data_files
where tablespace_name = 'TESTER';

RELATIVE_FNO
------------
          9
```

```
SQL> select phyrds, phyblkrd from v$filestat where file#=9;

   PHYRDS   PHYBLKRD
--------- ---------
        0         0

rem  Perform a full table scan:

SQL> select count(*) from testing;

 COUNT(*)
---------
    49999

select phyrds, phyblkrd from v$filestat where file#=9;

   PHYRDS   PHYBLKRD
--------- ---------
      154      1220

drop tablespace tester including contents;
```

Dividing the PhyBlkRd column by the PhyRds column yields a result of 7.92; the effective multiblock read count is 8. If the tablespace was not new, you would need to subtract the initial statistics (step 3) from the ending statistics (step 5) to determine the statistics change during the test. You can then change the DB_FILE_MULTIBLOCK_READ_COUNT parameter value at the session level and repeat the test. Do not set the parameter file's DB_FILE_MULTIBLOCK_READ_COUNT parameter to a value higher than the value you calculate.

When creating buffer pools, you can specify the size of the *keep area* and the size of the *recycle area*. Like the reserved area of the Shared Pool, the keep area retains entries, while the recycle area is more frequently recycled. You can specify the size of the keep area via the DB_KEEP_CACHE_SIZE parameter, as shown in the following listing:

```
DB_KEEP_CACHE_SIZE=20M
DB_RECYCLE_CACHE_SIZE=4m
```

In versions before Oracle9i, the size of the KEEP and RECYCLE buffer pools reduced the available space in the data block buffer cache because all three areas were part of the area defined by the initialization parameter DB_BLOCK_BUFFERS. In Oracle9i, the memory areas defined by DB_KEEP_CACHE_SIZE and DB_RECYCLE_CACHE_SIZE are in addition to the area defined by DB_CACHE_SIZE. For a table to use one of the new buffer pools, specify the name of the buffer pool via the **buffer_pool** parameter within the table's **storage** clause. For example, if you want a table to be quickly removed from memory, assign it to the RECYCLE pool. The default pool is named DEFAULT, so you can use the **alter table** command to redirect a table to the DEFAULT pool at a later date.

Specifying the Size of the SGA

To create the SGA, you should specify values for the following initialization parameters:

SGA_MAX_SIZE	As of Oracle9*i*, you can specify the maximum size to which the SGA can grow. The size of the Shared Pool and data block buffer cache can be changed dynamically.
SHARED_POOL_SIZE	The size of the Shared Pool.
DB_BLOCK_SIZE	This will be the default database block size for the database as established during database creation.
DB_CACHE_SIZE	This parameter replaces the DB_BLOCK_BUFFERS parameter used in earlier versions of the Oracle RDBMS. The cache size is specified in bytes rather than in blocks. Oracle rounds the size to units of 4MB if the SGA_MAX_ SIZE < 128MB; otherwise, it will be 16MB.
DB_*n*K_CACHE_SIZE	If you will be using multiple database block sizes within a single database, you must specify a DB_CACHE_SIZE parameter value and at least one DB_*n*K_CACHE_SIZE parameter value. For example, if your standard database block size is 4KB, you can also specify a cache for the 8KB block size tablespaces via the DB_8K_CACHE_SIZE parameter.

For example, you may specify

```
MAX_SGA_SIZE=500M
SHARED_POOL_SIZE=80M
DB_BLOCK_SIZE=8192
DB_CACHE_SIZE=160M
DB_4K_BLOCK_SIZE=4M
```

Within the SGA, 4MB will be available for data queried from objects in tablespaces with 4KB block sizes. Objects using the standard 8KB block size will use the 160MB cache. While the database is open, you can change the SHARED_POOL_SIZE and DB_CACHE_SIZE parameter values via the **alter system** command.

Using the Cost-Based Optimizer

With each release of its software, Oracle has added new features to its optimizer and improved its existing features. As a result, performance when using the cost-based optimizer (CBO) should be consistently improving. Although the RULE hint and rule-based optimization is available in Oracle8, the role of rule-based optimization will probably diminish over time, and you should begin converting to cost-based optimization if you have not already done so.

Effective use of the cost-based optimizer requires that the tables and indexes in your application be analyzed regularly. The frequency with which you analyze the objects depends on the rate of change within the objects. For batch transaction applications, you should reanalyze the objects after each large set of batch transactions. For OLTP applications, you should reanalyze the objects on a time-based schedule (such as via a weekly or nightly process).

Statistics on objects are gathered via the DBMS_STATS or DBMS_UTILITY packages (the **analyze** command is being deprecated in Oracle9i). If you analyze a table, then its associated indexes are automatically analyzed as well.

You can view the statistics on the COMPANY table and its indexes via DBA_ TABLES, DBA_TAB_COL_STATISTICS, and DBA_INDEXES. Some column-level statistics are still provided in DBA_TAB_COLUMNS, but they are provided there strictly for backward compatibility. The statistics for the columns of partitioned tables are found in DBA_PART_COL_STATISTICS.

Analyzing tables generates histograms of the tables' data. A histogram reflects the distribution of data values within a table. For example, there may be many distinct values for a column, in which case the column may seem ideal as a limiting value for a query. However, 90 percent of those values may all be clustered together, with the remaining 10 percent of the values outside the cluster. If your query performs a range scan with a limiting value inside the cluster, the index may not help the performance of your query. The use of an index for values outside the cluster would have a greater performance impact.

How does the optimizer know where data value clusters are? When you run the **analyze** command, you can tell Oracle to generate a histogram for the cluster. By default, Oracle will create a histogram that divides the data values into 75 *buckets*. Each bucket has the same number of records as every other bucket. The more buckets you create, the better the distribution of database values will be reflected via the histogram. You can specify the number of buckets to use via the **size** parameter of the **analyze** command. The maximum number of buckets per table is 254.

To analyze all objects in a schema, you can use the ANALYZE_SCHEMA procedure within the DBMS_UTILITY package. As shown in the following listing, it has two parameters: the name of the schema and the analyze option used (COMPUTE or ESTIMATE).

```
execute DBMS_UTILITY.ANALYZE_SCHEMA('APPOWNER','COMPUTE');
```

When the command in the preceding listing is executed, all of the objects belonging to the APPOWNER schema will be analyzed, using the **compute statistics** option. If you are using rule-based optimization, then the statistics, although not used during the optimization process, will provide useful information to the developers during the query tuning process.

You can use the DBMS_STATS package to analyze schemas, tables, columns, and indexes. The procedures within the DBMS_STATS package store statistics in a local table for later movement to the data dictionary. For the optimizer to use the statistics, you must move them to the data dictionary. You can create multiple sets of statistics for use during performance testing.

Within the DBMS_STATS package, you can use the GATHER_TABLE_STATS procedure to collect table, column, and index statistics. For index statistics, use the GATHER_INDEX_STATS procedure. The GATHER_SCHEMA_STATS, GATHER_DATABASE_STATS, and GATHER_SYSTEM_STATS collect statistics for the schema, database, and system I/O, respectively.

For example, the following command collects the statistics for the PERFTEST.EMP table. To see the collected statistics, query DBA_TABLES.

```
begin
DBMS_STATS.GATHER_TABLE_STATS('perftest','emp');
end;
```

NOTE
*During the creation or rebuild of an index, you can use the **compute statistics** clause to gather statistics as the index is being populated.*

Implications of Compute Statistics

In the examples in the preceding section, the **compute statistics** option of the **analyze** command was used to gather statistics about objects. Oracle also provides an **estimate statistics** option, which samples random blocks from several different blocks spread across all of the segment's extents. If you choose to use **estimate statistics**, analyze as much of the table as possible (you can specify a percentage of the rows to analyze).

To generate the most accurate statistics, you should use the **compute statistics** option wherever possible. For most environments, the **estimate statistics** option generates acceptable statistics if 6 percent to 8 percent of the table is analyzed. For indexes, use a higher percentage when using the **estimate statistics** option.

There are management issues associated with the **compute statistics** option. Specifically, it can require large amounts of temporary segment space (up to four times the size of the table). You need to make sure that the user performing the analysis has the proper temporary tablespace settings and that the temporary tablespace can handle the space requirements. As the table grows over time, the temporary segment space requirements of **compute statistics** will grow. If you have partitioned the table or index, you can analyze individual partitions, avoiding the recomputation of statistics for static data in other partitions.

Tuning Data Storage

How the database actually *stores* data also has an effect on the performance of queries. If the data is fragmented into multiple extents, then resolving a query may cause the database to look in several physical locations for related rows. The official statement from Oracle is that there is no noticeable overhead to access objects with 4096 or fewer extents. You actually want a large number of extents on different files for best performance of parallel queries.

Free space fragmentation may slow performance when storing new records. If the free space in a tablespace is fragmented, then the database may have to dynamically combine neighboring free extents to create a single extent that is large enough to handle the new space requirements. Tuning data storage thus involves tuning both used space and free space, as described in the next sections. DBAs should be using locally managed tablespaces starting with Oracle8i to totally avoid this problem.

Most enterprise database platforms use RAID (redundant array of independent disks) technologies to improve the system's I/O performance. RAID systems distribute data from a single file over multiple disks. Requests for data from a file are distributed over multiple disks, reducing the I/O burden on any single disk. As a result, fewer I/O bottlenecks will be encountered.

Defragmentation of Segments

As described in Chapter 4, when a database object (such as a table or index) is created, it is assigned to a tablespace via user defaults or specific instructions. A *segment* is created in that tablespace to hold the data associated with that object. The space that is allocated to the segment is never released until the segment is dropped or truncated.

A segment is made up of sections called *extents*. The extents themselves are contiguous sets of Oracle blocks. Once the existing extents can no longer hold new data, the segment will obtain another extent. This extension process will continue until no more free space is available in the tablespace's datafiles, or until an internal maximum number of extents per segment is reached. To simplify the management of segments, you should use a consistent set of extent sizes. The sizes you choose should be multiples of the operating system's I/O size, and should be multiples of each other. For example, you may create all of your small tables with 1MB extent sizes, medium-sized tables with 4MB extent sizes, and large tables with 16MB extent sizes. If your extents are properly sized, then table lookups will not be impacted by the number of extents in the table. DDL operations, however, may be impacted.

Oracle supports two types of internal space management: dictionary managed tablespaces and locally managed tablespaces. In dictionary managed tablespaces, the space management data is stored in the data dictionary, in tables called SYS.UET$ and SYS.FET$. In locally managed tablespaces, the space management data is stored in a bitmap within the tablespace's datafiles.

When an object allocates an extent in a dictionary managed tablespace, Oracle **update**s the entries in the used extents table, SYS.UET$. At the same time, it **update**s the entries in the free extents table, SYS.FET$. The SYS.UET$ table has one record for every extent in the database, and SYS.FET$ has one row for every free extent in the database. If you have a large number of extents in a table or index, then DDL commands that **update** SYS.UET$ and SYS.FET$ may impact the performance of your commands.

For example, consider a table that has 10,000 extents (either by itself or as a collection of partitions that together have 10,000 extents). When you drop that table, Oracle will need to perform 10,000 **update**s of SYS.UET$ (since the data in SYS.UET$ must always be consistent for everyone in the database). At the same time, Oracle must **update** SYS.FET$ and the other data dictionary tables used for object maintenance (for privileges, columns, etc.). SYS.UET$ is not tuned to support the drops of tables with thousands of extents. In a test environment, a **drop table** of a 5000 extent table took two minutes to complete. In the same environment, a **drop table** of a 10,000 extent table took ten minutes to complete. As more extents were added, the time required to drop the table grew exponentially worse.

> **NOTE**
> *Although the number of extents per segment is unlimited, a more practical extent limit for dictionary managed tablespaces is 10,000.*

When considering the impact of the number of extents on your DDL commands' performance, you should consider not only your tables but also the indexes, partitions, and index partitions that will be dropped along with the table. If you have a table with 100 partitions, and each of the partitions has 300 extents, and each of the partitions has a local index that in turn has 300 extents, then dropping the table will require dropping 60,000 extents—and that may cause performance problems. To resolve this problem, Oracle8i introduced locally managed tablespaces, in which the extent usage information is stored in a bitmap in the datafile header rather than in the data dictionary. Locally managed tablespaces are covered in more detail shortly.

The monitoring system provided in Chapter 6 checks the DBA_SEGMENTS data dictionary view to determine which segments have ten or more extents. A general query of the DBA_SEGMENTS view is shown in the following listing. The following query will retrieve the tablespace name, owner, segment name, and segment type for each segment in the database along with the segment's number of extents and blocks used.

```
select
        Tablespace_Name,    /*Tablespace name*/
        Owner,              /*Owner of the segment*/
        Segment_Name,       /*Name of the segment*/
        Segment_Type,       /*Type of segment (ex. TABLE, INDEX)*/
        Extents,            /*Number of extents in the segment*/
        Blocks,             /*Number of db blocks in the segment*/
        Bytes               /*Number of bytes in the segment*/
from DBA_SEGMENTS
/
```

Segment types include TABLE, TABLE PARTITION, INDEX, INDEX PARTITION, LOBINDEX, LOBSEGMENT, NESTED TABLE, CLUSTER, ROLLBACK, TEMPORARY, DEFERRED ROLLBACK, TYPE2 UNDO (new for Oracle9i), and CACHE. The DBA_ SEGMENTS view does not list the size of the individual extents in a segment. To see the size of each extent, query the DBA_EXTENTS view, as shown in the following listing:

```
select
        Tablespace_Name,    /*Tablespace name*/
        Owner,              /*Owner of the segment*/
        Segment_Name,       /*Name of the segment*/
        Segment_Type,       /*Type of segment (ex. TABLE, INDEX)*/
        Extent_ID,          /*Extent number in the segment*/
        Block_ID,           /*Starting block number for the extent*/
        Bytes,              /*Size of the extent, in bytes*/
        Blocks              /*Size of the extent, in Oracle blocks*/
  from DBA_EXTENTS
where Segment_Name = 'segment_name'
order by Extent_ID;
```

The query in the preceding listing selects the extent information for a single segment (identified via the **where** clause). It returns the storage information associated with the segment's extents, including the size and location of each data extent. A similar query shown later in this chapter is used when mapping the distribution of free extents and used extents in a tablespace.

If the table is an index-organized table, it may be rebuilt online via the **move** clause of the **alter table** command. If the table is a standard table, rebuilding it requires either using Export/Import or using the object rebuild options described in Chapter 5.

As noted in Chapter 11, the Export command has a COMPRESS flag. The COMPRESS flag will cause Export, when reading a table, to determine the total amount of space allocated to that table. It will then write to the export dump file a new **initial**

storage parameter—equivalent to the total of the allocated space—for the table. If
the table is then dropped, and Import is used to re-create it, then its data should all
fit in the new, larger initial extent.

Note that it is the *allocated,* not the *used,* space that is compressed. An empty
table with 300MB allocated to it in three 100MB extents will be compressed into a
single, empty 300MB extent. No space will be reclaimed. Also, the database will not
check to see if the new **initial** extent size is greater than the size of the largest datafile
for the tablespace. Since extents cannot span datafiles, attempting to create an extent
larger than a datafile will result in an error during import.

Evaluating Index Usage

As of Oracle9*i* you can enable monitoring of indexes to determine if they are being
used. If an index is not being used, you can drop it, saving space and improving
performance by eliminating unnecessary overhead during DML operations. The
number of unused indexes you can drop will reduce the number of indexes that
must be rebuilt when you rebuild a schema.

Because index monitoring is turned on or off at the system level, you should
turn this feature on or off when your database activity is lightest or when you start
your database. You must issue the command to turn index monitoring on or off on
an index-by-index basis; a schema-level command is not available. The following
listing shows the command to enable index monitoring for the EMPLOYEE_IDX index:

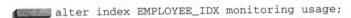
```
alter index EMPLOYEE_IDX monitoring usage;
```

To turn index usage monitoring off, issue the command:

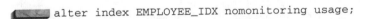
```
alter index EMPLOYEE_IDX nomonitoring usage;
```

> **NOTE**
> *When you enable index usage monitoring, you
> do so for your specific session and not for the
> entire database.*

To view the results of the monitoring session, use the V$OBJECT_USAGE view.
The view displays information about the index and table names, whether monitoring
is on, if the indexes are used, and the times when monitoring was started and/or
stopped. Each time you enable monitoring for usage, the view is reset for the
specified index and the previous usage information is cleared or reset. The view
information remains unchanged once you end monitoring of an index until you
either enable monitoring of the usage of that index again or drop the index. The
V$OBJECT_USAGE view is *dynamic*; that is, the contents displayed depend on

the identity and privileges of the user querying the view, but the view is based on a real data dictionary table so the contents are preserved and consistent even after a database crash.

Let's say that you have previously enabled monitoring on the indexes PK_EMPL and PK_DEP. In this example, monitoring is still enabled on the PK_DEP index but has been disabled on the PK_EMPL index. You can use the following query to see the results stored in the V$OBJECT_USAGE view:

```
select
        Index_Name,      /* The name of the index*/
        Table_Name,      /* The name of the table */
        Monitoring,      /* Whether enabled (YES/NO)*/
        Used,            /* Whether index is used (YES/NO)*/
        Start_Monitoring, /* Timestamp when monitoring began*/
        End_Monitoring   /* Timestamp when monitoring stopped*/
  from V$OBJECT_USAGE;

INDEX_NAME TABLE_NAME MON USE START_MONITORING     END_MONITORING
---------- ---------- --- --- ------------------   ------------------
PK_DEP     DEPARTMENT YES YES 08/21/2001 14:36:08
PK_EMPL    EMPLOYEES  NO  NO  08/21/2001 14:35:55 08/21/2001 14:38:10
```

As you can see, during the period of time that monitoring has been enabled, the PK_DEP index has been used but the PK_EMPL index has not.

NOTE
You will only be able to see the information stored in V$OBJECT_USAGE from the session in which you enable monitoring. If you enable index usage monitoring from the HR schema, you will not be able to see the results from the SYSTEM schema.

Locally Managed Tablespaces

As of Oracle8i, locally managed tablespaces are available to handle extent management within the tablespaces themselves. In locally managed tablespaces, the tablespace manages its own space by maintaining a bitmap in each datafile of the free and used blocks or sets of blocks in the datafile. Each time an extent is allocated or freed for reuse, Oracle **update**s the bitmap to show the new status.

When you use locally managed tablespaces, the dictionary is not **update**d and rollback activity is not generated. Locally managed tablespaces automatically track adjacent free space, so there is no need to coalesce extents. Within a locally managed tablespace, all extents can have the same size, or the system can automatically determine the size of extents.

To use local space management, you specify the **local** option for the **extent management** clause in the **create tablespace** command (as of Oracle9i, this is the default type of extent management). An example of the **create tablespace** command declaring a locally managed tablespace is shown here:

```
create tablespace CODES_TABLES
datafile '/u01/oracle/VLDB/codes_tables.dbf'
size 10M
extent management local uniform size 256K;
```

Assuming that the block size for the database in which this tablespace is created is 8KB, in this example, the tablespace is created with the extent management declared as **local** and with a uniform size of 256KB. Each bit in the bitmap describes 32 blocks (256/8). If the **uniform size** clause is omitted, the default is **autoallocate**. The default **size** for **uniform** is 1MB.

> **NOTE**
> *If you specify **local** in a **create tablespace** command, you cannot specify a **default storage** clause, **minextents**, or **temporary**. If you use the **create temporary tablespace** command to create the tablespace, you must specify **extent_management local**.*

As your database objects grow in extents, locally managed tablespaces become more important. As noted previously, DDL space management operations on tables with many thousands of extents may perform poorly due to the data dictionary management involved. If you use locally managed tablespaces, that performance penalty is significantly reduced.

Defragmentation of Free Extents

As noted in Chapter 4, a free extent in a tablespace is a collection of contiguous free blocks in the tablespace. When a segment is dropped, its extents are deallocated and marked as free. However, these free extents are not always recombined with neighboring free extents; the barriers between these free extents may be maintained.

> **NOTE**
> *To avoid most space fragmentation issues, use locally managed tablespaces in Oracle8i and Oracle9i databases.*

The SMON background process periodically coalesces neighboring free extents if the default **pctincrease** setting for the tablespace is nonzero. If the default **pctincrease** setting for a tablespace is zero, then the free space in the tablespace will not be coalesced automatically by the database. You can use the **coalesce** option of the **alter tablespace** command to force neighboring free extents to be coalesced, regardless of the default **pctincrease** setting for the tablespace.

NOTE
*The SMON background process only coalesces tablespaces whose default **pctincrease** value is nonzero. A **pctincrease** of 1 will force SMON to **coalesce** the adjacent free space in a tablespace but will only perform eight coalesces at a time for each tablespace. For best space usage, use locally managed tablespaces so that the tablespace never needs to be coalesced.*

Not forcing the coalescing of free extents affects the allocation of space within the tablespace during the next space request (such as by the creation or expansion of a table). In its quest for a large enough free extent, the database will not merge contiguous free extents unless there is no other alternative; thus, the large free extent at the rear of the tablespace tends to be used, while the smaller free extents toward the front of the tablespace are relatively unused, becoming "speed bumps" in the tablespace because they are not, by themselves, of adequate size to be of use. As this usage pattern progresses, the database thus drifts further and further from its ideal space allocation. Free space fragmentation is particularly prevalent in environments in which database tables and indexes are frequently dropped and re-created in dictionary managed tablespaces, especially if their storage parameters are changed in the process. Using locally managed tablespaces totally removes this problem.

You can force the database to recombine the contiguous free extents, thus emulating the SMON functionality. Coalescing the free extents will increase the likelihood of the free extents near the front of the file being reused, thus preserving the free space near the rear of the tablespace file. As a result, new requests for extents are more likely to meet with success.

Before attempting to defragment a tablespace, you should first generate a mapping of space usage in the tablespace. The following script will show all space marked as free or used by database objects. This is useful to show the distribution and size of the free extents and to determine which database objects are barriers between free extents. This script is most useful for dictionary managed tablespaces, as locally managed tablespaces will not exhibit the space allocation problems illustrated in the following example.

```
rem
rem    file: mapper.sql
rem    Parameters: the tablespace name being mapped
rem
rem    Sample invocation:
rem    @mapper DEMODATA
rem
rem    This script generates a mapping of the space usage
rem    (free space vs used) in a tablespace. It graphically
rem    shows segment and free space fragmentation.
rem
set pagesize 60 linesize 132 verify off
column file_id heading "File|Id"

select
       'free space' Owner,      /*"owner" of free space*/
       '  '  Object,             /*blank object name*/
       File_ID,                  /*file ID for the extent header*/
       Block_ID,                 /*block ID for the extent header*/
       Blocks                    /*length of the extent, in blocks*/
  from DBA_FREE_SPACE
where Tablespace_Name = UPPER('&&1')
union
select
       SUBSTR(Owner,1,20),        /*owner name (first 20 chars)*/
       SUBSTR(Segment_Name,1,32),  /*segment name*/
       File_ID,                    /*file ID for extent header*/
       Block_ID,                   /*block ID for block header*/
       Blocks                      /*length of the extent in blocks*/
  from DBA_EXTENTS
where Tablespace_Name = UPPER('&&1')
order by 3,4

spool &&1._map.lst
/
spool off
undefine 1
```

Sample output from this mapping query for a dictionary managed tablespace is shown in the following listing. The query output displays the owner and segment name for each extent in the tablespace. If the extent is a free extent, then the owner is listed as "free space," and the segment name (the Object column) is left blank.

```
File
Owner                OBJECT                Id  BLOCK_ID   Blocks
------------------   ------------------   ---  --------   -------
OPS$CC1              FILES                  6         2        20
OPS$CC1              SPACES                 6        22        20
OPS$CC1              EXTENTS                6        42        20
OPS$CC1              FILES                  6        62        20
free space                                  6        82         5
free space                                  6        87         5
free space                                  6        92         5
OPS$CC1              SPACES                 6        97        20
OPS$CC1              EXTENTS                6       117        20
free space                                  6       137        10
OPS$CC1              FILES                  6       147        20
free space                                  6       167    14,833
```

The output in the preceding listing shows 12 rows. Five of them are of free space extents, and seven are from data segments. The first three free space extents are contiguous. Following two more data extents, there is another free space extent. Because it is separated from the other free extents in the tablespace, the fourth free extent cannot be combined with any of the other free extents unless the tablespace is defragmented.

Combining the Free Extents

If a tablespace would benefit from having its free extents coalesced, you should either manually coalesce the extents or enable the SMON process to coalesce the extents.

To enable the SMON process to coalesce the extents, you should set the default **pctincrease** value for the tablespace to a nonzero value. In the following listing, the default storage for the DEMONDX tablespace is altered to use a **pctincrease** of 1.

```
alter tablespace DEMONDX
default storage (pctincrease 1);
```

If an object is created in the DEMONDX without a specified **pctincrease** value, then the object will use the default **pctincrease** (50 percent) value for the tablespace. In general, low **pctincrease** values accurately reflect the normal linear growth in the number of rows in the database. Therefore, the lowest allowable nonzero value (1) was used for the **pctincrease** value. You can override the default via the **storage** clause of the object you create.

To manually coalesce the free extents of the tablespace, use the **coalesce** option of the **alter tablespace** command.

```
alter tablespace DEMONDX coalesce;
```

The neighboring free extents will then be coalesced and a maximum of eight coalesces will take place, so you may have to run this statement several times to coalesce all of the free extents within a tablespace. You can reexecute the mapper.sql script shown earlier in this chapter to see the new structure of used and free extents in the tablespace. If there are many free extents located between data extents, then you will need to re-create the tablespace (for example, by exporting and importing its data) in order to be able to coalesce the free extents. If possible, use locally managed tablespaces to avoid the need for this type of defragmentation.

Identifying Chained Rows

When a data segment is created, a **pctfree** value is specified. The **pctfree** parameter tells the database how much space should be kept free in each data block. The free space is used when rows that are already stored in the data block extend in length via **update**s.

If a row no longer completely fits in a single data block because of an **update**, then that row may be moved or migrated to another data block, or the row may be *chained* to another block. If you are storing rows whose length is greater than the Oracle block size, then you will automatically have chaining, and it cannot be eliminated. Also, tables containing over 255 columns will always have chained rows. Chaining affects performance because it requires Oracle to look in multiple physical locations for data from the same logical row. By eliminating unnecessary chaining, you reduce the number of physical reads needed to return data from a datafile.

You can avoid migration by setting the proper value for **pctfree** during creation of data segments. For instructions for setting this value, see the "Estimating the Proper **pctfree**" section of Chapter 5.

You can use the **analyze** command to collect statistics about database objects. The cost-based optimizer can use these statistics to determine the best execution path to use. The **analyze** command has an option that detects and records chained rows in tables. Its syntax is

```
analyze table TABLE_NAME list chained rows into CHAINED_ROWS;
```

The **analyze** command will put the output from this operation into a table called CHAINED_ROWS in your local schema. The SQL to create the CHAINED_ROWS table is in a file named utlchain.sql, in the /rdbms/admin subdirectory under your Oracle software home directory. The following query will select the most significant columns from the CHAINED_ROWS table:

```
select
        Owner_Name,       /*Owner of the data segment*/
        Table_Name,       /*Name of the table with the chained rows*/
        Cluster_Name,     /*Name of the cluster, if it is clustered*/
        Head_RowID        /*Rowid of the first part of the row*/
from CHAINED_ROWS;
```

The output will show the RowIDs for all chained rows, allowing you to quickly see how many of the rows in the table are chained. If chaining is prevalent in a table, then that table should be rebuilt with a higher value for **pctfree**.

You can see the impact of row chaining by querying V$SYSSTAT. The V$SYSSTAT entry for the "table fetch continued row" statistic will be incremented each time Oracle selects data from a chained row. This statistic will also be incremented when Oracle selects data from a *spanned row*—a row that is chained because it is greater than a block in length. Tables with LONG, BLOB, CLOB, and NCLOB datatypes are likely to have spanned rows.

In addition to chaining rows, Oracle will occasionally move rows. If a row exceeds the space available to its block, the rows may be **insert**ed into a different block. The process of moving a row from one block to another is called *row migration*, and the moved row is called a *migrated row*. During row migration, Oracle has to dynamically manage space in multiple blocks and access the free list (the list of blocks available for **insert**s). A migrated row appears as a chained row in the chained rows table when the table is analyzed to list chained rows. Chained rows impact the performance of your transactions.

Increasing the Oracle Block Size

The effect of increasing the database block size is significant. In most environments, at least four block sizes are supported—for example, 2KB, 4KB, 8KB, and 16KB. Most of the installation routines are set to use 8KB block size. However, using the next higher value for the block size may improve the performance of query-intensive operations by up to 50 percent.

The performance benefit has few costs. Since there will be more rows per database block, there is a greater likelihood of block-level contention during data manipulation commands. To address the contention problems, increase the settings for **freelists**, **maxtrans**, and **initrans** at the table and index level. In general, setting **freelists** to greater than 4 will not yield much additional benefit. The **initrans** and **maxtrans** settings should reflect the number of concurrent transactions expected within a block.

To increase the database block size, the entire database must be rebuilt, and all of the old database files have to be **delete**d. The new files can be created in the same location as the old files, with the same size, but will be managed more efficiently by the database. The performance savings comes from the way that Oracle manages the block header information. More space is used by data, improving the ability of multiple users to access the same block of data in memory. Doubling the size of the Oracle blocks has little effect on the block header; thus, a smaller percentage of space is used to store block header information. For a Windows NT environment, a 4KB block size aligns nicely with the NTFS and is recommended.

The database block size is set during creation, via the DB_BLOCK_SIZE parameter. The DB_BLOCK_SIZE parameter may be specified in the initialization parameter file. As of Oracle9i, you can specify the block size at the tablespace level.

Be careful when setting DB_BLOCK_SIZE if you are still using the DB_BLOCK_BUFFERS parameter that is required for databases prior to Oracle9i. DB_BLOCK_BUFFERS, deprecated in Oracle9i, sets the number of blocks assigned to the data block buffer cache. As an alternative, Oracle9i databases should use the DB_CACHE_SIZE initialization parameter.

Using Index-Organized Tables

An index-organized table (IOT) is an index in which an entire row is stored, not just the key values for the row. Instead of storing a RowID for the row, the primary key for the row is treated as the logical identifier for the row. Rows in IOTs do not have RowIDs.

Within the IOT, the rows are stored sorted by their primary key values. Thus, any range query that is based on the primary key may benefit, since the rows are stored near each other (see the "Tuning SQL" section earlier in this chapter for the steps involved in ordering the data within normal tables). Additionally, any equivalence query based on the primary key may benefit, since the table's data is all stored in the index. In the traditional table/index combination, an index-based access requires an index access followed by a table access. In an IOT, only the IOT is accessed; there is no companion index.

However, the performance gains from a single index access in place of a normal index/table combination access may be minimal—any index-based access should be fast. To help improve performance further, index-organized tables offer additional features:

- **An overflow area** By setting the **pctthreshold** parameter when the IOT is created, you can store the primary key data apart from the row data. If the row's data exceeds the threshold of available space in the block, then it will dynamically be moved to an overflow area. You can designate the overflow area to be in a separate tablespace, improving your ability to distribute the I/O associated with the table.

- **Secondary indexes** As of Oracle8i, you can create secondary indexes on the IOT. Oracle will use the primary key values as the logical RowID for each row.

- **Key compression** If the same data is repeated in the same columns of multiple rows, then you can configure the IOT to store the repeated data once. Via key compression, Oracle creates a one-to-many relationship between the unique column values and those that are repeated.

- **Reduced storage requirements** In a traditional table/index combination, the same key values are stored in two places. In an IOT, they are stored once, reducing the storage requirements.

To create an IOT, use the **organization index** clause of the **create table** command. You must specify a primary key when creating an IOT. Within an IOT, you can drop columns or mark them as inactive via the **set unused** clause of the **alter table** command. See Chapter 5 for details concerning column management.

Tuning Issues for Index-Organized Tables
Like indexes, IOTs may become internally fragmented over time as values are **insert**ed, **update**d, and **delete**d. In the following example, the EMPLOYEE_IOT table is rebuilt, along with its overflow area:

```
alter table EMPLOYEE_IOT
  move tablespace DATA
overflow tablespace DATA_OVERFLOW;
```

You should avoid storing long rows of data in IOTs. In general, you should avoid using an IOT if the data is longer than 75 percent of the database block size. If the database block size is 4KB, and your rows will exceed 3KB in length, you should investigate the use of normal tables and indexes instead of IOTs. The longer the rows are, and the more transactions are performed against the IOT, the more frequently it will need to be rebuilt.

As noted earlier in this chapter, indexes impact data load rates. For best results, the primary key index of an index-organized table should be loaded with sequential values to minimize the costs of index management. Load rates for index-organized tables tend to be lower than those for normal tables.

Tuning Data Manipulation
There are several data manipulation tasks—usually involving manipulation of large quantities of data—that may involve the DBA. You have several options when loading and deleting large volumes of data, as described in the following sections.

You can improve the performance of database writes by creating multiple DBWR (Database Writer) processes. Creating multiple DBWR processes will prevent access requests against multiple disks from causing performance bottlenecks. The number of DBWR processes that should be created for an instance is set via the DB_WRITER_ PROCESSES parameter in the database's initialization parameter file. If you use a single DBWR process, you can create multiple I/O slaves for it via the DBWR_IO_SLAVES parameter. Use DB_WRITER_PROCESSES if your system supports ASYNC I/O and DBWR_IO_SLAVES if it does not.

In addition to creating I/O slaves for DBWR, you can create I/O slaves for the LGWR and ARCH processes in Oracle8 only. The LGWR_IO_SLAVES and ARCH_IO_ SLAVES parameters are desupported as of Oracle8i and are no longer used. You can use the LOG_ARCHIVE_MAX_PROCESSES initialization parameter starting in Oracle8i to set the number of ARCH processes initiated.

Bulk Inserts: Using the SQL*Loader Direct Path Option

When used in the Conventional Path mode, SQL*Loader reads a set of records from a file, generates **insert** commands, and passes them to the Oracle kernel. Oracle then finds places for those records in free blocks in the table and **update**s any associated indexes.

In Direct Path mode, SQL*Loader creates formatted data blocks within the server process and writes them directly to the datafiles. This requires occasional checks with the database to get new locations for data blocks, but no other I/O with the database kernel is required. The result is a data load process that is dramatically faster than Conventional Path mode.

If the table is indexed, then the indexes will be placed in DIRECT PATH state during the load. After the load is complete, the new keys (index column values) will be sorted and merged with the existing keys in the index. To maintain the temporary set of keys, the load will create a temporary index segment that is at least as large as the largest index on the table. The space requirements for this can be minimized by presorting the index and using the SORTED INDEXES clause in the SQL*Loader control file.

To use the Direct Path option, a series of views must be created in the database. These views are created during database creation via the script catldr.sql, located in $ORACLE_HOME/rdbms/admin.

To minimize the amount of dynamic space allocation necessary during the load, the data segment that you are loading into should already be created, with all of the space it will need previously allocated. You should also presort the data on the columns of the largest index in the table. Sorting the data and leaving the indexes on the table during a Direct Path load will usually yield better performance than if you were to drop the indexes before the load and then re-create them after it completed.

To take advantage of the Direct Path option, the table cannot be clustered, and there can be no other active transactions against it. During the load, only NOT NULL, UNIQUE, and PRIMARY KEY constraints will be enforced; after the load has completed, the CHECK and FOREIGN KEY constraints can be automatically reenabled. To force this to occur, use the

```
REENABLE DISABLED_CONSTRAINTS
```

clause in the SQL*Loader control file.

The only exception to this reenabling process is that table insert triggers, when reenabled, are not executed for each of the new rows in the table. A separate process must manually perform whatever commands were to have been performed by this type of trigger.

The SQL*Loader Direct Path loading option provides significant performance improvements over the SQL*Loader Conventional Path loader in loading data into Oracle tables by bypassing SQL processing, buffer cache management, and unnecessary reads for the data blocks. The Parallel Data Loading option of SQL*Loader allows multiple loading processes to work on loading the same table, utilizing spare resources on the system, and thereby reducing the overall elapsed times for loading. Given enough CPU and I/O resources, this can significantly reduce the overall loading times.

To use Parallel Data Loading, start multiple SQL*Loader sessions using the **parallel** keyword (otherwise, SQL*Loader puts an exclusive lock on the table). Each session is an independent session requiring its own control file. The following listing shows three separate Direct Path loads, all using the PARALLEL=TRUE parameter on the command line:

```
sqlload USERID=ME/PASS CONTROL=PART1.CTL DIRECT=TRUE PARALLEL=TRUE
sqlload USERID=ME/PASS CONTROL=PART2.CTL DIRECT=TRUE PARALLEL=TRUE
sqlload USERID=ME/PASS CONTROL=PART3.CTL DIRECT=TRUE PARALLEL=TRUE
```

Each session creates its own log, bad, and discard files (part1.log, part2.log, part3.log, part1.bad, part2.bad, etc.) by default. Since you have multiple sessions loading data into the same table, only the APPEND option is allowed for Parallel Data Loading. The SQL*Loader REPLACE, TRUNCATE, and INSERT options are not allowed for Parallel Data Loading. If you need to **delete** the table's data before starting the load, you must manually **delete** the data (via **delete** or **truncate** commands). You cannot use SQL*Loader to **delete** the records automatically if you are using Parallel Data Loading.

NOTE
*If you use Parallel Data Loading, indexes are not maintained by the SQL*Loader session. Before starting the loading process, you must drop all indexes on the table and disable all of its PRIMARY KEY and UNIQUE constraints. After the loads complete, you can re-create the table's indexes.*

In serial Direct Path Loading (PARALLEL=FALSE), SQL*Loader loads data into extents in the table. If the load process fails before the load completes, some data could be **commit**ted to the table prior to the process failure. In Parallel Data Loading, each load process creates temporary segments for loading the data. The temporary segments are later merged with the table. If a Parallel Data Load process fails before the load completes, the temporary segments will not have been merged with the table. If the temporary segments have not been merged with the table being loaded, then no data from the load will have been **commit**ted to the table.

You can use the SQL*Loader FILE parameter to direct each data loading session to a different datafile. By directing each loading session to its own datafile, you can balance the I/O load of the loading processes. Data loading is very I/O intensive and must be distributed across multiple disks for parallel loading to achieve significant performance improvements over serial loading.

After a Parallel Data Load, each session may attempt to reenable the table's constraints. As long as at least one load session is still under way, attempting to reenable the constraints will fail. The final loading session to complete should attempt to reenable the constraints, and should succeed. You should check the status of your constraints after the load completes. If the table being loaded has PRIMARY KEY and UNIQUE constraints, you can create the associated indexes in parallel prior to enabling the constraints.

Bulk Inserts: Common Traps and Successful Tricks

If your data is not being inserted from a flat file, SQL*Loader will not be a useful solution. For example, if you need to move a large set of data from one table to another, you will likely want to avoid having to write the data to a flat file and then read it back into the database. The fastest way to move data in your database is to move it from one table to another without going out to the operating system.

When moving data from one table to another, there are four common methods for improving the performance of the data migration:

- Tuning the structures—removing indexes and triggers

- Disabling constraints during the data migration

- Using hints and options to improve the transaction performance

- Isolating the rollback segments for the large transaction

The first of the four tips, tuning the structures, involves disabling any triggers or indexes that are on the table into which data is being loaded. For example, if you have a row-level trigger on the target table, that trigger will be executed for every row **insert**ed into the table. If possible, disable the triggers prior to the data load. If the trigger should be executed for every **insert**ed row, then you may be able to do a bulk operation once the rows have been **insert**ed, rather than a repeated operation during each **insert**. If properly tuned, the bulk operation will complete faster than the repeated trigger executions. You will need to be sure that the bulk operations execute for all rows that have not already been processed by the triggers.

In addition to disabling triggers, you should drop the indexes on the target table prior to starting the data load. If the indexes are left on the table, Oracle will dynamically manage the indexes as each row is **insert**ed. Rather than continuously manage the index, drop it prior to the start of the load and re-create it when the load has completed.

NOTE
*Dropping indexes and disabling triggers resolves
most of the performance problems associated with
large table-to-table data migration efforts.*

In addition to disabling indexes, you should consider disabling constraints on the table. If the source data is already in a table in the database, you can check that data for its adherence to your constraints (such as foreign keys or CHECK constraints) prior to loading it into your target table. Once the data has been loaded, reenable the constraints.

If none of those options gives you adequate performance, you should investigate the options Oracle has introduced for data migration tuning. Those options include the following:

- **The APPEND hint for insert commands**   Like the Direct Path Loader, the APPEND hint loads blocks of data into a table, starting at the high-water mark for the table (see Chapter 4). Use of the APPEND hint may increase your space usage.

- **The nologging option**   If you are performing a **create table as select** command, use the **nologging** option to avoid writing to the redo logs during the operation.

- **The parallel options**   The Parallel Query Options use multiple processes to accomplish a single task. For a **create table as select**, you can parallelize both the **create table** portion and the query. If you use the parallel options, you should also use the **nologging** option; otherwise the parallel operations will have to wait due to serialized writes to the online redo log files.

Before using any of these three advanced options, you should first investigate the target table's structures to make sure you have avoided the common traps cited earlier in this section.

The fourth tip for improving performance, isolating the rollback segment activity for the transaction, may require the creation of a new tablespace. For example, you can create a new tablespace for rollback segments and create one or more large rollback segments within it. The datafiles associated with that tablespace should be placed on disks that are isolated from the rest of the database. Create one rollback segment for each of the concurrent data migration transactions. You can then use the **set transaction use rollback segment** command to force the transaction to use the new rollback segment. If you cannot use this command, you may need to take the rest of the rollback segments offline before starting the large data migration transactions. To minimize the size of the rollback segments required, perform **commit**s frequently during the transaction.

You can also use programming logic to force **insert**s to be processed in arrays rather than as an entire set. For example, COBOL and C support array **insert**s, reducing the size of the transactions required to process a large set of data. See Chapter 15 for additional tips on supporting large transactions.

Bulk Deletes: The truncate Command

Occasionally, users attempt to **delete** all of the records from a table at once. When they encounter errors during this process, they complain that the rollback segments are too small, when in fact their transaction is too large.

A second problem occurs once the records have all been **delete**d. Even though the segment no longer has any records in it, it still maintains all of the space that was allocated to it. Thus, deleting all those records saved you not a single byte of allocated space.

The **truncate** command resolves both of these problems. It is a DDL command, not a DML command, *so it cannot be rolled back*. Once you have used the **truncate** command on a table, its records are gone, and none of its **delete** triggers are executed in the process. However, the table retains all of its dependent objects, such as grants, indexes, and constraints.

The **truncate** command is the fastest way to **delete** large volumes of data. Since it will **delete** all of the records in a table, this may force you to alter your application design so that no protected records are stored in the same table as the records to be **delete**d. If you use partitions, you can **truncate** one partition of a table without affecting the rest of the table's partitions (see Chapter 15).

A sample **truncate** command for a table is shown in the following listing:

```
truncate table EMPLOYEE drop storage;
```

The preceding example, in which the EMPLOYEE table's records are **delete**d, shows a powerful feature of **truncate**. The **drop storage** clause is used to deallocate the non-**initial** space from the table (this is the default option). Thus, you can **delete** all of a table's rows, and reclaim all but its initial extent's allocated space, without dropping the table.

The **truncate** command also works for clusters. In the next example, the **reuse storage** option is used to leave all allocated space empty within the segment that acquired it:

```
truncate cluster EMP_DEPT reuse storage;
```

When this example command is executed, all of the records in the EMP_DEPT cluster will be instantly **delete**d.

To **truncate** partitions, you need to know the name of the partition. In the following example, the partition named PART3 of the EMPLOYEE table is **truncate**d via the **alter table** command:

```
alter table EMPLOYEE
truncate partition PART3
drop storage;
```

The rest of the partitions of the EMPLOYEE table will be unaffected by the truncation of the PART3 partition. See Chapter 15 for details on creating and managing partitions.

As an alternative, you can create a PL/SQL program that uses dynamic SQL to divide a large **delete** operation into multiple smaller transactions. See Chapter 15 for an example of a program that forces **commit**s during a large **delete**.

Partitions

You can use partitions to isolate data physically. For example, you can store the data from one department in a separate partition of the EMPLOYEE table. If you perform a bulk data load or deletion on the table, you can customize the partitions to tune the data manipulation operation. For example:

■ You can **truncate** a partition and its indexes without affecting the rest of the table.

■ You can drop a partition, via the **drop partition** clause of the **alter table** command.

■ You can drop a partition's local index.

■ You can set a partition to **nologging**, reducing the impact of large inserts.

From a performance perspective, the chief advantage of partitions lies in their ability to be managed apart from the rest of the table. For example, being able to **truncate** a partition enables you to **delete** a large amount of data from a table (but not all of the table's data) without generating any redo information. In the short term, the beneficiary of this performance improvement is the DBA; in the longer term, the entire enterprise benefits from the improved availability of the data. See Chapter 15 for details on implementing partitions and subpartitions.

Tuning Physical Storage

The physical I/O for the databases must be evenly distributed and handled correctly. Chapter 4 describes a process for planning file distribution across disks. Planning file distribution involves understanding the interactions of the DBWR, LGWR, and ARCH background processes. A means of verifying the adequacy of the final layouts is also provided in Chapter 4.

In addition to that level of physical storage tuning, several other factors should be considered. The following sections address factors that are external to the database but may have a profound impact on its ability to access data quickly.

Using Raw Devices

Raw devices are available with some UNIX operating systems. When they are used, the DBWR process bypasses the UNIX buffer cache and eliminates the file system overhead. For I/O-intensive applications, the use of raw devices may result in a performance improvement of around 2 percent over traditional file systems. Recent file system enhancements have largely overcome this performance difference, and the overhead of maintaining raw devices is commonly believed to outweigh any performance benefit.

Raw devices cannot be managed with the same commands as file systems. For example, the **tar** command cannot be used to back up individual files; instead, the **dd** command must be used. This is a much less flexible command to use and limits your recovery capabilities. Raw devices are most commonly used in environments supporting Oracle Real Application Clusters (previously known as Oracle Parallel Server), but with advances in disk access technologies, those clustered environments may not require raw devices in the very near future.

> **NOTE**
> *Oracle files should not reside on the same physical devices as non-Oracle files, particularly if you use raw devices. Mixing an active UNIX file system with an active Oracle raw device will cause I/O performance problems.*

Using RAID and Mirroring

See Chapter 4 for details concerning the use of RAID and mirroring technologies for performance enhancement. In general, RAID 0+1 will yield the best performance, while RAID-5 is the cheapest to implement. The performance benefit derived from a RAID implementation is directly related to the manner in which the system is implemented.

Tuning Logical Storage

From a logical standpoint, like objects should be stored together. As discussed in Chapter 3, objects should be grouped based on their space usage and user interaction characteristics. Based on these groupings, tablespaces should be created that cater to specific types of objects. See Chapter 3 for suggested distributions of objects across tablespaces. For information on detecting and managing contention for rollback segments, see Chapter 7.

As described in Chapter 3, materialized views can be used to aggregate data and improve query performance. A materialized view is identical in structure to a snapshot—it is a physical table that holds data that would usually be read via a view. When you create a materialized view, you specify the view's base query as well as a schedule for the refreshes of its data. You can then index the materialized view to enhance the performance of queries against it. As a result, you can provide data to your users in the format they need, indexed appropriately. For details on the implementation of materialized views, see Chapter 15.

Reducing Network Traffic

As databases and the applications that use them become more distributed, the network that supports the servers may become a bottleneck in the process of delivering data to the user. Since DBAs typically have little control over the network management, it is important to use the database's capabilities to reduce the number of network packets that are required for the data to be delivered. Reducing network traffic will reduce your reliance on the network, and thus eliminate a potential cause of performance problems.

Replication of Data

As described in Chapter 2 and Part III of this book, you can manipulate and query data from remote databases. However, it is not desirable to have large volumes of data constantly sent from one database to another. To reduce the amount of data being sent across the network, different data replication options should be considered.

In a purely distributed environment, each data element exists in one place, as shown in Figure 8-1. When data is required, it is accessed from remote databases via database links. In the example shown in Figure 8-1, the EMPLOYEE data is queried from the MASTER1 database, and the DEPT data is queried from the REMOTE1 database. Both databases are accessible via database links created within the REMOTE2 database.

This purist approach (having data stored in only one place) is similar to implementing an application in third normal form, and as stated earlier in this chapter, that approach will not support any major production application. Modifying the

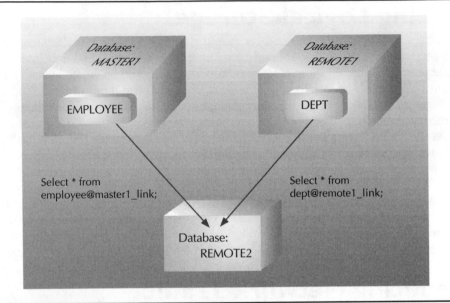

FIGURE 8-1. *Sample distributed environment*

application's tables to improve data retrieval performance involves denormalizing data. The denormalization process deliberately stores redundant data in order to shorten users' access paths to the data.

In a distributed environment, replicating data accomplishes this goal. Rather than force queries to cross the network to resolve user requests, selected data from remote servers is replicated to the local server. This can be accomplished via a number of means, as described in the following sections.

Using the copy Command to Replicate Data

In the first option, the data can be periodically copied to the local server. This is best accomplished via the SQL*Plus **copy** command, as described in Part III. The **copy** command allows selected columns and rows to be replicated to each server. This option is illustrated in Figure 8-2.

For example, the remote server may have a table called EMPLOYEE. The local server would be able to replicate the data that it needs by using the **copy** command to select records from the remote EMPLOYEE table. You can use the **copy** command to store those selected records in a table in the local database. The **copy** command includes a query clause; thus, it is possible to return only those rows that meet the specified criteria.

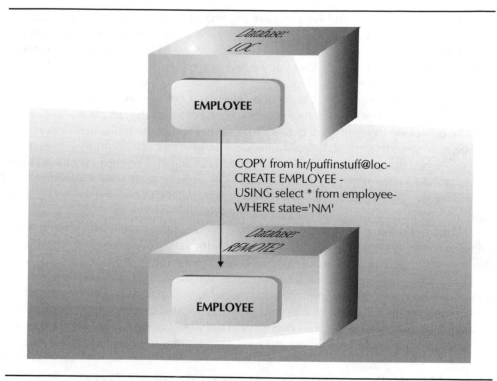

FIGURE 8-2. *Data replication using the* **copy** *command*

In this example, a portion of the EMPLOYEE table is copied down from the headquarters database to a local database. A **where** clause is used to restrict which records are selected.

```
set copycommit 1
set arraysize 1000
copy from HR/PUFFINSTUFF@loc -
create EMPLOYEE -
using -
select * from EMPLOYEE -
where State = 'NM'
```

The **copy from** clause in this example specifies the name of the remote database. In this case, the query is told to use the database identified by the service name LOC. During the connection, a session should be started by using the hr account, with the password puffinstuff.

The **set copycommit** and **set arraysize** commands specify the size of the data array. Setting the array size allows the DBA to force the database to **commit** during the data copy, thus reducing the size of the transactions to be supported. For more details on this capability and other **copy** options, see Part III.

As soon as the data is stored locally, it is accessible to the local users. They can thus query the data without traversing the network; a network access is performed during the **copy** instead of separate network accesses for each query.

The downside to replicating data in this manner is that the replicated data is out of date as soon as it is created. Replicating data for performance purposes is thus most effective when the source data is very infrequently changed. The **copy** command must be performed frequently enough so that the local tables contain useful, sufficiently accurate data. The **replace** option of the **copy** command can be used to replace the contents of the local tables during subsequent **copy**s.

Although the local table may be updatable, none of the changes made to it will be reflected in the source table. Thus, this scenario is only effective for improving the performance of query operations. If you need to be able to **update** the local data and have those changes sent back to the master database, then you will need to use some of the advanced replication options available within Oracle. Oracle supports multimaster configurations as well as read-only and updatable materialized views. The following section provides a brief overview of the use of materialized views from a performance standpoint; for a more detailed explanation, see Part III of this book.

Using Materialized Views/Snapshots to Replicate Data

Oracle's distributed capabilities offer means of managing the data replication within a database. Materialized views, known in previous versions as snapshots, replicate data from a master source to multiple targets. Oracle provides tools for refreshing the data and updating the targets at specified time intervals. A distributed environment option is illustrated in Figure 8-3.

Materialized views may be read-only or updatable. The management issues for materialized views are covered in Chapters 15 and 16; in this section, you will see their performance-tuning aspects.

Before creating a materialized view, a database link to the source database should first be created. The following example creates a private database link called HR_LINK, using the LOC service name:

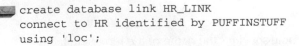

```
create database link HR_LINK
connect to HR identified by PUFFINSTUFF
using 'loc';
```

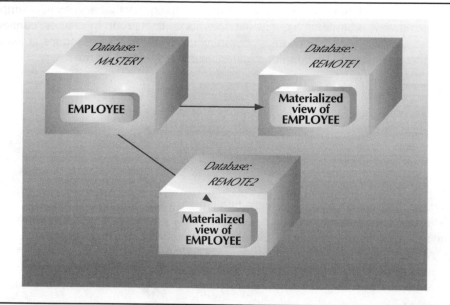

FIGURE 8-3. *Data replication using materialized views*

The **create database link** command, as shown in this example, has several parameters:

- The name of the link (HR_LINK, in this example).

- The account to connect to.

- The service name of the remote database (as found in the tnsnames.ora file for the server). In this case, the service name is LOC.

For more information on this command, see the entry for the **create database link** command in Appendix A.

There are two styles of materialized views available: *simple* and *complex*. The proper type to use for your environment depends on the amount of replicated data and the manner in which it is queried. The type of materialized views used affects which data-refresh options are available.

The type of materialized view is determined by the query that defines it. A simple materialized view is based on a query that does not contain **group by** clauses, **connect by** clauses, joins, or set operations. A complex materialized view contains at least one of these options. For example, a materialized view based on the query

```
select * from EMPLOYEE@HR_LINK;
```

would be simple, while one based on the query

```
select DEPT, MAX(Salary)
   from EMPLOYEE@HR_LINK
 group by DEPT;
```

would be complex because it uses grouping functions.

The syntax used to create the materialized view on the local server is shown in the following listing. In this example, the materialized view is given a name (LOCAL_EMP), and its storage parameters are specified. Its base query is given, as well as its refresh interval. In this case, the materialized view is told to immediately retrieve the master data, then to perform the refresh operation again in seven days (SysDate+7).

```
create materialized view LOCAL_EMP
pctfree 5
tablespace data_2
storage (initial 100K next 100K pctincrease 0)
refresh fast
      start with SysDate
      next SysDate+7
as select * from EMPLOYEE@HR_LINK;
```

The **refresh fast** clause tells the database to use a materialized view log to refresh the local materialized view. The ability to use materialized view logs during refreshes is only available with simple materialized views. When a materialized view log is used, only the changes to the master table are sent to the targets. If you use a complex materialized view, then the **refresh complete** clause must be used in place of the **refresh fast** clause. In a complete refresh, the refresh completely replaces the existing data in the materialized view's underlying table.

Materialized view logs must be created in the master database, via the **create materialized view log** command. An example of the **create materialized view log** command is shown in the following listing:

```
create materialized view log on EMPLOYEE
tablespace DATA
storage (initial 10K next 10K pctincrease 0);
```

The materialized view log must be created in the same schema as the master table.

You can use simple materialized views with materialized view logs to reduce the amount of network traffic involved in maintaining the replicated data. Since only the changes to the data will be sent via a materialized view log, the maintenance of simple materialized views should use fewer network resources than complex materialized views require, particularly if the master tables are large, fairly static tables. If the master tables are not static, then the volume of transactions sent via the materialized view log may not be any less than would be sent to perform a complete refresh.

Replication plays a part in your application design as well. If your data access paths require joining information from multiple remote tables, then you have two choices, as shown in Figure 8-4. The first option—see Figure 8-4a—is to create multiple simple materialized views and then perform the join query on the local server. The second option—see Figure 8-4b—is to create a single complex materialized view on the local server based on multiple remote tables.

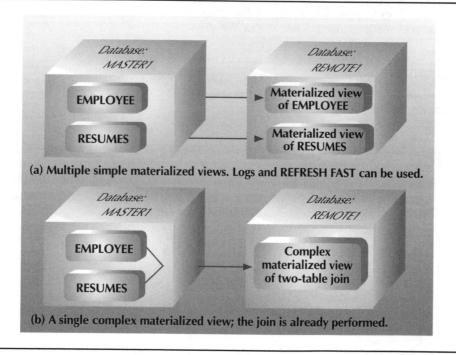

(a) Multiple simple materialized views. Logs and REFRESH FAST can be used.

(b) A single complex materialized view; the join is already performed.

FIGURE 8-4. *Data replication options for joins*

Which option will retrieve data faster? The answer to that depends on several factors:

- **Size of the master tables**   How long does a complete refresh take?

- **Volume of transactions against the master tables**   How large are the materialized view logs?

- **Frequency of the refreshes**   How often will the data be replicated?

If the data is rarely refreshed, and there are few transactions against the master tables, then it should be quicker to use a complex materialized view—see Figure 8-4*b*. If the data is frequently updated and refreshed, then the time savings from using fast refreshes should outweigh the cost of performing the join when the query is executed (rather than ahead of time via the materialized view). In that case, using a set of simple materialized views would result in a faster response time.

NOTE
In general, a fast refresh will outperform a complete refresh if fewer than 25 percent of the rows have changed. If more than 25 percent of the rows have changed, then you should consider using a complete refresh instead. Although a complete refresh may complete faster in that case, it will generate a greater volume of network traffic than a fast refresh will.

The tuning goal of data replication is to minimize the time it takes to satisfy the user's request for remote data. The decision on the proper type of materialized view configuration to use can only be made if you know most common joins ahead of time. For further information on the management of materialized views and their impact on the optimization of data warehouse queries, see Chapter 15.

Using Remote Procedure Calls

When using procedures in a distributed database environment, there are two options: to create a local procedure that references remote tables or to create a remote procedure that is called by a local application. These two options are illustrated in Figure 8-5.

The proper location for the procedure depends on the distribution of the data and the way the data is to be used. The emphasis should be on minimizing the amount of data that must be sent through the network in order to resolve the data request. The

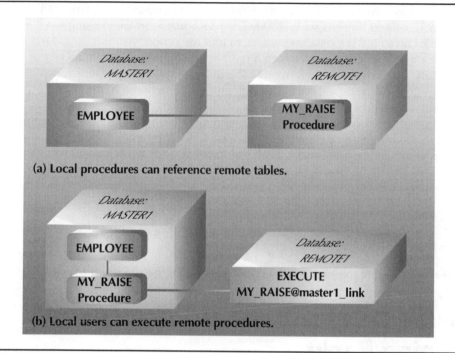

(a) Local procedures can reference remote tables.

(b) Local users can execute remote procedures.

FIGURE 8-5. *Options for procedure location*

procedure should reside within the database that contains most of the data that is used during the procedure's operations.

For example, consider this procedure:

```
create procedure MY_RAISE (My_Emp_No IN NUMBER, Raise IN NUMBER)
as begin
      update EMPLOYEE@HR_LINK
      set Salary = Salary+Raise
      where Empno = My_Emp_No;
end;
/
```

In this case, the procedure only accesses a single table (EMPLOYEE) on a remote node (as indicated by the database link HR_LINK). To reduce the amount of data sent across the network, move this procedure to the remote database identified by the database link HR_LINK and remove the reference to that database link from the **from** clause in the procedure. Then, call the procedure from the local database by using the database link, as shown in the following listing:

```
execute MY_RAISE@HR_LINK(1234,2000);
```

In this case, two parameters are passed to the procedure—My_Emp_No is set to 1234 and Raise is set to 2000. The procedure is invoked using a database link to tell the database where to find the procedure.

The tuning benefit of performing a remote procedure call is that all of the procedure's processing is performed in the database where the data resides. The remote procedure call minimizes the amount of network traffic necessary to complete the procedure's processing.

To maintain location transparency, you may create a local synonym that points to the remote procedure. The database link name will be specified in the synonym so that user requests will automatically use the remote database:

```
create synonym MY_RAISE for MY_RAISE@HR_LINK;
```

A user could then enter the command:

```
execute MY_RAISE(1234,2000);
```

and would execute the remote procedure defined by the synonym MY_RAISE.

Using OEM and the Performance Tuning Packs

Oracle supplies three packs that can be used in conjunction with the Oracle Enterprise Manager to perform tuning and change management control, and to generate system and database diagnostics.

There are two ways in which you can connect to the OEM console: as a stand-alone session or through the Oracle Management Server (OMS). Depending on the way you connect, the Tuning Pack option offers different options. For example, if you connect in stand-alone mode, you are offered four choices: Oracle Expert, Outline Management, SQL Analyze, and Tablespace Map. From the OMS, you are offered the four options available with the stand-alone version plus the Index Tuning Wizard and the Reorg Wizard.

We will examine the Oracle Expert option next. You can configure the Oracle Expert option to collect various forms of information, make suggestions about tuning steps, and create the SQL scripts to implement the tuning suggestions.

Within the Diagnostics pack, Performance Management and Performance Overview options are offered, as described in the later section "The Oracle Performance Manager Option."

The Oracle Expert Pack

When you access the Oracle Expert option for the first time, the only option offered is to load a sample tuning session, unless you have first established preferred credentials using the Preferences option under the OEM Console Administrator screen Configuration Option. Once you have established preferred credentials, you are given the options to either load the sample session or create a new session. Figure 8-6 shows the initial Tuning Session Wizard screen with Create a New Tuning Session selected.

After at least one session has been created, the option to connect to an existing session is also offered. To create a new tuning session, you are prompted to enter the database name and a tuning session name for your session. The name used for this example is "General Tuning 1" in the mydb9.world database.

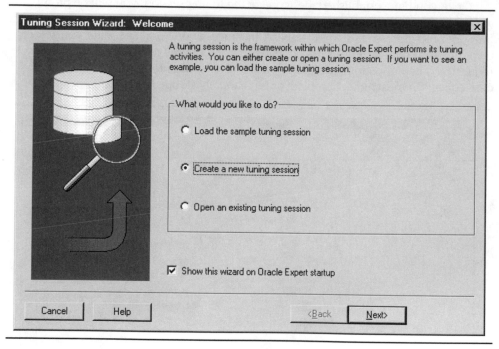

FIGURE 8-6. *Tuning Session Wizard Welcome screen*

The options associated with configuring a new session are Scope, Collect, Review, Recommendations, and Scripts. The first step in configuring a new session is setting the scope for the areas in which you want to perform tuning. Figure 8-7 shows the initial Oracle Expert screen with a new tuning session configured to check for the following items:

- Instance optimization

- SQL reuse opportunities

- Appropriate space management

- Optimal data access

Once you have established the scope of the tuning session, you will be prompted to choose the collection criteria. Figure 8-8 shows the collection criteria screen with four options selected: System, Database, Instance, and Workload. After you select the collection criteria, click on the Collect button and the tool will perform the requested data collection. In order to view suggestions and take further action, the data collection must either complete or be manually stopped. If you do not specify

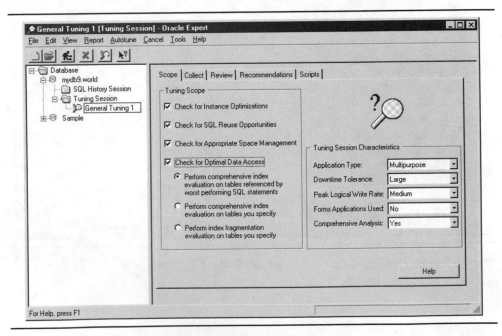

FIGURE 8-7. *Initial Oracle Expert screen*

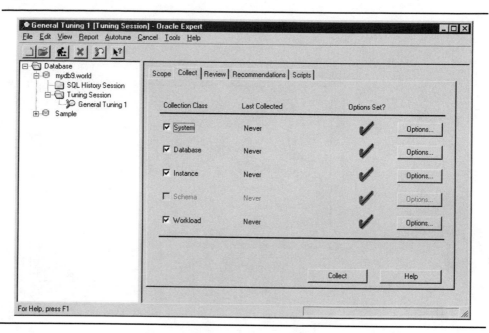

FIGURE 8-8. *Oracle Expert Collect screen*

a collection time range, the tool will continue to collect data at the specified intervals until you stop the process.

You can use the Review option to change various dynamic parameters within the database. Figure 8-9 shows the Review screen with some of the available areas in which parameters can be modified.

Once the data has been collected, you can select the Recommendations option shown in Figure 8-10 to view conclusions and suggestions for tuning the database. Finally, you can use the Scripts option to generate the scripts to implement the recommended database tuning suggestions. Figure 8-11 shows the Scripts screen. If you click on the Generate button of the Scripts screen, the tool will generate the scripts.

The Oracle Performance Manager Option

The Oracle Performance Manager option is available through the Diagnostics pack and enables the display of one or more performance charts to provide immediate feedback on the current state of the database.

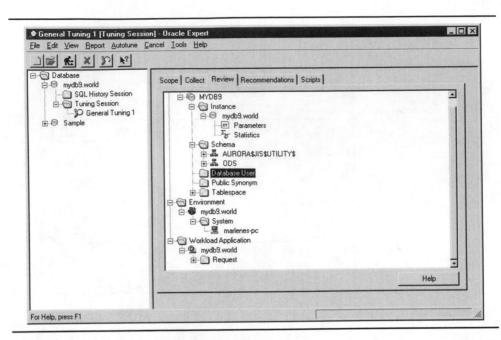

FIGURE 8-9. *Oracle Expert Review screen*

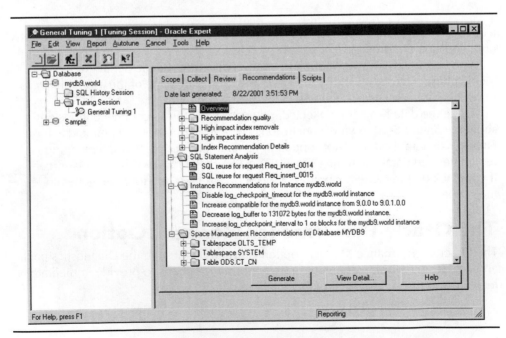

FIGURE 8-10. *Oracle Expert Recommendations screen*

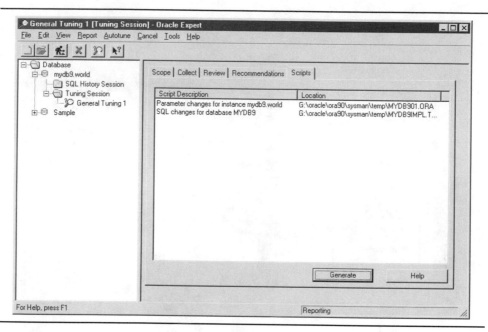

FIGURE 8-11. *Oracle Expert Scripts screen*

Figure 8-12 shows the initial Performance Manager screen with the Memory option selected. Within this option, the SGA Overview chart is selected, and the statistics chart is shown in Figure 8-13.

You can view the charts in several different chart forms, including pie, bar, strip, table, hierarchical, horizontal orientation, and vertical orientation. Not all of the chart types will be available for all of the chart options. When a chart type is unavailable for the selected option, the icon for that chart type will be grayed out and depressed so that it cannot be chosen.

The interval at which statistics are updated can be designated by either using the Stopwatch icon or by using the pull-down menu (see Figure 8-13). The statistics can be recorded for viewing at a later time.

This tool is designed to give you a quick look at the state of various database areas. One of the most useful areas is the Overview of Performance option, which enables you to get a quick summary view of several charts and graphs at once. Figure 8-14 shows the overview of the database statistics.

Another quick way to get just the performance overview of an entire database is to select the database of interest from the OEM Console and then select the Performance Overview option from the Diagnostics option. The same statistics screen displayed in Figure 8-14 is shown.

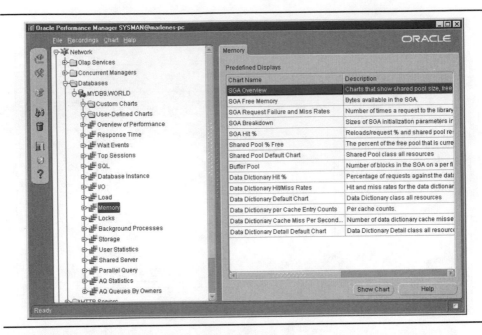

FIGURE 8-12. *Performance Manager initial screen*

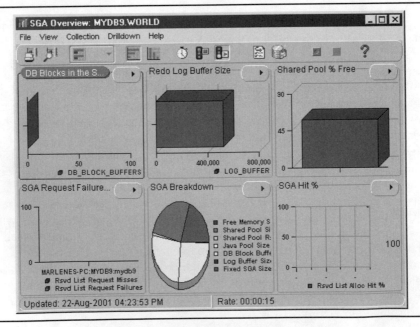

FIGURE 8-13. *Performance Manager SGA Overview chart*

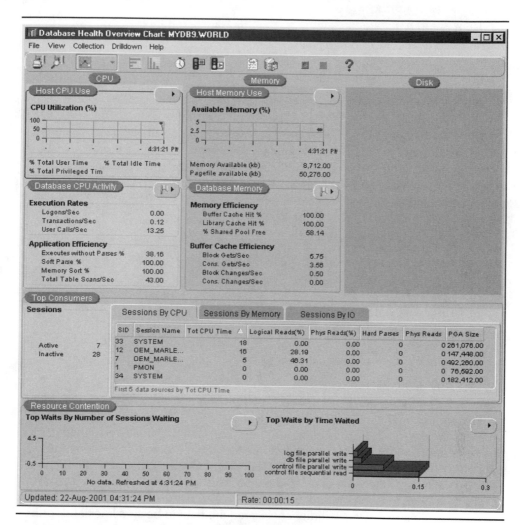

FIGURE 8-14. *Overview of Performance screen*

Tuning Solutions

There is an underlying approach to the techniques and tools presented throughout this chapter. Before spending your time and resources on the implementation of a new feature, you should first stabilize your environment and architecture—the server, the database, and the application. If the environment is stable, then you should be able to quickly accomplish two goals:

- Successfully re-create the performance problem
- Successfully isolate the cause of the problem

To achieve these goals, you may need to have a test environment available for your performance tests. See Chapter 5 for guidance on the creation of a test environment. Once the problem has been successfully isolated, you can apply the steps outlined in this chapter to the problem. In general, your tuning approach should mirror the order of the sections of this chapter:

1. Evaluate application design.

2. Tune SQL.

3. Tune memory usage.

4. Tune data storage.

5. Tune data manipulation.

6. Tune physical and logical storage.

7. Tune network traffic.

Depending on the nature of your application, you may choose a different order for the steps, or you may combine steps. For example, in a Web-based three-tier application, you may encounter performance problems during online data entry. In those environments, you should minimize the amount of interaction with the database. Often, the data validity checks (such as code table lookups) that perform well for server-based applications cause performance problems for three-tier applications. Data validity checks require data to be sent back and forth across the application's data components. In general, you should avoid querying data from the database that the application doesn't directly use.

How can you resolve this issue and still perform data validity checks? There are several options available:

- *Combine multiple data validity checks and perform a single query of the database rather than multiple queries.* Be sure to tune the combined query.

- *Use local variables or drop-down lists of choices at the application level to avoid querying the database.* For example, create a list of states or countries at the application level rather than querying the database for a list.

■ *Trust the users.* Rather than perform data validity at the instant the data is entered, perform the validity checks during the **commit** process. If you use constraints, the data will be checked during the **commit** anyway; the additional checks at the application level are usually in place to provide quicker feedback to the users. However, experienced users of an application don't make many data-related mistakes, so the cost of checking their work at the application level may not add any value to their work. If you remove the data checks from the application level, you may remove many of the performance bottlenecks from the data-entry portion of the application.

If the application design cannot be altered, and the SQL cannot be altered, then you can tune the memory and disk areas used by the application. As you alter the memory and disk area settings, you must be sure to revisit the application design and SQL implementation to be sure that your changes do not adversely impact the application. The need to revisit the application design process is particularly important if you choose to use a data replication method, since the timeliness of the replicated data may cause problems within the business process served by the application.

CHAPTER
9

Using STATSPACK

s of Oracle 8.1.6, you can use the STATSPACK utility to monitor the performance of your database. STATSPACK replaces the UTLBSTAT/UTLESTAT scripts available with earlier versions of Oracle and offers several significant enhancements to those scripts. In this chapter, you will see how to install STATSPACK, how to manage it, and how to run and interpret the generated reports.

Installing STATSPACK

STATSPACK must be installed in every database to be monitored. The installation script, named spcreate.sql, is found in the /rdbms/admin subdirectory under the Oracle software home directory. The spcreate.sql script creates a user named PERFSTAT and creates a number of objects under that schema.

> **NOTE**
> *You should allocate at least 100MB for the initial creation of the PERFSTAT schema's objects.*

To start the spcreate.sql script, change your directory to the ORACLE_HOME/ rdbms/admin directory and log into SQL*Plus in an account with SYSDBA privileges:

```
SQL> connect system/manager as SYSDBA
SQL> @spcreate
```

During the installation process, you will be prompted for a default tablespace for the PERFSTAT user (a list of available tablespaces will be displayed along with this prompt). You will also be asked to specify a temporary tablespace for the user. Once you have provided a default and temporary tablespace for the PERFSTAT account, it will be created, and the installation script will log in as PERFSTAT and continue to create the required objects. If there is not sufficient space to create the PERFSTAT objects in the specified default tablespace, the script will return an error.

> **NOTE**
> *Although you start the installation script while logged in as a SYSDBA-privileged user, the conclusion of the installation script will leave you logged in as the PERFSTAT user.*

If you want to drop the PERFSTAT user at a later date, you can run the spdusr.sql script located in the ORACLE_HOME/rdbms/admin directory.

Security of the PERFSTAT Account

The PERFSTAT account is created with the default password of PERFSTAT. Change the password after the installation process completes.

The PERFSTAT account is granted the SELECT_CATALOG_ROLE and HS_ADMIN_ROLE roles, along with several system privileges (CREATE/ALTER SESSION, CREATE TABLE, CREATE/DROP PUBLIC SYNONYM, CREATE SEQUENCE, and CREATE PROCEDURE). Any user who can access your PERFSTAT account can select from all of the dictionary views. For example, such a user could query all of the database account usernames from DBA_USERS, all the segment owners from DBA_SEGMENTS, and the currently logged in sessions from V$SESSION. The PERFSTAT account, if left unprotected, provides a security hole that allows intruders to browse through your data dictionary and select targets for further intrusion.

In addition to the privileges it receives during the installation process, the PERFSTAT account will also have any privileges that have been granted to PUBLIC. If you use PUBLIC grants instead of roles for application privileges, you must secure the PERFSTAT account. You can lock database accounts and unlock them as needed; see Chapter 10 for details.

Postinstallation

Once the installation process is complete, the PERFSTAT account will own (in 9.0.1) 36 tables, 37 indexes, a sequence, and a package. You will use the package, named STATSPACK, to manage the statistics collection process and the data in the tables. The collection tables, whose names all begin with "STATS$," will have column definitions based on the V$ view definitions. For example, the columns in STATS$WAITSTAT are the columns found in V$WAITSTAT with three identification columns added at the top:

```
desc stats$waitstat
```

```
Name                       Null?      Type
-------------------------- --------   ------------
SNAP_ID                    NOT NULL   NUMBER(6)
DBID                       NOT NULL   NUMBER
INSTANCE_NUMBER            NOT NULL   NUMBER
CLASS                      NOT NULL   VARCHAR2(18)
WAIT_COUNT                            NUMBER
TIME                                  NUMBER
```

The Class, Wait_Count, and Time columns are based on the Class, Count, and Time columns from V$WAITSTAT. STATSPACK has added three identification columns:

SNAP_ID	An identification number for the collection. Each collection is called a snapshot and is assigned an integer value.
DBID	A numeric identifier for the database.
INSTANCE_NUMBER	A numeric identifier for the instance, for Real Application Cluster installations.

Each collection you perform is given a new Snap_ID value that is consistent across the collection tables. You will need to know the Snap_ID values when executing the statistics report provided with STATSPACK.

Gathering Statistics

Each collection of statistics is called a *snapshot*. Snapshots of statistics have no relation to snapshots or materialized views used in replication. Rather, they are a point-in-time collection of the statistics available via the V$ views, and are given a Snap_ID value to identify the snapshot. You can generate reports on the changes in the statistics between any two snapshots.

NOTE
As with the UTLBSTAT/UTLESTAT reports, the STATSPACK report will only be valid if the database was not shut down and restarted between the snapshots evaluated.

NOTE
Be sure the TIMED_STATISTICS database initialization parameter is set to TRUE prior to gathering statistics.

To generate a snapshot of the statistics, execute the SNAP procedure of the STATSPACK package, as shown in the following listing. You must be logged in as the PERFSTAT user to execute this procedure.

```
execute STATSPACK.SNAP;

PL/SQL procedure successfully completed.
```

When the SNAP procedure is executed, Oracle populates your SNAP$ tables with the current statistics. You can then query those tables directly, or you can use the standard STATSPACK report (to see the change in statistics between snapshots). Snapshots should be taken in one of two ways:

■   To evaluate performance during specific tests of the system. For these tests, you can execute the SNAP procedure manually, as shown in the prior example.

■   To evaluate performance changes over a long period of time. To establish a baseline of the system performance, you may generate statistics snapshots on a scheduled basis. For these snapshots, you should schedule the SNAP procedure execution via Oracle's internal DBMS_JOB scheduler or via an operating system scheduler.

For the snapshots related to specific tests, you may wish to increase the collection level, which lets you gather more statistics. As noted in the "Managing the STATSPACK Data" section later in this chapter, each snapshot has a cost in terms of space usage and query performance. For example, since V$SYSSTAT has (in Oracle 9.0.1) 255 rows, every snapshot generates 255 rows in STATS$SYSSTAT. Avoid generating thousands of rows of statistical data with each snapshot unless you plan to use them.

To support differing collection levels, STATSPACK provides a **level** parameter. By default, the **level** value is set to 5. Prior to changing the **level** value, generate several snapshots and evaluate the reports generated. The default **level** value is adequate for most reports. Alternative **level** values are listed in the following table:

Level	Description
0 to 4	General performance statistics on all memory areas, latches, pools, and events.
5 to 9	Same statistics from the lower levels, plus the most resource-intensive SQL statements.
10 and greater	Same statistics from the lower levels, plus the most resource-intensive SQL statements and parent/child latch data.

The greater the collection level, the longer the snapshot will take. The default value (5) offers a significant degree of flexibility during the queries for the most resource-intensive SQL statements. The parameters used for the resource-intensive SQL portion of the snapshot are stored in a table named STATS$STATSPACK_PARAMETER. You can query STATS$STATSPACK_PARAMETER to see the settings for the different thresholds during the SQL statement gathering. Its columns include Snap_Level (the snapshot level), Executions_Th (threshold value for the number of executions), Disk_Reads_Th (threshold value for the number of disk reads), and Buffer_Gets_Th (threshold value for the number of disk reads).

For a level 5 snapshot using the default thresholds, SQL statements are stored if they meet any of the following criteria:

- The SQL statement has been executed at least 100 times.

- The number of disk reads performed by the SQL statement exceeds 1000.

- The number of parse calls performed by the SQL statement exceeds 1000.

- The number of buffer gets performed by the SQL statement exceeds 10,000.

- The sharable memory used by the SQL statement exceeds 1MB.

- The version count for the SQL statement exceeds 20.

When evaluating the snapshot's data and the performance report, keep in mind that the SQL threshold parameter values are cumulative. A very efficient query, if executed enough times, will exceed 10,000 buffer gets. Compare the number of buffer gets and disk reads to the number of executions to determine the activity each time the query is executed.

To modify the default settings for the thresholds, use the MODIFY_STATSPACK_ PARAMETER procedure of the STATSPACK package. Specify the snapshot level via the **i_snap_level** parameter, along with the parameters to change. Table 9-1 lists the available parameters for the MODIFY_STATSPACK_PARAMETER procedure.

To increase the Buffer_Gets threshold for a level 5 snapshot to 100,000, issue the following command:

```
execute STATSPACK.MODIFY_STATSPACK_PARAMETER -
  (i_snap_level=>5, i_buffer_gets_th=>100000);
```

If you plan to run the SNAP procedure on a scheduled basis, you should pin the STATSPACK package following database startup. The following listing shows a trigger that will be executed each time the database is started. The KEEP procedure of the DBMS_SHARED_POOL procedure pins the package in the Shared Pool. As an alternative to pinning, you can use the SHARED_POOL_RESERVED_SIZE initialization parameter to reserve Shared Pool area for large packages.

```
create or replace trigger PIN_ON_STARTUP
after startup on database
begin
   DBMS_SHARED_POOL.KEEP ('PERFSTAT.STATSPACK', 'P');
end;
/
```

Parameter Name	Range of Values	Default	Description
i_snap_level	0, 5, 10	5	Snapshot level
i_ucomment	Any text	blank	Comment for the snapshot
i_executions_th	Integer >=0	100	Threshold for the cumulative number of executions
i_disk_reads_th	Integer >=0	1000	Threshold for the cumulative number of disk reads
i_parse_calls_th	Integer >=0	1000	Threshold for the cumulative number of parse calls
i_buffer_gets_th	Integer >=0	10000	Threshold for the cumulative number of buffer gets
i_sharable_mem_th	Integer >=0	1048576	Threshold for the amount of sharable memory allocated
i_version_count_th	Integer >=0	20	Threshold for the number of versions of the SQL statement
i_session_id	Valid SID from V$SESSION	0	Session ID of an Oracle session, if you wish to gather session-level statistics
i_modify_parameter	TRUE or FALSE	FALSE	Set to TRUE if you wish to save your changes for future snapshots

TABLE 9-1.   *Modification Parameters*

Running the Statistics Report

If you have generated more than one snapshot, you can report on the statistics for the period between the two snapshots. The database must not have been shut down between the times the two snapshots were taken. When you execute the report, you will need to know the Snap_ID values for the snapshots. If you run the report interactively, Oracle will provide a list of the available snapshots and the times they were created.

To execute the report, go to the /rdbms/admin directory under the Oracle software home directory. Log into SQL*Plus as the PERFSTAT user and run the spreport.sql file found there.

```
SQL> @spreport
```

Oracle will display the database and instance identification information from V$INSTANCE and V$DATABASE and will then call a second SQL file, sprepins.sql.

The sprepins.sql generates the report of the changes in the statistics during the snapshot time interval. The available snapshots will be listed, and you will be prompted to enter a beginning and ending snapshot ID. Unless you specify otherwise, the output will be written to a file named sp_*beginning_ending*.lst (sp_1_2.lst for a report between Snap_ID values of 1 and 2).

The first portion of the report output provides an overview of the cache areas and their usage. The following listing shows sample output for this section, showing the cache sizes and the load profile.

```
Cache Sizes (end)
~~~~~~~~~~~~~~~~~
         Buffer Cache:      160M      Std Block Size:        8K
    Shared Pool Size:       64M         Log Buffer:        512K


Load Profile
~~~~~~~~~~~~                    Per Second          Per Transaction
                            ---------------        ---------------
          Redo size:          2,270.95              333,830.00
      Logical reads:             15.77                2,318.00
      Block changes:              3.83                  562.50
      Physical reads:             0.00                    0.50
     Physical writes:             0.72                  106.50
          User calls:             0.10                   14.50
             Parses:              0.27                   39.00
        Hard parses:              0.07                   10.00
              Sorts:              0.30                   44.50
             Logons:              0.00                    0.00
           Executes:              0.64                   94.50
       Transactions:              0.01


  % Blocks changed per Read:    24.27   Recursive Call %:     98.14
  Rollback per transaction %:    0.00     Rows per Sort:      86.06
```

The load profile helps to identify the type of activity being performed. In this example, the activity recorded was primarily performing queries. The next sections of the report show the instance efficiency percentages (such as the buffer hit ratio and library cache hit ratio) followed by the Shared Pool statistics. The Shared Pool statistics show the percentage of the Shared Pool in use and the percentage of SQL statements that have been executed multiple times (as desired). The following listing shows sample Shared Pool statistics from the report:

```
Shared Pool Statistics        Begin    End
                              ------   ------
           Memory Usage %:     28.37    29.17
     % SQL with executions>1:  27.77    30.45
  % Memory for SQL w/exec>1:   56.64    67.74
```

Based on the data in the preceding listing, at the time of the second snapshot, 29.17% of the Shared Pool's memory was in use. Of the statements in the Shared Pool, only 30% had been executed more than once, indicating a potential need to improve cursor sharing in the application.

NOTE
The section of the report showing the percentage of Shared Pool memory in use is new with the Oracle9i version of STATSPACK.

The next portion of the generated report shows the top five wait events, the full list of wait events, and the background wait events. Identifying major wait events may help to target your tuning efforts.

The most resource-intensive SQL statements in the database are then listed, in descending order of buffer gets. Since the buffer gets statistic is cumulative, the query with the most buffer gets may not be the worst-performing query in the database; it may just have been executed enough times to earn the highest ranking. Compare the cumulative number of buffer gets to the cumulative number of disk reads for the queries; if the numbers are close, then you should evaluate the explain plan for the query.

NOTE
If the Shared Pool is flushed between the execution times of the two snapshots, the SQL portion of the output report will not necessarily contain the most resource-intensive SQL executed during the period.

Following the SQL statement listing, you will see the list of changes to statistics from V$SYSSTAT, entitled "Instance Activity Stats." The V$SYSSTAT statistics are useful for identifying performance issues not shown in the prior sections. For example, you should compare the number of sorts performed on disk to the number performed in memory; increase the sort area size to reduce disk sorts. If there is a significant number of full table scans of large tables, evaluate the most-used queries. The following listing shows four rows from this section of the report:

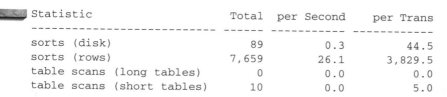

Statistic	Total	per Second	per Trans
sorts (disk)	89	0.3	44.5
sorts (rows)	7,659	26.1	3,829.5
table scans (long tables)	0	0.0	0.0
table scans (short tables)	10	0.0	5.0

The next section of the report provides the I/O statistics by tablespace and by datafile. If the I/O is not properly distributed among your files, you many encounter performance bottlenecks during periods of high activity. You can use this section of the report to identify such bottlenecks and to measure how effectively you have resolved those problems. See Chapter 4 for further details on I/O distribution across files.

Following the I/O statistics, the report lists the buffer cache statistics by pool (default, keep, and recycle), instance recovery statistics (the number of redo blocks), and the PGA memory statistics. After those sections, the report provides rollback segment statistics. First, it lists the activity in the rollback segment (writes, wraps, shrinks, extends) and the waits encountered, as shown in the following example:

RBS No	Trans Table Gets	Pct Waits	Undo Bytes Written	Wraps	Shrinks	Extends
0	2.0	0.00	0	0	0	0
1	4.0	0.00	0	0	0	0
2	2.0	0.00	0	0	0	0
3	13.0	0.00	0	0	0	0
4	6.0	0.00	0	0	0	0
5	4.0	0.00	0	0	0	0
6	7.0	0.00	1,824	0	0	0
7	10.0	0.00	202	0	0	0
8	96.0	0.00	207,234	5	0	5
9	8.0	0.00	0	0	0	0
10	32.0	0.00	10,856	0	0	0

If rollback segment waits are occurring, you may need to add more rollback segments to your database. The next section after the rollback segment statistics shows the storage allocations for your rollback segments, providing a guideline for the creation of additional rollback segments. Following the rollback segment sections, the report lists the undo segment statistics for environments using system-managed undo (see Chapter 7).

Latch activity and dictionary cache statistics are then presented, followed by the library cache activity. If your "Pct Miss" value is high, you may need to improve cursor sharing in your application or increase the size of the Shared Pool.

Namespace	Get Requests	Pct Miss	Pin Requests	Pct Miss	Reloads	Invali- dations
BODY	4	0.0	5	0.0	0	0
CLUSTER	3	0.0	3	0.0	0	0
JAVA DATA	1	0.0	4	0.0	0	0
SQL AREA	84	7.1	493	11.4	0	0
TABLE/PROCEDURE	298	1.7	408	17.2	0	0
TRIGGER	3	0.0	3	0.0	0	0

Following an SGA memory summary (from V$SGA) and a listing of the memory changes during the snapshot interval, the report lists the database initialization parameters in use at the beginning and end of the report.

Taken as a whole, the report generates a significant amount of data, allowing you to develop a profile of the database and its usage. Based on the initialization, file I/O, and SGA data, you can develop an understanding of the major components in the database configuration. Since it generates so much data, you should be careful not to generate more statistics than you plan to use. The following sections of this chapter address the management of the gathered data.

Managing the STATSPACK Data

You should manage the data generated by STATSPACK to guarantee that the space usage and performance of the STATSPACK application meets your requirements as the application data grows. Managing STATSPACK data includes the following steps:

1. Regularly analyze the STATSPACK data. At a minimum, you should analyze the STATSPACK table prior to running the spreport.sql report:

```
execute DBMS_UTILITY.ANALYZE_SCHEMA('PERFSTAT','COMPUTE');
```

2. Purge old data. Since you cannot generate valid interval reports across database shutdown/startup actions, data prior to the last database startup may not be as useful as the most current data. When the data is no longer needed, purge it from the tables. Oracle provides a script, sppurge.sql, to facilitate purges. The sppurge.sql script, located in the /rdbms/admin directory under the Oracle software home directory, lists the currently stored snapshots and prompts you for two input parameters: the beginning and ending snapshot numbers for the purge. The related records in the STATS$ tables will then be **delete**d. Due to the size of the transactions involved, databases using rollback segments should force the session to use a large rollback segment during the **delete**s:

```
SQL> commit;
SQL> set transaction use rollback segment roll_large;
SQL> @sppurge
```

The sppurge script prompts you to back up your old statistics before purging them. You can back up the data by exporting the PERFSTAT schema.

3. Truncate the STATSPACK tables when the data is not needed. Old statistical data may no longer be relevant, or you may have imported the old statistics during database migrations or creations. To truncate the old tables, execute the sptrunc.sql SQL*Plus script from within the PERFSTAT account. The script is located in the /rdbms/admin directory under the Oracle software home directory.

Deinstalling STATSPACK

Since STATSPACK includes public synonyms as well as private objects, you should remove the application via a SYSDBA privileged account. Oracle provides a script, spdrop.sql, to automate the deinstallation process. From within the /rdbms/admin directory under the Oracle software home directory, log into SQL*Plus and execute the script as shown in the following listing:

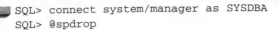

```
SQL> connect system/manager as SYSDBA
SQL> @spdrop
```

The spdrop.sql script calls scripts that will drop the tables, package, public synonyms, and the PERFSTAT user. To reinstall STATSPACK, execute the spcreate.sql script as shown earlier in this chapter.

CHAPTER
10

Database Security
and Auditing

reating and enforcing security procedures helps to protect what is rapidly becoming the most important corporate asset: data. And while storing that data in a database makes it more useful and available companywide, it also makes it susceptible to unauthorized access. Such access attempts must be detected and prevented.

The Oracle database has several layers of security and gives you the ability to audit each level. In this chapter, you will see descriptions for each layer in the auditing process. You will also see methods for setting impossible passwords and forcing passwords to expire.

Security Capabilities

Oracle makes several levels of security available to the DBA:

- Account security for validation of users
- Access security for database objects
- System-level security for managing global privileges

Each of these capabilities is described in the following sections; the "Implementing Security" section of this chapter provides details for effectively using the available options.

Account Security

In order to access data in an Oracle database, you must have access to an account in that database. This access can be direct—via user connections into a database—or indirect. Indirect connections include access via preset authorizations within database links. Each account must have a password associated with it. A database account can also be tied to an operating system account.

Passwords are set for a user when the user's account is created and may be altered after the account is created. A user's ability to alter the account password will be limited by the tools to which he or she is granted access. The database stores an encrypted version of the password in a data dictionary table. If the account is directly related to an operating system account, it is possible to bypass the password check and rely on the operating system authentication instead.

As of Oracle8, passwords can expire, and the DBA can establish the conditions under which a password can be reused (via a database setting for password history). Also, you can use profiles to enforce standards for the passwords (such as minimum length), and you can automatically lock accounts if there are multiple consecutive failures to connect to the account.

Object Privileges

Access to objects within a database is enabled via *privileges*. These allow specific database commands to be used against specific database objects via the **grant** command. For example, if the user THUMPER owns a table called EMPLOYEE, and executes the command

```
grant select on EMPLOYEE to PUBLIC;
```

then all users (PUBLIC) will be able to select records from THUMPER's EMPLOYEE table. You can create *roles*—named groups of privileges—to simplify the administration of privileges. For applications with large numbers of users, roles greatly reduce the number of **grant** commands needed. Since roles can be password protected and can be dynamically enabled or disabled, they add an additional layer of security to the database.

System-Level Roles and Privileges

You can use roles to manage the system-level commands available to users. These commands include **create table** and **alter index**. Actions against each type of database object are authorized via separate privileges. For example, a user may be granted the CREATE TABLE privilege or CREATE INDEX privilege. You can create customized system-level roles that grant users the exact privileges they need without granting them excessive authority within the database. As noted in Chapter 5, the CONNECT and RESOURCE roles are useful for the basic system privileges required by end users and developers, respectively.

Users who have the RESOURCE role are also granted the UNLIMITED TABLESPACE system privilege, enabling them to create objects anywhere in the database. Because of this additional privilege, you should restrict the use of the RESOURCE role to development and test environments.

Implementing Security

The security capabilities in Oracle include roles, profiles, and direct grants of privileges. The Oracle Enterprise Manager toolset provides a Security Manager tool to enable the management of user accounts, roles, privileges, and profiles. In the following sections you will see the usage of all of these features, including several undocumented capabilities.

The Starting Point: Operating System Security

You cannot access a database unless you can first access, either directly or indirectly, the server on which the database is running, The first step in securing your database is to secure the platform and network on which it resides. Once that has been accomplished, the operating system security must be considered.

Oracle uses a number of files that its users do not require direct access to. For example, the datafiles and the online redo log files are written and read via Oracle's background processes. Only DBAs who will be creating and dropping these files require direct access to them at the operating system level. Export dump files and other backup files must also be secured.

Your data may be copied to other databases—either as part of a replication scheme or to populate a development database. To secure your data, you will need to secure each of the databases in which your data resides, along with the backups of each of those databases. If someone can walk off with the backup tapes from a database that contains a copy of your data, then all of the security you've implemented in your database is worthless. You must prevent unauthorized access to all copies of your data.

Creating Users

When creating a user, your goal is to establish a secure, useful account that has adequate privileges and proper default settings. You can use the **create user** command to create a new database account. When the account is created, it will not have any capabilities, and users will not even be able to log in until that privilege is granted.

All of the necessary settings for a user account can be specified within a single **create user** command. These settings include values for all of the parameters listed in Table 10-1.

Parameter	Usage
Username	Name of the schema.
Password	Password for the account; may also be tied directly to the operating system host account name or authenticated via a network authentication service. For host-based authentication, use **identified externally**. For network-based authentication, use **identified globally as**.
Default tablespace	The default tablespace in which objects created in this schema will be stored. This setting does not give the user rights to create objects; it only sets a default value.
Temporary tablespace	The tablespace in which temporary segments used during sorting transactions will be stored.

TABLE 10-1. *Parameters for the **create user** Command*

Parameter	Usage
Quota [on tablespace]	Allows the user to store objects in the specified tablespace, up to the total size specified as the quota.
Profile	Assigns a profile to the user. If none is specified, then the default profile is used. Profiles are used to restrict the usage of system resources and to enforce password management rules.
Password	Preexpire the password.
Account	Sets the account to either locked or unlocked.
Default role[s]	Sets the default roles to be enabled for the user.

TABLE 10-1. *Parameters for the **create user** Command* (continued)

NOTE
You cannot set default roles during create:

```
create user FRED identified by FRED default role ABC;
ORA-01954: DEFAULT ROLE clause not valid for CREATE USER
```

The following listing shows a sample **create user** command. In this example, the user THUMPER is created, with a password of R3BB#T, a default tablespace of USERS, a temporary tablespace of TEMP, no quotas, and the default profile.

```
create user THUMPER
identified by R3BB#T
default tablespace USERS
temporary tablespace TEMP;
```

Since no profile is specified, the default profile for the database will be used. This is an actual profile named DEFAULT; its initial settings are for all resource consumption limits to be set to UNLIMITED. See the "User Profiles" section of this chapter for further details on profiles.

Since no quotas are specified, the user cannot create objects in the database.

To grant resource quotas, use the **quota** parameter of the **create user** or **alter user** command, as shown in the following listing. In this example, THUMPER is granted a quota of 100MB in the USERS tablespace.

```
alter user THUMPER
quota 100M on USERS;
```

The THUMPER user can now create up to 100MB worth of segments in the USERS tablespace.

> **NOTE**
> *Users do not need space quotas on the TEMP tablespace in order for their queries to create temporary segments there.*

Except for the username, all of the parameters in the **create user** command may be altered via the **alter user** command.

From the OEM Security Manager screen, you can create a new user or create a user "like" another user. This feature enables you to create a new user with the same attributes as an existing user. Figure 10-1 shows the initial Security Manager screen with the user THUMPER selected. With the OEM tool, roles, system privileges, object privileges, and quotas can be assigned as the user is created. On the first user screen, in Figure 10-1, the password authentication enables the designation of a

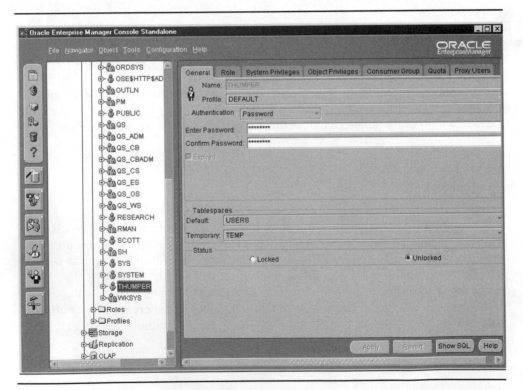

FIGURE 10-1. *Password authentication*

specific password, the designation that the account is to be global—used for remote database administration—or the account is to be identified externally. The option to preexpire the password is available, and the account can be created locked or unlocked (see the "Password Management" section later in this chapter for details on password expirations and account locking).

You can create a new user in OEM by selecting the General tab and clicking the right mouse button or by selecting the Create option from the Object menu while the Users area of the screen is selected. When you select the Create or Create Like option, a User Creation Wizard is activated and you can fill in the roles, privileges, and so on, that you want for the user you are creating. By default, there are no privileges or roles assigned to the new user. You must grant, at a minimum, the CREATE_SESSION privilege for the user to be able to connect to the database. If a default user tablespace has been declared, it will be assigned to the new user.

The temporary tablespace is set to <System Assigned> for the user, but a pull-down list enables you to select a temporary tablespace. Figure 10-2 shows the Create User

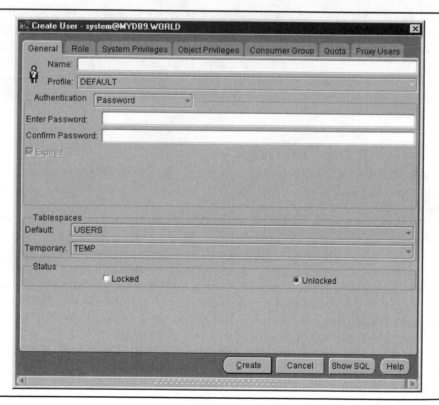

FIGURE 10-2. *Create User window, General tab*

window with the options available for creating a new user like the user THUMPER. Since THUMPER's default tablespace was selected as USERS and his temporary tablespace was designated as TEMP, the new user, by default, has the tablespace assignments as well as all of the other grants and privileges that THUMPER has. The only information that needs to be filled out to create the new user is the user's name, password, and anything different from THUMPER's information that is required.

Dropping Users

You can drop a user from the database via the **drop user** command. The **drop user** command has one parameter, **cascade**, which drops all objects in the user's schema before dropping the user. If the user owns objects, you must specify **cascade** in order to drop the user. A sample **drop user** command is shown in the following listing:

```
drop user THUMPER cascade;
```

Any views, synonyms, procedures, functions, or packages that reference objects in the schema of the dropped user will be marked as INVALID. If another user with the same name is created at a later date, there will be nothing for the new user to inherit from the previous user with that name. The OEM tool provides a **remove** capability through the Security Manager option that enables a user to be dropped. Within OEM, a confirmation screen is displayed to verify that the user should really be dropped.

System-Level Privileges

You can use system-level roles to distribute the availability of system-level commands used to manage the database. You can either create customized system-level roles or use the ones that come with the database. The available privileges that can be granted via system-level roles are listed in Appendix A under the "GRANT (System Privileges and Roles)" entry.

You can use the **with grant option** clause of the **grant** command to pass along to the grantee the ability to grant the privilege to other users.

Table 10-2 lists 15 system-level roles provided with Oracle. Using these roles allows you to limit the system-level privileges granted to database management roles. In addition to the roles shown in Table 10-2, your database may include roles generated in support of the Advanced Queuing Option (AQ_USER_ROLE, GLOBAL_ AQ_USER_ROLE, and AQ_ADMINISTRATOR_ROLE), Java development (JAVAUSERPRIV, JAVAIDPRIV, JAVASYSPRIV, JAVADEBUGPRIV, JAVA_ADMIN, and JAVA_DEPLOY), for Oracle Context Management (CTXAPP), and for use by the OEM Intelligent Agents (the OEM_MANAGER role).

Role Name	Privileges Granted to Role
CONNECT	ALTER SESSION, CREATE CLUSTER, CREATE DATABASE LINK, CREATE SEQUENCE, CREATE SESSION, CREATE SYNONYM, CREATE TABLE, CREATE VIEW
RESOURCE	CREATE CLUSTER, CREATE PROCEDURE, CREATE SEQUENCE, CREATE TABLE, CREATE TRIGGER
DBA	All system privileges WITH ADMIN OPTION
EXP_FULL_DATABASE	SELECT ANY TABLE, BACKUP ANY TABLE, INSERT, DELETE, AND UPDATE ON THE TABLES SYS.INCVID, SYS.INCFIL, AND SYS.INCEXP
WM_ADMIN_ROLE	All Workspace Manager privileges with GRANT OPTION
IMP_FULL_DATABASE	BECOME USER
DELETE_CATALOG_ROLE	DELETE on all dictionary packages
EXECUTE_CATALOG_ROLE	EXECUTE on all dictionary packages
SELECT_CATALOG_ROLE	SELECT on all catalog tables and views
CREATE TYPE	CREATE TYPE, EXECUTE, EXECUTE ANY TYPE, ADMIN OPTION, GRANT OPTION
RECOVERY_CATALOG_OWNER	DROP ROLE, CREATE ROLE, CREATE TRIGGER, CREATE PROCEDURE
OLAP_DBA	ALTER ANY DIMENSION, ALTER ANY TABLE, ANALYZE ANY, CREATE ANY DIMENSION, CREATE ANY INDEX, CREATE ANY TABLE, CREATE ANY VIEW, DROP ANY DIMENSION, DROP ANY TABLE, DROP ANY VIEW, LOCK ANY TABLE, SELECT ANY DICTIONARY, SELECT ANY TABLE

TABLE 10-2. *System-Level Roles Provided in Oracle9i*

Role Name	Privileges Granted to Role
HS_ADMIN_ROLE	HS_EXTERNAL_OBJECT, HS_EXTERNAL_USER
WKADMIN	CREATE ANY DIRECTORY, CREATE CLUSTER, CREATE PROCEDURE, CREATE TABLE, CREATE TRIGGER, CREATE TYPE, DROP ANY DIRECTORY
WKUSER	CREATE ANY DIRECTORY, CREATE CLUSTER, CREATE PROCEDURE, CREATE TABLE, CREATE TRIGGER, CREATE TYPE, DROP ANY DIRECTORY

TABLE 10-2. *System-Level Roles Provided in Oracle9i* (continued)

NOTE
In addition to the privileges listed in Table 10-2, users of the DBA and RESOURCE roles also receive the UNLIMITED TABLESPACE system privilege.

The CONNECT role is typically granted to end users. Although it does have some object creation abilities (including the CREATE TABLE privilege), it does not give users any quotas on any tablespace. Since users will not have tablespace quotas unless you grant them to users, they will not be able to create tables.

The RESOURCE role is granted to developers. As described in Chapter 5, the RESOURCE role gives developers the most-used application development privileges. The DBA role includes all 124 of the system-level privileges, with the option to grant those privileges to other users.

NOTE
Oracle Corporation recommends that you create your own roles rather than rely on these supplied roles. CONNECT, RESOURCE, and DBA may not be automatically created in future versions.

The IMP_FULL_DATABASE and EXP_FULL_DATABASE roles are used during Import and Export, respectively, when you perform a full database Import or Export (see Chapter 11). These roles are part of the DBA role; you can use these roles to grant users limited database management privileges.

The roles SELECT_ CATALOG_ ROLE, EXECUTE_CATALOG_ROLE, and DELETE_ CATALOG_ROLE were introduced in Oracle8.

The SELECT_CATALOG_ROLE and EXECUTE_CATALOG_ROLE roles grant users privileges to select from data dictionary tables like DBA_TABLES or execute exportable data dictionary objects. That is, not every database object is exported during a full system export (see Chapter 11). For example, the dynamic performance views (see Chapter 6) are not exported. Thus, SELECT_CATALOG_ROLE does not give the user the ability to select from the dynamic performance tables like V$ROLLSTAT; it does, however, give the user the ability to query from most of the data dictionary. Similarly, EXECUTE_CATALOG_ROLE grants users the ability to execute procedures and functions that are part of the data dictionary.

The CREATE TYPE role is enabled if you use the Objects option. Users who have the CREATE TYPE role enabled can create new abstract datatypes.

Given the system-level privileges and roles available, you may wish to reexamine your account creation process. Like the database backup process, DBA-level privileges are required to perform account creation. However, you can select out a subset of privileges that are needed to create new users.

For example, you can create a new system-level role called ACCOUNT_ CREATOR. It will only be able to create users; it will not be able to perform any other DBA-level commands. The commands that create this role are shown in the following listing:

```
create role ACCOUNT_CREATOR;
grant CREATE SESSION, CREATE USER, ALTER USER
    to ACCOUNT_CREATOR;
```

The first command in this listing creates a role called ACCOUNT_CREATOR. The second command grants that role the ability to log in (CREATE SESSION) and create and alter accounts (CREATE USER and ALTER USER). The ACCOUNT_ CREATOR role can then be granted to a centralized help desk, which will be able to coordinate the creation of all new accounts. You can create this role using the OEM tool by selecting the Create Role option and filling in the appropriate information. Figure 10-3 shows the ACCOUNT_CREATOR role being created using the OEM Security Manager tool, while Figure 10-4 shows the assignment of the privileges to the role.

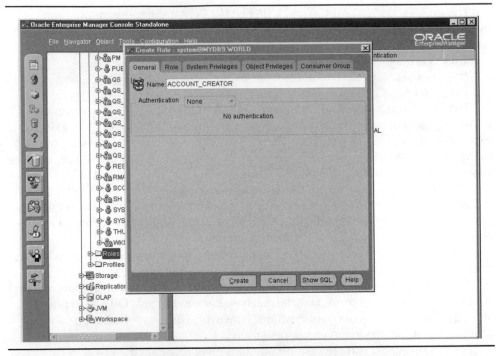

FIGURE 10-3. *Creating the ACCOUNT_CREATOR role*

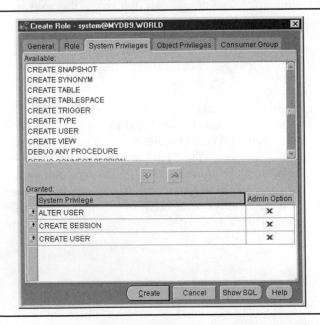

FIGURE 10-4. *Assigning system privileges to the ACCOUNT_CREATOR role*

Centralizing account creation helps to ensure that proper authorization procedures are followed when accounts are requested. The flexibility of system-level privileges and roles allows this capability to be given to a user—in this case, a help desk— without also giving that user the ability to query data from the database.

The ability to create an ACCOUNT_CREATOR role is particularly useful when you are implementing packaged software. Many third-party packaged applications assume they will have full DBA authority in your database, when in fact they only need the ability to execute **create user** and **alter user** commands. By creating an ACCOUNT_CREATOR role, you can limit the package schema owner's privileges in the rest of your database.

By default, your roles are enabled each time you log in. You can alter the default role for a user via the **default role** clause of the **alter user** command. For example, you can alter a user to have no roles enabled by default:

```
alter user THUMPER default role NONE;
```

You can specify the roles to enable:

```
alter user THUMPER default role CONNECT;
```

And you can specify the roles that should not be enabled when the session starts:

```
alter user THUMPER default role all except ACCOUNT_CREATOR;
```

If the specified roles have not been granted to the user, then the **alter user** commands will fail. If the user has not been granted a specified system-level role such as CONNECT, then attempting to set that role as a default role for a user will result in the following error:

```
ORA-01919: role 'CONNECT' does not exist
```

If the specified role is a database-specific role that has not been granted to the user, the **alter user** command will fail with the following error:

```
ORA-01955: DEFAULT ROLE 'ACCOUNT_CREATOR' not granted to user
```

You must grant the roles to the users before establishing the users' default roles.

If you use the **default role all** clause, then all of a user's roles will be enabled when the user's session begins. If you plan to dynamically enable and disable roles at different parts of an application (via **set role** commands), then you should control which of the roles are enabled by default.

NOTE
The MAX_ENABLED_ROLES init.ora parameter limits the number of roles any user can have enabled simultaneously. The default is 20 for Oracle9i.

NOTE
When you create a role, it is enabled for you by default. If you create many roles, then you may exceed the MAX_ENABLED_ROLES setting even if you are not the user of those roles.

User Profiles

You can use profiles to place limits on the amount of system and database resources available to a user and to manage password restrictions. If no profiles are created in a database, then the default profile, which specifies unlimited resources for all users, will be used.

The resources that can be limited via profiles are listed in Table 10-3.

Resource	Description
SESSIONS_PER_USER	The number of concurrent sessions a user can have in an instance.
CPU_PER_SESSION	The CPU time, in hundredths of seconds, that a session can use.
CPU_PER_CALL	The CPU time, in hundredths of seconds, that a parse, execute, or fetch can use.
CONNECT_TIME	The number of minutes a session can be connected to a database.
IDLE_TIME	The number of minutes a session can be connected to the database without being actively used.
LOGICAL_READS_PER_SESSION	The number of database blocks that can be read in a session.
LOGICAL_READS_PER_CALL	The number of database blocks that can be read during a parse, execute, or fetch.
PRIVATE_SGA	The amount of private space a session can allocate in the SGA's Shared SQL Pool (for Shared Server).
COMPOSITE_LIMIT	A compound limit, based on the preceding limits.

TABLE 10-3. *Resources Limited by Profiles*

Resource	Description
FAILED_LOGIN_ATTEMPTS	The number of consecutive failed login attempts that will cause an account to be locked.
PASSWORD_LIFE_TIME	The number of days a password can be used before it expires.
PASSWORD_REUSE_TIME	The number of days that must pass before a password can be reused.
PASSWORD_REUSE_MAX	The number of times a password must be changed before a password can be reused.
PASSWORD_LOCK_TIME	The number of days an account will be locked if the FAILED_LOGIN_ATTEMPTS setting is exceeded.
PASSWORD_GRACE_TIME	The length, in days, of the grace period during which a password can still be changed when it has reached its PASSWORD_LIFE_TIME setting.
PASSWORD_VERIFY_FUNCTION	The name of a function used to evaluate the complexity of a password; Oracle provides one that you can edit.

TABLE 10-3.   *Resources Limited by Profiles* (continued)

NOTE
PASSWORD_REUSE_MAX and PASSWORD_REUSE_TIME are mutually exclusive. If one of these resources is set to a value, the other must be set to UNLIMITED.

As shown in Table 10-3, a number of resources may be limited. However, all of these restrictions are *reactive*—no action takes place until the user has exceeded the resource limit. Thus, profiles will not be of much assistance in preventing runaway queries from using large amounts of system resources before they reach their defined limit. Once the limit is reached, the SQL statement will be stopped.

Profiles are created via the **create profile** command. The **alter profile** command, shown in the following example, is used to modify existing profiles. In this example, the DEFAULT profile for the database is altered to allow a maximum idle time of one hour.

```
alter profile DEFAULT
limit idle_time 60;
```

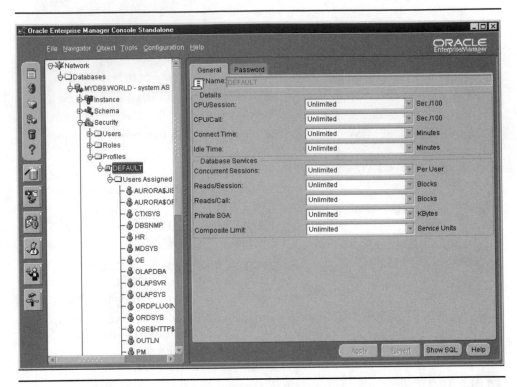

FIGURE 10-5. *DEFAULT profile settings*

The OEM Security Manager tool provides a GUI approach to creating and managing profiles. Figure 10-5 shows the default profile screen with the resources allocated to the profile.

You can use profiles to manage password complexity and lifetime, as described in the next section.

Password Management

You can use profiles to manage the expiration, reuse, and complexity of passwords. For example, you can limit the lifetime of a password and lock an account whose password is too old. You can also force a password to be at least moderately complex and lock any account that has repeated failed login attempts.

For example, if you set the FAILED_LOGIN_ATTEMPTS resource of the user's profile to 5, then five consecutive failed login attempts will be allowed for the account; the sixth will cause the account to be locked.

NOTE
If the correct password is supplied on the fifth attempt, then the "failed login attempt count" is reset to 0, allowing for five more consecutive unsuccessful login attempts before the account is locked.

In the following listing, the LIMITED_PROFILE profile is created, for use by the JANE user:

```
create profile LIMITED_PROFILE limit
FAILED_LOGIN_ATTEMPTS 5;

create user JANE identified by EYRE
profile LIMITED_PROFILE;

grant CREATE SESSION to JANE;
```

If there are five consecutive failed connects to the JANE account, the account will be automatically locked by Oracle. When you then use the correct password for the JANE account, you will receive an error.

```
connect jane/eyre
ERROR: ORA-28000: the account is locked
```

To unlock the account, use the **account unlock** clause of the **alter user** command (from a DBA account), as shown in the following listing:

```
alter user JANE account unlock;
```

Following the unlocking of the account, connections to the JANE account will once again be allowed. You can manually lock an account via the **account lock** clause of the **alter user** command:

```
alter user JANE account lock;
```

If an account becomes locked due to repeated connection failures, it will automatically become unlocked when its profile's PASSWORD_LOCK_TIME value is exceeded. For example, if PASSWORD_LOCK_TIME is set to 1, then the JANE account in the previous example would be locked for one day, at which point the account would be unlocked.

You can establish a maximum lifetime for a password via the PASSWORD_ LIFE_ TIME resource within profiles. For example, you could force users of the LIMITED_ PROFILE profile to change their passwords every 30 days:

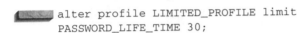
```
alter profile LIMITED_PROFILE limit
PASSWORD_LIFE_TIME 30;
```

In this example, the **alter profile** command is used to modify the LIMITED_ PROFILE profile. The PASSWORD_LIFE_TIME value is set to 30, so each account that uses that profile will have its password expire after 30 days. If your password has expired, you must change it the next time you log in unless the profile has a specified grace period for expired passwords. The grace period parameter is called PASSWORD_GRACE_TIME. If the password is not changed within the grace period, the account expires.

NOTE
If you are going to use the PASSWORD_LIFE_TIME parameter, then you need to give the users a way to change their passwords easily and interactively.

An *expired* account is different from a *locked* account. A locked account, as shown earlier in this section, may be automatically unlocked by the passage of time. An expired account, however, requires manual intervention by the DBA to be reenabled.

NOTE
If you use the password expiration features, make sure the accounts that own your applications have different profile settings; otherwise, they may become locked and the application may become unusable.

To reenable an expired account, you will need to execute the **alter user** command, as shown in the following example. In this example, the user JANE first has her password expired manually by the DBA.

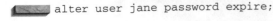
```
alter user jane password expire;

User altered.
```

Next, JANE attempts to connect to her account. When she provides her
password, she is immediately prompted for a new password for the account.

```
connect jane/eyre
ERROR: ORA-28001: the account has expired

Changing password for jane
Old password:
New password:
Retype new password:
Password changed
Connected.
SQL>
```

You can also force users to change their passwords when they first access their
accounts, via the **password expire** clause of the **create user** command. The **create
user** command does not, however, allow you to set an expiration date for the new
password set by the user; to do that, you must use the PASSWORD_LIFE_TIME
profile parameter shown in the previous examples.

To see the password expiration date of any account, query the Expiry_Date
column of the DBA_USERS data dictionary view. Users who wish to see the
password expiration date for their accounts can query the Expiry_Date column
of the USER_USERS data dictionary view (via either SQL*Plus or a client-based
query tool).

Preventing Password Reuse

To prevent a password from being reused, you can use one of two profile parameters:
PASSWORD_REUSE_MAX or PASSWORD_REUSE_TIME. These two parameters
are mutually exclusive; if you set a value for one of them, the other must be set to
UNLIMITED.

The PASSWORD_REUSE_TIME parameter specifies the number of days that
must pass before a password can be reused. For example, if you set PASSWORD_
REUSE_TIME to 60, then you cannot reuse the same password within 60 days.

The PASSWORD_REUSE_MAX parameter specifies the number of password
changes that must occur before a password can be reused. If you attempt to reuse
the password before the limit is reached, Oracle will reject your password change.

For example, you can set PASSWORD_REUSE_MAX for the LIMITED_PROFILE
profile created earlier in this chapter.

```
alter profile LIMITED_PROFILE limit
PASSWORD_REUSE_MAX 3
PASSWORD_REUSE_TIME UNLIMITED;
```

If the user JANE now attempts to reuse a recent password, the password change attempt will fail. For example, suppose she changes her password, as below:

```
alter user JANE identified by AUSTEN;
```

and then changes it again:

```
alter user JANE identified by EYRE;
```

During her next password change, she attempts to reuse a recent password, and the attempt fails.

```
alter user JANE identified by AUSTEN;
alter user JANE identified by AUSTEN
*
ERROR at line 1:
ORA-28007: the password cannot be reused
```

She cannot reuse any of her recent passwords; she will need to come up with a new password.

Password histories are stored in the table named USER_HISTORY$ under the SYS schema. In this table, Oracle stores the userid, encrypted password value, and the date/timestamp for the creation of the password. When the PASSWORD_REUSE_TIME value is exceeded or the number of changes exceeds PASSWORD_REUSE_MAX, the old password records are deleted from the SYS.USER_HISTORY$ table. If a new encryption matches an existing encryption, the new password is rejected.

Because the old passwords are stored in a table owned by SYS, the data is stored in the SYSTEM tablespace. If operating system storage space is a major consideration, and you will maintain a very large password history for a very large number of users who are forced to change passwords frequently, the space requirements of the password history table (SYS.USER_HISTORY$) may impact the space requirements of your SYSTEM tablespace.

Setting Password Complexity

You can force users' passwords to meet standards for complexity. For example, you can require that they be of at least a minimum length, that they not be simple words, and that they contain at least one number or punctuation mark. The PASSWORD_VERIFY_FUNCTION parameter of the **create profile** and **alter profile** commands specifies the name of the function that will evaluate the passwords. If a user's proposed password does not meet the criteria, it is not accepted. For example, you could have rejected "austen" and "eyre" as passwords since they do not contain any numeric values.

To simplify the process of enforcing password complexity, Oracle provides a function called VERIFY_FUNCTION. By default, this function is *not* created. The

VERIFY_FUNCTION function is only created if you run the utlpwdmg.sql script located in the /rdbms/admin subdirectory under the Oracle software home directory. In the following listing, an abridged version of this file is shown. The sections shown in bold will be referenced in the description following the listing.

```
Rem utlpwdmg.sql
Rem
Rem  Copyright (c) Oracle Corporation 1996. All Rights Reserved.
Rem
Rem    NAME
Rem      utlpwdmg.sql - script for Default Password Resource Limits
Rem
Rem    DESCRIPTION
Rem      This is a script for enabling the password management
Rem      features by setting the default password resource limits.
Rem
Rem    NOTES
Rem      This file contains a function for minimum checking of
Rem      password complexity. This is more of a sample function that
Rem      the customer can use to develop the function for actual
Rem      complexity checks that the customer wants to make on the new
Rem      password.
Rem
Rem    asurpur     12/12/96 - Changing the name of
Rem    password_verify_function
-- This script sets the default password resource parameters
-- This script needs to be run to enable the password features.
-- However the default resource parameters can be changed based
-- on the need.
-- A default password complexity function is also provided.
-- This function makes the minimum complexity checks like
-- the minimum length of the password, password not same as the
-- username, etc. The user may enhance this function according to
-- the need.
-- This function must be created in SYS schema.
-- connect sys/<password> as sysdba before running the script

CREATE OR REPLACE FUNCTION verify_function
(username varchar2,
  password varchar2,
  old_password varchar2)
  RETURN boolean IS
   n boolean;
   m integer;
   differ integer;
   isdigit boolean;
   ischar  boolean;
```

```
    ispunct boolean;
    digitarray varchar2(20);
    punctarray varchar2(25);
    chararray varchar2(52);

BEGIN
    digitarray:= '0123456789';
    chararray:=
    'abcdefghijklmnopqrstuvwxyzABCDEFGHIJKLMNOPQRSTUVWXYZ';
    punctarray:='!"#$%&()''*+,-/:;<>?_';

— Check if the password is same as the username
IF password = username THEN
raise_application_error(-20001, 'Password same as user');
END IF;

    — Check for the minimum length of the password
IF length(password) < 4 THEN<
        raise_application_error
            (-20002,'Password length less than 4');
    END IF;

    — Check if the password is too simple. A dictionary of words
    — may be maintained and a check may be made so as not to
    — allow the words that are too simple for the password.
    IF password IN ('welcome', 'password', 'oracle', 'computer',
'abcd') THEN
        raise_application_error(-20002, 'Password too simple');
    END IF;

    — Check if the password contains at least one letter, one digit and
    — one punctuation mark.
    — 1. Check for the digit
    isdigit:=FALSE;
    m := length(password);
    FOR i IN 1..10 LOOP
        FOR j IN 1..m LOOP
            IF substr(password,j,1) = substr(digitarray,i,1) THEN
                isdigit:=TRUE;
                GOTO findchar;
            END IF;
        END LOOP;
    END LOOP;
    IF isdigit = FALSE THEN
        raise_application_error(-20003, 'Password should contain at
least one digit, one character and one punctuation');
    END IF;
    -- 2. Check for the character
```

```
<<<findchar>>>
ischar:=FALSE;
FOR i IN 1..length(chararray) LOOP
   FOR j IN 1..m LOOP
      IF substr(password,j,1) = substr(chararray,i,1) THEN
         ischar:=TRUE;

            GOTO findpunct;
      END IF;
   END LOOP;
END LOOP;
IF ischar = FALSE THEN
   raise_application_error(-20003,
   'Password should contain at least one digit, one
    character and one punctuation');
END IF;
-- 3. Check for the punctuation
<<<findpunct>>>
ispunct:=FALSE;
FOR i IN 1..length(punctarray) LOOP
   FOR j IN 1..m LOOP
      IF substr(password,j,1) = substr(punctarray,i,1) THEN
         ispunct:=TRUE;
           GOTO endsearch;
      END IF;
   END LOOP;
END LOOP;
IF ispunct = FALSE THEN
   raise_application_error(-20003,
      'Password should contain at least one digit, one
        character and one punctuation');
END IF;


<<<endsearch>>>
-- Check if the password differs from the previous password
-- by at least 3 letters
IF old_password = '' THEN
   raise_application_error(-20004, 'Old password is null');
END IF;
- Everything is fine; return TRUE ;
RETURN(TRUE);
differ := length(old_password) - length(password);

IF abs(differ) < 3 THEN
   IF length(password) < length(old_password) THEN
      m := length(password);
   ELSE
      m := length(old_password);
```

```
        END IF;
        differ := abs(differ);
        FOR i IN 1..m LOOP
            IF substr(password,i,1) != substr(old_password,i,1) THEN
                differ := differ + 1;
            END IF;

        END LOOP;
        IF differ < 3 THEN
            raise_application_error(-20004, 'Password should differ by at
            least 3 characters');
        END IF;
    END IF;
    — Everything is fine; return TRUE ;
    RETURN(TRUE);
END;
/

— This script alters the default parameters for Password Management

— This means that all the users on the system have Password Management
— enabled and set to the following values unless another profile is
— created with parameter values set to different value or UNLIMITED
— is created and assigned to the user.

ALTER PROFILE DEFAULT LIMIT
PASSWORD_LIFE_TIME 60
PASSWORD_GRACE_TIME 10
PASSWORD_REUSE_TIME 1800
PASSWORD_REUSE_MAX UNLIMITED
FAILED_LOGIN_ATTEMPTS 3
PASSWORD_LOCK_TIME 1/1440
PASSWORD_VERIFY_FUNCTION verify_function;
```

NOTE
*The VERIFY_FUNCTION function must be created
under the SYS schema.*

The first three **if** clauses in the function check if the password is the same as the username, if the password is fewer than four characters, and if the password is in a set of specific words. You can modify any of these checks or add your own. For example, your corporate security guideline may call for passwords to have a minimum of six characters; simply update that portion of the utlpwdmg.sql file prior to running it.

The next major section of the function is a three-part check of the contents of the password string. In order to pass these checks, the password must contain at least one character, number, and punctuation mark. As with the earlier checks, these can be edited. For example, you may not require your users to use punctuation marks in their passwords; simply bypass that part of the password check.

The next section of the function compares the old password to the new password on a character-by-character basis. If there are not at least three differences, the new password is rejected.

NOTE
The verifications provided by the VERIFY_ FUNCTION are not as robust as those that serve the same function at the operating system level. If you need a more sophisticated password complexity checking routine, you can modify the VERIFY_FUNCTION procedure shown in the previous listing.

The last command in the script is not part of the function; it is an **alter profile** command that changes the DEFAULT profile. If you change the DEFAULT profile, then every user in your database who uses the DEFAULT profile will be affected. The command shown in the listing creates the following limits: password lifetimes of 60 days, with a 10-day grace period; no password reuse for 1800 days; and account locks after three failed attempts, with automatic unlocking of the account after one minute (1/1,440 of a day). These parameters may not reflect the settings you want. The most important setting is the last one—it specifies that the PASSWORD_ VERIFY_FUNCTION to use is the VERIFY_FUNCTION function created by the utlpwdmg.sql script.

NOTE
This function will only apply to the users of the specified profile.

Notice that the VERIFY_FUNCTION function does not make any database accesses and does not update any database values. If you modify the function, you should make sure that your modifications do not require database accesses or modifications.

You can alter the default profile to use the VERIFY_FUNCTION without altering the password expiration parameters:

```
alter profile DEFAULT limit
PASSWORD_VERIFY_FUNCTION VERIFY_FUNCTION;
```

If you alter the DEFAULT profile, you need to make sure that all users of the profile can successfully use it. For example, the SYS and SYSTEM users use DEFAULT; can you manage their passwords according to the settings specified here? You may wish to create a new profile and assign the new profile to non-DBA users and nonapplication owners to simplify profile management. The problem with that approach is that you will need to remember to assign the new profile to all new users. The more you standardize your user administration activities, the better your chances of implementing this process.

The name of the password verification function does not have to be VERIFY_FUNCTION. As shown in the preceding listing, you pass the name of the function as a parameter in the **alter profile** command. Since the name VERIFY_FUNCTION could apply to almost any function, you should change it to a name that makes sense for your database. For example, you could change it to VERIFY_ORACLE _PASSWORD. You should give it a name that is descriptive and easy to remember; doing so will improve the likelihood of other DBAs understanding what functions the program performs.

The OEM Security Manager tool enables the creation of profiles. You can use this tool to easily define the limits both for the general profile-controlled resources and the password resources. Figure 10-6 shows the general profile values while Figure 10-7 shows the password values screen.

Additional management options for passwords are described in the "Password Encryption and Trickery" section later in this chapter.

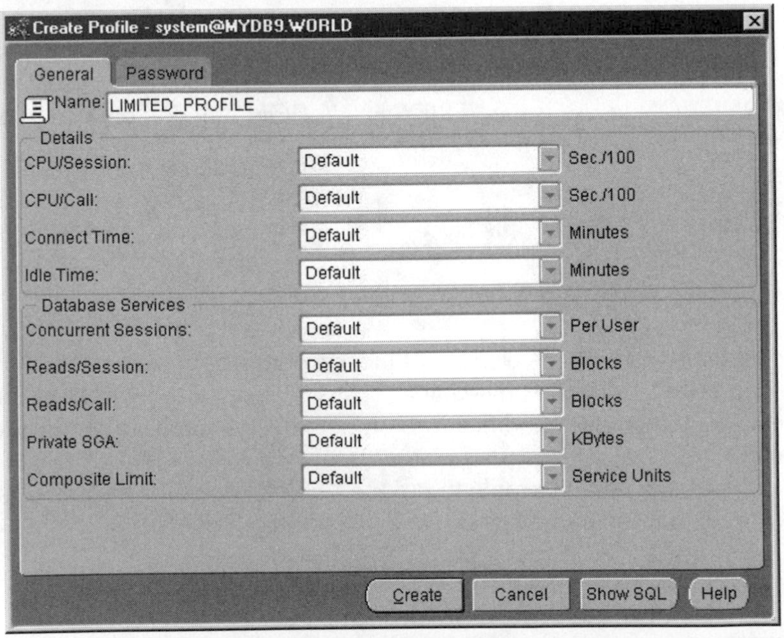

FIGURE 10-6.   *LIMITED_PROFILE general settings*

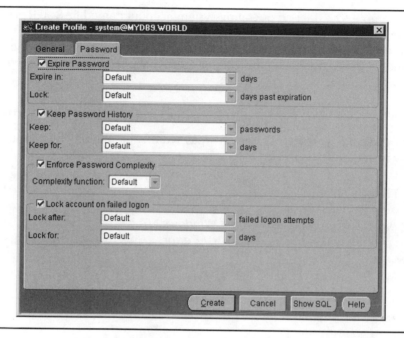

FIGURE 10-7. *LIMITED_PROFILE password settings*

Tying Database Accounts to Host Accounts

Users are allowed to access a database once they have entered a valid username and password for that database. However, it is possible to take advantage of the operating system to provide an additional level of user authentication.

A database account may be paired with an operating system account on the same server. The two account names will differ only in the prefix of the database account name. The prefix defaults to OPS$, but can be set to another value via the OS_AUTHENT_PREFIX parameter of the database's initialization parameter file. This prefix can even be set to a null string, so that no prefix will be used.

NOTE
If you change the OS_AUTHENT_PREFIX to anything other than OPS$, then the database accounts can either be used as autologin accounts or accessed via username/password—but not both ways. If you use OPS$ as the authentication prefix, then you can access the account both as an autologin account and via a username/password combination. Most installations use OPS$.

For example, consider an operating system account named FARMER. The matching database account name for this user is OPS$FARMER. When the FARMER user is logged in to his or her operating system account, he or she can access the OPS$FARMER account without specifying a password, as shown in the following listing:

```
> sqlplus /
```

The **/** takes the place of the username/password combination that would normally be required for access.

> **NOTE**
> *The autologin feature is not supported on all platforms. Entering* **sqlplus /** *from a Windows NT DOS prompt will return an ORA-01017 error message.*

Accounts may be created with passwords. Consider the OPS$FARMER account again. Its creation command may be in the following format:

```
create user OPS$FARMER
identified by SOME_PASSWORD
default tablespace USERS
temporary tablespace TEMP;
```

Even though the password will not be used, it still may be specified. Because the account has a password, it is possible to access the OPS$FARMER database account from a different operating system account if you know the password for the database account. The following listing shows a sample connection to the OPS$FARMER account from a different operating system account:

```
> sqlplus ops$farmer/some_password
```

There are two ways around this potential problem. First, you can create the account without a specific password, using the **identified externally** clause, as shown in the following listing. This clause bypasses the need for an explicit password for the account while keeping the connection between the host account name and the database account name.

```
create user OPS$FARMER
identified externally
default tablespace USERS
temporary tablespace TEMP;
```

When you use the **identified externally** clause, you force the database to validate the operating system account being used to access the database. The operating system account name and the database account name must be identical (except for the database account name prefix).

The second option is to create the account with an impossible password. This method, described in the "Setting Impossible Passwords" section of this chapter, prevents the user from logging into any database account other than through the operating system account associated with it.

There is one situation in which you may want to allow users to have an OPS$ account with a usable password. If the user will both log on directly from the operating system level and from a remote account via Oracle Net, the use of an account that has a password for remote access may be advantageous. If a developer is connecting to the database at the operating system level, she will not want to display her password in order to test a script, and the OPS$ autologin feature supports that need. If she is connecting via remote access (and REMOTE_OS_AUTHENT is not set to TRUE in the parameter file), she will need a password to be able to access the database.

How to Use a Password File for Authentication

In most situations, your DBA users can be authenticated by your operating system. For example, on UNIX systems, a member of the DBA group in the /etc/group file can use **connect internal** if the database is an Oracle8 or an Oracle8i database or **connect / as sysdba** in Oracle9i. **Connect internal** is not supported in Oracle9i. If your DBA users cannot be authenticated by the operating system, you will need to create and maintain a password file.

To create a password file, follow these steps:

1. Create the password file using the ORAPWD utility.

   ```
   > ORAPWD FILE=filename PASSWORD=password ENTRIES=max_users
   ```

   ORAPWD is an Oracle utility that generates the password file. When you execute ORAPWD, you specify the name of the password file to be created, along with the password for SYS access. The ENTRIES parameter tells Oracle how many entries you will be creating in the password file. You cannot expand the file at a later date, so set the ENTRIES value high. If the password file entries limit is exceeded, you will receive an ORA-1996 error. When you re-create the password file, you will need to regrant the SYSDBA and SYSOPER privileges.

2. Set the REMOTE_LOGIN_PASSWORDFILE initialization parameter to EXCLUSIVE in your init.ora file. Shut down and restart the database so the changed parameter takes effect.

3. Grant the SYSOPER and SYSDBA privileges to each user who needs to perform database administration, as shown in the following examples. SYSDBA gives the user DBA authority; SYSOPER lets the user perform support activities for database operations. In order to grant a user SYSOPER or SYSDBA privilege, you must be connected as SYSDBA. Privileged users should now be able to connect to the database by using a command similar to the one shown below:

```
connect george/mch11@PROD.world AS SYSDBA
```

You can use the **revoke** command to revoke the SYSDBA or SYSOPER system privilege from a user, as shown in the following example:

```
revoke SYSDBA from George;
```

To see users who have the SYSDBA and SYSOPER system privileges, query V$PWFILE_USERS. V$PWFILE_USERS will have a value of TRUE in its SysDBA column if the user has the SYSDBA privilege, and a value of TRUE in its SysOper column if the user has SYSOPER privilege.

Password Protection

Both accounts and roles can be protected via passwords. Passwords for both are set when they are created, and may be modified via the **alter user** and **alter role** commands.

The initial password for an account is set via the **create user** command, as shown in the following listing. In this example, the THUMPER account is created with an initial password of R3BB#T.

```
create user THUMPER
identified by R3BB#T;
```

Passwords for accounts should be changed via the **alter user** command. A sample **alter user** command is shown in the following listing:

```
alter user THUMPER identified by NEWPASSWORD;
```

You can use the SQL*Plus **password** command to change a user's password. The **password** command will prompt you for the old password, a new password, and a verification of the new password. The password values entered are not echoed to the screen.

To change your own password within SQL*Plus, type the **password** command, as shown in the following listing:

```
password
```

To change another user's password, use the **password** command followed by the username.

`password JANE`

You will be prompted for JANE's new password and a verification. The **password** command is very useful for your end users, since it greatly simplifies the commands they need to use when changing passwords. If they do not use the **password** command, then they will need to use the following command:

`alter user USERNAME identified by NEWPASSWORD;`

NOTE
*The **alter user** command does not fully enforce the password verification function shown earlier in this chapter. Oracle recommends using the **password** command when changing passwords.*

Passwords for roles are set at the time the role is created, via the **create role** command. You do not need to set a password for a role; if one is specified, the password must be entered when the role is enabled by the user.

`create role ACCOUNT_CREATOR identified by HELPD2SK_ONLY;`

You can use the **alter role** command to change the password associated with roles. Like user passwords, roles can also be **identified externally**, thereby enforcing a link between the host account name and the role name. Unlike user accounts, it is possible to have roles with no passwords (the default). You can remove a password from a role via the **not identified** clause, as shown in the following example:

`alter role ACCOUNT_CREATOR not identified;`

After this command has been executed, the ACCOUNT_CREATOR role will not be password protected.

Roles can be tied to operating system privileges. If this capability is available on your operating system, then you invoke it by using the **identified externally** clause of the **alter role** command. When the role is enabled, Oracle will check the operating system to verify your access. Altering a role to use this security feature is shown in the following example:

`alter role MANAGER identified externally;`

In most UNIX systems, the verification process uses the /etc/group file. In order to use this for any operating system, the OS_ROLES database startup parameter in the database parameter file must be set to TRUE.

The following example of this verification process is for a database instance called Local on a UNIX system. The server's /etc/group file may contain the following entry:

```
ora_local_manager_d:NONE:1:dora
```

This entry grants the MANAGER role to the account named Dora. The _d suffix indicates that this role is to be granted by default when Dora logs in. An _a suffix would indicate that this role is to be enabled **with admin option**. If this role were also the user's default role, then the suffix would be _ad. If more than one user were granted this role, then the additional usernames would be appended to the /etc/group entry, as shown in the following listing:

```
ora_local_manager_d:NONE:1:dora,judy
```

If you use this option, then all roles in the database will be enabled via the operating system.

Object-Level Privileges

Object-level privileges give users access to data that they do not own. You can use roles to ease the administration of privileges. Explicit privileges are also available, and are in fact necessary in some circumstances.

Privileges are created via the **grant** command and are recorded in the data dictionary. Access to tables, views, sequences—as well as synonyms for these—plus the ability to execute procedures, functions, packages, and types can be granted to users. The privileges that may be granted on objects are listed in Table 10-4.

Privilege	Capabilities Granted
ALTER	Can alter the object.
DEBUG*	Can enable the debug facility for Java programs (granted to the JAVADEBUGPRIV role).
DELETE	Can delete rows from the object.

TABLE 10-4. *Available Object Privileges*

Privilege	Capabilities Granted
DEQUEUE*	Can dequeue a message (used with the DBMS_AQ package).
ENQUEUE*	Can enqueue a message (used with the DBMS_AQ package).
EXECUTE	Can execute the function, package, procedure, library, or type.
INDEX	Can create indexes on the table.
INSERT	Can insert rows into the object. This privilege may be granted for specific columns of the object.
ON COMMIT REFRESH	Can create a refresh-on-commit materialized view on the specified table.
QUERY REWRITE	Can create a materialized view for query rewrite using the specified table.
READ	Can access the directory.
REFERENCE	Can create foreign keys that reference the table.
SELECT	Can query the object.
UNDER	Can create a subview or subtype under the current view or type.
UPDATE	Can update rows in the object. This privilege may be granted for specific columns of the object.
WRITE	Can write files in a directory.

TABLE 10-4.   *Available Object Privileges* (continued)

NOTE
In Table 10-4, privileges designated with an asterisk (*) indicate that the privilege is specific to the package mentioned in the description.

You can use the **with grant option** clause to pass along to the grantee the ability to make further grants on the base object. The following listing from SQL*Plus shows an example of this. In this example, the user named THUMPER grants the user named MCGREGOR both SELECT and partial UPDATE access on a table called EMPLOYEE, **with grant option**. This user then grants one of these privileges to another user (named JFISHER).

```
grant select, update (Employee_Name, Address)
on EMPLOYEE to MCGREGOR
with grant option;

connect MCGREGOR/FARMER
grant select on THUMPER.EMPLOYEE to JFISHER;
```

NOTE
*Granting the privileges to PUBLIC makes them
available to all users in the database.*

If EMPLOYEE is a partitioned table, you cannot grant SELECT access to just one partition of it. However, you can create a view that selects data just from one partition, and then grant SELECT access on that view to your users. The view will be an additional object to manage, but you can use it to enforce partition-level data security.

The management of privileges can quickly become a time-consuming task. Each user must be granted the appropriate privileges for each object in a database application. Consider a small application that has 20 tables and 30 users; 600 privileges (20 tables times 30 users) must be managed.

With the advent of roles, the management of such privileges became much easier. Roles are groups of privileges; the roles are then granted to users, greatly simplifying the privilege management process.

The following listing shows an example of the usage of roles. In this example, two roles are created. The first, APPLICATION_USER, is given the system-level privilege CREATE SESSION; a user who has been granted this role will be able to log into the database. The second role, DATA_ENTRY_CLERK, is granted privileges on tables.

```
create role APPLICATION_USER;
grant CREATE SESSION to APPLICATION_USER;

create role DATA_ENTRY_CLERK;
connect THUMPER/R3BB#T
grant select, insert on THUMPER.EMPLOYEE to DATA_ENTRY_CLERK;
grant select, insert on THUMPER.TIME_CARDS to DATA_ENTRY_CLERK;
grant select, insert on THUMPER.DEPARTMENT to DATA_ENTRY_CLERK;
```

Roles can be granted to other roles. For example, you can grant the APPLICATION_ USER role to the DATA_ENTRY_CLERK role, as shown in this example:

```
grant APPLICATION_USER to DATA_ENTRY_CLERK;
```

The role can then be granted to a user. This role can be dynamically enabled and disabled during the user's session via the **set role** command.

```
grant DATA_ENTRY_CLERK to MCGREGOR;
```

From the OEM Security Manager tool, select the specific user or role to whom object grants are to be given and use the Object Privileges window to select the schema and grants. Figure 10-8 shows the user THUMPER being granted SELECT, INSERT, and UPDATE privileges on the HR.LOCATIONS table.

Roles and system privileges (such as CREATE TABLE) may be granted to users with the privilege to pass them on to other users. For roles, the **with admin option**

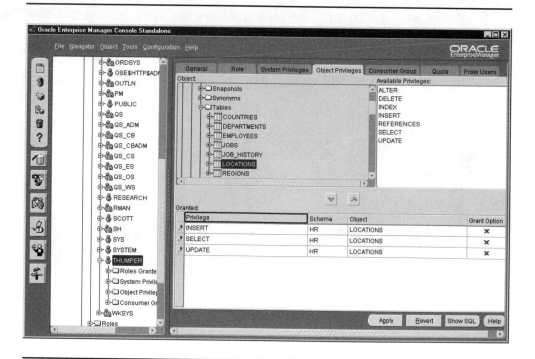

FIGURE 10-8. *Granting object privileges to a user*

clause is used. In the following listing, the DATA_ENTRY_CLERK role created earlier is granted to a user (BPOTTER), along with the privilege to administer the role:

```
grant DATA_ENTRY_CLERK to BPOTTER with admin option;
```

Given this privilege, the user BPOTTER can now **grant** and **revoke** the role to and from other users, and can drop the role as well.

NOTE
Users who have table privileges via roles cannot create views or procedures based on those tables. This restriction is needed because the grants made via a role are only valid while the user is logged in and the role is enabled. The creation of views by nonowners requires explicit privileges on the tables.

The dynamic nature of roles is very useful for restricting users' privileges. If a role is enabled when a user starts an application (via the **set role** command), and then disabled upon leaving the application, the user cannot take advantage of the role's privileges except when using the application.

For example, when MCGREGOR logs into an application, the command

```
set role DATA_ENTRY_CLERK;
```

may be executed. When this user leaves the application, the command

```
set role NONE;
```

will disable any privileges that had been granted via roles.

You can use the **revoke** command to revoke privileges and roles from users. You may either revoke some of a user's privileges (by explicitly listing them) or all of the user's privileges (via the **all** keyword). In the following example, a specific privilege is revoked for the EMPLOYEE table from one user, while another user's privileges are completely revoked:

```
revoke delete on EMPLOYEE from PETER;
revoke all on EMPLOYEE from MCGREGOR;
```

In the following example, the role ACCOUNT_CREATOR is revoked from the user account named HELPDESK:

```
revoke ACCOUNT_CREATOR from HELPDESK;
```

Because user accounts can be completely deleted via the following command,

```
drop user USERNAME cascade;
```

privilege cleanup of deleted accounts is not required. The **revoke** command is thus used mostly when users change status, or when applications move from one environment (such as acceptance test) to another (such as production).

There is an important distinction between **revoke**s of privileges granted **with grant option** and those granted **with admin option**. Suppose THUMPER grants MCGREGOR access to the EMPLOYEE table **with grant option**:

```
grant SELECT on EMPLOYEE to MCGREGOR with grant option;
```

MCGREGOR can now pass on that grant to the BPOTTER user, along with the **with grant option** privilege:

```
grant SELECT on THUMPER.EMPLOYEE to BPOTTER with grant option;
```

If THUMPER now **revoke**s the earlier grant to MCGREGOR:

```
revoke SELECT on EMPLOYEE from MCGREGOR;
```

then what privilege does BPOTTER have, since BPOTTER received access to the EMPLOYEE table via MCGREGOR? BPOTTER can no longer access THUMPER's EMPLOYEE table since MCGREGOR can no longer access that table.

Revokes of privileges granted **with admin option** function differently. If you grant MCGREGOR a system privilege **with admin option**, then MCGREGOR can grant that system privilege to BPOTTER. If you then **revoke** MCGREGOR's privilege, then BPOTTER *retains* the new system privilege.

Listing the Privileges

Information about privileges that have been granted is stored in the data dictionary. This data is accessible via data dictionary views.

You can use the data dictionary views listed in Table 10-5 to list the privileges that have been granted within the database. User-level views are also available.

Data Dictionary View	Contents
DBA_ROLES	Names of roles and their password status
DBA_ROLE_PRIVS	Users who have been granted roles
DBA_SYS_PRIVS	Users who have been granted system privileges

TABLE 10-5. *Privilege-Related Data Dictionary Views*

Data Dictionary View	Contents
DBA_TAB_PRIVS	Users who have been granted privileges on tables
DBA_COL_PRIVS	Users who have been granted privileges on columns
ROLE_ROLE_PRIVS	Roles that have been granted to other roles
ROLE_SYS_PRIVS	System privileges that have been granted to roles
ROLE_TAB_PRIVS	Table privileges that have been granted to roles

TABLE 10-5.   *Privilege-Related Data Dictionary Views* (continued)

For example, you may wish to display which system privileges have been granted to which roles. In that case, the following query would display that information:

```
select
      Role,                /*Name of the role*/
      Privilege,           /*System privilege*/
      Admin_Option         /*Was admin option granted?*/
 from ROLE_SYS_PRIVS;
```

To retrieve table grants for users, you now have to look for two types of grants: explicit grants of privileges to users and those that are granted via roles. To view the grants made via explicit grants, query the DBA_TAB_PRIVS view, as shown in the following listing:

```
select
      Grantee,             /*Recipient of the grant*/
      Owner,               /*Owner of the object*/
      Table_Name,          /*Name of the object*/
      Grantor,             /*User who made the grant*/
      Privilege,           /*Privilege granted*/
      Grantable            /*Was admin option granted?*/
 from DBA_TAB_PRIVS;
```

To view the table privileges granted via a role, find the user's records in DBA_ROLE_PRIVS and compare those to the role's table privileges (which are listed in ROLE_TAB_PRIVS).

```
select
      DBA_ROLE_PRIVS.Grantee,         /*Recipient of the grant*/
      ROLE_TAB_PRIVS.Owner,           /*Owner of the object*/
      ROLE_TAB_PRIVS.Table_Name,      /*Name of the object*/
```

```
        ROLE_TAB_PRIVS.Privilege,        /*Privilege granted*/
        ROLE_TAB_PRIVS.Grantable         /*Was admin option granted?*/
  from DBA_ROLE_PRIVS, ROLE_TAB_PRIVS
 where DBA_ROLE_PRIVS.Granted_Role = ROLE_TAB_PRIVS.Role
   and DBA_ROLE_PRIVS.Grantee = 'some username';
```

This query will retrieve the role-granted table privileges for a particular user.

To view the profile limits that are in place for your current session, you can query USER_RESOURCE_LIMITS. Its columns are

Resource_Name	The name of the resource (for example, SESSIONS_PER_USER)
Limit	The limit placed upon this resource

USER_PASSWORD_LIMITS describes the password profile parameters for the user. It has the same columns as USER_RESOURCE_LIMITS.

There is no "DBA" version of the USER_PASSWORD_LIMITS view; it is strictly limited to the user's current session. To see the cost associated with each available resource, you can query the RESOURCE_COST view. DBAs can access the DBA_PROFILES view to see the resource limits for all profiles. The Resource_Type column of DBA_PROFILES indicates whether the resource profile is a PASSWORD or KERNEL profile.

In addition to these views, there are two views, each with a single column, that list the privileges and roles currently enabled for the current session. They are

SESSION_PRIVS	The Privilege column lists all system privileges available to the session, whether granted directly or via roles.
SESSION_ROLES	The Role column lists all roles that are currently enabled for the session.

SESSION_PRIVS and SESSION_ROLES are available to all users.

Limiting Available Commands: Product User Profiles

Within SQL*Plus, an additional level of security is provided—individual commands may be disabled for specific users. That way, users with the UPDATE privilege on a table can be prevented from using the SQL*Plus command-line interface to update the table in an uncontrolled fashion. This capability allows DBAs to prevent users from accessing the operating system from within SQL*Plus (via the **host** command).

This prevention is useful when an application includes an option to access SQL*Plus and you do not want the users to have access to the operating system.

In addition to revoking users' ability to use the **host** command from within SQL*Plus, you may also revoke their use of the **connect** command. Eliminating the access to those commands will force users to stay within their own accounts. The following listing shows the results of these commands when this level of security is in place:

```
SQL> host
invalid command: host
SQL> connect system/manager
invalid command: connect
```

In each case, the "invalid command" message is returned. The user must remain in his or her own account.

To create this level of security, the Product User Profile tables must be created. The script for creating them is called pupbld.sql, and it is found in the /sqlplus/ admin subdirectory under the Oracle software home directory. This script creates several tables and views, and should be run from within the SYSTEM account. Beginning with Oracle8i, the script is run automatically when you create a database.

For SQL*Plus, the most important table is accessed via a synonym named PRODUCT_USER_PROFILE. The key columns for security purposes are listed in Table 10-6. Insert records into this table to create the desired level of security.

You can also use the Product User Profile tables to disable roles. To disable a role, set the Attribute column to ROLES, and place the role name in the Char_Value column. Disabling of roles is usually done in coordination with the disabling of the **set** command (see Table 10-6).

Column Name	Description
Product	Set to SQL*Plus. The name must be in mixed case, as shown here.
Userid	Username, in uppercase, for users whose commands are being disabled. The % wildcard may be used to specify multiple users. An entry for % used by itself will apply to all users.
Attribute	The name, in uppercase, of the command being disabled. Disabling the SET command in SQL*Plus also disables **set role** and **set transaction**.
Char_Value	Set to DISABLED, in uppercase.

TABLE 10-6. *Columns in PRODUCT_USER_PROFILE*

Password Security During Logins

When you connect to a database server from a client machine, or from one database to another via a database link, Oracle transmits the password you enter in an unencrypted format unless you specify otherwise. You can set parameters that force Oracle to encrypt the password values prior to transmitting them. To enable password encryption, set the following parameters:

- For your client machines, set the ORA_ENCRYPT_LOGIN parameter in your sqlnet.ora file to TRUE.

- For your server machines, set the DBLINK_ENCRYPT_LOGIN parameter in your init.ora file to TRUE.

Once these parameters are set (and the database is shut down and restarted), your passwords will be sent from client to server and server to server in an encrypted form.

Password Encryption and Trickery

Knowing how the database encrypts and sets passwords enables DBAs to perform a number of otherwise impossible tasks. These tasks include the setting of impossible passwords and the ability to become other users, as described in the following sections.

How Passwords Are Stored

When a password is specified for a user account or a role, the database stores the *encrypted* version of that password in the data dictionary. Setting the same password for two different accounts will result in different encryptions. For all passwords, the encrypted value is 16 characters long and contains numbers and capital letters.

How are passwords validated? When a password is entered during a user validation, that password is encrypted, and the encryption that is generated is compared to the one in the data dictionary for that account. If they match, then the password is correct and the authorization succeeds.

Setting Impossible Passwords

Knowing how the database stores passwords is important because it adds new options to account security. What would happen if you could specify the *encryption* of a password, rather than the password itself? And what if the encryption you generated did not follow the format rules for encrypted passwords? The result would be an account that could never be logged into, since no password could generate the invalid encryption.

Consider the accounts and encrypted passwords selected by the following query. The query selects the Username and Password fields from the DBA_USERS view.

```
select
        Username,          /*Username*/
        Password           /*Encrypted password*/
from DBA_USERS
where Username in ('MCGREGOR','THUMPER','OPS$FARMER');


USERNAME            PASSWORD
----------------    ----------------
MCGREGOR            1A2DD3CCEE354DFA
THUMPER             F3DE41CBB3AB4452
OPS$FARMER          4FF2FF1CBDE11332
```

Note that each of the encrypted passwords in the output is 16 characters in length.

Since the password is not stored in the data dictionary—but its encryption is—how does Import know what the passwords are? After all, when a full import is done from an export dump file, the passwords are imported as well.

Import executes SQL commands. During a full import, Import executes an undocumented version of the **create user** command. Importing the MCGREGOR user from the database shown in the preceding listing would generate the following **create user** command:

```
create user MCGREGOR identified by VALUES '1A2DD3CCEE354DFA';
```

In other words, Import uses the undocumented **values** clause within the **identified by** clause to specify the *encrypted* password for the user it is creating.

Import shouldn't get to have all the fun. You can use this same command to set an encryption for any account. As long as the encryption you set violates the encryption rules (16 characters, all capitals), it will be impossible to match during user authentication. The result will be an account that is only accessible from the correct operating system account on the server. In the following listing, the encryption is set to the phrase "no way." The DBA_USERS view is then queried.

```
alter user OPS$FARMER identified by VALUES 'no way';

select
      Username,              /*Username*/
      Password               /*Encrypted password*/
from DBA_USERS
where Username in ('MCGREGOR','THUMPER','OPS$FARMER');

USERNAME             PASSWORD
---------------- ----------------
MCGREGOR             1A2DD3CCEE354DFA
THUMPER              F3DE41CBB3AB4452
OPS$FARMER           no way
```

It is now impossible to access the OPS$FARMER account except via the FARMER account on the server, and even then it is only accessible via the /autologin. Impossible passwords are useful for locking non-OPS$ accounts that should never be logged into directly, such as SYS.

Becoming Another User

Since the encrypted passwords can be set, you can temporarily take over any account and then set it back to its original password without ever knowing the account's password. This capability allows you to become another user (which is very useful when testing applications or troubleshooting problems in production).

Temporarily becoming another user requires going through the following steps:

1. Query DBA_USERS to determine the current encrypted password for the account.

2. Generate the **alter user** command that will be needed to reset the encrypted password to its current value after you are done.

3. Spool the **alter user** command to a file.

4. Change the user's password.

5. Access the user's account and perform your testing.

6. When the testing is complete, run the file containing the **alter user** command to reset the user's encrypted password to its original value.

This process is automated via the following SQL*Plus script. This script automatically generates the command necessary to reset the user's account once your testing is complete.

```
REM*   become_another_user.sql
REM*
REM*   This script generates the commands necessary to allow
REM*   you to temporarily become another user.
REM*
REM*   It MUST be run from a DBA account.
REM*
REM*   Input variable: The username of the account to be taken
REM*   over.
REM*
REM*   Steps 1, 2, and 3: Query DBA_USERS. Generate the ALTER USER
REM*   command that will be necessary to reset the password to its
REM*   present value.
REM*
set pagesize 0 feedback off verify off echo off termout off
REM*
REM*   Create a file called reset.sql to hold the commands
REM*   generated
REM*
spool reset.sql
REM*
REM*   Select the encrypted password from DBA_USERS.
REM*
SELECT 'alter user &&1 identified by values '||''''||
password||''''||' profile '||profile||';'
FROM dba_users WHERE username = upper('&&1');

prompt 'host rm -f reset.sql'
prompt 'exit'
spool off
exit
```

NOTE
*In the **select** statement, there are two sets of four single quotes.*

This script generates as its output a script called reset.sql. This file will have three lines in it. The first line will contain the **alter user** command, with the **values** clause followed by the encrypted password. The second line will contain a **host** command that deletes the reset.sql file (since it will not be needed after it is used in step 6). The third line contains an **exit** command to leave SQL*Plus. A sample reset.sql file is shown in the following listing:

```
alter user MCGREGOR identified by values '1A2DD3CCEE354DFA' profile DEFAULT;
host rm -f reset.sql
exit
```

The **rm -f** command in the second line should be replaced by the appropriate file deletion command for your operating system.

You may now proceed with steps 4 and 5, which involve changing the user's password (via the **alter user** command) and accessing the account. These actions are shown in the following listing:

```
alter user MCGREGOR identified by MY_TURN;
connect MCGREGOR/MY_TURN
```

You will now be logged into the MCGREGOR account. When you have completed your testing, log into SQL*Plus and run the reset.sql script shown above. The execution of the reset.sql script is shown in the following listing:

```
sqlplus system/manager @reset
```

If you are testing multiple accounts simultaneously, you may wish to embed the username in the reset.sql filename; otherwise, the first reset.sql file may be overwritten by later versions. If you are doing this for OPS$ accounts, be careful, since **$** is a special character in some operating systems (such as UNIX).

The account will now be reset to its original encrypted password—and thus its original password. The testing of the account took place without your needing to know what its password was and without its password being destroyed.

Overriding Password Restrictions During "Become Another User" Operations

You can prevent users from reusing old passwords (see the "Preventing Password Reuse" section earlier in this chapter). Preventing the reuse of old passwords may impact your ability to become other users. As shown previously, the standard set of steps for becoming another user is as follows:

1. Query DBA_USERS to determine the current encrypted password for the account.

2. Generate the **alter user** command that will be needed to reset the encrypted password to its current value after you are done.

3. Spool the **alter user** command to a file.

4. Change the user's password.

5. Access the user's account and perform your testing.

6. When the testing is complete, run the file containing the **alter user** command to reset the user's encrypted password to its original value.

What if the user is not allowed to reuse the old password? Step 6 will fail, and you will be unable to set the user's password back to its original value. You will need to set a new password for the user—significantly reducing the effectiveness of the "become another user" procedure.

To avoid this situation, create a profile that does not enforce a password history constraint. Prior to becoming the user, assign the new profile to the user. When you have completed your session as the user, assign the original profile to the user. In the script provided in the preceding section, the user's **profile** setting is captured and is integrated into the **alter user** command that resets the user's password. The steps are as follows:

1. Check the profile settings for the user.

2. Assign the user to a profile that does not have a password history limit, does not have a password verification function, and has unlimited password reuse times. For example, the profile creation command could be

```
create profile temp_profile limit
password_verify_function    null
password_reuse_time         unlimited
password_reuse_max          unlimited;
```

3. Query DBA_USERS to determine the current encrypted password and profile for the account.

4. Generate the **alter user** command that will be needed to reset the encrypted password and profile to their current values after you are done.

5. Spool the **alter user** command to a file.

6. Change the user's password.

7. Access the user's account and perform your testing.

8. When the testing is complete, run the file containing the **alter user** command to reset the user's encrypted password and profile to their original values.

Virtual Private Databases

Oracle introduced the Virtual Private Database (VPD) to provide fine-grained access control coupled with a secure application context in Oracle8i, Release 3. With VPD you establish policies in the form of predicates (**where** clauses) that are attached to every query that users present to the database. An organization using VPD only needs to build a security structure once in the data server. Since the security policies are attached to the data instead of the application, security rules are enforced at all times and from any access approach. Thus, the data presented from a query is identical regardless of the connection mode: from an application, SQL*Plus, or an ODBC driver. VPD relies on several mechanisms to ensure data privacy for each user. To accomplish data separation, ensure that your tables are designed to enable restriction of data access according to the values in one or more columns.

One common approach for ensuring privacy of data where several companies are involved is to define a company key field on each table to identify each individual organization. Associate users with a particular key, and then establish a policy that says users can only access rows that correspond to their designated key. When a query is submitted, the appropriate **where** clause is automatically attached, restricting the user to see and manipulate only her data. Thus, fine-grained access control is automatically implemented and assured.

For example, let's say that you select from the Medical Records database using the following query:

```
select * from PATIENTS;
```

If the PATIENTS table has a security policy associated with it that restricts patients from seeing any information other than their own, the query would be automatically rewritten as

```
select *
  from PATIENTS
 where PATIENT_ID = sys_context('PATIENT_CONTEXT','ALL_PATIENT_ID')
/
```

In this example, the **where** clause that is automatically appended to the user's query by the policy ensures that users can only see their data no matter what data is in the table and how they construct their queries. The patient's ID is obtained from the user-defined application context, PATIENT_CONTEXT. The system function **sys_context** returns the value for the attribute ALL_PATIENT_ID in the PATIENT_CONTEXT.

Within VPD, you must still grant users the appropriate privileges for each table, but you do not need to create views and procedures to prevent users from accessing other users' data. Thus, using VPD, you no longer have to worry about users accessing the database through SQL*Plus with different privileges than they have through an application.

Creating a VPD

Creating an Oracle VPD is very different from installing and configuring most Oracle tools. The VPD is not actually an application unto itself, but rather is installed with the database. To create a VPD, follow these steps to

1. Determine the database objects and their relationships

2. Define your security policy objectives

3. Create the application context

4. Create a package that sets the context

5. Create the policy function

6. Associate the policy function with a table or view

There are different ways to perform several of these steps. We present the approach that we believe will yield the most robust, scalable, and secure implementation.

Determine the Database Objects and Their Relationships

To begin creating your VPD, you must determine the database objects involved, their relationship to each other, and the keys on which the security approach will be built. For example, in the Medical Records department, patients can view and gain copies of their own medical information electronically but not access anyone else's information.

Keeping each patient's information secure and private is of major importance. The primary key that links patient information together is the patient's unique ID number. In our example (which is overly simplified), there are only two tables in which data is stored: PATIENT_PERSONAL_INFORMATION and MEDICAL_INFORMATION. The PATIENT_PERSONAL_INFORMATION table stores information about each patient's address, phone number, and so on, while the MEDICAL_INFORMATION table, as the name implies, stores the associated medical data. The PATIENT_ID is used to link all of the information together.

Here is the composition of the two tables:

```
create table PATIENT_PERSONAL_INFORMATION
(Patient_Id            NUMBER(10) primary key,
 Physician_Id          NUMBER(6) not null,
 Patient_Username      VARCHAR2(10),
 Patient_Name          VARCHAR2(20),
 Patient_Address1      VARCHAR2(20),
 Patient_Address2      VARCHAR2(20),
 Patient_Phone         NUMBER(10)
);
create table MEDICAL_INFORMATION
(Patient_Id            NUMBER(10) primary key,
 Test_Performed        VARCHAR2(30),
 Test_Results          VARCHAR2(50),
 Diagnosis             VARCHAR2(500)
);
```

Define Your Security Policy Objectives

The security policy for our example is simply stated as "Patients can only see their own information." Your policy objectives will generally be more complex, and you can have several security policies associated with a table or view. Be very clear on how you phrase your policies because each security policy that you define must be translated into PL/SQL function code that will be attached to the specified application table or view.

Create the Application Context

An application context is a named set of attributes and values that you can set and then associate with the current user's session. Oracle provides the default context, USERENV, which contains system information about the current session such as the username, host, and program name. If you want to define other attributes for a user, such as PATIENT_ID, you can do so using application contexts.

Using the privilege CREATE ANY CONTEXT, you can create the application context. You supply a unique context name and then associate the name with the package that implements the context. Context names must be unique across the entire database. Therefore, if you attempt to create a context using a name that already exists, you will receive an error.

To create the context, you must have the CREATE ANY CONTEXT privilege granted to you. For this example, you will create a context called MEDICAL_SEC_CTX that will belong to our PL/SQL package stored in the MEDICAL_DEPT schema and named MEDICAL_SEC. The syntax follows:

```
create context MEDICAL_SEC_CTX using MEDICAL_DEPT.MEDICAL_SEC;
```

Create a Package That Sets the Context

Once the context is created, create the package and functions that set the context. The example below shows how you set the PATIENT_ID context attributes using the current user's username obtained from the default context, USERENV. The function uses the username to look up the necessary attributes in the table.

```
create or replace package MEDICAL_SEC is
    procedure GET_PATIENT_ID;
end MEDICAL_SEC;
/
create or replace package body MEDICAL_SEC is
    procedure GET_PATIENT_ID
    is
    PATIENT_ID_VAR number;
    begin
      select PATIENT_ID
        into PATIENT_ID_VAR from PATIENT_PERSONAL_INFORMATION
       where PATIENT_USERNAME = SYS_CONTEXT('USERENV','SESSION_USER');
      dbms_session.set_context('MEDICAL_SEC_CTX', 'PATIENT_ID',
          PATIENT_ID_VAR);
    end GET_PATIENT_ID;
end MEDICAL_SEC;
/
```

Oracle supplies the predefined function SYS_CONTEXT and the built-in context USERENV so that you can return the name of the user executing the procedure. There are many other values that you can obtain from the SYS_CONTEXT function. Displayed in Table 10-7 are some of the more security-oriented values.

Parameter	Value Returned
authentication_data	The data being used to authenticate the login user.
authentication_type	The method used to authenticate the user. The available values are as follows: Database: username/password authentication OS: operating system external user authentication Network: network protocol or ANO authentication Proxy: OCI proxy connection authentication
bg_job_id	If an Oracle background process established the current session, the job ID of the job will be returned.

TABLE 10-7. *SYS_CONTEXT Parameters*

Parameter	Value Returned
client_info	Used in conjunction with the DBMS_APPLICATION_INFO package to store information, this parameter returns up to 64 bytes of user session information.
current_schema	Name of the default schema being used as the current schema.
current_user	Name of the user whose privileges the current session is under.
current_userid	ID of the user whose privileges the current session is under.
db_domain	Database domain as specified in the DB_DOMAIN initialization parameter.
db_name	Database name as specified in the DB_NAME initialization parameter.
entryid	Available auditing entry identifier. Set if the AUDIT_TRAIL parameter is set to TRUE in the initialization parameter file.
external_name	External name of the database user. The distinguished name stored in the user certificate is returned for SSL authenticated sessions using v.503 certificates.
fg_job_id	If an Oracle foreground process established the current session, the job ID of the job will be returned.
host	Name of the host machine the client connected from.
instance	The instance identification number of the current instance.
isdba	If you have the DBA role enabled, TRUE will be returned. If you do not, FALSE will be returned.
network_protocol	Network protocol being used for communication.

TABLE 10-7. *SYS_CONTEXT Parameters* (continued)

Parameter	Value Returned
os_user	Operating system username of the client process that initiated the database session.
proxy_user	Name of the database user who opened the session on behalf of the SESSION_USER.
proxy_userid	Identifier of the database user who opened the session on behalf of the SESSION_USER.
session_user	Database username by which the current user is authenticated. This value remains the same throughout the session.
session_userid	Identifier of the database username by which the current user is authenticated.
sessionid	Auditing session identifier.
terminal	Operating system identifier for the client of the current session.

TABLE 10-7. *SYS_CONTEXT Parameters* (continued)

To set the context for a user session, call the function that was associated with the context when the context was created. You can do this from your application or, perhaps, by using a login trigger. Using a login trigger ensures that the context is set no matter how the user logs into the database. To set a login trigger, use the **on logon** trigger, available in Oracle8i, version 8.1.5 and beyond.

Create the Security Policy Functions

Next, a PL/SQL function to implement the policy is required. The function will then be associated with the MEDICAL_INFORMATION table.

Here is the process that occurs to impose fine-grained security on a query once the function is in place. By the way, the word "query" as used here means any form of information access from a table or view, including but not limited to **select**, **insert**, **delete**, **update**, and subquery statements. Once a security policy is associated with a table or view, when a user presents a query, the query processor calls the policy function and the function returns a value in the form of an access control condition, or *predicate*.

In reality, the predicate is a **where** clause that is appended to the user's SQL statement to limit the rows that will be returned, updated, or deleted depending on the type of statement that is used. The modified query is evaluated and optimized during statement parse time and can be shared and reused to help improve performance.

Our goal is to enable patients to view only their own information based on their own PATIENT_ID. Here's a sample PL/SQL procedure to accomplish that goal:

```
create or replace package MEDICAL_SEC as
  function MEDICAL_ID_SEC return varchar2;
  END MEDICAL_SEC;
/
create or replace package body MEDICAL_SEC as
/* LIMITS SELECT STATEMENTS BASED ON PATIENT_ID VALUE */
function MEDICAL_ID_SEC return varchar2
  is
    MY_PREDICATE varchar2 (2000);
    begin
      MY_PREDICATE := 'PATIENT_ID=SYS_CONTEXT
          (''MEDICAL_SEC_CTX'',''PATIENT_ID'')';
      return MY_PREDICATE;
    end MEDICAL_ID_SEC;
end MEDICAL_SEC;
/
```

To conserve space, no error handling is shown within the procedure.

In this code example, we retrieve the PATIENT_ID from the application context MEDICAL_SEC_CTX and generate the predicate to be appended to a query on the MEDICAL_INFORMATION table. To see how the predicate will look, let's say that the PATIENT_ID is 2435678987. The returned predicate will read

```
PATIENT_ID = 2435678987;
```

This predicate will be used in the **where** clause to ensure that the only information this patient will see is data that matches the correct PATIENT_ID.

Associate the Policy Function with a Table or View
Oracle provides a PL/SQL package called DBMS_RLS to manage security policy administration. Anyone creating or administering policies must have **execute** granted for this package through the SYS user. Table 10-8 shows the four procedures available in the package.

Procedure	Function
ADD_POLICY	Add a policy to a table or view.
DROP_POLICY	Remove a policy from a table or view.
REFRESH_POLICY	Force a reparse of open cursors associated with a policy to immediately take advantage of a new or changed policy.
ENABLE_POLICY	Enable or disable a policy that has been previously added to a table or view.

TABLE 10-8. *DBMS_RLS Package Procedures*

Use the DBMS_RLS package to associate a policy function to a table or view. There are different arguments that you use with each of the procedures. Table 10-9 shows the arguments.

Parameter	Description
object_schema	Name of the schema containing the table or view.
object_name	Name of the table or view.
policy_name	Name of the policy to be added or dropped; must be unique for the table or view.
function_schema	Schema of the policy function.
policy_function	Name of a function, which generates a predicate for the policy. If the function is defined within a package, the name of the package must be present.
statement_types	Statement types to which the policy will apply. Can be any combination of **select**, **insert**, **update**, and **delete**. The default is to apply to all of these types.
update_check	When set to TRUE, the value will be checked against security policies after insert or update (optional argument).
enable	Indicates whether the policy is enabled when added; default is TRUE.

TABLE 10-9. *DBMS_RLS Parameters for ADD_POLICY*

Object_schema, object_name, and policy_name are required for the DROP_POLICY, REFRESH_POLICY, and ENABLE_POLICY procedures as well. Enable is the only other required parameter for the ENABLE_POLICY procedure.

For this example, you can add the policy named MEDICAL_POLICY to the MEDICAL_INFORMATION table as follows:

```
execute DBMS_RLS.ADD_POLICY
('MEDICAL_DEPT','MEDICAL_INFORMATION','MEDICAL_POLICY','MEDICAL_DEPT',
   'MEDICAL_SEC.MEDICAL_ID_SEC','SELECT',FALSE,TRUE);
```

The statement creates the policy MEDICAL_POLICY that causes the MEDICAL_SEC.MEDICAL_ID_SEC function to be run when **select** statements are executed against the MEDICAL_INFORMATION table in the MEDICAL_DEPT schema.

Statements are parsed and placed in the Shared Pool for use by other users with the same access privileges. If one of your business policies says that a table can only be accessed during regular business hours, say from 9:00 A.M. to 5:00 P.M., then along with coding your procedure to limit access to the table, you will want to set up a job to run each evening at close of business to invalidate the shared SQL code. You can have your job run code like the following:

```
execute DBMS_RLS.REFRESH_POLICY
('<schema where policy is stored>','<table_name>','<policy_name>';
```

In our example, the policy function is in the same schema as the actual application tables. In practice, keep your policy functions in a schema area owned by your company's security officer to prevent anyone from inadvertently or intentionally removing a policy from a table or view.

Create the Trigger

Once all of the pieces are in place, you must create a trigger to enforce the policy. We recommend that you use a **logon** trigger to accomplish this task so that the policy will be activated regardless of the approach a user takes to connect to the database.

One word of warning though: if your trigger does not function properly, you could end up in a situation where no one can log onto your database. In that case, you must connect as a user with SYSDBA privileges and remove the trigger until you can correct the error. In Oracle9i, the syntax you use from the SQL*Plus GUI logon box is as follows: Enter the SYSTEM account with the password MANAGER. The required phrase "as sysdba" is appended after the connect string. In the example shown here, the instance name is MYDB9.WORLD.

```
User Name: SYSTEM
Password:  MANAGER
Host String: MYDB9.WORLD AS SYSDBA
```

Auditing

The database has the ability to audit all actions that take place within it. Audit records may be written to either the SYS.AUD$ table or the operating system's audit trail. The ability to use the operating system's audit trail is operating system dependent.

Three different types of actions may be audited: login attempts, object accesses, and database actions. Each of these action types will be described in the following sections. When performing audits, the database's default functionality is to record both successful and unsuccessful commands; this may be modified when each audit type is set up.

To enable auditing in a database, the init.ora file for the database must contain an entry for the AUDIT_TRAIL parameter. The AUDIT_TRAIL values are as follows:

NONE	Disables auditing
DB	Enables auditing, writing to the SYS.AUD$ table
OS	Enables auditing, writing to the operating system's audit trail (operating system dependent)

The **audit** commands described in the following sections can be issued regardless of the setting of the AUDIT_TRAIL parameter. They will not be activated unless the database is started using an init.ora AUDIT_TRAIL value that enables auditing.

If you elect to store the audit records in the SYS.AUD$ table, then that table's records should be periodically archived, and the table should then be **truncate**d. Since it is in the data dictionary, this table is in the SYSTEM tablespace and may cause space problems if its records are not periodically cleaned out. You can grant DELETE_CATALOG_ROLE to a user to give the user the ability to delete from the SYS.AUD$ table.

Login Audits

Every attempt to connect to the database can be audited. The command to begin auditing of login attempts is

```
audit session;
```

To audit only those connection attempts that result in successes or failures, use one of the commands shown in the following listing:

```
audit session whenever successful;
audit session whenever not successful;
```

If the audit records are stored in the SYS.AUD$ table, then they may be viewed via the DBA_AUDIT_SESSION data dictionary view of that table.

The query shown in the following listing retrieves login audit records from the DBA_AUDIT_SESSION view. It lists the operating system account that was used (OS_Username), the Oracle account name (Username), and the terminal ID that was used (Terminal). The Returncode column is evaluated: if it is 0, the connection attempt succeeded; otherwise, two common error numbers are checked to determine the cause of the failure. The login timestamp and logoff times are also displayed.

```
select
    OS_Username,                /*Operating system username used.*/
    Username,                   /*Oracle username of the account used.*/
    Terminal,                   /*Terminal ID used.*/
    DECODE(Returncode,'0','Connected',
              '1005','FailedNull',
              '1017','Failed',Returncode),      /*Failure check*/
    TO_CHAR(Timestamp,'DD-MON-YY HH24:MI:SS'),  /*Login time*/
    TO_CHAR(Logoff_Time,'DD-MON-YY HH24:MI:SS') /*Logoff time*/
    from DBA_AUDIT_SESSION;
```

The error numbers that are checked are ORA-1005 and ORA-1017. These two error codes cover most of the login errors that occur. ORA-1005 is returned when a user enters a username but no password. ORA-1017 is returned when a user enters an invalid password.

To disable session auditing, use the **noaudit** command, as shown in this example:

```
noaudit session;
```

Action Audits

Any action affecting a database object—such as a table, database link, tablespace, synonym, rollback segment, user, or index—can be audited. The possible actions—such as **create**, **alter**, and **drop**—that can affect those objects can be grouped together during auditing. This grouping of commands reduces the amount of administrative effort necessary to establish and maintain the audit settings.

All of the system-level commands can be audited, and groups of commands are provided. For example, to audit all commands that affect roles, enter the command

```
audit role;
```

To disable this setting, enter the command

```
noaudit role;
```

The SQL command groupings for auditing are listed in Appendix A, under the entry for "AUDIT (SQL Statements)." Each group can be used to audit all of the SQL commands that affect it (see Table 10-2 for a detailed listing of the related privileges). For example, the **audit role** command shown earlier will audit **create role**, **alter role**, **drop role**, and **set role** commands.

In addition to the core audit options shown in Appendix A, you may audit each individual command covered (such as **create table**). Oracle also provides the following groups of statement options:

CONNECT	Audits Oracle logons and logoffs
DBA	Audits commands that require DBA authority, such as **grant, revoke, audit, noaudit, create**, or **alter tablespace**; and **create** or **drop public synonym**
RESOURCE	Audits **create** and **drop** for tables, clusters, views, indexes, tablespaces, types, and synonyms
ALL	Audits all of these commands
ALL PRIVILEGES	All of the preceding commands plus **delete**s, **insert**s, **update**s, and several other commands; see Appendix A

Each action that can be audited is assigned a numeric code within the database. These codes are accessible via the AUDIT_ACTIONS view. The following query will display the available action codes for your database:

```
select
      Action,        /*Action code.*/
      Name           /*Name of the action, such as ALTER USER.*/
from AUDIT_ACTIONS;
```

Once the action code is known, you can use the DBA_AUDIT_OBJECT view to determine how an object was affected by the action. The query shown in the following listing retrieves login audit records from the DBA_AUDIT_OBJECT view. It lists the operating system account that was used (OS_Username), the Oracle account name (Username), and the terminal ID that was used (Terminal). The object owner (Owner) and name (Obj_Name) are selected, along with the action code (Action_Name) for the action performed. The Returncode column is evaluated: if it is 0, then the connection attempt succeeded; otherwise, the error number is reported. The login and logoff times are also displayed.

```
select
   OS_Username,          /*Operating system username used.*/
   Username,             /*Oracle username of the account used.*/
```

```
Terminal,                /*Terminal ID used.*/
Owner,                   /*Owner of the affected object.*/
Obj_Name,                /*Name of the affected object.*/
Action_Name,             /*Numeric code for the action.*/
DECODE(Returncode,'0','Success',Returncode),   /*Failure check*/
TO_CHAR(Timestamp,'DD-MON-YYYY HH24:MI:SS')        /*Timestamp*/
from DBA_AUDIT_OBJECT;
```

You can also specify particular users to audit, using the **by *username*** clause of the **audit** command, as shown in the following listing. In this example, all **update** actions by the user MCGREGOR will be audited.

```
audit update table by MCGREGOR;
```

Object Audits

In addition to system-level actions on objects, data manipulation actions to objects can be audited. These may include auditing **select**, **insert**, **update**, and **delete** operations against tables. Actions of this type are audited in a manner that is very similar to the action audits described in the previous section. The only difference is the addition of a new clause in the **audit** command.

Audit by Session or by Access

The additional clause for object audits is the **by session** or **by access** clause. This clause specifies whether an audit record should be written once for each session (**by session**) or once for each time an object is accessed (**by access**). For example, if a user executed four different **update** statements against the same table, auditing **by access** would result in four audit records being written—one for each table access. Auditing the same situation **by session** would result in only one audit record being written.

Auditing **by access** can therefore dramatically increase the rate at which audit records are written. The **by access** option is generally used on a limited basis to gauge the number of separate actions taking place during a specific time interval; when that testing is done, the auditing should be reverted to **by session** status.

Examples of these options are shown in the following listing. In the first command, all **insert** commands against the EMPLOYEE table are audited. In the second command, every command that affects the TIME_CARDS table is audited. In the third command, all **delete** operations against the DEPARTMENT table are audited, on a per-session basis.

```
audit insert on THUMPER.EMPLOYEE;
audit all on THUMPER.TIME_CARDS;
audit delete on THUMPER.DEPARTMENT by session;
```

The resulting audit records can be viewed via the query against the DBA_AUDIT_OBJECT view shown in the previous section.

Fine-Grained Object Auditing

One failing of object auditing is that although you can see that the object was accessed and see who accessed it, you cannot see what values were changed and what the old values were. Oracle9*i* provides a PL/SQL package to enable fine-grained object auditing that helps you track accessed information in your database and how the information has been modified.

To enable fine-grained object auditing, create a SQL predicate to describe the conditions under which an audit record should be logged. The SQL predicate defines the data access conditions that should trigger an audit event. You use the PL/SQL package DBMS_FGA to administer the fine-grained audit policies. The actions you can take using DBMA_FGA are

add_policy	Add a fine-grained auditing policy to a table or view.
drop_policy	Drop a fine-grained auditing policy from a table or view.
enable_policy	Enable a security policy for a table or view.
disable_ policy	Disable a security policy for a table or view.

Let's say that Farmer McGregor wants to audit anyone checking on the current number of carrots in stock. He would create a procedure to define how he wants to be notified of anyone querying the PRODUCE table and then create an audit policy to establish the audit criteria.

```
/* add the policy */
exec DBMS_FGA.ADD_POLICY( -
object_schema => 'FM', -
object_name   => 'PRODUCE', -
policy_name   => 'CHK_CARROT_COUNT', -
audit_condition => 'VEGETABLE = ''CARROTS'' ', -
audit_column => 'QUANTITY', -
handler_schema => 'SEC', -
handler_module => 'LOG_ACTION', -
enable                => TRUE);
```

In this example, an audit policy is created to capture anyone who selects the quantity value associated with the CARROTS entry from the PRODUCE table. You must also create an error handler, such as a trigger, to activate when the audit policy condition is met. In this case, the trigger LOG_ACTION in the SEC schema was used.

Protecting the Audit Trail

Since the database audit trail table, SYS.AUD$, is stored within the database, any audit records that are written there must be protected. Otherwise, a user may attempt to delete his or her audit trail records after attempting unauthorized actions within the database.

The ability to write audit records to the operating system audit trail helps to get around this problem by storing the records external to the database. However, this option is not available for all operating systems.

If you must store the audit trail information in SYS.AUD$, then you *must* protect that table. Start with audit actions against the table via the following command:

```
audit all on SYS.AUD$ by access;
```

If any actions are made against the SYS.AUD$ table (**insert**s generated via audits of other tables don't count), then those actions will be recorded in the audit trail. Not only that, but actions against SYS.AUD$ can only be deleted by users who have the ability to CONNECT <username/password> AS SYSDBA (they are in the DBA group). Any actions made while connected AS SYSDBA are automatically written to the audit trail.

Wherever possible, coordinate your database auditing and your operating system auditing. This will make it easier to track problems and coordinate security policies across the two environments. Since the system managers will most likely not want to see reams of audit trail entries, it also forces the DBA to analyze exactly which actions are the most critical to audit. Your aim should be to have an audit trail in which every record is significant. If it is not, then use the commands given in this chapter to modify the auditing options to reflect the true actions of interest.

Security in a Distributed Environment

Opening up a database to access from other servers also opens it up to potential security threats from those servers. Since such access comes via Oracle Net, modifications to Oracle Net parameters can provide most of the protection against unauthorized remote access. For details on the security aspects of Oracle Net, see Part III of this book. As a guiding principle, all access to data should be on a need-to-know basis. Extending this principle, all access to your server and operating system and network should be on a need-to-know basis. You should periodically review the current access privilege within the database and at the operating system level, and work with the systems management team to evaluate current network access privileges.

Solutions

Effective security management in an Oracle database requires resolving all known security issues and auditing attempted breaches of security. Your security plan should include, at a minimum, the following:

1. Change the passwords of the SYS and SYSTEM accounts from their default values right after database creation.

2. Change the password for all unlocked DBA-privileged accounts on a regular basis.

3. Drop any of the demo accounts that were created (such as SCOTT/TIGER).

4. Change the password on the DBSNMP account, and put the new password in the snmp.ora file.

5. Set the proper protection levels for all database files.

6. If your development database contains data from your production database, make sure the security rules enforced for production are also enforced for development.

7. Audit all access to SYS.AUD$.

8. Audit all failed connection attempts.

9. Audit all DBA actions.

10. Regularly generate audit reports and clean out old records from SYS.AUD$.

11. Secure your database backups.

12. Secure the physical facility in which your database server and backups are stored.

If you follow these 12 steps, you will be able to secure your database. As noted earlier in this chapter, you will still need to work with the system administration and network administration teams to eliminate any unauthorized access to the server's operating system.

CHAPTER
11

Backup and
Recovery Options

racle provides a variety of backup procedures and options that help protect an Oracle database. If they are properly implemented, these options will allow you to effectively back up your databases and recover them easily and efficiently.

Oracle's backup capabilities include logical and physical backups, both of which have a number of options available. This chapter will not detail every possible option and recovery scenario; Oracle's documentation has already accomplished that. Rather, the focus in this chapter is on using the best options in the most effective manner possible. You will see how to best integrate the available backup procedures with each other and with the operating system backups.

Capabilities

There are three standard methods of backing up an Oracle database: exports, offline backups, and online backups. An export is a *logical* backup of the database; the other two backup methods are *physical* file backups. In the following sections, you will see each of these options fully described. Physical backups may be executed via user scripts or Oracle's Recovery Manager (RMAN) utility. See Chapter 12 for details on the implementation and usage of RMAN.

A robust backup strategy includes both physical and logical backups. In general, production databases rely on physical backups as their primary backup method, while logical databases serve as the secondary method. For development databases and for some small data movement processing, logical backups offer a viable solution. You should understand the implications and uses of both physical and logical backups in order to develop the most appropriate solution for your applications.

Logical Backups

A *logical backup* of the database involves reading a set of database records and writing them to a file. These records are read independently of their physical location. In Oracle, the Export utility performs this type of database backup. To recover using the file generated from an export, Oracle's Import utility is used.

The Export/Import Process

Oracle's Export utility queries the database, including the data dictionary, and writes the output to a binary file called an *export dump file*. You can export the full database, specific users, or specific tables. During exports, you may choose whether or not to export the data dictionary information associated with tables, such as the grants, indexes, and constraints associated with them. The file written by Export will contain the commands necessary to completely re-create all of the chosen objects and data.

As of Oracle9i, you can perform tablespace-level exports to export all of the objects contained in a tablespace. Any indexes defined on the exported tables would also be exported. Tablespace-level exports use the **tablespaces** clause of the Export utility, as described later in this chapter.

Once data has been exported, it may be imported via Oracle's Import utility. The Import utility reads the binary export dump file created by Export and executes the commands found there. For example, these commands may include a **create table** command, followed by an **insert** command to load data into the table.

The data that has been exported does not have to be imported into the same database, or the same schema, as was used to generate the export dump file. You may use the export dump file to create a duplicate set of the exported objects under a different schema or in a separate database.

You can import either all or part of the exported data. If you import the entire export dump file from a Full export, then all of the database objects—including tablespaces, datafiles, and users—will be created during the import. However, it is often useful to precreate tablespaces and users in order to specify the physical distribution of objects in the database.

If you are only going to import part of the data from the export dump file, then the tablespaces, datafiles, and users that will own and store that data should be set up prior to the import.

Exported data may be imported into an Oracle database created under the next higher version of the Oracle software. The reverse capability—importing from an export file created by a more recent major release—is commonly supported, but extra actions may be required to support the older version of the views Export uses. The README.doc files that accompany Oracle releases detail the requirements for using Export and Import across specific versions.

Physical Backups

Physical backups involve copying the files that constitute the database. These backups are also referred to as *file system backups* since they involve using operating system file backup commands. Oracle supports two different types of physical file backups: the *offline backup* and the *online backup* (also known as the *cold* and *hot backups*, respectively).

Offline Backups

Consistent offline backups occur when the database has been shut down normally (that is, not due to instance failure). While the database is offline, the following files should be backed up:

- All datafiles
- All control files

- All online redo logs

- The init.ora file and spfile.ora (optional)

It is easiest to back up the datafiles if the database file architecture uses a consistent directory structure. A sample of such an architecture is shown in the "Database File Layout" section of Chapter 4.

Having all of these files backed up while the database is closed provides a complete image of the database as it existed at the time it was closed. The full set of these files could be retrieved from the backups at a later date and the database would be able to function. It is *not* valid to perform a file system backup of the database while it is open unless an online backup is being performed. Offline backups that occur following database aborts will also be considered inconsistent and may require more effort to use during recoveries—if they are usable.

Online Backups

You can use online backups for any database that is running in ARCHIVELOG mode. In this mode, the online redo logs are archived, creating a log of all transactions within the database.

Oracle writes to the online redo log files in a cyclical fashion: after filling the first log file, it begins writing to the second until that one fills, and then begins writing to the third. Once the last online redo log file is filled, the LGWR (Log Writer) background process begins to overwrite the contents of the first redo log file.

When Oracle is run in ARCHIVELOG mode, the ARCH (Archiver) background process makes a copy of each redo log file before overwriting it. These archived redo log files are usually written to a disk device. The archived redo log files may also be written directly to a tape device, but this tends to be very operator intensive.

NOTE
Most production databases, particularly those that support transaction processing applications, must be run in ARCHIVELOG mode.

You can perform file system backups of a database while that database is open, provided the database is running in ARCHIVELOG mode. An online backup involves setting each tablespace into a backup state, backing up its datafiles, then restoring the tablespace to its normal state.

NOTE
When using the Oracle-supplied Recovery Manager (RMAN) utility, you do not have to manually place each tablespace into a backup state. RMAN reads the data blocks in the same manner Oracle uses for queries.

The database can be fully recovered from an online backup, and can, via the archived redo logs, be rolled forward to any point in time. When the database is then opened, any committed transactions that were in the database at that time will have been restored, and any uncommitted transactions will have been rolled back.

While the database is open, the following files can be backed up:

- All datafiles

- All archived redo log files

- One control file, via the **alter database** command

Online backup procedures are very powerful for two reasons. First, they provide full point-in-time recovery. Second, they allow the database to remain open during the file system backup. Even databases that cannot be shut down due to user requirements can still have file system backups. Keeping the database open also keeps the System Global Area (SGA) of the database instance from being reset during database startups. Keeping the memory from being reset will improve the database's performance since it will reduce the number of physical I/Os required by the database.

Implementations

In this section, you will find the commands and procedures necessary to use each of the backup methods available in Oracle, as well as sample command files for performing them.

Export

The Export utility has four levels of functionality: Full mode, Tablespace mode, User mode, and Table mode. You can export partitions via a modified version of Table mode exports.

In Full mode, the full database is exported. The entire data dictionary is read, and the DDL needed to re-create the full database is written to the export dump file.

This file includes creation commands for all tablespaces, all users, and all of the objects, data, and privileges in their schemas.

In Tablespace mode, all of the objects contained in the specified tablespace(s) will be exported, including the definition of indexes on the contained objects, even if they are in another tablespace.

In User mode, a user's objects are exported, as well as the data within them. All grants and indexes created by the user on the user's objects are also exported. Grants and indexes created by users other than the owner are not exported.

In Table mode, a specified table is exported. The table's structure, indexes, and grants are exported along with or without its data. Table mode can also export the full set of tables owned by a user (by specifying the schema owner but no table names). You can also specify partitions of a table to export.

Export can be run interactively, through OEM, or via command files. The run-time options that can be specified for Export are listed in Table 11-1, along with their default values in Oracle9*i*.

Keyword	Description
userid	Username/password of the account running the export. **Userid** must be the first parameter on the command line.
buffer	Size of the buffer used to fetch data rows. The default is system dependent; this value is usually set to a high value (> 64,000).
file	Name of the export dump file; default is expdat.dmp.
compress	A Y/N flag to indicate whether export should compress fragmented segments into single extents. This affects the **storage** clauses that will be stored in the export file for those objects. Default is Y. Having objects in one large extent is not always the best choice. For large tables, you should use **compress = N**.
grants	A Y/N flag to indicate whether **grant**s on database objects will be exported. Default is Y.
indexes	A Y/N flag to indicate whether indexes on tables will be exported. Default is Y.
direct	A Y/N flag to indicate if a direct export should be performed. A direct export bypasses the buffer cache during the export, generating significant performance gains for the export process. Default is N.
log	The name of a file to which the log of the export will be written.

TABLE 11-1. *Export Run-Time Options*

Keyword	Description
rows	A Y/N flag to indicate whether rows should be exported. If this is set to N, then only the DDL for the database objects will be created in the export file. Default is Y.
consistent	A Y/N flag to indicate whether a read-consistent version of all exported objects should be maintained. This is needed when tables that are related to each other are being modified by users during the export process.
full	If set to Y, then a Full database export is performed. Default is N.
owner	A list of database accounts to be exported; User exports of those accounts may then be performed.
tables	A list of tables to be exported; Table exports of those tables may then be performed. As of Oracle9i, this parameter supports the use of the % and _ wildcards for pattern matching.
recordlength	The length, in bytes, of the export dump file record. Usually not specified unless you are going to transfer the export file between different operating systems.
triggers	A Y/N flag to indicate if triggers should be exported. Default is Y.
statistics	A parameter to indicate whether **analyze** commands for the exported objects should be written to the export dump file. Valid values are COMPUTE, ESTIMATE (the default), and N. In earlier versions of Oracle, this parameter was called **analyze**.
parfile	The name of a parameter file to be passed to Export. This file may contain entries for all of the parameters listed here.
constraints	A Y/N flag to indicate whether constraints on tables are exported. Default is Y.
feedback	The number of rows after which to display progress during Table exports. The default value is 0, so no feedback is displayed until a table is completely exported.
filesize	The maximum size for an export dump file. If multiple files are listed in the **file** entry, the export will be directed to those files based on the **filesize** setting.
flashback_scn	Specifies the SCN Export will use to enable flashback. The export is performed with data consistent as of this SCN.

TABLE 11-1. *Export Run-Time Options* (continued)

Keyword	Description
flashback_ time	Time used to get the SCN closest to the specified time. The export is performed with data consistent as of this SCN.
query	A **where** clause that will be applied to each table during the export.
resumable	A Y/N flag to indicate if the session is resumable following errors. Default is N.
resumable_ name	The specified value is inserted into the DBA_RESUMABLE view to help identify the resumable statement.
resumable_ timeout	The wait time for resumable statements.
tts_full_check	Perform full or partial dependency check for transportable tablespaces.
volsize	Number of bytes to write to each tape volume.
tablespaces	In Oracle9i, the tablespaces whose tables should be exported, including all tables that have a partition located in the specified tablespaces.
transport_table space	Set to Y if you are using the pluggable tablespace option available as of Oracle8i. Use in conjunction with the **tablespaces** keyword. Default is N.
template	Template name used to invoke iAS mode export.

TABLE 11-1. *Export Run-Time Options* (continued)

A number of the parameters conflict with each other or may result in inconsistent instructions for Export. For example, setting **full=y** and **owner=hr** would fail, since the **full** parameter calls for a Full export, while the **owner** parameter specifies a User export.

NOTE
The default values and available parameters may change with each release of Oracle.

You can display the Export parameters online via the following command:

```
exp help=Y
```

The **compress=y** option alters the **initial** parameter of the **storage** clause for segments that have multiple extents. During a subsequent import, the total allocated space for that segment will be compressed into a single extent. There are two important points to note concerning this functionality:

- First, it is the *allocated,* not the *used,* space that is compressed. An empty table with 300MB allocated to it in three 100MB extents will be compressed into a single empty 300MB extent. No space will be reclaimed.

- Second, if the tablespace has multiple datafiles, a segment may allocate space that is greater than the size of the largest datafile. In that case, using **compress=y** would change the **storage** clause to have an **initial** extent size that is greater than any datafile size. Since a single extent cannot span more than one datafile, the object creation will fail during import.

In the following example, the **compress=y** option is used, as the HR and THUMPER owners are exported:

```
exp system/manager file=expdat.dmp compress=Y owner=(HR,THUMPER)
```

NOTE
You can avoid space fragmentation problems through the use of locally managed tablespaces.

Consistent Exports

During the process of writing the database's data to the export dump file, Export reads one table at a time. Thus, although Export started at a specific point in time, each table is read at a different time. The data as it exists in each table at the moment Export starts to read *that table* is what will be exported. Since most tables are related to other tables, this may result in inconsistent data being exported if users are modifying data during the export. The export dump file may contain inconsistent data, such as foreign key records from one table without matching primary key records from a related table.

To avoid inconsistency in your exports, there are two options:

- First, you should schedule exports to occur when no one is making modifications to tables. If feasible, you can use the **startup restrict** option to make sure only DBAs are logged in while the export is occurring.

- Second, you can use the **consistent** parameter. This parameter is only available for complete exports. During a consistent export, Oracle will try to create a read-consistent version of the exported data as of the time the export started. You will get "snapshot too old" errors if Oracle cannot re-create the read-consistent version of the tables. To guarantee you will not encounter "snapshot too old" errors, you must create large rollback segments because Oracle will overwrite old rollback segment entries without regard to your **consistent=y** setting.

Whenever possible, guarantee the consistency of exported data by running exports while the database is not being used or is mounted in restricted mode. If you are unable to do this, restrict the database usage during the export and perform a **consistent=y** export.

Another alternative is to create two parameter files (**parfile**). One file will contain the names of the majority of tables within your database or schema. You can use this file for your first export with the default of **consistent=n**. The second file, containing the names of the tables whose consistency must be maintained, is used to perform an export with **consistent=y**. Using this approach, the size of your rollback segments will not need to be as large, and the performance of your system will not suffer as much.

Exporting Tablespaces

The better you have distributed your application schema owners and their objects across tablespaces, the easier it will be to export them. For example, if you wish to export all of the objects in the AP_DATA schema, you can execute a User export if only a single user owns objects in that tablespace. If multiple users own objects in the DATA tablespace, you can export all of the objects within the tablespace using one command (starting with Oracle9i) regardless of which schema owns the object:

```
exp demo/demo tablespaces=DATA
```

The following query maps users to tablespaces to determine the distribution of their tables and indexes:

```
break on Owner on Tablespace_Name
column Objects format A20
select
      Owner,
      Tablespace_Name,
      COUNT(*)||' tables' Objects
 from DBA_TABLES
where Owner <> 'SYS'
group by
      Owner,
      Tablespace_Name
union
select
      Owner,
```

```
        Tablespace_Name,
        COUNT(*)||' indexes' Objects
  from DBA_INDEXES
where Owner <> 'SYS'
group by
        Owner,
        Tablespace_Name;
```

Sample output from this query is shown in the following listing:

```
OWNER           TABLESPACE_NAME    OBJECTS
------------    ----------------   --------------------
FLOWER          USERS              3 tables
                                   2 indexes
HR              HR_TABLES          27 tables
                HR_INDEXES         35 indexes
THUMPER         USERS              5 tables
```

The sample output shown in the preceding listing shows that the user account FLOWER owns tables and indexes in the USERS tablespace, and that THUMPER owns several tables in that tablespace as well. The user HR owns objects in both the HR_TABLES and the HR_INDEXES tablespaces.

Before determining the proper combinations of users to export for a tablespace, the inverse mapping—of tablespaces to users—should be reviewed via the following query:

```
break on Tablespace_Name on Owner
column Objects format A20
select
        Tablespace_Name,
        Owner,
        COUNT(*)||' tables' Objects
  from DBA_TABLES
where Owner <> 'SYS'
group by
        Tablespace_Name,
        Owner
union
select
        Tablespace_Name,
        Owner,
        COUNT(*)||' indexes' Objects
  from DBA_INDEXES
where Owner <> 'SYS'
group by
        Tablespace_Name,
        Owner;
```

Sample output from this query is shown in the following listing:

```
TABLESPACE_NAME     OWNER        OBJECTS
---------------     ----------   --------------------
HR_INDEXES          HR           35 indexes
HR_TABLES           HR           27 tables
USERS               FLOWER       3 tables
                                 2 indexes
                    THUMPER      5 tables
```

The sample output shown in the preceding listing shows that the HR_TABLES tablespace contains objects from just one user (the HR account). The HR_INDEXES tablespace is similarly isolated. The USERS tablespace, on the other hand, contains both tables and indexes from several accounts.

The results of the preceding queries illustrate the importance of properly distributing users' objects among tablespaces. Since the HR_TABLES tablespace only contains tables owned by the HR account (from the second query), exporting the HR tables will export all of the objects in the HR_TABLES tablespace. As seen from the first query, HR does not own any tables anywhere else in the database. Because HR's tables are isolated to the HR_TABLES tablespace, and because that tablespace is only used by the HR account, a User export of HR will export all of the tables in HR_TABLES. Since the indexes on those tables are stored in HR_INDEXES, that tablespace can be re-created at the same time from the same export dump file.

As of Oracle9*i*, you can use the **tablespaces** parameter to export all tables located in a specific tablespace. If any table has a partition in the specified tablespace, the entire table will be exported. If you set **indexes=y**, the tables' associated indexes will be exported regardless of their tablespace location.

Third-Party Objects

As noted previously, User exports do not export "third-party" grants and indexes created by users other than the table owners. To determine if third-party grants or indexes exist, query the data dictionary views, as shown in the following queries.

The first set of queries searches for third-party grants.

```
break on Grantor skip 1 on Owner on Table_Name
select
        Grantor,          /*Account that made the grant*/
        Owner,            /*Account that owns the table*/
        Table_Name,       /*Name of the table*/
        Grantee,          /*Account granted access*/
        Privilege,        /*Privilege granted*/
        Grantable         /*Granted with admin option?*/
from DBA_TAB_PRIVS
```

```
where Grantor ! = Owner
order by Grantor, Owner, Table_Name, Grantee, Privilege;
```

As shown in the following listing, the search for third-party indexes queries the DBA_INDEXES data dictionary view to retrieve those records in which the index owner and the table owner columns do not have the same value.

```
select
        Owner,                  /*Owner of the index*/
        Index_Name,             /*Name of the index*/
        Table_Owner,            /*Owner of the table*/
        Table_Name              /*Name of the indexed table*/
from DBA_INDEXES
where Owner != Table_Owner;
```

If these queries show that third-party indexes or grants exist, and you plan to rely on User exports, then you must supplement those exports with scripts that generate the third-party grants and indexes. If you use the **tablespaces** option during your export, all of the tables' indexes will be exported regardless of their schemas.

Exporting Partitions

You can reference partitions and subpartitions within tables when you perform Table exports. For example, if the SALES table in the THUMPER schema is partitioned into PART1, PART2, and PART3, then you can export the entire table or its partitions.

To export the entire table, use the **tables** parameter of Export:

```
exp system/manager FILE=expdat.dmp TABLES=(Thumper.SALES)
```

To export a specific partition or subpartition, list the partition or subpartition name following the table name. The table name and the partition name should be separated by a colon (:). In the following listing, the PART1 partition is exported:

```
exp system/manager FILE=expdat.dmp TABLES=(Thumper.SALES:Part1)
```

If you export a partition, all of its subpartitions will be exported.

Partial Table Export Using OEM

You can use the OEM Server Manager Export Wizard to export a subset of rows for a table. In Figure 11-1, the EMPLOYEES table has been selected from the HR schema. However, making this selection will not influence the Export Wizard; it is shown to illustrate that there are times when making selections from the Navigator will not affect the task that you want to perform.

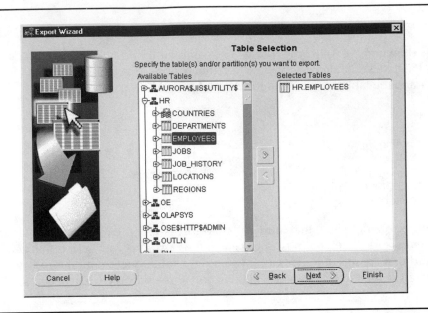

FIGURE 11-1. *Selecting the HR.EMPLOYEES table*

The next Export Wizard screen presents the export details as shown in Figure 11-2. The Advanced button on the right side of the screen is important because you will use this button to access the Query option.

The Advanced Options screen offers three tabs: General, Tuning, and Query. The General tab enables you to specify what form of statistics gathering you want, whether you want to have the export performed using direct-path mode, and log file location. The Tuning tab enables you to specify whether you want a read-consistent view of the data (**consistent=y**), whether you want the extents merged (**compress=y**), and whether you want to change the default record length and/or buffer size. Figure 11-3 shows the Query tab in which you can enter a **where** clause to limit the rows to be exported from the table. The query has been entered to select only the rows where the DEPARTMENT_ID is between the values 10 and 30.

The next two screens enable you to specify when you want to run the export job and what the filename and location are. After the job scheduler and summary screens have been displayed and approved, the export is performed.

Partial Table Export from the Operating System
As of Oracle8*i*, you can use the **query** option to apply a **where** clause while exporting data. The **query** parameter value is a text string that will be appended to the **select**s that Export executes. For example, you may be exporting an

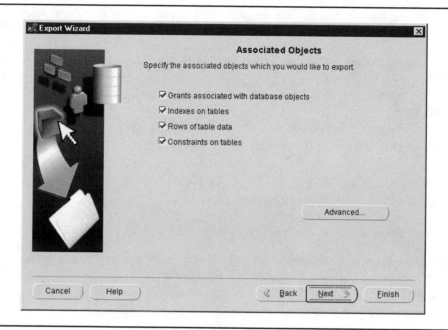

FIGURE 11-2. *Export Wizard, Objects option*

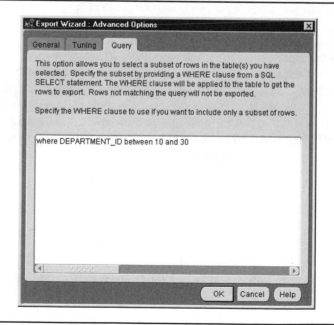

FIGURE 11-3. *Export Wizard: Advanced Options, Query tab*

unpartitioned table of SALES data and only want the data for the "North" sales region. You can export the "North" data via the following command:

```
exp system/manager FILE=expdat.dmp TABLES=(THUMPER.SALES) QUERY=\"where
region=\'North\'\"
```

NOTE
*In this example, the backslashes are added before
special characters so UNIX will process them correctly.*

The **query** text will be appended to Export's query of the SALES table, effectively creating the following query during the export:

```
select * from SALES where region = 'NORTH';
```

The text string in the **query** parameter value must be applicable to every table being exported. The export dump file will not contain any indication that a **query** clause was used to generate it, so you should be careful when using this option. You cannot use the **query** clause during a direct path export.

Creative Uses of the query Parameter

The **query** parameter gives you the ability to customize the SQL that Oracle executes against tables during exports. You can take advantage of this capability to perform exports of data that has changed since a particular date. If you create and maintain timestamp fields that capture the time when a transaction is entered, you can use that field in your **query** clause to export rows from specific business days.

You can use the **query** parameter to order the rows of a table as it is exported. In place of a **where** clause, use an **order by** clause in the **query** parameter value. When the rows are written to the export dump file, they will be ordered by the specified columns. During a subsequent import, the rows will be **insert**ed in that order. Queries that perform range scans should perform more efficiently when the data is sorted by the queried columns.

Import

The Import utility reads the export dump file and runs the commands stored there. Import may be used to selectively bring back objects or users from the export dump file.

You can run Import either interactively or via command files. The run-time options that can be specified for Import and their default values are listed in Table 11-2.

Keyword	Description
userid	Username/password of the account running the import; this must be the first parameter, and the "**userid=**" text is optional.
buffer	Size of the buffer used to fetch data rows. The default is system dependent; this value is usually set to a high value (>100,000).
file	Name of the export dump file to be imported.
show	A Y/N flag to specify whether the file contents should be displayed rather than executed. Default is N.
ignore	A Y/N flag to indicate whether the import should ignore errors encountered when issuing **create** commands. This flag is used if the objects being imported already exist. Default is N.
grants	A Y/N flag to indicate whether grants on database objects will be imported.
indexes	A Y/N flag to indicate whether indexes on tables will be imported. Default is Y.
rows	A Y/N flag to indicate whether rows should be imported. If this is set to N, then only the DDL for the database objects will be executed. Default is Y.
log	The name of a file to which the log of the import will be written.
full	A Y/N flag; if set to Y, then the Full export dump file is imported. Default is N.
fromuser	A list of database accounts whose objects should be read from the export dump file (when **full=n**).
touser	A list of database accounts into which objects in the export dump file will be imported. **fromuser** and **touser** do not have to be set to the same value.
tables	A list of tables to be imported. As of Oracle9i, the % and _ wildcards are supported for table names.
recordlength	The length, in bytes, of the export dump file record. Usually left at the default value unless you are going to transfer the export file between different operating systems.

TABLE 11-2. *Import Parameters and Default Values*

Keyword	Description
commit	A Y/N flag to indicate whether Import should **commit** after each array (whose size is set by **buffer**). If this is set to N (the default), then Import will **commit** after every table is imported. For large tables, **commit=N** requires equally large undo segments.
parfile	The name of a parameter file to be passed to Import. This file may contain entries for all of the parameters listed here.
constraints	A Y/N flag to indicate whether constraints on tables will be imported. Default is Y.
destroy	A Y/N flag to indicate whether the **create tablespace** commands found in dump files from Full exports will be executed (thereby destroying the datafiles in the database being imported into). Default is N.
indexfile	This option writes all of the **create table**, **create cluster**, and **create index** commands to a file, rather than running them. All but the **create index** commands will be commented out. If **constraints=y**, then constraints will be written to the file as well. This file can then be run (with slight modifications) after importing with **indexes=n**. It is useful for separating tables and indexes into separate tablespaces.
skip_unusable _indexes	A Y/N flag that indicates if Import should skip partition indexes marked as "unusable." You may wish to skip the indexes during import and manually create them later to improve index creation performance. Default is N.
feedback	The number of rows after which to display progress during table imports. The default value is 0, so no feedback is displayed until a table is completely imported.
toid_ novalidate	Enables Import to skip validation of specified object types.
filesize	The maximum dump size that was specified on export if the parameter **filesize** was used on export.
statistics	A flag to indicate if precomputed statistics should be imported. Default is ALWAYS; other values are NONE, SAFE (for nonquestionable statistics), and RECALCULATE (recalculate during the import).

TABLE 11-2. *Import Parameters and Default Values* (continued)

Keyword	Description
resumable	A Y/N flag to indicate if the session is resumable following errors. Default is N.
resumable_ name	The specified value is inserted into the DBA_RESUMABLE view to help identify the resumable statement.
resumable_ timeout	The wait time for resumable statements.
compile	A Y/N flag to indicate if procedures, functions, and packages should be recompiled during import. Default is Y.
volsize	Maximum number of bytes in a file on each volume of tape.
transport_ tablespace	A Y/N flag to indicate that transportable tablespace metadata is to be imported into the database. Default is N.
tablespaces	The name or list of names of tablespaces to be transported into the database.
datafiles	The list of datafiles to be transported into the database.
tts_owners	The name or list of names of owners of data in the transportable tablespace.

TABLE 11-2.   *Import Parameters and Default Values* (continued)

A number of the Import parameters conflict with each other or may result in inconsistent instructions for Import. For example, setting **full=y** and **owner=hr** would fail, since the **full** parameter calls for a Full import, while the **owner** parameter specifies a User import.

The **destroy** parameter is very useful for DBAs who run multiple databases on a single server. Since Full database exports record the entire data dictionary, the tablespace and datafile definitions are written to the export dump file. The datafile definitions will include the full path name for the files. If this export dump file is used to migrate data to a separate database on the same server, a problem may arise.

NOTE
Tablespace names are exported as part of an object's definition. If you are importing data from one instance into a separate instance, be sure to create tablespaces with the target database that have the same names as those in the source instance.

The problem is that when importing into the second database from the Full export of the first database, Import will execute the **create tablespace** commands found in the export dump file. These commands will instruct the database to create files in the same directory, with the same name, as the files from the first database. Without using **destroy=n** (the default option), the first database's datafiles may be overwritten.

Undo Segment Requirements

By default, the database will issue a **commit** after every table is completely imported. As a result, the rollback segment will contain a RowID for each row imported. To reduce the sizes of the undo segment entries, specify **commit=y** along with a value for **buffer**. A **commit** will then be executed after every **buffer** worth of data, as shown in the following example. In the first **import** command shown, a **commit** is executed after every table is loaded. In the second command shown, a **commit** is executed after every 64,000 bytes of data are inserted.

```
imp system/manager file=expdat.dmp
imp system/manager file=expdat.dmp buffer=64000 commit=Y
```

How large should **buffer** be? It should be large enough to handle the largest single row to be imported. If you do not know the longest row length that was exported, start with a reasonable value (such as 50,000) and run the import. If an IMP-00020 error is returned, then the **buffer** size is not large enough. Increase it and try the import again.

When using **commit=y**, remember that a **commit** is being performed for each **buffer** array. This implies that if the import of a table fails, it is possible that some of the rows in that table may have already been imported and **commit**ted. The partial load may then be either used or **delete**d prior to running the import again.

In tables with BFILE, LONG, LOB, REF, ROWID, and UROWID columns, rows are inserted individually. The **buffer** value does not have to accommodate the LONG and LOB portions of the row; Import will attempt to allocate additional buffer areas as needed for those portions.

Importing into Different Accounts

To move objects from one user to another user via Export/Import, perform a User export of the owner of the objects. During the import, specify the owner as the **fromuser** and the account that is to own the objects as the **touser**.

For example, to copy THUMPER's objects into the FLOWER account, you could execute the following commands. The first command exports the THUMPER owner, and the second command imports the THUMPER objects into the FLOWER account.

```
exp system/manager file=thumper.dat owner=thumper grants=N
   indexes=Y compress=Y rows=Y
```

```
imp system/manager file=thumper.dat FROMUSER=thumper TOUSER=flower
     rows=Y indexes=Y
```

Importing Structures That Failed to Import

You can use the **rows** parameter to re-create just the database structure, without the tables' data, even if that data was exported. The **rows** parameter is also useful during successive imports to recover objects that were not created during a prior import attempt. Multiple imports may be necessary if errors are encountered during the first import. During a second import into the same schema, you will usually need to specify **ignore=y** to avoid terminating the import due to the preexistence of the tables.

The following example shows this usage. The first import attempts to bring in the entire export dump file. If there are failures during this import, then a second pass is made to attempt to bring in those structures that failed the first time.

```
imp system/manager file=expdat.dmp full=Y commit=Y buffer=64000
```

During the import, unrecoverable errors are encountered with indexes after the data has been inserted. Now run the import a second time, with **ignore=y** and **rows=n.**

```
imp system/manager file=expdat.dmp ignore=Y rows=N commit=Y
   buffer=64000
```

The **ignore=y** parameter in the second command tells Import to ignore any objects that were created during the first pass. It will only import those objects that do not already exist in the schema.

NOTE
If a table referenced by a view is dropped, the view definition stays in the data dictionary. This definition can be exported, and the view creation will fail during an import. In that case, since the view was invalid to begin with, a second import attempt for the view will fail as well.

You may need to run multiple imports with **rows=n** in order to successfully re-create all of your database objects.

Using Import to Separate Tables and Indexes

You can use two import options—**indexfile** and **indexes**—to reorganize the tablespace assignments of tables and indexes during export/import operations.

NOTE
See Chapter 5 for details on reorganizing tables and indexes during normal database maintenance.

Using the **indexfile** option during an import will result in the export dump file being read, and instead of being imported, its table and index creation scripts will be written to an output file. You can edit this file to alter the **tablespace** and **storage** parameters of the tables and indexes listed there. You can then run the altered file via SQL*Plus either to precreate all objects prior to importing their data or to create only specified objects (such as indexes).

When the indexfile is created, the **create index** scripts are the only commands in the file that are not commented out via the **rem** command. This default functionality allows DBAs to separate a user's tables and indexes into separate tablespaces during import. Create the indexfile and alter the **tablespace** clauses for the indexes. Then import the user, with **indexes=n**, so that the user's indexes will not be imported. Once the tables have been created, run the altered indexfile to create the indexes in their new tablespace.

Note that the indexfile may contain entries for multiple users (if multiple users were exported). In practice, it is useful to separate the indexfile into multiple files, one for each user, to simplify the tablespace assignment management. The following steps show this process. In this example, THUMPER's objects are being copied into the FLOWER account, and the indexes are being separated from the tables in the process.

NOTE
*The **indexfile** parameter requires that either **full=y** or a **fromuser** value is specified.*

1. Export the user.

   ```
   exp system/manager file=expdat.dmp owner=thumper
   ```

2. Create the indexfile from this export dump file.

   ```
   imp system/manager file=expdat.dmp indexfile=indexes.sql full=Y
   ```

3. Edit the indexfile to change the **tablespace** settings of the indexes. Be careful performing global edits on the indexfile, since the **tablespace** keyword and the tablespace name may be split over two lines.

4. Import the user, without its indexes.

```
imp system/manager file=expdat.dmp fromuser=thumper
touser=flower
    indexes=N commit=Y buffer=64000
```

5. Log into SQL*Plus as the user and run the altered indexfile to create the indexes.

```
sqlplus flower/password
SQL> @indexes
```

If you are separating a small number of indexes from their tables, you should investigate the use of the **rebuild** option of the **alter index** command instead of using Export/Import. See Chapter 3 and Chapter 5 for details on this alternative method of moving indexes.

Implementing Offline Backups

An offline backup (sometimes called a cold backup, as mentioned at the beginning of this chapter) is a physical backup of the database files, made after the database has been shut down via either a **shutdown normal**, a **shutdown immediate**, or a **shutdown transactional**. While the database is shut down, each of the files that is actively used by the database is backed up. These files provide a complete image of the database as it existed at the moment it was shut down.

NOTE
*You should not rely on an offline backup performed following a **shutdown abort**, since it may be inconsistent. If you must perform a **shutdown abort**, you should restart the database and perform a normal **shutdown** or a **shutdown immediate** or a **shutdown transactional** prior to beginning your offline backup.*

The following files should be backed up during cold backups:

- All datafiles
- All control files
- All online redo logs

You may optionally choose to back up the database initialization parameter file, particularly if the backup will serve as the basis for a disaster recovery process.

To simplify the backup process, use a consistent directory structure for your datafiles. A sample of such an architecture is shown in the "Database File Layout" section of Chapter 4. In that architecture, all of the datafiles are located in directories at the same level on each device. The following listing shows a sample directory tree for a data disk named /db01:

```
/db01
          /oracle
                    /CASE
                              control1.dbf
                              sys01.dbf
                              tools.dbf
                    /CC1
                              control1.dbf
                              sys01.dbf
                              tools.dbf
                    /DEMO
                              control1.dbf
                              sys01.dbf
```

In the sample directory tree, all database files are stored in an instance-specific subdirectory under an /oracle directory for the device. Directories such as these should contain all of the datafiles, redo log files, and control files for a database.

If you use the directory structure in the prior example, your backup commands are greatly simplified. The following listing shows a sample UNIX **tar** command, which is used here to back up files to a tape drive called /dev/rmt/0hc. Because the directory structure is consistent and the drives are named /db01 through /db09, the following command will back up all of the CC1 database's datafiles, redo log files, and control files:

```
> tar -cvf /dev/rmt/0hc /db0[1-9]/oracle/CC1
```

> **NOTE**
> *Oracle's RMAN utility simplifies the backup process. See Chapter 12 for details on RMAN. The examples in this chapter feature user-managed backup procedures.*

The **-cvf** flag creates a new **tar** saveset. In many production systems, the database backup writes files to a separate file system area, and the database is then restarted. The disk-to-disk backup method is significantly faster than the disk-to-tape method, allowing the database to be shut down for a shorter period of time. After the database has been restarted, the backup copies of the files may be written to tape without impacting the availability of the database.

NOTE
If you use disk-to-disk backups as part of your backup strategy, the backup disks must be separate from the production disks. Otherwise, a failure of your production database disks may also affect your most recent backups.

Since offline backups involve changes to the database's availability, they are usually scheduled to occur at night. A command file to automate these backups would resemble the following listing. In this example, the ORACLE_SID and ORACLE_HOME environment variables are set to point to the CC1 database. This database is then shut down and the backup commands are executed. The database is then restarted.

```
ORACLE_SID=cc1; export ORACLE_SID
ORAENV_ASK=NO; export ORAENV_ASK
. oraenv
sqlplus <<EOF1
connect / as sysdba
shutdown immediate;
exit
EOF1
insert backup commands like the "tar" commands here
sqlplus <<EOF2
connect / as sysdba
startup
EOF2
```

These examples are generic so that non-UNIX operating systems can use them with little modification.

NOTE
This example uses SQL*Plus to start up and shut down Oracle9i. For Oracle8i, use Server Manager's line mode interface, svrmgrl.

During a recovery, an offline backup can restore the database to the point in time at which the database was shut down. Offline backups commonly play a part in disaster recovery planning, since they are self-contained and may be simpler to restore on a disaster recovery server than other types of backups. If the database is running in ARCHIVELOG mode, you can apply archived redo logs to the restored offline backup.

Implementing Online Backups

Consistent offline backups can only be performed while the database is shut down. However, you can perform physical file backups of a database while the database is open—provided the database is running in ARCHIVELOG mode and the backup is performed correctly. These backups are referred to as online backups, also known as hot backups.

Oracle writes to the online redo log files in a cyclical fashion: after filling the first log file, it begins writing the second until that one fills, and it then begins writing to the third. Once the last online redo log file is filled, the LGWR (Log Writer) background process begins to overwrite the contents of the first redo log file.

When Oracle is run in ARCHIVELOG mode, the ARCH background process makes a copy of each redo log file after the LGWR process finishes writing to it. These archived redo log files are usually written to a disk device. They may instead be written directly to a tape device, but this tends to be very operator intensive.

Getting Started

To make use of the ARCHIVELOG capability, the database must first be placed in ARCHIVELOG mode. The following listing shows the steps needed to place a database in ARCHIVELOG mode. For versions prior to Oracle9i, use Server Manager in place of SQL*Plus.

```
SQL> connect / as sysdba
SQL> startup mount cc1;
SQL> alter database archivelog;
SQL> alter database open;
```

The following command will display the current ARCHIVELOG status of the database from within Server Manager:

```
archive log list
```

NOTE
To see the currently active online redo log and its sequence number, query the V$LOG dynamic view.

To change a database back to NOARCHIVELOG mode, use the following set of commands after shutting down the database:

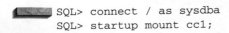

```
SQL> connect / as sysdba
SQL> startup mount cc1;
```

```
SQL> alter database noarchivelog;
SQL> alter database open;
```

A database that has been placed in ARCHIVELOG mode will remain in that mode until it is placed in NOARCHIVELOG mode. The location of the archived redo log files is determined by the settings in the database's parameter file. The parameters to note in Oracle9i are as follows (with sample values):

```
log_archive_dest_1        = /db01/oracle/arch/CC1/arch
log_archive_dest_state_1  = ENABLE
log_archive_start         = TRUE
```

In this example, the archived redo log files are being written to the directory /db01/oracle/arch/CC1. The archived redo log files will all begin with the letters "arch," followed by a sequence number. For example, the archived redo log file directory may contain the following files:

```
arch_170.arc
arch_171.arc
arch_172.arc
```

Each of these files contains the data from a single online redo log. They are numbered sequentially, in the order in which they were created. The size of the archived redo log files varies, but does not exceed the size of the online redo log files.

If the destination directory of the archived redo log files runs out of space, then ARCH will stop processing the online redo log data and the database will stop itself. This situation can be resolved by adding more space to the archived redo log file destination disk or by backing up the archived redo log files and then removing them from this directory.

> **NOTE**
> *Never delete archived redo log files until you have backed them up and verified that you can restore them successfully.*

In a database that is currently running, you can show the current ARCHIVELOG settings (including the destination directory) via the **archive log list** command within Server Manager, as shown earlier in this section. You can also query the parameter settings from the V$PARAMETER dynamic performance view.

```
select Name,
       Value
  from V$PARAMETER
 where Name like 'log_archive%';
```

Although the **log_archive_start** parameter may be set to TRUE, the database will *not* be in ARCHIVELOG mode unless you have executed the **alter database archivelog** command shown earlier in this section. Once the database is in ARCHIVELOG mode, it will remain in that mode through subsequent database shutdowns and startups until you explicitly place it in NOARCHIVELOG mode via the **alter database noarchivelog** command.

Automating Multiplexing of Archived Redo Log Files

As of Oracle8, you can instruct the database to write to multiple separate archived redo log file destination areas simultaneously. Writing to separate destination areas allows you to recover in the event that one of those destination disks fails. The archiving process must be able to write to at least one location in order for the database to continue functioning; you can specify the number of writes that must succeed.

NOTE
Oracle writes to multiple archived redo log file destination areas simultaneously, not consecutively.

In Oracle8.0, the LOG_ARCHIVE_DUPLEX_DEST init.ora parameter specifies the second destination area for archived redo log files. A second parameter, LOG_ ARCHIVE_MIN_SUCCEED_DEST, specifies the minimum number of archived redo log destination areas that must be successfully written to during an ARCH write. Both of these parameters are supported in Oracle8i, but they are officially obsolete and have been superseded by a new set of options.

As of Oracle8i, you can use the LOG_ARCHIVE_DEST_*n* parameter to specify up to five locations for your archived redo log files (LOG_ARCHIVE_DEST_1, LOG_ ARCHIVE_DEST_2, etc.). The ARCH process will write files to all of the specified locations simultaneously. Each of the archive destinations has a corresponding "state" set via the LOG_ARCHIVE_DEST_STATE_*n* parameter. An archive destination's state may be either ENABLED, in which case files are written there, or DEFER, in which case the destination is not presently active. You should create a LOG_ ARCHIVE_ DEST_ STATE_*n* entry (such as LOG_ARCHIVE_DEST_STATE_1, LOG_ ARCHIVE_ DEST_ STATE_2, etc.) for each LOG_ARCHIVE_DEST_*n* entry in your init.ora file.

The LOG_ARCHIVE_DEST_*n* parameter replaces the LOG_ARCHIVE_DEST parameter supported in earlier versions of Oracle.

Using OEM to Get Started

From the Instance Manager screen of the OEM tool, you can see whether or not ARCHIVELOG mode has been enabled. Figure 11-4 shows this screen with the General tab selected. The database is not in ARCHIVELOG mode in Figure 11-4. In order to use the startup, shutdown, and ARCHIVELOG options within Instance Manager, you must connect through the Management Server using an account with preferred credentials enabled and the SYSDBA role available.

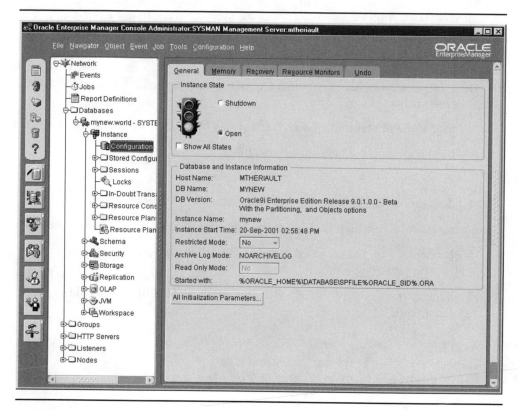

FIGURE 11-4. *OEM Console, Instance Configuration, General tab*

Performing Online Database Backups

Once a database is running in ARCHIVELOG mode, you can back it up while it is open and available to users. This capability allows round-the-clock database availability to be achieved while still guaranteeing the recoverability of the database.

Although hot backups can be performed during normal working hours, they should be scheduled for the times of the least user activity for several reasons. First, the hot backups will use operating system commands to back up the physical files, and these commands will use the available I/O resources in the system (impacting the system performance for interactive users). Second, while the tablespaces are being backed up, the manner in which transactions are written to the archived redo log files changes. When you put a tablespace in "hot backup" mode, the DBWR process writes all of the blocks in the buffer cache that belong to any file that is part of the tablespace back to disk. When the blocks are read back into memory and then changed, they will be copied to the log buffer the first time that a change is made to them. As long as they stay in the buffer cache, they will not be recopied to the online redo log file. This will use a great deal more space in the archived redo log file destination directory.

The command file for a hot backup has three parts:

1. A tablespace-by-tablespace backup of the datafiles, which in turn consists of

   a. Setting the tablespace into backup state

   b. Backing up the tablespace's datafiles

   c. Restoring the tablespace to its normal state

2. Backup of the archived redo log files, which consists of

   a. Recording which files are in the archived redo log destination directory

   b. Backing up the archived redo log files, then (optionally) deleting or compressing them

3. Backup of the control file via the **alter database backup controlfile** command.

NOTE
The online backup process is automated via the RMAN utility. See Chapter 12 for details on RMAN.

A command file to perform a hot backup of a database will resemble the following listing. It is structured the same as the description just given. This example is for a UNIX database. In the first section, the environment variables ORACLE_SID and ORACLE_HOME are set for the database. Each tablespace is then placed in **begin backup** state. The datafiles associated with each tablespace are then backed up.

When the datafiles are being backed up, there are two choices available: they may be backed up directly to tape, or they may be backed up to disk. If you have enough disk space available, choose the latter option since it will greatly reduce the time necessary for the backup procedures to complete. Be sure the backup destination areas are on different devices than the production files. For this example, the datafiles will be written directly to disk. This example shows the use of the svrmgrl utility provided with Oracle8i.

NOTE
You can simplify this script significantly, as described in the "Automation of the Backup Scripts" section later in this chapter.

```
#
# Sample Hot Backup Script for a UNIX File System database
#
# Set up environment variables:
ORACLE_SID=cc1; export ORACLE_SID
ORAENV_ASK=NO; export ORAENV_ASK
. oraenv
#
#   Step 1. Perform a tablespace-by-tablespace backup
#   of the datafiles. Set each tablespace, one at a time,
#   into begin backup state. Then back up its datafiles
#   and return the tablespace to its normal state.
#
# Note for UNIX: Set up an indicator for SQL*Plus or SVRMGRL
# (called EOFarch1 here).
#
svrmgrl <<EOFarch1
connect / as sysdba
REM
REM    Back up the SYSTEM tablespace
REM
alter tablespace SYSTEM begin backup;
!cp /db01/oracle/CC1/sys01.dbf /bckp/db01/oracle/CC1
alter tablespace SYSTEM end backup;
REM
REM    Back up the RBS tablespace
REM
alter tablespace RBS begin backup;
!cp /db02/oracle/CC1/rbs01.dbf /bckp/db02/oracle/CC1
alter tablespace RBS end backup;
REM
REM    Back up the DATA tablespace
REM    For the purposes of this example, this tablespace
REM    will contain two files, data01.dbf and data02.dbf.
REM    The * wildcard will be used in the filename.
REM
alter tablespace DATA begin backup;
!cp /db03/oracle/CC1/data0*.dbf /bckp/db03/oracle/CC1
alter tablespace DATA end backup;
REM
REM    Back up the INDEXES tablespace
REM
alter tablespace INDEXES begin backup;
!cp /db04/oracle/CC1/indexes01.dbf /bckp/db04/oracle/CC1
alter tablespace INDEXES end backup;
REM
REM    Back up the TEMP tablespace
REM
```

```
alter tablespace TEMP begin backup;
!cp /db05/oracle/CC1/temp01.dbf /bckp/db05/oracle/CC1
alter tablespace TEMP end backup;
REM
REM   Follow the same pattern to back up the rest
REM   of the tablespaces.
REM
exit
EOFarch1
# REM        Step 2. Back up the archived redo log files.
#
#   Record which files are in the destination directory.
#   Do this by setting an environment variable that is
#   equal to the directory listing for the destination
#   directory.
#   For this example, the log_archive_dest_1 is
#   /db01/oracle/arch/CC1.
#
FILES='ls /db01/oracle/arch/CC1/arch*.dbf'; export FILES
#
#   Now back up the archived redo logs to the tape
#   device via the "tar" command, then delete them
#   from the destination device via the "rm" command.
#   You may choose to compress them instead.
#
cp $FILES /bckp/db01/oracle/CC1/arch
rm -f $FILES
#
#       Step 3. Back up the control file to a disk file.
#
svrmgrl <<EOFarch3
connect / as sysdba
alter database backup controlfile to
   '/bckp/db01/oracle/CC1/CC1controlfile.bck';
alter database backup controlfile to trace;
exit
EOFarch3
#
#
#   End of hot backup script. The disk-based backups
#   can now be backed up to tape.
```

During the backup of the control file, two separate commands are executed. The first command copies the control file to a separate file on the server. The second backs up the control file **to trace**. When the second command is executed, Oracle will create a trace file in the user dump file destination area. The trace file will contain header information followed by the **create controlfile** command for the database. In addition to being a great source of information about the database's files, the trace file can be used in the event your recovery requires you to execute a **create controlfile** command. It is much simpler to generate the proper command in this fashion than to type it in by hand.

Automation of the Backup Scripts

The preceding backup script explicitly lists each datafile within each tablespace, so this backup script must be altered each time a datafile is added to the database. To simplify the backup process, you can consolidate the operations against the tablespaces. If your hardware environment uses mirroring or RAID technologies to safeguard against media failures, and if the backup is occurring at a time of few transactions, you can place a small set of the tablespaces into **begin backup** state concurrently. Your goal should be to have as few tablespaces in backup mode for as short a time as possible.

In the revised backup script, the order of events will be

1. Backup of all datafiles, which consists of

   a. Setting a set of tablespaces into backup state. You can dynamically select the names of tablespaces from DBA_TABLESPACE or V$TABLESPACE.

   b. Backing up all of the datafiles for those tablespaces. You can dynamically select the names of the datafiles from V$DATAFILE or DBA_DATA_FILES.

   c. Restoring the tablespaces to their normal state, using the list of tablespaces generated in step 1a.

   d. Repeating the cycle until all sets of tablespaces have been backed up.

2. Backup of the archived redo log files, which consists of

   a. Recording which files are in the archived redo log destination directory

   b. Backing up the archived redo log files, then (optionally) deleting or compressing them

3. Backup of the control file via the **alter database backup controlfile** commands.

The differences between this order of commands and the commands given earlier in this chapter are found in step 1. Instead of placing tablespaces into **begin backup** state one at a time, all of the tablespaces are placed into **begin backup** state at the same time. To automatically generate the commands needed to alter the tablespaces, query DBA_TABLESPACES as shown in the following listing:

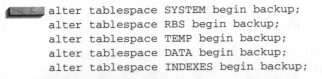

```
set pagesize 0 feedback off

select
    'alter tablespace '||Tablespace_Name||' begin backup;'
  from DBA_TABLESPACES
 where Status <> 'INVALID'

spool alter_begin.sql
/
spool off
```

The output of this query will be a command named alter_begin.sql. Its entries will resemble the following:

```
alter tablespace SYSTEM begin backup;
alter tablespace RBS begin backup;
alter tablespace TEMP begin backup;
alter tablespace DATA begin backup;
alter tablespace INDEXES begin backup;
```

NOTE
Since the TEMP tablespace contains only temporary objects, it is not required as part of a backup set; during recovery, you could simply drop that tablespace and create a new TEMP tablespace. However, having TEMP in your backup set greatly simplifies disaster recoveries, in which the persons performing the recovery may not be your usual DBAs.

NOTE
If you use a temporary tablespace created via the **create temporary tablespace** *command, it will never participate in recovery; you just alter the tablespace to add a tempfile if it is lost.*

When you execute this command file, all of the tablespaces will be placed into **begin backup** state. You can now back up all of the datafiles. Instead of backing up specific datafiles, you can back up all datafiles in the proper directories without regard to their tablespace affiliations. In the following listing, the datafiles from disks /db01 to /db09 are backed up to tape via a single UNIX **tar** command:

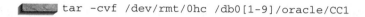

```
tar -cvf /dev/rmt/0hc /db0[1-9]/oracle/CC1
```

NOTE
You may want to exclude the archived redo log file directory from this backup step since those files will be backed up via step 2 of the backup procedure.

Once the datafiles are backed up, you can change them from **begin backup** state to their normal state. You can automatically generate the script to perform this change, as shown in the following listing:

```
set pagesize 0 feedback off

select
    'alter tablespace '||Tablespace_Name||' end backup;'
  from DBA_TABLESPACES
 where Status <> 'INVALID'

spool alter_end.sql
/
spool off
```

When you execute the alter_end.sql script generated by this query, your tablespaces will be back in their normal state and you can now proceed to steps 2 (archived redo log file backups) and 3 (control file backup) of the backup process.

NOTE
*For larger databases, it is more appropriate to issue the **alter tablespace begin backup** commands on a tablespace-by-tablespace basis or on a very small set of tablespaces at a time.*

The automation of backup scripts generates the greatest benefit when you have many databases that are changing frequently. If you rely on automated backup scripts, you should make sure your server hardware is very reliable. As of Oracle7.2, you can alter a tablespace to **end backup** state prior to opening the database if the database shut down abnormally while the tablespace was in **begin backup** state. Ideally, you should avoid server activity—and server failures—during your database backup process.

Archived Redo Log File Backups
Since the archived redo log file destination directory may become full before the hot backup procedure is run, you should have a separate backup procedure that only

backs up that directory. The files in that directory can then be deleted, leaving space for new archived redo log files.

> **NOTE**
> *If you have multiple archive log destination areas, you may be able to defer writes to a filled destination while writes continue to a second destination.*

The archived redo log file backup procedure is simply a portion of the full hot backup process:

1. Record which files are in the archived redo log destination directory.

2. Back up the archived redo log files.

3. Delete those files from the destination directory.

The following script performs this process for UNIX databases using file systems. The **tar** command is used to back up the files to tape. Note that if you are not concerned with stopping the archiver during this process (such as if it is already stuck), you do not need to log into the database.

```
#     Step 1: IF NEEDED, stop the archiving process. This
#     will keep additional archived redo log files from
#     being written to the destination directory for several
#     seconds while file names are collected during this
#     process.
#
#     If you need this step, uncomment the following 7 lines
#svrmgrl <<EOFarch1
#connect / as sysdba
#archive log stop;
#REM
#REM  Exit Server Manager using the indicator set earlier.
#exit
#EOFarch1
#
#     Step 2: Record which files are in the destination
#     directory.
#     Do this by setting an environment variable that is
#     equal to the directory listing for the destination
#     directory.
#     For this example, the log_archive_dest_1 is
```

```
#   /db01/oracle/arch/CC1.
#
FILES='ls /db01/oracle/arch/CC1/arch*.dbf'; export FILES
#
#   Step 3: IF YOU STOPPED THE ARCHIVER IN STEP 1, go back
#   into Server Manager and restart the archiving process.
#   Set an indicator (called EOFarch2 in this example).
#
#   If you need to execute this step, uncomment the
#   following 5 lines.
#svrmgrl <<EOFarch2
#connect / as sysdba
#archive log start;
#exit
#EOFarch2
#
#     Step 4. Back up the archived redo logs to the tape
#   device via the "tar" command, then delete them
#   from the destination device via the "rm" command.
#
#   Edit the following command to reflect your tape device
#   name.
tar -rvf /dev/rmt/0hc $FILES
#
#     Step 5. Delete those files from the destination directory.
#
rm -f $FILES
#
#     End of archived redo log file backup script.
```

The archived redo logs that are backed up via this procedure should be stored with the last previous hot backup. As an alternative to backing them up to tape, you can move them to a separate directory and compress them. During recoveries, you may need to move the files after restoring them so the recovery process can find them.

Alternatives to Stopping the Archiver

As part of the backup process shown in the preceding section, the ARCH process may be temporarily stopped via the **archive log stop** command. Once a directory of files in the archive log destination area is generated, the ARCH process is restarted via the **archive log start** command. The ARCH process is temporarily stopped because the backup scripts in the preceding sections all end by deleting the old archived redo log files. You need to be sure that you do not delete a file that has not been backed up. By temporarily disabling archiving, no new files will be created for a few seconds and you can generate a consistent listing of the archive destination directory. This method assumes that if any file is currently being written to the archive destination directory, it will be closed by the time the file is backed up.

As an alternative, you can query the V$LOG dynamic dictionary view. The Archived column of the V$LOG view will contain a value of YES if the log has been completely archived. You can select the highest archived log from V$LOG (using the Sequence# column) and use that as the basis for your listing of files to be backed up. For example, if V$LOG says that Sequence# 2334 was the last log file to be archived, then you can successfully back up all of the files in your archived redo log destination directory that have sequence numbers of 2334 and below. If you attempt to back up #2335, your backup may succeed at an operating system level, but since the file is not yet fully archived, that backup may be only half-written and therefore may not be useful during a recovery operation.

You can choose not to delete the old archived redo log files. If you have enough space available on your disk arrays, keep several days' worth of archived redo log files available on your servers. You can compress the older files to reduce the amount of space required, but you will need to have enough space available to uncompress them during a recovery operation.

Ideally, you should maintain enough free space in your archive destination area to store enough compressed archived redo logs to enable you to perform a recovery without needing to recover archived redo log files from tape.

Using LogMiner

Oracle uses online redo log files to track every change that is made to user data and the data dictionary. The information stored in the redo log files is used to re-create the database, in part or in full, during recovery. To enable recovery of the database to a point in time after the database backup was made, archived copies of the redo log files can be maintained.

In Oracle8i, the ability to examine redo log files and archived log files became available. A new tool, called LogMiner, provides a vital view into the modifications that have occurred within your database.

When you use LogMiner, you see both the changes that have been made (the SQL_*redo*) and the SQL you can use to reverse those changes (the SQL_*undo*). Thus, you can review the history of the database, without actually applying any redo logs, and obtain the code to reverse any problematic transactions. Until the advent of LogMiner, DBAs had to rely on users telling them the time at which problems were noted or use a best-guess estimate of when to stop a database recovery. Using LogMiner, you can pinpoint the transaction under which corruption first occurred so you can determine the correct point in time to recover your database just prior to the corruption.

If there were a small number of transactions that required rolling back, prior to LogMiner, you would have to restore the table to an earlier state and apply archived log files to bring the table forward to just before the corruption. When restoring the table and applying the archived log files, you would risk losing later transactions that you would like to retain. You can now use LogMiner to roll back only the transactions that are problematic without losing later, valid transactions.

LogMiner in its original form has had some limitations associated with its use. With the original approach, you could only review one log file at a time, and the interface to the tool was cumbersome to use. In Oracle9i, a major overhaul of the interface has been implemented, and the functionality has been greatly enhanced, including a LogMiner Viewer for use with the Oracle Enterprise Manager. Both the manual approach to using LogMiner and the OEM LogMiner Viewer are presented within this section.

How LogMiner Works

Although LogMiner can be used with databases that are running Oracle version 8.0 or higher, some of the newest features may only be available with Oracle9i databases. You must have either EXECUTE privilege on the DMBS_LOGMNR package or the EXECUTE_CATALOG_ROLE role to run LogMiner. LogMiner requires a data dictionary to fully translate the redo log file contents and translate internal object identifiers and datatypes to object names and external data formats. If a data dictionary is not available, LogMiner will return the data in hex format and the object information as internal object IDs.

You have three choices for obtaining a data dictionary for LogMiner use as follows:

- Extract the data dictionary information to a flat file.

- Extract the data dictionary to redo log files.

- Use the online data dictionary from the current database.

The LogMiner analysis usually requires that the data dictionary in use was generated from the same database that generated the redo log files. However, if you are using a flat file format or are using the data dictionary from redo log files, you can analyze the redo log files either from the database on which LogMiner is running or from another database. If, however, you are using the online catalog from the current database, you can only analyze redo log files from the current database.

Since you can run LogMiner from one database against the redo log files in another database, the character sets used on both databases must match. The hardware platform must also match the one used when the redo log files were generated.

Extracting the Data Dictionary

When you perform analysis of the redo log files using LogMiner, you must have a data dictionary available. To run LogMiner to analyze the redo log files, a data dictionary that was used when the redo log files were generated must be available. If you do not want to impact your current production database and platform, you can extract the data dictionary into either a flat file or into redo log files and use a different database to analyze the redo log files.

One potential problem with extracting the data dictionary to a flat file is that while you are extracting the data dictionary, someone else could be issuing DDL statements. Therefore, the extracted data dictionary could be out of sync with the database. When you use a flat file to store the data dictionary, fewer system resources are required than when you use redo log files.

When you extract the data dictionary to redo log files, no DDL statements can be processed during the time in which the data dictionary is extracted. Therefore, the dictionary will be in sync with the database; the extraction is more resource intensive, but the extraction process is faster.

To extract the data dictionary to either a flat file or to redo log files, you use the procedure DBMS_LOGMNR_D.BUILD. The data dictionary file is placed in a directory. Thus, you must have write permission of the directory in which the file will be placed. To define the location of the directory, use the initialization parameter UTL_FILE_DIR. For example, to specify the location D:\Oracle\Ora90\database as the location for the LogMiner output, you place the following entry in the parameter file:

```
UTL_FILE_DIR= D:\Oracle\Ora90\database
```

NOTE
*You cannot dynamically change the UTL_FILE_DIR parameter using the **alter system** command. You must modify the initialization file and stop and restart the database.*

To execute the DBMS_LOGMNR_D.BUILD procedure, you must specify a filename for the dictionary, the directory path name for the file, and whether you want the dictionary written to a flat file or redo log files. To extract the data dictionary to a flat file located in the directory G:\Oracle\Ora90\database with the filename mydb_dictionary, you issue the following command:

```
execute DBMS_LOGMNR_D.BUILD
('mydb_dictionary.ora',
'G:\Oracle\Ora90\database',
options=>DBMS_LOGMNR_D.STORE_IN_FLAT_FILE);
```

You can use DBMS_LOGMNR_D.STORE_IN_FLAT_FILE as the other option.

NOTE
Although the command is shown on several lines here, you must enter it on one continuous line, or you will receive error messages.

Once you have the dictionary stored in a flat file, you can copy it to another platform to run LogMiner. You may need to run dbmslmd.sql on the other database to establish the correct environment. The dbmslmd.sql file can be found in the $ORACLE_HOME\rdbms\admin directory on a UNIX system.

Analyzing One or More Redo Log Files

To analyze redo log files using LogMiner, follow these steps:

1. Obtain a list of the available redo log files using V$LOGMNR_LOGS.

2. Start the LogMiner utility using the DBMS_LOGMNR.START_LOGMNR procedure.

3. Query V$LOGMNR_CONTENTS to see the results.

4. Once you have finished viewing the redo logs, issue the following command to end the session:

```
execute DBMS_LOGMNR.END_LOGMNR;
```

The available subprograms for the DBMS_LOGMNR package are described in Table 11-3.

Subprogram	Description
ADD_LOGFILE	Adds a file to the list of archive files to process
START_LOGMNR	Initializes the LogMiner utility
END_LOGMNR	Completes and ends a LogMiner session
MINE_VALUE (*function*)	Returns the undo or redo column value of the column name specified by the COLUMN_NAME parameter for any row returned from V$LOGMNR_CONTENT
COLUMN_PRESENT (*function*)	Determines if undo or redo column values exist for the column name specified by the COLUMN_NAME parameter for any row returned from V$LOGMNR_CONTENT

TABLE 11-3. *DBMS_LOGMNR Subprograms*

There are several options available for the DBMS_LOGMNR.START_LOGMNR package and several parameters that you can use to specify the range of redo logs you want to analyze. Table 11-4 shows the available options, and Table 11-5 shows the parameters.

To create a list of the redo log files that are available for analysis, you run the procedure DBMS_LOGMNR.ADD_LOGFILE with the NEW option as follows:

```
execute DBMS_LOGMNR.ADD_LOGFILE(
LogFileName=> '/oracle/ora90/redo01.ora',
Options=> DBMS_LOGMNR.NEW);
execute DBMS_LOGMNR.ADD_LOGFILE(
LogFileName=> '/oracle/ora90/redo02.ora',
Options=> DBMS_LOGMNR.NEW);
```

You can specify the location of the data dictionary file as follows:

```
execute DBMS_LOGMNR.ADD_LOGFILE(
DictFileName=> '/oracle/ora90/dictionary.ora',
```

After you've told LogMiner the location of the data dictionary and added the redo log files, you can begin analyzing the redo log files using the DBMS_ LOGMNR .START_LOGMNR package. For example, the following command analyzes log files over a range of times:

```
execute DBMS_LOGMNR.START_LOGMNR(
DictFileName => '/oracle/dictionary.ora',
StartTime => TO_DATE('01-JUNE-2001 12:31:00', DD-MON-YYYY HH:MI:SS'),
EndTime => TO_DATE('01-JULY-2001 00:00:00', DD-MON-YYYY HH:MI:SS'));
```

Options Flag	Description
NEW	Places the specified redo log file in the list of log files to be analyzed and purges the existing logs, if any exist
ADDFILE	Adds the specified redo log file in the list of log files to be analyzed
REMOVEFILE	Removes the specified redo log file in the list of log files to be analyzed

TABLE 11-4. *DBMS_LOGMNR Options to Add or Remove a File*

Options	Description
COMMITTED_DATA_ONLY	Only DMLs corresponding to committed transactions are returned if this option is set.
SKIP_CORRUPTION	Skips any corruption encountered in the redo log file during a select from V$LOGMNR_CONTENTS. This option works only if a block in the actual redo log file is corrupted and does not work if the corruption is in the header block.
DDL_DICT_TRACKING	Enables LogMiner to update the internal data dictionary if a DDL event occurs, to ensure that SQL_REDO and SQL_UNDO information is maintained and correct.
NO_DICT_RESET_ONSELECT	Prevents LogMiner from reloading its internal data dictionary each time a new select statement is issued (only available if DDL_DICT_TRACKING is enabled).
DICT_FROM_ONLINE_CATALOG	Instructs LogMiner to use the online data dictionary instead of a flat file or redo log file stored dictionary.
DICT_FROM_REDO_LOGS	Instructs LogMiner to use the data dictionary stored in one or more redo log files.

TABLE 11-5. *START_LOGMNR Options Values*

NOTE
Using the timestamp will not ensure ordering of the redo records. You must use the SCN numbers to ensure the order of the records.

You can use the SCN values to filter data as follows:

```
execute DBMS_LOGMNR.START_LOGMNR(
DictFileName => '/oracle/dictionary.ora',
StartScn => 125,
EndScr => 300);
```

If you do not enter a start and end time or range of SCN numbers, the entire file is read for every select statement that you issue.

To look at the redo and undo code, you select the Sql_Redo and Sql_Undo columns as follows:

```
select Sql_Redo, Sql_Undo
  from V$LOGMNR_CONTENTS;
```

You can use the options shown in Table 11-5 to limit the returned values.

Using the Oracle Enterprise Manager LogMiner Viewer

You can use the OEM Server Manager Console to launch the LogMiner Viewer to view redo and archived redo logs. To launch the LogMiner Viewer on a Windows platform, use the Start | Programs | Oracle_Home | Oracle Enterprise Manager Console option. Once you have connected to the OEM Server Console, select the database on which you want to run the LogMiner Viewer. Ensure that the database has been started.

To start the LogMiner Viewer, highlight the database and right-click. Move the cursor to the Related Tools option, and then move to the LogMiner Viewer option, as shown in Figure 11-5.

If this is the first time you are accessing the Oracle LogMiner Viewer for the database, the following informational message is displayed:

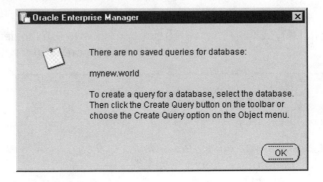

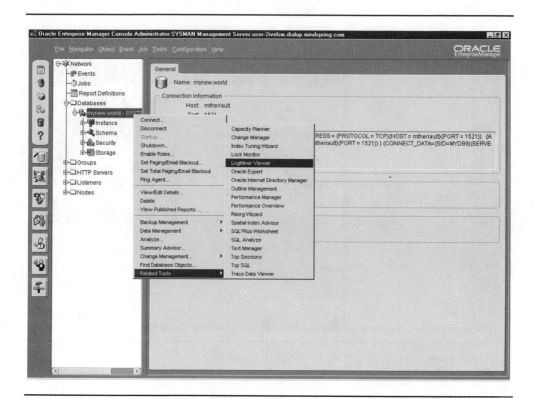

FIGURE 11-5.   *OEM Console with LogMiner Viewer option*

After you acknowledge the message, the LogMiner Viewer Console screen displays as shown in Figure 11-6.

To create an object query, either click on the top icon in the icon panel or select Create Query from the Object pull-down menu. The LogMiner Viewer automatically looks for available archived redo log files from which to create a query. If there are no archived redo log files available, you receive an error message.

You can review the commands that have been issued by selecting the Application SQL History option from the View pull-down menu, as shown in Figure 11-7.

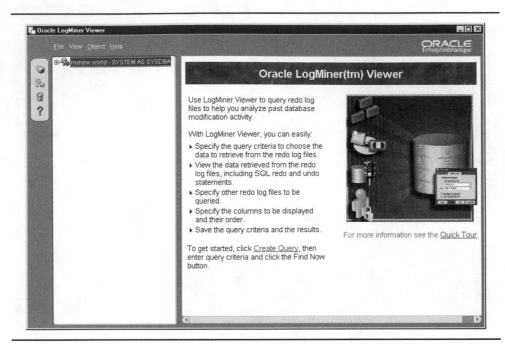

FIGURE 11-6. *LogMiner Viewer Console screen*

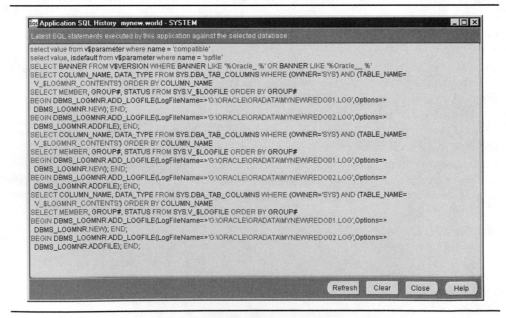

FIGURE 11-7. *Application SQL History screen*

FIGURE 11-8.   *Create Query, Query Criteria tab*

When you select the Create Query option, the Create Query screen displays with three tabs: Query Criteria, Redo Log Files, and Display Options. Figure 11-8 shows the Create Query screen with the Query Criteria tab.

The Query Criteria tab enables you to specify the filtering options for the log mining operation. By default, the NEW option is selected so that you can create a new query. With the Graphical Filter option selected, you can limit your query by Username, Operation, Owner, Table, Tablespace, Timestamp, SCN, and so on. The most frequently used filters are at the top of the list of values. In Figure 11-8, the Username filter has been selected with the name SCOTT entered.

Using the Textual Filter, you can manually enter a **where** clause. The Column values are displayed with an explanation of what each contains, as shown in Figure 11-9.

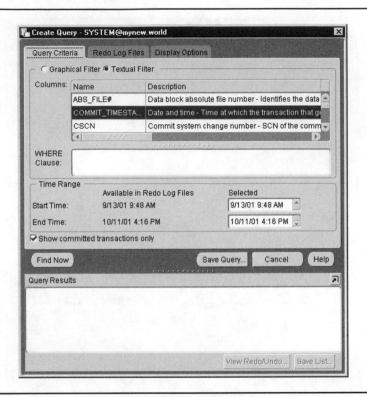

FIGURE 11-9. *Create Query, Query Criteria tab with Textual Filter option*

The available Time Range is displayed in the middle of the screen, and the Query Results are displayed after you click on the Find Now button. If the query will return more than 100 rows, a warning is displayed, and you are given the option to restrict the number of rows or continue, as shown in the following illustration.

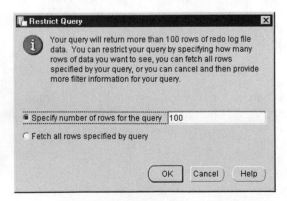

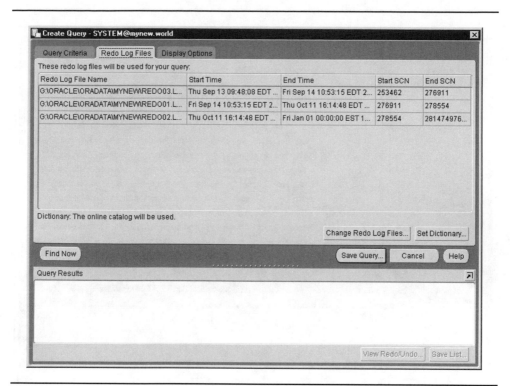

FIGURE 11-10. *Create Query, Redo Log Files tab*

The Redo Log Files tab enables you to view the start SCN number and stop SCN number for each redo log file that is available. You can use the information displayed in the Redo Log Files tab to limit the query. Figure 11-10 shows the Redo Log Files tab and the data dictionary being used.

The Display Options tab enables you to quickly choose the columns you want to use and the order in which they are to be displayed, along with the display name. Figure 11-11 shows the Display Options tab with several columns selected. If you want to have the columns in a specific order, deselect all of the columns, and then click in the box under Is Visible for each column in the order in which you want them displayed.

Once you have selected all of the criteria, click on the Find Now button to execute the LogMiner query. You can save the query for reuse and save the returned list to use for database recovery.

Using the new OEM LogMiner Viewer makes the job of sifting through redo log files much quicker and easier.

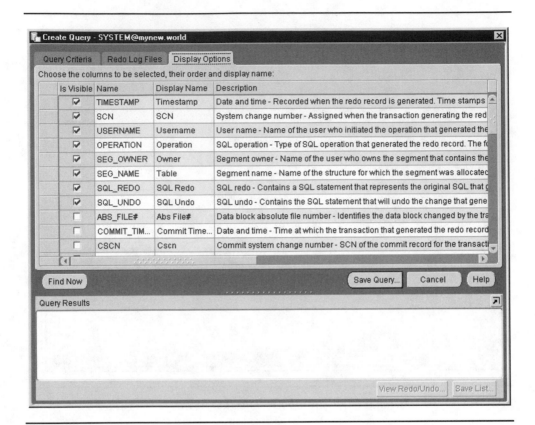

FIGURE 11-11. *Create Query, Display Options tab*

Standby Databases

You can maintain a *standby database* for quick disaster recovery. A standby database maintains a copy of the production database in a permanent state of recovery. In the event of a disaster in the production database, the standby database can be opened with a minimal amount of recovery necessary. You may, however, lose the contents of your online redo log files in your production database during the switch to the standby database. As of Oracle7.3, the management of standby databases is greatly simplified, and with Oracle8i the management has become fully automatic.

The standby database must use the same version of the kernel that the production system uses. You can create a standby database from a copy of the current production database (generated via either an offline backup or an online backup). As archived redo log files are generated by the production instance in Oracle8i, they will be copied to the standby system and applied to the standby database automatically.

Maintaining a standby database requires keeping the file structures and software versions of the production and standby databases continuously synchronized. See the *Oracle Server Administrator's Guide* for detailed directions for setting up and maintaining standby databases.

As of Oracle8i, you can use the standby database as a read-only database to enable large queries to be run in a nontransaction processing database. However, while the database is in read-only mode, redo log files will not be automatically applied to the database. The database could be placed in read-only mode during the day and then placed into standby mode at night and the redo logs resynchronized. If the standby database—in read-only mode—is needed for recovery during the day, the redo log files must be applied before the standby database can be made available.

In Oracle8i, Release 3, a scripted-based implementation called the Oracle8i Data Guard was introduced to enable easier standby database management. Tasks such as managing the production database, the physical standby database, associated applications, and the log transport services are performed through a command-line interface. Oracle9i Data Guard is used to automate many of the tasks handled by the Oracle8i version using both a GUI interface and the DGMGRL command-line interface.

Each tool is used for different tasks. You use the GUI tool, the Data Guard Manager, for configuration, setup, and operational tasks. Use the command-line interface, DGMGRL, for basic monitoring using some of the V$ views, to issue role changes to fail over from one machine to another, and to establish the Data Guard environment. See the *Oracle Server Administrator's Guide* for further directions for setting up and maintaining standby databases and using Oracle9i Data Guard.

As of Oracle9i, the ability to fail over to the standby database and later fail back to the primary database has been greatly enhanced. However, you should not plan on actively using the standby database, either as a reporting database or as a temporary transaction processing database. Standby databases support the ability for your business processes to continue in the wake of a disaster. Standby databases are seldom the best fits for reporting needs, as they will have the same table and index structures as the primary database.

Integration of Backup Procedures

Since there are multiple methods for backing up the Oracle database, there is no need to have a single point of failure in your backup strategy. Depending on your database's characteristics, one method should be chosen, and at least one of the remaining methods should be used as a backup to your primary backup method.

NOTE
When considering physical backups, you should also evaluate the use of RMAN to perform incremental physical backups.

In the following sections, you will see how to choose the primary backup method for your database, how to integrate logical and physical backups, and how to integrate database backups with file system backups.

For backup strategies specific to very large databases, see Chapter 15. For details on RMAN, see Chapter 12.

Integration of Logical and Physical Backups

Which backup method is appropriate to use as the primary backup method for your database? When deciding, you should take into account the characteristics of each method:

Method	Type	Recovery Characteristics
Export	Logical	Can recover any database object to its status as of the moment it was exported.
Offline backups	Physical	Can recover the database to its status as of the moment it was shut down; if the database is run in ARCHIVELOG mode, you can recover the database to its status at any point in time.
Online backups	Physical	Can recover the database to its status at any point in time.

Offline backups are the least flexible method of backing up the database if the database is running in NOARCHIVELOG mode. Offline backups are a point-in-time snapshot of the database; and since they are a physical backup, DBAs cannot selectively recover logical objects (such as tables) from them. Although there are times when they are appropriate (such as for disaster recovery), offline backups should normally be used as a fallback position in the event that the primary backup method fails. If you are running the database in ARCHIVELOG mode, you can use the offline backups as the basis for a media recovery, but an online backup would normally be more appropriate for that situation.

Of the two remaining methods, which one is more appropriate? For production environments, the answer is almost always online backups. Online backups, with the database running in ARCHIVELOG mode, allow you to recover the database to the point in time immediately preceding a system fault or a user error. Using an Export-based strategy would limit you to only being able to go back to the data as it existed the last time the data was exported.

Consider the size of the database and what objects you will likely be recovering. Given a standard recovery scenario—such as the loss of a disk—how long will it take for the data to be recovered? If a file is lost, the quickest way to recover it is usually via a physical backup, which again favors online backups over exports.

If the database is small, transaction volume is very low, and availability is not a concern, then offline backups may serve your needs. If you are only concerned about one or two tables, then you could use Export to selectively back them up. However, if the database is large, then the recovery time needed for Export/Import may be prohibitive. For large, low-transaction environments, offline backups may be appropriate.

Regardless of your choice for primary backup method, the final implementation should include a physical backup and some sort of logical backup, either via Export or via replication. This redundancy is necessary because these methods validate different aspects of the database: Export validates that the data is logically sound, and physical backups that it is physically sound. Three sample integrations of these methods are shown here:

Database Type	Online Backups	Offline Backups	Exports
All sizes, transaction intensive	Nightly	Weekly	Weekly
Small, mostly read-only	Not done	Nightly	Nightly
Large, mostly read-only	Not done	Nightly	Weekly

As shown in these solutions, a good database backup strategy integrates logical and physical backups. The frequency and type of backup performed will vary based on the database's usage characteristics.

Other database activities may call for ad hoc backups. Ad hoc backups may include offline backups before performing database upgrades and exports during application migration between databases.

Integration of Database and Operating System Backups

As described in this chapter, the DBA's backup activities involve a number of tasks normally assigned to a systems management group: monitoring disk usage, maintaining tapes, and so on. Rather than duplicate these efforts, it is best to integrate them; focus on a process-based alignment of your organization. The database backup strategy should be modified so that the systems management personnel's file system backups will take care of all tape handling, allowing you to centralize the production control processes in your environment.

Centralization of production control processes is usually accomplished by dedicating disk drives as destination locations for physical file backups. Instead of backing up files to tape drives, the backups will instead be written to other disks on the same server. Those disks should be targeted for backups by the systems management personnel's regular file system backups. The DBA does not have to run a separate tape backup job. However, the DBA does need to verify that the systems management team's backup procedures executed correctly and completed successfully.

CHAPTER
12

Using Recovery Manager (RMAN)

ne of your primary duties as a database administrator is to ensure the protection and recoverability of your company's data. Problems that you can encounter that lead to data loss are

- Hardware failure

- Damage caused by people within or outside your organization (accidental or intentional)

- Faulty software

- Catastrophic weather conditions such as a fire or flood

Beginning in Oracle8.0, a Recovery Manager toolset called RMAN has been supplied to enable you to back up and recover your databases in an automated manner using either a command-line mode or the Recovery Manager from within the Oracle Enterprise Manager. You can use either approach to back up, restore, and recover database files.

In Chapter 11, we told you about the different forms of backup and recovery. We described how to perform database backup and recovery manually. In this chapter we'll examine the RMAN tool architecture and show you how to perform each of the available backup and recovery options using the OEM toolset.

About Recovery Manager

Although RMAN provides you with a wonderful tool for protecting your databases and ensuring successful recovery, using Recovery Manager does not diminish your backup planning issues. For example, what type of datafile backup will you use? What are the implications for your recovery procedures? What tapes and backup media will you need to have available in order to perform a recovery? Will you have the catalog data placed in your control file (the default in Oracle9*i*) or use a recovery catalog instead?

NOTE
You should only use backup procedures that fit your specific database backup performance and capability requirements.

Starting with Oracle9*i*, Recovery Manager now stores its catalog of information in the database control files, and you must allot adequate storage retention to ensure a complete backup history for database recovery. If you opt to store the catalog information within a database, you must ensure that the database holding the catalog is protected and backed up frequently.

But, the primary question for you to ask is "Why should I use RMAN instead of user-management methods?" RMAN provides you with a media management API so that you can incorporate your third-party vendor media management software easily. As RMAN performs online backups, each fractured data block is reread to ensure data consistency. As backups are performed, RMAN calls the same kernel utilities that all other processes use to validate the integrity of Oracle data blocks.

During incremental backups, RMAN captures only blocks that have been changed since the previous backup. You can recover a database using incremental backups even if the database is in NOARCHIVELOG mode. You must ensure that the incremental backups of a database in NOARCHIVELOG mode have been taken after a consistent shutdown.

If you establish an RMAN repository, you can use it to report information such as

- What files need to be backed up

- Which files have not been backed up for a specific number of days

- Which backups can be deleted

- Current RMAN persistent settings

When performing database recovery, you often need to restore files either from disk locations or from tape before the recovery process can begin. The RMAN tool provides automatic parallelization of backup and restore operations. RMAN is also an effective tool for creating duplicate or standby databases easily.

Another feature available through RMAN is the ability for the tool to perform automatic archived log failover if it encounters a missing or corrupt log during a backup. In the event of a missing or corrupt log, RMAN will evaluate the other log copies listed in the repository as alternative candidates for the backup.

Recovery Manager Architecture

There are four components within the Recovery Manager: the RMAN executable, one or more target databases, the recovery catalog database, and the media management software. The only components that you must have are the RMAN executable and a target database. Since RMAN automatically stores its metadata in the target database's control file, you do not have to have a recovery catalog. However, because you can gain much additional benefit from having a recovery catalog, we recommend that you include one. Media management software is supplied by third-party vendors and will not be discussed here.

A Look at the RMAN Executable and Target Database

The RMAN executable is generally located in the $ORACLE_HOME/bin directory on a UNIX system and in ORACLE_HOME\bin in a Windows environment, but the location may vary based on the operating system involved. To manually run RMAN, enter the following command at the operating system prompt:

```
$ rman
RMAN>
```

The initial arguments you can use when accessing RMAN from an operating system prompt are shown in Table 12-1. You can see the set of arguments for your specific version of RMAN by typing **rman help** at the operating system command-line prompt (such as the Windows DOS prompt).

The arguments can be used when you access the RMAN tool. For example, you can specify the target you want to connect to by typing

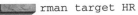
```
rman target HR
```

Argument	Value	Description
target	quoted-string	Connect string for target database
catalog	quoted-string	Connect string for recovery catalog
nocatalog	none	If specified, then no recovery catalog is used
cmdfile	quoted-string	Name of input command file
log	quoted-string	Name of output message log file
trace	quoted-string	Name of output debugging message log file
append	none	If specified, log is opened in append mode
debug	optional-args	Activate debugging
msgno	none	Show RMAN-nnnn prefix for all messages
send	quoted-string	Send a command to the media manager
pipe	string	Building block for pipe names
timeout	integer	Number of seconds to wait for pipe input

TABLE 12-1. *RMAN Access Arguments*

In this example, the database HR is specified as the target database for backing up, restoring, or recovering. When you enter this command, you are prompted for the password for the target database.

Using an RMAN Repository

If you choose to create and enable an RMAN repository, you gain the benefits of having a set of metadata in which information about the target database and its backup and recovery operations are stored. You can store information for multiple databases within one recovery catalog. Some of the information that RMAN stores is about image and proxy copies, backup sets and pieces, archived redo logs, target database schema, and persistent configuration settings. Scripts and operating system files can also be stored within the repository.

You can obtain reports and view metadata only if you enable and use a repository.

NOTE
You can have RMAN store configuration values in the control file and resynchronize them to the repository as necessary.

To see the configurable parameters, issue a **show all** command from the RMAN prompt with the target database running. The configurable parameters with their default values are shown in Table 12-2.

Parameter	Default Value
RETENTION POLICY TO REDUNDANCY	1
BACKUP OPTIMIZATION	OFF
DEFAULT DEVICE TYPE TO	DISK
CONTROLFILE AUTOBACKUP	OFF
CONTROLFILE AUTOBACKUP FORMAT FOR DEVICE TYPE DISK TO	'%F'
DEVICE TYPE DISK PARALLELISM	1

TABLE 12-2.   *RMAN Configuration Parameters*

Parameter	Default Value
DATAFILE BACKUP COPIES FOR DEVICE TYPE DISK TO	1
ARCHIVELOG BACKUP COPIES FOR DEVICE TYPE DISK TO	1
MAXSETSIZE TO	UNLIMITED
SNAPSHOT CONTROLFILE NAME TO	'<ORACLE_HOME>/dbs/snapcf_<DBNAME>.f'

TABLE 12-2.   *RMAN Configuration Parameters* (continued)

You can use the command **configure** to override the default parameters persistently. That is, the parameters can be set once and then used for subsequent jobs. One of the parameters you can set is the RETENTION POLICY. As you can see in Table 12-2, the parameter defaults to REDUNDANCY, which defines a fixed number of backups to be retained. Any backups in excess of this number can be deleted. The default value of 1 says that as soon as a new backup is created, the old one is no longer needed and can be deleted. The other option for RETENTION POLICY is RECOVERY WINDOW, specified in days, to define a period of time in which point-in-time recovery must be possible. The RECOVERY WINDOW is the best way to specify how long backups should be retained, but does not really control how many copies of the backup are created or kept. The REDUNDANCY option enables you to specify a number of backups to be cataloged before any backup is considered to be obsolete. There are two other commands associated with the RETENTION POLICY. The first command is

```
configure retention policy to none;
```

This command tells RMAN that there is no retention policy. Backups are never expired using this command. The other command is

```
configure retention policy clear;
```

This command resets the RETENTION POLICY value to REDUNDANCY with a value of 1.

Creating a Recovery Catalog

A recovery catalog should be created in its own schema within its own tablespace in a database that is separate from all of the target databases you intend to back up. Installing the recovery catalog in a target database defeats the purpose of having a recovery catalog because, if you lose the database, you lose not only your catalog but the ability to restore the target database as well. Although you can use the SYSTEM tablespace to store the recovery catalog, we strongly recommend that you use a totally separate tablespace to help ensure less tablespace contention.

If you use the Oracle Database Configuration Assistant, described in Chapter 1, to create your database, an RMAN account, with password RMAN, is automatically created with account locked and password expired. There are 29 tables, 63 indexes, 2 packages with 2 package bodies, 1 sequence, and 25 views created for a total of 122 objects used to constitute the recovery catalog.

To create the recovery catalog, if you do not have an RMAN account within your database, first create the user in which the catalog will be stored and grant the privileges RECOVERY_CATALOG_OWNER, CONNECT, and RESOURCE. For example, you can use the following commands to create the user:

```
connect SYSTEM/MANAGER as sysdba
create user RMAN identified by RMAN temporary tablespace TEMP
default tablespace CATTBS;
grant CONNECT, RESOURCE, RECOVERY_CATALOG_OWNER to RMAN;
```

Once the RMAN schema has been created and the appropriate privileges (CONNECT, RESOURCE, RECOVERY_CATALOG_OWNER) granted, you can connect to the RMAN executable as described earlier in this chapter and create the recovery catalog by issuing the following commands:

```
% rman target / catalog RMAN/RMAN@HR
RMAN> create catalog
```

Once the catalog is created, you can register a database by issuing the following command:

```
RMAN> register database;
```

Storing Recovery Information in the Target Control Files

You have the choice of having the Recovery Manager store recovery information within a recovery catalog or completely within the target database control file. RMAN can perform all of the necessary backup and recovery operations using just control file information, but you will not be able to take advantage of RMAN repository capabilities like the following:

- Store manually created scripts for backup, restore, or recovery
- Store copies of operating system backup files
- Restore and recover a target database if its control files become lost or damaged

RMAN uses the database structure, archived redo logs, backup sets, and datafile copy information stored in the control files to populate the recovery catalog. If your target database is small and it does not make sense to support a separate database solely to house the recovery catalog, RMAN can just use the target's control file for backup and recovery purposes. When using the control file exclusively, RMAN stores two types of records: *circular reuse records* and *noncircular reuse records*. Noncircular records include datafile and log file information; circular information includes archived redo logs.

Circular reuse records contain noncritical information that can be overwritten when necessary, such as log history, archived redo logs, and backups. The records are written to the control file in a logical ring. Oracle can either expand the ring or overwrite records when all of the available record slots are full. The parameter CONTROL_FILE_RECORD_KEEP_TIME defines the minimum amount of time in days that a record should be retained without being overwritten. Noncircular reuse records such as datafiles, online redo logs, and redo threads contain critical information that cannot be overwritten.

When you intend to restore and recover a database from the control file using RMAN, you should ensure that there are at least two or three copies of the control file retained on different disks and on different controllers. To have RMAN automatically create copies of the control file, use the command **configure controlfile autobackup**. When you issue the command with the parameter set to ON, you ensure that RMAN will make and retain backup copies of the control file. RMAN can use the automatic copies of the control file that it has made, without using the actual database control file or accessing a repository. If you use the **configure controlfile autobackup** command, you must ensure that all of the Recovery Manager backup logs are kept.

In the next section, you'll see the complete list of RMAN commands with examples of how to use many of them.

Using the Recovery Manager and RMAN

The most significant capability provided via Recovery Manager is the ability to perform incremental physical backups of your datafiles. During a full (called a *level 0*) datafile backup, all of the blocks ever used in the datafile are backed up. During a cumulative (*level 1*) datafile backup, all of the blocks used since the last full datafile backup are backed up. An incremental (*level 2*) datafile backup backs up only those blocks that have changed since the most recent cumulative or full backup. You can define the levels used for incremental backups.

If you do not use the OEM tools during database recovery using RMAN, you will need to know which files are current, which are restored, and the backup method you plan to use. In its present form, Recovery Manager does not completely shield you from the commands needed to recover the database.

The ability to perform incremental and cumulative backups of datafiles may greatly improve the performance of your backups. The greatest performance improvements will be realized by very large databases in which only a small subset of a large tablespace changes. Using the traditional backup methods, you would need to back up all of the datafiles in the tablespace. Using Recovery Manager, you only back up the blocks that have changed since the last backup.

RMAN Commands and Their Usage

There are many commands that you can use in RMAN to back up, restore, and recover your database. The commands are shown in Table 12-3.

Command	Purpose
@	Run a command file.
@@	Run a command file in the same directory as another command file that is currently running. The @@ command differs from the @ command only when run from within a command file.
allocate channel	Establish a channel, which is a connection between RMAN and a database instance.
allocate channel for maintenance	Allocate a channel in preparation for issuing maintenance commands such as **delete**.
alter database	Mount or open a database.
backup	Back up a database, tablespace, datafile, archived log, or backup set.

TABLE 12-3.   *Summary of RMAN Commands*

Command	Purpose
blockrecover	Recover an individual data block or set of data blocks within one or more datafiles.
catalog	Add information about a datafile copy, archived redo log, or control file copy to the repository.
change	Mark a backup piece, image copy, or archived redo log as having the status UNAVAILABLE or AVAILABLE; remove the repository record for a backup or copy; override the retention policy for a backup or copy.
configure	Configure persistent RMAN settings. These settings apply to all RMAN sessions until explicitly changed or disabled.
connect	Establish a connection between RMAN and a target, auxiliary, or recovery catalog database.
copy	Create an image copy of a datafile, control file, or archived redo log.
create catalog	Create the schema for the recovery catalog.
create script	Create a stored script and store it in the recovery catalog.
crosscheck	Determine whether files managed by RMAN, such as archived logs, datafile copies, and backup pieces, still exist on disk or tape.
delete	Delete backups and copies, remove references to them from the recovery catalog, and update their control file records to status DELETED.
delete script	Delete a stored script from the recovery catalog.
drop catalog	Remove the schema from the recovery catalog.
duplicate	Use backups of the target database to create a duplicate database that you can use for testing purposes or to create a standby database.

TABLE 12-3. *Summary of RMAN Commands* (continued)

Command	Purpose
execute script	Run an RMAN stored script.
exit	Quit the RMAN executable.
host	Invoke an operating system command-line subshell from within RMAN, or run a specific operating system command.
list	Produce a detailed listing of backup sets or copies.
print script	Display a stored script.
quit	Exit the RMAN executable.
recover	Apply redo logs or incremental backups to a restored backup set or copy in order to update it to a specified time.
register	Register the target database in the recovery catalog.
release channel	Release a channel that was allocated with an **allocate channel** command.
replace script	Replace an existing script stored in the recovery catalog. If the script does not exist, then **replace script** creates it.
replicate	Copy the control file to all the locations specified in the CONTROL_FILES initialization parameter.
report	Perform detailed analyses of the content of the recovery catalog.
reset database	Inform RMAN that the SQL statement **alter database open resetlogs** has been executed and that a new incarnation of the target database has been created, or reset the target database to a prior incarnation.
restore	Restore files from backup sets or from disk copies to the default or a new location.

TABLE 12-3. *Summary of RMAN Commands* (continued)

Command	Purpose
resync	Perform a full resynchronization, which creates a snapshot control file and then copies any new or changed information from that snapshot control file to the recovery catalog.
run	Execute a sequence of one or more RMAN commands, which are one or more statements executed within the braces of **run**.
send	Send a vendor-specific quoted string to one or more specific channels.
set	Make the following session-level settings: Control whether RMAN commands are displayed in the message log. Set the DBID when restoring a control file. Specify new filenames for restored datafiles. Specify a limit for the number of permissible block corruptions. Override default archived redo log destinations. Specify the number of copies of each backup piece. Determine which server session corresponds to which channel. Control where RMAN searches for backups when using an Oracle Real Application Clusters configuration. Override the default format of the control file autobackup.
show	Display the current **configure** settings.
shutdown	Shut down the target database. This command is equivalent to the SQL*Plus **shutdown** command.
spool	Write RMAN output to a log file.
sql	Execute a SQL statement from within Recovery Manager.
startup	Start up the target database. This command is equivalent to the SQL*Plus **startup** command.

TABLE 12-3. *Summary of RMAN Commands* (continued)

Command	Purpose
switch	Specify that a datafile copy is now the current datafile—that is, the datafile pointed to by the control file. This command is equivalent to the SQL statement **alter database rename file** as it applies to datafiles.
upgrade catalog	Upgrade the recovery catalog schema from an older version to the version required by the RMAN executable.
validate	Examine a backup set and report whether its data is intact. RMAN scans all of the backup pieces in the specified backup sets and looks at the checksums to verify that the contents can be successfully restored.

TABLE 12-3.   *Summary of RMAN Commands* (continued)

NOTE
Oracle has put emphasis on simplifying RMAN, and you can now back up a database with the single command **backup database**.

Before showing you examples of how to use the commands presented in Table 12-3, look at the subclauses available for use with various RMAN commands, as shown in Table 12-4. This table shows the subclauses, their purpose, and the commands they can be used with. Where a subclause can be used with most of the available commands, the word "Many" has been inserted into the Used With column.

Subclause	Purpose	Used With
allocOperandList	Specifies channel control options such as PARMS, FORMAT, and MAXOPENFILES.	**allocate channel, allocate channel for maintenance, configure**

TABLE 12-4.   *RMAN Command Specifiers*

Subclause	Purpose	Used With
archivelogRecordSpecifier	Specifies a range of archived redo log files based on time range, SCN, or sequence.	**archivelog**
completedTimeSpec	Specifies a time range during which the backup or copy completed.	Many
connectStringSpec	Specifies the username, password, and net service name for connecting to a target, recovery catalog, or auxiliary database. The connection is necessary to authenticate the user and identify the database.	**connect target**
datafileSpec	Specifies a datafile by filename or absolute file number.	**copy**
deviceSpecifier	Specifies the type of storage device to be used for a backup or copy.	**backup, copy**
keepOption/nokeepOption	Specifies that a backup or copy should or should not be exempt from the current retention policy. Keywords are **until time**, **forever**, **logs**, **nologs**.	**backup, change copy**
listObjList	Specifies which items will be displayed by the **list** command. Keywords are **datafile**, **tablespace**, **database**, and **controlfile**.	**list, crosscheck, delete**

TABLE 12-4.   *RMAN Command Specifiers* (continued)

Subclause	Purpose	Used With
maintQualifier	Specifies additional options for maintenance commands such as **delete** and **change**. Keywords are **tag**, **like**, and **device type**.	**list**, **crosscheck**, **delete**
obsOperandList	Determines which backups and copies are obsolete. Keywords are **redundancy**, **recovery window of**, and **orphan**.	**delete**, **report**
recordSpec	Specifies which objects the maintenance commands should operate on. Keywords are **backuppiece**, **proxy**, **backupset**, **controlfilecopy**, **datafilecopy**, **archivelog**.	**crosscheck**, **delete**, **list**
releaseForMaint	Releases a channel allocated with an **allocate channel for maintenance** command.	**allocate channel for maintenance**
untilClause	Specifies an upper limit by time, SCN, or log sequence number. This clause is usually used to specify the desired point in time for an incomplete recovery.	**backup**, **restore**, **recovery**, **report**

TABLE 12-4. *RMAN Command Specifiers* (continued)

To let RMAN know you want to begin a command, you use the word "RUN" followed by an open brace ({). To begin the backup, restore, or recovery process, you must establish some kind of connection between RMAN and the target database instance. The connection you establish is called a *channel*. When you allocate a channel, Oracle creates a server session to perform the work. There is always a

case-sensitive channel ID or name associated with the channel to be used by RMAN
for error reporting. You specify a device type as well to indicate the storage device
RMAN is to use in performing the backup, restore, or recover operation.

The following code allocates a channel called DefaultChannel using a device
type of disk. Since a disk is going to be used, the directory location where the file
will be placed or read from is also listed. You must next tell RMAN what action you
want taken. In this example, RMAN is instructed to make a backup of the database
and include a copy of the current control file within the backup set. The directory
specified in the first command is to be the location for the backup set. End the
command with a closing brace (}).

```
RUN {
allocate channel DefaultChannel type disk
'G:\ORACLE\ORADATA\MYDB9\b_%u_%s_%p';
backup (database include current controlfile);
}
```

In Oracle9*i*, once you have configured channels using the **configure** command,
RMAN will automatically allocate the channel if one is not specified in the RMAN
command. You can use this feature to your advantage by configuring a channel for
maintenance actions like **change**, **delete**, or **crosscheck**. Normally, if a channel has
not been configured, you must use the **allocate channel for maintenance** command
before issuing one of the maintenance commands. You can take more than one
maintenance action in one command. For example, to delete four backups from
both a disk and a tape drive, you can issue the following command:

```
RUN {
set allocate on;
allocate channel for maintenance device type disk;
allocate channel for maintenance device type sbt;
delete backupset 2,4,6,7;
}
```

Earlier, the use of a retention policy was shown. If you want to ensure that a
backup is archived and retained for a longer time than specified in your retention
policy, use the following command:

```
RUN {
...
backup...KEEP [until 'date' | FOREVER |][NOLOGS | LOGS]
}
```

You can specify KEEP with either the **backup** or **copy** command when you
create a backup, or with the **change** command when you alter the retention or
recoverability time for an existing backup. If you use the parameter FOREVER, the
backup is marked never to expire, but you must use a recovery catalog with this

setting since the information would eventually get aged out of a control file. When you use the LOGS parameter, you specify that the backup and associated archive logs can be used to recover the database to any point in time within the scope of the backup and archive logs. Therefore, all of the archive logs for the backup must be retained and remain available. Likewise, when you use NOLOGS, you specify that only the backup itself can be used for recovery to the point when the backup was captured. No archive logs can be used to recover the database past the backup time. The NOKEEP parameter is the default and tells Oracle to follow the declared retention policy.

You can use the **delete obsolete** command to delete backup sets that are no longer needed. If you have identified a backup set as never expired, that set will be unaffected when the **delete obsolete** command is issued.

The **crosscheck** command is used to verify that files referenced in the recovery catalog still exist on disk or tape. Although RMAN does not remove the references from the catalog for files that no longer exist, the entries are marked EXPIRED. To use the **crosscheck** command to verify all of the backups that were written to tape between 01-FEB-2001 and 01-MAR-2001, for example, issue the command

```
RUN {
allocate channel for maintenance device type sbt;
crosscheck backup device type sbt completed between '01-FEB-2001' and '01-MAR-2001';
}
```

As you can see from the list in Table 12-3, there are many more commands that you can use with RMAN. A complete explanation of the commands can be found in the *Oracle9i Recovery Manager Reference* guide.

Using the OEM Backup Manager

To use the Backup Manager, you must enter the tool using the Oracle Enterprise Manager's Management Server Console. Before connecting to the Management Server Console for the first time, run the Oracle Enterprise Management Configuration Assistant to configure the OEM repository. This repository will house OEM information and is not the repository that will be used by RMAN. Once the OEM repository is created, ensure that the Management Server service is started.

NOTE
The sequence required to successfully bring up the OEM Server Manager Console is to start the OEM repository database service and database, start the OEM Server Manager service, and then access the console. If the Server Manager service is not running, you will receive a misleading listener error message.

Performing a Backup Using OEM

To perform any level backup using the OEM tool, connect to the OEM Server Manager Console, select the appropriate database, and right-click to bring up the database options. From the database options, select Backup from the Backup Manager menu. The Backup Wizard will activate. Figure 12-1 shows the OEM Console with a database selected and the backup/recovery options on the pop-up menu.

Alternately, you can select the target database and use the pull-down menu options Tools | Database Wizards | Backup Management | Backup. To perform a backup operation, the target database must be running and available. After the initial Welcome screen, you are prompted to select a Strategy choice. You can select a predefined backup strategy or customize your own backup strategy. For this example, the predefined backup strategy is selected, as shown in Figure 12-2.

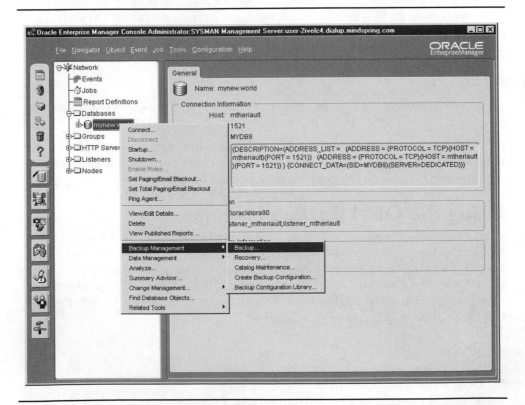

FIGURE 12-1. *OEM Console, Backup option*

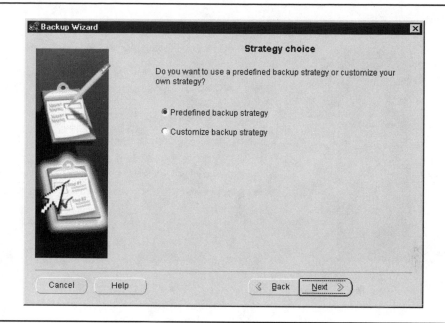

FIGURE 12-2.   *Backup Wizard, Strategy Choice*

Figure 12-3 displays the Backup Frequency options screen with three choices:

- A Decision Support System (DSS) with a backup frequency of once a week

- A moderately updated system (OLTP) that is not very large, with a backup frequency of every day

- A frequently updated, medium to large database, with a backup frequency of full backups weekly and incremental backups nightly

The default option is a DSS backed up once a week on Sunday. For the once-a-week backup, the next screen enables you to select an appropriate time for the backup to be performed. Figure 12-4 shows the Backup Time screen. The message at the bottom of the screen shows that the target database is not in ARCHIVELOG mode and, therefore, will be shut down with a cold backup and then restarted.

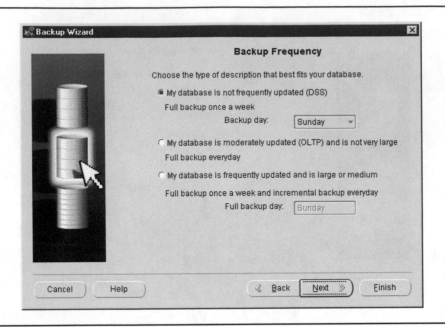

FIGURE 12-3. *Backup Wizard, Backup Frequency screen*

The default time value is 12:00 A.M. The screen shown in Figure 12-5 shows the selected configuration. You can use the Launch Wizard button on the Configuration screen to examine the configuration settings for Channels, Recovery Catalog, Backup Parameters, and Preferred Credentials, but you cannot change any of the settings from this option.

Once the configuration is accepted, the tool enables you to declare whether the configuration should be used on multiple destinations. For this example, only one database is available and has been preselected by the tool. The only choices from this screen are Back, Finish, Cancel, and Help. When Finish is selected, a summary sheet is presented. Figure 12-6 displays the summary sheet. At the bottom of the screen, not shown in the figure, is the script that will be used, as follows:

```
Recovery Manager Script:
run {
allocate channel DefaultChannel type disk format
'G:\ORACLE\ORADATA\MYNEW\b_%u_%s_%p';
backup ( database include current controlfile );
}
```

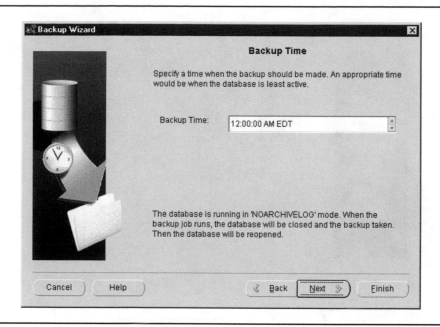

FIGURE 12-4.   *Backup Wizard, Backup Time screen*

To verify that the backup job has been stored in the Backup Manager, right-click from the Databases option in the OEM Server Manager Console to enable selecting the Backup Configuration Library screen under the Backup Manager option. The following illustration shows the Backup Configuration Library screen with a default backup entered:

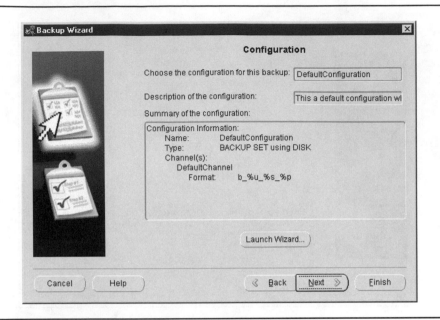

FIGURE 12-5. *Backup Wizard, Configuration screen*

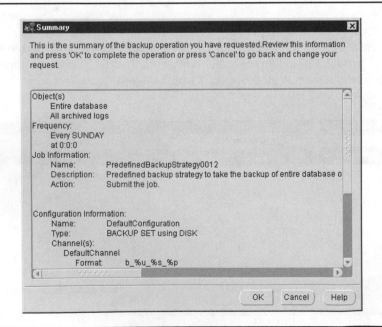

FIGURE 12-6. *Backup Wizard, Summary screen*

To perform an immediate backup, you can choose the Customize option. The option, although not selected, is shown in Figure 12-2.

When you perform a backup with ARCHIVELOG enabled using the Customize option, the choices presented are to back up the entire database (as just shown) or back up tablespaces, datafiles, or archive logs.

When you select the Tablespaces option, a screen with a list of the available tablespaces is presented with the check box "Include control files with this backup" selected. Figure 12-7 shows the Tablespaces screen with the DRSYS tablespace selected.

Once you have selected the tablespace(s) to back up, the Archive Logs screen is displayed. You can choose one of three options: include all of the archive logs, exclude all of the archive logs, or select a subset of archive logs to back up. As with the entire database backup, you are presented with a Configuration screen. A Schedule screen is displayed to enable you either to run the job immediately or select a scheduled run time. Figure 12-8 shows the Schedule screen with the Immediately option selected.

After you define your schedule for the backup, a Job Information screen, as shown in Figure 12-9, is displayed. A default job name and description are displayed, as well as the options to submit the job now, not submit the job now but save the job to the job library, or submit the job and save it to the job library.

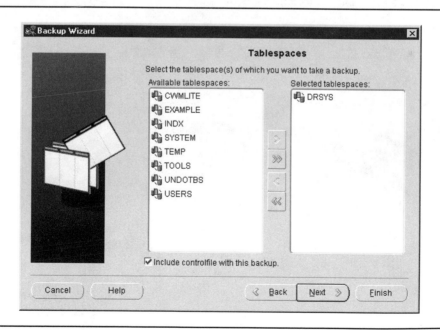

FIGURE 12-7. *Backup Wizard, Tablespaces screen*

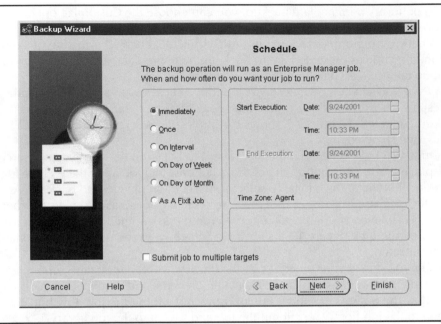

FIGURE 12-8. *Backup Wizard, Schedule screen*

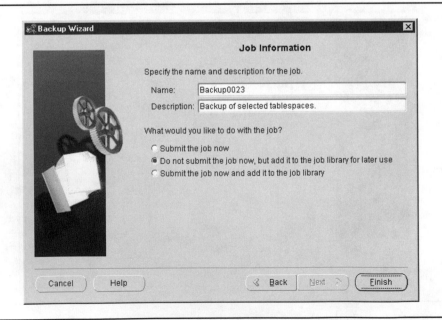

FIGURE 12-9. *Backup Wizard, Job Information screen*

Finally, a Summary screen is displayed, as shown earlier in Figure 12-6. The script created for the tablespace backup in this example is as follows:

```
Recovery Manager Script:
run {
allocate channel DefaultChannel type disk format 'G:\ORACLE\ORADATA\MYNEW\b_%u_%s_%p';
backup
    (tablespace 'DRSYS' include current controlfile );
}
```

When you choose to back up datafiles from the Customize option with ARCHIVELOG mode enabled for your database, you see a Datafiles screen with a list of all of the datafiles in your database. You can select one or more of the datafiles for backup. Figure 12-10 shows the Datafiles screen with the datafile for the DRSYS tablespace selected.

As in the tablespaces backup example, the Archive Logs screen is displayed, followed by the Configuration screen, the Schedule screen, the Job Information screen, and the Summary screen. The script to run the datafiles backup is as follows:

```
Recovery Manager Script:
run {
allocate channel DefaultChannel type disk format 'G:\ORACLE\ORADATA\MYNEW\b_%u_%s_%p';
backup
    (datafile 'G:\ORACLE\ORADATA\MYNEW\DRSYS01.DBF' include current controlfile);
}
```

If you choose the archive log backup option, the Archive Logs screen is displayed with the options described earlier. The Configuration, Schedule, Job Information, and Summary screens are then displayed in that order. The script that is created to back up the archive logs is as follows:

```
Recovery Manager Script:
run {
allocate channel DefaultChannel type disk format 'G:\ORACLE\ORADATA\MYNEW\b_%u_%s_%p';
backup (archivelog all delete input);
}
```

This script instructs RMAN to back up all of the archive logs and then delete them from the system. If you have multiple copies of the archive logs in multiple directories, only one copy of each distinct archive log is made when the ALL option is specified. However, the DELETE option tells RMAN to delete every copy of the archive log from every directory location.

Multiple Backup Copies

In Oracle8i, the ability to make more than one copy of each backup piece became available using the **set duplex** command. In Oracle9i, the feature is enhanced to increase the number of backup piece copies you can have and to let you specify the directory where you want the copies to be written using the FORMAT option.

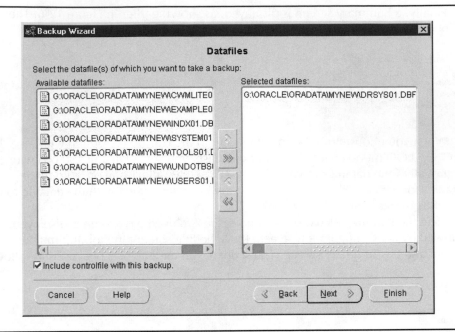

FIGURE 12-10. *Backup Wizard, Datafiles screen*

With the enhanced features, you can specify up to four values for the locations for backup pieces. You use the **set backup copies #** command with a number from 1 to 4 to describe the first, second, third, and fourth location values. For example, if you want to have three copies of the backup pieces written to three different directories, you use the following command:

```
run {
   set backup copies 3
   backup database
   format '/dir1/%U','/dir2/%U','/dir3/%U';
}
```

If you specify fewer directory values than the number of copies requested, RMAN will cycle through the values beginning with the first one entered. In our preceding example, if the following command is entered, dir1 will be used for the location of the first and third backup piece copies.

```
run {
   set backup copies 3
   backup database
```

```
format '/dir1/%U','/dir2/%U';
}
```

If you enter more directory locations than the number of copies specified, the extra locations will be ignored.

Restarting Failed Backups

In pre-Oracle9i versions of RMAN, if a backup failed, you had to start from the beginning and re-back up all of the files of interest. With Oracle9i, you can restart an unsuccessful backup attempt where the backup left off; only missing or incomplete files will be backed up. RMAN bases its decision to back up a file on the backup time of the existing files. You can use the new option **not backed up** with the optional command **since time 'TIMESTAMP'** to restart a backup that has failed. If a backup failed on December 22, 2001, at 10:15 A.M., for example, you would issue the following command to resume the failed backup:

```
RUN {
...
backup database not backed up since time '22-DEC-01 10:15:00';
}
```

If you do not specify a date and time, only files that have never been backed up will be captured. Thus, if you have just created new datafiles, you can use the **backup database not backed up** command, as described in Table 12-3, to have them backed up. In any case, RMAN takes the date you have entered and compares it to the backup set completion time. The entire backup set will carry the time that the last file in the set was backed up, and RMAN will look at the most recent backup when doing its comparisons.

You can back up archive logs using the option **plus archivelog** with the **backup datafile** command.

If the Recovery Manager encounters blocks that fail logical validation during backup, the information is written to the V$BACKUP_CORRUPTION or V$COPY_CORRUPTION views. If the block is not recognized at all, the header and footer of the block do not match, or the block contains all zeros, information will be written to one of these views based on whether a backup or copy action was being performed. The other situation under which corruption is recorded is when the contents of a block are logically inconsistent. In this case, the header and footer of the block match and the checksum can be valid, but corruption exists and will be noted.

Recovery Using OEM

You can use RMAN directly through command-line prompts or through the OEM tool to perform recovery. Using RMAN, you can recover datafiles, tablespaces, full databases, control files, and/or archive logs. The Recovery Manager will select the best strategy for recovery. If a copy is available, it will be chosen over a backup set. The types of recovery that can be performed are database, tablespace, and datafile. The **set newname** command can be used to restore files to a different location, and if a control file is being restored, a destination must be supplied.

To ensure that the backup is restorable, you can use the command **restore database validate**. This command will read all of the backups and validate the tape for I/O errors but will not perform an actual restore operation. By periodically running the **restore database validate** command, you will get a validation of your backups and a general indication of the amount of time it will take to restore the files from tape. The files must be restored from tape before recovery can be performed. The restore and recovery can be combined in one routine to make the entire process automatic.

The view V$RECOVERY_FILE_STATUS provides information about the particular files that need recovery, while the view V$RECOVER_FILE shows which datafiles need recovery. The view V$RECOVERY_STATUS provides overall recovery information.

You can track the progress of the recovery using the view V$SESSION_LONGOPS while using the following query, and look for increasing values:

```
select ROUND(Sofar/Totalwork*100,2)
   from V$SESSION_LONGOPS;
```

Your recovery job should be the only job running at the time, so the query result will show the percentage of the recovery that has completed.

Whether you use RMAN directly or through the OEM facility, you need to ensure that the recovery catalog remains synchronized with any files that have been changed outside of the Recovery Manager's control. For example, if an archived redo log file is moved or a file-level backup is performed manually, the recovery catalog will need to be resynchronized to reflect the change. You should store copies of your scripts outside of the Recovery Manager facility so that you can manually run them if you need to. Be sure to periodically test the scripts to ensure that they will operate properly when needed.

You can perform recovery tests using a new TEST option of the **recover** command to verify whether there are going to be problems recovering your database. The recovery applies redo information as it would for a normal recovery, but changes are held in memory and no updated blocks are written back to disk. To use the TEST option, simply add the word "TEST" to the end of your **recover** command. For example, to test recovery for the database named MYDB9 you enter the command

```
RUN {
...
recover database MYDB9 test;
}
```

RMAN offers support for Oracle Managed Files as well as backup and recovery of multiple block sizes.

If you find that there is corruption within specific blocks, RMAN supplies a command called **blockrecover** (shown in Table 12-3) to perform recovery on one or more individual blocks within a datafile. You can issue a **blockrecover** command and specify the datafile number and block number to be recovered. Since block recovery is performed independently, you can list several different datafile and block numbers within one command as follows:

```
RUN {
...
blockrecover datafile 5 block 6, datafile 8 block 7, 10, datafile 10 block 15, 67, 78;
}
```

In this example, three datafiles with various blocks are specified for recovery.

NOTE
RMAN will not detect all forms of corruption.

Using the Recovery Wizard
When you invoke the Recovery option from the OEM Management Server Console to perform recovery, the tool verifies that the target database is started and mounted but not opened before it begins. You can use the Object pull-down menu to start up and mount the database. Once the database is started and mounted, you can start the Recovery Wizard from the Tools | Database Wizards | Backup Management | Recovery pull-down menu. The Recovery Wizard's initial screen is shown in Figure 12-11.

Because the database used in this example is not in ARCHIVELOG mode, the next screen advises you that only an entire database recovery can be performed. The screen is shown in Figure 12-12.

The Configuration screen is displayed next, showing you the proposed configuration. The Launch Wizard button in the middle of the screen can be used to display the configuration parameters for the channels, recovery catalog, backup parameters, and preferred credentials that will be used. Figure 12-13 shows the Configuration screen with the Launch Wizard option.

Finally, the Summary screen is displayed with the details of the intended recovery job displayed. At the bottom of the details information is the script that the job will run. For our example, the script is as follows:

```
Recovery Manager Script:
run {
allocate channel DefaultChannel type disk format 'G:\ORACLE\ORADATA\MYNEW\b_%u_%s_%p';
restore (database);
recover database ;
}
```

The script first performs a **restore** operation, and then a **recover** command is issued.

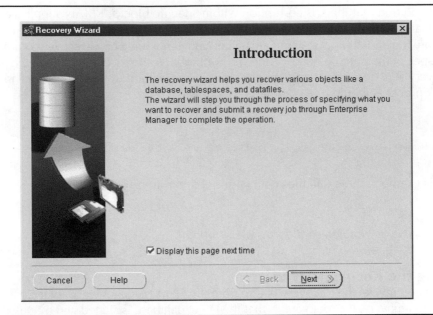

FIGURE 12-11. *Recovery Wizard, Introduction screen*

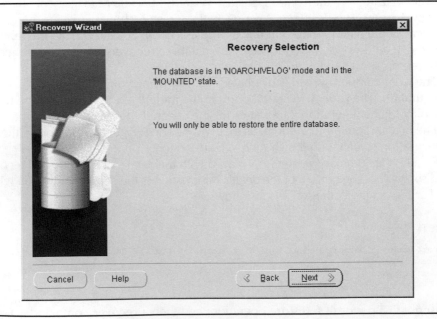

FIGURE 12-12. *Recovery Wizard, Recovery Selection screen,*
NOARCHIVELOG mode

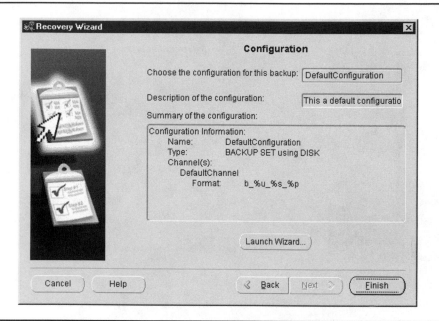

FIGURE 12-13. *Recovery Wizard, Configuration screen*

With ARCHIVELOG enabled and the database mounted but not opened, the Recovery Selection screen offers three recovery options: Entire Database, Tablespaces, or Datafiles. Figure 12-14 shows the Recovery Selection screen with the Tablespaces option selected. If the database is open, only the Tablespaces and Datafiles options are available.

Notice the check box labeled "Perform recovery without restoring the datafiles" in the lower part of the screen. By default, the check box is deselected. If you select the check box, the recover action is performed without a restore. You use this option to apply the redo logs when you do not need to restore the datafile because it already exists. If the datafile does not exist or exists but is corrupted, do not select this check box.

If you select the Entire Database option, the wizard proceeds as shown in the NOARCHIVELOG example. If you select the Tablespaces option, a screen showing all of the tablespaces within the database is displayed with the DRSYS tablespace selected, as shown in Figure 12-15.

You are next given the option to restore the associated datafile(s) for the tablespace to another location. If you have selected the "Perform recovery without restoring the datafiles" check box, as shown earlier, this screen will not be displayed. Figure 12-16 shows the Rename screen.

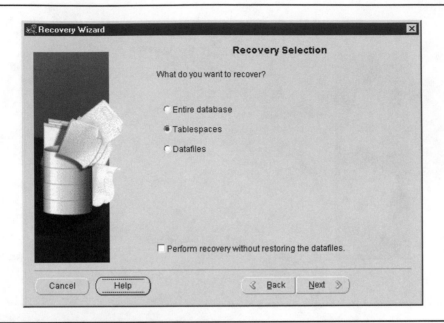

FIGURE 12-14. *Recovery Wizard, Recovery Selection screen, ARCHIVELOG mode*

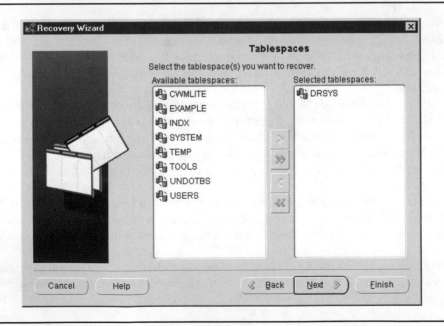

FIGURE 12-15. *Recovery Wizard, Tablespaces screen*

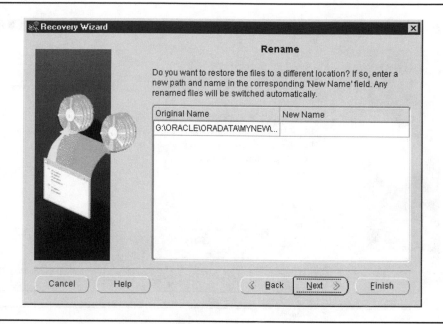

FIGURE 12-16. *Recovery Wizard, Rename screen*

As with the Backup Wizard and previously shown Recovery Wizard screens, a Configuration screen and Summary screen are displayed to enable you to modify the configuration and verify the job summary before the job is submitted to the job library, or submitted to run. The proposed recovery script is shown at the bottom of the Summary as follows:

```
Recovery Manager Script:
run {
allocate channel DefaultChannel type disk format
'G:\ORACLE\ORADATA\MYNEW\b_%u_%s_%p';
restore ( tablespace 'DRSYS'  );
recover  tablespace 'DRSYS' ;
}
```

When the Datafiles option is selected for recovery, instead of the Tablespaces list (as shown in Figure 12-15), a Datafiles screen with all of the available datafiles is displayed. Figure 12-17 shows the Datafiles screen with the DRSYS datafile selected.

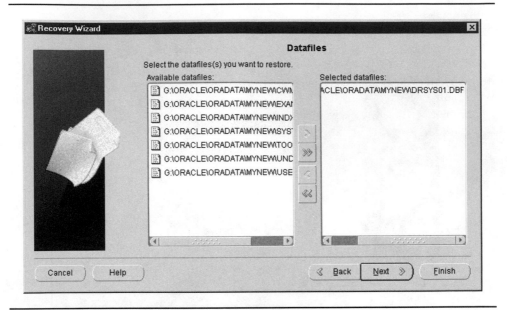

FIGURE 12-17. *Recovery Wizard, Datafiles screen*

The same file rename option is offered next (as shown in Figure 12-16), as well as the Configuration and Summary screens shown earlier. The proposed script for the datafile recovery in our example is as follows:

```
Recovery Manager Script:
run {
allocate channel DefaultChannel type disk format 'G:\ORACLE\ORADATA\MYNEW\b_%u_%s_%p';
restore (datafile 'G:\ORACLE\ORADATA\MYNEW\DRSYS01.DBF');
recover datafile 'G:\ORACLE\ORADATA\MYNEW\DRSYS01.DBF';
}
```

Generating Lists and Reports

An advantage of using a recovery catalog instead of relying on the subset of information stored in the target database control files is that you can use the full complement of parameters available to generate lists of information about backup sets, proxy copies, and image copies contained within the repository. You can generate lists of some of the information even if NOCATALOG has been specified. You can also obtain reports on files that require backup, have become obsolete, or are unrecoverable.

Using the list Command

Of the enhancements for Oracle9i RMAN, the commands used for catalog maintenance are **list, crosscheck, delete expired**, and **change**. There are a number of changes that have been made to improve consistency across these commands, and they all now use similar syntax and the same output formats and status codes when possible.

Using the **list** command, you can have output written to either the terminal screen or the message log. You can organize the output BY BACKUP or BY FILE, and you can specify the level of detail to be presented: either VERBOSE or SUMMARY. The **list** command enables you to view the following information:

- Expired backups and copies within the RMAN catalog

- Datafile backups and copies that can be used in a restore operation

- Archive logs, backup sets and pieces, control file copies, datafile copies, and proxy copies

- Backups and copies that are restricted by either tag, completion time, recoverability, or device type

- Either incarnations of a specific database or information on all databases known within the catalog

NOTE
*You must be connected to a target database to use the **list** command.*

To obtain a list of all of the backups available in the catalog, in the default VERBOSE mode, you can issue the following command:

```
list backup;

List of Backup Sets
===================
BS Key  Device Type Elapse Time Completion Time
-------  ----------- ----------- ---------------
366     DISK        00:00:10    25-SEP-01 BP
        Key: 367      Status: AVAILABLE  Tag:
        Piece Name: /oracle/dbs/09c5unih_1_1
    List of Archived Logs in backup set 366
    Thrd Seq     Low SCN    Low Time   Next SCN   Next Time
    ---- -------  ---------- ---------  ---------- ---------
    1    282     34567      25-SEP-01 35678      26-SEP-01
    1    284     35678      25-SEP-01 36122      26-SEP-01
```

```
BS Key   Type LV Size        Device Type Elapse Time Completion Time
-------  ---- -- ----------  ----------- ----------- ---------------
384      Full 92M           DISK         00:00:37    15-SEP-01
         BP Key: 345   Status: AVAILABLE  Tag:
         Piece Name: /oracle/dbs/0ac5unj5_1_1
  Controlfile Included: Ckp SCN: 51554      Ckp time: 25-SEP-01
  List of Datafiles in backup set 344
  File LV Type Ckp SCN    Ckp Time   Name
  ---- -- ---- ---------- --------- ----
   1      Full 62345      25-SEP-01 /oracle/dbs/tbs_01.f
   2      Full 62345      25-SEP-01 /oracle/dbs/tbs_02.f
List of Proxy Copies
====================
PCKey File Status    Completion time    Ckp SCN Ckp time
----- ---- --------- ----------------- ------- -----------------
678   1    AVAILABLE 9/26/2001 01:55:32 78022   9/26/2001 01:55:42
           Datafile name: /oracle/dbs/tbs_01.f
           Handle: 0kb90b85_1_0
689   1    AVAILABLE 9/26/2001 02:05:18 78025   9/26/2001 02:38:01
           Datafile name: /oracle/dbs/tbs_01.f
           Handle: 0mb91c60_1_0
           Tag: wklybkup
```

The same command, in summary mode, produces the following listing:

```
LIST BACKUP SUMMARY;
List of Backups
===============
Key      TY LV S Device Type Completion Time #Pieces #Copies Tag
-------  -- -- - ----------- --------------- ------- ------- ---
232      B     A DISK        23-SEP-01       1       1
341      B     A DISK        23-SEP-01       1       1
```

There are many options available for the **list** command that you can view in the *Oracle9i Recovery Manager Reference* documentation. You will also find many excellent examples to study there.

Using the report Command

The RMAN **report** command is used to perform detailed analysis of the RMAN repository and present the output to either the user's terminal or the message log file. You can only issue the **report** command from the RMAN prompt. You can request reports to find the following information:

- Files requiring backup

- Files that have not been backed up for a specific period of time

- Unrecoverable files

- Files to delete because they are obsolete

- The physical schema of the database at a previous time

NOTE
*You need to be connected to a recovery catalog to issue the **report schema** command AT TIME, AT SCN, or AT SEQUENCE; all other **report** commands can be issued without a recovery catalog present.*

Based on your established retention policy being set to a value other than none, you can use the **report need backup** command to display which files require backup. The command can be used with either a specified limiting number of incremental backups, a number of days since the last backup, or a redundancy value of the number of backup copies required for the file to be considered not to need backing up. If, for example, the application of each incremental backup takes 10 minutes and you do not want your database to be unavailable for more than 30 minutes, you must ensure that no more than three incremental backups are needed at any one time to recover your database. You can issue the following command to see which files require more than three incremental backups to be applied during recovery:

```
report need backup increments 3 database;
```

A new option, RECOVERY WINDOW, is available for the **report need backup** command and is used to specify a window of time in which the database must be recoverable. For example, if your retention policy states that you must have backups that are less than three days old, you can issue the following command:

```
report need backup recovery window 3 days;
```

The results will display any files that need to be backed up because they are more than three days old.

You can also use the RECOVERY WINDOW option with the **report obsolete** command mentioned earlier to display files that are obsolete because they are older than the specified window.

Some RMAN Recommendations

Matthew Reagan and Kevin Gilpin supplied the following recommendations. Some of the suggestions are commonsense approaches.

RMAN requires a database in which it stores its recovery information. Don't use a database on the same node as the ones you are backing up with RMAN. After all, how can you use the recovery information when the database must be recovered before you can use it for recovery? An alternative solution is to have two RMAN databases on two separate nodes. Use one to back up the other, so the RMAN databases are also protected.

Don't use the default account and password, for obvious security reasons.

Make sure the version of RMAN you are using is the version that matches the latest DB version you are using. RMAN versions are backward compatible, but not forward compatible.

In some circumstances, it may be beneficial to use "classical" backup techniques as the main recovery option, and use RMAN as a rapid recovery option. This is certainly the case when first deploying the Recovery Manager.

Make sure you completely understand the classical backup and recovery procedures. RMAN is a great enhancement to your backup approach, but if you don't understand what it's doing, you won't be able to handle the bumps that come up. RMAN's methodology is a little different from the classical backup, but the basic concept is still valid.

Don't forget to back up the control file. The rules for when to back up the control file have not changed. When you change your structure—add a datafile, add a tablespace, and so on—back up the control file.

Quantum's SNAPSERVER (http://www.snapserver.com) makes a great place to put the compressed output from RMAN for your development and test databases. No matter what your developers do, you can recover to the point in time just prior to the error in a matter of minutes. However, don't do this with your production databases, unless you then back up the SNAPSERVER.

Ensure that you are backing up files that RMAN does not back up. Use conventional methods to back up these files:

- alert.log

- init.ora

- Oracle Net and/or Net8 configuration files

- oratab

- crontab (or other schedule file)

- Relevant scripts (backups, database DDL scripts, etc.)

RMAN backs up raw datafiles with no change in configuration. With conventional backups, you may need to use an alternate backup command, such as **dd**.

You can use RMAN to clone a database. If you clone a database using conventional methods of copying datafiles and creating a control file, the original and clone databases will have the same database ID and cannot be backed up using the same recovery catalog because of conflicting database IDs.

MetaLink note 148138.1 has some good Oracle9i RMAN information. It describes how you can use RMAN to clean up old archive log files. With conventional backups, this must be performed manually.

RMAN can be used as a diagnostic tool. If you perform backups with RMAN, RMAN checks for and reports block-level corruption. The time to catch corruption is during backup, not recovery.

If you use RMAN to back up files to disk rather than directly to tape, you do not have to perform the configuration of the MML (media management layer) or worry about the version compatibility of RMAN and your MML software when you upgrade the database. If you perform your RMAN backups directly to disk, then you should configure the backup of these backed-up files (pieces) to tape with some other means that are specific to your backup software. If your backup software backs up the backup piece files residing on disk, then your backup software is dependent on your operating system version and hardware, but not on your database version.

When you use RMAN, you must resynchronize the recovery catalog from time to time. It is recommended that you perform this step whenever there is a change to the file layout of the database.

The database storing your recovery catalog can be backed up by a third database containing another recovery catalog, or it can be backed up using conventional means. It should not take long to back up the database containing the recovery catalog because this database will be small, particularly if you age-out old backup entries in your recovery catalog regularly. Shutting down the recovery catalog database and taking a cold backup of it does not impact the availability of the databases for which the recovery catalog is storing backup information. The disadvantage of backing up this file with conventional means is that you do not get the block corruption benefit of backing up with RMAN.

You should not rely on using a PC to do production backups (and restores/ recoveries) because that PC then becomes as critical a component as anything else, since the ability to do reliable backup and restore/recovery is the most important part of any database. Ask yourself if you want this PC to become the single point of failure for backups/restores/recoveries.

Avoid placing the recovery catalog database on the same server as the databases for which it is storing backup information. If it must be on the same server, then avoid putting the database files of the recovery catalog database on the same physical disks as those containing database files for the databases for which the recovery catalog database is storing backup information.

When you use RMAN, pay attention to V$LONGOPS to guard against long-running backup sessions.

No matter what tool you use, you should ensure that your backups accurately reflect your recovery requirements. Once you have established your backup procedures and scripts, test them and document your recovery procedures and the performance you experienced. You will then be able to implement the available procedures in a way that makes the most sense for your installation. The result should be a well-protected database and quick, efficient recoveries. And that, in turn, should lead to fewer calls to Oracle Support at 3:00 A.M.

PART

III

Networked
Oracle

CHAPTER
13

Oracle Net

t's hard to find a computer these days that isn't tied into a network. Distributing computing power across servers and sharing information across networks greatly enhances the value of the computing resources available. Instead of being a stand-alone server, the server becomes an entry point for intranets, the Internet, and its associated Web sites.

Originally released as SQL*Net, renamed to Net8, and now known as *Oracle Net*, Oracle's networking tool can be used to connect to distributed databases. Oracle Net facilitates the sharing of data between databases, even if those databases are on different types of servers running different operating systems and communications protocols. It also allows for client/server applications to be created; the server can then function primarily for database I/O, while the application can be fielded to a middle-tier application server, and the data presentation requirements of an application can be moved to front-end client machines.

Oracle Net and Net8 support Oracle7, Oracle8.0, and Oracle8i, but Oracle Net is only compatible back to Oracle7, Version 7.3.4. Thus, you can use Oracle Net to access your Oracle7.3.4, Oracle8, and Oracle8i databases while you migrate your applications to Oracle9i. Once the migration to Oracle9i is completed, the Oracle Net toolset should be used. In this chapter, you will see how to configure and administer Oracle Net and the Oracle Net Services.

The installation and configuration instructions for Oracle Net depend on the particular hardware, operating system, and communications software you are using. The material provided here will help you get the most out of your database networking, regardless of your configuration. Although much of the information presented can be applied to Net8, the emphasis within this chapter is on the Oracle9i implementation of Oracle Net.

Overview of Oracle Net

Using Oracle Net distributes the workload associated with database applications. Since many database queries are performed via applications, a server-based application forces the server to support both the CPU requirements of the application and the I/O requirements of the database (see Figure 13-1*a*). Using a client/server configuration (also referred to as a *two-tier architecture*) allows this load to be distributed between two machines. The first, called the *client*, supports the application that initiates the request from the database. The back-end machine on which the database resides is called the *server*. The client bears the burden of presenting the data, while the database server is dedicated to supporting queries, not applications. This distribution of resource requirements is shown in Figure 13-1*b*.

When the client sends a database request to the server, the server receives and executes the SQL statement that is passed to it. The results of the SQL statement, plus any error conditions that are returned, are then sent back to the client. The

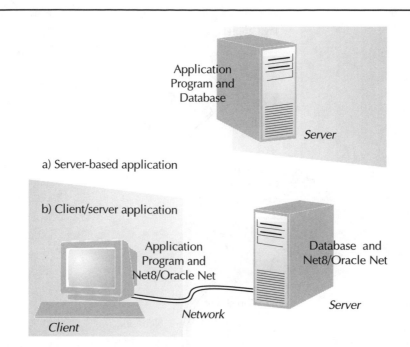

a) Server-based application

b) Client/server application

FIGURE 13-1. *Client/server architecture*

client/server configuration needs a fairly robust workstation with a large hard drive (8GB or more) and large memory requirements (usually over 256MB of RAM). The resources required have caused the client/server configuration to sometimes be dubbed *fat-client* architecture. Although workstation costs have dropped appreciably over recent years, the cost impact to a company can still be substantial.

The more common, cost-effective architecture used with Oracle Net is a *thin-client* configuration (also referred to as a *three-tier architecture*). The application code is housed and executed using Java scripts on a separate server from the database server. The client resource requirements become very low and the cost is reduced dramatically. The application code becomes isolated from the database. Figure 13-2 shows the thin-client configuration.

The client connects to the application server. Once the client is validated, display management code is downloaded to the client in the form of Java applets. A database request is sent from the client through the application server to the database server; the database server then receives and executes the SQL statement that is passed to it. The results of the SQL statement, plus any error conditions that are returned, are then sent back to the client through the application server. In some

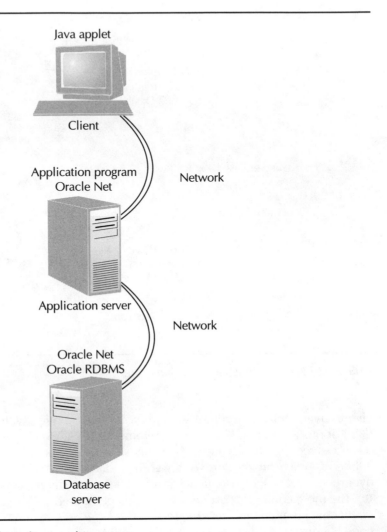

FIGURE 13-2. *Thin-client architecture*

versions of the three-tier architecture, some of the application processing is performed on the application server and the rest is performed on the database server. The advantage of a thin-client architecture is that you have low resource requirements and maintenance on the client side, medium resource requirements and central maintenance on the application server, and high resource but lower maintenance requirements on one or more back-end database servers.

In addition to client/server and thin-client implementations, *server/server* configurations are often needed. In this type of environment, databases on separate servers share data with each other. You can then physically isolate each server from every other server without logically isolating the servers. A typical implementation of this type involves corporate headquarters servers that communicate with departmental servers in various locations. Each server supports client applications, but it also has the ability to communicate with other servers in the network. This architecture is shown in Figure 13-3.

When one of the servers sends a database request to another server, the sending server acts like a client. The receiving server executes the SQL statement that is passed to it, and returns the results plus error conditions to the sender.

Oracle Net allows these architectures to become reality. When run on the clients and the servers, Oracle Net allows database requests made from one database (or application) to be passed to another database on a separate server. In most cases, machines can function both as clients and servers; the only exceptions are operating systems with single-user architectures, such as network appliances. In such cases, those machines can only function as clients.

The end result of an Oracle Net implementation is the ability to communicate with all databases that are accessible via the network. You can then create synonyms that give applications true network transparency: the user who submits the query will not know the location of the data that is used to resolve it. In this chapter, you will see the main configuration methods and files used to manage interdatabase communications, along with usage examples. You will see more detailed examples of distributed database management in Chapter 16.

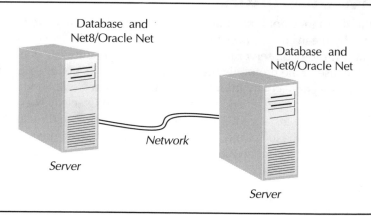

FIGURE 13-3. *Server/server architecture*

Each object in a database is uniquely identified by its owner and name. For example, there will only be one table named EMPLOYEE owned by the user HR; there cannot be two tables of the same name and type within the same schema.

Within distributed databases, two additional layers of object identification must be added. First, the name of the instance that accesses the database must be identified. Next, the name of the server on which that instance resides must be identified. Putting together these four parts of the object's name—its server, its instance, its owner, and its name—results in a *global object name*. In order to access a remote table, the table's global object name must be known. DBAs and application administrators can set up access paths to automate the selection of all four parts of the global object name. In the following sections, you will see how to set up the access paths used by Oracle Net.

The foundation of Oracle Net is the Transparent Network Substrate (TNS), which resolves all server-level connectivity issues. Oracle Net relies on configuration files on the client and the server to manage the database connectivity. If the client and server use different communications protocols, the Oracle Connection Manager (described in a later section of this chapter) manages the connections. The combination of the Oracle Connection Manager and the TNS allows Oracle Net connections to be made independent of the operating system and communications protocol run by each server.

Oracle Net also has the capability to send and receive data requests in an asynchronous manner; this allows it to support the shared server (formerly known as the Multithreaded Server (MTS)) architecture. The Oracle Net Connection Manager replaces the MultiProtocol Interchange architecture. As mentioned earlier, Oracle Net supports connections to databases running version 7.3.4 or higher.

Connect Descriptors

The server and instance portions of an object's global object name in Oracle Net are identified by means of a *connect descriptor*. A connect descriptor specifies the communications protocol, server name, and instance name to use when performing the query. Because of the protocol independence of Oracle Net, the descriptor also includes hardware connectivity information. Introduced in Net8, Service names can be used to identify a database. Previously, the format for an Oracle network connection descriptor included the instance name or SID. The format for an Oracle Net connect descriptor is shown in the following listing. The example shown here uses the TCP/IP protocol, and specifies a connection to an instance named LOC on a server named HQ. The keywords are protocol specific.

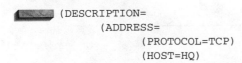

```
(DESCRIPTION=
    (ADDRESS=
        (PROTOCOL=TCP)
        (HOST=HQ)
```

```
                (PORT=1521))
       (CONNECT DATA=
              (SID=LOC)))
```

In this connect descriptor, the protocol is set to TCP/IP, the server (HOST) is set to HQ, and the port on that host that should be used for the connection is port 1521 (which is the Oracle registered port assignment for Oracle Net). The instance name is specified in a separate part of the descriptor as the SID assignment.

The structure for this descriptor is consistent across all protocols. Also, the descriptors can be automatically generated via the Net8 Assistant tool for Oracle8 and Oracle8i and the Net Configuration Assistant for Oracle9i. As previously noted, the keywords used by the connect descriptors are protocol specific. The keywords to use and the values to give them are provided in the operating-system-specific documentation for Oracle Net.

Service Names

Users are not expected to type in a connect descriptor each time they want to access remote data. Instead, the DBA can set up *service names* (aliases), which refer to these connect descriptors. Service names are stored in a file called tnsnames.ora. This file should be copied to all servers on the database network. Every client and application server should have a copy of this file.

On the server, the tnsnames.ora file should be located in the directory specified by the TNS_ADMIN environment variable. The file is usually stored in a common directory, such as the $ORACLE_HOME/network/admin directory on UNIX systems, or for a Windows NT/2000 server or client, in the \network\admin subdirectory under your Oracle software home directory.

A sample entry in the tnsnames.ora file is shown in the following listing. This example assigns a service name of LOC to the connect descriptor given above.

```
LOC =(DESCRIPTION=
      (ADDRESS=
            (PROTOCOL=TCP)
            (HOST=HQ)
            (PORT=1521))
      (CONNECT DATA=
            (SERVICE_NAME=LOC)))
```

A user wishing to connect to the LOC instance on the HQ server can now use the LOC service name, as shown in this example:

```
sqlplus hr/puffinstuff@LOC;
```

The @ sign tells the database to use the service name that follows it to determine which database to log into. If the username and password are correct for that database, then a session is opened there and the user can begin using the database.

Service names create aliases for connect descriptors, so you do not need to give the service name the same name as the instance. For example, you could give the LOC instance the service name PROD or TEST, depending on its use within your environment. The use of synonyms to further enhance location transparency will be described in the "Usage Example: Database Links" section of this chapter.

Replacing tnsnames.ora with the Oracle Internet Directory

A directory is a specialized electronic database in which you store information about one or more objects. Your electronic mail address book is an example of a directory. Within each of your email address entries is information about the contact's name, email address, home and business addresses, and so on. You can use the address book to locate a specific person with whom you want to correspond.

Oracle provides an electronic database tool called the Oracle Internet Directory (OID) for use in resolving user, server, and database locations as well as password and other important information storage. Within Oracle9*i*, the emphasis has moved from supporting many separate tnsnames.ora files on distributed machines to supporting one or more directories on centralized machines. See the section "Directory Naming with Oracle Internet Directory" later in this chapter for more information about OID.

Listeners

Each database server on the network must contain a listener.ora file. The listener.ora file lists the names and addresses of all of the listener processes on the machine and the instances they support. Listener processes receive connections from Oracle Net and Net8 clients.

A listener.ora file has four parts:

- Header section
- Protocol address list
- Instance definitions
- Operational parameters

The listener.ora file is automatically generated by the Network Manager (Oracle Net) and Net8 Assistant tools. You can edit the resulting file as long as you follow its syntax rules. The following listing shows sample sections of a listener.ora file—an address definition and an instance definition:

```
LISTENER =
    (ADDRESS_LIST =
        (ADDRESS=
          (PROTOCOL=IPC)
          (KEY= loc.world)
        )
        (ADDRESS=
          (PROTOCOL=TCP)
          (HOST= HR)
          (POER=1521)
        )
    )
SID_LIST_LISTENER =
  (SID_DESC =
      (GLOBAL_DBNAME = loc.world)
      (ORACLE_HOME = D:\oracle\ora90)
      (SID_NAME = loc)
    )
  )
```

The first portion of this listing contains the protocol address list—one entry per instance. The protocol address list defines the protocol addresses on which a listener is accepting connections, including an interprocess calls (IPC) address-definition section. In this case, the listener is listening for connections to the service identified as loc.world as well as any requests coming from the HR machine on PORT 1521 using the TCP/IP protocol. The .world suffix is the default domain name for Oracle Net connections. As of Net8, the default domain name was changed to be a NULL string.

The second portion of the listing, beginning with the SID_LIST_LISTENER clause, identifies the global database name as defined in the init.ora file for that database, the Oracle software home directory for each instance the listener is servicing, and the instance name or SID. The GLOBAL_DBNAME comprises the database name and database domain. The SID_LIST descriptor is retained for static database registration, backward compatibility with earlier versions, and for use by the Oracle Enterprise Manager. In Oracle8i and Oracle9i, databases dynamically register with the listener on database startup.

NOTE
If you change the Oracle software home directory for an instance, you need to change the listener.ora file for the server.

Additional listener.ora Parameters

The listener.ora file supports a number of additional parameters. The parameters should each be suffixed with the listener name. For example, the default listener name is LISTENER, so the LOG_FILE parameter is named LOG_FILE_LISTENER. The additional listener.ora parameters are listed in Table 13-1.

Parameter	Description
CONNECT_TIMEOUT	Time, in seconds, that the listener will wait for a valid connection request after the listener has started. Default is 10.
LOG_DIRECTORY	The directory for the listener log file.
LOG_FILE	The name of the listener log file.
LOGGING	A flag to set logging ON or OFF.
PASSWORDS	The password for the listener. Default is LISTENER.
PRESENTATION	Typical Net8 clients use a presentation of two-task communication (TTC). Java clients use General Inter-ORB Protocol (GIOP).
PROTOCOL_STACK	The presentation and session layer information for a connection. New in 8i.
SAVE_CONFIG_ON_STOP	Available as of Net8. A flag to indicate if changes made to the listener while it is running should be saved to the listener.ora file.
SERVICE_LIST	The services list supported by the listener (more general than the SID_LIST shown in the example).
SESSION	A virtual pipe that carries data requests. Can be NS or RAW.
STARTUP_WAIT_TIME	The number of seconds the listener sleeps before responding to a startup command.
TRACE_DIRECTORY	The directory for the listener trace file.

TABLE 13-1.   *listener.ora Parameters*

Parameter	Description
TRACE_FILE	The name of the listener trace file.
TRACE_LEVEL	The level of tracing (ADMIN, USER, SUPPORT, or OFF).
USE_PLUG_AND_PLAY	A flag (ON or OFF) to instruct the listener to register with a Names server.

TABLE 13-1. *listener.ora Parameters* (continued)

You can modify the listener parameters after the listener has been started. If you use the SAVE_CONFIG_ON_STOP option (available as of Net8), then any changes you make to a running listener will be written to its listener.ora file. See examples of controlling the listener behavior later in this chapter.

Listeners in Oracle9i

Prior to Oracle8i, the listener was configured using static entries in the listener.ora file. In Oracle8i and beyond, the database instances register themselves with the listener upon database startup. The database instance registration consists of the following two types of information:

- **Service information** The database service names and instance names
- **Shared server dispatcher registration** The dispatcher information

If an instance is unavailable, database instance registration provides automatic failover to another listener for a client connection. Database instance registration also provides connection load balancing by balancing the number of active connections among all of the available instances and dispatchers for the same service.

Prior to Oracle8i, the tnsnames.ora file is mined for the SID, which Oracle uses in the connection attempt. From Oracle8i forward, Oracle uses either the SID or the service names in tnsnames.ora or through the OID to resolve its connection. The SID or service name and connection information is passed to the listener for verification. Once the listener verifies the information, the connection is either accepted or denied.

To support the new approach, the parameters listed in Table 13-2 were added to the tnsnames.ora file.

The SERVICE_NAME and INSTANCE_NAME parameters are also placed in the init.ora file for the database, and the values are established at database startup.

Parameter	Description
SERVICE_NAME	Set to a service name value.
INSTANCE_NAME	Set to the name of the instance.
LOAD_BALANCE	Set to ON to activate load balancing.
FAILOVER	Set to ON to activate listener failover.

TABLE 13-2.   *tnsnames.ora Parameters*

Using the Oracle Net Configuration Assistant

In Oracle9i, a new tool, the Oracle Net Configuration Assistant, has been added to replace the Oracle Net8 toolset. The Oracle Net Configuration Assistant performs the initial network configuration steps after the Oracle software installation and automatically creates the default, basic configuration files. The tool has a graphical user interface for configuring the following elements:

- Listener
- Naming methods
- Local net service names
- Directory usage

In the Oracle8i Net8 version, net service names replace the use of service name aliases. For the net service name LOC on the HQ server, the net service name maps to a connect server using the following syntax:

```
LOC=
   (DESCRIPTION=
   (ADDRESS =
       (PROTOCOL = TCP)
```

```
      (HOST = HQ)
      (PORT = 1521))
  )
  (CONNECT_DATA =
    (SERVICE_NAME = loc)
    (INSTANCE_NAME = loc)
  )
)
```

In this example, the service name and the instance name match. However, they can be different names. The client will connect to a server using the net service name just as the client connected using the service name in earlier versions.

`sqlplus hr/puffinstuff@LOC`

Figure 13-4 shows the initial screen of the Oracle Net Configuration Assistant. As shown in Figure 13-4, Listener Configuration is the default option.

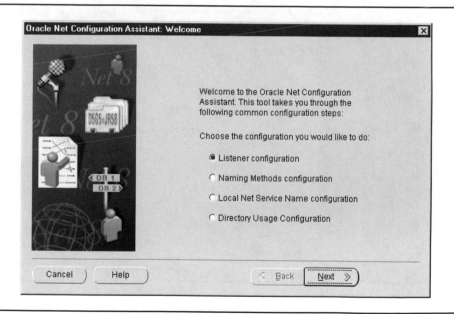

FIGURE 13-4.   *Oracle Net Configuration Assistant Welcome screen*

Configuring the Listener

Using the Oracle Net Configuration Assistant, you can configure a listener easily and quickly. When you select the Listener Configuration options, you are given the choice to add, reconfigure, delete, or rename a listener. After selecting the Add option, the first step is to select a listener name. Figure 13-5 shows the Listener Name screen with the default listener name, LISTENER, displayed.

After selecting a listener name, you must select a protocol. The default protocol selected is TCP. Figure 13-6 shows the protocol selection screen.

Once a protocol has been selected, you must designate a port number on which the new listener will listen. The default port number presented is 1521, but you are given the option to designate another port. As shown in Figure 13-7, the port 1526 has been designated for the new listener.

The next three screens, not shown here, are a prompt to configure another listener (response is No or Yes), a request to indicate a listener you want to start, and a confirmation that the listener configuration is completed for this listener.

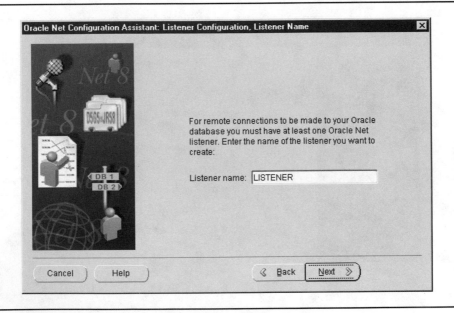

FIGURE 13-5. *Listener Configuration, Listener Name screen*

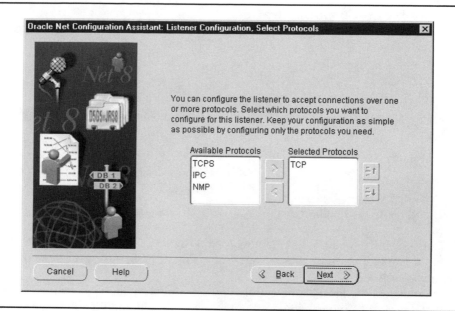

FIGURE 13-6. *Listener Configuration, Select Protocols screen*

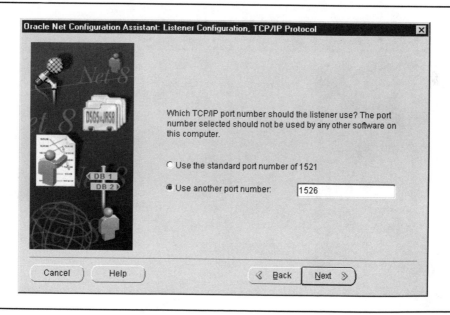

FIGURE 13-7. *Listener Configuration, TCP/IP Protocol screen*

Naming Methods Configuration

The Naming Methods Configuration option of the Oracle Net Configuration Assistant configures net service names. There are many options available for naming methods. A few of them are listed here:

Local	The tnsnames.ora file.
Oracle Names	An Oracle Names server for use by Oracle Names.
Host name	Uses a TCP naming service. You cannot use connection pooling or the Oracle Connection Manager with this option.
Sun NIS, DCE CDS, Directory	External naming services.

Figure 13-8 shows the Select Naming Methods screen. The Local, Oracle Names, and Host Name options are preselected, but in Figure 13-8, the Host Name option has been deselected.

If you accept the Host Name option, you see an informational screen advising you that the Host Name naming does not require any additional configuration "at this time." You are instructed that any time you add a database service in the future, you must make an entry in your TCP/IP host name resolution system.

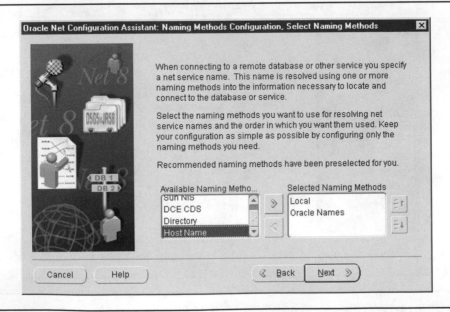

FIGURE 13-8. *Naming Methods Configuration, Select Naming Methods screen*

Once you have selected the naming methods, the Oracle Net Configuration Assistant displays a Confirmation screen.

Local Net Service Name Configuration

You can use the Oracle Net Configuration Assistant's Local Net Service Name configuration options to manage net service names. For the Oracle Net Configuration Assistant, Local Net Service Name configuration tool, five options are available:

- Add
- Reconfigure
- Delete
- Rename
- Test

For the Add option, you must first specify the database version you are going to access. Your options are Oracle8i or Later Database or Service, or Oracle8, Release 8.0, Database or Service. Based on your choice, you will be prompted for the database global service name for configurations using the Oracle8i or later database and for the instance name (SID) for an Oracle8, Release 8.0, database. Once you have entered the global service name or SID, you are prompted to enter the protocol, as shown in Figure 13-9.

You must specify the machine name of the host and designate the listener port, as shown in Figure 13-10. In this example, the host is HR and the port selected is the default port 1521.

The next screen offers you the option to verify that the Oracle database you have specified can be successfully reached. You can choose to skip or perform the connection test. Once you have either chosen to test the connection and it has completed successfully, or opted to skip the test, you are prompted to specify the net service name for the new net service. By default, the service name you entered earlier is used, but you can specify a different name if you so choose. Finally, you are notified that your new local net service name has been successfully created, and you are asked if you want to configure another one.

You can use the Reconfigure option to select and modify an existing net service name. You are prompted to select an existing net service name. The Database Version screen, the service name screen (Figure 13-8), and the Select Protocols (Figure 13-9) screen are used as well as the TCP/IP Protocol screen shown in Figure 13-10. The option to test the database connection is offered as well as the Net Service Name screen to enable you to rename the net service you are reconfiguring.

The Delete option displays the Select Net Service Name screen and, once a service name is selected, prompts with a Verification screen to confirm that the

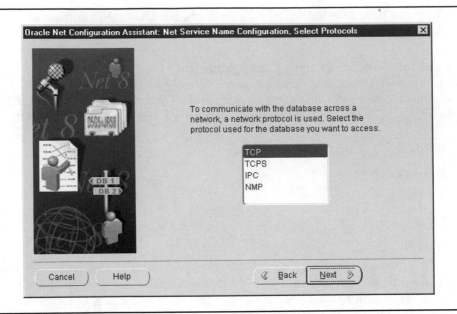

FIGURE 13-9. *Net Service Name Configuration, Select Protocols*

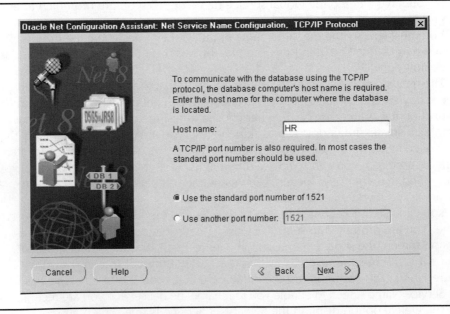

FIGURE 13-10. *Net Service Name Configuration, TCP/IP Protocol*

service name is to be deleted. A Deletion Confirmation screen and the general Net Service Name Completion screen complete the Delete option.

The Rename option displays the Select Net Service Name screen from which a service name is selected. The next screen prompts for a new name for the service. A Net Service Name Renamed Confirmation screen and the general Net Service Name Completion screen complete the Rename option.

The Test option enables you to verify that your configuration information is correct, that the database specified can be reached, and that a successful connection can be made.

Directory Usage Configuration

A directory service provides a central repository of information for the network. The most common directory forms support the Lightweight Directory Access Protocol (LDAP). An LDAP server can provide the following features:

- Store net service names and their location resolution

- Provide global database links and aliases

- Act as a clearinghouse for configuration information for clients across the entire network

- Aid in configuring other clients

- Update client configuration files automatically

- House client information such as usernames and passwords

The Directory Usage Configuration option supports both Oracle Internet Directory and the Microsoft Active Directory. The actions that you can take are shown in Figure 13-11.

When you select the first option, "Select the directory server you want to use...," you are asked to select the type of directory you have: either OID or Microsoft Active Directory. If you select OID, you are prompted to supply the directory service location host name, port, and SSL port. By default, the port is 389 and the SSL port is 636. Once you have specified this information, the tool attempts to connect to your directory repository and verify that you have already established a schema and context. If you have not, you will receive an error message instructing you to do so. Figure 13-12 shows the schema error message, and Figure 13-13 shows the context error message.

From the second option, "Select the directory server you want to use, and configure the directory server for Oracle usage...," you receive the same initial prompts to select the directory type and enter the host name and ports. Once the information is verified, if your directory does not contain the required schema, you

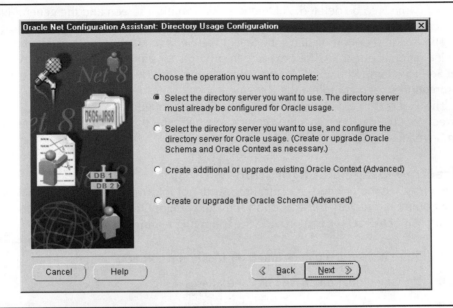

FIGURE 13-11. *Directory Usage Configuration*

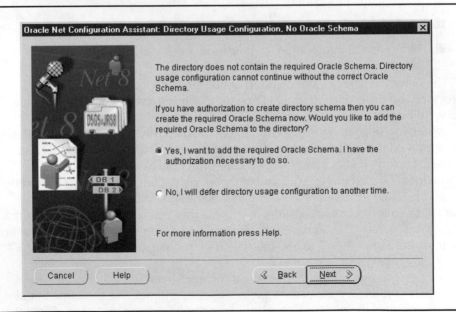

FIGURE 13-12. *Directory Usage Configuration, No Oracle Schema*

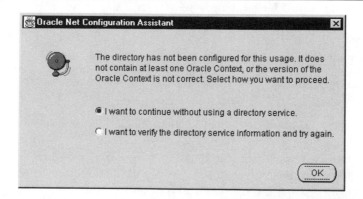

FIGURE 13-13. *"Directory service not configured" warning message*

are given the opportunity to create the directory schema. You must have the appropriate privileges to perform this task. By default, the initial username with the appropriate privileges for schema creation for the Oracle Internet Directory is "cn=orcladmin," and the password is "welcome." You should change the password at your earliest opportunity.

The third and fourth options enable you to individually configure a schema and a context.

Using the Oracle Net Manager

When the Oracle Names server was first introduced, a 16-bit application called the Configuration Manager was provided to use in generating the Names server configuration. This application can still be used to configure the Oracle Names server for version 7. With Net8, you can use the Net8 Assistant to manage your configuration files. For Oracle9i, you can use the Oracle Net Manager, found under the Programs | Oracle OracleHome90 | Management Tools menu option in a Windows environment.

There is some overlap between the Oracle Net Configuration Assistant shown in the previous section and the new Oracle Net Manager functionality. Both tools can be used to configure a listener or a net service name. Both provide ease in configuring a Names service, local profile, and directory service. However, the Oracle Net Manager is the only tool that enables you to create and configure an Oracle Names server. The Oracle Net Configuration Assistant is a GUI tool that guides you through the configuration process step-by-step. The Oracle Net Manager is not quite as user friendly but provides a more in-depth configuration alternative. Which is better? The choice really is one of personal preference.

As shown in Figure 13-14, the opening screen of the Oracle Net Manager lists the basic functionality it provides, as follows:

- **Naming** Defines simple names to identify the location of a service
- **Naming Methods** Defines the way the simple names map to connect descriptors
- **Listeners** Supports the creation and configuration of listeners

You can use the Oracle Net Manager to manage your configuration files and test your connections. For example, Figure 13-15 shows the different types of profile methods you can change and the naming types under the Local/Profile option: either via tnsnames.ora files, Oracle Names, or using a host name. Options such as Oracle Advanced Security can be managed via the Oracle Net Manager. The Oracle Advanced Security option provides end-to-end encryption of data in a distributed environment. By default, your data will travel in clear text across the network unless you use Oracle's encryption or a hardware-based encryption.

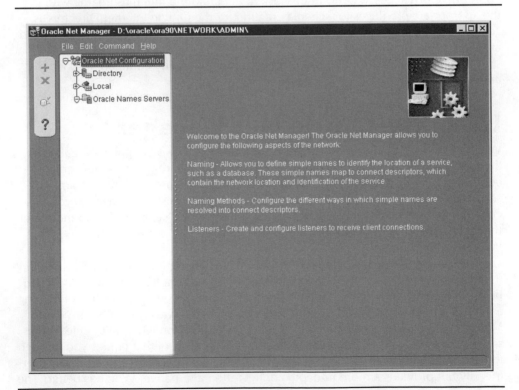

FIGURE 13-14. *Oracle Net Manager Console screen*

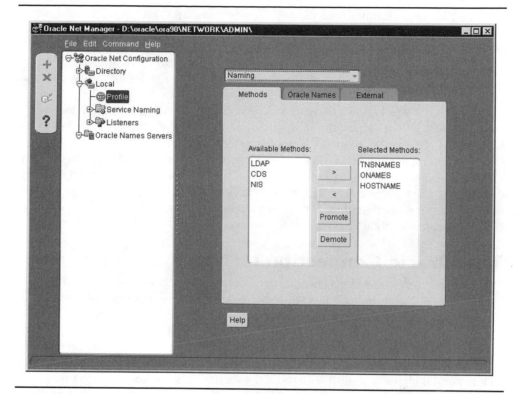

FIGURE 13-15.   *Oracle Net Manager Profile options*

You can create a new net service name for your tnsnames.ora file via the Oracle Net Service Names Wizard. Once you have specified a net service name, you are prompted to select the network protocol you want to use. The options are as follows:

- TCP/IP (Internet Protocol)
- TCP/IP with SSL (Secure Internet Protocol)
- Named Pipes (Microsoft Networking)
- IPC (Local Database)

The Oracle Net Manager will prompt you for each of the parameters required to establish a database connection and will modify your local tnsnames.ora file to reflect the information you provide. The information you will be prompted for is host, port number, service or SID name depending on the Oracle version, and the connection type: database default, shared server, or dedicated server. Finally, you are given the opportunity to test the new service name. You can also test existing net service names by selecting the net service name from the displayed list of services and selecting the Test Connection option from the menu options.

When you test your connections, the Oracle Net Manager will attempt to log into the database using the default username SCOTT with the default password TIGER and will report the result of the connection attempt.

The simpler you keep your client and server configurations, and the closer you adhere to the default values, the simpler the management of your configuration files will be. The Oracle Net Manager simplifies your configuration file administration. One word of caution: if you are using your listener to listen for connections from the Internet through a firewall, be sure that you do not leave a listener listening on the default port 1521, since a hole through your firewall can leave you open to potential remote listener reconfiguration. An unsecured listener using default values can enable a hacker to obtain database information that could compromise your site.

The Oracle Connection Manager

The Oracle Connection Manager portion of Oracle Net acts as a router used to establish database communication links between otherwise incompatible network protocols as well as take advantage of multiplexing and access control.

The advantage of an Oracle Connection Manager is that all servers do not have to use the same communications protocol. Because of this, each server can use the communications protocol that is best suited to its environment, and can still be able to transfer data back and forth with other databases. This communication takes place regardless of the communications protocols used on the remote servers; the Oracle Connection Manager takes care of the differences between the protocols.

Multiple access paths can be used to handle different client requests. The Oracle Connection Managers will select the most appropriate path based on path availability and network load. The relative cost of each path is specified via the Network Manager utility when the Oracle Connection Managers are set up.

In an intranet environment, the Oracle Connection Manager can be used as a firewall for Oracle Net traffic. You can establish filtering rules to enable or disable specific client access using the Oracle Connection Manager. The filtering rules can be based on any of the following criteria:

- Destination host names or IP addresses for servers

- Destination database service name

- Source host names or IP addresses for clients

- Whether the client is using the Oracle Advanced Security option

The Oracle Connection Manager is used to enhance your firewall security by filtering out client access based on one or more aspects of the filtering rules that you create. For example, you could specify that an IP address is to be refused access using the CMAN_RULES parameter within the cman.ora file.

The file sqlnet.ora may be used to specify additional diagnostics beyond the default diagnostics provided.

Using Connection Manager

Oracle Net uses the Connection Manager to support connections within homogenous networks, reducing the number of physical connections maintained by the database. There are two main processes and a control utility associated with the Connection Manager, as follows:

CMGW	The gateway process that acts as a hub for the Connection Manager.
CMADMIN	A multithreaded process responsible for all administrative tasks and issues.
CMCTL	A utility that enables basic management functions for Oracle Control Manager administration.

The CMGW Process

The Connection Manager Gateway (CMGW) process registers itself with the CMADMIN process and listens for incoming connection requests. By default, this process listens on port 1630 using the TCP/IP protocol. The CMGW process initiates connection requests to listeners from clients and relays data between the client and server.

The CMADMIN Process

The multithreaded Connection Manager Administrative (CMADMIN) process performs many tasks and functions. The CMADMIN processes CMGW registrations and registers source route addressing information about the CMGW and listeners. The CMADMIN process is tasked with identifying all listener processes that support at least one database. Using the Oracle Names servers or Oracle Internet Directory, the CMADMIN performs the following tasks:

- Locates local Oracle Names servers

- Monitors registered listeners

- Maintains client address information

- Periodically updates the Connection Manager's cache of available services

The CMADMIN handles source route information about the CMGW and listeners.

Configuring the Oracle Connection Manager

The cman.ora file, located by default in the $ORACLE_HOME/network/admin directory on a UNIX system, or ORACLE_HOME\network\admin on a Windows system, contains the configuration parameters for the Oracle Connection Manager. The file contains protocol addresses of the listening gateway process, access control parameters, and profile or control parameters. Here is a sample cman.ora file:

```
CMAN=
  (ADDRESS=(PROTOCOL=tcp)(HOST=proxysvr)(PORT=1630))
  (ADDRESS=(PROTOCOL=tcps)(HOST=192.23.34.234)(PORT=2484))
CMAN_ADMIN=
  (ADDRESS=(PROTOCOL=tcp)(HOST=proxysvr)(PORT=1830))
CMAN_RULES=
  (RULE=(SRC=194.34.228.123)(DST=HR)(SRV=*)(ACT=accept)))
  (RULE=(SRC=194.34.228.124)(DST=HR)(SRV=*)(ACT=reject)))
CMAN_PROFILE=
  (PARAMETER_LIST=
    (LOG_LEVEL=2)
    (TRACING=on))
```

In this example, there are two ports the CMAN process is listening for: 1630 for TCP protocol unencrypted requests and 2484 for secure, TCPS protocol encrypted requests. The CMAN_ADMIN process is listening for TCP protocol requests on port 1830. According to the CMAN_RULES, any request coming from the source IP address 194.34.228.123 for the HR server is to be accepted, while the requests coming from IP address 194.34.228.124 are to be rejected. The logging level is set to 2, which means that any connection request matching the RULE_LIST criteria is to be logged. Tracing is turned on.

The complete set of cman.ora parameters is shown in Table 13-3.

Parameter	Description
answer_timeout	Determines the number of seconds the Oracle Connection Manager uses to time out a protocol handshake for an incoming request. Values: [0 – n] Default: 0
authentication_level	Determines the level of security. Values: 0 = Reject connect requests that are not using SNS 1 = Don't check for SNS Default: 0

TABLE 13-3. *cman.ora Parameters*

Parameter	Description
log_level	Specifies the level of logging to the file cmadm_<pid>.log. Values: 0 = No log output 2 = Output RULE_LIST matching 3 = Output relay blocking 4 = Output relay I/O counts Default: 0
max_freelist_buffers	Determines the maximum number of buffers kept on the freelist for reuse by the Transparent Network Substrate (TNS) once a relay is closed. Values: [0 – 10240] Default: 0
maximum_connect_ data	Limits the connect data string length of incoming connection requests. Values: [257 – 4096] Default: 1024
maximum_relays	Specifies the maximum number of concurrent connections. Values: [1 – 2048] Default: 128
relay_statistics	Determines if I/O statistics are recorded. The statistics that are captured are the number of incoming and outgoing bytes and packets. Values: [YES | TRUE | ON | 1 | NO | FALSE | OFF | 0] Default: NO
remote_admin	Determines if remote access to an Oracle Connection Manager is to be permitted. Values: [YES | TRUE | ON | 1 | NO | FALSE | OFF | 0] Default: NO
show_tns_info	Instructs the Oracle Connection Manager to include TNS information in the log. Values: [YES | TRUE | ON | 1 | NO | FALSE | OFF | 0] Default: NO

TABLE 13-3.   *cman.ora Parameters* (continued)

Parameter	Description
trace_directory	The directory in which to store the trace files. Values: A directory default: $ORACLE_HOME/network/trace for UNIX, ORACLE_HOME\network\trace for Windows
trace_filelen	Specifies the size of the trace file. Values: Size of file in kilobytes Default: unlimited
trace_fileno	Specifies the number of trace files to track. The files are written in a cyclical fashion. Values: [1 – 8] Default: 1
trace_timestamp	When enabled, adds a timestamp to each trace event. Values: [YES | TRUE | ON | 1 | NO | FALSE | OFF | 0] Default: NO
tracing	Specifies whether tracing is enabled. Values: [YES | TRUE | ON | 1 | NO | FALSE | OFF | 0] Default: NO
use_async_call	Specifies whether asynchronous functions are enabled during the answering or calling phase of connection establishment. Values: [YES | TRUE | ON | 1 | NO | FALSE | OFF | 0] Default: YES

TABLE 13-3.   *cman.ora Parameters* (continued)

The Connection Manager Control Utility (CMCTL)

The Connection Manager Control Utility provides administrative access to CMADMIN and CMGW. The Connection Manager is started via the **cmctl** command. The command syntax is

```
cmctl command process_type
```

The default startup command from an operating system prompt is

```
cmctl start cman
```

The commands are broken into four basic types:

- Operational commands such as **start**
- Modifier commands such as **set**
- Informational commands such as **show**
- Command utility operations such as **exit**

Using the parameter REMOTE_ADMIN, you can control, but not start, remote managers. Unlike the Listener utility discussed later in this chapter, you cannot interactively set a password for the Oracle Connection Manager. To set a password for this tool, you put a plain-text password in the cman.ora file. The available command options for the **cmctl** command are shown in Table 13-4.

Option	Description
accept_connections	Enable or disable accepting new connections. Existing connections are unaffected. Values: ON or OFF
close_relay	Shut down a connection identified by a relay number.
exit	Disconnect from the CMCTL process.
help	Provide a list of CMCTL commands.
quit	Exit the utility and return to the operating system prompt.
set	Alter a parameter's value while the Oracle Connection Manager is running. To make the connection permanent, modify the cman.ora file.
set authentication_level	Set the level of security for the Oracle Connection Manager. Values: 0 = no authentication required from the client (default) 1 = reject connections not using Secure Network Socket (SNS) encryption

TABLE 13-4. *cman Command Options*

Option	Description
set display_mode	Change the level of detail or format for the commands **start**, **stats**, **status**, **stop**, and **version**.
set log_level	Set the log level for the Oracle Connection Manager.
set relay_statistics	Turn on or off statistic collection for I/O of connections. When on, inbound and outbound bytes and packets are tracked.
show	Display the current setting for the requested parameter, including address, ALL, displaymode, profile, relay, and rules.
shutdown	Shut down the Oracle Connection Manager process.
start	Start the CMCTL process (process must not be running).
stats	Provide statistic for total_relays, active_delays, most_relays, out_of_relay, and total_refused for the CMCTL process.
status	Provide basic status information about version, start time, and current statistics.
stop	Stop a specific CMCTL process—either CMGW or CMADMIN.
stop now	Stop all CMCTL processes (at least one process must be running).
version	Display the current version and name of the CMCTL.

TABLE 13-4. *cman Command Options* (continued)

There are three process_type options for the **cmctl** command:

cman	Controls both the CMGW and CMADMIN processes
adm	Controls just the CMADMIN process
cm	Controls just the CMGW process

If the Connection Manager has been started, any client that has SOURCE_ROUTE set to YES in its tnsnames.ora file can use the Connection Manager. The Connection Manager reduces system resource requirements by maintaining logical connections while reusing physical connections.

Directory Naming with Oracle Internet Directory

With the release of Oracle8i, the Oracle Internet Directory was introduced to facilitate support for LDAP-compliant directory servers for centralized network names resolution management in a distributed Oracle network. For localized management, the tnsnames.ora file is still available.

The file ldap.ora, located in the $ORACLE_HOME/network/admin directory on a UNIX system and ORACLE_HOME\network\admin in a Windows environment, is used to store the configuration parameters to access a directory server. Oracle supports both the Oracle Internet Directory and Microsoft Active Directory.

To resolve a connect descriptor using a centralized directory server, the steps are as follows:

1. Oracle Net, on behalf of the client, contacts the directory server to obtain the resolution for the connect identifier to a connect descriptor.

2. The directory server takes the connect identifier, locates the associated connect descriptor, and returns the descriptor to Oracle Net.

3. Oracle Net uses the resolved descriptor to make the connection request to the correct listener.

The directory server uses a tree structure in which to store its data. Each node in the tree is an *entry*. A hierarchical structure of entries is used, called a *directory information tree* (DIT), and each entry is identified by a unique *distinguished name* (DN) that tells the directory server exactly where the entry resides. DITs can be structured to use existing Domain Name System (DNS), organizational or geographical lines, or Internet naming scheme.

Using a DIT that is organized along organizational lines, for example, the DN for the HR server could be (dn: cn=HR, cn=OracleContext, dc=us, dc=ourcompany, dc=com). The lowest component of a DN is placed at the leftmost location of the DIT and moved progressively up the tree. The following illustration shows the DIT for this example:

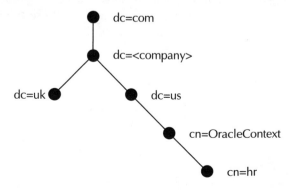

The commonly used LDAP attributes are

CommonName (cn)	Common name of an entry
Country (c)	Name of country
Domain component (dc)	Domain component
Organization (o)	Name of organization
OrganizationalUnitName (ou)	Name of unit within the organization

NOTE
The value cn=OracleContext is a special entry in the directory server that supports directory-enabled features such as directory naming. The Oracle Context is created using the Oracle Net Configuration Assistant discussed earlier in this chapter.

Setting Up an Oracle Internet Directory

As detailed earlier, you can use the Oracle Net Configuration Assistant or the Oracle Net Manager to perform the initial configuration tasks. Once the directory schema and Oracle Context have been established, you can begin to register service names with the directory service using the Oracle Net Manager. The Oracle Context area is the root of the directory subtree where all information relevant to Oracle software is stored.

When the Oracle Context is installed, two entities are created: OracleDBCreators and OracleNetAdmins. The OracleDBCreators entity with a DN of (cn=OracleDBCreators, cn=OracleContext) is created. Any user who is a member of the OracleDBCreators can register a database server entry or directory client entry using the Oracle Database Configuration Assistant. A user assigned as a member of the OracleNetAdmins can create, modify, and delete net service names and modify Oracle Net attributes of database servers using the Oracle Net Manager. If you are a directory administrator, you can add users to these groups.

Clients who want to look up information in the directory must meet minimum requirements; they must

- Be configured to use the directory server

- Be able to access the Oracle Net entries in the Oracle Context

- Have anonymous authentication with the directory server

The clients can either use the common names of database servers and net service entries to perform the lookups, or additional directory location information may be required in the connection string.

Using Oracle Names

With Oracle Names, all of the tasks of managing distributed databases are handled via a global naming service available to all servers in a network that are running Oracle. The service is used to store information about the following:

- Connect descriptors
- Database links
- Object aliases

NOTE
Oracle Corporation intends to desupport the Oracle Names Server in a future release and recommends that the directory server be used instead. A migration tool is available to aid in the migration from Oracle Names to the directory server.

As of Oracle8i, Oracle Names resolves database links by first looking at the user's private database links. If none with the matching name is found, then the available public database links are checked. If the first two checks do not return a match for the database link name, the Oracle Names server's list of global database link names is searched for the database link. If the link name is found there, Oracle Names returns the link's specifications and resolves the query.

Oracle Names greatly simplifies the administration of location transparency in a distributed environment. The information related to remote data access is now stored in a central location. The impact of this is felt every time a part of a global object name is modified. For example, if there were multiple links using specific connections to a single remote database, then a pre-Names modification to the user's password would require dropping and re-creating multiple database links. With Names, this change is made once.

Oracle Names also supports the Domain Name System (DNS) structure that Oracle introduced with Net8. Oracle's DNS allows network hierarchies to be specified; thus, a server may be identified as HR.HQ.ACME.COM, which would be interpreted as the HR server in the HQ network of the ACME company.

If connect descriptors are also stored in Oracle Names, the need for manually maintaining multiple copies of the tnsnames.ora file diminishes. The centralized Oracle Names server defines the relationships among the network objects. The database network may be divided into administrative regions, and the management tasks may be likewise divided. A change to one region will be transparently propagated to the other regions.

You can control an Oracle Names server via the **namesctl** utility, and you can configure it via the Oracle Net Manager.

Starting the Listener Server Process

The listener process is controlled by the Listener Control utility, executed via the **lsnrctl** command. The options available for the **lsnrctl** command are described in the next section. To start the listener, use the command

 > lsnrctl start

This command will start the default listener (named LISTENER). If you wish to start a listener with a different name, include that listener's name as the second parameter in the **lsnrctl** command. For example, if you created a listener called MY_LSNR, then you could start it via the following command:

> lsnrctl start my_lsnr

In the next section you will find descriptions of the other parameters available for the Listener Control utility.

After starting a listener, you can check that it is running by using the **status** option of the Listener Control utility. The following command can be used to perform this check:

> lsnrctl status

Sample output for this command is shown in the following listing:

```
LSNRCTL for 32-bit Windows: Version 9.0.1.0.0 - Production on 07-SEP-2001 16:53:20
Copyright(c) 1991, 2001 Oracle Corporation. All rights reserved.
Connecting to (DESCRIPTION=(ADDRESS=(PROTOCOL=IPC)(KEY=EXTROC0)))
STATUS of the LISTENER
----------------------
Alias                     LISTENER
Version                   TNSLSNR for 32-bit Windows: Version 9.0.1.0.0 - Production
Start Date                07-SEP-2001 13:21:53
Uptime                    0 days 3 hr. 31 min. 37 sec
Trace Level               off
Security                  OFF
SNMP                      OFF
Listener Parameter File   D:\oracle\ora90\network\admin\listener.ora
Listener Log File         D:\oracle\ora90\network\log\listener.log
Services Summary...
Service "loc" has 1 instance(s).
  Instance "loc", status UNKNOWN, has 1 handler(s) for this service...
The command completed successfully
```

The status output in the preceding listing shows that the listener has been started, and that it is currently supporting only one service (loc), as defined by its listener.ora file. The listener parameter file is identified as /etc/listener.ora, and its log file location is shown.

If you wish to see the operating system–level processes that are involved, use the following command. This example uses the UNIX **ps -ef** command to list the system's active processes. The **grep tnslsnr** command then eliminates those rows that do not contain the term "tnslsnr."

```
> ps -ef | grep tnslsnr
```

Sample output for this command:

```
oracle  4022    1  0 13:36:53 ?        0:00 /oracle/products/901/bin/tnslsnr
                                        LISTENER -inherit
oracle  5469 2419  1 13:56:23 ttypc    0:00 grep tnslsnr
```

This output shows two processes: the listener process and the process that is checking for it. The first line of output is wrapped to the second line and may be truncated by the operating system.

Controlling the Listener Server Process

You can use the Listener Control utility, **lsnrctl**, to start, stop, and modify the listener process on the database server. Its command options are listed in Table 13-5. Each of these commands may be accompanied by a value; for all except the **set password** command, that value will be a listener name. If no listener name is specified, then the default (LISTENER) will be used. Once within **lsnrctl**, you can change the listener being modified via the **set current_listener** command.

Command	Description
change_password	Sets a new password for the listener. You will be prompted for the old password for the listener.
exit	Exits **lsnrctl**.
help	Displays a list of the **lsnrctl** command options. You can also see additional options via the **help set** and **help show** commands.
quit	Exits **lsnrctl**.

TABLE 13-5.   *Listener Control Utility Parameters*

Command	Description
reload	Allows you to modify the listener services after the listener has been started. It forces Oracle Net to read and use the most current listener.ora file.
save_config	New as of Net8. Creates a backup of your existing listener.ora file, then updates your listener.ora with parameters you have changed via **lsnrctl**.
services	Displays services available, along with its connection history. It also lists whether each service is enabled for remote DBA or autologin access.
set	Sets parameter values. Options are **current_listener** changes the listener process whose parameters are being set or shown. **displaymode** changes the format and level of detail for the **services** and **status** commands. **log_directory** sets the directory for the listener log file. **log_file** sets the name of the listener log file. **log_status** sets whether logging is ON or OFF. **password** sets the listener password **save_config_on_stop** saves your configuration changes to your listener.ora file when you exit **lsnrctl** (new as of Net8). **startup_waittime** sets the number of seconds the listener sleeps before responding to a **lsnrctl start** command. **trc_directory** sets the directory for the listener trace file. **trc_file** sets the name for the listener trace file. **trc_level** sets the trace level (ADMIN, USER, SUPPORT, or OFF). See **lsnrctl trace**.
show	Shows current parameter settings. Options are the same as the **set** options with the sole omission of the **password** command.
spawn	Spawns a program that runs with an alias in the listener.ora file.

TABLE 13-5. *Listener Control Utility Parameters* (continued)

Command	Description
start	Starts the listener.
status	Provides status information about the listener, including the time it was started, its parameter filename, its log file, and the services it supports. This can be used to query the status of a listener on a remote server.
stop	Stops the listener.
trace	Sets the trace level of the listener to one of four choices: OFF; USER (limited tracing); ADMIN (high level of tracing); and SUPPORT (for ORACLE Support).
version	Displays version information for the listener, TNS, and the protocol adapters.

TABLE 13-5.   *Listener Control Utility Parameters* (continued)

NOTE
*Options for **lsnrctl** may be introduced or removed with each new version of Oracle Net.*

You can enter the **lsnrctl** command by itself and enter the **lsnrctl** utility shell, from which all other commands can then be executed.

The command options listed in Table 13-5 give you a great deal of control over the listener process, as shown in the following examples. In most of these examples, the **lsnrctl** command is first entered by itself. This places the user in the **lsnrctl** utility (as indicated by the LSNRCTL prompt). The rest of the commands are entered from within this utility. The following examples show the use of the **lsnrctl** utility to stop, start, and generate diagnostic information about the listener.

To stop the listener:

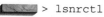
```
> lsnrctl
LSNRCTL> set password lsnr_password
LSNRCTL> stop
```

To list status information for the listener:

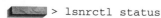
```
> lsnrctl status
```

To list the status of a listener on another host, add a service name from that host as a parameter to the **status** command. The following example uses the HQ service name shown earlier in this chapter:

```
> lsnrctl status hq
```

To list version information about the listener:

```
> lsnrctl version
```

To list information about the services supported by the listener:

```
> lsnrctl
LSNRCTL> set password lsnr_password
LSNRCTL> services
```

Usage Example: Client/Server Applications

There are several ad hoc query tools available that work in a client/server fashion. Consider the example of a query tool operating on a PC. The PC is connected via a network card to a TCP/IP network and is running a TCP/IP software package and Oracle Net or Net8. The database that it will be accessing resides on a UNIX server on the same network. This configuration is depicted in Figure 13-16.

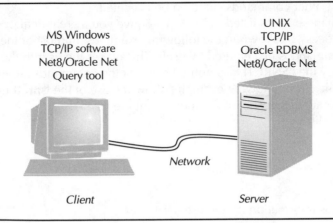

FIGURE 13-16. *Example client/server configuration*

When users run the tool on the PC, a username, password, and service name for a database must be specified. When users are connected to the database, they may then query from the tables available there. Every time a query is executed, the SQL statement for the query is sent to the server and executed. The data is then returned via Oracle Net or Net8 and displayed on the client PC.

Usage Example: Database Links

For frequently used connections to remote databases, *database links* should be established. Database links specify the connect descriptor to be used for a connection, and may also specify the username to connect to in the remote database.

A database link is typically used to create local objects (such as views or synonyms) that access remote databases via server/server communications. The local synonyms for remote objects provide location transparency to the local users. When a database link is referenced by a SQL statement, it opens a session in the remote database and executes the SQL statement there. The data is then returned, and the remote session may stay open in case it is needed again. Database links can be created as public links (by DBAs, making the link available to all users in the local database) or as private links.

The following example creates a private database link called HR_LINK:

```
create database link HR_LINK
connect to HR identified by PUFFINSTUFF
using 'loc';
```

The **create database link** command, as shown in this example, has three parameters:

- The name of the link (HR_LINK, in this example)
- The account to connect to
- The service name

A public database link can be created by adding the keyword **public** to the **create database link** command, as shown in the following example:

```
create public database link HR_LINK
connect to HR identified by PUFFINSTUFF
using 'loc';
```

If the LOC instance is moved to a different server, then the database links can be redirected to LOC's new location simply by distributing a tnsnames.ora file that contains the modification or by revising the listing in the directory server. You can generate the revised entry for the tnsnames.ora file or directory server by using either the Oracle Net Configuration Assistant tool or the Oracle Net Manager described previously in this chapter.

To use these links, simply add them as suffixes to table names in commands. The following example creates a local view of a remote table, using the HR_LINK database link:

```
create view LOCAL_EMPLOYEE_VIEW
as
select * from EMPLOYEE@HR_LINK
where Office='ANNAPOLIS';
```

The **from** clause in this example refers to EMPLOYEE@HR_LINK. Since the HR_LINK database link specifies the server name, instance name, and owner name, the global object name for the table is known. If no account name had been specified, the user's account name would have been used instead.

In this example, a view was created in order to limit the records that users could retrieve. If no such restriction is necessary, a synonym can be used instead. This is shown in the following example:

```
create public synonym EMPLOYEE for EMPLOYEE@HR_LINK;
```

Local users who query the local public synonym EMPLOYEE will automatically have their queries redirected to the EMPLOYEE table in the LOC instance on the HQ server. Location transparency has thus been achieved.

By default, a single SQL statement can use up to four database links. This limit can be increased via the OPEN_LINKS parameter in the database's init.ora file.

Usage Example: The copy Command

The SQL*Plus **copy** command is an underutilized, underappreciated command. You can use the **copy** command to copy data between databases (or within the same database) via SQL*Plus. Although it allows the user to select which columns to **copy**, it works best when all of the columns of a table are being chosen. The greatest benefit of this command is its ability to **commit** after each array of data has been processed; this in turn generates transactions that are of a manageable size.

Consider the case of a large table (again, using EMPLOYEE as the example). What if the EMPLOYEE table has 100,000 rows that use a total of 100MB of space, and you need to make a copy of that table into a different database? The easiest option, using a database link, involves the following steps:

```
create database link HR_LINK
connect to HR identified by PUFFINSTUFF
using 'loc';

create table EMPLOYEE
as
select * from EMPLOYEE@HR_LINK;
```

The first command creates the database link, and the second command creates a new table based on all of the data in the remote table.

To break the transaction into smaller entries, use the SQL*Plus **copy** command. The syntax for this command is

```
copy from
remote_username/remote_password@service_name
to
username/password@service_name
[append|create|insert|replace]
TABLE_NAME
using subquery;
```

If the current account is to be the destination of the copied data, then the local username, password, and service name are not necessary.

To set the transaction entry size, use the SQL*Plus **set** command to set a value for the **arraysize** parameter. This determines the number of records that will be retrieved in each "batch." The **copycommit** parameter tells SQL*Plus how many batches should be **commit**ted at one time. Thus, the following SQL*Plus script accomplishes the same data-copying goal that the **create table as** command met; however, it breaks up the single transaction into multiple transactions. In this example, the data is committed after every 1000 records. This reduces the transaction's rollback segment entry size needed from 100MB to 1MB—a much more manageable transaction size.

```
set copycommit 1
set arraysize 1000
copy from HR/PUFFINSTUFF@loc -
create EMPLOYEE -
using -
select * from EMPLOYEE
```

Except for the last line, each line in the **copy** command must be terminated with a dash, since this is a SQL*Plus command.

The different data options within the **copy** command are described in Table 13-6.

Option	Description
append	Inserts the rows into the destination table. Automatically creates the table if it does not exist.
create	Creates the table, then inserts the rows.
insert	Inserts the rows into the destination table if it exists; otherwise, returns an error. When using INSERT, all columns must be specified in the **using** subquery.
replace	Drops the existing destination table and replaces it with a new table containing the copied data.

TABLE 13-6. *copy Command Data Options*

The feedback provided by this command is confusing at first. After the final **commit** is complete, the database reports to the user the number of records that were **commit**ted in the *last* batch. The command feedback does not report the total number of records **commit**ted (unless they are all **commit**ted in a single batch).

Oracle Names Server Versus Client Configurations or Directory Servers

The decision to use Oracle Names server or rely on distributing and maintaining the current tnsnames.ora file for each client, or to migrate to a directory server is a choice that every DBA faces. There are many considerations to weigh. Factors that will play a part in the decision are as follows:

■ The number of clients on the system

■ The number of servers on the system

■ The number of different locations that are accessed

■ The frequency at which databases are added or removed from the system

Each time a database is added or removed from the system, a new tnsnames.ora entry should be generated to reflect the system change. In an environment where only a few clients are accessing only one or a few databases, it is easy to maintain the tnsnames.ora file and keep it current and disseminated to the clients. As the user base grows and the number of development, test, and production databases grows, tracking the specific clients who should receive connection information for specific databases becomes more complicated. Over time, the task of ensuring that each client's configuration is accurate for his or her needs becomes very complex. If there are servers in different locations across the country or around the world, ensuring that all of the correct connection information will get to all of the clients can be a daunting task.

If an Oracle Names server approach is chosen, you have one centralized place where changes to the connection configuration are made. Once the modifications are completed, the new configuration is sent to each Names server in the network, and the changes become available to clients without having to redistribute a tnsnames.ora file to each user.

Configuring the initial Oracle Names server has become easier over time, and the reward of getting the Names server working is the ease of enabling all clients to access the correct connection information rapidly. However, the Oracle Names server is an Oracle-specific solution. Also, Oracle Corporation has stated that the intent is to desupport Oracle Names in a future release. Therefore, the solution for supporting distributed names resolution in the future is to go with a directory server, as described earlier in this chapter.

Since the directory server will interact with and support both Names server resolution and user name/password support for authentication, we recommend using the Oracle Internet Directory solution.

Tuning Oracle Net

Tuning Oracle Net applications is fairly straightforward: wherever possible, reduce the amount of data that is sent across the network, particularly for online transaction-processing applications. Also, reduce the number of times data is requested from the database. The basic procedures that should be applied include the following:

- The use of distributed objects, such as materialized views, to replicate static data to remote databases.

- The use of procedures to reduce the amount of data sent across the network. Rather than sending data back and forth, only the procedure's error status is returned.

- The use of the highest buffer size available for Oracle Net buffering.

- The use of homogenous servers wherever possible to eliminate the need for connection managers.

- The use of shared servers to support more clients with less processes.

The buffer size used by Oracle Net and Net8 should take advantage of the packet sizes used by the network protocols (such as TCP/IP). If you send large packets of data across the network, then the packets may be fragmented. Since each packet contains header information, reducing packet fragmentation reduces network traffic.

You can tune the size of the service layer and transport layer buffer sizes. The specification for the service layer data buffer is called SDU; it may be specified in your tnsnames.ora and listener.ora files. For example, the following listing shows a section of tnsnames.ora file for the LOC service name. In this example, the service layer buffer size is set to 2KB via the SDU parameter.

```
LOC =(DESCRIPTION=
        (SDU=2048)
        (ADDRESS=
                (PROTOCOL=TCP)
                (HOST=HQ)
                (PORT=1521))
        (CONNECT DATA=
                (SID=loc)))
```

The listener.ora file must contain matching entries.

```
LISTENER =
    (ADDRESS_LIST =
        (ADDRESS=
            (PROTOCOL=IPC)
            (KEY= loc.world)
        )
    )
SID_LIST_LISTENER =
    (SID_LIST =
      (SID_DESC =
        (SDU=2048)
        (SID_NAME = loc)
        (Oracle_HOME = /orasw/app/oracle/product/9.0.1.0)
      )
    )
```

The listener.ora and tnsnames.ora SDU settings do not have to be identical; if they are different, the lower of the two will be used for the communications. The default size of the SDU setting is 2KB, as shown in the preceding listings.

The impact of changing the SDU settings is a reduction in network traffic and a shortening of the time required to connect to the database. However, you will need to know the size of the data being transferred in order to know whether increasing the SDU parameter can affect your performance. The buffer size for TCP/IP is 1500 bytes; if your data exceeds this value, you will be using multiple network packets no matter what the values are for the other parameters. The amount of data transferred at a time is determined by your **arraysize** setting and the size of the rows being read.

For example, if you **set arraysize 100** in SQL*Plus, and query rows that are 100 bytes each, then your data will require 10,000 bytes—so you will be using multiple packets. If you use an array size of 10 instead, you will be transferring 1000 bytes each time. Given the smaller array size, you can eliminate or reduce packet fragmentation by setting the SDU parameter to 2KB, as shown in the previous examples. Setting SDU to higher values will not have a noticeable effect on your network traffic, since you will be limited by the buffer size supported by the underlying network protocol. If you regularly query tables with large row sizes, you may not be able to reduce the network traffic generated.

UNIX and Oracle Net

UNIX is the operating system of choice for many Oracle installations; it supports small Oracle databases as well as extremely large databases. The combination of operating system flexibility, tuning options, and scalability make UNIX a solid foundation for an Oracle installation. In this section, you will see instructions for implementing Oracle Net in UNIX. You can use Oracle Net to access Oracle8, Oracle8i, and Oracle9i databases. For Oracle9i, Oracle Net will work with versions from 7.3.4 forward. Since the TCP/IP communications protocol is commonly used for UNIX servers, that protocol will be featured in the examples in this section.

Before a process can connect to a database on a server, there are several steps that the DBA must take in conjunction with the UNIX system administrator. The following sections describe each of these steps.

Identification of Hosts

A *host,* for the purposes of this section, will be defined as a server that is capable of communicating with another server via a network. Each host maintains a list of the hosts with which it can communicate. This list is maintained in a file called /etc/hosts. The "/etc" portion of the filename signifies that it is located in the /etc directory. This file contains the Internet address for the hosts, plus the host names.

It may optionally include an alias for each host name. A sample portion of an /etc/hosts file is shown in the following listing:

```
127.0.0.1 localhost
130.110.238.109 nmhost
130.110.238.101 txhost
130.110.238.102 azhost   arizona
```

Your UNIX implementation may use the Domain Name System (DNS), in which case the host IP addresses may not all be listed in the /etc/hosts file. If DNS is in use, you can use the **nslookup** command to query the IP address of a known host name (or vice versa). The following listing shows a sample lookup of an IP address from DNS:

```
> nslookup txhost
Server:  txhost.company.com
Address: 130.110.238.101
```

In this example, there are four hosts listed. The first entry is the "loopback" entry for the server. The next two entries assign host names (nmhost and txhost) to Internet addresses. The last entry assigns both a host name (azhost) and an alias (arizona) to an Internet address.

Most networking software for PC clients uses a similar file, either located on the PC or on a shared network drive. Within the network software directory structure, a hosts file is maintained. This file lists the IP address and host name for each host that the client can directly reach. The file is identical in structure to the UNIX /etc/hosts file shown in the preceding listing.

Whenever possible, use the host names rather than IP addresses in the Oracle Net configuration files. UNIX servers may use DHCP, a protocol that assigns IP addresses to hosts during each server startup. Servers that use DHCP may have different IP addresses each time they start up, so any connection based on a hard-coded IP address would fail.

Identification of Databases

All databases that are run on a host and are accessible to the network must be listed in a file, usually named /etc/oratab. The "/etc" portion of the filename signifies that it is located in the /etc directory. This file is maintained by the DBA.

NOTE
Depending on the version of UNIX in use, the name and location of the /etc/oratab file may vary. See your operating system–specific Oracle installation guide for details.

The components of an entry in this file are listed in Table 13-7.

The Startup_Flag component doesn't seem to fit; after all, why should a network connection care about the startup schedule for an instance? This flag is part of the entry because this file is also used (by default; it can be changed) during system startup to start the server's Oracle databases.

Component	Description
ORACLE_SID	Instance name (server ID).
ORACLE_HOME	Full path name of the root directory of the Oracle software used by the database.
STARTUP_FLAG	Flag to indicate whether the instance should be started when the host is started. If set to Y, then it will be started. If set to N, then it will not be started. This flag is used by the db_startup command file provided by Oracle.

TABLE 13-7. *etc/oratab Components*

The three components are listed all on one line, separated only by colons (:). A sample /etc/oratab file is shown in the following listing:

```
loc:/orasw/app/oracle/product/9.0.1.0:Y
cc1:/orasw/app/oracle/product/9.0.1.0:N
old:/orasw/app/oracle/product/9.0.1.0:Y
```

This example shows entries for three instances, named loc, cc1, and old. The first two instances have the same Oracle_HOME; the third uses an older version of the Oracle kernel. Both loc and old will be automatically started when the server starts; cc1 will have to be manually started. To access the instances, you will first need to start the listener process; the next section describes the configuration of the listener process in UNIX.

Debugging Connection Problems

As shown in the preceding examples, Oracle Net connections in UNIX require that a number of communication mechanisms be properly configured. The connections involve host-to-host communication, proper identification of services and databases, and proper configuration of the listener server processes. In the event of connection problems when using Oracle Net, it is important to eliminate as many of these components as possible.

Start by making sure that the host the connection is trying to reach is accessible via the network. This can be checked via the following command:

```
> telnet host_name
```

If this command is successful, you will be prompted for a username and password on the remote host. If the **ping** command is available to you, then you may use it instead. This command, shown in the following listing, will check to see if the remote host is available and will return a status message:

```
> ping host_name
```

If the host is available on the network, the next step is to check if the listener is running. At the same time, you can check to see what parameters it is currently using; this is important if you are attempting a remote autologin access. The **lsnrctl status** command will provide this information:

```
> lsnrctl status net_service_name
```

The *net_service_name* clause should refer to the name of a service on the remote server. If the *net_service_name* clause is not used, then the command will return the status of the listener on the local server.

These two checks—of host availability and listener availability—will resolve over 95 percent of Oracle Net connection problems in server/server communications. The rest of the problems will result from difficulties with the database specification that is being used. These problems include invalid username/password combinations, down databases, and databases in need of recovery.

In client/server communications, the same principles for debugging connection problems apply. First, verify that the remote host is accessible; most communications software for clients includes a **telnet** or **ping** command. If it is not accessible, the problem may be on the client side. Verify that *other* clients are able to access the host on which the database resides. If they can, the problem is isolated to the client. If they cannot, the problem lies on the server side, and the server, its listener processes, and its databases should be checked.

From the client, you can use the **tnsping** command to test connection to a listener. Execute the **tnsping** command with two parameters: the name of the service name to check and the number of connections to attempt. For example, if you run the command **tnsping hq 20**, then Oracle will attempt to connect to the hq service 20 consecutive times. The multiple connections are used because the output of the **tnsping** command may be displayed very quickly, and forcing it through multiple tests gives you time to read the output. The **tnsping** command is provided as part of the Windows client Oracle Net and Net8 connectivity software. The Net8 Assistant contains a connection test component that performs the same function as **tnsping**.

CHAPTER
14

Tuning 9iAS

racle 9iAS is Oracle's application server. As the middle tier of a three-tier architecture, 9iAS is a set of services that allow browser-based applications to interact with Oracle databases. Unlike the previous version of Oracle's application server (called OAS), 9iAS is based on the Apache Web server.

Oracle classifies the 9iAS services into several groups according to the type of support they provide:

- **Communication Services**   Web servers to handle requests to and from the Web

- **Business Logic Services**   Development tools and languages for building custom applications

- **Presentation Services**   Dynamic Web page development tools

- **Caching Services**   Tools to improve Web site performance by caching common data or pages

- **Content Management Services**   IFS for managing documents in the database

- **Portal Services**   Tools for publishing links, content, and applications to which the end user can subscribe

- **Business Intelligence Services**   Tools for creating reports and ad hoc queries of user activity on your sites

- **Database Services**   The Oracle9i database for storing your application data

As part of the 9iAS Suite, Oracle also provides several developer's kits to aid in creating dynamic, flexible applications, and tools to manage the database and security once the Web sites are deployed.

In this chapter, you will see guidance for tuning 9iAS, with emphasis on the Communication Services and the Caching Services. Even if the database is running with no significant wait events occurring, a poor application design or an untuned application server implementation may severely hamper the application performance. DBAs should take on the ownership of the 9iAS environment to ensure it will be properly tuned for the business needs.

NOTE
Thanks to Brad Brown, Randall Swanson, Kamila Bajaria, and Matt Malcheski of TUSC for their contributions to this chapter. For further details on the development of 9iAS-based applications, see Brad's book Oracle9i Web Development *(McGraw-Hill/Osborne [Oracle Press], 2001).*

Starting, Stopping, and Restarting iAS (Apache)

The 9iAS control program is named **apache** on NT and **apachectl** on UNIX. To start 9iAS on NT at the command line, check to see that the **apache** executable is in the system PATH environment variable. To check this, find the **apache** executable, typically located in the ORACLE_HOME\Apache\Apache directory, and then check the path by selecting the system icon in the Control Panel and selecting the Environment tab (NT) or Advanced tab (Win 2000). Add the directory for the **apache** executable in the PATH environment variable if it is not set.

To start 9iAS from the command line, enter the following:

```
apache -k start
```

To stop 9iAS from the command line, enter the following:

```
apache -k shutdown
```

You can also start and stop 9iAS using the Oracle HTTP Server shortcuts under Start | Programs | Oracle. Additionally, the Services icon in the Control Panel has an entry for Oracle HTTP Server, allowing you to start and stop 9iAS here, or you can set the service startup to automatic and have the Oracle HTTP Server started at system startup.

To start 9iAS on UNIX, use the following command to check if your path has been set containing the directory that holds the **httpd** executable:

```
echo $PATH
```

To start 9iAS on UNIX from the command line, enter

```
apachectl
```

or enter

```
httpd
```

To have 9iAS start automatically when the server is rebooted, edit the /etc/rc.d/rc.local file and add the following command:

```
$ORACLE_HOME/Apache/Apache/bin/httpd
```

To shut down 9iAS, enter

```
apachectl shutdown
```

You can also use the following command to shut down 9iAS:

```
kill -9 'cat $ORACLE_HOME/Apache/Apache/logs/httpd.pid`
```

Command-line syntax for **apache** and **apachectl** is

```
Usage: APACHE [-D name] [-d directory] [-f file] [-n service]
              [-C "directive"] [-c "directive"] [-k signal]
              [-v] [-V] [-h] [-l] [-L] [-S] [-t] [-T]
```

Command-line options for UNIX and NT are shown in Table 14-1.

Option	Description
-D *name*	Define a name for use in <IfDefine *name*> directives.
-d *directory*	Specify an alternate initial ServerRoot.
-f *file*	Specify an alternate ServerConfigFile.
-c or **-C** *"directive"*	Process directive before reading config files.
-v	Show version number.
-V	Show compile settings.
-h	List available command-line options.
-l	List compiled-in modules.
-L	List available configuration directives.
-S	Show parsed settings (currently only vhost settings).
-t or **-T**	Run syntax check for config files (with docroot check).
-n *name*	Name the 9iAS service for **-k** options.
-k stop|shutdown	Tell running 9iAS to shut down.
-k restart	Tell running 9iAS to do a graceful restart.
-k start	Tell 9iAS to start.
-k install | -I	Install a 9iAS service.
-k config	Reconfigure an installed 9iAS service.
-k uninstall | -u	Uninstall a 9iAS service.

TABLE 14-1. *UNIX and NT Apache Command-Line Options*

Tuning Apache and TCP

When tuning Apache for 9iAS applications, you should first verify that the environment is robust enough to support your processing requirements. Apache tuning commonly begins with increasing the RAM available to Apache. The more memory available, the more data Apache can cache to improve performance. Increasing the available memory also enhances the performance of many of the 9iAS modules (such as mod_plsql). Apache Web servers commonly use a minimum memory of 512MB. In benchmark tests, adding memory beyond 768MB does not significantly enhance the number of requests per second processed.

Tuning Apache involves manipulating the configuration parameters specified in the httpd.conf configuration file. The settings for ServerRoot, DocumentRoot, and LogLevel, as described in the following sections, may directly impact your performance.

ServerRoot is the default location where the configuration, error, and log files are kept. For example:

```
ServerRoot "D:\Oracle\Ora90\Apache\Apache"
```

DocumentRoot is the default location where Web pages reside (commonly a directory named htdocs). By default, 9iAS looks for the htdocs directory under ServerRoot. DocumentRoot sets the virtual root for the initial HTML document directory. For example:

```
DocumentRoot "D:\Oracle\Ora90\Apache\Apache\htdocs"
```

To enhance performance, keep your URL directories as shallow as possible. When a service is requested, each level of a directory structure needs to be traversed. Create a symbolic link /www to point to the location of your DocumentRoot directory, and then use /www as your DocumentRoot in the Apache configuration file:

```
DocumentRoot "/www"
```

The LogLevel setting controls the type of logging Apache performs (error, warn, or debug). For best performance, streamline the logging performed. Apache logging should be set to a minimum, and the logs should be written to fast, dedicated disks. Using "LogLevel error" in place of the default logging level ("LogLevel warn") may more than double the number of requests per second processed. Host names should never be stored in the logs, as this requires a DNS lookup for each request. Logs are stored in the $ORACLE_HOME/Apache/Apache/logs directory on UNIX or ORACLE_HOME\Apache\Apache\logs on a Windows system.

In addition to tuning Apache, you should tune your environment's TCP parameters. Note that modifying these parameters may require kernel rebuilds in some environments. Work with your system administrators to determine the most efficient settings for these parameters in your environment. The TCP parameters most frequently changed from their defaults on common UNIX platforms are listed in Table 14-2. These parameters are commonly modified via the tcpset.sh file located in $ORACLE_HOME/Apache/Apache/bin.

Enhancing Security of the Apache Installation

As part of your security plan for a 9iAS installation, you protect the location from which the Apache server will serve its content. You must protect not only the directory in which the startup commands reside but the parent directories as well. Regardless of the directory in which you define ServerRoot, you must ensure that only the root user has access to write or modify the files. On a UNIX system, you can protect the files by changing the owner and group to root for the files and changing the mode to 755 on the files. The following example illustrates these steps:

```
mkdir /usr/local/apache
cd /usr/local/apache
mkdir bin conf logs
chown root . bin conf logs
chgrp root . bin conf logs
chmod 755 . bin conf logs
```

Likewise, you should protect the **httpd** executable and any other associated sensitive files and directories from nonprivileged users writing to files.

Tuning the Oracle HTTP Server Configuration

The httpd.conf file, located in the $ORACLE_HOME/Apache/Apache/conf directory, contains the configuration settings for 9iAS. The following httpd.conf entries can significantly impact your performance.

HostNameLookup
Looking up the host name for every client that accessed 9iAS is time consuming and resource intensive. Set the HostNameLookup parameter to off.

SymLinksIfOwnerMatch
Options SymLinksIfOwnerMatch causes Apache to check file system permissions every time the symbolic link is traversed, slowing response times. If possible, use Options FollowSymLinks, which will avoid the extra permission check, in place of Options SymLinksIfOwnerMatch.

Sun Solaris	Compaq Tru64	HP/UX	IBM AIX	Linux
tcp_conn_hash_size	tcbhashsize	tcp_time_wait_interval	rfc1323	rmem_default
tcp_close_wait_interval	tcbhashnum	tcp_conn_req_max	sb_max	rmem_max
tcp_time_wait_interval	tcp_keepalive_default	tcp_ip_abort_interval	tcp_mssdflt	wmem_default
tcp_conn_req_max_q	tcp_sendspace	tcp_keepalive_interval	lpqmaxlen	wmem_max
tcp_conn_req_max_q0	tcp_recvspace	tcp_rexmit_interval_initial	tcp_sendspace	tcp_timestamps
tcp_slow_start_initial	somaxconn	tcp_rexmit_interval_max	tcp_recvspace	tcp_windowscaling
tcp_xmit_hiwat	sominconn	tcp_rexmit_interval_min	xmt_que_size	tcp_sack
tcp_recv_hiwat	sbcompress_threshold	tcp_xmit_hiwater_def		
		tcp_recv_hiwater_def		

TABLE 14-2. *TCP Parameters for Major UNIX Platforms*

AllowOverride

The AllowOverride All setting will access the .htaccess file in each level of the URL's directory structure to look for additional access restrictions, causing a significant performance drain. Use AllowOverride None where possible to eliminate the additional overhead.

MinSpareServers, MaxSpareServers, and StartServers

The MinSpareServers, MaxSpareServers, and StartServers parameters affect the prespawning of Apache server processes. For best performance, you should set MinSpareServers to at least 5. In addition, MaxSpareServers should be set to the expected number of concurrent requests during a busy period, not necessarily the absolute peak. StartServers should be set to the same value of MaxSpareServers.

MaxClients

The MaxClients parameter controls the maximum number of concurrent requests that Apache will service at one time. MaxClients defaults to 150 and can be increased to 1024.

Using the Oracle Caching Services

Caches store data that will be used repeatedly, with their primary purpose being to improve the access to that data. A cache can exist anywhere between the user's browser and the back-end database that stores the data used by the browser-based application. 9iAS applications can take advantage of the Oracle Web Cache and the Oracle9iAS Database Cache. In the following sections, you will see descriptions of the functionality and implementation of these caches.

Oracle Web Cache

The Oracle Web Cache can be thought of as a reverse proxy server. By storing URLs in the cache, the Web Cache bypasses the Apache Web server's need to reprocess requests. Requests that would have been processed by the Apache Web server are instead handled by the Web Cache without accessing the Apache Web server. As a result, the performance, scalability, and availability of busy Web sites will be enhanced.

In the simplest case, you can deploy the Oracle Web Cache on the same node as the Web server. In this scenario, both the Web Cache and the Web server have the same host name. You can optionally place the Oracle Web Cache on a separate server apart from the Web server, in which case the domain would be registered to the IP address of the Oracle Web Cache, not the Web server.

In addition to Apache's static object caching, the Oracle Web Cache allows for the caching of dynamic content such as JSPs (Java Server Pages). The Oracle Web Cache serves cached content in compressed (gzip) format to greatly reduce network load, the memory required on the cache server, and the load on communication lines. The client's browser will dynamically uncompress the compressed content.

The Oracle Web Cache architecture allows for user-customized caching; two users using the same URL to access an application's home page may see different pages. These different pages can be cached; when the user requests the page again, the user-specific cached version will be displayed.

The Oracle Web Cache also acts as a load balancer that will intercept requests to the application server. If the page requested is not found in the cache, the Oracle Web Cache can distribute the load across several application servers. The Oracle Web Cache load balancing capability may obviate the need to purchase load balancing hardware for your environment.

Using the Oracle Web Cache

To administer the Oracle Web Cache, use the browser-based Oracle Web Cache Manager tool. The administration server process must be running to use the administration interface. Once the Oracle Web Cache is configured, the cache server process performs the actual caching function. An optional watchdog server process can be started to automatically detect if the Oracle Web Cache fails and to attempt to restart the failed processes.

To start and stop the server processes, use the **webcachectl** command-line utility. If you are running the Oracle Web Cache on Windows NT, you can also start, stop, and view the status of the server processes using the Services window. Once the administration server process is running, you can use the Oracle Web Cache Manager to stop and start the cache process.

The webcachectl Utility

The **webcachectl** utility is used only to administer the server processes and doesn't provide the configuration functions available using the Oracle Web Cache Manager. The **webcachectl** utility takes only one parameter: either **start**, **stop**, **status**, or **repair**:

- **start**   Start the administration and cache processes.

- **stop**   Stop the administration and cache processes, and the watchdog process.

- **status**   Display messages for the administration, cache, and watchdog processes, showing whether each process is running.

- **repair**   Restore the previous version of the configuration. The Oracle Web Cache Manager doesn't provide the same level of consistency checking as the administration process. Consequently, it's possible for the administrator to enter bad configuration values that can prevent the administration process from starting. If this occurs, use **webcachectl repair** to restore the previous version of the configuration.

For example, to start the Oracle Web Cache processes, enter the following at a command prompt:

```
webcachectl start
```

Starting and Stopping Processes in Windows NT

Within Windows NT, the Oracle Web Cache services have the value of the associated Oracle installation identifier as part of the process names. The administration service is named Oracle*ORACLE_HOME*WebCacheAdmin, the cache service is named Oracle*ORACLE_HOME*WebCache, and the watchdog service is named Oracle*ORACLE_HOME*WebCacheMon. For example, if the Oracle installation home identifier is MyDb, the service names, respectively, are OracleMyDbWebCacheAdmin, OracleMyDbWebCache, and OracleMyDbWebCacheMon.

Oracle Web Cache Manager

Once the administration server process is running, start the Oracle Web Cache Manager using your Web browser. For example:

```
http://webcachehost:4000/webcacheadmin
```

When prompted for the administrator ID and password, enter **administrator** for the userid and enter the administrator's password (the default initial password is the same as the username). A separate invalidation administrator user named INVALIDATOR is set up with its initial password the same as the username.

From within the Oracle Web Cache Manager, select the desired option on the Navigator frame to configure, administer, and monitor the performance of the Oracle Web Cache and the application Web servers for which it accelerates content delivery. The main categories are

- Administering Oracle Web Cache
- Administering Web Sites
- Monitoring Oracle Web Cache
- Monitoring Application Web Servers

You need to click Apply Changes after modifying any configuration parameters, and then restart the cache process.

Administering Oracle Web Cache

The first option within the Administering Oracle Web Cache section, Web Cache Operations, enables the administrator to stop and start the cache process or change the administration port. Figure 14-1 shows the Administration Port screen with the Change Administration Port options.

The administrator can also change the invalidation port, used to invalidate pages in the cache, and the statistics port, used to monitor Oracle Web Cache performance. The default values of the invalidation and statistics ports are 4001 and 4002, respectively.

Using the Security options, listed in the left panel of the screen, the administrator can change the passwords for the ADMINISTRATOR and INVALIDATOR users, as

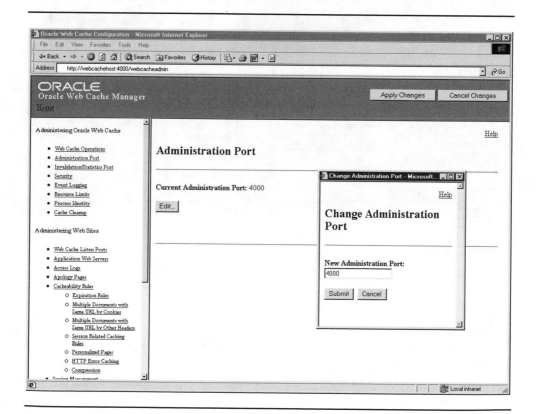

FIGURE 14-1. *Administration Port, Change Administration Port*

shown in Figure 14-2. The Security link also enables the administrator to change the trusted subnets that define the computers from which the administrator can administer and invalidate cached objects (All Subnets, This Machine Only, or a list of IP addresses).

Events and errors are stored in an event log that is configured using the Event Logging option (also in the left panel). The event log file, named event_log, is located in the /webcache/logs directory under the Oracle home directory. All events are in the format "timestamp Information/Warning/Error Message." The administrator configures whether the timestamp values are in the local time zone or GMT. The *Oracle Web Cache Administration and Deployment Guide* recommends using GMT to improve performance. The administrator can also

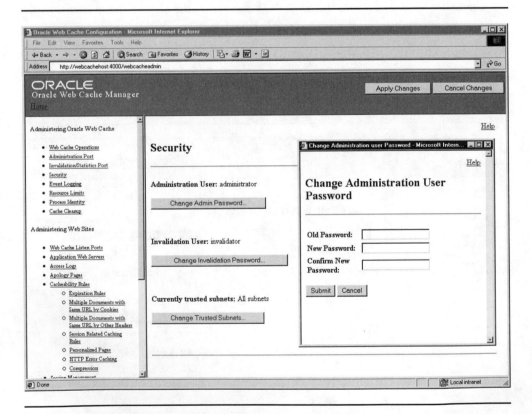

FIGURE 14-2. *Administering user security*

select whether to use Verbose Logging to log only typical events (set to No) or to log typical events plus application Web server events (set to Yes).

To tune the Oracle Web Cache performance, use the Resource Limits option to configure the cache size and connection limits, as shown in Figures 14-3 and 14-4. The cache size defines the amount of memory in which the Oracle Web Cache can store documents. Once the cache is full, the Oracle Web Cache performs garbage collection to remove the less popular and less valid documents. To minimize swapping documents in and out of the cache, set the cache size as large as possible within the operating system resource limit.

The connection limit is the sum of the number of incoming open connections to the Oracle Web Cache and the number of outgoing open connections to the application Web servers. Carefully analyze site use to configure an appropriate

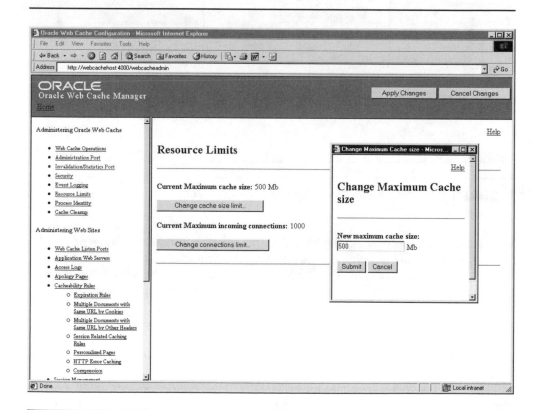

FIGURE 14-3. *Maximum Cache Size*

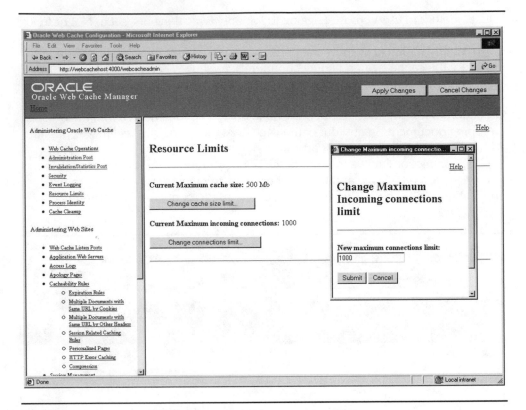

FIGURE 14-4. *Maximum Incoming Connections Limit*

connection limit, because setting the value too low causes refused connections, and setting the value too high causes performance degradation.

If the Oracle Web Cache is running on a UNIX platform, the administrator can select the Process Identity option to change the userid and groupid values of the Oracle Web Cache executables. The values aren't changeable if the installation is on Windows NT.

Finally, the Cache Cleanup option, as shown in Figure 14-5, provides a simple means to invalidate cached pages manually. The administrator can select to invalidate all pages in the cache, pages for a specific URL, or pages that begin with a specified URL prefix. This option generates the HTTP POST invalidation requests to reduce the chances of error. Entering the HTTP header fields, especially the Base64 encoding values, plus the XML can be tricky, so the cache cleanup feature can isolate the administrator from the low-level protocol details.

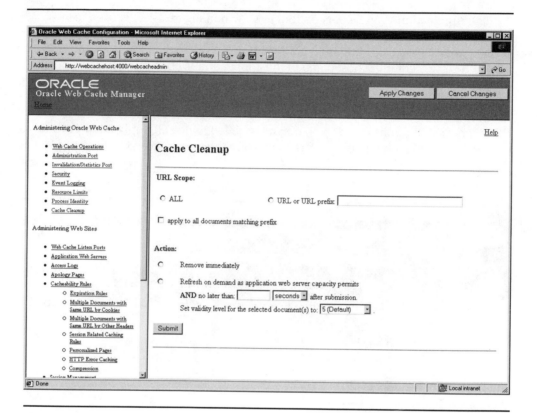

FIGURE 14-5.   *Cache Cleanup*

Administering Web Sites

By default, Oracle Web Cache listens for browser requests on port 1100. The first option in the Administering Web Sites section, Web Cache Listen Ports, enables the administrator to configure an additional listening port from which Oracle Web Cache receives browser requests.

NOTE
You typically want to change this from port 1100 to port 80. If both the application server and the Web Cache are on the same server, move your iAS default port to 8080 and make the Web Cache's default port 80.

The Application Web Servers option, as shown in Figure 14-6, is used to manage the application Web servers for which the Oracle Web Cache accelerates content. You can use this option to configure up to 100 application Web servers. For each server, enter the host name of the application Web server, listening port, capacity in terms of the number of connections that the server can sustain at one time, failover threshold, ping URL, and the ping interval. The *failover threshold* determines the number of times the application Web server doesn't respond to a request before it is considered to be down/has failed. Once an application Web server has failed, it no longer sends requests, and the Oracle Web Cache pings

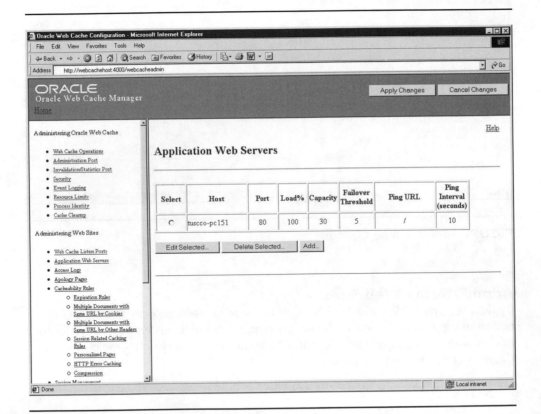

FIGURE 14-6. *Application Web Servers*

the specified URL periodically as defined by the ping interval until it resumes responding to requests.

NOTE
The Application Web Servers option page is where you configure Web Cache to point to all the servers for which it should serve as a cache.

The Access Logs option allows you to control the storage of information about HTTP requests sent to the Oracle Web Cache. The default location for the access log, named access_log, is the same directory as the event log, $ORACLE_HOME/ webcache/logs. Requests are buffered in memory until they're written to the log when the buffer is full. You can define whether logging is enabled, the logging directory, whether times are in the local time zone or GMT, the rollover frequency in which the log is archived, and the desired fields to include in the log entries. Several available fields are part of the Extended LogFile Format (XLF), a superset of the Common LogFile Format (CLF). The default fields are **c-ip** (browser IP address), **cauth-id** (username if authentication required), **clf-date** (date and time), **"request line"** (the HTTP request), **sc-status** (status code), and **bytes** (content length).

As with all caches, a set of cacheability rules defines which pages are cached and which are excluded from the cache. You should work closely with the Oracle Web Cache administrator to define a complete set of cacheability rules to optimize the number of cached pages and to ensure content that shouldn't be cached is excluded. If a page request isn't covered by one of the cacheability rules, the page is cached according to the HTTP header information, which typically only caches static pages.

The cacheability rules are defined within the Oracle Web Cache Manager, as shown in Figure 14-7, using a series of prioritized, POSIX 1003 regular expressions. These expressions are similar to the pattern-matching expressions used by UNIX utilities, such as **sed**. The ^ denotes the start of a URL, **$** denotes the end of a URL, **.** is a wildcard for any single character, ***** denotes any number of the previous character, **?** indicates the previous character is optional, and the backslash \ is used to escape special characters, such as the period (.), asterisk (*), and question mark (?). For example, to cache all files that end in .htm or .html, enter the URL expression:

```
\.html?$
```

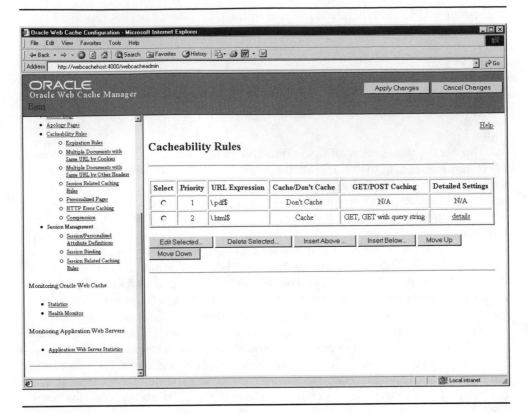

FIGURE 14-7. *Cacheability Rules*

In the preceding example, the backslash escapes the period to indicate that a URL matching the pattern must contain a period. If the period is followed by htm or, optionally, html at the end of the URL, the page should follow the cacheability rule.

TIP
Be sure to add a cache rule to cache Java Server Pages (that is, \.jsp) and/or PL/SQL code (that is, ^/pls/examples/) for your dynamic pages.*

For each regular expression, specify whether a URL matching the expression is or is not cached. If the URL should be cached, specify whether documents are retrieved from the cache in response to GET, GET with query string, POST, or any combination of these three HTTP methods. Also, specify an expiration rule, as shown in Figure 14-8, for matching documents, whether to cache multiple copies of a document based on the contents of a cookie or HTTP headers, how to track sessions using a session cookie or URL parameter, how to process personalized in-cache content, the HTTP error codes to cache, and whether to compress the documents in the cache.

TIP

Don't cache documents requested through GET with query string or POST if these documents update the database.

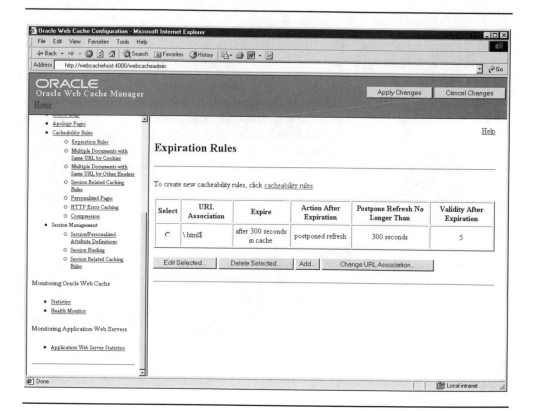

FIGURE 14-8. *Expiration Rules*

You have three choices to define an expiration date on the cached content:

- **Expire after cache entry**   Enter the number of seconds after the document is placed in the cache for when the document expires.

- **Expire after document creation**   Enter the number of seconds after the document is created for when the document expires.

- **Expire as per HTTP Expires header**   Set the expiration date in the HTTP Expires header. This is the default option.

You have two choices for specifying how to handle expired documents in the cache. Expired documents are assigned a validity level that defines the time the cache could return a stale document before receiving an updated page from the Web server. The choices are

- **Remove immediately**   Expired documents are removed from the cache and a stale cached copy is never returned to the browser, equivalent to a validity level of 0.

- **Refresh on demand as application Web server capacity permits *and* no later than the specified number of seconds after expiration**   Allows the Oracle Web Cache to return stale cached copies of the requested document while waiting for the application server to create a fresh copy of the document. Returning stale documents only occurs if the document's expiration date, plus the number of seconds allowed, is still within the specified window. Documents with a lower validity level (1 is the lowest) are returned stale for less time than documents with a higher validity level (9 is the highest).

You can use the Multiple Documents with Same Selector by Cookies option to configure pages when different versions of the page should be cached based on the contents of a cookie. Enter the cookie name, whether to cache a copy of the page for browsers that don't send the cookie with the request, and the URLs associated with the cookie. You can also cache pages based on their HTTP request header, their session parameters, or personalization information.

The Session Related Caching Rules area, in the left panel, enables the administrator to configure caching behavior of session parameters, as shown in Figure 14-9. For each rule, select or create a new session parameter associated with a cookie, URL parameter, or both. Define whether to cache documents whose requests contain the session parameter and whether to cache documents whose requests don't contain the session parameter. Specify the URLs associated with this rule.

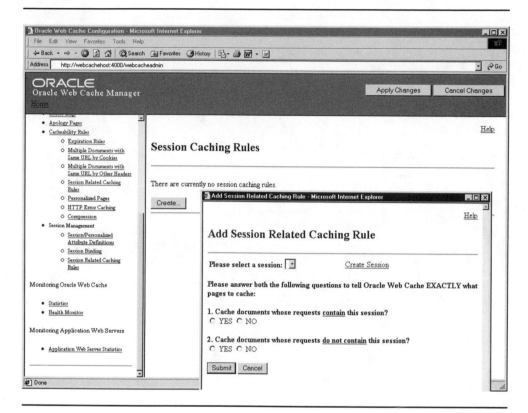

FIGURE 14-9.   *Session Related Caching Rule*

You can also use the Session/Personalized Attribute Definitions area to define session parameters, as shown in Figure 14-10. Each session parameter is associated with a cookie name, a URL parameter, or both. You can enter up to 20 session parameters for each cached page.

Monitoring Oracle Web Cache

The Monitoring Oracle Web Cache section of the Web Cache Manager, as shown in Figure 14-11, contains options to gather performance statistics and monitor the overall health of the Oracle Web Cache. Monitored statistics include

- **Last Modified**   The time the statistics page was created.

- **Oracle Web Cache Start Timestamp**   The time the Oracle Web Cache was started.

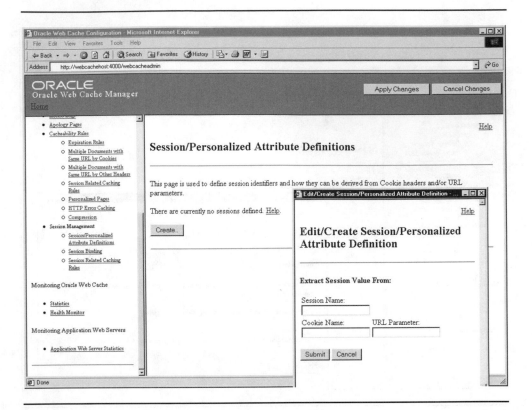

FIGURE 14-10. *Session/Personalized Attribute Definitions*

- **Time Since Start**   The elapsed time since Oracle Web Cache was started, expressed as days/hours/minutes/seconds.

- **Number of Documents in Cache**   The number of documents stored in the Oracle Web Cache, plus the number of documents that are in transit and may be cached, depending on the cacheability rules.

- **Cache Size (in bytes)**   The current size of the cache.

- **Total Number of Bytes Written**   The total number of bytes written to the cache.

- **Current Number of Open Connections**   The sum of the number of incoming open connections from browsers and the number of outgoing open connections to the application Web servers.

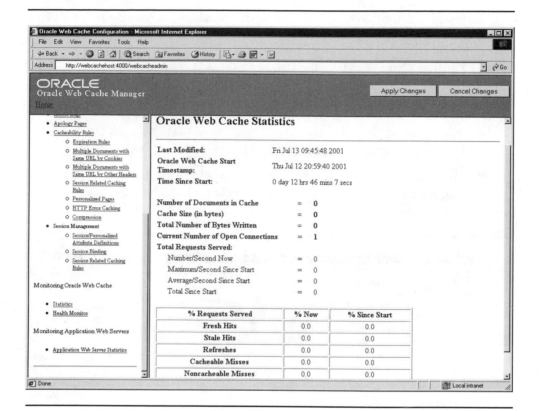

FIGURE 14-11.   *Oracle Web Cache Statistics*

- **Total Requests Served**   A table containing information on the total number of requests served to the browsers. Information includes the number of current requests for each second, maximum number of requests for each second since the Oracle Web Cache was started, the average number of requests for each second since the Oracle Web Cache was started, and the total number of requests served since the Oracle Web Cache was started.

- **Percentage Requests Served**   A table containing information on the cache performance in terms of the hit ratio. Information includes the percentage of fresh hits, the percentage of stale hits, the percentage of documents refreshed with new information from the application Web servers, the percentage of missed requests for cacheable documents, and the percentage of requests for noncacheable documents.

The Health Monitor, as seen in Figure 14-12, provides information on overall cache performance. Statistics include the following:

■ **Current Time**   The time the statistics page was created.

■ **Oracle Web Cache Start Timestamp**   The time the Oracle Web Cache was started.

■ **Time Since Start**   The elapsed time since Oracle Web Cache was started, expressed as days/hours/minutes/seconds.

■ **Total Number of Requests Served by Oracle Web Cache**   The total number of requests served since the Oracle Web Cache was started.

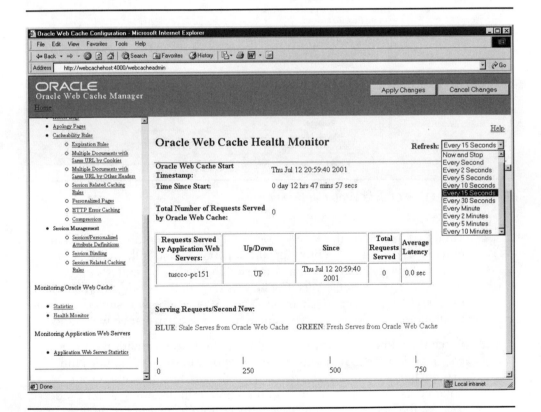

FIGURE 14-12.   *Health Monitor*

■ **Requests Served by Application Web Servers** A table containing information on the application Web servers for which the Oracle Web Cache accelerates content delivery. Information includes the name of the application Web server, whether the application Web server is up, how long the application Web server has been up, the total number of requests resolved by the application Web server, and the average amount of time required for the application Web server to resolve requests.

■ **Serving Requests/Second Now** A graphical bar that shows the number of browser requests resolved for each second. The bar shows the number of documents in the cache that are expired or invalidated and are waiting to be refreshed, and the number of documents in the cache that are still valid.

Monitoring Application Web Servers

The Oracle Web Cache lists detailed statistics about the application Web servers it services. The Application Web Server Statistics table, as shown in Figure 14-13, contains columns including the following:

■ **Application Web Server** The name of the application Web server.

■ **Up/Down Time** The status of the application Web server (up or down) and the time the application Web server was started or stopped.

■ **Completed Requests** The current, maximum, and average number of requests for each second the application Web server is processing, plus the total number of requests processed by the application Web server.

■ **Latency** The average time to process requests in ten-second intervals and the overall average time to process requests since the application Web server was started.

■ **Load** The current and maximum number of connections from the Oracle Web Cache that the application Web server has open, or has had open at one time.

■ **Active Sessions** The current and maximum number of active sessions from the Oracle Web Cache to the application Web server.

Apology pages are sent when a network error occurs or a site is too busy. The Apology Pages Served information shows the current number of apology pages being returned to browsers this second, plus the total number of apology pages returned to browsers.

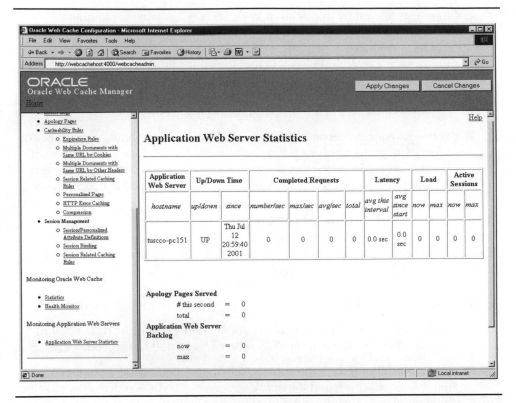

FIGURE 14-13. *Application Web Server Statistics*

The Application Web Server Backlog information shows the current number of requests the application Web server is processing and the maximum number of requests the application Web server has processed for the Oracle Web Cache.

Invalidating Cached Documents

When the data in a database is updated, any cached documents built on the changed data must be invalidated. The pages can still be returned stale for the amount of time defined in the cacheability rule while waiting for the application server to create a fresh copy of the document. The Oracle Web Cache listens for HTTP requests whose request method is POST on the defined invalidation request port. The default invalidation request port is 4001, and can be changed on the Oracle Web Cache Invalidation/Statistics Port page.

Invalidation requests are written in XML, where the XML message body contains the instructions for marking the appropriate cached documents as invalid. These HTTP POST requests can be sent manually using the Oracle Web Cache Manager or using the command line, or they can be generated automatically using triggers, scripts, or application code.

Manual Invalidation Using the Command Line

You can **telnet** into the Oracle Web Cache's invalidation port and directly enter the contents of the POST request. The format of the XML message is as follows:

```
<?xml version="1.0"?>
<!DOCTYPE INVALIDATION SYSTEM "internal:///invalidation.dtd">
<INVALIDATION>
   <URL EXP="url" PREFIX="YES|NO">
      <VALIDITY LEVEL="validity" REFRESHTIME="seconds"/>
      <COOKIE NAME="cookie_name" VALUE="value" NONEXIST="YES|NO"/>
      <HEADER NAME="HTTP_request_header" VALUE="value"/>
   </URL>
</INVALIDATION>
```

The **exp** parameter shown in the prior listing specifies one or more URLs to invalidate. If the value of the **prefix** parameter is YES, the URL can contain a regular expression. Otherwise, the URLs listed in the **exp** parameter must match exactly.

The format of the XML response is as follows:

```
<?xml version="1.0"?>
<!DOCTYPE INVALIDATIONRESULT [
<!ELEMENT INVALIDATIONRESULT (URL+)>
<!ELEMENT URL    EMPTY>
<!ATTLIST URL
            EXPR        CDATA     #REQUIRED
            ID          CDATA     #REQUIRED
            STATUS      CDATA     #REQUIRED
            NUMINV      CDATA     #REQUIRED
>
]>
<INVALIDATIONRESULT>
   <URL EXPR="url" ID="id" STATUS="status" NUMINV="number">
</INVALIDATIONRESULT>
```

The *id* parameter shown in the preceding listing specifies a sequence number if multiple URLs are in the invalidation response. The *status* attribute returns 'SUCCESS', 'URL NOT CACHEABLE', or 'URL NOT FOUND'. The *numinv* attribute contains the number of documents invalidated by the request.

Manual Invalidation Using the Oracle Web Cache Manager

To invalidate cached documents within the Oracle Web Cache Manager, simply select the Cache Cleanup option within the Administering Oracle Web Cache section (see Figure 14-1).

Automatic Invalidation Using Scripts

If you use a script to load data into the database, you can add logic at the end of the script to create and send the appropriate invalidation messages to the Oracle Web Cache. Performance assurance mechanisms built into the Oracle Web Cache allow the script to send general invalidation messages without having to specify each row that has changed in the database.

Load Balancing among Application Servers

Most Web sites use multiple application servers on separate computers to increase reliability and distribute the load of servicing incoming requests. The Oracle Web Cache provides the capability to balance the load of requests that cannot be serviced by the cache for up to 100 application Web servers. The administrator defines the weighted load percentage for each application Web server based on the server's capacity. See Figure 14-6.

If you prefer, you can use a third-party load balancer to distribute the incoming requests among the application Web servers. The Oracle Web Cache sends all requests it cannot service to the load balancer, which distributes the requests among the application Web servers.

Regardless of the caching choices used, be sure there is not a network bottleneck between the application server and the database server. No configuration parameter setting or Oracle enhancement can overcome a significant network hardware limitation.

Oracle9iAS Database Cache

In addition to caching Web pages, you can create a cache of tables. The tables will be stored in a database that exists between the application server and the back-end database. You can choose which tables to include in the cache. Oracle's database cache, called the Oracle9iAS Database Cache, contains copies of selected tables along with recently processed queries accessing the cached tables. If a query is submitted to the database and it exists in the Database Cache, the result set is retrieved by using the cached data instead of by sending the query to the database. Because the database wasn't needed to check the syntax and parse the query, the result set is returned more quickly to the user. Changes to the data in the cache are periodically updated using a schedule defined by the administrator. The administrator can also define an expiration date for the data, during which time the cached data can be used to satisfy queries even if it is no longer current.

The Oracle9iAS Database Cache builds on Oracle's replication technology by storing materialized views of the data between the application server and the back-end database. Using a shadow connection to the Oracle9iAS Database Cache for each database connection, Oracle determines if the data needed to create a result set for a read-only query is available in the cache (a cache "hit") or if it must be retrieved from the database. Query routing is transparent to OCI applications provided the applications use dynamic linking to the libclntsh.so library, which references the new library wtc8.so containing the routing logic. Applications that are statically linked with this library must be relinked to use the enhanced version of this library.

How the Database Cache Works

The Oracle9iAS Database Cache contains *data sets,* which consist of replicas of tables from the origin database. The Oracle9iAS Database Cache also stores information about previous queries to determine which queries were satisfied by data available in the cached data sets. Using the Java-based DBA Studio Cache Manager component or the supplied DBMS_ICACHE PL/SQL package, you define the tables to cache, the cache properties, and the synchronization policy.

The synchronization policy determines how often the cached data sets are refreshed with current data in the origin database. For each table, specify whether the cached object is updated with incremental changes or completely refreshed. You can also choose to schedule the incremental or complete synchronization, or perform the task manually. The synchronization options are based on the materialized view refresh methods described in Chapter 16.

When a query or PL/SQL subprogram is executed, the Oracle9iAS Database Cache attempts to execute the query using the data sets stored in the cache. When the query can be satisfied using the cached data sets, the cache returns the result set without using resources on the source database. If the query cannot be satisfied using the cached data sets, the query is routed to the origin server. **Insert**, **update**, and **delete** statements are always routed to the origin database for processing.

Developers should work closely with DBAs to determine which tables contain the most frequently requested data, which PL/SQL objects should be cached, and whether each data set should be refreshed using incremental updates or completely recopied from the corresponding table in the origin database.

Enable Caching for All Applications

To enable the Oracle9iAS Database Cache to service all applications that reside on the same server, simply define the ORA_OCI_CACHE environment variable with a value of 1.

Specify Connections to Cache or Not Cache

To allow caching by the Oracle9iAS Database Cache for any connection, the ORA_OCI_CACHE environment variable must be defined. Within an OCI application, you can specify whether caching is enabled or disabled for a connection using the *mode* parameter of the OCIEnvCreate() function. You can either set the *mode* to

OCI_CACHE to specify that the connection uses the Oracle9iAS Database Cache, or to OCI_NO_CACHE to specify that the connection does not use the Oracle9iAS Database Cache.

For example, to specify that a connection uses the Oracle9iAS Database Cache:

```
OCIEnvCreate((dvoid**)&envhp,
    (ub4) OCI_DEFAULT | OCI_CACHE,
    (dvoid *)0,
    (dvoid * (*)(dvoid *, size_t))0,
    (dvoid * (*)(dvoid *, dvoid *, size _t))0,
    (void (*)(dvoid , dvoid *))0,
    (size_t)0,
    (dvoid **)0))
```

Specifying Statements Not to Cache

For an even lower level of control, you can use the OCIAttrGet() function to specify which statements should be routed directly to the database, even if the connection specifies that the cache should be used.

For example, to specify that a statement does not use the cache:

```
OCIAttrSet((dvoid *)stmthp1,
    (ub4)OCI_HYPE_STMT,
    (dvoid *)&rem,
    (ub4)0,
    (ub4)OCI_ATTR_NO_CACHE,
    errhp1)
```

Taking Advantage of the Oracle9iAS Database Cache

If your application is capable of using the Oracle9iAS Database Cache, use it. The cache can dramatically improve response times for the end user and reduce loads on the database server, allowing database-driven Web sites to scale more efficiently. Both data and PL/SQL procedures may be cached.

Oracle Enterprise Manager provides a management interface to the Oracle Database Cache to report on cache statistics and statements that are executed to aid in determining which objects should be cached. Items that are largely read-only in nature are the best candidates for using the Database Cache. Queries of static data may run over 100 times faster when using Oracle9iAS Database Cache.

CHAPTER
15

Managing
Large Databases

hen managing a large database, you need to view the database from a nonstandard perspective. In this chapter, you will see management advice specific to large databases, including the following:

- Setting up the environment, including partitions and materialized views

- Managing transactions, including data loads

- Implementing backup strategies

- Tuning

- Using transportable tablespaces for data movement

Some of the advice in this chapter will not be applicable for smaller systems. If you are managing a smaller database, follow the advice found in the other chapters of this book.

Setting Up the Environment

Within a large database, a small number of tables typically use the majority of the space allocated to tables. For example, in a large database used for decision support purposes, you may have 100 tables, 5 of which account for over 90 percent of the records in the database. The remaining 95 tables are used for codes tables or special reporting functions. To improve the performance of queries against the application, you may choose to create tables that contain aggregations of data from the largest table; each of those aggregation tables will be small relative to the largest table. Codes tables will be even smaller. If the application and the end users access the aggregation tables instead of the large transaction tables, your tuning efforts will be focused on tuning access to the aggregation tables.

When you create and manage a large database, the bulk of your effort will likely be devoted to managing the few very large tables that account for the majority of the rows. The database configuration tips provided in this section include methods for transparently splitting the large table into smaller (more easily managed) tables and distributing the I/O requirements of the large table across many devices.

Sizing Large Databases

When creating a large database, categorize each table you will be creating according to the following types:

- **Small codes table**   A codes table rarely increases in size.

- **Large business transactions table**   This type of table accounts for the majority of the records in the database. It may increase in size over time.

Even if it does not increase in size over time, it experiences a high volume of transactions.

- **Aggregation table** This type of table may increase in size over time or may remain at a constant size, depending on your application design. Ideally, it does not increase in size over time. Its data is based on aggregations of data from the large transaction tables.

- **Temporary work table** A temporary work table is used during data load processing and bulk data manipulation.

In the following sections, you will see sizing and configuration advice for each type of table.

Sizing Codes Tables

A codes table contains a list of codes and descriptions, such as a list of country abbreviations and country names. A codes table should be fairly constant in size.

Since a codes table's data may be very static, you should be able to properly size the codes table and not have to worry about it becoming fragmented over time. If the codes tables are small, you should be able to create them with the proper storage parameters so that each table fits in a single extent. If there are multiple codes tables with the same relative size, you can place them in a tablespace whose default storage parameters are correct for the codes tables. For example, if all of your codes tables require between 500KB and 1MB, you may store them all in the CODES_TABLES tablespace.

```
create tablespace CODES_TABLES
datafile '/u01/oracle/VLDB/codes_tables.dbf'
size 10M
extent management local uniform size 1M;
```

If you create a table in the CODES_TABLES tablespace, the table will use the default storage parameters for the tablespace unless you specify values of your own. In this example, each table created in CODES_TABLES that uses the default storage values will have an initial extent 1MB in size, and all subsequent extents will be 1MB in size. Having all of the extents the same size maximizes the likelihood that a dropped extent will be reused. If you must use differently sized extents, they should be sized to maximize the reuse of dropped extents. A common strategy for extent sizing is to use extent sizes of 1MB, 2MB, 4MB, 8MB, 16MB, and so on.

As part of the **default storage** clause for the CODES_TABLES tablespace, the **pctfree** setting is set very low. The low setting for **pctfree** means that very little space will be held free in each database block for subsequent **update**s. In general, codes table values are rarely **update**d (for example, country names do not change frequently). If one of your codes tables has values that are frequently **update**d, then you will need to set **pctfree** to a higher value to support the space requirements of the **update**s.

Because they have similar storage and usage characteristics, codes tables are frequently stored together. If you have multiple sets of codes tables with varying usage rates, you may need to store them in multiple tablespaces to minimize contention.

You may choose to eliminate codes tables from your database and store static codes values as arrays in your programs. If the codes table data is small and static, then hardcoding the values into programs will have little impact on your long-term maintenance costs. For example, you may have a table that tracks units of measure:

Abbreviation	Unit of Measure
V	Volt
KW	Kilowatt
F	Degrees Fahrenheit

Rather than storing this data in an Oracle table, you can store it in arrays in your programs. In C and C++, you can store the array data in a header file. When the data is stored as arrays, no database access is required to reference the units of measure. If the application required a new unit of measure, the header file for the program would need to be amended and the code regenerated. Modifying the programs to accommodate code value changes may not be a significant maintenance cost, since the programs may have to be edited to create new functions, classes, and procedures to handle the new unit of measure. If you hardcode static code values into your programs, you remove them entirely from the database. You will need to weigh the costs and benefits of this approach for your environment, based on the volatility of your codes table data.

You can use the **cache** option to store such tables in memory, but for a client/server or three-tier application this may be only part of the solution. Even if the data is cached, each access of the database may encounter network latency. A large number of efficient queries, executed repeatedly, can impact the users' perceived performance of the transaction processing system.

Sizing Business Transaction Tables

The business transaction tables store the majority of the data in the database. They store the raw data on which the aggregation tables are based. When sizing the business transaction tables, you first need to understand how historical data is handled within the application. Does the application always store the same volume of data in its transaction tables, or are past records kept indefinitely?

If the business transaction tables always store the same volume of data, sizing the tables is straightforward. You should be able to estimate the number of rows in the table and the size of each row. In large databases, the business transaction tables are typically loaded via batch programs. Thus, you know two things about the data: the size of the input file and the source of data changes.

By analyzing the input file, you should be able to estimate the size of the rows in the business transaction tables. The source of data changes is equally important. If the table is **truncate**d and reloaded with each subsequent data load, then there is no need for a high **pctfree** setting for the table. If records are **update**d, however, you will need to set **pctfree** high enough so that an **update**d row can still fit in its original block. If a row cannot fit in its original block, then Oracle may migrate the row to a new block or cause the row to span multiple blocks.

NOTE
You can use locally managed tablespaces to further ease the space management concerns.

The **pctincrease** value for a table should support the growth pattern of the table. If the table grows at a constant rate, you should use a **pctincrease** of 0. If the table's data volume grows geometrically, you should use a nonzero value for **pctincrease**. For most tables, a **pctincrease** setting of 0 correctly mirrors their growth.

NOTE
In most tables, the number of rows grows at a linear rate—such as 10 rows, then 20, then 30, then 40 for the cumulative number of records. In each case, a constant volume of 10 rows was added. If the number of records increases at a geometric rate, then the number of records added each time could be 10, then 20, then 40, then 80, yielding a cumulative total of 10, then 30, then 70, then 150. For linear growth in the table's space allocation, use a **pctincrease** *value close to 0.*

As of Oracle8, you can partition a large business transaction table into multiple smaller tables. When you split a table into partitions, you need to size each of the partitions. Correctly sizing partitions requires that you know the distribution of data values within the table. Since the data is typically loaded in batches, the data distribution information may already be available to you prior to loading the data. The creation of partitions is described in the "Partitions" section later in this chapter.

Sizing Aggregation Tables
An aggregation table stores summaries of the data in the business transaction table. Materialized views are commonly used as the basis for the aggregations. Aggregations are usually designed to improve the performance of frequently accessed screens or

reports within an application. Most users of an application rarely need to see the detailed business transaction data. By storing the aggregations of the business transaction tables' data in aggregation tables, you can achieve two goals:

- Improving the performance of queries against the application. You don't want your database to have to support users who frequently perform aggregation operations (**SUM**, **MIN**, **MAX**, **AVG**, for example) of the largest table in your database. If you store the aggregated data in its own set of tables, then the users query the smaller, customized aggregation tables instead of the huge transaction data.

- Reducing the number of times the business transaction tables are accessed. The aggregation tables are created and refreshed via batch processes, so the business transaction tables are only accessed via batch programs. The reduction in the number of accesses significantly improves your ability to maintain, load, alter, and manage the business transaction tables. For example, if users only directly access aggregation tables, you can **truncate** or index the business transaction table without affecting the availability of the application.

If the business transaction table grows in size over time, then the aggregation tables may grow in size over time. However, it is more common for the aggregation tables to grow in number, not size, over time. For example, you may create an aggregation table that holds the sales data for a particular time period, such as the first sales period after a product is launched. Where do you store data for the next time period? You can either expand the existing aggregation table, or you can create a new table to hold the new data. If the data is placed in a new table (as is often the case), you should be able to accurately predict the data volume of the new table based on the storage requirements of the existing aggregation tables. If the new data is stored in an existing aggregation table, you will need to estimate the number of periods' worth of data to be stored in a single aggregation table. If there is no limit to the data volume in the aggregation tables, those tables will eventually become large and the performance and management of those tables may become problematic.

Sizing Temporary Work Tables
A temporary work table is used during the processing of batch data loads. For example, you may use a loading process that performs no constraint checking of the incoming data. Prior to loading the new data into the business transaction table, you should "clean" the data to make sure it is correct and acceptable. Since batch loads typically use outside data sources, some of the records to be inserted may fail your system's criteria. You can either apply the logic checks during the data load or, if you use temporary work tables, following the data load.

Applying the data-cleaning logic following the data load allows you to tune the data load for very rapid processing of rows. However, it increases the amount of space required within the database since the data must be stored in a separate table prior to being loaded into the production business transaction tables. The temporary work tables should be stored in a tablespace apart from any production tables, and their size should match the space required to hold the records from a data load.

In addition to allocating space for the temporary work tables, you should allocate space for any indexes you will create on those tables during the data loading and validation process.

Sizing Other Database Areas

In addition to the space required by the production tables and their associated indexes, you also need to provide adequate space for other core database objects: the data dictionary, rollback segments (or undo tablespace), and temporary segments.

The data dictionary is stored in the SYSTEM tablespace. The source code for packages, procedures, functions, triggers, and methods is stored in the data dictionary tables. If your application makes extensive use of these objects, you may need to increase the space available to the SYSTEM tablespace. The use of auditing (see Chapter 10) also increases the potential space usage within the SYSTEM tablespace. The SYSTEM tablespace should be created with **autoextend** on so it can grow as necessary.

Rollback segments and undo tablespaces support the transactions within the database. In a large database, there are typically three distinct types of transactions: large batch loads, batch aggregations, and small user-generated transactions. The batch transactions should be supported by large, dedicated tablespaces (such as dedicated rollback segments that are offline at other times). See Chapter 7 for information on determining the required number, size, and structure of objects needed to support your transactions. As of Oracle9i, you can use System Managed Undo instead of rollback segments to simplify undo management.

Oracle creates temporary segments during the processing of sorting operations. The initial data load may use temporary segments if you use the SQL*Loader Direct Path option and the loaded table is indexed. In general, most of the temporary segment activity in a large database comes from the aggregation processing and the creation of indexes. When estimating the required size of a temporary segment, first estimate the size of the table or index being created. For instance, suppose the aggregation table being created will be 50MB in size. Next, multiply that size by four. For the aggregation table being created, you should be able to support a temporary segment that is 200MB in size. The temporary segment will be created in the user's temporary tablespace, using the default storage parameters for the tablespace, so you need to make sure that those storage values are large enough to support the aggregations and sorting operations performed.

NOTE
If you are using the SQL*Loader Direct Path loading option, your temporary segments must be large enough to store the indexes used by the tables being loaded.

Sizing Support Areas

Outside of the database, there are several types of files that may use considerable disk space; you need to plan for this area prior to implementing your system.

- You may need space for the raw datafiles to be loaded. Unless you are loading data directly from a tape or CD, you will likely be storing raw datafiles on the disks of your system.

- You may need space for file processing that occurs before the data is loaded into the database. For example, it is common to sort the data prior to loading it; you therefore need space for both the original file and the sorted version of that file.

- You may be required to keep the files online for a set period of time. Ensure there is enough space to hold multiple sets of files, and that old files are removed when they are no longer required to be online.

- You may choose to use the external table capability introduced in Oracle9*i*. When using external tables, the data is stored in files outside of the database.

- Depending on your backup strategy, you may need disk space available for archived redo log files or export files. You will see details on backup strategies for large databases in the "Backups" section of this chapter.

The sizes for these support areas vary depending on your implementation of your application and your backup strategies. Prior to finalizing your space estimate for the new system, be sure to finalize the size of the nondatabase areas you will need.

Choosing a Physical Layout

In implementing the physical layout for a large database, you should have two primary objectives:

- Spread the I/O burden across as many disks as possible.

- Reduce I/O contention among dissimilar types of objects.

In order to spread the I/O burden across many disks, many large systems use RAID arrays of disks. A RAID array treats a set of disks as a single logical volume;

when a file is created within that volume, the operating system spreads the file across the disks. For example, if there are four disks in the RAID array, then the first disk may contain the first block of a file, the second disk may contain the second block, the third disk may contain the third block, and the fourth disk may contain a parity block. If one of the disks is lost due to a media failure, the RAID unit can use the existing disks to reconstruct the missing data.

The more disks there are in the RAID array, the more the I/O burden is distributed. Because they involve writing and maintaining parity information, RAID arrays are usually most effective for write-once, read-many applications. If the data will frequently be updated, you should consider an alternative storage mechanism (such as mirroring, described presently). During an **update** to a data value, for example, a RAID system would need to read the original data block, read the original parity block, and update and write both blocks back to the disk. Many large RAID systems use a disk cache to improve the performance of such operations, but they still may experience performance degradation.

An alternative architecture uses *mirroring*. In a mirrored system, there are multiple copies of each disk maintained by the operating system. For example, there may be Disk1 and a second disk that is a duplicate of Disk1. During reads and writes, the operating system may read or write to either copy of Disk1. The operating system maintains the read consistency of the files on the mirrored disks. Mirroring is effective (for writes as well as for reads), but you will need to double your disk space availability in order to use it.

To reduce I/O contention between dissimilar types of objects, use the strategies described in Chapter 4 to categorize the types of files you will be storing. Then, categorize the tables within your application based on the categories described earlier in this chapter (codes tables, aggregation tables, etc.). You should separate the temporary work tables from their data source (the external data files). You should store the business transaction tables apart from their data source (either the temporary work tables or the external data files). You should store the aggregation tables apart from their data source (the business transaction tables). All of the data tables should be separated from the rollback segments, data dictionary, and temporary segments.

What if you are using RAID devices? In that case, treat each set of RAID disks as a single disk. Store the business transaction tables on a different RAID set than the aggregation tables are stored on. Store the tables' indexes on a different RAID set than the tables.

NOTE
Determining the optimal RAID configuration may require a great deal of interaction with the system administration team. You need to explain the file access patterns of your database to the system administrators, and you need to understand their approach for distributing the I/O burden.

Partitions

You can use partitions to make large tables easier to manage. Partitions dynamically separate the rows in your table into smaller tables. You can query the partitioned data; the data will appear to be together logically, although it is separated physically. Splitting a large table into multiple smaller partitions may improve the performance of maintenance operations, backups, recoveries, transactions, and queries.

The criteria used to determine which rows are stored in which partitions are specified as part of the **create table** command. Dividing a table's data across multiple tables in this manner is called *partitioning* the table; the table that is partitioned is called a *partitioned table*, and the parts are called *partitions*.

The Oracle optimizer will know that the table has been partitioned; as you will see later in this section, you can also specify the partition to use as part of the **from** clause of your queries.

Creating a Partitioned Table

As of Oracle9*i*, Oracle supports multiple types of partitioning: range partitioning, hash partitioning, list partitioning, and composite partitioning. To create a range partitioned table, you must specify the ranges of values to use for the partitions as part of the **create table** command.

Consider the EMPLOYEE table:

```
create table EMPLOYEE (
EmpNo          NUMBER(10) primary key,
Name           VARCHAR2(40),
DeptNo         NUMBER(2),
Salary         NUMBER(7,2),
Birth_Date     DATE,
Soc_Sec_Num    VARCHAR2(9),
State_Code     CHAR(2),
constraint FK_DeptNO foreign key (DeptNo)
   references DEPT(DeptNo),
constraint FK_StateCode foreign key (State_Code)
   references State(State_Code)
);
```

If you will be storing a large number of records in the EMPLOYEE table, you may want to separate the EMPLOYEE rows across multiple tables. To partition the table's records by range, use the **partition by range** clause of the **create table** command. The ranges will determine the values stored in each partition.

The column used as the basis for the partition logic is rarely the primary key for the table. More often, the basis for partitioning is one of the foreign key columns in the table. In the EMPLOYEE table, the DeptNo and State_Code columns are foreign keys. If you frequently query by the DeptNo column, and it makes sense to split the data based on that column, then use it as the partition key. In a system that tracks historical data (such as sales history or salary history), it may be more appropriate to partition the data based on one of the time-based columns (such as sales period or effective date of salary change).

```
create table EMPLOYEE (
EmpNo           NUMBER(10) primary key,
Name            VARCHAR2(40),
DeptNo          NUMBER(2),
Salary          NUMBER(7,2),
Birth_Date      DATE,
Soc_Sec_Num     VARCHAR2(9),
 constraint FK_DeptNO foreign key (DeptNo)
   references DEPT(DeptNo)
)
partition by range (DeptNo)
 (partition PART1   values less than (11)
   tablespace PART1_TS,
  partition PART2   values less than (21)
   tablespace PART2_TS,
  partition PART3   values less than (31)
   tablespace PART3_TS,
  partition PART4   values less than (MAXVALUE)
   tablespace PART4_TS)
;
```

The EMPLOYEE table will be partitioned based on the values in the DeptNo column:

```
partition by range (DeptNo)
```

For any DeptNo values less than 11, the record will be stored in the partition named PART1. The PART1 partition will be stored in the PART1_TS tablespace. Any DeptNo in the range between 11 and 20 will be stored in the PART2 partition; values between 21 and 30 will be stored in the PART3 partition. Any value greater than 30 will be stored in the PART4 partition. Note that in the PART4 partition definition, the range clause is

```
partition PART4   values less than (MAXVALUE)
```

You do not need to specify a maximum value for the last partition; the **maxvalue** keyword tells Oracle to use the partition to store any data that could not be stored in the earlier partitions. For each partition, you only specify the maximum value for the range. The minimum value for the range is implicitly determined by Oracle.

When partitioning a table, you should store the partitions in separate tablespaces. Separating them by tablespace allows you to control their physical storage location and avoid contention between the partitions. Concurrent **insert**s into multiple partitions of the same table will cause performance degradation.

How many partitions should you have? You should have as many partitions as are required to logically separate your data. The additional maintenance work involved in having many partitions is negligible. Focus on dividing the rows of your table into logical groups. If the partition ranges make sense for your application, then they are the ones you should use. If your largest table is 1 terabyte in size, using 100 evenly sized partitions generates 100 partitions that are each 10GB in size. Although a 10GB table is not always simple to manage, it is certainly simpler to manage than a 1 terabyte table is. Use enough partitions to reduce the size of the tables to a size that is easily manageable in your operating system and hardware configuration.

> **NOTE**
> *You cannot partition object tables or tables that use LOB datatypes.*

QUERYING DIRECTLY FROM PARTITIONS   If you know the partition from which you will be retrieving your data, you can specify the name of the partition as part of the **from** clause of your query. For example, what if you wanted to query the records for the employees in Departments 11 through 20? The optimizer should be able to use the partition definitions to determine that only the PART2 partition could contain data that can resolve this query. If you wish, you can tell Oracle to use PART2 as part of your query.

```
select *
  from EMPLOYEE partition (PART2)
 where DeptNo between 11 and 20;
```

This example explicitly names the partition in which Oracle is to search for the matching employee records. If the partition is modified (for example, if its range of values is altered), then PART2 may no longer be the partition that contains the needed records. Thus, you should use great care when using this syntax. You can obtain a list of partition names from the USER_TAB_PARTITIONS view if you own the base table or from ALL_TAB_PARTITIONS if you do not own the table.

In general, listing the partition name explicitly is not necessary because Oracle knows the highest value that can be in each partition (via the HiBoundVal column value in SYS.TABPART$). When you query from the partitioned table, Oracle uses the partition range value information to determine which partitions should be involved in resolving the query. Partition elimination may result in a small number of rows being searched for the query, improving query performance. Additionally, the partitions may be stored in different tablespaces (and thus on separate disk devices), helping to reduce the potential for disk I/O contention during the processing of the query.

During an **insert** into the partitioned table, Oracle uses the partitions' range constraints to determine which partition the record should be inserted into. Thus, you can use a partitioned table as if it were a single table, and rely on Oracle to manage the internal separation of the data.

Indexing Partitions

When you create a partitioned table, you should create an index on the table. The index may be partitioned according to the same range values that were used to partition the table. In the following listing, the **create index** command for the EMPLOYEE table is shown:

```
create index EMPLOYEE_DEPTNO
   on EMPLOYEE(DeptNo)
    local
    (partition PART1
      tablespace PART1_NDX_TS,
     partition PART2
      tablespace PART2_NDX_TS,
     partition PART3
      tablespace PART3_NDX_TS,
     partition PART4
      tablespace PART4_NDX_TS);
```

Notice the **local** keyword. In this **create index** command, no ranges are specified. Instead, the **local** keyword tells Oracle to create a separate index for each partition of the EMPLOYEE table. There were four partitions created on EMPLOYEE. The EMPLOYEE_DEPTNO index will create four separate indexes—one for each partition. Since there is one index per partition, the indexes are "local" to the partitions.

Local indexes mimic the way indexes traditionally work in Oracle; a single index applies to only one table. If you use local partitions, you can manage the index along with its matching table.

You can also create "global" indexes. A global index may contain values from multiple partitions. The index itself may be partitioned, as shown in this example:

```
create index EMPLOYEE_DEPTNO
 on EMPLOYEE(Name)
  global partition by range (Name)
  (partition PART1   values less than ('J')
    tablespace PART1_NDX_TS,
   partition PART2   values less than ('N')
    tablespace PART2_NDX_TS,
```

```
partition PART3   values less than ('R')
 tablespace PART3_NDX_TS,
partition PART4   values less than (MAXVALUE)
 tablespace PART4_NDX_TS);
```

NOTE
*You would not normally create global indexes
partitioned on the same column and with the same
range as the table is partitioned. Local indexes
would be much better, with fewer invalidations.*

The **global** clause in this **create index** command allows you to specify ranges
for the index values that are different from the ranges for the table partitions. In this
case, the same partition ranges were used. Even though the same partition ranges
are used for both the table and the global index, the index partitions are not directly
related to the table partitions. Instead, the index partitions are part of a global index
whose values span all of the table partitions. There is a direct relationship between
table partitions and index partitions only when the index is a local index.

In most cases, you should use local index partitions. If you use local partitions of
your indexes, you will be able to easily relate index partitions to table partitions.
Local indexes are simpler to manage than global indexes since they represent only a
portion of the data in the partitioned table. In the next section, you will see other
aspects of partition management.

Managing Partitions

You can use the **alter table** command to **add**, **drop**, **exchange**, **move**, **modify**,
rename, **split**, and **truncate** partitions. These commands allow you to alter the
existing partition structure, as may be required after a partitioned table has been
used heavily. For example, the distribution of the DeptNo values within the
partitioned table may have changed or the maximum value may have increased.
Note that when you **split** a partition without using the **into** clause to specify
partition characteristics, Oracle will create two new partitions in its place, and
neither will have the same name as the old partition.

For the full syntax of the **alter table** command, see Appendix A.

You can use the **alter table** command to manage the storage parameters of the
partitions. When the EMPLOYEE table was partitioned earlier in this chapter, no
storage parameters were specified for its partitions. For example, the first partition,
PART1, was assigned to the PART1_TS tablespace, with no **storage** clause.

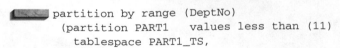

```
partition by range (DeptNo)
  (partition PART1   values less than (11)
    tablespace PART1_TS,
```

The PART1 partition will use the default storage for the PART1_TS tablespace. If you wish to use different storage parameters, you must either specify them when the table is created (via a **storage** clause) or alter the partition's storage after it has been created.

For example, the following command changes the storage parameters for the PART1 partition of the EMPLOYEE table:

```
alter table EMPLOYEE
    modify partition PART1
    storage (next 1M pctincrease 0);
```

You can **truncate** partitions, leaving the rest of the table's partitions unaffected, as shown here:

```
alter table EMPLOYEE
   truncate partition PART3
   drop storage;
```

When you **truncate** a partition, its local indexes are also **truncate**d.

You can also use the **alter table** command to move partitions to new tablespaces, split existing partitions into multiple new partitions, exchange partitions, drop partitions, and add new partitions.

For index partitions, the options are more limited. The partition-related syntax for the **alter index** command is shown in Appendix A. You can use the **alter index** command to modify an index partition's storage or rename, drop, split, or rebuild the partition. You can use the partition-related extensions to the **alter index** command to manage the index partitions the same way you manage normal indexes. For example, you can rebuild an existing index partition via the **rebuild partition** clause of the **alter index** command.

```
alter index EMPLOYEE_DEPTNO
rebuild partition PART4
storage (initial 2M next 2M pctincrease 0);
```

When you use the **rebuild** option for an index or an index partition, you must have enough storage space available to simultaneously hold both the old index and the new index and additional space to hold transaction information if you rebuild it online.

Managing Subpartitions

You can create subpartitions—partitions of partitions. You can use subpartitions to combine two separate types of partitions: range partitions and hash partitions.

A hash partition, like a hash cluster, determines the physical placement of data by performing a hash function on the values of the partition key. In range partitioning, consecutive values of the partition key are usually stored in the same partition. In hash partitioning, consecutive values of the partition key are not necessarily stored in the same partition. Hash partitioning distributes a set of records over a greater set of partitions than range partitioning does, potentially decreasing the likelihood for I/O contention.

To create a hash partition, use the **partition by hash** clause in place of the **partition by range** clause, as shown in the following listing:

```
create table EMPLOYEE (
EmpNo           NUMBER(10) primary key,
Name            VARCHAR2(40),
DeptNo          NUMBER(2),
Salary          NUMBER(7,2),
Birth_Date      DATE,
Soc_Sec_Num     VARCHAR2(9),
 constraint FK_DeptNO foreign key (DeptNo)
   references DEPT(DeptNo)
)
partition by hash (DeptNo)
partitions 10;
```

You can name each partition and specify its tablespace, just as you would for range partitioning, as shown here:

```
create table EMPLOYEE (
EmpNo           NUMBER(10) primary key,
Name            VARCHAR2(40),
DeptNo          NUMBER(2),
Salary          NUMBER(7,2),
Birth_Date      DATE,
Soc_Sec_Num     VARCHAR2(9),
 constraint FK_DeptNO foreign key (DeptNo)
   references DEPT(DeptNo)
)
partition by hash (DeptNo)
partitions 2
store in (PART1_TS, PART2_TS);
```

Following the **partition by hash (DeptNo)** line, you have two choices for format:

■ As shown in the preceding listing, you can specify the number of partitions and the tablespaces to use:

```
partitions 2
store in (PART1_TS, PART2_TS);
```

This method will create partitions with system-generated names of the format SYS_P*nnn*. The number of tablespaces specified in the **store in** clause does not have to equal the number of partitions. If more partitions than tablespaces are specified, the partitions will be assigned to the tablespaces in a round-robin fashion.

■ You can specify named partitions:

```
partition by hash (DeptNo)
(partition P1 tablespace P1_TS,
 partition P2 tablespace P2_TS);
```

In this method, each partition is given a name and a tablespace, with the option of using an additional **lob** or **varray** storage clause. Specifying named partitions gives you more control over the location of the partitions, with the added benefit of letting you specify meaningful names for the partitions.

NOTE
You cannot create global indexes for hash partitions.

You can use hash partitions in combination with range partitions, creating hash partitions of the range partitions. For very large tables, this composite partitioning may be an effective way of separating the data into manageable and tunable divisions.

The following example range partitions the EMPLOYEE table by the DeptNo column, and hash partitions the DeptNo partitions by Name values:

```
create table EMPLOYEE (
EmpNo           NUMBER(10) primary key,
Name            VARCHAR2(40),
DeptNo          NUMBER(2),
Salary          NUMBER(7,2),
Birth_Date      DATE,
Soc_Sec_Num     VARCHAR2(9),
 constraint FK_DeptNO foreign key (DeptNo)
   references DEPT(DeptNo)
)
partition by range (DeptNo)
subpartition by hash (Name)
subpartitions 10
 (partition PART1   values less than (11)
   tablespace PART1_TS,
  partition PART2   values less than (21)
   tablespace PART2_TS,
  partition PART3   values less than (31)
   tablespace PART3_TS,
  partition PART4   values less than (MAXVALUE)
   tablespace PART4_TS);
```

The EMPLOYEE table will be range partitioned into four partitions, using the ranges specified for the four named partitions. Each of those partitions will be hash partitioned on the Name column.

List Partitions

As of Oracle9*i*, you can use list partitioning—partitioning rows based on a list of values rather than a range of values. As shown in the following listing, list partitioning is a limited version of range partitioning. In this example, state and province codes are grouped according to geographic region.

```
create table LOCATIONS
  ( Location_ID     NUMBER,
    Street_Address VARCHAR2(25),
    Postal_Code     NUMBER(10),
    City            VARCHAR2(25),
    State_Province VARCHAR2(2),
    Country_ID      VARCHAR2(10))
partition by list (State_Province)
  ( partition REGION_EAST
    VALUES ('MA','NY','CT','NH','ME','MD','VA','PA','NJ')
  , partition REGION_WEST
    VALUES ('CA','AZ','NM','OR','WA','UT','NV','CO')
  , partition REGION_SOUTH
    VALUES ('TX','KY','TN','LA','MS','AR','AL','GA')
  , partition REGION_CENTRAL
    VALUES ('OH','ND','SD','MO','IL','MI', NULL, 'IA')
  );
```

When partitioning a table based on a list, you can only specify one partitioning key column in the **partition by list** clause. You cannot specify **maxvalue** as a list partition value.

NOTE
You cannot list partition an index-organized table.

Creating Materialized Views

A materialized view is a table that stores derived data. During its creation, you specify the SQL used to populate the materialized view. Materialized views are useful as aggregations, since they store replicated data and provide an internal data refresh capability.

For a large database, a materialized view may offer several performance advantages. Depending on the complexity of the base SQL, you may be able to populate the materialized view with incremental changes (via a materialized view log) instead of completely re-creating it during data refreshes.

Materialized views can be used dynamically by the optimizer to change the execution paths for queries. This feature, called query rewrite, enables the optimizer to use a materialized view in place of the table queried by the materialized view, even if the materialized view is not named in the query. For example, if you have a large SALES table, you may create a materialized view that sums the SALES data by region. If a user queries the SALES table for the sum of the SALES data for a region, Oracle can redirect that query to use your materialized view in place of the SALES table. As a result, you can reduce the number of accesses against your largest tables, improving the system performance.

To enable a materialized view for query rewrite, all of the master tables for the materialized view must be in the materialized view's schema, and you must have the QUERY REWRITE system privilege. If the view and the tables are in separate schemas, you must have the GLOBAL QUERY REWRITE system privilege. In general, you should create materialized views in the same schema as the tables on which they are based; otherwise, you will need to manage the permissions and grants required to create and maintain the materialized view.

A materialized view creates a local table to store the data and a view that accesses that data. Depending on the complexity of the materialized view, Oracle may also create an index on the materialized view's local table. You can index the materialized view's local table to improve the performance of queries against the materialized view.

To create a materialized view, use the **create materialized view** command (see Appendix A for the full syntax of this command). The example shown in the following listing creates a materialized view against the SALES table:

```
create materialized view SALES_MONTH_MV
tablespace AGG_DATA
refresh complete
start with sysdate
next sysdate+1
enable query rewrite
as
select  SALES.Sales_Month,
        PRODUCT.Product_Type,
        CUSTOMER.Customer_Type,
        SUM(SALES.Amount)
  from SALES, PRODUCT, CUSTOMER
 where SALES.Product_ID=PRODUCT.Product_ID
   and SALES.Customer_ID=CUSTOMER.Customer_ID
 group by SALES.Sales_Month,
        PRODUCT.Product_Type, CUSTOMER.Customer_Type;
```

As shown in the preceding listing, the **create materialized view** command specifies the name of the view and its refresh schedule. In this example, a complete refresh of the view is chosen—each time the view is refreshed, its data will be completely deleted and re-created. For views that are not based on aggregations, you can use fast refreshes in combination with materialized view logs to send only incremental changes to the materialized view. The **start with** and **next** clauses tell Oracle when to schedule refreshes of the data. The data will be automatically refreshed if you have enabled background job processes (via the JOB_QUEUE_ PROCESSES initialization parameter). The **tablespace** clause tells Oracle where to store the local table for the materialized view. The **enable query rewrite** clause enables the optimizer to redirect queries of SALES to SALES_MONTH_MV if appropriate.

To enable query rewrites to occur, set the QUERY_REWRITE_ENABLED initialization parameter to TRUE. If the database is currently open, you can change the QUERY_REWRITE_ENABLED parameter value via the **alter session** and **alter system** commands.

Fast refreshes of materialized views use *materialized view logs*. A materialized view log is a table stored along with the master table for the materialized view. As rows change in the master table, the changes are written to the materialized view log. During a fast refresh, the changed rows from the master table, as identified via the materialized view log, are sent to the materialized view. If the changes account for less than 25 percent of the rows in the master table, a fast refresh is generally faster than a complete refresh. For the full syntax of the **create materialized view log** command, see Appendix A.

Creating and Managing Index-Organized Tables

An *index-organized table* keeps its data sorted according to the primary key column values for the table. Index-organized tables store their data as if the entire table was stored in an index. A normal index only stores the indexed columns in the index; an index-organized table stores all of the table's columns in the index.

Because the table's data is stored as an index, the rows of the table do not have RowIDs. Therefore, you cannot select the RowID pseudocolumn values from an index-organized table. As of Oracle8*i*, you can create secondary indexes on an index-organized table.

To create an index-organized table, use the **organization index** clause of the **create table** command, as shown in the following example:

```
create table STATE (
State_Code      CHAR(2) primary key,
Description     VARCHAR2(25)
)
organization index;
```

In order to create STATE as an index-organized table, you must create a PRIMARY KEY constraint on it, as shown in the example. When you create STATE as an index-organized table, its data is stored in sorted order (sorted by the primary key values).

An index-organized table will require less space than if the data were stored in a normal table. Within the index, no RowID values are stored (since the table has none), so it also takes less space than an index would if the index contained all of the columns of the table.

Creating and Managing External Tables

As of Oracle9i, you can create metadata pointing to external files. Based on the metadata definitions, you can then access the data within the external files as if it exists in read-only tables within the database. You can define loading parameters for the data (very similar to SQL*Loader), enabling you to perform **insert as select** operations based on the external data. Because the data is accessed via a table structure, you can apply **where** clauses to the data during queries.

To access external data, you must first create a directory within the database, as you would if you use the BFILE datatype. The **create directory** command, as shown in the following listing, allows Oracle to find files in specific operating system directories. Oracle does not manage the files in those directories.

```
create directory state_dir as '/u01/files';
```

To create an external table, use the **organization external** option of the **create table** command. Following the **organization external** clause, specify the parameters used to separate the data within the file. For STATE data that has two characters (the state abbreviation) followed by comma and the description, the **create table** command may be

```
create table STATE_EXTERNAL
(State_Code CHAR(2),
Description VARCHAR2(25))
organization external
 ( type ORACLE_LOADER
   default directory (state_dir)
   access parameters ( FIELDS TERMINATED BY ','
                       BADFILE 'files/bad_states'
   logfile 'files/log_states' ( State_Code CHAR, DESCRIPTION CHAR))
   location ('state_dir/state.txt') )
reject limit 25;
```

The **reject limit** clause sets the maximum number of errors that can be encountered before a query fails. Once the STATE_EXTERNAL table has been created, you can select data from it into relational tables. For best performance, you should order the external data by the indexed columns in the database tables prior to starting the load.

Creating and Managing Global Temporary Tables

You can create temporary tables whose data is only accessible by the session that creates the data. The **create global temporary table** command accepts the standard column definitions used for creating tables, along with the **on commit delete rows** or **on commit preserve rows** clauses. If you elect to delete rows on commit, the table's data will be transaction specific and each **commit** will be followed by a **truncate**. If the rows are preserved on commit, they will not be truncated until the session ends. You can index temporary tables.

The command shown in the following listing creates a temporary table used as a work area for a data loading session:

```
create global temporary table STATE_WORK
(State_Code CHAR(2),
Description VARCHAR2(25))
on commit preserve rows;
```

For transactions increasing in number of rows and row length, the redo generated for a global temporary tables remains fairly constant, while the redo generated for standard tables increases.

Creating and Managing Bitmap Indexes

Normally, indexes are created on columns that are very selective; that is, there are very few rows that have the same value for the column. A column whose values are only ever Y or N is a very poor candidate for B*-tree index because the index contains only two unique values, so any access via that column will return an average of half of the table. However, if the values in those columns belong to a fairly static group of values, then you should consider using bitmap indexes for them.

For example, if there are very few distinct State_Code values in a very large EMPLOYEE table, then you would not usually create a B*-tree index on State_Code, even if it is commonly used in **where** clauses. However, State_Code may be able to take advantage of a bitmap index.

Internally, a bitmap index maps the distinct values for the columns to each record. For this example, assume there are only two State_Code values (NH and DE) in a very large EMPLOYEE table. Since there are two State_Code values, there are two separate bitmap entries for the State_Code bitmap index. If the first five rows in the table have a

State_Code value of DE and the next five have a State_Code value of NH, the
State_Code bitmap entries would resemble those shown in the following listing:

```
State_Code bitmaps:
     DE:  < 1 1 1 1 1 0 0 0 0 0 >
     NH:  < 0 0 0 0 0 1 1 1 1 1 >
```

In the preceding listing, each number represents a row in the EMPLOYEE table.
Since there are ten rows considered, there are ten bitmap values shown. Reading
the bitmap for State_Code, the first five records have a value of DE (the 1 values),
and the next five do not (the 0 values). You could have more than two possible
values for the column, in which case there would be a separate bitmap entry for
each possible value.

The Oracle optimizer can dynamically convert bitmap index entries to RowIDs
during query processing. This conversion capability allows the optimizer to use
indexes on columns that have many distinct values (via B*-tree indexes) and those
that have few distinct values (via bitmap indexes).

To create a bitmap index, use the **bitmap** clause of the **create index** command,
as shown in the following listing. You should indicate its status as a bitmap index
within the index name so that it will be easy to detect during tuning operations.

```
create bitmap index EMPLOYEE$STATE_CODE$BMAP
    on EMPLOYEE(State_Code);
```

If you choose to use bitmap indexes, you will need to weigh the performance
benefit during queries against the performance cost during data manipulation
commands. The more bitmap indexes there are on a table, the greater the cost will be
during each transaction. You should not use bitmap indexes on a column that
frequently has new values added to it. Each addition of a new value to the State_Code
column will require that a new bitmap be created for the new State_Code value.

When creating bitmap indexes, Oracle compresses the bitmaps that are stored. As
a result, the space required for a bitmap index may be only 20 to 30 percent of the
space required for a normal B*-tree index. You should consider using bitmap indexes
for any nonselective column that is frequently used in **where** clauses, provided the set
of values for the column is limited. If there are new values frequently added to the
column's list of values, then the bitmaps will have to be constantly adjusted.

Within a large database, bitmap indexes will yield the biggest impact when
used on columns in the business transaction and aggregation tables; larger tables
typically benefit from bitmap indexing strategies. You can create both bitmap
indexes and normal (B*-tree) indexes on the same table, and Oracle will perform
any necessary index conversions dynamically during query processing.

Bitmap indexes are usually not suitable for tables that are involved in many **insert**, **update**, and **delete** operations. A single bitmap index entry against a column with few unique values will contain references to several RowIDs, and thus several rows will be locked during transactions that **update** the bitmap. The locking of rows for bitmap index **update**s may significantly degrade performance of DML operations. The same performance penalty is not suffered when bitmap indexes are used as part of query-intensive decision support systems.

Using Bitmap Join Indexes

As of Oracle9*i*, you can create bitmap join indexes. A bitmap join index is similar in concept to a cluster of two indexes; RowIDs from multiple tables are stored prejoined in an index. For data warehouses with static data, bitmap join indexes offer an efficient way of processing query requests that frequently span a small set of tables. If your fact tables are frequently joined to a set of dimension tables, you may create bitmap join indexes that join the key values from the fact to dimension tables. Queries that use those joins will then be able to take advantage of the bitmap join index and avoid more costly table or index lookups.

Managing Transactions

In a large database, batch data loads usually account for the bulk of the transactions. There may be small transactions within your large database, but most of the transactions will not be generated by individual users. When managing the transactions within a large database, you should pay special attention to the batch transactions involved in loading and aggregating the data.

The timing of your batch transactions is critical. Executing large batch operations concurrently with small online transactions is a common cause of rollback segment–related problems in the database. Additionally, a batch process (such as SQL*Loader Direct Path loading or the OCI direct loading option) using a direct load option will put indexes into a load state. While the indexes are in a load state, online **update**s to the table will fail.

Ideally, the batch loads should be executed when there is no online processing occurring. The more you can isolate the batch-load transactions, the more likely they will be to succeed.

Configuring the Batch Transaction Environment

In the following sections, you will see management advice for loading and deleting data from the large tables in your database. Prior to performing large batch transactions, you must create an environment that is capable of supporting the transactions.

Create Dedicated Rollback Segments

The rollback segments used by batch transactions have different characteristics than those used by transactions entered by online application users. Instead of having many small transactions, batch systems tend to have few, larger transactions. Therefore, your rollback segments that support the batch transactions will typically be few in number and have larger extent sizes than those that support online users. For example, you may have ten rollback segments with 20 extents each to support your online users, but only a single large rollback segment with 10 extents to support the batch transaction.

To force a transaction to use a particular rollback segment, use the

```
set transaction use rollback segment SEGMENT_NAME;
```

command within SQL*Plus. This command should immediately follow logging onto a session or issuing a **rollback** or **commit** command. You will need to provide the name of the rollback segment you will be using for the transaction. If you are working with multiple databases, you should standardize the names of your batch transaction rollback segments to simplify your load processing. For example, you could call the batch data load rollback segment ROLL_BATCH in each database. If you use a consistent naming standard, you won't have to alter your data loading programs as you move from one database to another.

Disable Archiving of Redo Logs

Archiving the contents of your online redo log files allows you to recover in the event of a media failure. However, consider the transactions that are being written to the online redo log files during the batch load: they are the **insert**s that are occurring because of the data load. If you can completely re-create those **insert**s by reexecuting your data load, then you do not need to enable archiving of the transactions.

For example, if you are already running in ARCHIVELOG mode, you could shut the database down prior to the data load (which we'll call time T1). Start the database in NOARCHIVELOG mode (point in time T2). Execute the data load until it completes (time T3). Then, shut down and restart the database in ARCHIVELOG mode. If a media failure occurs prior to time T1, you can use the archived redo log files to recover your data. If it fails between time T2 and time T3, you can recover from that as well: recover to time T1 and reexecute the data load. At time T3, take a new backup of the database.

If you turn off the archiving of online redo log files during your data load, you need to make sure that no other transactions are occurring during your data load. If other transactions are occurring at the same time, their data may be lost during a recovery. You can use the **nologging** parameter to avoid logging transactions against specific tables or parts of tables, as described in the next section.

Disable Logging for the Large Tables

When you create a table using the **nologging** keyword, the transactions that initially populate the table are not written to the online redo log when you use commands like **create table as select**. Additionally, any subsequent SQL*Loader Direct Path loads and any **insert** commands using the APPEND hint will not write redo log entries to the online redo log files.

> **NOTE**
> *You do not have to create the table with the*
> ***nologging*** *option to bypass logging when doing*
> *direct loads; it is automatic.*

You can target specific tables (such as your large business transaction tables or the aggregation tables) for no logging. Being able to avoid writing these transactions to the online redo log files allows you to keep the full database in ARCHIVELOG state while the largest tables are essentially in NOARCHIVELOG state. You can also specify **nologging** for the LOB portions of tables that use BLOB or CLOB datatypes if you specify **nocache** in the LOB storage clause.

Rebuild Indexes after Data Loads

Efficient indexes are the key to fast data access in a large database. To maximize their efficiency, you should rebuild your indexes after every major data load. You can use the **rebuild** clause of the **alter index** command to build a new index that uses the old index as its data source.

Even if you use the SQL*Loader Direct Path option (while leaving the indexes on during the data load), you should still periodically rebuild your indexes. If you are not using that load option, then you should drop your indexes prior to the data load and then re-create them once the load completes.

The same advice holds true for mass deletions and **update**s: if many index values have been **delete**d or **update**d, you should rebuild the indexes. The better organized an index is, the faster the associated data access will be.

Loading Data

When loading data from files into your business transaction tables, you should try to eliminate factors that can slow down **insert**s. You should disable the constraints on the table and disable any triggers on the table (although batch-loaded tables should typically not have triggers), and you should drop indexes prior to the data load. If you do not drop the indexes and the data is sorted prior to loading, you can use the SQL*Loader Direct Path option. In addition to managing indexes, this option allows you to insert entire blocks at a time rather than performing one **insert** per row. If the partition or table being loaded via the Direct Path load is marked as **nologging**, the loaded blocks are not written to the redo log files.

During a normal **insert** of a row, Oracle checks the list of free blocks in the table—those new blocks that have more than **pctfree** space left in them. Oracle finds the first block that can hold the record and **insert**s it. For the next record, Oracle performs the search for free space again. The search is repeated for each record. SQL*Loader Direct Path avoids the cost of these searches by inserting entire blocks of data at a time.

To know where to load data, SQL*Loader first determines the *high-water mark* of the table. The high-water mark is the highest-numbered block that has ever held data in the table. For example, if you load 1000 blocks' worth of rows into the table and then **delete** the rows, the high-water mark will point to block number 1000. During a SQL*Loader Direct Path insert, Oracle does not search for open space in currently used blocks. Instead, it loads blocks of data at the first block after the high-water mark. If there is space available below the high-water mark, the SQL*Loader Direct Path option will not use it.

There are only two ways to reset the high-water mark for a table: drop and re-create the table or **truncate** the table. Thus, you need to be aware of the methods used to **delete** records from a table. If you load 1000 blocks' worth of rows into a table and later **delete** them, the high-water mark is left unchanged. A subsequent SQL*Loader Direct Path load of the same data would use 1000 blocks—starting at block 1001. Instead of using 1000 blocks, the table would now use 2000 blocks.

In addition to allowing you to use the very efficient Direct Path option, SQL*Loader also has options for parallel operations and unlogged operations. See the "Tuning" section later in this chapter for further details on parallel operations. See the "Disable Logging for the Large Tables" section earlier in this chapter for information on the **nologging** parameter.

Inserting Data

If the data being **insert**ed is from another table (such as an **insert as select** used to populate an aggregation table), you can take advantage of the APPEND hint. APPEND uses the high-water mark as the basis for **insert**s of blocks of data, the same way SQL*Loader Direct Path does (see the previous section of this chapter for a discussion of high-water marks).

The APPEND hint tells Oracle to find the last block into which the table's data has been **insert**ed. The new records will be **insert**ed starting in the next block following the high-water mark.

For instance, if a table had previously used 20 blocks within the database, an **insert** command that used the APPEND hint would start writing its data in the 21st block. Since the data is being written into new blocks of the table, there is much less space management work for the database to do during the **insert**. Therefore, the

insert may complete faster when the APPEND hint is used. The table's space requirements may increase because of unused space below the high-water mark.

You specify the APPEND hint within the **insert** command. A hint looks like a comment—it starts with **/*** and ends with ***/**. The only difference in syntax is that the starting set of characters includes a **+** before the name of the hint. The following example shows an **insert** command whose data is appended to the table:

```
insert /*+ APPEND */ into SALES_PERIOD_CUST_AGG
select Period_ID, Customer_ID, SUM(Sales)
  from SALES
 group by Period_ID, Customer_ID;
```

The records from the SALES business transaction table will be **insert**ed into the SALES_PERIOD_CUST_AGG aggregation table. Instead of attempting to reuse previously used space within the SALES_PERIOD_CUST_AGG table, the new records will be placed at the end of the table's physical storage space.

Since the new records will not attempt to reuse available space that the table has already used, the space requirements for the SALES_PERIOD_CUST_AGG table may increase. In general, you should use the APPEND hint only when **insert**ing large volumes of data into tables with little reusable space.

The APPEND hint is ideal for the creation of aggregate tables, since their data source is a table stored elsewhere in the database. Since they store redundant data, aggregate tables are also good candidates for the **nologging** parameter discussed earlier in this chapter. Rows **insert**ed via the APPEND hint do not generate redo log entries if the table being loaded has the **nologging** parameter enabled.

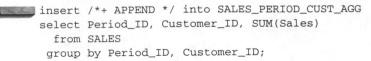

NOTE
Some purchased applications are designed to be database independent and may not use SQL*Loader for data loading. If the application provides an executable that performs loads, check with the vendor or the application support team to make sure array processing is performed during **insert***s. Avoid row-by-row* **insert***s, even in batch mode.*

Deleting Data

When managing large volumes of data, you should try to set up your tables so you can use the **truncate** command. If the data is all stored in a single large table, you should consider using partitions since you can **truncate** partitions via the **alter table** command shown earlier in this chapter. If you need to **delete** large volumes at once via the **delete** command, however, you will either need to configure your environment to support a large transaction, or you will need to use a procedural method to break the transaction into smaller pieces.

Configuring the Environment

The configuration requirements for large **delete**s are identical to those required for large **insert**s; you need to create and maintain a rollback segment that is large enough to support the transaction. To force the rollback segment to be used by the transaction, use the **set transaction use rollback segment** command immediately following a **commit**. You should schedule the bulk **delete** to occur during a time when there are few other transactions occurring in the database to avoid potential read concurrency problems.

Using a Procedural Method

You can use PL/SQL to break a single deletion into multiple transactions. You can create a PL/SQL block that takes as its input the **delete** command and the number of records to **commit** in each batch. For example, if there are one million records to **delete** and you cannot use the **truncate** command, you can force a **commit** after every 1000 records. To do this, you will need to use dynamic PL/SQL and loops. In the following PL/SQL procedure (developed and distributed by Oracle Support), the two input parameters are the SQL statement and the number of records to be committed in each batch. For example, suppose the **delete** command is

```
delete from SALES where Customer_ID=12;
```

and you want to **commit** after each 1000 rows committed. The procedure, named DELETE_COMMIT, will be called with those two parameters, as shown here:

```
execute DELETE_COMMIT('delete from SALES where Customer_ID=12',1000);
```

If the values in the **where** clause are character strings, enclose them in double sets of quotes:

```
execute DELETE_COMMIT('delete from SALES where State_Code = ''NH''',500)
```

The code for the DELETE_COMMIT procedure is shown here:

```
create or replace procedure DELETE_COMMIT
( p_statement in varchar2,
  p_commit_batch_size   in number default 10000)
is
        cid                             integer;
        changed_statement               varchar2(2000);
        finished                        boolean;
```

```
        nofrows                        integer;
        lrowid                         rowid;
        rowcnt                         integer;
        errpsn                         integer;
        sqlfcd                         integer;
        errc                           integer;
        errm                           varchar2(2000);
begin
        /* If the actual statement contains a WHERE clause, then
          append a rownum < n clause after that using N, else
          use WHERE rownum < n clause */
        if ( upper(p_statement) like '% WHERE %') then
                changed_statement := p_statement||' AND rownum < '
||to_char(p_commit_batch_size + 1);
        else
changed_statement := p_statement||' WHERE rownum <
'||to_char(p_commit_batch_size + 1);
        end if;
        begin
  cid := dbms_sql.open_cursor; -- Open a cursor for the task
                dbms_sql.parse(cid,changed_statement, dbms_sql.native);
                        -- parse the cursor.
  rowcnt := dbms_sql.last_row_count;
                        -- store for some future reporting
        exception
          when others then
                        errpsn := dbms_sql.last_error_position;
                        -- gives the error position in the changed sql
                        -- delete statement if anything happens
    sqlfcd := dbms_sql.last_sql_function_code;
                        --function code can be found in the OCI manual
                        lrowid := dbms_sql.last_row_id;
                        -- store all these values for error reporting.
                        -- However all these are really useful in a
                        -- stand-alone proc execution for dbms_output
                        -- to be successful, not possible when called
                        -- from a form or front-end tool.
                        errc := SQLCODE;
                        errm := SQLERRM;
                        dbms_output.put_line('Error '||to_char(errc)||
                                ' Posn '||to_char(errpsn)||
            ' SQL fCode '||to_char(sqlfcd)||
        ' rowid '||rowidtochar(lrowid));
                        raise_application_error(-20000,errm);
                        -- this will ensure the display of at least
                        -- the error message if something happens,
                        -- even in a front-end tool.
        end;
```

```
        finished := FALSE;
        while not (finished)
        loop -- keep on executing the cursor till there is no more
              -- to process.
                begin
    nofrows := dbms_sql.execute(cid);
                      rowcnt := dbms_sql.last_row_count;
              exception
                  when others then
                        errpsn := dbms_sql.last_error_position;
                      sqlfcd := dbms_sql.last_sql_function_code;
                        lrowid := dbms_sql.last_row_id;
                          errc := SQLCODE;
                          errm := SQLERRM;
                dbms_output.put_line('Error '||to_char(errc)||
                        ' Posn '||to_char(errpsn)||
              ' SQL fCode '||to_char(sqlfcd)||
        ' rowid '||rowidtochar(lrowid));
                            raise_application_error(-20000,errm);
                end;
                if nofrows = 0 then
                      finished := TRUE;
                else
                 finished := FALSE;
                end if;
                commit;
        end loop;
        begin
              dbms_sql.close_cursor(cid);
                    -- close the cursor for a clean finish
        exception
              when others then
                    errpsn := dbms_sql.last_error_position;
                    sqlfcd := dbms_sql.last_sql_function_code;
                    lrowid := dbms_sql.last_row_id;
    errc := SQLCODE;
                    errm := SQLERRM;
    dbms_output.put_line('Error '||to_char(errc)||
    ' Posn '||to_char(errpsn)||
                        ' SQL fCode '||to_char(sqlfcd)||
                        ' rowid '||rowidtochar(lrowid));
                  raise_application_error(-20000,errm);
        end;
end;
/
```

Much of the code in the DELETE_COMMIT procedure handles any exceptions that may be encountered during statement processing. Conceptually, the executable command section follows this logic: if the **delete** command contains a **where** clause already, append an **and** clause to the statement; otherwise, append a **where** clause. These clauses are used to limit the number of rows **delete**d at a time. Process and **commit** the **delete** for the specified number of records. The second time the **delete** is executed, a second set of rows will be **delete**d. Reexecute the **delete** until there are no more records that match the **where** clause criteria.

The exceptions that may be raised are documented within the procedure and are rarely encountered. For best performance, be sure that the **delete** command's **where** clause can use indexes. You can use the **explain plan** command prior to executing the command to determine if a **delete** command will use indexes. See Chapter 8 for information on the **explain plan** command.

Backups

Why bother backing up a large database?

That may seem a bit of a heretical question for a DBA to ask, but it is relevant and appropriate. Often, you can reload the database and re-create the aggregations in less time than it would take to recover the data using the Oracle backup and recovery utilities. If you can reload the data faster than you can recover it, do you need to back up the data at all? The answer depends on the way in which your data load processing occurs.

Evaluating Backup Needs and Strategies

As described earlier in this chapter, most large databases have four types of tables:

- Large business transaction tables, which contain the majority of the raw data in the database

- Aggregation tables, which store aggregated data from the business transaction tables

- Codes tables

- Temporary work tables

When evaluating your database's backup needs, you should evaluate the backup needs for each type of table.

The data load processing methods requirements for business transaction tables drive the backup processes. If the business transaction data is completely replaced with each data load, then you can use the data load process to recover the data; you do not need to rely on Oracle's tools. If the business transaction data is not completely replaced with each data load, you may be able to use a combination of backup methods to recover the data.

For example, if each data load consists of only one period's worth of data in the SALES table, you will need to back up the prior periods' data as well as the current period's data. There are two ways to do this:

■ Back up the old data and use the data load process to re-create the current period's data.

■ Save the old data files and during a recovery run the data load for each period separately.

Depending on your data load procedures, the second option may allow your recovery to complete faster. You can still use Oracle's utilities as a backup to your data load recovery method.

If the data in your business transaction tables can be updated after loading, you will need to be able to re-create those transactions. You can either export the data following the transactions, or you can run the database in ARCHIVELOG mode. If you are relying on the archived redo log files to re-create the transaction data, you cannot place the business transaction table in **nologging** mode. You can also use RMAN (see Chapter 12) to minimize the amount of data backed up during file system backups.

In an ideal scenario, the business transaction table is completely reloaded during each data load, and no **update**s occur following the data load. If you need to recover the business transaction table, you can simply reexecute the data load procedure and the table can be kept in **nologging** state. As an additional backup method, you can back up the data following each data load. If your data can be **update**d following a data load, or if the data load does not account for all of the data in the table, then you need to back up the user transactions or the historical data.

Aggregation tables store redundant data. All of the data in the aggregation tables can be generated by reexecuting the commands used to create them. If you lose an aggregation table (for example, if it is accidentally dropped), you can re-create it by executing the **create table as select** command used to populate it. You should not permit modifications to the aggregation tables following their creation. If data needs to be changed, it should be changed in the business transaction tables that are the data source of the aggregation tables, and the aggregation tables should then be re-created.

Given these characteristics of aggregation tables, there is no need to make backups for them. You may wish to export the data following the table creation, but you can usually re-create the table faster via SQL than via other methods.

Codes tables store static data. There should be very few transactions occurring in the codes tables, so exports are usually sufficient for the codes tables. Since there are so few transactions occurring, there is usually no need to use archived redo log files to recover them; if you time your export properly, you should be able to use the exports during recovery with no data loss.

Temporary work tables are used during data load processing and are typically not accessed as part of the production application. The only recovery needs for the temporary work tables arise as part of the data load process. For example, you may wish to back up the temporary work tables at different points in the data load in order to minimize the amount of recovery activity needed if the data load process fails. Since there are no online transactions occurring within the temporary work tables, exports are usually used to back up these tables.

Developing the Backup Plan

Consider a large database whose business transaction tables are fully reloaded during each load (with no subsequent transactions in them) and whose codes tables are unchanging. What is the appropriate backup strategy? For such a system, there is no need to use ARCHIVELOG mode anywhere; indeed, it may be appropriate to put many of the tables into **nologging** state. The backup strategy could be as follows:

1. Back up the business transaction tables following data loads. Rely primarily on the data load process for recovery.

2. Back up the aggregation tables following their creation. Rely primarily on table re-creation for recovery.

3. Back up the codes tables after major changes. If the tables are small enough, you can also create copies of the codes tables via **create table as select** commands. Rely primarily on the exports for recovery.

4. Back up the temporary work tables after critical steps in the data load process. Rely primarily on the data load process for recovery.

As described, the backups are performed at different times in the data processing. Only one of the table types (codes tables) relies on exports as its primary recovery method.

It is very likely that this kind of backup strategy is inconsistent with the backup strategy used on your other, online transactions systems. However, there are a few key similarities:

■ Each table has a primary backup method and a secondary backup method. If, for example, the **create table as select** for an aggregation table fails, you can rely on an export of that table as a secondary recovery method. Never rely on just one backup method.

■ Each recovery type should be fully tested. If you have not tested a recovery operation, then you cannot rely on it.

As you tune your data load process, you should be able to reduce the time required to recover the database, giving you greater flexibility in its management.

Tuning

Tuning a large database is a two-part process: first tune the environment; then tune the specific queries and transactions that place the largest performance burden on the database. The tuning of database environments was discussed in Chapter 8, and some transaction tuning tips were provided earlier in this chapter. For example, your data load processes should use the block insert methods found in the SQL*Loader Direct Path loader and the APPEND hint of the **insert** command.

For a large database, the data block buffer portion of the System Global Area (SGA) should be approximately 2 percent of the database size. An SGA that large implies that the database is being run on a host and operating system that can support the management of large memory areas.

When creating the database, you should set the database block size to the highest value supported by Oracle on your operating system. The larger the database block is, the more efficiently data is stored, both in the tables and in the indexes. Doubling the database block size typically results in performance gains of about 40 percent on most batch operations.

NOTE
As of Oracle9i, you can have differing database block sizes at the tablespace level.

You should consider partitioning the main tables of the large database as described in the "Partitions" section of this chapter. You can also use materialized views to automate the aggregation process and enable the query rewrite capability within the optimizer.

Outside of the database, you should take advantage of the available devices and disk storage architectures to properly distribute the system I/O requirements. See the "Choosing a Physical Layout" section earlier in this chapter for information on disk options and architectures such as RAID devices and disk mirroring.

If your host machine has multiple CPUs available, you may be able to take full advantage of Oracle's Parallel Query Option (PQO). When you use PQO, multiple processes are created to complete a single task—such as a query or an index creation. Because they involve large transactions and sorts, large databases typically benefit from the use of the PQO.

Tuning Queries of Large Tables

In addition to creating fully indexed tables, creating bitmap indexes, partitioning tables and indexes, and using the PQO for queries of large tables, you can further tune queries of large tables to minimize their impact on the rest of the database. Whereas multiple users can benefit from sharing data from small tables in the SGA, that benefit disappears when very large tables are accessed. For very large tables, index accesses can have a negative effect on the rest of the database.

When a table and its indexes are small, there can be a high degree of data sharing within the SGA. Multiple users performing table reads or index range scans can use the same blocks over and over. As a result of the reuse of blocks within the SGA, the *hit ratio*—a measure of the reuse of blocks within the SGA—increases.

As a table grows, the table's indexes grow too. If a table and its indexes grow much larger than the available space in the SGA, it becomes less likely that the next row needed by a range scan will be found within the SGA. The reusability of data within the SGA's data block buffer cache will diminish. The hit ratio for the database will decrease. Eventually, each logical read will require a separate physical read.

The SGA is designed to maximize the reuse among multiple users of the blocks read from the datafiles. To maximize reuse, the SGA maintains a list of the blocks that have been read; if the blocks were read via index accesses or via table access by RowID, those blocks are kept in the SGA the longest. If a block is read into the SGA via a full table scan, that block is the first to be removed from the SGA when more space is needed in the data block buffer cache.

For applications with small tables, the data block buffer cache management in the SGA maximizes the reuse of blocks and increases the hit ratio. What happens, though, if an index range scan is performed on a very large table? The index's blocks will be kept for a long time in the SGA, even though it is likely that no other users will be able to use the values in the index's blocks. Since the index is large, many of its blocks may be read, consuming a substantial portion of the available space in the SGA's data block buffer cache. A greater amount of space will be consumed by the table blocks accessed by RowID, and those blocks will be even less likely to be reused. The hit ratio will begin to drop—ironically, because index scans are being performed. The tuning methods used for very large tables therefore focus on special indexing techniques and on alternatives to indexes.

Manage Data Proximity

If you intend to continue using indexes during accesses of very large tables, you must be concerned about *data proximity*—the physical relationship between logically related records. To maximize data proximity, **insert** records into the table sequentially, ordered by columns commonly used in range scans of the table. For example, the primary key of the large SALES table is the combination of Period_ID,

Customer_ID, and Sale_No. Accesses that use Period_ID as a limiting condition will be able to use the unique index on the primary key; but if range scans are commonly performed on the SALES.Customer_ID column, the data should be stored in order of Customer_ID.

If the data is stored in an ordered format, then during range searches, such as

```
where Customer_ID between 123 and 241
```

you will more likely be able to reuse the table and index blocks read into the SGA because all of the Customer_ID values with a value of 123 will be stored together. Fewer index and table blocks will be read into the SGA's data block buffer cache, minimizing the impact of the index range scan on the SGA. Storing data in an ordered fashion helps range scans regardless of the size of the table, but it is particularly critical for large tables due to the negative implications of large range scans.

You can also specify multiple buffer pools and assign objects to those pools. For example, you can create a RECYCLE pool, and assign your largest tables to that pool. Using a RECYCLE pool will minimize the impact of scans of the large table on the memory management within the SGA.

Favoring full table scans is not a typical tuning method. However, if a table is so large that its index-based accesses will override the SGA, you should consider using a full table scan for queries of very large tables in multiuser environments. To improve the performance of the full table scan, consider parallelizing the operation, which bypasses the buffer cache.

Using Transportable Tablespaces

Oracle has introduced a significant number of features designed to improve the performance of data movement operations. As highlighted in the earlier sections of this chapter, these data movement features include the following:

- The **truncate** command for bulk **delete**s

- The APPEND hint and SQL*Loader Direct Path loads for **insert**s

- Partitions for dividing tables and indexes into smaller sets of data

- **nologging** operations

You can use another feature—transportable tablespaces—to improve the performance of data movement operations. Transportable tablespaces should improve the performance of operations that move large amounts of data between databases. You can transport both data and indexes, but you cannot transport bitmap indexes or tables containing collectors (nested tables and varying arrays).

To transport tablespaces, you need to generate a tablespace set, move that tablespace set to the new database, and plug the set into the new database. In the following section, you will see the steps to follow along with implementation tips. The databases should be on the same operating system, with the same version of Oracle and character set. Prior to Oracle9i, the databases should also have the same database block size.

Generating a Transportable Tablespace Set

A transportable tablespace set contains all of the datafiles for the tablespaces being moved, along with an export of the metadata for those tablespaces. The tablespaces being transported should be self-contained—they should not contain any objects that are dependent on objects outside of the tablespaces. For example, if you want to move a table, you must also transport the tablespace that contains the table's indexes. The better you have organized and distributed your objects among tablespaces (see Chapter 3), the easier it is to generate a self-contained set of tablespaces to transport.

You can optionally choose whether to include referential integrity constraints as part of the transportable tablespace set. If you choose to use referential integrity constraints, the transportable tablespace set will increase to include the tables required to maintain the key relationships. Referential integrity is optional because you may have the same codes tables in multiple databases. For example, you may be planning to move a tablespace from your test database to your production database. If you have a COUNTRY table in the test database, then you may already have an identical COUNTRY table in the production database. Since the codes tables are identical in the two databases, you do not need to transport that portion of the referential integrity constraints. You could transport the tablespace and then reenable the referential integrity in the target database once the tablespace has been moved, simplifying the creation of the transportable tablespace set.

To determine if a tablespace set is self-contained, you can execute the TRANSPORT_SET_CHECK procedure of the DBMS_TTS package. This procedure takes two input parameters: the set of tablespaces and a Boolean flag set to TRUE if you want referential integrity constraints to be considered. In the following example, referential integrity constraints are not considered for the combination of the AGG_DATA and AGG_INDEXES tablespaces:

```
execute DBMS_TTS.TRANSPORT_SET_CHECK('AGG_DATA,AGG_INDEXES',FALSE);
```

If there are any self-containment violations in the specified set, Oracle will populate the TRANSPORT_SET_VIOLATIONS data dictionary view. If there are no violations, the view will be empty.

Once you have selected a self-contained set of tablespaces, make the tablespaces read-only, as shown here:

```
alter tablespace AGG_DATA read only;
alter tablespace AGG_INDEXES read only;
```

Next, export the metadata for the tablespaces, using the TRANSPORT_TABLESPACE and TABLESPACES export parameters:

```
exp TRANSPORT_TABLESPACE=Y TABLESPACES=(AGG_DATA,AGG_INDEXES)
CONSTRAINTS=N GRANTS=Y TRIGGERS=N
```

As shown in the example, you can specify whether triggers, constraints, and grants are exported along with the tablespace metadata. You should also note the names of the accounts that own objects in the transportable tablespace set. You can now copy the tablespaces' datafiles to a separate area. If needed, you can put the tablespaces back into read-write mode in their current database. After you have generated the transportable tablespace set, you can move its files (including the export) to an area that the target database can access.

Plugging in the Transportable Tablespace Set

Once the transportable tablespace set has been moved to an area accessible to the target database, you can plug the set into the target database. First, use Import to import the exported metadata:

```
imp TRANSPORT_TABLESPACE=Y DATAFILES=(agg_data.dbf, agg_indexes.dbf)
```

In the import, you specify the datafiles that are part of the transportable tablespace set. You can optionally specify the tablespaces (via the TABLESPACES parameter) and the object owners (via the OWNERS parameter).

After the import completes, all tablespaces in the transportable tablespace set are left in read-only mode. You can issue the **alter tablespace read write** command in the target database to place the new tablespaces in read-write mode.

```
alter tablespace AGG_DATA read write;
alter tablespace AGG_INDEXES read write;
```

Note that you cannot change the ownership of the objects being transported.

Transportable tablespaces support very fast movement of large datasets. In a data warehouse, you could use transportable tablespaces to publish aggregations from core warehouse to data marts, or from the data marts to a global data warehouse. Any read-only data can be quickly distributed to multiple databases—instead of sending SQL scripts, you can send datafiles and exported metadata. This modified data movement process may greatly simplify your procedures for managing remote databases, remote data marts, and large data movement operations.

Locally Managed Tablespaces

You can use two different methods to track free and used space in a tablespace. The first method, which has been available since the advent of tablespaces, is to handle extent management via the data dictionary (dictionary managed tablespaces). In a dictionary managed tablespace, each time an extent is allocated or freed for reuse in a tablespace, the appropriate entry is **update**d in the data dictionary table. Rollback information is also stored about each **update** of the dictionary table. Dictionary tables and rollback segments are part of the database, and the rules that apply to other data activity apply to them as well. Therefore, recursive space management operations can occur as extents are acquired and released.

The second method, available as of Oracle8*i* and the default method in Oracle9*i*, handles extent management within the tablespaces themselves (locally managed tablespaces). In locally managed tablespaces, the tablespace manages its own space by maintaining a bitmap in each datafile of the free and used blocks or sets of blocks in the datafile. Each time an extent is allocated or freed for reuse, Oracle **update**s the bitmap to show the new status.

When you use locally managed tablespaces, the dictionary is not **update**d and rollback activity is not generated. Locally managed tablespaces automatically track adjacent free space, so there is no need to coalesce extents. Within a locally managed tablespace, all extents can have the same size or the system can automatically determine the size of extents.

To use this feature, you must specify the **local** option for the **extent management** clause in the **create tablespace** command. An example of the **create tablespace** command declaring a locally managed tablespace is shown here:

```
create tablespace CODES_TABLES
datafile '/u01/oracle/VLDB/codes_tables.dbf'
size 10M
extent management local uniform size 256K;
```

Assuming that the block size for the database in which this tablespace is created is 4KB, in this example, the tablespace is created with the extent management declared as **local** and with a uniform size of 256KB. Each bit in the bitmap describes

64 blocks (256/4). If the **uniform size** clause is omitted, the default is **autoallocate**. The default **size** for **uniform** is 1MB.

NOTE
*If you specify **local** in a **create tablespace** command, you cannot specify a **default storage** clause, **minextents**, or **temporary**. If you use the **create temporary tablespace** command to create the tablespace, you can specify **extent_management local**.*

In the case of the SYSTEM tablespace, you can declare the extent management as **local** in the **create database** statement. Even though it is documented, you cannot create the SYSTEM tablespace as locally managed. However, any of the other tablespaces in the database can have dictionary managed extents.

As your database objects grow in extents, locally managed tablespaces become more important. As noted in Chapter 4, DDL space management operations on tables with thousands of extents perform poorly due to the data dictionary management involved. If you use locally managed tablespaces, that performance penalty is significantly reduced. See Chapter 4 for additional details concerning locally managed tablespaces.

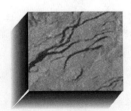

CHAPTER
16

Managing Distributed Databases

he distributed database architecture is based on the server/server
configurations described in Chapter 13. In a distributed environment,
databases on separate servers (hosts) may be accessed during a single
transaction or query. Each server can be physically isolated without
being logically isolated from other servers.

A typical replication implementation involves corporate headquarters servers
that communicate with departmental servers in various locations. Each server
supports client applications, but it also has the ability to communicate with other
servers in the network. This architecture is shown in Figure 16-1.

When one of the servers sends a database request to another server, the sending
server acts like a client. The receiving server executes the SQL statement that is
passed to it and returns the results plus error conditions to the sender.

Oracle Net (known previously as SQL*Net and Net8) allows this architecture to
become reality. When run on all of the servers, Oracle Net allows database requests
made from one database (or application) to be passed to another database on a
separate server. Both distributed queries and distributed updates are supported.
With this functionality, you can communicate with all of the databases that are
accessible via your network. You can then create synonyms that give applications
true network transparency; the user who submits a query will not know the location
of the data that is used to resolve it.

You can configure Oracle to support multi-master replication (in which all
databases involved own the data and can serve as the source for data propagation)

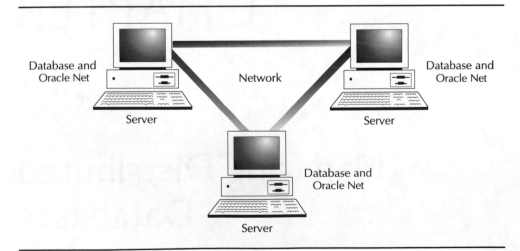

FIGURE 16-1. *Server/server architecture*

or single-master replication (in which only one database owns the data). When designing a replication configuration, you should try to restrict the ownership of data as much as possible. As the number of sources for propagation increase, the potential for errors to occur increases dramatically. In the following sections, you will see examples of the different replication capabilities available, followed by management techniques.

Remote Queries

To query a remote database, you must create a database link in the database in which the query will originate. The database link specifies the service name to use and may also specify the username to connect to in the remote database. When a database link is referenced by an SQL statement, Oracle opens a session in the remote database and executes the SQL statement there. The data is then returned, and the remote session stays open for the duration of the user's session. You can create database links as public links (created by DBAs, making the link available to all users in the local database) or as private links.

The following example creates a public database link called HR_LINK:

```
create public database link HR_LINK
connect to HR identified by PUFFINSTUFF
using 'hq';
```

The **create database link** command shown in this example has several parameters:

- The optional keyword **public**, which allows DBAs to create links for all users in a database. An additional optional keyword, **shared**, is described later in this chapter.

- The name of the link (HR_LINK, in this example).

- The account to connect to. You can configure the database link to use the local username and password in the remote database. This link connects to a fixed username in the remote database.

- The service name (hq).

To use the newly created link, simply add it as a suffix to table names in commands. The following example queries a remote table by using the HR_LINK database link:

```
select * from EMPLOYEE@HR_LINK
 where Office='ANNAPOLIS';
```

When you execute this query, Oracle will establish a session via the HR_LINK database link and query the EMPLOYEE table in that database. The **where** clause will be applied to the EMPLOYEE rows, and the matching records will be returned. The execution of the query is shown graphically in Figure 16-2.

The **from** clause in this example refers to EMPLOYEE@HR_LINK. Since the HR_LINK database link specifies the server name, instance name, and owner name, the full name of the table is known. If no account name had been specified in the database link, the user's account name and password in the local database would have been used when attempting to log into the remote database.

The management of database links is described in the "Managing Distributed Data" section later in this chapter.

Remote Data Manipulation: Two-Phase Commit

To support data manipulation across multiple databases, Oracle relies on Two-Phase Commit (2PC). 2PC allows groups of transactions across several nodes to be treated as a unit: either the transactions all **commit** or they all get rolled back. A set of distributed transactions is shown in Figure 16-3. In the figure, two **update** transactions are performed. The first **update** goes against a local table (EMPLOYEE); the second, against a remote table (EMPLOYEE@HR_LINK). After the two transactions

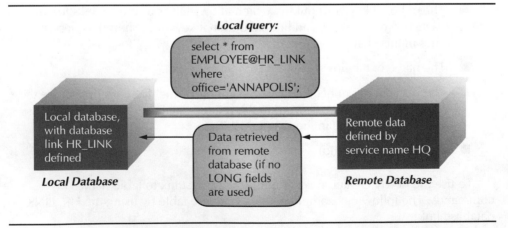

FIGURE 16-2.   *Sample remote query*

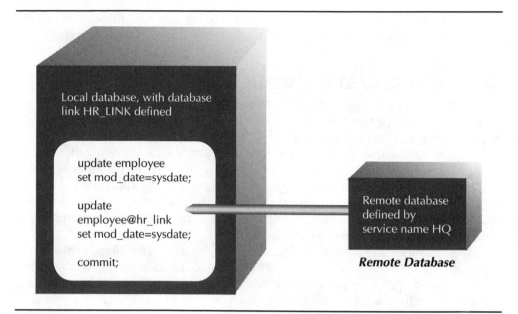

FIGURE 16-3. *Sample distributed transaction*

are performed, a single **commit** is then executed. If either transaction cannot **commit**, both transactions will be rolled back.

Distributed transactions yield two important benefits. One is that databases on other servers can be **update**d, and those transactions can be grouped together with others in a logical unit. The second benefit occurs because of the database's use of 2PC. Its two phases are

- **The prepare phase** An initiating node called the *global coordinator* notifies all sites involved in the transaction to be ready either to **commit** or roll back the transaction.

- **The commit phase** If there is no problem with the prepare phase, then all sites **commit** their transactions. If a network or node failure occurs, then all sites roll back their transactions.

The use of 2PC is transparent to the users. If the node that initiates the transaction forgets about the transaction, a third phase, the forget phase, is performed. The detailed management of distributed transactions is discussed in the "Managing Distributed Transactions" section later in this chapter.

Dynamic Data Replication

To improve the performance of queries that use data from remote databases, you may wish to replicate that data on the local server. There are several options for accomplishing this, depending on which Oracle features you are using.

You can use *database triggers* to replicate data from one table into another. For example, after every **insert** into a table, a trigger may fire to **insert** that same record into another table—and that table may be in a remote database. Thus, you can use triggers to enforce data replication in simple configurations. If the types of transactions against the base table cannot be controlled, the trigger code needed to perform the replication will be unacceptably complicated.

When using Oracle's distributed features, you can use *materialized views* to replicate data between databases. You do not have to replicate an entire table or limit yourself to data from just one table. When replicating a single table, you may use a **where** clause to restrict which records are replicated, and you may perform **group by** operations on the data. You can also join the table with other tables and replicate the result of the queries.

> **NOTE**
> *You cannot use materialized views to replicate data using LONG, LONG RAW, or datatypes.*

The data in the local materialized view of the remote table(s) will need to be refreshed. You can specify the refresh interval for the materialized view, and the database will automatically take care of the replication procedures. If the materialized view is a one-to-one replication of records in a remote table (called a *simple materialized view*), the database can use a *materialized view log* to send over only transaction data; otherwise, it is a *complex materialized view*, and, with some exceptions, the database will perform complete refreshes on the local materialized view. The dynamic replication of data via materialized views is shown in Figure 16-4.

Other methods may be used to replicate data, but they are not dynamically maintained by the database. For example, you can use the SQL*Plus **copy** command (see the "Usage Example: The **copy** Command" section of Chapter 13) to create copies of remote tables in local databases. However, the **copy** command would need to be repeated every time the data is changed; therefore, its use is limited to those situations in which large, static tables are replicated. Dynamic data requires dynamic replication.

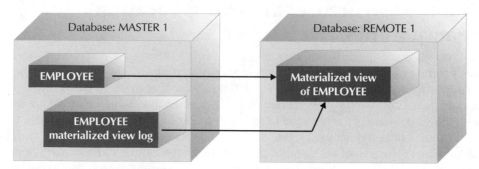

(a) A simple materialized view; materialized view logs can be used.

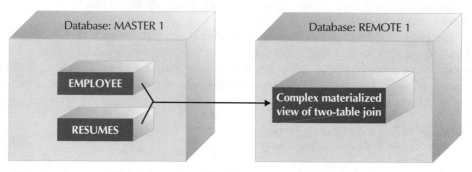

(b) A complex materialized view; the result of the join is replicated.

FIGURE 16-4.   *Simple and complex materialized views*

Managing Distributed Data

Before you can worry about managing transactions against remote databases, you have to get the data there and make it globally accessible to other databases. The following sections describe the requisite management tasks: enforcing location transparency and managing the database links, triggers, and materialized views that are used to access the data.

NOTE
The examples in this chapter assume that you are using tnsnames.ora files for your database service name resolution. See Chapter 13 for additional options.

The Infrastructure: Enforcing Location Transparency

To properly design your distributed databases for long-term use, you must start by making the physical location of the data transparent to the application. The name of a table within a database is unique within the schema that owns it. However, a remote database may have an account with the same name, which may own a table with the same name. How can the table name be properly qualified?

Within distributed databases, two additional layers of object identification must be added. First, the name of the instance that accesses the database must be identified. Next, the name of the host on which that instance resides must be identified. Putting together these four parts of the object's name—its host, its instance, its owner, and its name—results in a *global object name*. To access a remote table, that table's global object name must be known.

The goal of location transparency is to make the first three parts of the global object name—the host, the instance, and the schema—transparent to the user. The first three parts of the global object name are all specified via database links, so any effort at achieving location transparency should start there. First, consider a typical database link:

```
create public database link HR_LINK
connect to HR identified by PUFFINSTUFF
using 'hq';
```

> **NOTE**
> *If the GLOBAL_NAMES initialization parameter is set to TRUE, the database link name must be the same as the name of the remote database.*

By using a service name (hq), the host and instance names are kept transparent. They are translated into their actual values via the local host's tnsnames.ora file. A partial entry in this file, for this service name, is shown in the following listing:

```
hq =(DESCRIPTION=
        (ADDRESS=
              (PROTOCOL=TCP)
              (HOST=HQ)
              (PORT=1521))
        (CONNECT DATA=
              (SID=loc))))
```

The two lines in bold in this listing fill in the two missing pieces of the global object name: when the HQ service name is used, the host name is HQ, and the instance name is LOC. This tnsnames.ora file shows the parameters for the TCP/IP protocol; other protocols may use different keywords, but their usage is the same. The tnsnames.ora entries provide transparency for the server and instance names.

The HR_LINK database link created via the code given earlier in this section will provide transparency for the first two parts of the global object name. But what if the data moves from the HR schema, or the HR account's password changes? The database link would have to be dropped and re-created. The same would be true if account-level security was required; you may need to create and maintain multiple database links.

To resolve the transparency of the schema portion of the global object name, you can modify the database link syntax. Consider the database link in the following listing:

```
create public database link HR_LINK
connect to current_user
using 'hq';
```

This database link uses the **connect to current_user** clause. It will use what is known as a *connected user connection*, while the earlier example was a *fixed user connection*. An example of this link being used is shown in the following listing:

```
select * from EMPLOYEE@HR_LINK;
```

When HR_LINK is used, the database will resolve the global object name in the following manner:

1. It will search the local tnsnames.ora file to determine the proper host name, port, and instance name.

2. It will check the database link for a **connect to** specification. If the **connect to current_user** clause is found, it will attempt to connect to the specified database using the *connected user*'s username and password.

3. It will search the **from** clause of the query for the object name.

Connected user links are often used to access tables whose rows can be restricted based on the username that is accessing the table. For example, if the remote database had a table named HR.EMPLOYEE, and every employee was allowed to see his or her own record, then a database link with a specific connection, such as

```
create public database link HR_LINK
connect to HR identified by PUFFINSTUFF
using 'hq';
```

would log in as the HR account (the owner of the table). If this specific connection is used, you cannot restrict the user's view of the records on the remote host. However, if a connected user link is used, and a view is created on the remote host using the User pseudocolumn, then only that user's data would be returned from the remote host. A sample database link and view of this type is shown in the following listing:

```
REM   In the local database:
REM
create public database link HR_LINK
connect to current_user
using 'hq';

create view REMOTE_EMP
as select * from EMPLOYEE@HR_LINK
where Ename=User;
```

The User pseudocolumn's value is the current Oracle username. If you query the REMOTE_EMP view, you are using the HR_LINK database link. Since that link uses a default connection, your username and password will be used to connect to the hq service name's database. You will therefore retrieve only those records from EMPLOYEE@HR_LINK for which your username is equal to the value of the Ename column in that table.

Either way, the data being retrieved can be restricted. The difference is that when a connected user link is used, the data can be restricted based on the username in the remote database; if a fixed connection is used, then the data can be restricted after it has been returned to the local database. The connected user link reduces the amount of network traffic needed to resolve the query and adds an additional level of location transparency to the data.

Connected user database links raise a different set of maintenance issues. The tnsnames.ora files must be synchronized across the servers, and the username/password combinations in multiple databases must be synchronized. These issues are addressed in the next sections.

If you are using Oracle Names server, an additional type of database link is available. Called a *global link*, it has only a **using** clause, with no connection information. The user must be authenticated externally; see the *Oracle9i Advanced Security Administrator's Guide* for further details on authentication.

Database Domains

A *Domain Name Service* (DNS) allows hosts within a network to be hierarchically organized. Each node within the organization is called a *domain*, and each domain is labeled by its function. These functions may include COM for companies and EDU for schools. Each domain may have many subdomains. Therefore, each host will be given a unique name within the network; its name contains information about how it fits into the network hierarchy. Host names within a network typically have up to four parts: the leftmost portion of the name is the host's name, and the rest of the name shows the domain to which the host belongs.

For example, a host may be named HQ.MYCORP.COM. In this example, the host is named HQ. It is identified as being part of the MYCORP subdomain of the COM domain.

The domain structure is significant for two reasons. First, the host name is part of the global object name. Second, Oracle allows you to specify the DNS version of the host name in database link names, simplifying the management of distributed database connections.

To use DNS names in database links, you first need to add two parameters to your initialization file for the database. The first of these, DB_NAME, may already be there; it should be set to the instance name. The second parameter, DB_DOMAIN, is set to the DNS name of the database's host. DB_DOMAIN specifies the network domain in which the host resides. If a database named LOC is created on the HQ.MYCORP.COM server, its entries will be

```
DB_NAME = loc
DB_DOMAIN = hq.mycorp.com
```

To enable the usage of the database domain name, the GLOBAL_NAMES parameter must be set to TRUE in your parameter file, as shown in the following listing:

```
GLOBAL_NAMES = true
```

Once these parameters have been set, the database must be shut down and restarted using this parameter file for the settings to take effect.

NOTE
If you set GLOBAL_NAMES to TRUE, then all of your database link names must follow the rules described in this section.

When using this method of creating global database names, the names of the database links that are created are the same as the databases to which they point. Thus, a database link that pointed to the LOC database listed earlier would be named LOC.HQ.MYCORP.COM. This is shown in the following listing:

```
CREATE PUBLIC DATABASE LINK loc.hq.mycorp.com
USING 'service name';
```

Oracle may append the local database's DB_DOMAIN value to the name of the database link. For example, if the database was within the HQ.MYCORP.COM domain and the database link was named LOC, the database link name, when used, would be automatically expanded to LOC.HQ.MYCORP.COM.

Using global database names establishes a link between the database name, database domain, and database link names. This, in turn, may make it easier to identify and manage database links. For example, you can create a public database link (with no connect string, as shown in the preceding example) in each database that points to every other database. Users within a database no longer need to guess at the proper database link to use; if they know the global database name, they know the database link name. If a table is moved from one database to another, or if a database is moved from one host to another, it is easy to determine which of the old database links must be dropped and re-created. Using global database names is part of migrating from stand-alone databases to true networks of databases.

Using Shared Database Links

If you use the Shared Server option for your database connections and your application will employ many concurrent database link connections, you may benefit from using *shared database links*. A shared database link uses shared server connections to support the database link connections. If you have multiple concurrent database link accesses into a remote database, you can use shared database links to reduce the number of server connections required.

To create a shared database link, use the **shared** keyword of the **create database link** command. As shown in the following listing, you will also need to specify a schema and password for the remote database:

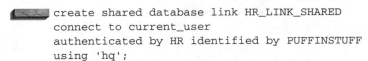

```
create shared database link HR_LINK_SHARED
connect to current_user
authenticated by HR identified by PUFFINSTUFF
using 'hq';
```

The HR_LINK_SHARED database link uses the connected user's username and password when accessing the 'hq' database, as specified via the **connect to current_user** clause. In order to prevent unauthorized attempts to use the shared link, shared links require the **authenticated by** clause. In this example, the account used for authentication is an application account, but you can also use an empty schema for authentication. The authentication account must have the CREATE SESSION system privilege. During usage of the HR_LINK_SHARED link, connection attempts will include authentication against the HR link account.

NOTE
The authentication username and password are visible to users with access to the SYS.LINK$ table.

If you change the password on the authentication account, you will need to drop and re-create each database link that references it. To simplify maintenance, create an account that is only used for authentication of shared database link connections. The account should have only the CREATE SESSION system privilege, and should not have any privileges on any of the application tables.

If your application uses database links infrequently, you should use traditional database links without the **shared** clause. Without the **shared** clause, each database link connection requires a separate connection to the remote database.

Managing Database Links

You can retrieve information about public database links via the DBA_DB_LINKS data dictionary view. You can view private database links via the USER_DB_LINKS data dictionary view. Whenever possible, separate your users among databases by application so that they may all share the same public database links. As a side benefit, these users will usually be able to share public grants and synonyms.

The columns of the DBA_DB_LINKS data dictionary view are listed in the following table. The password for the link to use is not viewable via DBA_DB_LINKS; it is stored unencrypted in the SYS.LINK$ table.

Column Name	Description
OWNER	Owner of the database link
DB_LINK	Name of the database link (such as HR_LINK in this chapter's examples)
USERNAME	The name of the account to use to open a session in the remote database, if a specific connection is used
HOST	The connect string that will be used to connect to the remote database
CREATED	A timestamp that marks the creation date for the database link

NOTE
The number of database links that can be used by a single query is limited by the OPEN_LINKS parameter in the database's initialization file. Its default value is 4.

The managerial tasks involved for database links depend on the level to which you have implemented location transparency in your databases. In the best-case scenario, connected user links are used along with service names or aliases. In that scenario, the only requirements for successful maintenance are that the tnsnames.ora file be consistent across hosts and that user account/password combinations be maintained globally.

Synchronizing account/password combinations across databases may be difficult, but there are several alternatives. First, you may force all changes to user account passwords to go through a central authority. This central authority would have the responsibility for updating the password for the account in all databases in the network—a time-consuming task, but a valuable one.

Second, you may audit user password changes made via the **alter user** command by auditing the usage of that command (see Chapter 10). If a user's password changes in one database, it must be changed on all databases available in the network that are accessed via connected user links.

If any part of the global object name—such as a username—is embedded in the database link, a change affecting that part of the global object name requires that the database link be dropped and re-created. For example, if the HR user's password were changed, the HR_LINK database link with a specific connection defined earlier would be dropped with

```
drop database link HR_LINK;
```

and the link would then be re-created, using the new account password:

```
create public database link HR_LINK
connect to HR identified by NEWPASSWORD
using 'hq';
```

You cannot create a database link in another user's account. If you attempt to create a database link in SCOTT's account, as shown here,

```
create database link SCOTT.HR_LINK
connect to HR identified by PUFFINSTUFF
using 'hq';
```

then Oracle will not create the HR_LINK database link in SCOTT's account. Instead, Oracle will create a database link named SCOTT.HR_LINK in the account that executed the **create database link** command. To create private database links, you must be logged into the database in the account that will own the link.

NOTE
To see which links are presently in use in your database, query V$DBLINK.

Managing Database Triggers

If your data replication needs are fairly limited, you can use database triggers to replicate data from one table into another. In general, this method is used when the only type of data being sent to the remote database is either an **insert** or a **delete**. The code necessary to support **update** transactions is usually much more complex than a comparable materialized view (see the following sections for details on implementing materialized views).

Database triggers are executed when specific actions happen. They can be executed for each row of a transaction, for an entire transaction as a unit, or when systemwide events occur. When dealing with data replication, you will usually be concerned with triggers affecting each row of data.

Before creating a replication-related trigger, you must create a database link for the trigger to use. In this case, the link is created in the database that *owns* the data, accessible to the owner of the table being replicated.

```
create public database link TRIGGER_LINK
connect to current_user
using 'remote1';
```

This link, named TRIGGER_LINK, uses a service name (remote1) to specify the connection to a remote database. The link will attempt to log into the remote1 database using the same username and password as the account that calls the link.

The trigger shown in the following listing uses this link. The trigger is fired after every row is **insert**ed into the EMPLOYEE table. Since the trigger executes after the row has been **insert**ed, the row's data has already been validated in the local database. The trigger **insert**s the same row into a remote table with the same structure, using the TRIGGER_LINK database link just defined. The remote table must already exist.

```
create trigger COPY_DATA
after insert on EMPLOYEE
for each row
begin
    insert into EMPLOYEE@TRIGGER_LINK
    values
    (:new.Empno, :new.Ename, :new.Deptno,
    :new.Salary, :new.Birth_Date, :new.Soc_Sec_Num);
end;
/
```

This trigger uses the **new** keyword to reference the values from the row that was just **insert**ed into the local EMPLOYEE table.

NOTE
*If you use trigger-based replication, your trigger
code must account for potential error conditions at
the remote site, such as duplicate key values, space
management problems, or a shut-down database.*

To list information about triggers, use the DBA_TRIGGERS data dictionary view.
The following query will list the "header" information about the trigger—its type,
the statement that calls it, and the table on which it calls. This example shows the
header information for the COPY_DATA trigger just created:

```
select Trigger_Type,
       Triggering_Event,
       Table_Name
  from DBA_TRIGGERS
 where Trigger_Name = 'COPY_DATA';
```

Sample output from this query is shown here:

```
TYPE               TRIGGERING_EVENT       TABLE_NAME
---------------- ---------------------- ------------
AFTER EACH ROW   INSERT                  EMPLOYEE
```

You can query the text of the trigger from DBA_TRIGGERS, as shown in the
following listing:

```
set long 1000
select Trigger_Body
  from DBA_TRIGGERS
 where Trigger_Name = 'COPY_DATA';
```

Sample output from this query is shown in the following listing:

```
TRIGGER_BODY
--------------------------------------------------------
begin
    insert into EMPLOYEE@TRIGGER_LINK
    values
    (:new.Empno, :new.Ename, :new.Deptno,
    :new.Salary, :new.Birth_Date, :new.Soc_Sec_Num);
end;
```

It is theoretically possible to create a trigger to replicate all possible
permutations of data manipulation actions on the local database, but this quickly

becomes difficult to manage. For a complex environment, you should consider the use of materialized views or manual data copies. For the limited circumstances described earlier, triggers are a very easy solution to implement.

NOTE
If you use triggers for your data replication, the success of a transaction in the master database is dependent on the success of the remote transaction.

Managing Materialized Views

Data generally flows from an online transaction processing database into a data warehouse. Normally the data is prestaged, cleansed or otherwise processed, and then moved into the data warehouse. From there, the data may be fielded to other databases or data marts. Prior to Oracle8i, summaries of the data involving joins or aggregates like sums or counts had to be precalculated to help improve performance. Users had to know each precalculated summary and understand which one to use to obtain their desired results. In Oracle8i, materialized views were introduced to provide a way to transparently provide summaries and other features to help improve query performance in both data warehouses and replication environments.

What Is a Materialized View?

Materialized views are generic objects used to summarize, precompute, replicate, or distribute data. You can use materialized views to precompute and store aggregate information within a database, to dynamically replicate data between distributed databases, and to synchronize data updates within replicated environments. In replication environments, materialized views enable local access to data that would normally have to be accessed remotely. A materialized view may be based on another materialized view.

In large databases, materialized views help to increase the response speed of queries that involve aggregates (including sum, count, average, variance, standard deviation, minimum, and maximum) or table joins. Using materialized views, you can precompute and store aggregate data within the database, and the query optimizer will automatically recognize that the materialized view should be used to satisfy the query as long as you have created statistics on the materialized view—a feature known as *query rewrite*.

NOTE
For best results, make sure the statistics on the materialized view are kept current.

You can use initialization parameters to configure the optimizer to automatically rewrite queries to use the materialized views whenever possible. Since materialized views are transparent to SQL applications, they can be dropped or created without impacting the execution code. You can create a partitioned materialized view, and you can base materialized views on partitioned tables.

Unlike regular views, materialized views store data and take up physical space in your database. Materialized views are populated with data generated from their base queries, and refreshed on demand or on a scheduled basis. Therefore, whenever the data accessed by the base query changes, the materialized views should be refreshed to reflect the data changes. The data refresh frequency depends on how much data latency your business can tolerate in the processes supported by the materialized views. You'll see how to establish your refresh rate later in this chapter.

In addition to *simple materialized views*—in which the rows in the materialized view map directly to one (usually remote) table—you can create materialized views with aggregates and materialized views that contain only joins. Materialized views in a data warehouse environment normally contain one or more aggregates. The valid aggregates are **SUM**, **COUNT**(*column*), **COUNT**(*), **AVG**, **VARIANCE**, **STDDEV**, **MIN**, and **MAX**. A materialized view's base query can also contain one or more table joins or subqueries. In some cases, the materialized view contains only joins and no aggregates.

The materialized view will create several objects in the database. The user creating the materialized view must have the CREATE MATERIALIZED VIEW, CREATE TABLE, and CREATE VIEW privileges as well as the SELECT privilege on any tables that are referenced but are owned by another schema. If the materialized view is going to be created in another schema, the user creating the materialized view must have CREATE ANY MATERIALIZED VIEW privilege and SELECT privilege to the tables that are referenced in the materialized view if the tables are owned by another schema. To enable query rewrite on a materialized view that references tables within another schema, the user enabling query rewrite must have the GLOBAL QUERY REWRITE privilege or be explicitly granted the QUERY REWRITE privilege on any referenced table within another schema. You must also have the UNLIMITED TABLESPACE privilege. Materialized views can be created in the local database, and pull data from the remote master database, or materialized views can reside on the same database server on which the data is located.

If you plan to use the query rewrite feature, you must put the following entry in your initialization parameter file:

```
QUERY_REWRITE_ENABLE=TRUE
```

Materialized View Decisions

Before you can create a materialized view, you must make several decisions, including:

- Whether the materialized view is to be populated with data during creation or after

- How often the materialized view is to be refreshed

- What type of refreshes to perform

- Whether to maintain a materialized view log

You can either have data loaded to the materialized view upon its creation using the **build immediate** command option of the **create materialized view** command, or you can precreate the materialized view, but not populate it until the first time it is used, by declaring **build deferred**. The advantage of populating the view on creation is that the data will be available immediately when you make the materialized view available. However, if the materialized view is not going to be used for some time and the data changes fairly rapidly, the data could become stale before the view is used. If you wait to have the materialized view populated, the view will not be populated with data until the package DBMS_MVIEW.REFRESH is executed and your user must wait for the view to populate before any data is returned, producing a performance degradation. If a view already exists and you want to convert it to a materialized view, you can use the **prebuilt** command option.

You must decide how much stale data is tolerable based on your company's needs. You can base your decision on how frequently the data changes in the table on which the materialized view is based. If your management does not have to have up-to-the-minute information on which to base decisions, you might only need to refresh your materialized view once an hour or once a day. If it is critical for the data to be absolutely accurate at all times, you may need to perform fast refreshes every five minutes throughout the day and night.

There are four forms of refresh: Complete, Fast, Force, and Never. In a Fast refresh, materialized view logs are used to track the data changes that have occurred within the table since the last refresh. Only changed information is populated back to the materialized view, on a periodic basis, based on the refresh criteria you have established. The materialized view log is maintained in the same database and schema as the master table for the materialized view. Because the fast refresh just applies changes made since the last refresh, the time taken to perform the refresh should generally be very short.

In a Complete refresh, the data within the materialized view is completely replaced each time the refresh is run. The time required to perform a complete refresh of the materialized view can be substantial. You can either have the refresh performed each time transactions are committed on the master table (**refresh on commit**) or only when the DBMS_MVIEW.REFRESH procedure is run (**refresh on demand**).

When you specify Force refresh, the refresh process first evaluates whether or not a Fast refresh can be run. If it can't, a Complete refresh will be performed. If you specify Never as the refresh option, the materialized view will not be refreshed.

If you do not have a materialized view log created and populated, only Complete refreshes can be executed.

Creating a Materialized View

The syntax used to create the materialized view is shown in the following listing. In this example, the materialized view is given a name (STORE_DEPT_SAL_MV), and its storage parameters are specified as well as its refresh interval and the time at which it will be populated with data. In this case, the materialized view is told to use the Complete refresh option and not populate the data until the DBMS_MVIEW.REFRESH procedure is run. Query rewrite is enabled. The materialized view's base query is then given.

```
create materialized view STORE_DEPT_SAL_MV
pctfree 0 tablespace MVIEWS
storage (initial 1M next 1M pctincrease 0)
build deferred
refresh complete
enable query rewrite
as
select d.DNAME, sum(SAL) as tot_sum
  from DEPT d, EMP e
where d.DEPTNO = e.DEPTNO
group by d.DNAME;
```

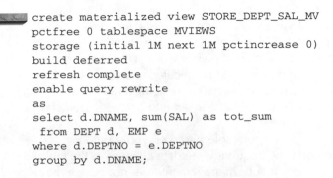

> **NOTE**
> *A materialized view query cannot reference tables or views owned by the user SYS.*

Here is another example of a materialized view creation, using **refresh fast on commit**. To support fast refreshes when commits occur, you will need to create a materialized view log on the base table. See "Managing Materialized View Logs" later in this chapter for details.

```
create materialized view STORE_DEPT_SAL_MV
pctfree 0 tablespace MYMVIEWS
storage (initial 20k next 20k pctincrease 0)
parallel
build immediate
refresh fast on commit
enable query rewrite
as
select d.DNAME, sum(SAL) as tot_sum
  from DEPT d, EMP e
where d.DEPTNO = e.DEPTNO
group by d.DNAME;
```

In this example, the same base query is used, but the materialized view name is created with a Fast refresh to be performed every time a transaction is committed in the master table. This materialized view will be populated with data on creation, and the inserted information will be loaded in parallel. Query rewrite is enabled.

NOTE
The fast refresh option will not be used unless a materialized view log is created on the base table for the materialized view. Oracle can perform fast refreshes of joined tables in materialized views.

See Appendix A for the full syntax options of the **create materialized view** command.

You can alter the materialized view's storage parameters via the **alter materialized view** command, as shown in the following listing:

```
alter materialized view STORE_DEPT_SAL_MV pctfree 5;
```

The two most frequently used operations against a materialized view are queries and refreshes. Each of these actions requires different resources and has different performance requirements. You may index the base table of the materialized view—for example, adding a bitmap index—to improve query performance. If you have a materialized view that uses join conditions, an index on the key columns may improve the Fast refresh operations. If your materialized view uses both joins and aggregates and is Fast refreshable, as shown in the earlier example, an index is automatically created for the view unless you specify **using no index** in the **create materialized view** command.

To drop a materialized view, use the **drop materialized view** command:

```
drop materialized view STORE_DEPT_SAL_MV;
```

Available Tools
There are two different packages that you can use to manage and evaluate your materialized views: DBMS_MVIEW and DBMS_OLAP. To create these packages for materialized views, you must run dbmssnap.sql and dbmssum.sql, respectively.

The DBMS_MVIEW package is used to perform management actions such as evaluating, registering, or refreshing a materialized view. The DBMS_MVIEW package options are shown in Table 16-1.

The DBMS_OLAP package can be used to determine whether a materialized view would enhance your database query performance, generate materialized view creation scripts, estimate the size the materialized view would be, and so on. The DBMS_OLAP package options are shown in Table 16-2.

Subprogram	Description
BEGIN_TABLE_REORGANIZATION	Performs a process to preserve the data needed for a materialized view refresh; used prior to reorganizing the master table.
END_TABLE_REORGANIZATION	Ensures that the materialized view master table is in the proper state and that the master table is valid, at the end of a master table reorganization.
EXPLAIN_MVIEW	Explains what is possible with an existing or proposed materialized view (is it Fast refreshable, is query rewrite available).
EXPLAIN_REWRITE	Explains why a query failed to rewrite, or which materialized views will be used if it rewrites.
I_AM_A_REFRESH	The value of the I_AM_A_REFRESH package state is returned; called during replication.
PMARKER	Used for partition change tracking; returns a partition marker from a RowID.
PURGE_DIRECT_LOAD_LOG	Used with data warehousing, this subprogram purges rows from the direct loader log after they are no longer needed by a materialized view.
PURGE_LOG	Purges a subset of rows from the materialized view log.
PURGE_MVIEW_FROM_LOG	Deletes all rows from the materialized view log for the specified materialized view.
REFRESH	Refreshes one or more materialized views that are not members of the same refresh group.
REFRESH_ALL	Refreshes all materialized views that do not reflect changes to their master table or master materialized view.

TABLE 16-1. *DBMS_MVIEW Subprograms*

Subprogram	Description
REFRESH_DEPENDENT	Refreshes all table-based materialized views that depend on either a specified master table or master materialized view. The list can contain one or more master tables or master materialized views.
REGISTER_MVIEW	Enable an individual materialized view's administration.
UNREGISTER_MVIEW	Used to unregister a materialized view at a master site or master materialized view site.

TABLE 16-1. *DBMS_MVIEW Subprograms* (continued)

Subprogram	Description
ADD_FILTER_ITEM	Filters the contents used during the recommendation process.
CREATE_ID	Creates an internal ID used by a new workload collection, a new filter, or a new advisor run.
ESTIMATE_MVIEW_SIZE	Estimates the size of a materialized view in bytes and rows that you could create.
EVALUATE_MVIEW_STRATEGY	Measures the utilization of each existing materialized view.
GENERATE_MVIEW_REPORT	Generates an HTML-based report on the given Advisor run.
GENERATE_MVIEW_SCRIPT	Generates a simple script containing the SQL commands to implement recommendations made in the Summary Advisor report.
LOAD_WORKLOAD_CACHE	Obtains a SQL cache workload.
LOAD_WORKLOAD_TRACE	Loads a workload collected by Oracle Trace.

TABLE 16-2. *DBMS_OLTP Subprograms*

Subprogram	Description
LOAD_WORKLOAD_USER	Loads a user-defined workload.
PURGE_FILTER	Deletes a specific filter or all filters.
PURGE_RESULTS	Removes all results or those for a specific run.
PURGE_WORKLOAD	Deletes a specific collection or all workloads.
RECOMMEND_MVIEW_STRATEGY	Generates a set of recommendations about which materialized views should be created, retained, or dropped.
SET_CANCELLED	If the Advisor is taking too long to report results, stops the Advisor.
VALIDATE_DIMENSION	Verifies that the relationships specified in a dimension are correct.
VALIDATE_WORKLOAD_CACHE	Validates the SQL Cache workload before performing load operations.
VALIDATE_WORKLOAD_TRACE	Validates the Oracle Trace workload before performing load operations.
VALIDATE_WORKLOAD_USER	Validates the user-supplied workload before performing load operations.

TABLE 16-2. *DBMS_OLTP Subprograms* (continued)

To refresh a single materialized view, use DBMS_MVIEW.REFRESH. Its two main parameters are the name of the materialized view to be refreshed and the method to use. For the method, you can specify 'c' for a Complete refresh, 'f' for Fast refresh, and '?' for Force. For example:

```
execute DBMS_MVIEW.REFRESH('store_dept_sal_mv','c');
```

If you are refreshing multiple materialized views via a single execution of DBMS_MVIEW.REFRESH, list the names of all of the materialized views in the first parameter, and their matching refresh methods in the second parameter, as shown here:

```
execute DBMS_MVIEW.REFRESH('mv1,mv2,mv3','cfc');
```

In this example, the materialized view named MV2 will be refreshed via a Fast refresh, while the others will use a Complete refresh.

You can use a separate procedure in the DBMS_MVIEW package to refresh all of the materialized views that are scheduled to be automatically refreshed. This procedure, named REFRESH_ALL, will refresh each materialized view separately. It does not accept any parameters. The following listing shows an example of its execution:

```
execute DBMS_MVIEW.REFRESH_ALL;
```

Since the materialized views will be refreshed via REFRESH_ALL consecutively, they are not all refreshed at the same time. Therefore, a database or server failure during the execution of this procedure may cause the local materialized views to be out of sync with each other. If that happens, simply rerun this procedure after the database has been recovered. As an alternative, you can create refresh groups, as described in the next section.

Enforcing Referential Integrity among Materialized Views

The referential integrity between two related tables, both of which have simple materialized views based on them, may not be enforced in their materialized views. If the tables are refreshed at different times, or if transactions are occurring on the master tables during the refresh, it is possible that the materialized views of those tables will not reflect the referential integrity of the master tables.

If, for example, EMPLOYEE and DEPT are related to each other via a primary key/ foreign key relationship, then simple materialized views of these tables may contain violations of this relationship, including foreign keys without matching primary keys. In this example, that could mean employees in the EMPLOYEE materialized view with DEPTNO values that do not exist in the DEPT materialized view.

There are a number of potential solutions to this problem. First, time the refreshes to occur when the master tables are not in use. Second, perform the refreshes manually (see the following section for information on this) immediately after locking the master tables or quiescing the database. Third, you may join the tables in the materialized view, creating a complex materialized view that will be based on the master tables (which will be properly related to each other).

Using refresh groups is a fourth solution to the referential integrity problem. You can collect related materialized views into *refresh groups*. The purpose of a refresh group is to coordinate the refresh schedules of its members. Materialized views whose master tables have relationships with other master tables are good candidates for membership in refresh groups. Coordinating the refresh schedules of the materialized views will maintain the master tables' referential integrity in the materialized view as well. If refresh groups are not used, the data in the materialized views may be inconsistent with regard to the master tables' referential integrity.

Manipulation of refresh groups is performed via the DBMS_REFRESH package. The procedures within that package are MAKE, ADD, SUBTRACT, CHANGE, DESTROY, and REFRESH, as shown in the following examples. Information about

existing refresh groups can be queried from the USER_REFRESH and
USER_REFRESH_CHILDREN data dictionary views.

NOTE
*Materialized views that belong to a refresh group do
not have to belong to the same schema, but they all
have to be stored within the same database.*

Create a refresh group by executing the MAKE procedure in the
DBMS_REFRESH package, whose structure is shown in the following listing:

```
DBMS_REFRESH.MAKE
(name IN VARCHAR2,
 list IN VARCHAR2, |
  tab IN DBMS_UTILITY.UNCL_ARRAY,
 next_date IN DATE,
 interval IN VARCHAR2,
 implicit_destroy IN BOOLEAN := FALSE,
 lax IN BOOLEAN := FALSE,
 job IN BINARY INTEGER := 0,
 rollback_seg IN VARCHAR2 := NULL,
 push_deferred_rpc IN BOOLEAN := TRUE,
 refresh_after_errors IN BOOLEAN := FALSE,
 purge_option IN BINARY_INTEGER := NULL,
 parallelism IN BINARY_INTEGER := NULL,
 heap_size IN BINARY_INTEGER := NULL);
```

All but the first four of the parameters for this procedure have default values that
are usually acceptable. The *list* and *tab* parameters are mutually exclusive. You can
use the following command to create a refresh group for materialized views named
LOCAL_EMP and LOCAL_DEPT. Note that although the command is shown here
separated across several lines, do not enter hard returns between the command lines.

```
execute DBMS_REFRESH.MAKE
(name => 'emp_group',
 list => 'local_emp, local_dept',
 next_date => SysDate,
 interval => 'SysDate+7');
```

NOTE
The list *parameter, which is the second parameter
in the listing, has a single quote at its beginning
and at its end, with none between. In this example,
two materialized views—LOCAL_EMP and
LOCAL_DEPT—are passed to the procedure via
a single parameter.*

The preceding command will create a refresh group named EMP_GROUP, with two materialized views as its members. The refresh group name is enclosed in single quotes, as is the *list* of members—but not each member.

If the refresh group is going to contain a materialized view that is already a member of another refresh group (for example, during a move of a materialized view from an old refresh group to a newly created refresh group), then you must set the *lax* parameter to TRUE. A materialized view can only belong to one refresh group at a time.

To add materialized views to an existing refresh group, use the ADD procedure of the DBMS_REFRESH package, whose structure is

```
DBMS_REFRESH.ADD
(name IN VARCHAR2,
 list IN VARCHAR2, |
  tab IN DBMS_UTILITY.UNCL_ARRAY,
 lax IN BOOLEAN := FALSE);
```

As with the MAKE procedure, the ADD procedure's *lax* parameter does not have to be specified unless a materialized view is being moved between two refresh groups. When this procedure is executed with the *lax* parameter set to TRUE, the materialized view is moved to the new refresh group and is automatically deleted from the old refresh group.

To remove materialized views from an existing refresh group, use the SUBTRACT procedure of the DBMS_REFRESH package, as in the following listing:

```
DBMS_REFRESH.SUBTRACT
(name IN VARCHAR2,
 list IN VARCHAR2, |
  tab IN DBMS_UTILITY.UNCL_ARRAY,
 lax IN BOOLEAN := FALSE);
```

As with the MAKE and ADD procedures, a single materialized view or a list of materialized views (separated by commas) may serve as input to the SUBTRACT procedure. You can alter the refresh schedule for a refresh group via the CHANGE procedure of the DBMS_REFRESH package:

```
DBMS_REFRESH.CHANGE
(name IN VARCHAR2,
 next_date IN DATE := NULL,
 interval IN VARCHAR2 := NULL,
 implicit_destroy IN BOOLEAN := NULL,
 rollback_seg IN VARCHAR2 := NULL,
 push_deferred_rpc IN BOOLEAN := NULL,
 refresh_after_errors IN BOOLEAN := NULL,
 purge_option IN BINARY_INTEGER := NULL,
 parallelism IN BINARY_INTEGER := NULL,
 heap_size IN BINARY_INTEGER := NULL);
```

The *next_date* parameter is analogous to the **start with** clause in the **create materialized view** command. The *interval* parameter is analogous to the **next** clause in the **create materialized view** command. For example, to change the EMP_GROUP's schedule so that it will be replicated every three days, you can execute the following command (which specifies a **NULL** value for the *next_date* parameter, leaving that value unchanged):

```
execute DBMS_REFRESH.CHANGE
(name => 'emp_group',
 next_date => null,
 interval => 'SysDate+3');
```

After this command is executed, the refresh cycle for the EMP_GROUP refresh group will be changed to every three days.

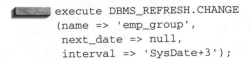

> **NOTE**
> *Refresh operations on refresh groups may take longer than comparable materialized view refreshes. Group refreshes may also require significant undo segment space to maintain data consistency during the refresh.*

You may manually refresh a refresh group via the REFRESH procedure of the DBMS_REFRESH package. The REFRESH procedure accepts the name of the refresh group as its only parameter. The command shown in the following listing will refresh the refresh group named EMP_GROUP:

```
execute DBMS_REFRESH.REFRESH('emp_group');
```

To delete a refresh group, use the DESTROY procedure of the DBMS_REFRESH package, as shown in the following example. Its only parameter is the name of the refresh group.

```
execute DBMS_REFRESH.DESTROY(name => 'emp_group');
```

You may also implicitly destroy the refresh group. If you set the *implicit_destroy* parameter to TRUE when you create the group with the MAKE procedure, the refresh group will be deleted (destroyed) when its last member is removed from the group (usually via the SUBTRACT procedure).

> **NOTE**
> *For performance statistics related to materialized view refreshes, query V$MVREFRESH.*

Managing Materialized View Logs

A materialized view log is a table that maintains a record of modifications to the master table in a materialized view. It is stored in the same database as the master table and is only used by simple materialized views. The data in the materialized view log is used during Fast refreshes. If you are going to use Fast refreshes, create the materialized view log before creating the materialized view.

To create a materialized view log, you must be able to create an AFTER ROW trigger on the table, so you need CREATE TRIGGER and CREATE TABLE privileges. You cannot specify a name for the materialized view log.

Since the materialized view log is a table, it has the full set of table storage clauses available to it. The example in the following listing shows the creation of a materialized view log on a table named EMPLOYEE:

```
create materialized view log on EMPLOYEE
tablespace DATA_2
storage(initial 1M next 1M pctincrease 0)
pctfree 5 pctused 90;
```

The **pctfree** value for the materialized view log can be set very low, and the **pctused** value should be set very high, as shown in this example. The size of the materialized view log depends on the number of changes that will be processed during each refresh. The more frequently the materialized view is refreshed, the less space needed for the log.

You can modify the storage parameters for the materialized view log via the **alter materialized view log** command. When using this command, specify the name of the master table. An example of altering the EMPLOYEE table's materialized view log is shown in the following listing:

```
alter materialized view log EMPLOYEE
pctfree 10;
```

To drop a materialized view log, use the **drop materialized view log** command, as shown in the following example:

```
drop materialized view log on EMPLOYEE;
```

This command will drop the materialized view log and its associated objects from the database.

Purging the Materialized View Log

The materialized view log contains transient data; records are **insert**ed into the log, used during refreshes, and then **delete**d. You should encourage reuse of the log's blocks by setting a high value for **pctused** when creating the log.

If multiple materialized views use the same master table, then they share the same materialized view log. If one of the materialized views is not refreshed for a long period, the materialized view log may never delete any of its records. As a result, the space requirements of the materialized view log will grow.

To reduce the space used by log entries, you can use the PURGE_LOG procedure of the DBMS_MVIEW package. PURGE_LOG takes three parameters: the name of the master table, a *num* variable, and a DELETE flag. The *num* variable specifies the number of least recently refreshed materialized views whose rows will be removed from the materialized view log. For example, if you have three materialized views that use the materialized view log and one of them has not been refreshed for a very long time, you would use a *num* value of 1.

The following listing shows an example of the PURGE_LOG procedure. In this example, the EMPLOYEE table's materialized view log will be purged of the entries required by the least recently used materialized view:

```
execute DBMS_MVIEW.PURGE_LOG
(master => 'EMPLOYEE',
   num => 1,
   flag => 'DELETE');
```

To further support maintenance efforts, Oracle provides two materialized view-specific options for the **truncate** command. If you want to **truncate** the master table without losing its materialized view log entries, you can enter the command

```
truncate table EMPLOYEE preserve materialized view log;
```

If the EMPLOYEE table's materialized view is based on primary key values (the default behavior), the materialized view log values will still be valid following an export/import of the EMPLOYEE tables. However, if the EMPLOYEE table's materialized views are based on RowID values, the materialized view log would be invalid following an export/import of the base table (since different RowIDs may be assigned during the import). In that case, you should **truncate** the materialized view log when you **truncate** the base table.

```
truncate table EMPLOYEE purge materialized view log;
```

Using OEM to Create a Materialized View

You can use the Oracle Enterprise Manager to create materialized views from either Standalone mode or from the Oracle Enterprise Manager Server Console. Creating a materialized view from the Standalone mode will be shown here; the procedure is the same from either mode.

Once you have connected to the OEM Console and ensured that the database on which you want to create the materialized view is running, from the right side of the Console screen, click on the plus sign (+) next to the database of choice to expand the navigation options. Click on the plus sign next to the Schema option to expand it, and click on the Materialized View entry. Figure 16-5 shows the OEM Console screen with the Materialized Views entry highlighted and the current materialized views displayed.

You can choose the Create option by any one of the following methods:

- Use the pull-down Object | Create menu option.

- Place the mouse cursor on the Materialized Views highlighted entry and click the right mouse button to select the Create option.

- Click on the green Create cube icon (the third icon from the top on the right side of the screen).

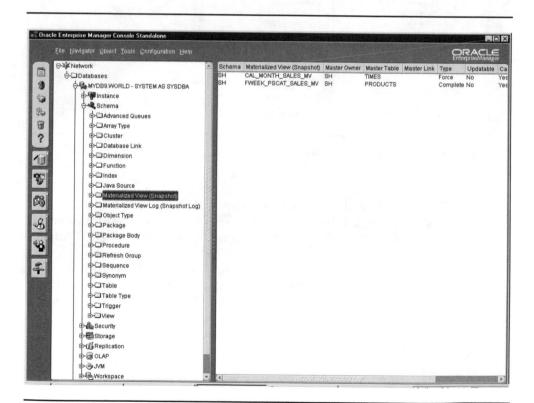

FIGURE 16-5. *OEM Console with Materialized View option highlighted*

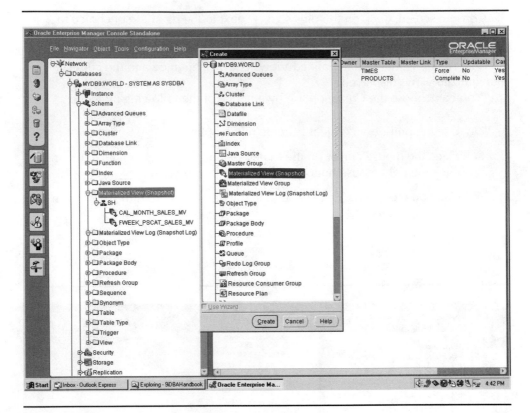

FIGURE 16-6. *OEM Create objects option screen*

Regardless of the method you choose, the Create object options box is displayed, as shown in Figure 16-6. The Materialized View object is highlighted. Once you have selected the object type that you want to create, click the Create button at the bottom of the screen.

After the Materialized View option has been selected and the Create button clicked, the Create Materialized View screen is displayed with five option tabs. The General tab is presented first, as shown in Figure 16-7. This tab enables you to enter a name and description for the new materialized view as well as names for the schema and tablespace you want to use. You can enable query rewrite from the General tab and, if the materialized view is to be used in an advanced replication environment, indicate whether the view should be updatable. If you have an existing table from

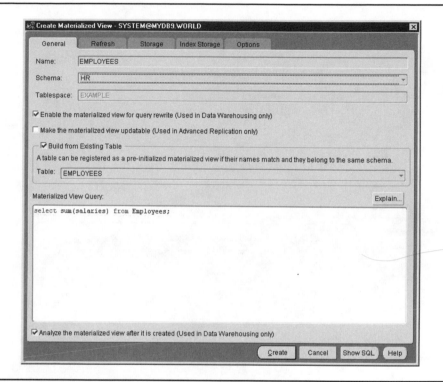

FIGURE 16-7. *Create Materialized View, General tab*

which you want the materialized view built, you can indicate this in the Build from Existing Table area of the tab. When you select this option, the list of values in the Table area becomes active, and you can select a table name from the schema you named in the second field of the General tab. If the view is to be used in a data warehouse environment, you can also indicate that you want the view analyzed after its creation. As with most OEM options, you can view the SQL that the tool is going to use by clicking the Show SQL button at the bottom of the screen.

If a materialized view is updatable, changes made to data in the materialized view can be propagated to the master table. To make a materialized view updatable, specify the **for update** clause. Updatable materialized views are part of multi-master environments—multiple sites serve as the data source for the same data. See the Oracle replication documentation for further details on creating and managing multi-master environments.

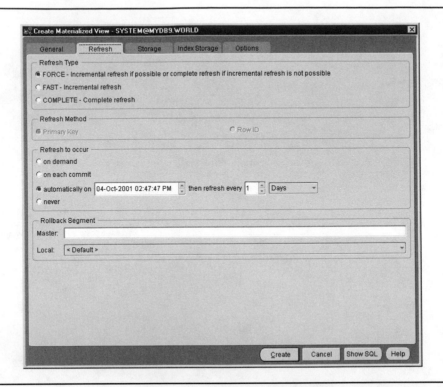

FIGURE 16-8. *Create Materialized View, Refresh tab*

The Refresh tab, shown in Figure 16-8, allows you to specify the following information:

■ The type of refresh you want for the new materialized view

■ The Refresh Method: Primary Key or Row ID

■ When the refresh should be performed: On Demand, On Each Commit, Automatically on a starting date and then automatically every *x* number of days, or Never

■ The name of the rollback segment to use either at the master site (Master) or local site (Local)

The Storage tab enables you to modify the storage parameters for the materialized view. In this example, the options shown in Figure 16-9 were not available for modification because the materialized view is being built on a preexisting table.

If both joins and aggregates are used in the materialized view query, an index is automatically created on the view. The Index Storage tab, shown in Figure 16-10, enables you to modify the storage location and parameters of the index. You can also designate that an index is not to be created.

The Options tab shown in Figure 16-11 enables you to request that the materialized view be loaded in parallel and lets you specify the logging characteristics. You can also designate that more frequently used data be placed at the top of the buffer cache.

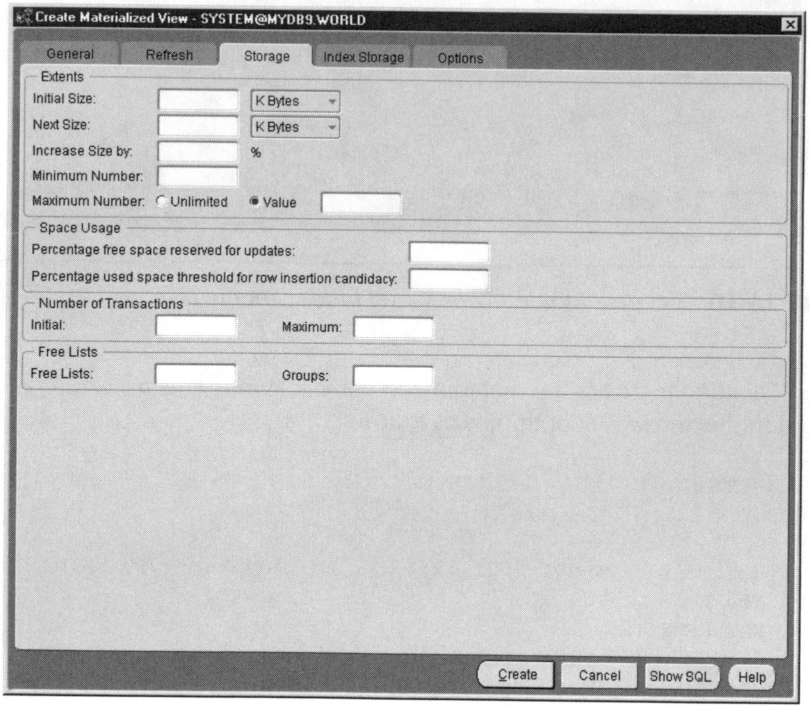

FIGURE 16-9.   *Create Materialized View, Storage tab*

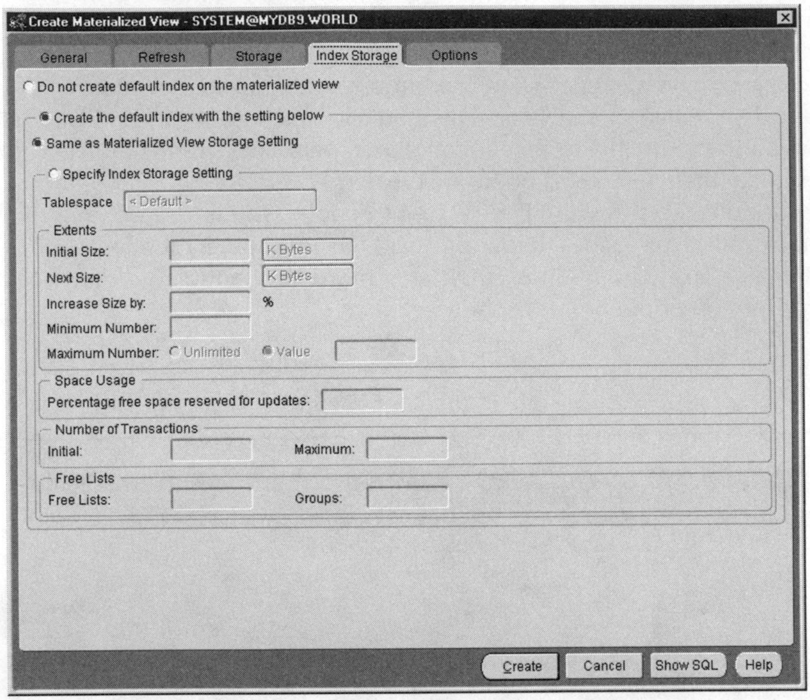

FIGURE 16-10. *Create Materialized View, Index Storage tab*

The SQL code to create the materialized view shown in this example, as displayed in the Show SQL option, is as follows:

```
CREATE MATERIALIZED VIEW "HR"."EMPLOYEES"
ON PREBUILT TABLE
REFRESH FORCE
START WITH to_date('04-Oct-2001 02:47:47 PM','dd-Mon-yyyy HH:MI:SS AM')
NEXT sysdate + 1
ENABLE QUERY REWRITE
AS
select sum(salaries) from Employees
BEGIN
    DBMS_STATS.GATHER_TABLE_STATS(
        ownname => 'HR',
        tabname => 'EMPLOYEES');
END;
```

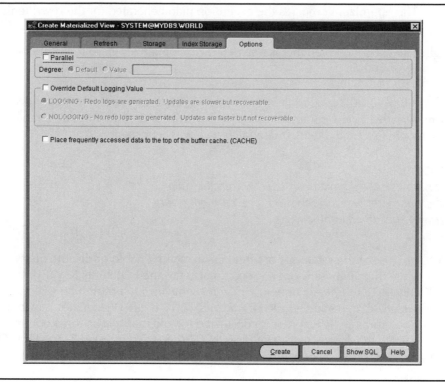

FIGURE 16-11. *Create Materialized View, Options tab*

About Query Rewrite

Using the query rewrite feature associated with materialized views, Oracle translates an SQL statement that references tables and views into one that accesses the materialized views defined on the tables that are transparent to the end-user application. Query rewrite works in conjunction with the cost-based optimizer and requires no references to the materialized view within the SQL statements.

The steps involved in the optimizer's decision to use query rewrite instead of going to the underlying tables or views are shown in Figure 16-12 and are as follows:

1. The user presents a query to the optimizer.

2. The optimizer generates the execution plan for the query as it has been presented. The query is rewritten and the execution plan is generated.

3. The optimizer compares the execution plan generated for the rewritten query with the execution plan generated for the original query.

4. The execution plan that is deemed by the optimizer to be the best one is executed.

If you have used the **build deferred** option of the **create materialized view** or **alter materialized view** command, the query rewrite feature will not be enabled until after the first time that the materialized view is refreshed.

> **NOTE**
> *If bind variables have been used within the query, the optimizer will not rewrite it even though query rewrite has been enabled.*

You can use **alter system set** or **alter session set** to enable or disable query rewrite while the database is open. You can also use the SQL hints REWRITE and NOREWRITE to influence the optimizer's behavior for a particular query.

The initialization parameter QUERY_REWRITE_INTEGRITY specifies how old a materialized view can be before it is considered too old to use. The three options associated with this parameter are ENFORCED, TRUSTED, and STALE_TOLERATED. When you use ENFORCE, consistency and integrity are enforced. With the TRUSTED

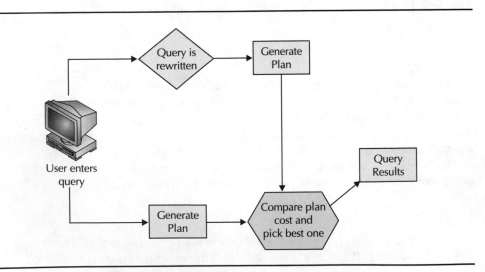

FIGURE 16-12. *Query rewrite flow*

option, the optimizer trusts that the data is fresh and that all of the relationships are correct and will use prebuilt materialized views or materialized views based on views. If you use STALE_TOLERATED, views that are inconsistent with the underlying detail tables can still be used for query rewrite.

When the optimizer rewrites a query, it uses a full text matching method where the entire text of the materialized view query is compared to the entire text of the submitted query. White spaces are ignored during the text matching operation. If the full text matching method fails, the optimizer will try to use a partial text match. In a partial text match, the submitted query is compared starting at the **from** clause to the materialized view starting at the **from** clause. When neither rewrite match succeeds, a general query rewrite is used. A general query rewrite will be used if any of the following criteria are met: Aggregate, Grouping, Join, or Selection compatibility or Data sufficiency. For more information on the query rewrite capabilities, see *Oracle9i Data Warehousing Guide* in the Oracle documentation set.

Managing Distributed Transactions

A single logical unit of work may include transactions against multiple databases. The example shown earlier in Figure 16-3 illustrates this: a **commit** is submitted after two tables in separate databases have been **update**d. Oracle will transparently maintain the integrity between the two databases by ensuring that all of the transactions involved either **commit** or roll back as a group. This is accomplished automatically via Oracle's Two-Phase Commit (2PC) mechanism.

In the first phase of the 2PC, the prepare phase, each node involved in a transaction prepares the data that it will need either to **commit** or roll back the data. Once prepared, a node is said to be *in doubt*. The nodes notify the initiating node for the transaction (known as the *global coordinator*) of their status.

Once all nodes are prepared, the transaction enters the commit phase, and all nodes are instructed to **commit** their portion of the logical transaction. The databases all **commit** the data at the same logical time, preserving the integrity of the distributed data.

Resolving In-Doubt Transactions

Transactions against stand-alone databases may fail due to problems with the database server; for example, there may be a media failure. Working with distributed databases increases the number of potential failure causes during a set of related transactions.

When a distributed transaction is pending, an entry for that transaction will appear in the DBA_2PC_PENDING data dictionary view. When the transaction completes, its DBA_2PC_PENDING record is removed. If the transaction is pending, but is not able to complete, then its record stays in DBA_2PC_PENDING.

The RECO (Recoverer) background process periodically checks the DBA_2PC_PENDING view for distributed transactions that failed to complete. Using the information there, the RECO process on a node will automatically attempt to recover the local portion of an in-doubt transaction. It then attempts to establish connections to any other databases involved in the transaction and resolves the distributed portions of the transaction. The related rows in the DBA_2PC_PENDING views in each database are then removed.

> **NOTE**
> *The RECO background process will not be started unless the DISTRIBUTED_TRANSACTIONS parameter in your database parameter file is set to a nonzero value prior to startup. This parameter should be set to the anticipated maximum number of concurrent distributed transactions.*

The recovery of distributed transactions is performed automatically by the RECO process. You can manually recover the local portions of a distributed transaction, but this will usually result in inconsistent data between the distributed databases. If a local recovery is performed, the remote data will be out of sync.

To minimize the number of distributed recoveries necessary, you can influence the way that the distributed transaction is processed. The transaction processing is influenced via the use of *commit point strengths* to tell the database how to structure the transaction.

Commit Point Strength

Each set of distributed transactions may reference multiple hosts and databases. Of those, one host and database can normally be singled out as being the most reliable, or as owning the most critical data. This database is known as the *commit point site*; if data is committed there, it should be committed for all databases. If the transaction against the commit point site fails, the transactions against the other nodes are rolled back. The commit point site also stores information about the status of the distributed transaction.

The commit point site will be selected by Oracle based on each database's commit point strength. This is set via the initialization file, as shown in the following listing:

```
COMMIT_POINT_STRENGTH=100
```

The values for the COMMIT_POINT_STRENGTH parameter are set on a relative scale, not on an absolute scale. In the preceding example, it was set to 100. If another database has a commit point strength of 200, then that database would be the commit point site for a distributed transaction involving those two databases. The COMMIT_POINT_STRENGTH value cannot exceed 255.

Since the scale is relative, set up a site-specific scale. Set the commit point on your most reliable database to 200. Then, grade the other servers and databases relative to that most reliable database. If, for example, another database is only 80 percent as reliable as the most reliable database, then assign it a commit point strength of 160 (80 percent of 200). Fixing a single database at a definite point (in this case, 200) allows the rest of the databases to be graded on an even scale. This scale should result in the proper commit point site being used for each transaction.

Monitoring Distributed Databases

Most database-level monitoring systems, such as the Command Center database described in Chapter 6, analyze the performance of databases without taking their environments into account. However, there are several other key performance measures that must be taken into account for databases:

- Performance of the host
- Distribution of I/O across disks and controllers
- Usage of available memory

For distributed databases, you must also consider the following:

- Capacity of the network and its hardware
- Load on the network segments
- Usage of different physical access paths between hosts

None of these can be measured from within the database. The focus of monitoring efforts for distributed databases shifts from being database-centric to network-centric. The database becomes one part of the monitored environment, rather than the only part that is checked.

You still need to monitor those aspects of the database that are critical to its success, such as the free space in tablespaces. However, the *performance* of distributed databases cannot be measured except as part of the performance of the network that supports them. Therefore, all performance-related tests, such as stress tests, must be coordinated with the network management staff. That staff may also be able to verify the effectiveness of your attempts to reduce the database load on the network.

The performance of the individual hosts can usually be monitored via a network monitoring package. This monitoring is thus performed in a top-down fashion—network to host to database. Use the monitoring system described in Chapter 6 as an extension to the network and host monitors.

Tuning Distributed Databases

When tuning a stand-alone database, the goal is to reduce the amount of time it takes to find data. As described in Chapter 8, you can use a number of database structures and options to increase the likelihood that the data will be found in memory or in the first place that the database looks.

When working with distributed databases, there is an additional consideration. Since data is now not only being found but also being shipped across the network, the performance of a query is made up of the performance of these two steps. You must therefore consider the ways in which data is being transferred across the network, with a goal of reducing the network traffic.

A simple way to reduce network traffic is to replicate data from one node to another. You can do this manually (via the SQL*Plus **copy** command) or automatically by the database (via materialized views). Replicating data improves the performance of queries against remote databases by bringing the data across the network once—usually during a slow period on the local host. Local queries can use the local copy of the data, eliminating the network traffic that would otherwise be required.

Two problems commonly arise with replicated solutions. First, the local data may become out of sync with the remote data. This is a standard problem with derived data; it limits the usefulness of this option to tables whose data is fairly static. Even if a simple materialized view is used with a materialized view log, the data will not be refreshed continuously—only when scheduled.

The second problem with the replicated data solution is that the copy of the table may not be able to pass **update**s back to the master table. That is, if a read-only materialized view is used to make a local copy of a remote table, then the snapshot cannot be **update**d. If you are using materialized views, you can use updatable materialized views to send changes back to the master site, or writable materialized views to support local ownership of data.

Any **update**s that must be processed against replicas must also be performed against the master tables. If the table is frequently **update**d, then replicating the data will not improve your performance unless you are using Oracle's multi-master replication options. When there is multisite ownership of data, users can make changes in any database designated as an owner of the data. The management of Oracle's multi-master replication is very involved, and requires creating a database environment (with database links, etc.) specifically designed to support multidirectional replication of data. See the Oracle replication documentation for details on implementing a multi-master environment.

In single-master environments, the type of materialized view to use depends on the nature of the application. Simple materialized views do not involve any data manipulation with the query; they are simply copies of rows from remote tables. Complex materialized views perform operations such as **group by**, **connect by**, or joins on the remote tables. Knowing which type of materialized view to use requires that you know the way in which the data is to be used by the local database.

If you use simple materialized views, you can use materialized view logs. When it is time to refresh that table's materialized views, only the transactions from the materialized view log are sent across the network. If the remote table is frequently modified, and you need frequent refreshes of less than 25 percent of the table's rows, then using a simple materialized view will improve the performance of the materialized view refresh process.

When a complex materialized view is refreshed, Oracle may have to completely **truncate** and repopulate the underlying tables. This seems at first like a tremendous burden to put on the system—why not find a way to use simple materialized views instead? However, there are potential advantages to complex materialized views:

- Tables chosen for replication are typically modified infrequently. Therefore, the refreshes can normally be scheduled for low-usage times in the local database, lessening the impact of full refreshes.

- Complex materialized views may replicate less data than simple materialized views.

The second point may seem a little cryptic. After all, a complex materialized view usually involves more processing than a simple materialized view, so shouldn't it require more work for the network? Actually, it may require *less* work for the network, because more work is being done by the database.

Consider the case of two tables being replicated via materialized views. The users on the local database will always query the two tables together, via a join. As shown in Figure 16-13, there are two options. You can either use two simple materialized views (Figure 16-13a), or you can perform the join via a complex materialized view (Figure 16-13b). What is the difference in performance between the two?

If the tables are joined properly, then the complex materialized view should not send any more data across the network than the two simple materialized views will when they are first created. In fact, it will most likely send less data during its

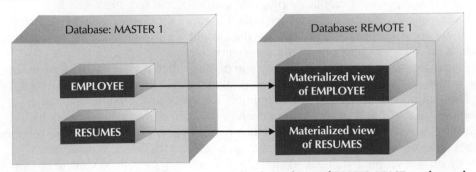

(a) Multiple simple materialized views; materialized view logs and REFRESH FAST can be used.

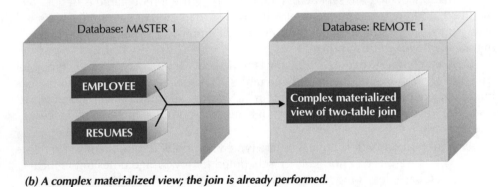

(b) A complex materialized view; the join is already performed.

FIGURE 16-13.   *Data replication options for joins*

creation. When choosing between these two alternatives on the basis of performance, you need to consider two factors:

- Performance of the refreshes
- Performance of queries against the materialized views

The second of these criteria is usually the more important of the two. After all, the data is being replicated to improve local processing performance. If the users only access the tables via a specific join, then the complex materialized view has already performed the join for them. Performing the join against two simple materialized views may take longer. You cannot determine which of these options is preferable until the access paths that the users will use have been fully defined. If the tables are sometimes queried separately, or via a different join path, then you will need to use simple materialized views or multiple complex materialized views.

The performance of the refreshes generally won't concern your users. What may concern them is the validity and timeliness of the data. If the remote tables are frequently modified, and are of considerable size, you are almost forced to use simple materialized views with materialized view logs to keep the data current. Performing complete refreshes in the middle of a workday is generally unacceptable. Thus, it is the *frequency* of the refreshes rather than the size of them that determines which type of materialized view will better serve the users. After all, users are most concerned about the performance of the system while they are using it; refreshes performed late at night do not directly affect them. If the tables need to be frequently synchronized, use simple materialized views with materialized view logs.

As was noted previously in this chapter, you may index the underlying tables that are created by the materialized view in the local database. Indexing should also help to improve query performance, at the expense of slowing down the refreshes.

Another means of reducing network traffic, via remote procedure calls, is described in Chapter 8. That chapter also includes information on tuning SQL and the application design. If the database was properly structured, tuning the way the application processes data will yield the most significant performance improvements.

Using the Job Queues

In order to support snapshot refreshes and other replication functions, Oracle manages a set of internal job queues. If you have enabled job queues within your database (via the JOB_QUEUE_PROCESSES initialization parameter), you can submit jobs of your own to the queues. You can use these queues in place of operating system job queues.

To manage the internal job queue, you can use the SUBMIT, REMOVE, CHANGE, WHAT, NEXT_DATE, INTERVAL, BROKEN, and RUN procedures of the DBMS_JOB package. The most important are the SUBMIT, REMOVE, and RUN procedures.

The SUBMIT procedure has seven parameters, as follows:

```
PROCEDURE SUBMIT
   ( job       OUT BINARY_INTEGER,
     what      IN  VARCHAR2,
     next_date IN  DATE DEFAULT sysdate,
     interval  IN  VARCHAR2 DEFAULT 'null',
     no_parse  IN  BOOLEAN DEFAULT FALSE,
     instance  IN  BINARY_INTEGER DEFAULT any_instance,
     force     IN  BOOLEAN DEFAULT FALSE);
```

The *job* parameter is an output parameter; Oracle generates a job number for the job via the SYS.JOBSEQ sequence. When you submit a job, you should first define a variable that will accept the job number as the output. For example, the following listing defines a variable and submits a job to execute 'myproc' every day:

```
variable jobno number;
begin
  DBMS_JOB.SUBMIT(:jobno,'myproc',SysDate,SysDate+1);
  commit;
end;
/

print jobno

JOBNO
-----------
      8791
```

The submitter of a job can later alter the job (via the BROKEN, CHANGE, INTERVAL, NEXT_DATE and WHAT procedures), remove it from the queue (the REMOVE procedure), or force it to run (the RUN procedure). For each of these procedures, you will need to know the job number.

If you did not record the job number when you submitted your job, you can query the DBA_JOBS view to see the jobs submitted in your database.

Managing Jobs

You can alter a job to "broken" state via the BROKEN procedure. If you mark a job as being broken, it will not be run the next time it is scheduled to run. The structure of the BROKEN procedure is

```
PROCEDURE BROKEN
( job        IN   BINARY_INTEGER,
  broken     IN   BOOLEAN,
  next_date  IN   DATE DEFAULT SYSDATE );
```

If you have previously set a job to be broken (by setting the *broken* variable to TRUE), then you can set it to be not broken by setting the *broken* variable to FALSE.

The CHANGE procedure lets you change the code you want to have executed via the *what* parameter, the next date on which the job will be run, and the interval between job runs. Its structure is

```
PROCEDURE CHANGE
( job        IN   BINARY_INTEGER,
  what       IN   VARCHAR2,
  next_date  IN   DATE,
  interval   IN   VARCHAR2,
  instance   IN   BINARY_INTEGER DEFAULT NULL,
  force      IN   BOOLEAN DEFAULT FALSE);
```

If you do not specify a value for the CHANGE variables (or set them to **NULL**), they will be left at their former settings. Thus, you can change part of the job specification via the CHANGE procedure without having to reset all of the job's settings.

If you only want to change the interval between job executions, you can use the INTERVAL procedure, whose two parameters are the job number and the new interval function. You can use the NEXT_DATE procedure to change the next date on which the job is to be run; its two parameters are the job number and the date on which the job should be run.

If you want to change the PL/SQL code that is executed, you can use the WHAT procedure. Its two parameters are the job number and the PL/SQL code to be executed. The INTERVAL, NEXT_DATE, and WHAT procedures do not provide any capabilities that are not already provided via the CHANGE procedure described previously. When using CHANGE, just set to **NULL** the variables you don't want to change.

You can remove a job from the job queue via the REMOVE procedure. The REMOVE procedure has the job number as its sole input parameter. If you have many features of the job to change, you may wish to completely remove the job from the job queue and resubmit it.

To force a job to run at any time, use the RUN procedure. The RUN procedure, which takes the job number as its first input variable, is the only way you can run a broken job. Its second input variable is *force*, which defaults to FALSE. If set to FALSE, the job can be run in the foreground only in the specified instance. Setting *force* to TRUE bypasses the instance affinity restriction.

Job queues are typically used to manage internal database functions (such as analyzing database objects). If the jobs are to be part of the regular production maintenance of the database, they should be run via the normal scheduling mechanism for the system on which the database resides. Depending on the nature of the work performed, it may be more appropriate to run some jobs via a centrally controlled job management facility that is maintained outside of the database. For further details on the DBMS_JOB procedures, see the dbmsjob.sql file, which is located in the /rdbms/admin subdirectory under the Oracle software home directory.

APPENDIX

A

SQL Reference for DBA Commands

ALTER DATABASE

PURPOSE
Use the ALTER DATABASE statement to modify, maintain, or recover an existing database.

PREREQUISITES
You must have the ALTER DATABASE system privilege. To specify the RECOVER clause, you must also have the SYSDBA system privilege.

SYNTAX
alter_database::=

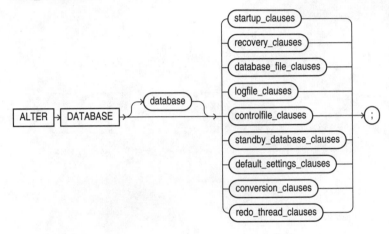

startup_clauses::=

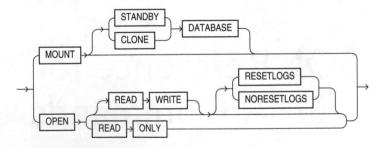

recovery_clauses::=

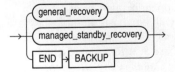

general_recovery::=

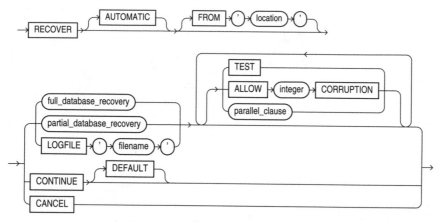

full_database_recovery::=

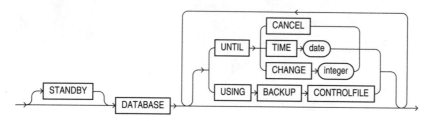

partial_database_recovery::=

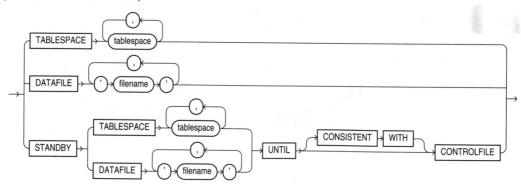

parallel_clause::=

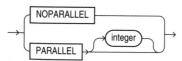

managed_standby_recovery::=

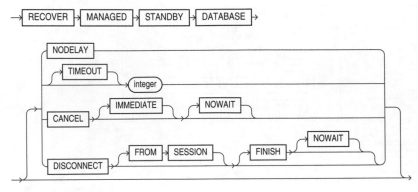

database_file_clauses::=

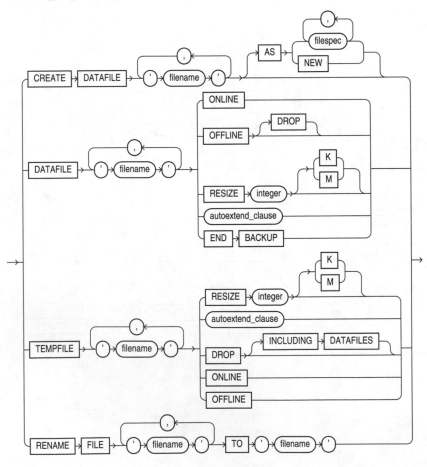

autoextend_clause::=

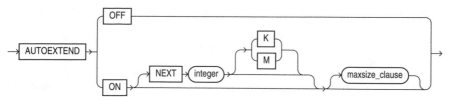

maxsize_clause::=

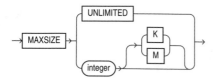

logfile_clauses::=

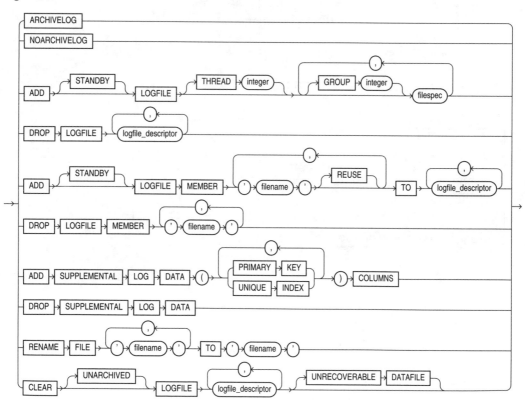

logfile_descriptor::=

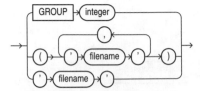

controlfile_clauses::=

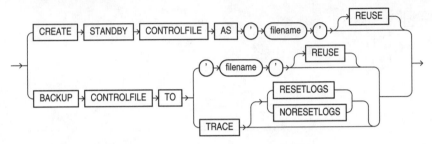

standby_database_clauses::=

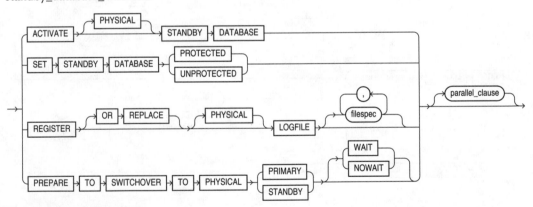

default_settings_clauses::=

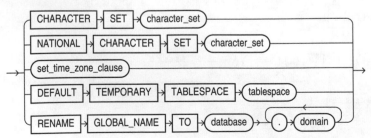

set_time_zone_clause::=

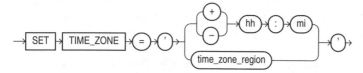

conversion_clauses::=

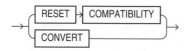

redo_thread_clauses::=

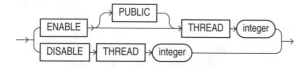

KEYWORDS AND PARAMETERS

database   Specify the name of the database to be altered. The database name can contain only ASCII characters. If you omit *database*, Oracle alters the database identified by the value of the initialization parameter DB_NAME. You can alter only the database whose control files are specified by the initialization parameter CONTROL_FILES. The database identifier is not related to the Oracle Net database specification.

startup_clauses   The *startup_clauses* let you mount and open the database so that it is accessible to users.

MOUNT Clause   Use the MOUNT clause to mount the database. Do not use this clause when the database is mounted.

MOUNT STANDBY DATABASE   Specify MOUNT STANDBY DATABASE to mount the standby database. As soon as this statement executes, the standby instance receives archived redo logs from the primary instance and archives the logs to the STANDBY_ARCHIVE_DEST location.

MOUNT CLONE DATABASE   Specify MOUNT CLONE DATABASE to mount the clone database.

OPEN Clause   Use the OPEN clause to make the database available for normal use. You must mount the database before you can open it. You must activate a standby database before you can open it.

   If you specify only OPEN, without any other keywords, the default is OPEN READ WRITE NORESETLOGS.

READ WRITE   Specify READ WRITE to open the database in read/write mode, allowing users to generate redo logs. This is the default.

RESETLOGS   Specify RESETLOGS to reset the current log sequence number to 1 and discards any redo information that was not applied during recovery, ensuring that it will never be applied. This effectively discards all changes that are in the redo log, but not in the database.

You must specify RESETLOGS to open the database after performing media recovery with an incomplete recovery using the RECOVER clause or with a backup control file. After opening the database with this clause, you should perform a complete database backup.

NORESETLOGS   Specify NORESETLOGS to retain the current state of the log sequence number and redo log files.

Restriction: You can specify RESETLOGS and NORESETLOGS only after performing incomplete media recovery or complete media recovery with a backup control file. In any other case, Oracle uses the NORESETLOGS automatically.

READ ONLY   Specify READ ONLY to restrict users to read-only transactions, preventing them from generating redo logs. You can use this clause to make a standby database available for queries even while archive logs are being copied from the primary database site.

Restrictions on the OPEN clause:

■   You cannot open a database READ ONLY if it is currently opened READ WRITE by another instance.

■   You cannot open a database READ ONLY if it requires recovery.

■   You cannot take tablespaces offline while the database is open READ ONLY. However, you can take datafiles offline and online, and you can recover offline datafiles and tablespaces while the database is open READ ONLY.

recovery_clauses   The *recovery_clauses* include post-backup operations.

general_recovery   The *general_recovery* clause lets you design media recovery for the database or standby database, or for specified tablespaces or files. You can use this clause when your instance has the database mounted, open or closed, and the files involved are not in use.

Restrictions:

■   You can recover the entire database only when the database is closed.

■   Your instance must have the database mounted in exclusive mode.

■   You can recover tablespaces or datafiles when the database is open or closed, provided that the tablespaces or datafiles to be recovered are offline.

■   You cannot perform media recovery if you are connected to Oracle through the Shared Server architecture.

NOTE
If you do not have special media requirements, Oracle Corporation recommends that you use the SQL*Plus RECOVER command rather than the general_recovery_clause.

AUTOMATIC   Specify AUTOMATIC if you want Oracle to automatically generate the name of the next archived redo log file needed to continue the recovery operation. If the LOG_ARCHIVE_DEST_*n* parameters are defined, Oracle scans those that are valid and enabled for the first local destination. It uses that destination in conjunction with LOG_ARCHIVE_FORMAT to generate the target redo log filename. If the LOG_ARCHIVE_DEST_*n* parameters are not defined, Oracle uses the value of the LOG_ARCHIVE_DEST parameter instead.

If the resulting file is found, Oracle applies the redo contained in that file. If the file is not found, Oracle prompts you for a filename, displaying the generated filename as a suggestion.

If you specify neither AUTOMATIC nor LOGFILE, Oracle prompts you for a filename, displaying the generated filename as a suggestion. You can then accept the generated filename or replace it with a fully qualified filename. If you know that the archived filename differs from what Oracle would generate, you can save time by using the LOGFILE clause.

FROM 'location'   Specify FROM *'location'* to indicate the location from which the archived redo log file group is read. The value of *location* must be a fully specified file location following the conventions of your operating system. If you omit this parameter, Oracle assumes that the archived redo log file group is in the location specified by the initialization parameter LOG_ARCHIVE_DEST or LOG_ARCHIVE_DEST_1.

full_database_recovery   The *full_database_recovery* clause lets you recover an entire database.

DATABASE   Specify the DATABASE clause to recover the entire database. This is the default. You can use this clause only when the database is closed.

STANDBY DATABASE   Specify the STANDBY DATABASE clause to recover the standby database using the control file and archived redo log files copied from the primary database. The standby database must be mounted but not open.

NOTE
This clause recovers only online datafiles.

- Use the UNTIL clause to specify the duration of the recovery operation.
    - CANCEL indicates cancel-based recovery. This clause recovers the database until you issue the ALTER DATABASE statement with the RECOVER CANCEL clause.
    - TIME indicates time-based recovery. This parameter recovers the database to the time specified by the date. The date must be a character literal in the format 'YYYY-MM-DD:HH24:MI:SS'.
    - CHANGE indicates change-based recovery. This parameter recovers the database to a transaction-consistent state immediately before the system change number (SCN) specified by *integer*.
- Specify USING BACKUP CONTROLFILE if you want to use a backup control file instead of the current control file.

partial_database_recovery   The *partial_database_recovery* clause lets you recover individual tablespaces and datafiles.

TABLESPACE   Specify the TABLESPACE clause to recover only the specified tablespaces. You can use this clause if the database is open or closed, provided the tablespaces to be recovered are offline.

DATAFILE   Specify the DATAFILE clause to recover the specified datafiles. You can use this clause when the database is open or closed, provided the datafiles to be recovered are offline.

STANDBY TABLESPACE   Specify STANDBY TABLESPACE to reconstruct a lost or damaged tablespace in the standby database using archived redo log files copied from the primary database and a control file.

STANDBY DATAFILE   Specify STANDBY DATAFILE to reconstruct a lost or damaged datafile in the standby database using archived redo log files copied from the primary database and a control file.

■ Specify UNTIL [CONSISTENT WITH] CONTROLFILE if you want the recovery of an old standby datafile or tablespace to use the current standby database control file. However, any redo in advance of the standby controlfile will not be applied. The keywords CONSISTENT WITH are optional and are provided for semantic clarity.

LOGFILE   Specify the LOGFILE '*filename*' to continue media recovery by applying the specified redo log file.

TEST   Use the TEST clause to conduct a trial recovery. A trial recovery is useful if a normal recovery procedure has encountered some problem. It lets you look ahead into the redo stream to detect possible additional problems. The trial recovery applies redo in a way similar to normal recovery, but it does not write changes to disk, and it rolls back its changes at the end of the trial recovery.

ALLOW ... CORRUPTION   The ALLOW *integer* CORRUPTION clause lets you specify, in the event of logfile corruption, the number of corrupt blocks that can be tolerated while allowing recovery to proceed.

When you use this clause during trial recovery (that is, in conjunction with the TEST clause), *integer* can exceed 1. When using this clause during normal recovery, *integer* cannot exceed 1.

parallel_clause   Use the PARALLEL clause to specify whether the recovery of media will be parallelized.

NOTE
The syntax of the parallel_clause *supersedes syntax appearing in earlier releases of Oracle. Superseded syntax is still supported for backward compatibility, but may result in slightly different behavior.*

NOPARALLEL   Specify NOPARALLEL for serial execution. This is the default.

PARALLEL   Specify PARALLEL if you want Oracle to select a degree of parallelism equal to the number of CPUs available on all participating instances times the value of the PARALLEL_THREADS_PER_CPU initialization parameter.

PARALLEL integer   Specification of *integer* indicates the **degree of parallelism**, which is the number of parallel threads used in the parallel operation. Each parallel thread may use one or two parallel execution servers. Normally Oracle calculates the optimum degree of parallelism, so it is not necessary for you to specify *integer*.

CONTINUE   Specify CONTINUE to continue multi-instance recovery after it has been interrupted to disable a thread.

Specify CONTINUE DEFAULT to continue recovery using the redo log file that Oracle would automatically generate if no other logfile were specified. This clause is equivalent to specifying AUTOMATIC, except that Oracle does not prompt for a filename.

CANCEL   Specify CANCEL to terminate cancel-based recovery.

managed_standby_recovery   The *managed_standby_recovery* clause specifies automated standby recovery mode. This mode assumes that the automated standby database is an active component of an overall standby database architecture. A primary database actively archives its redo log files to the standby site. As these archived redo logs arrive at the standby site, they become available for use by a managed standby recovery operation. Automated standby recovery is restricted to media recovery. You can use this clause when your instance has the database mounted, open or closed, and the files involved are not in use.

   Restrictions: The same restrictions apply as are listed under *general_recovery*.

NODELAY   Specify NODELAY if the need arises to apply a delayed archivelog immediately on the standby database. This clause overrides any setting of DELAY in the LOG_ARCHIVE_DEST_*n* parameter on the primary database. If you omit this clause, application of the archivelog is delayed according to the parameter setting. If DELAY was not specified in the parameter, the archivelog is applied immediately.

TIMEOUT   Use the TIMEOUT clause to specify in minutes the wait period of the managed recovery operation. The recovery process waits for *integer* minutes for a requested archived log redo to be available for writing to the automated standby database. If the redo log file does not become available within that time, the recovery process terminates with an error message. You can then issue the statement again to return to automated standby recovery mode.

   Restriction: You cannot specify TIMEOUT if you have specified DISCONNECT [FROM SESSION]. TIMEOUT applies only to foreground recovery operations, whereas the DISCONNECT clause initiates background recovery operations.

   If you do not specify TIMEOUT, the database remains in automated standby recovery mode until you reissue the statement with the RECOVER CANCEL clause or until instance shutdown or failure.

CANCEL   Specify CANCEL to terminate the managed standby recovery operation after applying all the redo in the current archived redo file. If you specify only CANCEL, session control returns when the recovery process actually terminates.

- ■ Specify CANCEL IMMEDIATE to terminate the managed recovery operation after applying all the redo in the current archived redo file or after the next redo log file read, whichever comes first. Session control returns when the recovery process actually terminates.

   Restriction: The CANCEL IMMEDIATE clause cannot be issued from the same session that issued the RECOVER MANAGED STANDBY DATABASE statement.

- ■ CANCEL IMMEDIATE NOWAIT is the same as CANCEL IMMEDIATE except that session control returns immediately, not after the recovery process terminates.

- ■ CANCEL NOWAIT terminates the managed recovery operation after the next redo log file read and returns session control immediately.

DISCONNECT   Specify DISCONNECT to indicate that the managed redo process (MRP), an Oracle background process, should apply archived redo files as a detached background process. Doing so leaves the current session available for other tasks. (The FROM SESSION keywords are optional and are provided for semantic clarity.)

FINISH   Specify FINISH to recover the current log standby logfiles of the standby database. This clause is useful in the event of the failure of the primary database, when the logwriter (LGWR) process has been transmitting redo to the standby current logs. This clause overrides any delay intervals specified for the archivelogs, so that Oracle applies the logs immediately.

NOWAIT   Specify NOWAIT to have control returned immediately rather than after the recovery process is complete.

END BACKUP Clause   Specify END BACKUP to take out of online backup mode any datafiles in the database currently in online backup mode. The database must be mounted but not open when you perform this operation.

You can end online ("hot") backup operations in three ways. During normal operation, you can take a tablespace out of online backup mode using the ALTER TABLESPACE ... END BACKUP statement. Doing so avoids the increased overhead of leaving the tablespace in online backup mode.

After a system failure, instance failure, or SHUTDOWN ABORT operation, Oracle does not know whether the files in online backup mode match the files at the time the system crashed. If you know the files are consistent, you can take either individual datafiles or all datafiles out of online backup mode. Doing so avoids media recovery of the files upon startup.

- To take an individual datafile out of online backup mode, use the ALTER DATABASE DATAFILE ... END BACKUP statement. See *database_file_clauses*.
- To take all datafiles in a tablespace out of online backup mode, use an ALTER TABLESPACE ... END BACKUP statement.

database_file_clauses   The *database_file_clauses* let you modify datafiles and tempfiles. You can use any of the following clauses when your instance has the database mounted, open or closed, and the files involved are not in use.

CREATE DATAFILE   Use the CREATE DATAFILE clause to create a new empty datafile in place of an old one. You can use this clause to re-create a datafile that was lost with no backup. The '*filename*' must identify a file that is or was once part of the database.

- Specify AS NEW to create an Oracle-managed datafile with a system-generated filename, the same size as the file being replaced, in the default file system location for datafiles.
- Specify AS *filespec* to assign a filename (and optional size) for the new datafile.

If you specify AS *filespec*, and *filename* is an existing Oracle-managed datafile, then Oracle deletes the old file. If you specify AS *filespec* and *filename* is an existing user-managed datafile, Oracle leaves the file as is and does not return an error.

If you omit the AS clause entirely, Oracle creates the new file with the same name and size as the file specified by '*filename*'.

During recovery, all archived redo logs written to since the original datafile was created must be applied to the new, empty version of the lost datafile.

Oracle creates the new file in the same state as the old file when it was created. You must perform media recovery on the new file to return it to the state of the old file at the time it was lost.

Restriction: You cannot create a new file based on the first datafile of the SYSTEM tablespace.

DATAFILE Clauses   The DATAFILE clauses affect your database files as follows:

ONLINE   Specify ONLINE to bring the datafile online.

OFFLINE   Specify OFFLINE to take the datafile offline. If the database is open, you must perform media recovery on the datafile before bringing it back online, because a checkpoint is not performed on the datafile before it is taken offline.

DROP   If the database is in NOARCHIVELOG mode, you must specify the DROP clause to take a datafile offline. However, the DROP clause does not remove the datafile from the database. To do that, you must drop the tablespace in which the datafile resides. Until you do so, the datafile remains in the data dictionary with the status RECOVER or OFFLINE.

If the database is in ARCHIVELOG mode, Oracle ignores the DROP keyword.

RESIZE   Specify RESIZE if you want Oracle to attempt to increase or decrease the size of the datafile to the specified absolute size in bytes. Use K or M to specify this size in kilobytes or megabytes. There is no default, so you must specify a size.

If sufficient disk space is not available for the increased size, or if the file contains data beyond the specified decreased size, Oracle returns an error.

END BACKUP   Specify END BACKUP to take the datafile out of online backup mode. The END BACKUP clause is described more fully at the top level of the syntax of ALTER DATABASE. See previous section on the END BACKUP clause.

TEMPFILE Clause   Use the TEMPFILE clause to resize your temporary datafile or specify the *autoextend_clause*, with the same effect as with a permanent datafile.

NOTE

On some operating systems, Oracle does not allocate space for the tempfile until the tempfile blocks are actually accessed. This delay in space allocation results in faster creation and resizing of tempfiles, but it requires that sufficient disk space is available when the tempfiles are later used. Please refer to your operating system documentation to determine whether Oracle allocates tempfile space in this way on your system.

Restriction: You cannot specify TEMPFILE unless the database is open.

DROP   Specify DROP to drop *tempfile* from the database. The tablespace remains.

If you specify INCLUDING DATAFILES, Oracle also deletes the associated operating system files and writes a message to the alert log for each such deleted file.

autoextend_clause   Use the *autoextend_clause* to enable or disable the automatic extension of a new datafile or tempfile. If you do not specify this clause, these files are not automatically extended.

ON   Specify ON to enable autoextend.

OFF   Specify OFF to turn off autoextend if is turned on.

NOTE

When you turn off autoextend, the values of NEXT and MAXSIZE are set to zero. If you turn autoextend back on in a subsequent statement, you must reset these values.

NEXT   Use the NEXT clause to specify the size in bytes of the next increment of disk space to be allocated automatically when more extents are required. Use K or M to specify this size in kilobytes or megabytes. The default is the size of one data block.

MAXSIZE   Use the MAXSIZE clause to specify the maximum disk space allowed for automatic extension of the datafile.

UNLIMITED   Use the UNLIMITED clause if you do not want to limit the disk space that Oracle can allocate to the datafile or tempfile.

RENAME FILE Clause   Use the RENAME FILE clause to rename datafiles, tempfiles, or redo log file members. You must create each filename using the conventions for filenames on your operating system before specifying this clause.

- To use this clause for datafiles and tempfiles, the database must be mounted. The database can also be open, but the datafile or tempfile being renamed must be offline.

- To use this clause for logfiles, the database must be mounted but not open.

This clause renames only files in the control file. It does not actually rename them on your operating system. The operating system files continue to exist, but Oracle no longer uses them. If the old files were Oracle managed, Oracle drops the old operating system file after this statement executes, because the control file no longer points to them as datafiles, tempfiles, or redo log files.

logfile_clauses   The logfile clauses let you add, drop, or modify log files.

ARCHIVELOG | NOARCHIVELOG   Use the ARCHIVELOG clause and NOARCHIVELOG clause only if your instance has the database mounted but not open, with Real Application Clusters disabled.

ARCHIVELOG   Specify ARCHIVELOG if you want the contents of a redo log file group to be archived before the group can be reused. This mode prepares for the possibility of media recovery. Use this clause only after shutting down your instance normally, or immediately with no errors, and then restarting it and mounting the database with Real Application Clusters disabled.

NOARCHIVELOG   Specify NOARCHIVELOG if you do not want the contents of a redo log file group to be archived so that the group can be reused. This mode does not prepare for recovery after media failure.

ADD [STANDBY] LOGFILE Clause   Use the ADD LOGFILE clause to add one or more redo log file groups to the specified thread, making them available to the instance assigned the thread. If you specify STANDBY, the redo log file created is for use by standby databases only.

To learn whether a logfile has been designated for online or standby database use, query the TYPE column of the V$LOGFILE dynamic performance view.

THREAD   The THREAD clause is applicable only if you are using Oracle with the Real Application Clusters option in parallel mode. *integer* is the thread number. The number of threads you can create is limited by the value of the MAXINSTANCES parameter specified in the CREATE DATABASE statement.

If you omit THREAD, the redo log file group is added to the thread assigned to your instance.

GROUP   The GROUP clause uniquely identifies the redo log file group among all groups in all threads and can range from 1 to the MAXLOGFILES value. You cannot add multiple redo log file groups having the same GROUP value. If you omit this parameter, Oracle generates its value automatically. You can examine the GROUP value for a redo log file group through the dynamic performance view V$LOG.

filespec   Each *filespec* specifies a redo log file group containing one or more members (that is, one or more copies).

ADD [STANDBY] LOGFILE MEMBER Clause   Use the ADD LOGFILE MEMBER clause to add new members to existing redo log file groups. Each new member is specified by *'filename'*. If the file already exists, it must be the same size as the other group members, and you must specify REUSE. If the file does not exist, Oracle creates a file of the correct size. You cannot add a member to a group if all of the group's members have been lost through media failure.

You can specify STANDBY for symmetry, to indicate that the logfile member is for use only by a standby database. However, this keyword is not required. If group *integer* was added for standby database use, all of its members will be used only for standby databases as well.

You can specify an existing redo log file group in one of two ways:

GROUP integer   Specify the value of the GROUP parameter that identifies the redo log file group.

filename(s)   List all members of the redo log file group. You must fully specify each filename according to the conventions of your operating system.

ADD SUPPLEMENTAL LOG DATA Clause   Specify the ADD SUPPLEMENTAL LOG DATA clause to place additional column data into the log stream any time an update operation is performed. This information can be used by LogMiner and any products building on LogMiner technology.

NOTE
You can issue this statement when the database is open. However, Oracle will invalidate all DML cursors in the cursor cache, which will have an effect on performance until the cache is repopulated.

PRIMARY KEY COLUMNS   When you specify PRIMARY KEY COLUMNS, Oracle ensures, for all tables with a primary key, that all columns of the primary key are placed into the redo log whenever an update operation is performed. If no primary key is defined, Oracle places into the redo log a set of columns that uniquely identifies the row. This set may include all columns with a fixed-length maximum size.

UNIQUE INDEX COLUMNS   When you specify UNIQUE INDEX COLUMNS, Oracle ensures, for all tables with a unique key, that if any unique key columns are modified, all other columns belonging to the unique are also placed into the redo log.

DROP LOGFILE Clause   Use the DROP LOGFILE clause to drop all members of a redo log file group. Specify a redo log file group as indicated for the ADD LOGFILE MEMBER clause.

- ■ To drop the current log file group, you must first issue an ALTER SYSTEM SWITCH LOGFILE statement.
- ■ You cannot drop a redo log file group if it needs archiving.
- ■ You cannot drop a redo log file group if doing so would cause the redo thread to contain less than two redo log file groups.

DROP LOGFILE MEMBER Clause   Use the DROP LOGFILE MEMBER clause to drop one or more redo log file members. Each *'filename'* must fully specify a member using the conventions for filenames on your operating system.

- ■ To drop a log file in the current log, you must first issue an ALTER SYSTEM SWITCH LOGFILE statement.

- ■ You cannot use this clause to drop all members of a redo log file group that contains valid data. To perform that operation, use the DROP LOGFILE clause.

DROP SUPPLEMENTAL LOG DATA Clause   Use the DROP SUPPLEMENTAL LOG DATA clause to instruct Oracle to stop placing additional log information into the redo log stream whenever an update operation occurs. This statement terminates the effect of a previous ADD SUPPLEMENTAL LOG DATA statement.

CLEAR LOGFILE Clause   Use the CLEAR LOGFILE clause to reinitialize an online redo log, optionally without archiving the redo log. CLEAR LOGFILE is similar to adding and dropping a redo log, except that the statement may be issued even if there are only two logs for the thread and also may be issued for the current redo log of a closed thread.

- ■ You must specify UNARCHIVED if you want to reuse a redo log that was not archived.

CAUTION
Specifying UNARCHIVED makes backups unusable if the redo log is needed for recovery.

- ■ You must specify UNRECOVERABLE DATAFILE if you have taken the datafile offline with the database in ARCHIVELOG mode (that is, you specified ALTER DATABASE ... DATAFILE OFFLINE without the DROP keyword), and if the unarchived log to be cleared is needed to recover the datafile before bringing it back online. In this case, you must drop the datafile and the entire tablespace once the CLEAR LOGFILE statement completes.

  Do not use CLEAR LOGFILE to clear a log needed for media recovery. If it is necessary to clear a log containing redo after the database checkpoint, you must first perform incomplete media recovery. The current redo log of an open thread can be cleared. The current log of a closed thread can be cleared by switching logs in the closed thread.

  If the CLEAR LOGFILE statement is interrupted by a system or instance failure, then the database may hang. If this occurs, reissue the statement after the database is restarted. If the failure occurred because of I/O errors accessing one member of a log group, then that member can be dropped and other members added.

controlfile_clauses   The *controlfile_clauses* let you create or back up a control file.

CREATE STANDBY CONTROLFILE Clause   Use the CREATE STANDBY CONTROLFILE clause to create a control file to be used to maintain a standby database. If the file already exists, you must specify REUSE.

BACKUP CONTROLFILE Clause   Use the BACKUP CONTROLFILE clause to back up the current control file.

TO 'filename'   Specify the file to which the control file is backed up. You must fully specify the *filename* using the conventions for your operating system. If the specified file already exists, you must specify REUSE.

TO TRACE   Specify TO TRACE if you want Oracle to write SQL statements to the database's trace file rather than making a physical backup of the control file. You can use SQL statements written to the trace file to start up the database, re-create the control file, and recover and open the database appropriately, based on the created control file. The database must be open or mounted when you specify this clause.

You can copy the statements from the trace file into a script file, edit the statements as necessary, and use the database if all copies of the control file are lost (or to change the size of the control file).

- ■ NORESETLOGS indicates that the SQL statement written to the trace file for starting the database is ALTER DATABASE OPEN NORESETLOGS. This is the default.

- ■ RESETLOGS indicates that the SQL statement written to the trace file for starting the database is ALTER DATABASE OPEN RESETLOGS.

standby_database_clauses   Use these clauses to activate the standby database or to specify whether it is in protected or unprotected mode.

ACTIVATE STANDBY DATABASE Clause   The ACTIVATE STANDBY DATABASE clause changes the state of a standby database to an active database and prepares it to become the primary database. The database must be mounted before you can specify this clause. The keyword PHYSICAL is optional.

SET STANDBY DATABASE Clause   The SET STANDBY DATABASE clause lets you specify whether your database environment is in **no-data-loss mode**. In this mode, Oracle places highest priority on maintaining an absolute match between the primary and standby databases. The standby database must be mounted, and no Real Application Clusters instance can have the primary database open, even in exclusive mode.

PROTECTED   Specify PROTECTED to indicate that the standby instance must contain at least one standby archivelog destination to be archived by the logwriter (LGWR) process in order for the primary database to be opened and to remain open in the event the last connection from primary to standby database is lost. In a Real Application Clusters environment, Oracle will verify that the LGWR processes of all instances that have the primary database open archive to the same standby databases.

If a connection to the last standby database is lost, Oracle will shut down the primary instance. Therefore, you should use this setting only if absolute correspondence between the primary and standby databases is more important than availability of the database.

UNPROTECTED   Specify UNPROTECTED to indicate that the instance does not require any standby databases to be maintained by the logwriter process. This is the default.

Use this setting if the absolute correspondence between the primary and standby databases is not as important as availability of the database.

To determine whether a database is in PROTECTED or UNPROTECTED mode, query the STANDBY_DATABASE column of the V$DATABASE dynamic performance view.

REGISTER LOGFILE Clause   Specify the REGISTER LOGFILE clause from the standby database to register log files from the failed primary. This operation is required unless missing log files from the failed primary have been copied to the directory specified in the STANDBY_ARCH_DEST initialization parameter.

OR REPLACE   Specify OR REPLACE to allow an existing archivelog entry in the standby database to be updated, for example, when its location or filespec changes. The SCNs of the entries must match exactly, and the original entry must have been created by the managed standby log transmittal mechanism.

PREPARE TO SWITCHOVER Clause   On the primary database, specify PREPARE TO SWITCHOVER TO STANDBY to prepare the current primary database for switchover to standby status. On one of the standby databases, issue a PREPARE TO SWITCHOVER TO PRIMARY statement to prepare the standby database for switchover to primary status.

default_settings_clauses   Use these clauses to modify the default settings of the database.

CHARACTER SET, NATIONAL CHARACTER SET   CHARACTER SET changes the character set the database uses to store data. NATIONAL CHARACTER SET changes the national character set used to store data in columns specifically defined as NCHAR, NCLOB, or NVARCHAR2. Specify *character_set* without quotation marks. The database must be open.

CAUTION
You cannot roll back an ALTER DATABASE CHARACTER SET or ALTER DATABASE NATIONAL CHARACTER SET statement. Therefore, you should perform a full backup before issuing either of these statements.

CAUTION
Oracle Corporation recommends that you use the Character Set Scanner (CSSCAN) to analyze your data before migrating your existing database character set to a new database character set. Doing so will help you avoid losing non-ASCII data that you might not have been aware was in your database. Please see Oracle9i Globalization Support Guide *for more information about CSSCAN.*

Notes on Changing Character Sets:
In Oracle 9i, CLOB data is stored as UCS-2 (two-byte fixed-width Unicode) for multibyte database character sets. For single-byte database character sets, CLOB data is stored in the database character set. When you change the database or national character set with an ALTER DATABASE statement, no data conversion is performed. Therefore, if you change the database character set from single byte to multibyte using this statement, CLOB columns will remain in the original database character set. This may introduce data inconsistency in your CLOB columns. Likewise, if

you change the national character set from one Unicode set to another, your SQL NCHAR columns (NCHAR, NVARCHAR2, NCLOB) may be corrupted.

The recommended procedure for changing database character sets is:

1. Export the CLOB and SQL NCHAR datatype columns.
2. Drop the tables containing the CLOB and SQL NCHAR columns.
3. Use ALTER DATABASE statements to change the character set and national character set.
4. Reimport the CLOB and SQL NCHAR columns.

Restrictions:

■   You must have SYSDBA system privilege, and you must start up the database in restricted mode (for example, with the SQL*Plus STARTUP RESTRICT command).

■   The current character set must be a strict subset of the character set to which you change. That is, each character represented by a codepoint value in the source character set must be represented by the same codepoint value in the target character set.

set_time_zone_clause   Use the SET TIME_ZONE clause to set the time zone of the database. You can specify the time zone in two ways:

■   By specifying a displacement from UTC (Coordinated Universal Time—formerly Greenwich Mean Time). The valid range of *hh:mm* is -12:00 to +14:00.

■   By specifying a time zone region. To see a listing of valid region names, query the TZNAME column of the V$TIMEZONE_NAMES dynamic performance view.

Oracle normalizes all new TIMESTAMP WITH LOCAL TIME ZONE data to the time zone of the database when the data is stored on disk. Oracle does not automatically update existing data in the database to the new time zone.

After setting or changing the time zone with this clause, you must restart the database for the new time zone to take effect.

DEFAULT TEMPORARY TABLESPACE Clause   Specify this clause to change the default temporary tablespace of the database. After this operation completes, Oracle automatically reassigns to the new default temporary tablespace all users who had been assigned to the old default temporary tablespace. You can then drop the old default temporary tablespace if you wish.

To learn the name of the current default temporary tablespace, query the PROPERTY_VALUE column of the DATABASE_PROPERTIES data dictionary table where the PROPERTY_NAME = 'DEFAULT_TEMP_TABLESPACE'.

Restriction: The tablespace you assign or reassign as the default temporary tablespace must have a standard block size.

conversion_clauses

RESET COMPATIBILITY Clause   Specify RESET COMPATIBILITY to mark the database to be reset to an earlier version of Oracle when the database is next restarted. Do not use this clause when the database is mounted.

NOTE
RESET COMPATIBILITY works only if you have successfully disabled Oracle features that affect backward compatibility.

CONVERT Clause   Use the CONVERT clause to complete the conversion of the Oracle7 data dictionary. After you use this clause, the Oracle7 data dictionary no longer exists in the Oracle database.

NOTE
Use this clause only when you are migrating to Oracle9i, and do not use this clause when the database is mounted.

redo_thread_clauses   Use these clauses to enable and disable the thread of redo log file groups.

ENABLE THREAD Clause   In an Oracle Real Application Clusters environment, specify ENABLE THREAD to enable the specified thread of redo log file groups. The thread must have at least two redo log file groups before you can enable it. The database must be open.

PUBLIC   Specify PUBLIC to make the enabled thread available to any instance that does not explicitly request a specific thread with the initialization parameter THREAD. If you omit PUBLIC, the thread is available only to the instance that explicitly requests it with the initialization parameter THREAD.

DISABLE THREAD Clause   Specify DISABLE THREAD to disable the specified thread, making it unavailable to all instances. The database must be open, but you cannot disable a thread if an instance using it has the database mounted.

RENAME GLOBAL_NAME Clause   Specify RENAME GLOBAL_NAME to change the global name of the database. The *database* is the new database name and can be as long as eight bytes. The optional *domain* specifies where the database is effectively located in the network hierarchy. Do not use this clause when the database is mounted.

NOTE
Renaming your database does not change global references to your database from existing database links, synonyms, and stored procedures and functions on remote databases. Changing such references is the responsibility of the administrator of the remote databases.

ALTER INDEX

PURPOSE
Use the ALTER INDEX statement to change or rebuild an existing index.

PREREQUISITES
The index must be in your own schema or you must have ALTER ANY INDEX system privilege. To execute the MONITORING USAGE clause, the index must be in your own schema. To modify a domain index, you must have EXECUTE object privilege on the indextype of the index. Schema object privileges are granted on the parent index, not on individual index partitions or subpartitions. You must have tablespace quota to modify, rebuild, or split an index partition or to modify or rebuild an index subpartition.

SYNTAX

alter_index::=

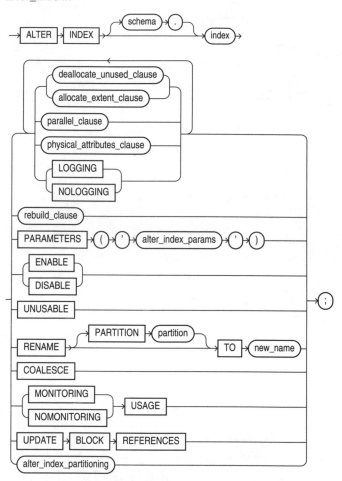

deallocate_unused_clause::=

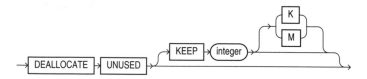

allocate_extent_clause::=

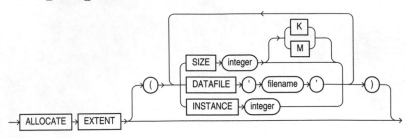

parallel_clause::=

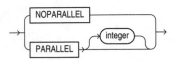

physical_attributes_clause::=

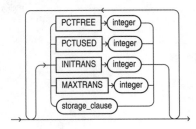

rebuild_clause::=

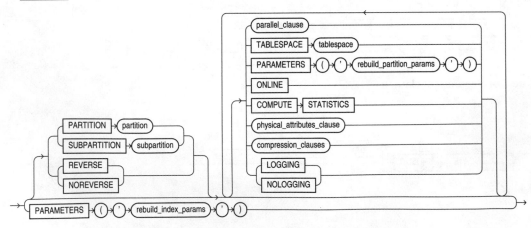

compression_clauses::=

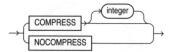

alter_index_partitioning::=

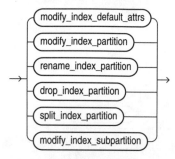

modify_index_default_attrs::=

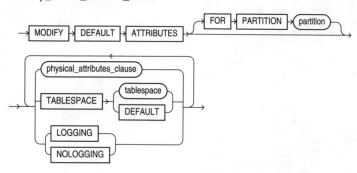

modify_index_partition::=

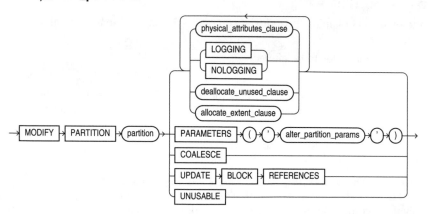

rename_index_partition::=

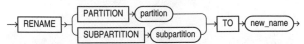

drop_index_partition::=

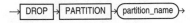

split_index_partition::=

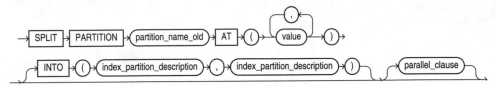

index_partition_description::=

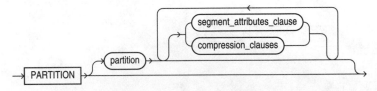

modify_index_subpartition::=

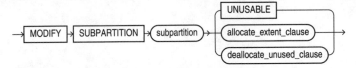

KEYWORDS AND PARAMETERS

schema   Specify the schema containing the index. If you omit *schema*, Oracle assumes the index is in your own schema.

index   Specify the name of the index to be altered.
  Restrictions:

  ■ If *index* is a domain index, you can specify only the PARAMETERS clause, the RENAME clause, or the *rebuild_clause* (with or without the PARAMETERS clause). No other clauses are valid.

  ■ You cannot alter or rename a domain index that is marked LOADING or FAILED. If an index is marked FAILED, the only clause you can specify is REBUILD.

deallocate_unused_clause   The *deallocate_unused_clause* lets you explicitly deallocate unused space at the end of the index and makes the freed space available for other segments in the tablespace. Only unused space above the high water mark can be freed.

If *index* is range-partitioned or hash-partitioned, Oracle deallocates unused space from each index partition. If *index* is a local index on a composite-partitioned table, Oracle deallocates unused space from each index subpartition.

Restrictions:

- You cannot specify this clause for an index on a temporary table.
- You cannot specify this clause and also specify the *rebuild_clause*.

KEEP integer   The KEEP clause lets you specify the number of bytes above the high water mark that the index will have after deallocation. If the number of remaining extents are less than MINEXTENTS, then MINEXTENTS is set to the current number of extents. If the initial extent becomes smaller than INITIAL, then INITIAL is set to the value of the current initial extent. If you omit KEEP, all unused space is freed.

allocate_extent_clause   The *allocate_extent_clause* lets you explicitly allocate a new extent for the index. For a local index on a hash-partitioned table, Oracle allocates a new extent for each partition of the index.

Restriction: You cannot specify this clause for an index on a temporary table or for a range-partitioned or composite-partitioned index.

SIZE   Specify the size of the extent in bytes. Use K or M to specify the extent size in kilobytes or megabytes. If you omit SIZE, Oracle determines the size based on the values of the index's storage parameters.

DATAFILE   Specify one of the datafiles in the index's tablespace to contain the new extent. If you omit DATAFILE, Oracle chooses the datafile.

INSTANCE   Use the INSTANCE clause to make the new extent available to the specified instance. An instance is identified by the value of its initialization parameter INSTANCE_NUMBER. If you omit this parameter, the extent is available to all instances. Use this parameter only if you are using Oracle with Real Application Clusters.

Explicitly allocating an extent with this clause does not change the values of the NEXT and PCTINCREASE storage parameters, so does not affect the size of the next extent to be allocated.

parallel_clause   Use the PARALLEL clause to change the default degree of parallelism for queries and DML on the index.

Restriction: You cannot specify this clause for an index on a temporary table.

NOTE
The syntax of the parallel_clause *supersedes syntax appearing in earlier releases of Oracle. Superseded syntax is still supported for backward compatibility, but may result in slightly different behavior than that documented.*

NOPARALLEL   Specify NOPARALLEL for serial execution. This is the default.

PARALLEL   Specify PARALLEL if you want Oracle to select a degree of parallelism equal to the number of CPUs available on all participating instances times the value of the PARALLEL_THREADS_PER_CPU initialization parameter.

PARALLEL integer   Specification of *integer* indicates the **degree of parallelism**, which is the number of parallel threads used in the parallel operation. Each parallel thread may use one or two parallel execution servers. Normally Oracle calculates the optimum degree of parallelism, so it is not necessary for you to specify *integer*.

physical_attributes_clause   Use the *physical_attributes_clause* to change the values of parameters for a nonpartitioned index, all partitions and subpartitions of a partitioned index, a specified partition, or all subpartitions of a specified partition.

Restrictions:

■ You cannot specify this clause for an index on a temporary table.

■ You cannot specify the PCTUSED parameter at all when altering an index.

■ You can specify the PCTFREE parameter only as part of the *rebuild_clause*, the *modify_index_default_attrs* clause, or the *split_partition_clause*.

storage_clause   Use the *storage_clause* to change the storage parameters for a nonpartitioned index, index partition, or all partitions of a partitioned index, or default values of these parameters for a partitioned index.

LOGGING | NOLOGGING   Use LOGGING or NOLOGGING to specify whether subsequent Direct Loader (SQL*Loader) and direct-path INSERT operations against a nonpartitioned index, a range or hash index partition, or all partitions or subpartitions of a composite-partitioned index will be logged (LOGGING) or not logged (NOLOGGING) in the redo log file.

In NOLOGGING mode, data is modified with minimal logging (to mark new extents invalid and to record dictionary changes). When applied during media recovery, the extent invalidation records mark a range of blocks as logically corrupt, because the redo data is not logged. Therefore, if you cannot afford to lose this index, you must take a backup after the operation in NOLOGGING mode.

If the database is run in ARCHIVELOG mode, media recovery from a backup taken before an operation in LOGGING mode will re-create the index. However, media recovery from a backup taken before an operation in NOLOGGING mode will not re-create the index.

An index segment can have logging attributes different from those of the base table and different from those of other index segments for the same base table.

Restriction: You cannot specify this clause for an index on a temporary table.

RECOVERABLE | UNRECOVERABLE   These keywords are deprecated and have been replaced with LOGGING and NOLOGGING, respectively. Although RECOVERABLE and UNRECOVERABLE are supported for backward compatibility, Oracle Corporation strongly recommends that you use the LOGGING and NOLOGGING keywords.

RECOVERABLE is not a valid keyword for creating partitioned tables or LOB storage characteristics. UNRECOVERABLE is not a valid keyword for creating partitioned or index-organized tables. Also, it can be specified only with the AS subquery clause of CREATE INDEX.

rebuild_clause   Use the *rebuild_clause* to re-create an existing index or one of its partitions or subpartitions. If index is marked UNUSABLE, a successful rebuild will mark it USABLE. For a function-based index, this clause also enables the index. If the function on which the index is based does not exist, the rebuild statement will fail.

Restrictions:

■ You cannot rebuild an index on a temporary table.

■ You cannot rebuild a bitmap index that is marked INVALID. Instead, you must drop and then re-create it.

- You cannot rebuild an entire partitioned index. You must rebuild each partition or subpartition, as described below.
- You cannot also specify the *deallocate_unused_clause* in this statement.
- You cannot change the value of the PCTFREE parameter for the index as a whole (ALTER INDEX) or for a partition (ALTER INDEX ... MODIFY PARTITION). You can specify PCTFREE in all other forms of the ALTER INDEX statement.
- For a domain index, you can specify only the PARAMETERS clause (either for the index or for a partition of the index). No other rebuild clauses are valid.
- You cannot rebuild a local index, but you can rebuild a partition of a local index (ALTER INDEX ... REBUILD PARTITION).

PARTITION Clause   Use the PARTITION clause to rebuild one partition of an index. You can also use this clause to move an index partition to another tablespace or to change a create-time physical attribute.

NOTE
The storage of partitioned database entities in tablespaces of different block sizes is subject to several restrictions. Please refer to Oracle9i Database Administrator's Guide *for a discussion of these restrictions.*

Restriction: You cannot specify this clause for a local index on a composite-partitioned table. Instead, use the REBUILD SUBPARTITION clause.

SUBPARTITION Clause   Use the SUBPARTITION clause to rebuild one subpartition of an index. You can also use this clause to move an index subpartition to another tablespace. If you do not specify TABLESPACE, the subpartition is rebuilt in the same tablespace.

NOTE
The storage of partitioned database entities in tablespaces of different block sizes is subject to several restrictions. Please refer to Oracle9i Database Administrator's Guide *for a discussion of these restrictions.*

Restrictions:

- The only parameters you can specify for a subpartition are TABLESPACE and the *parallel_clause.*
- You cannot rebuild the subpartition of a list partition.

REVERSE | NOREVERSE   Indicate whether the bytes of the index block are stored in reverse order:

- REVERSE stores the bytes of the index block in reverse order and excludes the rowid when the index is rebuilt.
- NOREVERSE stores the bytes of the index block without reversing the order when the index is rebuilt. Rebuilding a REVERSE index without the NOREVERSE keyword produces a rebuilt, reverse-keyed index.

Restrictions:

- You cannot reverse a bitmap index or an index-organized table.
- You cannot specify REVERSE or NOREVERSE for a partition or subpartition.

TABLESPACE Clause   Specify the tablespace where the rebuilt index, index partition, or index subpartition will be stored. The default is the default tablespace where the index or partition resided before you rebuilt it.

COMPRESS | NOCOMPRESS   Specify COMPRESS to enable key compression, which eliminates repeated occurrence of key column values. Use *integer* to specify the prefix length (number of prefix columns to compress).

- For unique indexes, the range of valid prefix length values is from 1 to the number of key columns minus 1. The default prefix length is the number of key columns minus 1.
- For nonunique indexes, the range of valid prefix length values is from 1 to the number of key columns. The default prefix length is number of key columns.

Oracle compresses only nonpartitioned indexes that are nonunique or unique indexes of at least two columns.

Restriction: You cannot specify COMPRESS for a bitmap index.

Specify NOCOMPRESS to disable key compression. This is the default.

ONLINE Clause   Specify ONLINE to allow DML operations on the table or partition during rebuilding of the index.

Restrictions:

- Parallel DML is not supported during online index building. If you specify ONLINE and then issue parallel DML statements, Oracle returns an error.
- You cannot specify ONLINE for a bitmap index or a cluster index.
- You cannot specify ONLINE when rebuilding an index that enforces a referential integrity constraint.

COMPUTE STATISTICS Clause   Specify COMPUTE STATISTICS if you want to collect statistics at relatively little cost during the rebuilding of an index. These statistics are stored in the data dictionary for ongoing use by the optimizer in choosing a plan of execution for SQL statements. The types of statistics collected depend on the type of index you are rebuilding.

NOTE
If you create an index using another index (instead of a table), the original index might not provide adequate statistical information. Therefore, Oracle generally uses the base table to compute the statistics, which will improve the statistics but may negatively affect performance.

Additional methods of collecting statistics are available in PL/SQL packages and procedures.

LOGGING | NOLOGGING   Specify whether the ALTER INDEX ... REBUILD operation will be logged.

PARAMETERS Clause   The PARAMETERS clause applies only to domain indexes. This clause specifies the parameter string for altering or rebuilding a domain index or a partition of a domain index. If index is marked UNUSABLE, modifying the parameters alone does not make it USABLE. You must also rebuild the UNUSABLE index to make it usable.

The maximum length of the parameter string is 1000 characters. This string is passed uninterpreted to the appropriate indextype routine.

NOTE
If you have installed Oracle Text, you can rebuild your Oracle Text domain indexes using parameters specific to that product. For more information on those parameters, please refer to Oracle Text Reference.

Restrictions:

- You cannot specify this clause for any indexes other than domain indexes.
- You can modify index partitions only if *index* is not marked IN_PROGRESS or FAILED, no index partitions are marked IN_PROGRESS, and the partition being modified is not marked FAILED.
- You can rebuild the index only if *index* is not marked IN_PROGRESS.
- You can rebuild the index partitions only if *index* is not marked IN_PROGRESS or FAILED and *partition* is not marked IN_PROGRESS.

ENABLE Clause   ENABLE applies only to a function-based index that has been disabled because a user-defined function used by the index was dropped or replaced. This clause enables such an index if these conditions are true:

- The function is currently valid
- The signature of the current function matches the signature of the function when the index was created
- The function is currently marked as DETERMINISTIC

Restriction: You cannot specify any other clauses of ALTER INDEX in the same statement with ENABLE.

DISABLE Clause   DISABLE applies only to a function-based index. This clause enables you to disable the use of a function-based index. You might want to do so, for example, while working on the body of the function. Afterward you can either rebuild the index or specify another ALTER INDEX statement with the ENABLE keyword.

UNUSABLE Clause   Specify UNUSABLE to mark the index or index partition(s) or index subpartition(s) UNUSABLE. An unusable index must be rebuilt, or dropped and re-created, before it can be used. While one partition is marked UNUSABLE, the other partitions of the index are still valid. You can execute statements that require the index if the statements do not access the unusable partition. You can also split or rename the unusable partition before rebuilding it.

Restriction: You cannot specify this clause for an index on a temporary table.

RENAME Clause   Specify RENAME TO to rename an index or a partition of an index. The *new_index_name* is a single identifier and does not include the schema name.

Restrictions:

■ For a domain index, *index* and any partitions of *index* must not be marked IN_PROGRESS or FAILED.

■ For a partition of a domain index, *index* must not be marked IN_PROGRESS or FAILED, none of the partitions can be marked IN_PROGRESS, and the partition you are renaming must not be marked FAILED.

COALESCE Clause   Specify COALESCE to instruct Oracle to merge the contents of index blocks where possible to free blocks for reuse.

Restriction:

■ You cannot specify this clause for an index on a temporary table.

■ Do not specify this clause for the primary key index of an index-organized table. Instead use the COALESCE clause of ALTER TABLE.

MONITORING USAGE | NOMONITORING USAGE   Use this clause to begin or end the collection of statistics on index usage. This clause is useful in determining whether an index is being used.

Specify MONITORING USAGE to begin statistics collection. Oracle first clears existing statistics on *index* and then begins to collect statistics on index usage. Statistics collection continues until a subsequent ALTER INDEX ... NOMONITORING USAGE statement is executed.

To terminate collection of statistics on index, specify NOMONITORING USAGE.

To see the statistics collected, query the ALL_, USER_, or DBA_INDEXES data dictionary views. To determine when the statistics collection began and ended, query the V$OBJECT_USAGE dynamic performance view.

UPDATE BLOCK REFERENCES Clause   The UPDATE BLOCK REFERENCES clause is valid only for normal and domain indexes on index-organized tables. Specify this clause to update all the stale "guess" data block addresses stored as part of the index row with the correct database address for the corresponding block identified by the primary key.

NOTE
For a domain index, Oracle executes the ODCIIndexAlter routine with the alter_option parameter set to AlterIndexUpdBlockRefs. This routine enables the cartridge code to update the stale "guess" data block addresses in the index.

Restriction: You cannot combine this clause with any other clause of ALTER INDEX.

alter_index_partitioning   The partitioning clauses of the ALTER INDEX statement are valid only for partitioned indexes.

NOTE
The storage of partitioned database entities in tablespaces of different block sizes is subject to several restrictions. Please refer to Oracle9i Database Administrator's Guide for a discussion of these restrictions.

Restrictions:

■ You cannot specify any of these clauses for an index on a temporary table.

■ You can combine several operations on the base index into one ALTER INDEX statement (except RENAME and REBUILD), but you cannot combine partition operations with other partition operations or with operations on the base index.

modify_index_default_attrs   Specify new values for the default attributes of a partitioned index.
     Restriction: The only attribute you can specify for an index on a hash-partitioned or composite-partitioned table is TABLESPACE.

TABLESPACE   Specify the default tablespace for new partitions of an index or subpartitions of an index partition.

LOGGING | NOLOGGING   Specify the default logging attribute of a partitioned index or an index partition.

FOR PARTITION   Use the FOR PARTITION clause to specify the default attributes for the subpartitions of a partition of a local index on a composite-partitioned table.
     Restriction: You cannot specify FOR PARTITION for a list partition.

modify_index_partition   Use the *modify_index_partition* clause to modify the real physical attributes, logging attribute, or storage characteristics of index partition *partition* or its subpartitions.

UPDATE BLOCK REFERENCES   The UPDATE BLOCK REFERENCES clause is valid only for normal indexes on index-organized tables. Use this clause to update all stale "guess" data block addresses stored in the secondary index partition.
     Restrictions:

■ You cannot specify the *physical_attributes_clause* for an index on a hash-partitioned table.

■ You cannot specify UPDATE BLOCK REFERENCES with any other clause in ALTER INDEX.

NOTE
If the index is a local index on a composite-partitioned table, the changes you specify here will override any attributes specified earlier for the subpartitions of index, as well as establish default values of attributes for future subpartitions of that partition. To change the default attributes of the partition without overriding the attributes of subpartitions, use ALTER TABLE ... MODIFY DEFAULT ATTRIBUTES OF PARTITION.

rename_index_partition   Use the *rename_index_partition* clauses to rename index partition or subpartition to *new_name*.
     Restriction: You cannot rename the subpartition of a list partition.

drop_index_partition   Use the *drop_index_partition* clause to remove a partition and the data in it from a partitioned global index. When you drop a partition of a global index, Oracle marks the index's next partition UNUSABLE. You cannot drop the highest partition of a global index.

split_index_partition   Use the *split_index_partition* clause to split a partition of a global partitioned index into two partitions, adding a new partition to the index.

Splitting a partition marked UNUSABLE results in two partitions, both marked UNUSABLE. You must rebuild the partitions before you can use them.

Splitting a usable partition results in two partitions populated with index data. Both new partitions are usable.

AT Clause   Specify the new noninclusive upper bound for *split_partition_1*. The *value_list* must evaluate to less than the presplit partition bound for *partition_name_old* and greater than the partition bound for the next lowest partition (if there is one).

INTO Clause   Specify (optionally) the name and physical attributes of each of the two partitions resulting from the split.

modify_index_subpartition   Use the *modify_index_subpartition* clause to mark UNUSABLE or allocate or deallocate storage for a subpartition of a local index on a composite-partitioned table. All other attributes of such a subpartition are inherited from partition-level default attributes.

Restriction: You cannot modify the subpartition of a list partition.

ALTER MATERIALIZED VIEW

PURPOSE
A materialized view is a database object that contains the results of a query. The FROM clause of the query can name tables, views, and other materialized views. Collectively these are called **master tables** (a replication term) or **detail tables** (a data warehouse term). This reference uses "master tables" for consistency. The databases containing the master tables are called the **master databases**.

Use the ALTER MATERIALIZED VIEW statement to modify an existing materialized view in one or more of the following ways:

- To change its storage characteristics
- To change its refresh method, mode, or time
- To alter its structure so that it is a different type of materialized view
- To enable or disable query rewrite.

NOTE
The keyword SNAPSHOT is supported in place of MATERIALIZED VIEW for backward compatibility.

PREREQUISITES
The privileges required to alter a materialized view should be granted directly, as follows: The materialized view must be in your own schema, or you must have the ALTER ANY MATERIALIZED VIEW system privilege.

To enable a materialized view for query rewrite:

- If all of the master tables in the materialized view are in your schema, you must have the QUERY REWRITE privilege.
- If any of the master tables are in another schema, you must have the GLOBAL QUERY REWRITE privilege.
- If the materialized view is in another user's schema, both you and the owner of that schema must have the appropriate QUERY REWRITE privilege, as described in the preceding two items. In addition, the owner of the materialized view must have SELECT access to any master tables that the materialized view owner does not own.

SYNTAX

alter_materialized_view::=

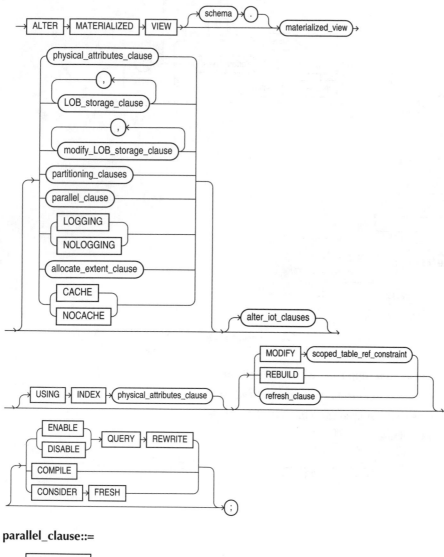

parallel_clause::=

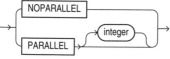

allocate_extent_clause::=

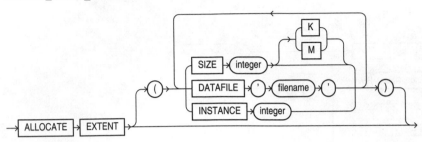

alter_iot_clauses::=

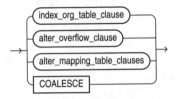

index_org_table_clause::=

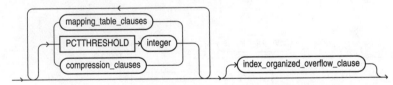

mapping_table_clauses: not supported with materialized views

compression_clauses: not supported with materialized views

alter_mapping_clauses: not supported with materialized views

index_org_overflow_clause::=

alter_overflow_clause::=

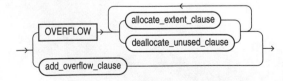

add_overflow_clause::=

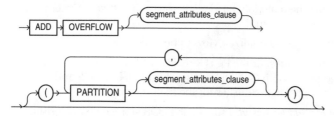

scoped_table_ref_constraint::=

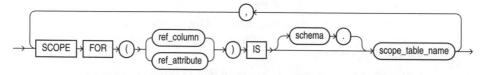

alter_mv_refresh_clause::=

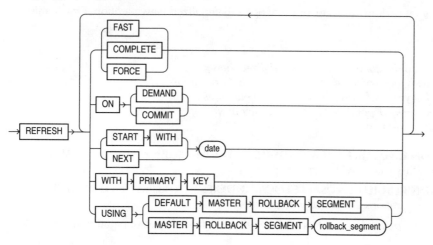

physical_attributes_clause::=

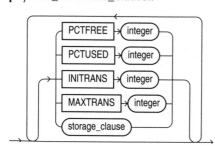

KEYWORDS AND PARAMETERS

schema   Specify the schema containing the materialized view. If you omit *schema*, Oracle assumes the materialized view is in your own schema.

materialized_view   Specify the name of the materialized view to be altered.

physical_attributes_clause   Specify new values for the PCTFREE, PCTUSED, INITRANS, and MAXTRANS parameters (or, when used in the USING INDEX clause, for the INITRANS and MAXTRANS parameters only) and the storage characteristics for the materialized view.

LOB_storage_clause   The *LOB_storage_clause* lets you specify the LOB storage characteristics.

modify_LOB_storage_clause   The *modify_LOB_storage_clause* lets you modify the physical attributes of the LOB attribute *lob_item* or LOB object attribute.

partitioning_clauses   The syntax and general functioning of the partitioning clauses for materialized views is the same as for partitioned tables.

> **Restrictions on *partitioning_clauses*:**
>
> - You cannot specify the *LOB_storage_clause* or *modify_LOB_storage_clause* within any of the *partitioning_clauses.*
> - If you attempt to drop, truncate, or exchange a materialized view partition, Oracle raises an error.

NOTE
If you wish to keep the contents of the materialized view synchronized with those of the master table, Oracle Corporation recommends that you manually perform a complete refresh of all materialized views dependent on the table after dropping or truncating a table partition.

MODIFY PARTITION UNUSABLE LOCAL INDEXES   Use this clause to mark UNUSABLE all the local index partitions associated with *partition*.

MODIFY PARTITION REBUILD UNUSABLE LOCAL INDEXES   Use this clause to rebuild the unusable local index partitions associated with *partition*.

parallel_clause   The *parallel_clause* lets you change the default degree of parallelism for the materialized view.

NOTE
The syntax of the parallel_clause *supersedes syntax appearing in earlier releases of Oracle. Superseded syntax is still supported for backward compatibility, but may result in slightly different behavior than that documented.*

NOPARALLEL   Specify NOPARALLEL for serial execution. This is the default.

PARALLEL   Specify PARALLEL if you want Oracle to select a degree of parallelism equal to the number of CPUs available on all participating instances times the value of the PARALLEL_THREADS_PER_CPU initialization parameter.

PARALLEL integer   Specification of *integer* indicates the **degree of parallelism**, which is the number of parallel threads used in the parallel operation. Each parallel thread may use one or two parallel execution servers. Normally Oracle calculates the optimum degree of parallelism, so it is not necessary for you to specify *integer.*

LOGGING | NOLOGGING   Specify or change the logging characteristics of the materialized view.

allocate_extent_clause   The *allocate_extent_clause* lets you explicitly allocate a new extent for the materialized view.

CACHE | NOCACHE   For data that will be accessed frequently, CACHE specifies that the blocks retrieved for this table are placed at the most recently used end of the LRU list in the buffer cache when a full table scan is performed. This attribute is useful for small lookup tables. NOCACHE specifies that the blocks are placed at the least recently used end of the LRU list.

alter_iot_clauses   Use the *alter_iot_clauses* to change the characteristics of an index-organized materialized view. The keywords and parameters of the components of the *alter_iot_clauses* have the same semantics as in ALTER TABLE, with the restrictions that follow.

   Restrictions: You cannot specify the *mapping_table_clauses* or the *compression_clauses* of the *index_org_table_clause.*

USING INDEX Clause   Use this clause to change the value of INITRANS, MAXTRANS, and STORAGE parameters for the index Oracle uses to maintain the materialized view's data.

   Restriction: You cannot specify the PCTUSED or PCTFREE parameters in this clause.

MODIFY scoped_table_ref_constraint   Use the MODIFY *scoped_table_ref_constraint* clause to rescope a REF column or attribute to a new table.

   Restrictions: You can rescope only one REF column or attribute in each ALTER MATERIALIZED VIEW statement, and this must be the only clause in this statement.

REBUILD Clause   Specify REBUILD to regenerate refresh operations if a type that is referenced in *materialized_view* has evolved.

   Restriction: You cannot specify any other clause in the same ALTER MATERIALIZED VIEW statement.

alter_mv_refresh_clause   Use the *alter_mv_refresh_clause* to change the default method and mode and the default times for automatic refreshes. If the contents of a materialized view's master tables are modified, the data in the materialized view must be updated to make the materialized view accurately reflect the data currently in its master table(s). This clause lets you schedule the times and specify the method and mode for Oracle to refresh the materialized view.

NOTE
This clause only sets the default refresh options.

FAST Clause   Specify FAST for incremental refresh method, which performs the refresh according to the changes that have occurred to the master tables. The changes are stored either in the materialized view log associated with the master table (for conventional DML changes) or in the direct loader log (for direct-path INSERT operations).

   For both conventional DML changes and for direct-path INSERTs, other conditions may restrict the eligibility of a materialized view for fast refresh.

   Restrictions:

   ■   When you specify FAST refresh at create time, Oracle verifies that the materialized view you are creating is eligible for fast refresh. When you change the refresh method to FAST in an ALTER MATERIALIZED VIEW statement, Oracle does not perform this verification. If the materialized view is not eligible for fast refresh, Oracle will return an error when you attempt to refresh this view.

- Materialized views are not eligible for fast refresh if the defining query contains an analytic function.

COMPLETE Clause   Specify COMPLETE for the complete refresh method, which is implemented by executing the materialized view's defining query. If you request a complete refresh, Oracle performs a complete refresh even if a fast refresh is possible.

FORCE Clause   Specify FORCE if, when a refresh occurs, you want Oracle to perform a fast refresh if one is possible or a complete refresh otherwise.

ON COMMIT Clause   Specify ON COMMIT if you want a fast refresh to occur whenever Oracle commits a transaction that operates on a master table of the materialized view.

Restriction: This clause is supported only for materialized join views and single-table materialized aggregate views.

ON DEMAND Clause   Specify ON DEMAND if you want the materialized view to be refreshed on demand by calling one of the three DBMS_MVIEW refresh procedures. If you omit both ON COMMIT and ON DEMAND, ON DEMAND is the default.

NOTE
If you specify ON COMMIT or ON DEMAND, you cannot also specify START WITH or NEXT.

START WITH Clause   Specify START WITH *date* to indicate a date for the first automatic refresh time.

NEXT Clause   Specify NEXT to indicate a date expression for calculating the interval between automatic refreshes.

Both the START WITH and NEXT values must evaluate to a time in the future. If you omit the START WITH value, Oracle determines the first automatic refresh time by evaluating the NEXT expression with respect to the creation time of the materialized view. If you specify a START WITH value but omit the NEXT value, Oracle refreshes the materialized view only once. If you omit both the START WITH and NEXT values, or if you omit the *alter_mv_refresh_clause* entirely, Oracle does not automatically refresh the materialized view.

WITH PRIMARY KEY Clause   Specify WITH PRIMARY KEY to change a rowid materialized view to a primary key materialized view. Primary key materialized views allow materialized view master tables to be reorganized without affecting the materialized view's ability to continue to fast refresh. The master table must contain an enabled primary key constraint.

USING ROLLBACK SEGMENT Clause   Specify USING ROLLBACK SEGMENT to change the remote rollback segment to be used during materialized view refresh, where *rollback_segment* is the name of the rollback segment to be used.

DEFAULT   Specify DEFAULT if you want Oracle to choose the rollback segment to use. If you specify DEFAULT, you cannot specify *rollback_segment.*

MASTER ... rollback_segment   Specify the remote rollback segment to be used at the remote master for the individual materialized view. (To change the local materialized view rollback segment, use the DBMS_REFRESH package, described in *Oracle9i Replication*.)

One master rollback segment is stored for each materialized view and is validated during materialized view creation and refresh. If the materialized view is complex, the master rollback segment, if specified, is ignored.

QUERY REWRITE Clause   Use this clause to determine whether the materialized view is eligible to be used for query rewrite.

ENABLE Clause   Specify ENABLE to enable the materialized view for query rewrite.
Restrictions:

- If the materialized view is in an invalid or unusable state, it is not eligible for query rewrite in spite of the ENABLE mode.

- You cannot enable query rewrite if the materialized view was created totally or in part from a view.

- You can enable query rewrite only if all user-defined functions in the materialized view are DETERMINISTIC.

- You can enable query rewrite only if expressions in the statement are repeatable. For example, you cannot include CURRENT_TIME or USER.

DISABLE Clause   Specify DISABLE if you do not want the materialized view to be eligible for use by query rewrite. (If a materialized view is in the invalid state, it is not eligible for use by query rewrite, whether or not it is disabled.) However, a disabled materialized view can be refreshed.

COMPILE   Specify COMPILE to explicitly revalidate a materialized view. If an object upon which the materialized view depends is dropped or altered, the materialized view remains accessible, but it is invalid for query rewrite. You can use this clause to explicitly revalidate the materialized view to make it eligible for query rewrite.

If the materialized view fails to revalidate, it cannot be refreshed or used for query rewrite.

CONSIDER FRESH   This clause lets you manage the staleness state of a materialized after changes have been made to its master tables. CONSIDER FRESH directs Oracle to consider the materialized view fresh and therefore eligible for query rewrite in the TRUSTED or STALE_TOLERATED modes. Because Oracle cannot guarantee the freshness of the materialized view, query rewrite in ENFORCED mode is not supported. This clause also sets the staleness state of the materialized view to UNKNOWN. The staleness state is displayed in the STALENESS column of the ALL_MVIEWS, DBA_MVIEWS, and USER_MVIEWS data dictionary views.

NOTE
A materialized view is stale if changes have been made to the contents of any of its master tables. This clause directs Oracle to assume that the materialized view is fresh and that no such changes have been made. Therefore, actual updates to those tables pending refresh are purged with respect to the materialized view.

ALTER MATERIALIZED VIEW LOG

PURPOSE
Use the ALTER MATERIALIZED VIEW LOG statement to alter the storage characteristics, refresh mode or time, or type of an existing materialized view log. A **materialized view log** is a table associated with the master table of a materialized view.

NOTE
*The keyword SNAPSHOT is supported in place of
MATERIALIZED VIEW for backward compatibility.*

PREREQUISITES

Only the owner of the master table or a user with the SELECT privilege on the master table and the ALTER privilege on the materialized view log can alter a materialized view log.

SYNTAX

alter_materialized_view_log::=

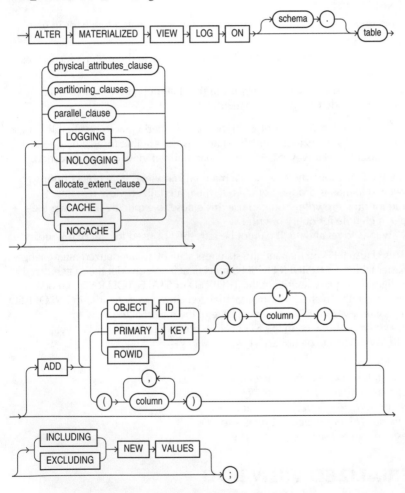

physical_attributes_clause::=

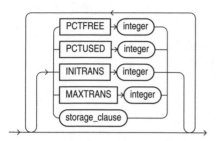

allocate_extent_clause::=

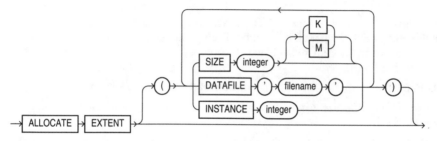

parallel_clause::=

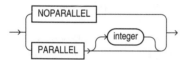

KEYWORDS AND PARAMETERS

schema   Specify the schema containing the master table. If you omit *schema*, Oracle assumes the materialized view log is in your own schema.

table   Specify the name of the master table associated with the materialized view log to be altered.

physical_attributes_clause   The *physical_attributes_clause* lets you change the value of PCTFREE, PCTUSED, INITRANS, and MAXTRANS parameters for the table, the partition, the overflow data segment, or the default characteristics of a partitioned table.

partitioning_clauses   The syntax and general functioning of the partitioning clauses is the same as described for the ALTER TABLE statement.

   Restrictions on *partitioning_clauses*:

   ■   You cannot use the *LOB_storage_clause* or *modify_LOB_storage_clause* when modifying partitions of a materialized view log.

   ■   If you attempt to drop, truncate, or exchange a materialized view log partition, Oracle raises an error.

parallel_clause   The *parallel_clause* lets you specify whether parallel operations will be supported for the materialized view log.

> **NOTE**
> *The syntax of the* parallel_clause *supersedes syntax appearing in earlier releases of Oracle. Superseded syntax is still supported for backward compatibility, but may result in slightly different behavior than that documented.*

NOPARALLEL   Specify NOPARALLEL for serial execution. This is the default.

PARALLEL   Specify PARALLEL if you want Oracle to select a degree of parallelism equal to the number of CPUs available on all participating instances times the value of the PARALLEL_THREADS_PER_CPU initialization parameter.

PARALLEL integer   Specification of *integer* indicates the **degree of parallelism**, which is the number of parallel threads used in the parallel operation. Each parallel thread may use one or two parallel execution servers. Normally Oracle calculates the optimum degree of parallelism, so it is not necessary for you to specify *integer*.

LOGGING | NOLOGGING   Specify the logging attribute of the materialized view log.

allocate_extent_clause   The *allocate_extent_clause* lets you explicitly allocate a new extent for the materialized view log.

CACHE | NOCACHE Clause   For data that will be accessed frequently, CACHE specifies that the blocks retrieved for this log are placed at the most recently used end of the LRU list in the buffer cache when a full table scan is performed. This attribute is useful for small lookup tables. NOCACHE specifies that the blocks are placed at the least recently used end of the LRU list.

ADD Clause   The ADD clause lets you augment the materialized view log so that it records the primary key values, rowid values, or object ID values when rows in the materialized view master table are changed. This clause can also be used to record additional columns.

To stop recording any of this information, you must first drop the materialized view log and then re-create it. Dropping the materialized view log and then re-creating it forces each of the existing materialized views that depend on the master table to complete refresh on its next refresh.

Restriction: You can specify only one PRIMARY KEY, one ROWID, one OBJECT ID and one column list for each materialized view log. Therefore, if any of these three values were specified at create time (either implicitly or explicitly), you cannot specify those values in this ALTER statement.

OBJECT ID   Specify OBJECT ID if you want the appropriate object identifier of all rows that are changed to be recorded in the materialized view log.

Restriction: You can specify OBJECT ID only for logs on object tables, and you cannot specify it for storage tables.

PRIMARY KEY   Specify PRIMARY KEY if you want the primary key values of all rows that are changed to be recorded in the materialized view log.

ROWID   Specify ROWID if you want the rowid values of all rows that are changed to be recorded in the materialized view log.

column   Specify the additional columns whose values you want to be recorded in the materialized view log for all rows that are changed. Typically these columns are filter columns (non-primary-key columns referenced by materialized views) and join columns (non-primary-key columns that define a join in the WHERE clause of the subquery).

NEW VALUES Clause   The NEW VALUES clause lets you specify whether Oracle saves both old and new values in the materialized view log. The value you set in this clause applies to all columns in the log, not only to primary key, rowid, or columns you may have added in this ALTER MATERIALIZED VIEW LOG statement.

INCLUDING   Specify INCLUDING to save both new and old values in the log. If this log is for a table on which you have a single-table materialized aggregate view, and if you want the materialized view to be eligible for fast refresh, you must specify INCLUDING.

EXCLUDING   Specify EXCLUDING to disable the recording of new values in the log. You can use this clause to avoid the overhead of recording new values. However, do not use this clause if you have a fast-refreshable single-table materialized aggregate view defined on this table.

ALTER OUTLINE

PURPOSE
Use the ALTER OUTLINE statement to rename a stored outline, reassign it to a different category, or regenerate it by compiling the outline's SQL statement and replacing the old outline data with the outline created under current conditions.

PREREQUISITES
To modify an outline, you must have the ALTER ANY OUTLINE system privilege.

SYNTAX
alter_outline::=

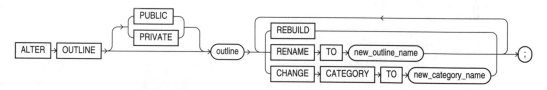

KEYWORDS AND PARAMETERS

PUBLIC | PRIVATE   Specify PUBLIC if you want to modify the public version of this outline. This is the default.

Specify PRIVATE if you want to modify the outline that is private to the current session and whose data is stored in the current parsing schema.

outline   Specify the name of the outline to be modified.

REBUILD   Specify REBUILD to regenerate the execution plan for *outline* using current conditions.

RENAME TO Clause   Use the RENAME TO clause to specify an outline name to replace *outline*.

CHANGE CATEGORY TO Clause   Use the CHANGE CATEGORY TO clause to specify the name of the category into which the *outline* will be moved.

ALTER PROFILE

PURPOSE
Use the ALTER PROFILE statement to add, modify, or remove a resource limit or password management parameter in a profile.

Changes made to a profile with an ALTER PROFILE statement affect users only in their subsequent sessions, not in their current sessions.

PREREQUISITES
You must have ALTER PROFILE system privilege to change profile resource limits. To modify password limits and protection, you must have ALTER PROFILE and ALTER USER system privileges.

SYNTAX

alter_profile::=

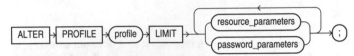

resource_parameters::=

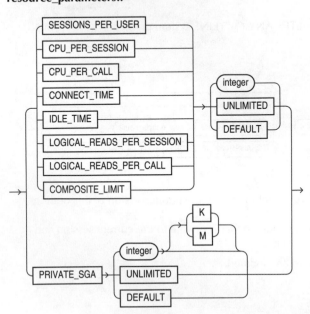

password_parameters::=

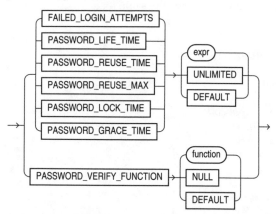

KEYWORDS AND PARAMETERS

The keywords and parameters in the ALTER PROFILE statement all have the same meaning as in the CREATE PROFILE statement.

NOTE
You cannot remove a limit from the DEFAULT profile.

ALTER ROLE

PURPOSE

Use the ALTER ROLE statement to change the authorization needed to enable a role.

PREREQUISITES

You must either have been granted the role with the ADMIN OPTION or have ALTER ANY ROLE system privilege.

Before you alter a role to IDENTIFIED GLOBALLY, you must:

- Revoke all grants of roles identified externally to the role and
- Revoke the grant of the role from all users, roles, and PUBLIC.

The one exception to this rule is that you should not revoke the role from the user who is currently altering the role.

SYNTAX

alter_role::=

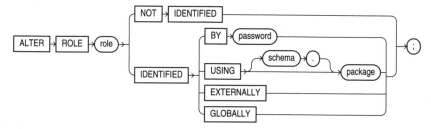

KEYWORDS AND PARAMETERS

The keywords and parameters in the ALTER ROLE statement all have the same meaning as in the CREATE ROLE statement.

NOTE

When you alter a role, user sessions in which the role is already enabled are not affected.

NOTE

If you change a role identified by password to an application role (with the USING package clause), password information associated with the role is lost. Oracle will use the new authentication mechanism the next time the role is to be enabled.

NOTE

If you have the ALTER ANY ROLE system privilege and you change a role that is IDENTIFIED GLOBALLY to IDENTIFIED BY password, IDENTIFIED EXTERNALLY, or NOT IDENTIFIED, then Oracle grants you the altered role with the ADMIN OPTION, as it would have if you had created the role identified nonglobally.

ALTER ROLLBACK SEGMENT

PURPOSE

Use the ALTER ROLLBACK SEGMENT statement to bring a rollback segment online or offline, to change its storage characteristics, or to shrink it to an optimal or specified size.

The information in this section assumes that your database is running in rollback undo mode (the UNDO_MANAGEMENT initialization parameter is set to MANUAL or not set at all).

If your database is running in Automatic Undo Management mode (the UNDO_MANAGEMENT initialization parameter is set to AUTO), then user-created rollback segments are irrelevant. In this case, Oracle returns an error in response to any CREATE ROLLBACK SEGMENT or ALTER ROLLBACK SEGMENT statement. To suppress these errors, set the UNDO_SUPPRESS_ERRORS parameter to TRUE.

PREREQUISITES

You must have ALTER ROLLBACK SEGMENT system privilege.

SYNTAX

alter_rollback_segment::=

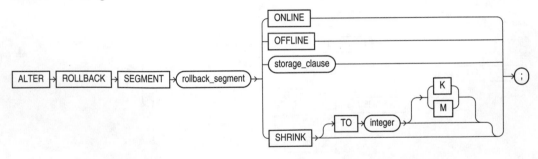

KEYWORDS AND PARAMETERS

rollback_segment   Specify the name of an existing rollback segment.

ONLINE   Specify ONLINE to bring the rollback segment online. When you create a rollback segment, it is initially offline and not available for transactions. This clause brings the rollback segment online, making it available for transactions by your instance. You can also bring a rollback segment online when you start your instance with the initialization parameter ROLLBACK_SEGMENTS.

OFFLINE   Specify OFFLINE to take the rollback segment offline.

- If the rollback segment does not contain any information needed to roll back an active transaction, Oracle takes it offline immediately.

- If the rollback segment does contain information for active transactions, Oracle makes the rollback segment unavailable for future transactions and takes it offline after all the active transactions are committed or rolled back.

Once the rollback segment is offline, it can be brought online by any instance.

To see whether a rollback segment is online or offline, query the data dictionary view DBA_ROLLBACK_SEGS. Online rollback segments have a STATUS value of IN_USE. Offline rollback segments have a STATUS value of AVAILABLE.

Restriction: You cannot take the SYSTEM rollback segment offline.

storage_clause   Use the *storage_clause* to change the rollback segment's storage characteristics.

Restriction: You cannot change the values of the INITIAL and MINEXTENTS for an existing rollback segment.

SHRINK Clause   Specify SHRINK if you want Oracle to attempt to shrink the rollback segment to an optimal or specified size. The success and amount of shrinkage depend on the available free space in the rollback segment and how active transactions are holding space in the rollback segment.

The value of *integer* is in bytes, unless you specify K or M for kilobytes or megabytes.

If you do not specify TO *integer*, then the size defaults to the OPTIMAL value of the *storage_clause* of the CREATE ROLLBACK SEGMENT statement that created the rollback segment. If OPTIMAL was not specified, then the size defaults to the MINEXTENTS value of the *storage_clause* of the CREATE ROLLBACK SEGMENT statement.

Regardless of whether you specify TO *integer*:

- The value to which Oracle shrinks the rollback segment is valid for the execution of the statement. Thereafter, the size reverts to the OPTIMAL value of the CREATE ROLLBACK SEGMENT statement.

- The rollback segment cannot shrink to less than two extents.

To determine the actual size of a rollback segment after attempting to shrink it, query the BYTES, BLOCKS, and EXTENTS columns of the DBA_SEGMENTS view.

Restriction: In a Real Application Clusters environment, you can shrink only rollback segments that are online to your instance.

ALTER SEQUENCE

PURPOSE

Use the ALTER SEQUENCE statement to change the increment, minimum and maximum values, cached numbers, and behavior of an existing sequence. This statement affects only future sequence numbers.

PREREQUISITES

The sequence must be in your own schema, or you must have the ALTER object privilege on the sequence, or you must have the ALTER ANY SEQUENCE system privilege.

SYNTAX

alter_sequence::=

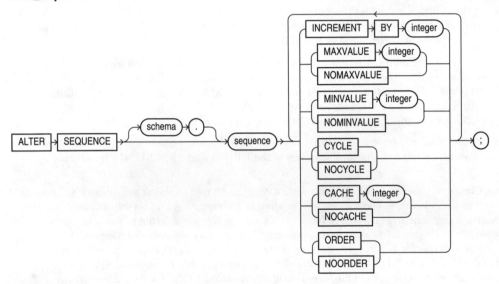

KEYWORDS AND PARAMETERS

The keywords and parameters in this statement serve the same purposes they serve when you create a sequence.

- ■ To restart the sequence at a different number, you must drop and re-create it.

- ■ If you change the INCREMENT BY value before the first invocation of NEXTVAL, some sequence numbers will be skipped. Therefore, if you want to retain the original START WITH value, you must drop the sequence and re-create it with the original START WITH value and the new INCREMENT BY value.

- ■ Oracle performs some validations. For example, a new MAXVALUE cannot be imposed that is less than the current sequence number.

ALTER SYSTEM

PURPOSE

Use the ALTER SYSTEM statement to dynamically alter your Oracle instance. The settings stay in effect as long as the database is mounted.

PREREQUISITES

You must have ALTER SYSTEM system privilege. To specify the *archive_log_clause*, you must have the SYSDBA or SYSOPER system privilege.

SYNTAX

alter_system::=

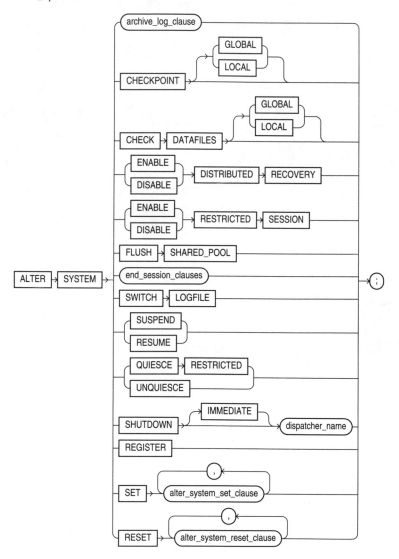

archive_log_clause::=

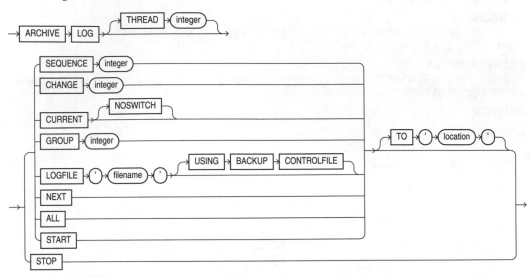

end_session_clauses::=

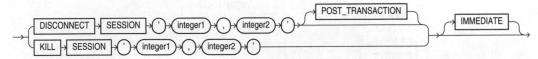

alter_system_set_clause::=

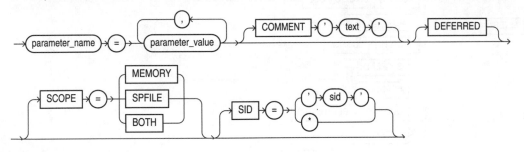

alter_system_reset_clause::=

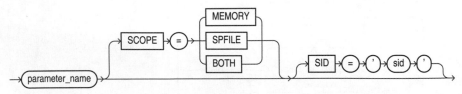

KEYWORDS AND PARAMETERS

archive_log_clause   The archive_log_clause manually archives redo log files or enables or disables automatic archiving. To use this clause, your instance must have the database mounted. The database can be either open or closed unless otherwise noted.

THREAD Clause   Specify THREAD to indicate the thread containing the redo log file group to be archived.

   Restriction: Set this parameter only if you are using Oracle with Real Application Clusters.

SEQUENCE Clause   Specify SEQUENCE to manually archive the online redo log file group identified by the log sequence number *integer* in the specified thread. If you omit the THREAD parameter, Oracle archives the specified group from the thread assigned to your instance.

CHANGE Clause   Specify CHANGE to manually archive the online redo log file group containing the redo log entry with the system change number (SCN) specified by *integer* in the specified thread. If the SCN is in the current redo log file group, Oracle performs a log switch. If you omit the THREAD parameter, Oracle archives the groups containing this SCN from all enabled threads.

   You can use this clause only when your instance has the database open.

CURRENT Clause   Specify CURRENT to manually archive the current redo log file group of the specified thread, forcing a log switch. If you omit the THREAD parameter, Oracle archives all redo log file groups from all enabled threads, including logs previous to current logs. You can specify CURRENT only when the database is open.

   Specify NOSWITCH if you want to manually archive the current redo log file group without forcing a log switch. You can use this clause only when your instance has the database mounted but not open. If the database is open, this operation closes the database automatically. You must then manually shut down the database before you can reopen it.

GROUP Clause   Specify GROUP to manually archive the online redo log file group with the GROUP value specified by *integer*. You can determine the GROUP value for a redo log file group by querying the data dictionary view DBA_LOG_FILES. If you specify both the THREAD and GROUP parameters, the specified redo log file group must be in the specified thread.

LOGFILE Clause   Specify LOGFILE to manually archive the online redo log file group containing the redo log file member identified by '*filename*'. If you specify both the THREAD and LOGFILE parameters, the specified redo log file group must be in the specified thread.

   If the database was mounted with a backup controlfile, specify USING BACKUP CONTROLFILE to permit archiving of all online logfiles, including the current logfile.

   Restriction: You must archive redo log file groups in the order in which they are filled. If you specify a redo log file group for archiving with the LOGFILE parameter, and earlier redo log file groups are not yet archived, Oracle returns an error.

NEXT Clause   Specify NEXT to manually archive the next online redo log file group from the specified thread that is full but has not yet been archived. If you omit the THREAD parameter, Oracle archives the earliest unarchived redo log file group from any enabled thread.

ALL Clause   Specify ALL to manually archive all online redo log file groups from the specified thread that are full but have not been archived. If you omit the THREAD parameter, Oracle archives all full unarchived redo log file groups from all enabled threads.

START Clause   Specify START to enable automatic archiving of redo log file groups.

   Restriction: You can enable automatic archiving only for the thread assigned to your instance.

TO *location* Clause   Specify TO '*location*' to indicate the primary location to which the redo log file groups are archived. The value of this parameter must be a fully specified file location following the conventions of your operating system. If you omit this parameter, Oracle archives the redo log file group to the location specified by the initialization parameters LOG_ARCHIVE_DEST or LOG_ARCHIVE_DEST_*n*.

STOP Clause   Specify STOP to disable automatic archiving of redo log file groups. You can disable automatic archiving only for the thread assigned to your instance.

CHECKPOINT Clause   Specify CHECKPOINT to explicitly force Oracle to perform a checkpoint, ensuring that all changes made by committed transactions are written to datafiles on disk. You can specify this clause only when your instance has the database open. Oracle does not return control to you until the checkpoint is complete.

   GLOBAL: In a Real Application Clusters environment, this setting causes Oracle to perform a checkpoint for all instances that have opened the database. This is the default.

   LOCAL: In a Real Application Clusters environment, this setting causes Oracle to perform a checkpoint only for the thread of redo log file groups for the instance from which you issue the statement.

CHECK DATAFILES Clause   In a distributed database system, such as a Real Application Clusters environment, this clause updates an instance's SGA from the database control file to reflect information on all online datafiles.

- Specify GLOBAL to perform this synchronization for all instances that have opened the database. This is the default.
- Specify LOCAL to perform this synchronization only for the local instance.

Your instance should have the database open.

end_session_clauses   The end_session_clauses give you several ways to end the current session.

DISCONNECT SESSION Clause   Use the DISCONNECT SESSION clause to disconnect the current session by destroying the dedicated server process (or virtual circuit if the connection was made by way of a Shared Server). To use this clause, your instance must have the database open. You must identify the session with both of the following values from the V$SESSION view:

- For *integer1*, specify the value of the SID column.
- For *integer2*, specify the value of the SERIAL# column.

If system parameters are appropriately configured, application failover will take effect.

- The POST_TRANSACTION setting allows ongoing transactions to complete before the session is disconnected. If the session has no ongoing transactions, this clause has the same effect as KILL SESSION, described below.
- The IMMEDIATE setting disconnects the session and recovers the entire session state immediately, without waiting for ongoing transactions to complete.
  - If you also specify POST_TRANSACTION and the session has ongoing transactions, the IMMEDIATE keyword is ignored.
  - If you do not specify POST_TRANSACTION, or you specify POST_TRANSACTION but the session has no ongoing transactions, this clause has the same effect as KILL SESSION IMMEDIATE, described below.

KILL SESSION Clause   The KILL SESSION clause lets you mark a session as dead, roll back ongoing transactions, release all session locks, and partially recover session resources. To use this clause, your instance must have the database open, and your session and the session to be killed must be on the same instance. You must identify the session with both of the following values from the V$SESSION view:

- For *integer1*, specify the value of the SID column.
- For *integer2*, specify the value of the SERIAL# column.

If the session is performing some activity that must be completed, such as waiting for a reply from a remote database or rolling back a transaction, Oracle waits for this activity to complete, marks the session as dead, and then returns control to you. If the waiting lasts a minute, Oracle marks the session to be killed and returns control to you with a message that the session is marked to be killed. The PMON background process then marks the session as dead when the activity is complete.

Whether or not the session has an ongoing transaction, Oracle does not recover the entire session state until the session user issues a request to the session and receives a message that the session has been killed.

IMMEDIATE: Specify IMMEDIATE to instruct Oracle to roll back ongoing transactions, release all session locks, recover the entire session state, and return control to you immediately.

DISTRIBUTED RECOVERY Clause   The DISTRIBUTED RECOVERY clause lets you enable or disable distributed recovery. To use this clause, your instance must have the database open.

ENABLE: Specify ENABLE to enable distributed recovery. In a single-process environment, you must use this clause to initiate distributed recovery.

You may need to issue the ENABLE DISTRIBUTED RECOVERY statement more than once to recover an in-doubt transaction if the remote node involved in the transaction is not accessible. In-doubt transactions appear in the data dictionary view DBA_2PC_PENDING.

DISABLE: Specify DISABLE to disable distributed recovery.

RESTRICTED SESSION Clause   The RESTRICTED SESSION clause lets you restrict logon to Oracle.

You can use this clause regardless of whether your instance has the database dismounted or mounted, open or closed.

ENABLE: Specify ENABLE to allows only users with RESTRICTED SESSION system privilege to log on to Oracle. Existing sessions are not terminated.

DISABLE: Specify DISABLE to reverse the effect of the ENABLE RESTRICTED SESSION clause, allowing all users with CREATE SESSION system privilege to log on to Oracle. This is the default.

FLUSH SHARED_POOL Clause   The FLUSH SHARED POOL clause lets you clear all data from the shared pool in the system global area (SGA). The shared pool stores

- Cached data dictionary information and
- Shared SQL and PL/SQL areas for SQL statements, stored procedures, function, packages, and triggers.

This statement does not clear shared SQL and PL/SQL areas for items that are currently being executed. You can use this clause regardless of whether your instance has the database dismounted or mounted, open or closed.

SWITCH LOGFILE Clause   The SWITCH LOGFILE clause lets you explicitly force Oracle to begin writing to a new redo log file group, regardless of whether the files in the current redo log file group are full. When you force a log switch, Oracle begins to perform a checkpoint but returns control to you immediately rather than when the checkpoint is complete. To use this clause, your instance must have the database open.

SUSPEND | RESUME   The SUSPEND clause lets you suspend all I/O (datafile, control file, and file header) as well as queries, in all instances, enabling you to make copies of the database without having to handle ongoing transactions.

> **Restrictions:**
>
> ■ Do not use this clause unless you have put the database tablespaces in hot backup mode.
>
> ■ If you start a new instance while the system is suspended, that new instance will not be suspended.

The RESUME clause lets you make the database available once again for queries and I/O.

QUIESCE RESTRICTED | UNQUIESCE   Use the QUIESCE RESTRICTED and UNQUIESCE clauses to put the database in and take it out of the **quiesced state**. This state enables database administrators to perform administrative operations that cannot be safely performed in the presence of concurrent transactions, queries, or PL/SQL operations.

If multiple QUIESCE RESTRICTED or UNQUIESCE statements issue at the same time from different sessions or instances, all but one will receive an error.

QUIESCE RESTRICTED   Specify QUIESCE RESTRICTED to put the database in the quiesced state. For all instances with the database open, this clause has the following effect:

> ■ Oracle instructs the Database Resource Manager in all instances to prevent all inactive sessions (other than SYS and SYSTEM) from becoming active. No user other than SYS and SYSTEM can start a new transaction, a new query, a new fetch, or a new PL/SQL operation.
>
> ■ Oracle waits for all existing transactions in all instances that were initiated by a user other than SYS or SYSTEM to finish (either commit or abort). Oracle also waits for all running queries, fetches, and PL/SQL procedures in all instances that were initiated by users other than SYS or SYSTEM and that are not inside transactions to finish. If a query is carried out by multiple successive OCI fetches, Oracle does not wait for all fetches to finish. It waits for the current fetch to finish and then blocks the next fetch. Oracle also waits for all sessions (other than those of SYS or SYSTEM) that hold any shared resources (such as enqueues) to release those resources. After all these operations finish, Oracle places the database into quiesced state and finishes executing the QUIESCE RESTRICTED statement.
>
> ■ If an instance is running in shared server mode, Oracle instructs the Database Resource Manager to block logins (other than SYS or SYSTEM) on that instance. If an instance is running in non-shared-server mode, Oracle does not impose any restrictions on user logins in that instance.

During the quiesced state, you cannot change the Resource Manager plan in any instance.

UNQUIESCE   Specify UNQUIESCE to take the database out of quiesced state. Doing so permits transactions, queries, fetches, and PL/SQL procedures that were initiated by users other than SYS or SYSTEM to be undertaken once again. The UNQUIESCE statement does not have to originate in the same session that issued the QUIESCE RESTRICTED statement.

SHUTDOWN Clause   The SHUTDOWN clause is relevant only if your system is using Oracle's shared server architecture. It shuts down a dispatcher identified by *dispatcher_name*.

The *dispatcher_name* must be a string of the form 'D*xxx*', where xxx indicates the number of the dispatcher. For a listing of dispatcher names, query the NAME column of the V$DISPATCHER dynamic performance view.

- If you specify IMMEDIATE, the dispatcher stops accepting new connections immediately and Oracle terminates all existing connections through that dispatcher. After all sessions are cleaned up, the dispatcher process literally shuts down.

- If you do not specify IMMEDIATE, the dispatcher stops accepting new connections immediately but waits for all its users to disconnect and for all its database links to terminate. Then it literally shuts down.

REGISTER Clause   Specify REGISTER to instruct the PMON background process to register the instance with the listeners immediately. If you do not specify this clause, registration of the instance does not occur until the next time PMON executes the discovery routine. As a result, clients may not be able to access the services for as long as 60 seconds after the listener is started.

alter_system_set_clause   The alter_system_set_clause lets you set or reset the value of any initialization parameter. The parameters are described in "Initialization Parameters and ALTER SYSTEM".

When setting the parameter's value, you can specify additional settings as follows:

COMMENT   The COMMENT clause lets you associate a comment string with this change in the value of the parameter. If you also specify SPFILE, this comment will appear in the parameter file to indicate the most recent change made to this parameter.

DEFERRED   The DEFERRED keyword sets or modifies the value of the parameter for future sessions that connect to the database. Current sessions retain the old value.

SCOPE   The SCOPE clause lets you specify when the change takes effect. Scope depends on whether you are started up the database using a parameter file (pfile) or server parameter file (spfile).

MEMORY: MEMORY indicates that the change is made in memory, takes effect immediately, and persists until the database is shut down. If you started up the database using a parameter file (pfile), this is the only scope you can specify.

SPFILE: SPFILE indicates that the change is made in the server parameter file. The new setting takes effect when the database is next shut down and started up again. You must specify SPFILE when changing the value of a static parameter.

BOTH: BOTH indicates that the change is made in memory and in the server parameter file. The new setting takes effect immediately and persists after the database is shut down and started up again.

If a server parameter file was used to start up the database, BOTH is the default. If a parameter file was used to start up the database, MEMORY is the default, as well as the only scope you can specify.

SID   The SID clause is relevant only in a Real Application Clusters environment. This clause lets you specify the SID of the instance where the value will take effect.

- Specify SID = '*' if you want Oracle to change the value of the parameter for all instances.

- Specify SID = *'sid'* if you want Oracle to change the value of the parameter only for the instance *sid*. This setting takes precedence over previous and subsequent ALTER SYSTEM SET statements that specify SID = '*'.

If you do not specify this clause:

- If the instance was started up with a pfile (client-side initialization parameter file), Oracle assumes the SID of the current instance.
- If the instance was started up with an spfile (server parameter file), Oracle assumes SID = '*'.

If you specify an instance other than the current instance, Oracle sends a message to that instance to change the parameter value in the memory of that instance.

alter_system_reset_clause   The alter_system_reset_clause is for use in a Real Application Clusters environments. It gives you separate control for an individual instance over parameters that may have been set for all instances in a server parameter file. The SCOPE clause has the same behavior as described for the alter_system_set_clause.

SID: Specify the SID clause to remove a previously specified setting of this parameter for your instance (that is, a previous ALTER SYSTEM SET ... SID = 'sid' statement). Your instance will assume the value of the parameter as specified in a previous or subsequent ALTER SYSTEM SET ... SID = '*' statement.

ALTER TABLE

PURPOSE
Use the ALTER TABLE statement to alter the definition of a nonpartitioned table, a partitioned table, a table partition, or a table subpartition. For object tables or relational tables with object columns, use ALTER TABLE to convert the table to the latest definition of its referenced type after the type has been altered.

PREREQUISITES
The table must be in your own schema, or you must have ALTER privilege on the table, or you must have ALTER ANY TABLE system privilege. For some operations you may also need the CREATE ANY INDEX privilege.

Additional Prerequisites for Partitioning Operations   If you are not the owner of the table, you need the DROP ANY TABLE privilege in order to use the *drop_table_partition* or *truncate_table_partition* clause.

You must also have space quota in the tablespace in which space is to be acquired in order to use the *add_table_partition*, *modify_table_partition*, *move_table_partition*, and *split_table_partition* clauses.

Additional Prerequisites for Constraints and Triggers   To enable a UNIQUE or PRIMARY KEY constraint, you must have the privileges necessary to create an index on the table. You need these privileges because Oracle creates an index on the columns of the unique or primary key in the schema containing the table.

To enable or disable triggers, the triggers must be in your schema or you must have the ALTER ANY TRIGGER system privilege.

Additional Prerequisites When Using Object Types   To use an object type in a column definition when modifying a table, either that object must belong to the same schema as the table being altered, or you must have either the EXECUTE ANY TYPE system privilege or the EXECUTE schema object privilege for the object type.

SYNTAX

alter_table::=

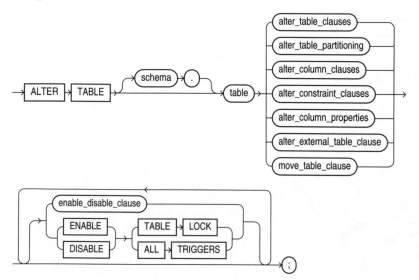

alter_table_clauses::=

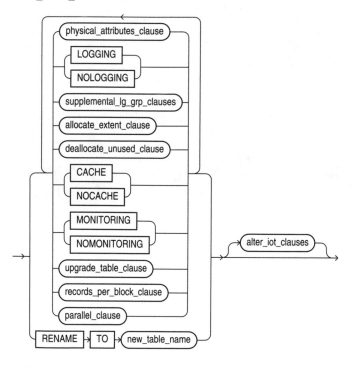

physical_attributes_clause::=

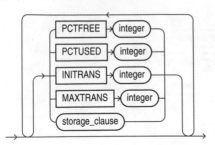

supplemental_lg_grp_clauses::=

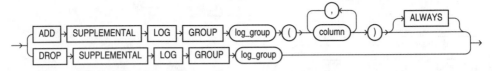

allocate_extent_clause::=

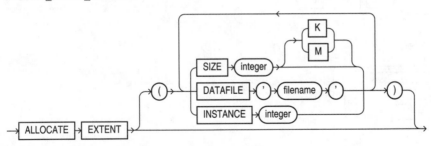

deallocate_unused_clause::=

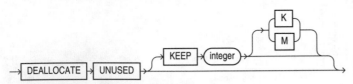

upgrade_table_clause::=

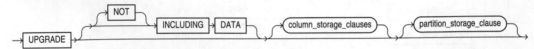

records_per_block_clause::=

alter_iot_clauses::=

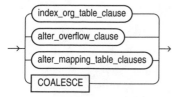

index_org_table_clause::=

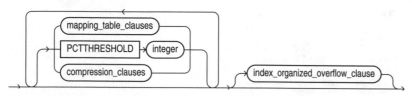

mapping_table_clauses::=

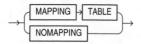

compression_clauses::=

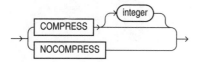

index_org_overflow_clause::=

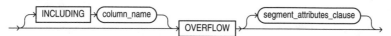

segment_attributes_clause::=

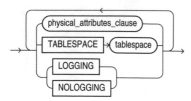

alter_overflow_clause::=

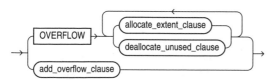

add_overflow_clause::=

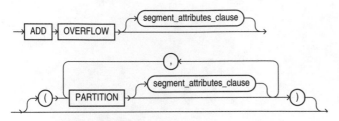

alter_mapping_table_clause::=

alter_table_partitioning::=

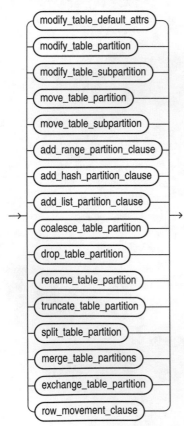

modify_table_default_attrs::=

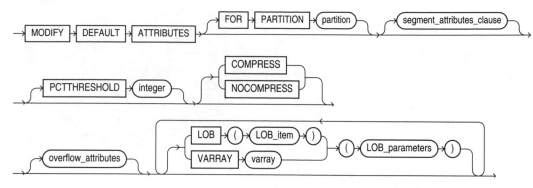

modify_table_partition::=

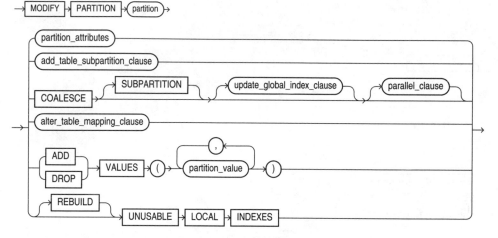

update_global_index_clause::=

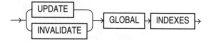

parallel_clause::=

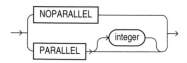

partition_attributes::=

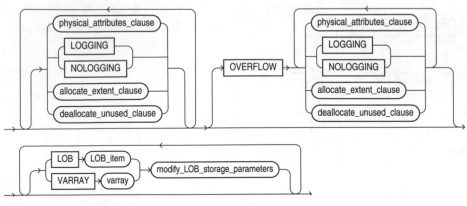

add_table_subpartition::=

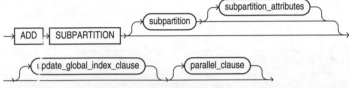

subpartition_attributes::=

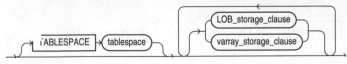

modify_table_subpartition::=

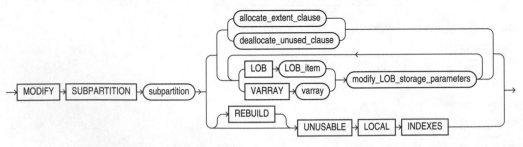

move_table_partition::=

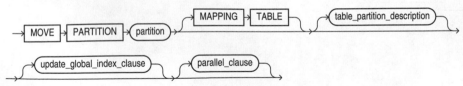

table_partition_description::=

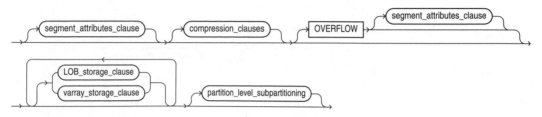

partition_level_subpartition::=

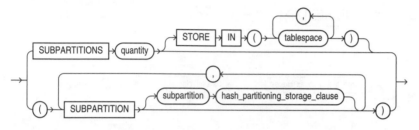

hash_partitioning_storage::=

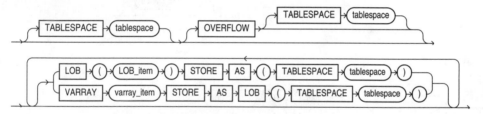

move_table_subpartition::=

add_range_partition_clause::=

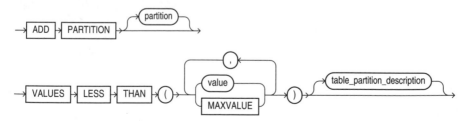

add_hash_partition_clause::=

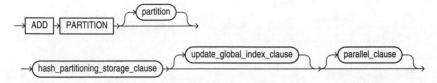

add_list_partition_clause::=

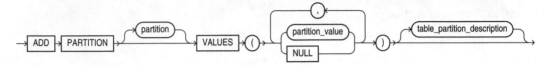

coalesce_table_partition::=

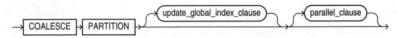

drop_table_partition::=

rename_table_partition::=

truncate_table_partition::=

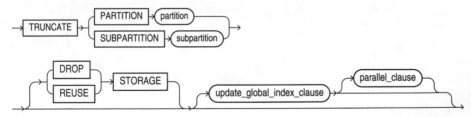

split_table_partition::=

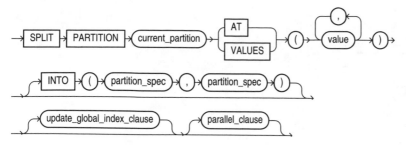

partition_spec::=

merge_table_partitions::=

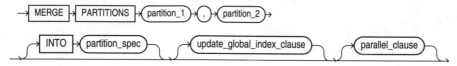

exchange_table_partition::=

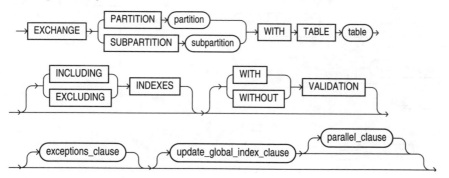

exceptions_clause::=

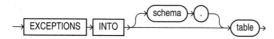

row_movement_clause::=

alter_column_clauses::=

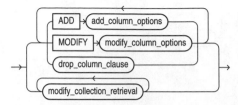

add_column_options::=

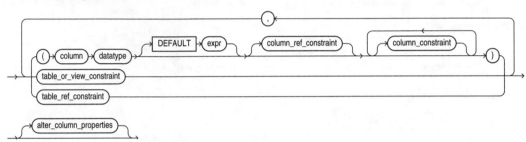

modify_column_options::=

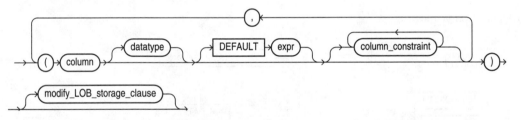

drop_column_clause::=

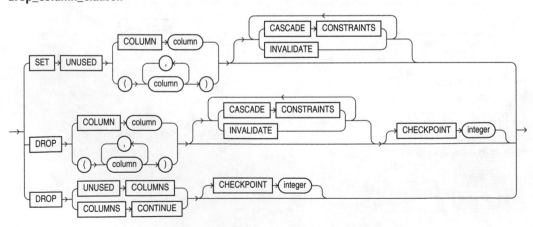

modify_collection_retrieval::=

alter_constraint_clauses::=

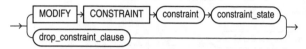

drop_constraint_clause::=

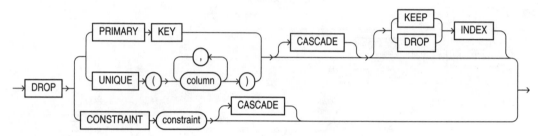

alter_column_properties::=

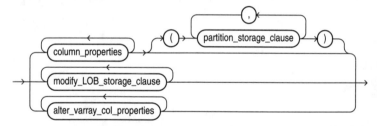

column_properties::=

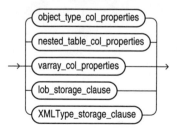

object_type_col_properties::=

substitutable_column_clause::=

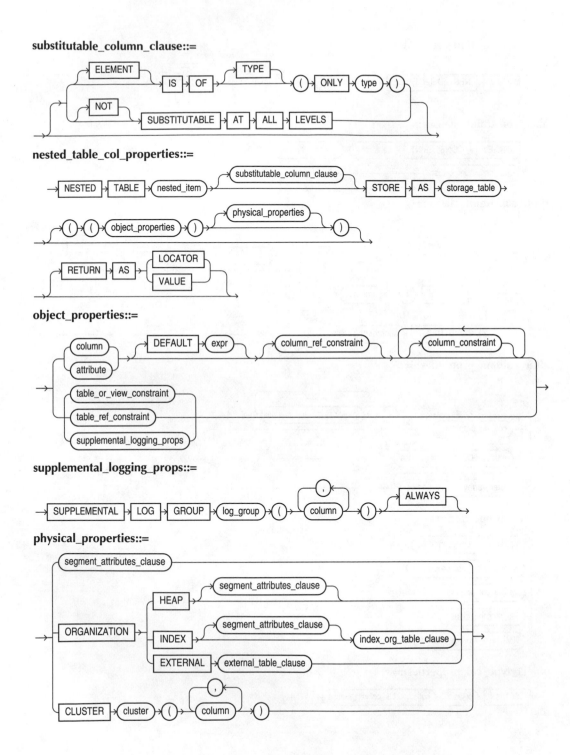

nested_table_col_properties::=

object_properties::=

supplemental_logging_props::=

physical_properties::=

varray_col_properties::=

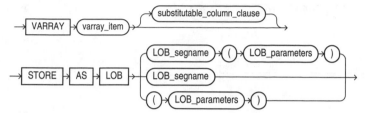

LOB_storage_clause::=

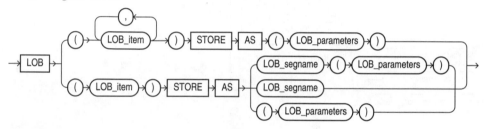

LOB_parameters::=

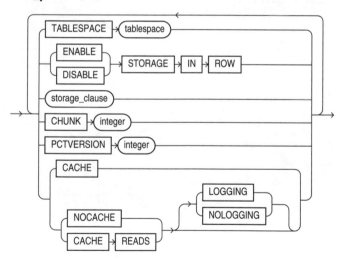

partition_storage_clause::=

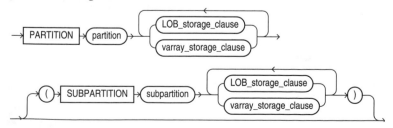

modify_lob_storage_clause::=

modify_lob_parameters::=

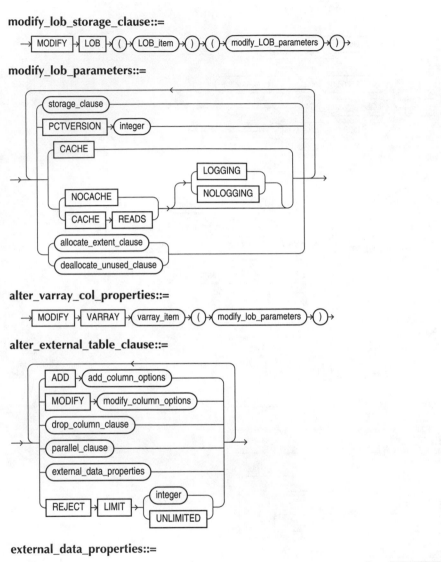

alter_varray_col_properties::=

alter_external_table_clause::=

external_data_properties::=

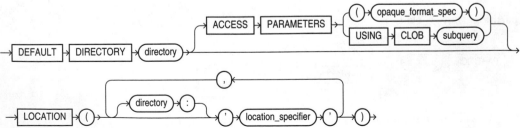

move_table_clause::=

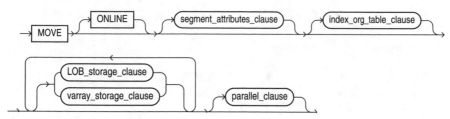

enable_disable_clause::=

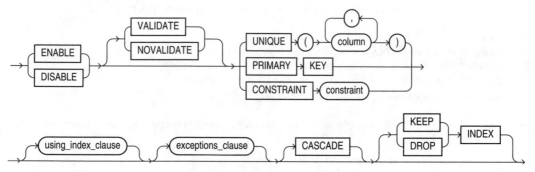

using_index_clause::=

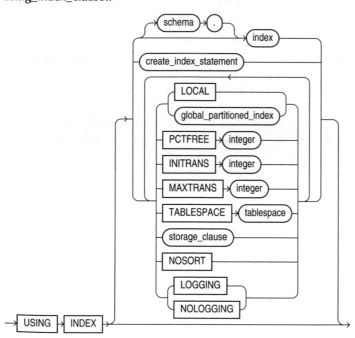

global_partitioned_index::=

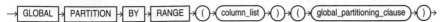

global_partitioning_clause::=

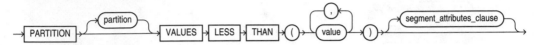

KEYWORDS AND PARAMETERS
Many clauses of the ALTER TABLE statement have the same functionality they have in a CREATE TABLE statement. For more information on such clauses, please see "CREATE TABLE".

NOTE
Operations performed by the ALTER TABLE statement can cause Oracle to invalidate procedures and stored functions that access the table. For information on how and when Oracle invalidates such objects, see Oracle 9i Database Concepts.

schema   Specify the schema containing the table. If you omit schema, Oracle assumes the table is in your own schema.

table   Specify the name of the table to be altered.
Restrictions on Temporary Tables:
You can modify, drop columns from, or rename a temporary table. However, for a temporary table you cannot:

- Add columns of nested table or varray type. You can add columns of other types.
- Specify referential integrity (foreign key) constraints for an added or modified column.
- Specify the following clauses of the LOB_storage_clause for an added or modified LOB column: TABLESPACE, storage_clause, LOGGING or NOLOGGING, or the LOB_index_clause.
- Specify the physical_attributes_clause, nested_table_col_properties, parallel_clause, allocate_extent_clause, deallocate_unused_clause, or any of the index organized table clauses.
- Exchange partitions between a partition and a temporary table.
- Specify LOGGING or NOLOGGING.
- Specify MOVE.

Restrictions on External Tables:
You can add, drop, or modify the columns of an external table. However, for an external table you cannot:

- Add a LONG, LOB, or object type column or change the datatype of an external table column to any of these datatypes.

- Add a constraint to an external table.
- Modify the storage parameters of an external table.
- Specify LOGGING or NOLOGGING.
- Specify MOVE

NOTE
If you alter a table that is a master table for one or more materialized views, Oracle marks the materialized views INVALID. Invalid materialized views cannot be used by query rewrite and cannot be refreshed. For information on revalidating a materialized view, see "ALTER MATERIALIZED VIEW".

alter_table_clauses
Use the alter_table_clauses to modify a database table.

physical_attributes_clause   The physical_attributes_clause lets you change the value of PCTFREE, PCTUSED, INITRANS, and MAXTRANS parameters and storage characteristics.
   Restrictions:

- You cannot specify the PCTUSED parameter for the index segment of an index-organized table.
- If you attempt to alter the storage attributes of tables in locally managed tablespaces, Oracle raises an error. However, if some segments of a partitioned table reside in a locally managed tablespace and other segments reside in a dictionary-managed tablespace, Oracle alters the storage attributes of the segments in the dictionary-managed tablespace but does not alter the attributes of the segments in the locally managed tablespace, and does not raise an error.
- For segments with automatic segment-space management, Oracle ignores attempts to change the PCTUSED setting. If you alter the PCTFREE setting, you must subsequently run the DBMS_REPAIR.segment_fix_status procedure to implement the new setting on blocks already allocated to the segment.

CAUTION
For a nonpartitioned table, the values you specify override any values specified for the table at create time.

CAUTION
For a range-, list-, or hash-partitioned table, the values you specify are the default values for the table and the actual values for every existing partition, overriding any values already set for the partitions. To change default table attributes without overriding existing partition values, use the modify_table_default_attrs clause.

CAUTION
*For a composite-partitioned table, the values you specify are the
default values for the table and all partitions of the table and the
actual values for all subpartitions of the table, overriding any
values already set for the subpartitions. To change default
partition attributes without overriding existing subpartition
values, use the modify_table_default_attrs clause with the FOR
PARTITION clause.*

LOGGING | NOLOGGING   Specify whether subsequent Direct Loader (SQL*Loader) and
direct-path INSERT operations against a nonpartitioned table, table partition, all partitions of a
partitioned table, or all subpartitions of a partition will be logged (LOGGING) or not logged
(NOLOGGING) in the redo log file.

When used with the *modify_table_default_attrs* clause, this clause affects the logging attribute
of a partitioned table.

LOGGING|NOLOGGING also specifies whether ALTER TABLE ... MOVE and ALTER TABLE ...
SPLIT operations will be logged or not logged.

For a table or table partition, if you omit LOGGING|NOLOGGING, the logging attribute of the
table or table partition defaults to the logging attribute of the tablespace in which it resides.

For LOBs, if you omit LOGGING|NOLOGGING,

- If you specify CACHE, then LOGGING is used (because you cannot have CACHE
  NOLOGGING).
- If you specify NOCACHE or CACHE READS, the logging attribute defaults to the logging
  attribute of the tablespace in which the LOB resides.

NOLOGGING does not apply to LOBs that are stored inline with row data. That is, if you
specify NOLOGGING for LOBs with values less than 4000 bytes and you have not disabled
STORAGE IN ROW, Oracle ignores the NOLOGGING specification and treats the LOB data the
same as other table data.

In NOLOGGING mode, data is modified with minimal logging (to mark new extents invalid and
to record dictionary changes). When applied during media recovery, the extent invalidation records
mark a range of blocks as logically corrupt, because the redo data is not logged. Therefore, if you
cannot afford to lose this table, it is important to back up the table after the NOLOGGING operation.

If the database is run in ARCHIVELOG mode, media recovery from a backup made before the
LOGGING operation will restore the table. However, media recovery from a backup made before
the NOLOGGING operation will not restore the table.

The logging attribute of the base table is independent of that of its indexes.

supplemental_lg_grp_clauses   The supplemental_lg_grp_clauses let you add and drop
supplemental redo log groups.

- Use the ADD LOG GROUP clause to add a redo log group.
- Use the DROP LOG GROUP clause to drop a redo log group when it is no longer needed.

allocate_extent_clause   The allocate_extent_clause lets you explicitly allocate a new extent for
the table, the partition or subpartition, the overflow data segment, the LOB data segment, or the
LOB index.

Restriction: You cannot allocate an extent for a range- or composite-partitioned table.

NOTE
Explicitly allocating an extent with this clause does not affect the size for the next extent to be allocated as specified by the NEXT and PCTINCREASE storage parameters.

SIZE integer: Specify the size of the extent in bytes. Use K or M to specify the extent size in kilobytes or megabytes. If you omit this parameter, Oracle determines the size based on the values of the STORAGE parameters of the table's overflow data segment or of the LOB index.

DATAFILE 'filename': Specify one of the datafiles in the tablespace of the table, overflow data segment, LOB data tablespace, or LOB index to contain the new extent. If you omit this parameter, Oracle chooses the datafile.

INSTANCE integer: Specifying INSTANCE integer makes the new extent available to the freelist group associated with the specified instance. If the instance number exceeds the maximum number of freelist groups, the former is divided by the latter, and the remainder is used to identify the freelist group to be used. An instance is identified by the value of its initialization parameter INSTANCE_NUMBER. If you omit this parameter, the space is allocated to the table but is not drawn from any particular freelist group. Instead, Oracle uses the master freelist and allocates space as needed.

NOTE
Use this parameter only if you are using Oracle with Real Application Clusters.

deallocate_unused_clause   Use the deallocate_unused_clause to explicitly deallocate unused space at the end of the table, partition or subpartition, overflow data segment, LOB data segment, or LOB index and make the space available for other segments in the tablespace. You can free only unused space above the high water mark (that is, the point beyond which database blocks have not yet been formatted to receive data).

Oracle credits the amount of the released space to the user quota for the tablespace in which the deallocation occurs.

Oracle deallocates unused space from the end of the object toward the high water mark at the beginning of the object. If an extent is completely contained in the deallocation, then the whole extent is freed for reuse. If an extent is partially contained in the deallocation, then the used part up to the high water mark becomes the extent, and the remaining unused space is freed for reuse.

The exact amount of space freed depends on the values of the INITIAL, MINEXTENTS, and NEXT storage parameters.

KEEP integer: Specify the number of bytes above the high water mark that the table, overflow data segment, LOB data segment, or LOB index is to have after deallocation.

- If you omit KEEP and the high water mark is above the size of INITIAL and MINEXTENTS, then all unused space above the high water mark is freed. When the high water mark is less than the size of INITIAL or MINEXTENTS, then all unused space above MINEXTENTS is freed.

- If you specify KEEP, then the specified amount of space is kept and the remaining space is freed. When the remaining number of extents is less than MINEXTENTS, then MINEXTENTS is adjusted to the new number of extents. If the initial extent becomes smaller than INITIAL, then INITIAL is adjusted to the new size.

- In either case, NEXT is set to the size of the last extent that was deallocated.

CACHE | NOCACHE

CACHE Clause: For data that is accessed frequently, this clause indicates that the blocks retrieved for this table are placed at the *most recently used* end of the least recently used (LRU) list in the buffer cache when a full table scan is performed. This attribute is useful for small lookup tables.

As a parameter in the *LOB_storage_clause*, CACHE specifies that Oracle places LOB data values in the buffer cache for faster access.

Restriction: You cannot specify CACHE for an index-organized table. However, index-organized tables implicitly provide CACHE behavior.

NOCACHE Clause: For data that is not accessed frequently, this clause indicates that the blocks retrieved for this table are placed at the *least recently used* end of the LRU list in the buffer cache when a full table scan is performed.

As a parameter in the *LOB_storage_clause*, NOCACHE specifies that the LOB value is either not brought into the buffer cache or brought into the buffer cache and placed at the least recently used end of the LRU list. (The latter is the default behavior.) NOCACHE is the default for LOB storage.

Restriction: You cannot specify NOCACHE for index-organized tables.

MONITORING | NOMONITORING

MONITORING Clause: Specify MONITORING if you want Oracle to collect modification statistics on *table*. These statistics are estimates of the number of rows affected by DML statements over a particular period of time. They are available for use by the optimizer or for analysis by the user.

NOMONITORING Clause: Specify NOMONITORING if you do not want Oracle to collect modification statistics on *table*.

Restriction: You cannot specify MONITORING or NOMONITORING for a temporary table.

upgrade_table_clause The upgrade_table_clause is relevant for object tables and for relational tables with object columns. It lets you instruct Oracle to convert the metadata of the target table to conform with the latest version of each referenced type. If table is already valid, then the table metadata remains unchanged.

INCLUDING DATA: Specify INCLUDING DATA if you want Oracle to convert the data in the table to the latest type version format (if it was not converted when the type was altered). You can define the storage for any new column while upgrading the table by using the column_properties and the partition_storage_clause. This is the default.

For information on whether a table contains data based on an older type version, refer to the DATA_UPGRADED column of the USER_TAB_COLUMNS data dictionary view.

NOT INCLUDING DATA: Specify NOT INCLUDING DATA if you want Oracle to leave column data unchanged.

Restriction: You cannot specify NOT INCLUDING DATA if the table contains columns in Oracle8 release 8.0.x image format. To determine whether the table contains such columns, refer to the V80_FMT_IMAGE column of the USER_TAB_COLUMNS data dictionary view.

records_per_block_clause The records_per_block_clause lets you specify whether Oracle restricts the number of records that can be stored in a block. This clause ensures that any bitmap indexes subsequently created on the table will be as small (compressed) as possible.

Restrictions:

- You cannot specify either MINIMIZE or NOMINIMIZE if a bitmap index has already been defined on table. You must first drop the bitmap index.
- You cannot specify this clause for an index-organized table or nested table.

MINIMIZE: Specify MINIMIZE to instruct Oracle to calculate the largest number of records in any block in the table, and limit future inserts so that no block can contain more than that number of records.

Restriction: You cannot specify MINIMIZE for an empty table.

NOMINIMIZE: Specify NOMINIMIZE to disable the MINIMIZE feature. This is the default.

RENAME TO   Use the RENAME clause to rename *table* to *new_table_name*.

Restriction: You cannot rename a materialized view.

NOTE

Using this clause invalidates any dependent materialized views. For more information on materialized views, see "CREATE MATERIALIZED VIEW" and Oracle9i Data Warehousing Guide.

ALTER_IOT_CLAUSES

index_org_table_clause   See index_org_table_clause in "CREATE TABLE".

alter_overflow_clause   The alter_overflow_clause lets you change the definition of an index-organized table. Index-organized tables keep data sorted on the primary key and are therefore best suited for primary-key-based access and manipulation.

NOTE

When you add a column to an index-organized table, Oracle evaluates the maximum size of each column to estimate the largest possible row. If an overflow segment is needed but you have not specified OVERFLOW, Oracle raises an error and does not execute the ALTER TABLE statement. This checking function guarantees that subsequent DML operations on the index-organized table will not fail because an overflow segment is lacking.

PCTTHRESHOLD integer: Specify the percentage of space reserved in the index block for an index-organized table row. PCTTHRESHOLD must be large enough to hold the primary key. All trailing columns of a row, starting with the column that causes the specified threshold to be exceeded, are stored in the overflow segment. PCTTHRESHOLD must be a value from 1 to 50. If you do not specify PCTTHRESHOLD, the default is 50.

Restriction: You cannot specify PCTTHRESHOLD for individual partitions of an index-organized table.

INCLUDING column_name: Specify a column at which to divide an index-organized table row into index and overflow portions. The primary key columns are always stored in the index. column_name can be either the last primary-key column or any non-primary-key column. All non-primary-key columns that follow column_name are stored in the overflow data segment.

Restriction: You cannot specify this clause for individual partitions of an index-organized table.

NOTE

If an attempt to divide a row at column_name causes the size of the index portion of the row to exceed the PCTTHRESHOLD value (either specified or default), Oracle breaks up the row based on the PCTTHRESHOLD value.

overflow_attributes: The overflow_attributes let you specify the overflow data segment physical storage and logging attributes to be modified for the index-organized table. Parameters specified in this clause are applicable only to the overflow data segment.

add_overflow_clause: The add_overflow_clause lets you add an overflow data segment to the specified index-organized table.

Use the STORE IN tablespace clause to specify tablespace storage for the entire overflow segment. Use the PARTITION clause to specify tablespace storage for the segment by partition.

For a partitioned index-organized table:

- If you do not specify PARTITION, Oracle automatically allocates an overflow segment for each partition. The physical attributes of these segments are inherited from the table level.

- If you wish to specify separate physical attributes for one or more partitions, you must specify such attributes for every partition in the table. You need not specify the name of the partitions, but you must specify their attributes in the order in which they were created.

You can find the order of the partitions by querying the PARTITION_NAME and PARTITION_POSITION columns of the USER_IND_PARTITIONS view.

If you do not specify TABLESPACE for a particular partition, Oracle uses the tablespace specified for the table. If you do not specify TABLESPACE at the table level, Oracle uses the tablespace of the partition's primary key index segment.

alter_mapping_table_clause   The alter_mapping_table_clause is valid only if table is index organized and has a mapping table.

UPDATE BLOCK REFERENCES: Specify UPDATE BLOCK REFERENCES to update all stale "guess" data block addresses stored as part of the logical ROWID column in the mapping table with the correct address for the corresponding block identified by the primary key.

allocate_extent_clause: Specify the allocate_extent_clause to allocate new extents at the end of the mapping table for the index-organized table.

deallocate_unused_clause: Specify the deallocate_unused_clause to deallocate unused space at the end of the mapping table of the index-organized table.

COALESCE   The keyword is relevant only if *table* is index organized. Specify COALESCE to instruct Oracle to combine the primary key index blocks of the index-organized table where possible to free blocks for reuse. You can specify this clause with the *parallel_clause*.

alter_table_partitioning: The following clauses apply only to partitioned tables. You cannot combine partition operations with other partition operations or with operations on the base table in one ALTER TABLE statement.

NOTES
The storage of partitioned database entities in tablespaces of different block sizes is subject to several restrictions. Please refer to Oracle 9i Database Administrator's Guide *for a discussion of these restrictions.*

- If you drop, exchange, truncate, move, modify, or split a partition on a table that is a master table for one or more materialized views, existing bulk load information about the table will be deleted. Therefore, be sure to refresh all dependent materialized views before performing any of these operations.

■ If a bitmap join index is defined on *table*, any operation that alters a partition of *table* causes Oracle to mark the index UNUSABLE.

modify_table_default_attrs   The modify_table_default_attrs lets you specify new default values for the attributes of table. Partitions and LOB partitions you create subsequently will inherit these values unless you override them explicitly when creating the partition or LOB partition. Existing partitions and LOB partitions are not affected by this clause.

Only attributes named in the statement are affected, and the default values specified are overridden by any attributes specified at the individual partition level.

■ FOR PARTITION applies only to composite-partitioned tables. This clause specifies new default values for the attributes of partition. Subpartitions and LOB subpartitions of partition that you create subsequently will inherit these values unless you override them explicitly when creating the subpartition or LOB subpartition. Existing subpartitions are not affected by this clause.

■ The PCTTHRESHOLD, COMPRESS, and OVERFLOW clauses are valid only for partitioned index-organized tables.

■ You cannot specify the PCTUSED parameter for the index segment of an index-organized table.

■ You can specify COMPRESS only if compression is already specified at the table level.

modify_table_partition   The modify_table_partition clause lets you change the real physical attributes of partition. This clause optionally modifies the storage attributes of one or more LOB items for the partition. You can specify new values for any of the following physical attributes for the partition: the logging attribute; PCTFREE, PCTUSED, INITRANS, or MAXTRANS parameter; or storage parameters.

If table is composite partitioned:

■ If you specify the allocate_extent_clause, Oracle allocates an extent for each subpartition of partition.

■ If you specify deallocate_unused_clause, Oracle deallocates unused storage from each subpartition of partition.

■ Any other attributes changed in this clause will be changed in subpartitions of partition as well, overriding existing values. To avoid changing the attributes of existing subpartitions, use the FOR PARTITION clause of modify_table_default_attrs.

Restriction: If table is hash partitioned, you can specify only the allocate_extent_clause and deallocate_unused_clause. All other attributes of the partition are inherited from the table-level defaults except TABLESPACE, which stays the same as it was at create time.

add_table_subpartition: The add_table_subpartition clause lets you add a hash subpartition to partition. Oracle populates the new subpartition with rows rehashed from the other subpartition(s) of partition as determined by the hash function.

If you do not specify subpartition, Oracle assigns a name in the form SYS_SUBPnnn.

If you do not specify TABLESPACE, the new subpartition will reside in the default tablespace of partition.

Oracle invalidates any global indexes on table. You can update these indexes during this operation using the update_global_index_clause.

Oracle adds local index partitions corresponding to the selected partition. Oracle marks UNUSABLE, and you must rebuild, the local index partitions corresponding to the added partitions.

Restriction: You cannot specify this clause for a list partition.

COALESCE SUBPARTITION: COALESCE applies only to hash partitions and subpartitions. Use the COALESCE SUBPARTITION clause if you want Oracle to select a hash subpartition, distribute its contents into one or more remaining subpartitions (determined by the hash function), and then drop the selected subpartition.

Oracle invalidates any global indexes on table. You can update these indexes during this operation using the update_global_index_clause.

Oracle drops local index partitions corresponding to the selected partition. Oracle marks UNUSABLE, and you must rebuild, the local index partitions corresponding to one or more absorbing partitions.

ADD | DROP VALUES Clauses: These clauses are valid only when you are modifying list partitions.

- Use the ADD VALUES clause to extend the partition_value list of partition to include additional values. The added partition values must comply with all rules and restrictions listed in the list_partitioning of CREATE TABLE

- Use the DROP VALUES clause to reduce the partition_value list of partition by eliminating one or more partition_value. When you specify this clause, Oracle checks to ensure that no rows with this value exist. If such rows do exist, Oracle returns an error.

NOTE
A DROP VALUES operation will be enhanced if you have a local prefixed index defined on the table.

UNUSABLE LOCAL INDEXES: The next two clauses modify the attributes of local index partitions corresponding to partition.

- UNUSABLE LOCAL INDEXES marks UNUSABLE all the local index partitions associated with partition.

- REBUILD UNUSABLE LOCAL INDEXES rebuilds the unusable local index partitions associated with partition.

Restrictions:

- You cannot specify this clause with any other clauses of the modify_table_partition_clause.

- You cannot specify this clause for partitions that are subpartitioned.

update_global_index_clause   When you perform DDL on a table partition, if a global index is defined on table, Oracle invalidates the entire index, not just the partitions undergoing DDL. This clause lets you update the global index partition you are changing during the DDL operation, eliminating the need to rebuild the index after the DDL.

UPDATE GLOBAL INDEXES: Specify UPDATE GLOBAL INDEXES to update the global indexes defined on table.

INVALIDATE GLOBAL INDEXES: Specify INVALIDATE GLOBAL INDEXES to invalidate the global indexes defined on table.

If you specify neither, Oracle invalidates the global indexes.

Restrictions: This clause supports only global indexes. Domain indexes and index-organized tables are not supported. In addition, this clause updates only indexes that are USABLE and VALID. UNUSABLE indexes are left unusable, and INVALID global indexes are ignored.

parallel_clause   The parallel_clause lets you change the default degree of parallelism for queries and DML on the table.

> **NOTE**
> *The syntax of the parallel_clause supersedes syntax appearing in earlier releases of Oracle. Superseded syntax is still supported for backward compatibility, but may result in slightly different behavior than that documented.*

NOPARALLEL: Specify NOPARALLEL for serial execution. This is the default.

PARALLEL: Specify PARALLEL if you want Oracle to select a degree of parallelism equal to the number of CPUs available on all participating instances times the value of the PARALLEL_THREADS_PER_CPU initialization parameter.

PARALLEL integer: Specification of integer indicates the degree of parallelism, which is the number of parallel threads used in the parallel operation. Each parallel thread may use one or two parallel execution servers. Normally Oracle calculates the optimum degree of parallelism, so it is not necessary for you to specify integer.

Restrictions:

- If table contains any columns of LOB or user-defined object type, subsequent INSERT, UPDATE, and DELETE operations on table are executed serially without notification. Subsequent queries, however, are executed in parallel.

- If you specify the parallel_clause in conjunction with the move_table_clause, the parallelism applies only to the move, not to subsequent DML and query operations on the table.

modify_table_subpartition   The modify_table_subpartition clause lets you allocate or deallocate storage for an individual subpartition of table.

UNUSABLE LOCAL INDEXES: UNUSABLE LOCAL INDEXES marks UNUSABLE all the local index subpartitions associated with subpartition.

REBUILD UNUSABLE LOCAL INDEXES: REBUILD UNUSABLE LOCAL INDEXES rebuilds the unusable local index subpartitions associated with subpartition.

Restrictions:

- The only modify_lob_parameters you can specify for subpartition are the allocate_extent_clause and deallocate_unused_clause.

- You cannot specify this clause for a list-partitioned table.

- You cannot specify either of the UNUSABLE LOCAL INDEXES clauses for list partitions.

rename_table_partition   Use the rename_table_partition clause to rename a table partition or subpartition current_name to new_name. For both partitions and subpartitions, new_name must be different from all existing partitions and subpartitions of the same table.

If table is index organized, Oracle assigns the same name to the corresponding primary key index partition as well as to any existing overflow partitions and mapping table partitions.

move_table_partition   Use the move_table_partition clause to move partition to another segment. You can move partition data to another tablespace, recluster data to reduce fragmentation, or change create-time physical attributes.

If the table contains LOB columns, you can use the LOB_storage_clause to move the LOB data and LOB index segments associated with this partition. Only the LOBs named are affected. If you do not specify the LOB_storage_clause for a particular LOB column, its LOB data and LOB index segments are not moved.

Oracle invalidates any global indexes on heap-organized tables. You can update these indexes during this operation using the update_global_index_clause. Global indexes on index-organized tables are primary key based, so they do not become unusable.

Oracle moves local index partitions corresponding to the selected partition. If the moved partitions are not empty, Oracle marks them UNUSABLE, and you must rebuild them.

When you move a LOB data segment, Oracle drops the old data segment and corresponding index segment and creates new segments even if you do not specify a new tablespace.

The move operation obtains its parallel attribute from the parallel_clause, if specified. If not specified, the default parallel attributes of the table, if any, are used. If neither is specified, Oracle performs the move without using parallelism.

Specifying the parallel_clause in MOVE PARTITION does not change the default parallel attributes of table.

NOTE
For index-organized tables, Oracle uses the address of the primary key, as well as its value, to construct logical rowids. The logical rowids are stored in the secondary index of the table. If you move a partition of an index-organized table, the address portion of the rowids will change, which can hamper performance. To ensure optimal performance, rebuild the secondary index(es) on the moved partition to update the rowids.

MAPPING TABLE: The MAPPING TABLE clause is relevant only for an index-organized table that already has a mapping table defined for it. Oracle moves the mapping table along with the index partition and marks all corresponding bitmap index partitions UNUSABLE.

Restrictions on Moving a Table Partition:

■   If partition is a hash partition, the only attribute you can specify in this clause is TABLESPACE.

■   You cannot specify this clause for a partition containing subpartitions. However, you can move subpartitions using the move_table_subpartition_clause.

move_table_subpartition   Use the move_table_subpartition clause to move subpartition to another segment. If you do not specify TABLESPACE, the subpartition remains in the same tablespace.

You can update global indexes on table during this operation using the update_global_index_clause. If the subpartition is not empty, Oracle marks UNUSABLE, and you must rebuild, all local index subpartitions corresponding to the subpartition being moved.

If the table contains LOB columns, you can use the LOB_storage_clause to move the LOB data and LOB index segments associated with this subpartition. Only the LOBs named are affected. If you do not specify the LOB_storage_clause for a particular LOB column, its LOB data and LOB index segments are not moved.

When you move a LOB data segment, Oracle drops the old data segment and corresponding index segment and creates new segments even if you do not specify a new tablespace.

Restriction: You cannot move a subpartition of a list partition.

ADD PARTITION Clauses   Use the ADD PARTITION clauses to add a hash, range, or list partition to table.

Oracle adds to any local index defined on table a new partition with the same name as that of the base table partition. If the index already has a partition with such a name, Oracle generates a partition name of the form SYS_Pn.

If table is index organized, Oracle adds a partition to any mapping table and overflow area defined on the table as well.

add_range_partition_clause   The add_range_partition_clause lets you add a new range partition to the "high" end of a partitioned table (after the last existing partition). You can specify any create-time physical attributes for the new partition. If the table contains LOB columns, you can also specify partition-level attributes for one or more LOB items.

If a domain index is defined on table, the index must not be marked IN_PROGRESS or FAILED. A table can have up to 64K-1 partitions.

Restrictions:

- If the upper partition bound of each partitioning key in the existing high partition is MAXVALUE, you cannot add a partition to the table. Instead, use the split_table_partition clause to add a partition at the beginning or the middle of the table.

- The compression_clause and OVERFLOW are valid only for a partitioned index-organized table. You can specify OVERFLOW only if the partitioned table already has an overflow segment. You can specify compression only if compression is enabled at the table level.

- You cannot specify the PCTUSED parameter for the index segment of an index-organized table.

VALUES LESS THAN (value_list): Specify the upper bound for the new partition. The value_list is a comma-separated, ordered list of literal values corresponding to column_list. The value_list must collate greater than the partition bound for the highest existing partition in the table.

partition_level_subpartition: The partition_level_subpartition clause is permitted only for a composite-partitioned table. This clause lets you specify hash subpartitions for a new range or list partition. You specify composite partitioning in one of two ways:

- You can specify individual subpartitions by name, and optionally the tablespace where each should be stored, or

- You can specify the number of subpartitions (and optionally one or more tablespaces where they are to be stored). In this case, Oracle assigns partition names of the form SYS_SUBPnnn. The number of tablespaces does not have to equal the number of subpartitions. If the number of subpartitions is greater than the number of tablespaces, Oracle cycles through the names of the tablespaces.

The subpartitions inherit all their attributes from any attributes specified for the new partition, except for TABLESPACE, which you can specify at the subpartition level. Any attributes not specified at the subpartition or partition level are inherited from table-level defaults.

This clause overrides any subpartitioning specified at the table level.

If you do not specify this clause but you specified default subpartitioning at the table level, the new partition inherits the table-level default subpartitioning.

add_hash_partition_clause   The add_hash_partition_clause lets you add a new hash partition to the "high" end of a partitioned table. Oracle will populate the new partition with rows rehashed from other partitions of table as determined by the hash function.

You can specify a name for the partition, and optionally a tablespace where it should be stored. If you do not specify a name, Oracle assigns a partition name of the form SYS_Pnnn. If you do not specify TABLESPACE, the new partition is stored in the table's default tablespace. Other attributes are always inherited from table-level defaults.

You can update global indexes on table during this operation using the update_global_index_clause. For a heap-organized table, if this operation causes data to be rehashed among partitions, Oracle marks UNUSABLE, and you must rebuild, any corresponding local index partitions. Indexes on index-organized tables are primary key based, so they do not become unusable.

parallel_clause: Use the parallel_clause to specify whether to parallelize the creation of the new partition.

add_list_partition_clause   The add_list_partition_clause lets you add a new partition to table using a new set of partition values. You can specify any create-time physical attributes for the new partition. If the table contains LOB columns, you can also specify partition-level attributes for one or more LOB items.

When you add a list partition to a table, Oracle adds a corresponding index partition with the same value list to all local indexes defined on the table. Global indexes are not affected.

coalesce_table_partition   COALESCE applies only to hash partitions and subpartitions. Use the coalesce_table_partition clause to indicate that Oracle should select a hash partition, distribute its contents into one or more remaining partitions (determined by the hash function), and then drop the selected partition.

Oracle invalidates any global indexes on heap-organized tables. You can update these indexes during this operation using the update_global_index_clause. Global indexes on index-organized tables are primary key based, so they do not become unusable.

Oracle drops local index partitions corresponding to the selected partition. Oracle marks UNUSABLE, and you must rebuild, the local index partitions corresponding to one or more absorbing partitions.

drop_table_partition   The drop_table_partition clause removes partition, and the data in that partition, from a partitioned table. If you want to drop a partition but keep its data in the table, you must merge the partition into one of the adjacent partitions.

If the table has LOB columns, Oracle also drops the LOB data and LOB index partitions (and their subpartitions, if any) corresponding to partition.

If table is index organized and has a mapping table defined on it, Oracle drops the corresponding mapping table partition as well.

Oracle drops local index partitions and subpartitions corresponding to partition, even if they are marked UNUSABLE.

You can update global indexes on heap-organized tables during this operation using the update_global_index_clause. If you specify the parallel_clause with the update_global_index_clause, Oracle parallelizes the index update, not the drop operation.

If you drop a partition and later insert a row that would have belonged to the dropped partition, Oracle stores the row in the next higher partition. However, if that partition is the highest partition, the insert will fail because the range of values represented by the dropped partition is no longer valid for the table.

Restrictions:

- You cannot drop a partition of a hash-partitioned table.
- If table contains only one partition, you cannot drop the partition. You must drop the table.

truncate_table_partition　　Specify TRUNCATE PARTITION to remove all rows from partition or, if the table is composite partitioned, all rows from partition's subpartitions. Specify TRUNCATE SUBPARTITION to remove all rows from subpartition. If table is index organized, Oracle also truncates any corresponding mapping table partitions and overflow area partitions.

If the partition or subpartition to be truncated contains data, you must first disable any referential integrity constraints on the table. Alternatively, you can delete the rows and then truncate the partition.

If the table contains any LOB columns, the LOB data and LOB index segments for this partition are also truncated. If table is composite partitioned, the LOB data and LOB index segments for this partition's subpartitions are truncated.

If a domain index is defined on table, the index must not be marked IN_PROGRESS or FAILED, and the index partition corresponding to the table partition being truncated must not be marked IN_PROGRESS.

For each partition or subpartition truncated, Oracle also truncates corresponding local index partitions and subpartitions. If those index partitions or subpartitions are marked UNUSABLE, Oracle truncates them and resets the UNUSABLE marker to VALID.

You can update global indexes on table during this operation using the update_global_index_clause. If you specify the parallel_clause with the update_global_index_clause, Oracle parallelizes the index update, not the truncate operation.

Restriction: You cannot truncate a subpartition of a list partition.

DROP STORAGE: Specify DROP STORAGE to deallocate space from the deleted rows and make it available for use by other schema objects in the tablespace.

REUSE STORAGE: Specify REUSE STORAGE to keep space from the deleted rows allocated to the partition or subpartition. The space is subsequently available only for inserts and updates to the same partition or subpartition.

split_table_partition　　The split_table_partition clause lets you create, from current_partition, two new partitions, each with a new segment and new physical attributes, and new initial extents. The segment associated with current_partition is discarded.

Restriction: You cannot specify this clause for a hash-partitioned table.

If you specify subpartitioning for the new partitions, you can specify only TABLESPACE for the subpartitions. All other attributes are inherited from the containing new partition.

If current_partition is subpartitioned and you do not specify any subpartitioning for the new partitions, the new partitions inherit the number and tablespaces of the subpartitions in current_partition.

If table is index organized, Oracle splits any corresponding mapping table partition and places it in the same tablespace as the parent index-organized table partition. Oracle also splits any corresponding overflow area, and you can specify segment attributes for the new overflow areas.

Oracle splits corresponding local index partitions, even if they are marked UNUSABLE.

Oracle invalidates any global indexes on heap-organized tables. You can update these indexes during this operation using the update_global_index_clause. Global indexes on index-organized tables are primary key based, so they do not become unusable.

Oracle drops local index partitions corresponding to the selected partition. Oracle marks UNUSABLE, and you must rebuild, the local index partitions corresponding to the split partitions.

If table contains LOB columns, you can use the LOB_storage_clause to specify separate LOB storage attributes for the LOB data segments resulting from the split. Oracle drops the LOB data and LOB index segments of current_partition and creates new segments for each LOB column, for each partition, even if you do not specify a new tablespace.

AT (value_list): The AT (value_list) clause applies only to range partitions. Specify the new noninclusive upper bound for the first of the two new partitions. The value_list must compare less than the original partition bound for current_partition and greater than the partition bound for the next lowest partition (if there is one).

VALUES (values_list): The VALUES (value_list) clause applies only to list partitions. Specify the partition values you want to include in the first of the two new partitions. Oracle creates the first new partition using the partition value list you specify and creates the second new partition using the remaining partition values from current_partition. The new partitions inherit all unspecified physical attributes from current_partition.

Oracle splits the corresponding partition in each local index defined on table, even if the index is marked UNUSABLE.

Restriction: The value_list cannot contain all of the partition values of current_partition, nor can it contain any partition values that do not already exist for current_partition.

INTO partition_spec, partition_spec: The INTO clause lets you describe the two partitions resulting from the split. The keyword PARTITION is required even if you do not specify the optional names and physical attributes of the two partitions resulting from the split. If you do not specify new partition names, Oracle assigns names of the form SYS_Pn. Any attributes you do not specify are inherited from current_partition.

Restrictions:

- You can specify the compression_clause and OVERFLOW only for a partitioned index-organized table.

- You cannot specify the PCTUSED parameter for the index segment of an index-organized table.

parallel_clause: The parallel_clause lets you parallelize the split operation, but does not change the default parallel attributes of the table.

merge_table_partitions   The merge_table_partitions clause lets you merge the contents of two partitions of table into one new partition, and then drops the original two partitions. The two partitions to be merged must be adjacent if they are range partitions. List partitions need not be adjacent in order to be merged.

Restriction: You cannot specify this clause for a hash-partitioned table.

The new partition inherits the partition-bound of the higher of the two original partitions.

Any attributes not specified in the segment_attributes_clause are inherited from table-level defaults.

If you do not specify a new partition_name, Oracle assigns a name of the form SYS_Pnnn. If the new partition has subpartitions, Oracle assigns subpartition names of the form SYS_SUBPnnn.

When you merge two list partitions, the resulting partition_value list is the union of the set of the two partition_value lists of the partitions being merged.

Oracle invalidates any global indexes on heap-organized tables. You can update these indexes during this operation using the update_global_index_clause. Global indexes on index-organized tables are primary key based, so they do not become unusable.

Oracle drops local index partitions corresponding to the selected partitions. Oracle marks UNUSABLE, and you must rebuild, the local index partitions corresponding to merged partition.

partition_level_subpartition: The partition_level_subpartition clause lets you specify hash subpartitioning attributes for the new merged partition. Any attributes not specified in this clause are inherited from table-level defaults. If you do not specify this clause, the new merged partition inherits subpartitioning attributes from table-level defaults.

parallel_clause: The parallel_clause lets you parallelize the merge operation.

exchange_table_partition   Use the EXCHANGE PARTITION or EXCHANGE SUBPARTITION clause to exchange the data and index segments of

- One nonpartitioned table with one hash, list, or range partition (or one hash subpartition)
- One hash-partitioned table with the hash subpartitions of a range partition of a composite-partitioned table

This clause facilitates high-speed data loading when used with transportable tablespaces.

If table contains LOB columns, for each LOB column Oracle exchanges LOB data and LOB index partition or subpartition segments with corresponding LOB data and LOB index segments of table.

All of the segment attributes of the two objects (including tablespace and logging) are also exchanged.

All statistics of the table and partition are exchanged, including table, column, index statistics, and histograms. The aggregate statistics of the table receiving the new partition are recalculated.

Oracle invalidates any global indexes on the objects being exchanged. If you specify the update_global_index_clause with this clause, Oracle updates the global indexes on the table whose partition is being exchanged. Global indexes on the table being exchanged remain invalidated. If you specify the parallel_clause with the update_global_index_clause, Oracle parallelizes the index update, not the exchange operation.

WITH TABLE: Specify the table with which the partition or subpartition will be exchanged.

INCLUDING INDEXES: Specify INCLUDING INDEXES if you want local index partitions or subpartitions to be exchanged with the corresponding table index (for a nonpartitioned table) or local indexes (for a hash-partitioned table).

EXCLUDING INDEXES: Specify EXCLUDING INDEXES if you want all index partitions or subpartitions corresponding to the partition and all the regular indexes and index partitions on the exchanged table to be marked UNUSABLE.

WITH VALIDATION: Specify WITH VALIDATION if you want Oracle to return an error if any rows in the exchanged table do not map into partitions or subpartitions being exchanged.

WITHOUT VALIDATION: Specify WITHOUT VALIDATION if you do not want Oracle to check the proper mapping of rows in the exchanged table.

exceptions_clause: Specify a table into which Oracle should place the rowids of all rows violating the constraint. If you omit schema, Oracle assumes the exceptions table is in your own schema. If you omit this clause altogether, Oracle assumes that the table is named EXCEPTIONS. The exceptions table must be on your local database.

You can create the EXCEPTIONS table using one of these scripts:

- UTLEXCPT.SQL uses physical rowids. Therefore it can accommodate rows from conventional tables but not from index-organized tables. (See the Note that follows.)
- UTLEXPT1.SQL uses universal rowids, so it can accommodate rows from both heap-organized and index-organized tables.

If you create your own exceptions table, it must follow the format prescribed by one of these two scripts.

NOTE
If you are collecting exceptions from index-organized tables based on primary keys (rather than universal rowids), you must create a separate exceptions table for each index-organized table to accommodate its primary key storage. You create multiple exceptions tables with different names by modifying and resubmitting the script.

Restrictions on the exceptions_clause:

- This clause is not valid with subpartitions.
- The partitioned table must have been defined with a UNIQUE constraint, and that constraint must be in DISABLE VALIDATE state.

If these conditions are not true, Oracle ignores this clause.

Restrictions on Exchanging Partitions:

- You cannot exchange subpartitions of list partitions.
- Both tables involved in the exchange must have the same primary key, and no validated foreign keys can be referencing either of the tables unless the referenced table is empty.
- When exchanging between a hash-partitioned table and the range partition of a composite-partitioned table, the following restrictions apply:
  - The partitioning key of the hash-partitioned table must be identical to the subpartitioning key of the composite-partitioned table.
  - The number of partitions in the hash-partitioned table must be identical to the number of subpartitions in the range partition of the composite-partitioned table.
- For partitioned index-organized tables, the following additional restrictions apply:
  - The source and target table/partition must have their primary key set on the same columns, in the same order.
  - If compression is enabled, it must be enabled for both the source and the target, and with the same prefix length.
  - Both the source and target must be index organized.
  - Both the source and target must have overflow segments, or neither can have overflow segments. Also, both the source and target must have mapping tables, or neither can have a mapping table.
  - Both the source and target must have identical storage attributes for any LOB columns.

row_movement_clause　　The row_movement_clause determines whether a row can be moved to a different partition or subpartition because of a change to one or more of its key values.

　　Restriction: You can specify this clause only for partitioned tables.

　　ENABLE: Specify ENABLE to allow Oracle to move a row to a different partition or subpartition as the result of an update to the partitioning or subpartitioning key.

CAUTION

Moving a row in the course of an UPDATE operation changes that row's rowid.

　　DISABLE: Specify DISABLE to have Oracle return an error if an update to a partitioning or subpartitioning key would result in a row moving to a different partition or subpartition. This is the default.

alter_column_clauses

add_column_options　　ADD add_column_options lets you add a column or integrity constraint to a table.

　　If you add a column, the initial value of each row for the new column is null unless you specify the DEFAULT clause. In this case, Oracle updates each row in the new column with the value you specify for DEFAULT. This update operation, in turn, fires any AFTER UPDATE triggers defined on the table.

NOTE

If a column has a default value, you can use the DEFAULT clause to change the default to NULL, but you cannot remove the default value completely. That is, if a column has ever had a default value assigned to it, the DATA_DEFAULT column of the USER_TAB_COLUMNS data dictionary view will always display either a default value or NULL.

　　You can add an overflow data segment to each partition of a partitioned index-organized table.

　　You can add LOB columns to nonpartitioned and partitioned tables. You can specify LOB storage at the table and at the partition or subpartition level.

　　If you previously created a view with a query that used the "SELECT *" syntax to select all columns from table, and you now add a column to table, Oracle does not automatically add the new column to the view. To add the new column to the view, re-create the view using the CREATE VIEW statement with the OR REPLACE clause.

　　Restrictions:

- ■　You cannot add a LOB column to a clustered table.

- ■　If you add a LOB column to a hash-partitioned table, the only attribute you can specify for the new partition is TABLESPACE.

- ■　You cannot add a column with a NOT NULL constraint if table has any rows unless you also specify the DEFAULT clause.

- ■　If you specify this clause for an index-organized table, you cannot specify any other clauses in the same statement.

DEFAULT: Use the DEFAULT clause to specify a default for a new column or a new default for an existing column. Oracle assigns this value to the column if a subsequent INSERT statement omits a value for the column. If you are adding a new column to the table and specify the default value, Oracle inserts the default column value into all rows of the table.

The datatype of the default value must match the datatype specified for the column. The column must also be long enough to hold the default value.

Restrictions:

■   A DEFAULT expression cannot contain references to other columns, the pseudocolumns CURRVAL, NEXTVAL, LEVEL, and ROWNUM, or date constants that are not fully specified.

■   The expression can be of any form except a scalar subquery expression.

table_ref_constraint, column_ref_constraint: These clauses let you further describe a column of type REF. The only difference between these clauses is that you specify table_ref from the table level, so you must identify the REF column or attribute you are defining. You specify column_ref after you have already identified the REF column or attribute.

column_constraint: Use column_constraint to add or remove a NOT NULL constraint to or from an existing column. You cannot use this clause to modify any other type of constraint using ALTER TABLE.

table_or_view_constraint: Use table_or_view_constraint to add or modify an integrity constraint on the table.

modify_column_options   Use MODIFY modify_column_options to modify the definition of an existing column. Any of the optional parts of the column definition (datatype, default value, or column constraint) that you omit from this clause remain unchanged.

datatype: You can change any column's datatype if all rows for the column contain nulls. However, if you change the datatype of a column in a materialized view container table, the corresponding materialized view is invalidated.

You can omit the datatype only if the statement also designates the column as part of the foreign key of a referential integrity constraint. Oracle automatically assigns the column the same datatype as the corresponding column of the referenced key of the referential integrity constraint.

You can always increase the size of a character or raw column or the precision of a numeric column, whether or not all the columns contain nulls. You can reduce the size of a column's datatype as long as the change does not require data to be modified. Oracle scans existing data and returns an error if data exists that exceeds the new length limit.

You can modify a DATE column to TIMESTAMP or TIMESTAMP WITH LOCAL TIME ZONE. You can modify any TIMESTAMP WITH LOCAL TIME ZONE to a DATE column.

NOTE
When you modify a TIMESTAMP WITH LOCAL TIME ZONE column to a DATE column, the fractional seconds and time zone adjustment data is lost.

■   If the TIMESTAMP WITH LOCAL TIME ZONE data has fractional seconds, Oracle updates the row data for the column by rounding the fractional seconds.

■   If the TIMESTAMP WITH LOCAL TIME ZONE data has the minute field greater than equal to 60 (which can occur in a boundary case when the daylight savings rule switches), Oracle updates the row data for the column by subtracting 60 from its minute field.

If the table is empty, you can increase or decrease the leading field or the fractional second value of a datetime or interval column. If the table is not empty, you can only increase the leading field or fractional second of a datetime or interval column.

You can change a LONG column to a CLOB or NCLOB column, and a LONG RAW column to a BLOB column.

■ The modified LOB column inherits all constraints and triggers that were defined on the original LONG column. If you wish to change any constraints, you must do so in a subsequent ALTER TABLE statement.

■ If any domain indexes are defined on the LONG column, you must drop them before modifying the column to a LOB.

■ After the modification, you will have to rebuild all other indexes on all columns of the table.

For CHAR and VARCHAR2 columns, you can change the length semantics by specifying CHAR (to indicate character semantics for a column that was originally specified in bytes) or BYTE (to indicate byte semantics for a column that was originally specified in characters). To learn the length semantics of existing columns, query the CHAR_USED column of the ALL_, USER_, or DBA_TAB_COLUMNS data dictionary view.

column_constraint: The only type of integrity constraint that you can add to an existing column using the MODIFY clause with the column constraint syntax is a NOT NULL constraint, and only if the column contains no nulls. To define other types of integrity constraints (UNIQUE, PRIMARY KEY, referential integrity, and CHECK constraints) on existing columns, using the ADD clause and the table constraint syntax.

Restrictions:

■ You cannot modify a column of a table if a domain index is defined on the column. You must first drop the domain index and then modify the column.

■ You cannot specify a column of datatype ROWID for an index-organized table, but you can specify a column of type UROWID.

■ You cannot change a column's datatype to REF.

drop_column_clause   The drop_column_clause lets you free space in the database by dropping columns you no longer need, or by marking them to be dropped at a future time when the demand on system resources is less.

■ If you drop a nested table column, its storage table is removed.

■ If you drop a LOB column, the LOB data and its corresponding LOB index segment are removed.

■ If you drop a BFILE column, only the locators stored in that column are removed, not the files referenced by the locators.

■ If you drop (or mark unused) a column defined as an INCLUDING column, the column stored immediately before this column will become the new INCLUDING column.

SET UNUSED Clause: Specify SET UNUSED to mark one or more columns as unused. Specifying this clause does not actually remove the target columns from each row in the table (that is, it does not restore the disk space used by these columns). Therefore, the response time is faster than it would be if you execute the DROP clause.

You can view all tables with columns marked UNUSED in the data dictionary views USER_UNUSED_COL_TABS, DBA_UNUSED_COL_TABS, and ALL_UNUSED_COL_TABS.

Unused columns are treated as if they were dropped, even though their column data remains in the table's rows. After a column has been marked UNUSED, you have no access to that column. A "SELECT *" query will not retrieve data from unused columns. In addition, the names and types of columns marked UNUSED will not be displayed during a DESCRIBE, and you can add to the table a new column with the same name as an unused column.

NOTE
Until you actually drop these columns, they continue to count toward the absolute limit of 1000 columns in a single table. However, as with all DDL statements, you cannot roll back the results of this clause. That is, you cannot issue SET USED counterpart to retrieve a column that you have SET UNUSED.

Also, if you mark a column of datatype LONG as UNUSED, you cannot add another LONG column to the table until you actually drop the unused LONG column.

DROP Clause: Specify DROP to remove the column descriptor and the data associated with the target column from each row in the table. If you explicitly drop a particular column, all columns currently marked UNUSED in the target table are dropped at the same time.

When the column data is dropped:

■ All indexes defined on any of the target columns are also dropped.

■ All constraints that reference a target column are removed.

■ If any statistics types are associated with the target columns, Oracle disassociates the statistics from the column with the FORCE option and drops any statistics collected using the statistics type.

NOTE
If the target column is a parent key of a nontarget column, or if a check constraint references both the target and nontarget columns, Oracle returns an error and does not drop the column unless you have specified the CASCADE CONSTRAINTS clause. If you have specified that clause, Oracle removes all constraints that reference any of the target columns.

DROP UNUSED COLUMNS Clause: Specify DROP UNUSED COLUMNS to remove from the table all columns currently marked as unused. Use this statement when you want to reclaim the extra disk space from unused columns in the table. If the table contains no unused columns, the statement returns with no errors.

column: Specify one or more columns to be set as unused or dropped. Use the COLUMN keyword only if you are specifying only one column. If you specify a column list, it cannot contain duplicates.

CASCADE CONSTRAINTS: Specify CASCADE CONSTRAINTS if you want to drop all referential integrity constraints that refer to the primary and unique keys defined on the dropped columns, and drop all multicolumn constraints defined on the dropped columns. If any constraint is referenced by columns from other tables or remaining columns in the target table, then you must specify CASCADE CONSTRAINTS. Otherwise, the statement aborts and an error is returned.

INVALIDATE: The INVALIDATE keyword is optional. Oracle automatically invalidates all dependent objects, such as views, triggers, and stored program units. Object invalidation is a recursive process. Therefore, all directly dependent and indirectly dependent objects are invalidated. However, only local dependencies are invalidated, because Oracle manages remote dependencies differently from local dependencies.

An object invalidated by this statement is automatically revalidated when next referenced. You must then correct any errors that exist in that object before referencing it.

CHECKPOINT: Specify CHECKPOINT if you want Oracle to apply a checkpoint for the DROP COLUMN operation after processing integer rows; integer is optional and must be greater than zero. If integer is greater than the number of rows in the table, Oracle applies a checkpoint after all the rows have been processed. If you do not specify integer, Oracle sets the default of 512. Checkpointing cuts down the amount of undo logs accumulated during the DROP COLUMN operation to avoid running out of rollback segment space. However, if this statement is interrupted after a checkpoint has been applied, the table remains in an unusable state. While the table is unusable, the only operations allowed on it are DROP TABLE, TRUNCATE TABLE, and ALTER TABLE DROP COLUMNS CONTINUE (described below).

You cannot use this clause with SET UNUSED, because that clause does not remove column data.

DROP COLUMNS CONTINUE Clause: Specify DROP COLUMNS CONTINUE to continue the drop column operation from the point at which it was interrupted. Submitting this statement while the table is in a valid state results in an error.

Restrictions on the drop_column_clause:

- Each of the parts of this clause can be specified only once in the statement and cannot be mixed with any other ALTER TABLE clauses. For example, the following statements are not allowed:

  ```
  ALTER TABLE t1 DROP COLUMN f1 DROP (f2);
  ALTER TABLE t1 DROP COLUMN f1 SET UNUSED (f2);
  ALTER TABLE t1 DROP (f1) ADD (f2 NUMBER);
  ALTER TABLE t1 SET UNUSED (f3)
     ADD (CONSTRAINT ck1 CHECK (f2 > 0));
  ```

- You can drop an object type column only as an entity. To drop an attribute from an object type column, use the ALTER TYPE ... DROP ATTRIBUTE statement with the CASCADE INCLUDING TABLE DATA clause. Be aware that dropping an attribute affects all dependent objects.

- You can drop a column from an index-organized table only if it is not a primary key column. The primary key constraint of an index-organized table can never be dropped, so you cannot drop a primary key column even if you have specified CASCADE CONSTRAINTS.

- You can export tables with dropped or unused columns. However, you can import a table only if all the columns specified in the export files are present in the table (that is, none of those columns has been dropped or marked unused). Otherwise, Oracle returns an error.

- You cannot drop a column on which a domain index has been built.

- You cannot use this clause to drop:
  - A pseudocolumn, cluster column, or partitioning column. (You can drop nonpartitioning columns from a partitioned table if all the tablespaces where the partitions were created are online and in read/write mode.)
  - A column from: a nested table, an object table, or a table owned by SYS.

modify_collection_retrieval   Use the modify_collection_retrieval clause to change what Oracle returns when a collection item is retrieved from the database.

collection_item: Specify the name of a column-qualified attribute whose type is nested table or varray.

RETURN AS: Specify what Oracle should return as the result of a query:

- LOCATOR specifies that a unique locator for the nested table is returned.
- VALUE specifies that a copy of the nested table itself is returned.

alter_constraint_clauses

Use the alter_constraint_clauses to modify the state of a constraint or to drop a constraint.

MODIFY CONSTRAINT constraint   MODIFY CONSTRAINT lets you change the state of an existing constraint.

Restrictions on Modifying Constraints:

- You cannot modify the datatype or length of a column that is part of a table or index partitioning or subpartitioning key.
- You can change a CHAR column to VARCHAR2 (or VARCHAR) and a VARCHAR2 (or VARCHAR) to CHAR only if the column contains nulls in all rows or if you do not attempt to change the column size.
- You cannot change a LONG or LONG RAW column to a LOB if it is part of a cluster. If you do change a LONG or LONG RAW column to a LOB, the only other clauses you can specify in this ALTER TABLE statement are the DEFAULT clause and the LOB_storage_clause.
- You can specify the LOB_storage_clause as part of modify_column_options only when you are changing a LONG or LONG RAW column to a LOB.
- If you specify this clause for an index-organized table, you cannot specify any other clauses in the same statement.

drop_constraint_clause   The drop_constraint_clause lets you drop an integrity constraint from the database. Oracle stops enforcing the constraint and removes it from the data dictionary. You can specify only one constraint for each drop_constraint_clause, but you can specify multiple drop_constraint_clauses in one statement.

PRIMARY KEY: Specify PRIMARY KEY to drop the table's primary key constraint.

UNIQUE: Specify UNIQUE to drop the unique constraint on the specified columns.

NOTE
If you drop the primary key or unique constraint from a column on which a bitmap join index is defined, Oracle invalidates the index. See "CREATE INDEX" for information on bitmap join indexes.

CONSTRAINT: Specify CONSTRAINT constraint to drop an integrity constraint other than a primary key or unique constraint.

CASCADE: Specify CASCADE if you want all other integrity constraints that depend on the dropped integrity constraint to be dropped as well.

KEEP | DROP INDEX: Specify KEEP or DROP INDEX to indicate whether Oracle should preserve or drop the index it has been using to enforce the PRIMARY KEY or UNIQUE constraint.

Restrictions on the drop_constraint_clause:

- You cannot drop a primary key or unique key constraint that is part of a referential integrity constraint without also dropping the foreign key. To drop the referenced key and the foreign key together, use the CASCADE clause. If you omit CASCADE, Oracle does not drop the primary key or unique constraint if any foreign key references it.

- You cannot drop a primary key constraint (even with the CASCADE clause) on a table that uses the primary key as its object identifier (OID).

- If you drop a referential integrity constraint on a REF column, the REF column remains scoped to the referenced table.

- You cannot drop the scope of the column.

alter_column_properties
The alter_column_properties clause lets you change the storage characteristics of a column or partition.

column_properties   The column_properties determine the storage characteristics of an object, nested table, varray, or LOB column.

object_type_col_properties: Use the object_type_col_properties to specify storage characteristics of an object column or attribute or an element of a collection column or attribute.

column: For column, specify an object column or attribute.

substitutable_column_clause: The substitutable_column_clause indicates whether object columns or attributes in the same hierarchy are substitutable for each other. You can specify that a column is of a particular type, or whether it can contain instances of its subtypes, or both.

- If you specify ELEMENT, you constrain the element type of a collection column or attribute to a subtype of its declared type.

- The IS OF [TYPE] (ONLY type) clause constrains the type of the object column to a subtype of its declared type.

- NOT SUBSTITUTABLE AT ALL LEVELS indicates that the object column cannot hold instances corresponding to any of its subtypes. Also, substitution is disabled for any embedded object attributes and elements of embedded nested tables and varrays. The default is SUBSTITUTABLE AT ALL LEVELS.

Restrictions on the substitutable_column_clause:

- You can specify this clause only for top-level object columns, not for attributes of object columns.

- For a collection type column, the only part of this clause you can specify is [NOT] SUBSTITUTABLE AT ALL LEVELS.

nested_table_col_properties: The nested_table_col_properties clause lets you specify separate storage characteristics for a nested table, which in turn lets you to define the nested table as an index-organized table. You must include this clause when creating a table with columns or column attributes whose type is a nested table. (Clauses within this clause that function the same way they function for parent object tables are not repeated here.)

- For nested_item, specify the name of a column (or a top-level attribute of the table's object type) whose type is a nested table.

- For storage_table, specify the name of the table where the rows of nested_item reside. The storage table is created in the same schema and the same tablespace as the parent table.

Restrictions:

- You cannot specify the parallel_clause.

- You cannot specify TABLESPACE (as part of the segment_attributes_clause) for a nested table. The tablespace is always that of the parent table.

varray_col_properties: The varray_col_properties clause lets you specify separate storage characteristics for the LOB in which a varray will be stored. If you specify this clause, Oracle will always store the varray in a LOB, even if it is small enough to be stored inline.

Restriction: You cannot specify TABLESPACE as part of LOB_parameters for a varray column. The LOB tablespace for a varray defaults to the containing table's tablespace.

LOB_storage_clause: Use the LOB_storage_clause to specify the LOB storage characteristics for a newly added LOB column. You cannot use this clause to modify an existing LOB column. Instead, you must use the modify_lob_storage_clause.

CACHE READS Clause: CACHE READS applies only to LOB storage. It indicates that LOB values are brought into the buffer cache only during read operations, but not during write operations.

- For lob_item, specify the LOB column name or LOB object attribute for which you are explicitly defining tablespace and storage characteristics that are different from those of the table.

- For lob_segname, specify the name of the LOB data segment. You cannot use lob_segname if more than one lob_item is specified.

When you add a new LOB column, you can specify the logging attribute with CACHE READS, as you can when defining a LOB column at create time.

When you modify a LOB column from CACHE or NOCACHE to CACHE READS, or from CACHE READS to CACHE or NOCACHE, you can change the logging attribute. If you do not specify the LOGGING or NOLOGGING, this attribute defaults to the current logging attribute of the LOB column.

For existing LOBs, if you do not specify CACHE, NOCACHE, or CACHE READS, Oracle retains the existing values of the LOB attributes.

Restrictions:

- The only parameter of LOB_parameters you can specify for a hash partition or hash subpartition is TABLESPACE.

- You cannot specify the LOB_index_clause if table is partitioned.

ENABLE | DISABLE STORAGE IN ROW: Specify whether the LOB value is to be stored in the row (inline) or outside of the row (out of line). (The LOB locator is always stored inline regardless of where the LOB value is stored.)

■ ENABLE specifies that the LOB value is stored inline if its length is less than approximately 4000 bytes minus system control information. This is the default.

■ DISABLE specifies that the LOB value is stored out of line regardless of the length of the LOB value.

Restriction: You cannot change STORAGE IN ROW once it is set. Therefore, you cannot specify this clause as part of the modify_column_options clause. However, you can change this setting when adding a new column (add_column_options) or when moving the table (move_table_clause).

CHUNK integer: Specify the number of bytes to be allocated for LOB manipulation. If integer is not a multiple of the database block size, Oracle rounds up (in bytes) to the next multiple. For example, if the database block size is 2048 and integer is 2050, Oracle allocates 4096 bytes (2 blocks).The maximum value is 32768 (32 K), which is the largest Oracle block size allowed. The default CHUNK size is one Oracle database block.

Restrictions:

■ You cannot change the value of CHUNK once it is set.

■ The value of CHUNK must be less than or equal to the value of NEXT (either the default value or that specified in the storage clause). If CHUNK exceeds the value of NEXT, Oracle returns an error.

PCTVERSION integer: Specify the maximum percentage of overall LOB storage space to be used for creating new versions of the LOB. The default value is 10, meaning that older versions of the LOB data are not overwritten until 10% of the overall LOB storage space is used.

LOB_index_clause: This clause has been deprecated since Oracle8i. Oracle generates an index for each LOB column. The LOB indexes are system named and system managed, and they reside in the same tablespace as the LOB data segments.

It is still possible for you to specify this clause in some cases. However, Oracle Corporation strongly recommends that you no longer do so. In any event, do not put the LOB index in a different tablespace from the LOB data.

partition_storage_clause   The partition_storage_clause lets you specify a separate LOB_storage_clause or varray_col_properties clause for each partition. You must specify the partitions in the order of partition position. You can find the order of the partitions by querying the PARTITION_NAME and PARTITION_POSITION columns of the USER_IND_PARTITIONS view.

If you do not specify a LOB_storage_clause or varray_col_properties clause for a particular partition, the storage characteristics are those specified for the LOB item at the table level. If you also did not specify any storage characteristics for the LOB item at the table level, Oracle stores the LOB data partition in the same tablespace as the table partition to which it corresponds.

Restriction: You can specify only one list of partition_storage_clauses in a single ALTER TABLE statement, and all LOB_storage_clauses and varray_col_properties clause must precede the list of partition_storage_clauses.

modify_lob_storage_clause   The modify_lob_storage_clause lets you change the physical attributes of the LOB lob_item. You can specify only one lob_item for each modify_lob_storage_clause.
> **Restrictions**:
>
> ■ You cannot modify the value of the INITIAL parameter in the storage_clause when modifying the LOB storage attributes.
>
> ■ You cannot specify both the allocate_extent_clause and the deallocate_unused_clause in the same statement.

alter_varray_col_properties   The alter_varray_col_properties clause lets you change the storage characteristics of an existing LOB in which a varray is stored.
> **Restriction:** You cannot specify the TABLESPACE clause of LOB_parameters as part of this clause. The LOB tablespace for a varray defaults to the tablespace of the containing table.

alter_external_table_clause
Use the alter_external_table_clause to change the characteristics of an external table. This clause has no affect on the external data itself. The syntax and semantics of the parallel_clause, enable_disable_clause, external_data_properties, and REJECT LIMIT clause are the same as described for CREATE TABLE. See the external_table_clause of "CREATE TABLE".
> **Restrictions**:
>
> ■ You cannot modify an external table using any clause outside of this clause.
>
> ■ You cannot add a LONG, LOB, or object type column to an external table, nor can you change the datatype of an external table column to any of these datatypes.
>
> ■ You cannot add a constraint to an external table.
>
> ■ You cannot modify the storage parameters of an external table.

move_table_clause
The move_table_clause lets you relocate data of a nonpartitioned table into a new segment, optionally in a different tablespace, and optionally modify any of its storage attributes.
> You can also move any LOB data segments associated with the table using the LOB_storage_clause and varray_col_properties clause. LOB items not specified in this clause are not moved.

index_organized_table_clause   For an index-organized table, the index_org_table_clause of the syntax lets you additionally specify overflow segment attributes. The move_table_clause rebuilds the index-organized table's primary key index. The overflow data segment is not rebuilt unless the OVERFLOW keyword is explicitly stated, with two exceptions:
> ■ If you alter the values of PCTTHRESHOLD or the INCLUDING column as part of this ALTER TABLE statement, the overflow data segment is rebuilt.
>
> ■ If you explicitly move any of out-of-line columns (LOBs, varrays, nested table columns) in the index-organized table, then the overflow data segment is also rebuilt.

The index and data segments of LOB columns are not rebuilt unless you specify the LOB columns explicitly as part of this ALTER TABLE statement.
> **ONLINE Clause:** Specify ONLINE if you want DML operations on the index-organized table to be allowed during rebuilding of the table's primary key index.

Restrictions:

- You cannot combine this clause with any other clause in the same statement.
- You can specify this clause only for a nonpartitioned index-organized table.
- Parallel DML is not supported during online MOVE. If you specify ONLINE and then issue parallel DML statements, Oracle returns an error.

mapping_table_clauses: Specify MAPPING TABLE if you want Oracle to create a mapping table if one does not already exist. If it does exist, Oracle moves the mapping table along with the index-organized table, and marks any bitmapped indexes UNUSABLE. The new mapping table is created in the same tablespace as the parent table.

Specify NOMAPPING to instruct Oracle to drop an existing mapping table.

Restriction: You cannot specify NOMAPPING if any bitmapped indexes have been defined on table.

compression_clause: Use the compression_clause to enable or disable key compression in an index-organized table.

- COMPRESS enables key compression, which eliminates repeated occurrence of primary key column values in index-organized tables. Use integer to specify the prefix length (number of prefix columns to compress).

  The valid range of prefix length values is from 1 to the number of primary key columns minus 1. The default prefix length is the number of primary key columns minus 1.

- NOCOMPRESS disables key compression in index-organized tables. This is the default.

TABLESPACE tablespace: Specify the tablespace into which the rebuilt index-organized table is stored.

Restrictions on the move_table_clause:

- If you specify MOVE, it must be the first clause, and the only clauses outside this clause that are allowed are the physical_attributes_clause, the parallel_clause, and the LOB_storage_clause.
- You cannot move a table containing a LONG or LONG RAW column.
- You cannot MOVE an entire partitioned table (either heap or index organized). You must move individual partitions or subpartitions.

NOTE
For any LOB columns you specify in a move_table_clause: (1) Oracle drops the old LOB data segment and corresponding index segment and creates new segments, even if you do not specify a new tablespace. (2) If the LOB index in table resided in a different tablespace from the LOB data, Oracle collocates the LOB index with the LOB data in the LOB data's tablespace after the move.

enable_disable_clause
The enable_disable_clause lets you specify whether and how Oracle should apply an integrity constraint. The DROP and KEEP clauses are valid only when you are disabling a unique or primary key constraint.

TABLE LOCK

Oracle permits DDL operations on a table only if the table can be locked during the operation. Such table locks are not required during DML operations.

NOTE
Table locks are not acquired on temporary tables.

ENABLE TABLE LOCK: Specify ENABLE TABLE LOCK to enable table locks, thereby allowing DDL operations on the table.

DISABLE TABLE LOCK: Specify DISABLE TABLE LOCK to disable table locks, thereby preventing DML operations on the table.

ALL TRIGGERS Use the ALL TRIGGERS clause to enable or disable all triggers associated with the table.

ENABLE ALL TRIGGERS: Specify ENABLE ALL TRIGGERS to enable all triggers associated with the table. Oracle fires the triggers whenever their triggering condition is satisfied.

To enable a single trigger, use the enable_clause of ALTER TRIGGER.

DISABLE ALL TRIGGERS: Specify DISABLE ALL TRIGGERS to disable all triggers associated with the table. Oracle will not fire a disabled trigger even if the triggering condition is satisfied.

ALTER TABLESPACE

PURPOSE

Use the ALTER TABLESPACE statement to alter an existing tablespace or one or more of its datafiles or tempfiles.

PREREQUISITES

If you have ALTER TABLESPACE system privilege, you can perform any of this statement's operations. If you have MANAGE TABLESPACE system privilege, you can only perform the following operations:

- Take the tablespace online or offline
- Begin or end a backup
- Make the tablespace read only or read write

Before you can make a tablespace read only, the following conditions must be met:

- The tablespace must be online.
- The tablespace must not contain any active rollback segments. For this reason, the SYSTEM tablespace can never be made read only, because it contains the SYSTEM rollback segment. Additionally, because the rollback segments of a read-only tablespace are not accessible, Oracle recommends that you drop the rollback segments before you make a tablespace read only.
- The tablespace must not be involved in an open backup, because the end of a backup updates the header file of all datafiles in the tablespace.

Performing this function in restricted mode may help you meet these restrictions, because only users with RESTRICTED SESSION system privilege can be logged on.

SYNTAX

alter_tablespace::=

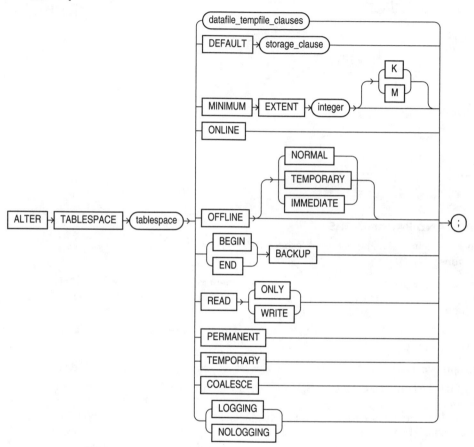

datafile_tempfile_clauses::=

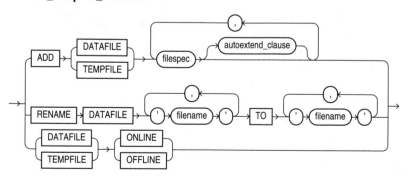

autoextend_clause::=

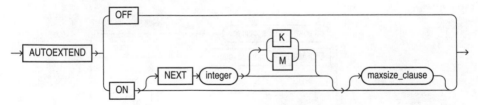

maxsize_clause::=

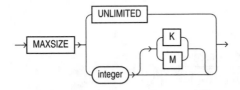

KEYWORDS AND PARAMETERS

tablespace   Specify the name of the tablespace to be altered.
   Restrictions:

- If tablespace is an undo tablespace, the only other clauses you can specify in this statement are ADD DATAFILE, RENAME DATAFILE, DATAFILE ... ONLINE | OFFLINE, and BEGIN | END BACKUP.

- For locally managed temporary tablespaces the only clause you can specify in this statement is the ADD clause.

datafile_tempfile_clauses   The tablespace file clauses let you add or modify a datafile or tempfile.

ADD DATAFILE | TEMPFILE Clause   Specify ADD to add to the tablespace a datafile or tempfile specified by *filespec*.
   You can add a datafile or tempfile to a locally managed tablespace that is online or to a dictionary managed tablespace that is online or offline. Be sure the file is not in use by another database.
   Restriction: For locally managed temporary tablespaces, this is the only clause you can specify at any time.

NOTE
On some operating systems, Oracle does not allocate space for the tempfile until the tempfile blocks are actually accessed. This delay in space allocation results in faster creation and resizing of tempfiles, but it requires that sufficient disk space is available when the tempfiles are later used. Please refer to your operating system documentation to determine whether Oracle allocates tempfile space in this way on your system.

RENAME DATAFILE Clause   Specify RENAME DATAFILE to rename one or more of the tablespace's datafiles. The database must be open, and you must take the tablespace offline before renaming it. Each '*filename*' must fully specify a datafile using the conventions for filenames on your operating system.

This clause merely associates the tablespace with the new file rather than the old one. This clause does not actually change the name of the operating system file. You must change the name of the file through your operating system.

DATAFILE | TEMPFILE ONLINE | OFFLINE   Use this clause to take all datafiles or tempfiles in the tablespace offline or put them online. This clause has no effect on the ONLINE/OFFLINE status of the tablespace.

The database must be mounted. If tablespace is SYSTEM, or an undo tablespace, or the default temporary tablespace, the database must not be open.

autoextend_clause

NOTE
This clause is valid only when you are adding a new datafile or tempfile. To enable or disable AUTOEXTEND for an existing datafile, use the ALTER DATABASE DATAFILE clause.

Use the autoextend_clause to enable or disable the automatic extension of a new datafile or tempfile. If you do not specify this clause, these files are not automatically extended.

ON: Specify ON to enable autoextend.

OFF: Specify OFF to turn off autoextend if is turned on.

NOTE
When you turn off autoextend, the values of NEXT and MAXSIZE are set to zero. If you turn autoextend back on in a subsequent statement, you must reset these values.

NEXT: Use the NEXT clause to specify the size in bytes of the next increment of disk space to be allocated automatically when more extents are required. Use K or M to specify this size in kilobytes or megabytes. The default is the size of one data block.

MAXSIZE: Use the MAXSIZE clause to specify the maximum disk space allowed for automatic extension of the datafile.

UNLIMITED: Use the UNLIMITED clause if you do not want to limit the disk space that Oracle can allocate to the datafile or tempfile.

DEFAULT storage_clause   DEFAULT *storage_clause* lets you specify the new default storage parameters for objects subsequently created in the tablespace. For a dictionary-managed temporary table, Oracle considers only the NEXT parameter of the *storage_clause*.

Restriction: You cannot specify this clause for a locally managed tablespace.

MINIMUM EXTENT   The MINIMUM EXTENT clause lets you control free space fragmentation in the tablespace by ensuring that every used or free extent in a tablespace is at least as large as, and is a multiple of, *integer*. This clause is not relevant for a dictionary-managed temporary tablespace.

Restriction: You cannot specify this clause for a locally managed tablespace.

ONLINE   Specify ONLINE to bring the tablespace online.

OFFLINE   Specify OFFLINE to take the tablespace offline and prevent further access to its segments. When you take a tablespace offline, all of its datafiles are also offline.

TIP
Before taking a tablespace offline for a long time, you may want to alter the tablespace allocation of any users who have been assigned the tablespace as either a default or temporary tablespace. When the tablespace is offline, these users cannot allocate space for objects or sort areas in the tablespace.

Restriction: You cannot take a temporary tablespace offline.

NORMAL: Specify NORMAL to flush all blocks in all datafiles in the tablespace out of the SGA. You need not perform media recovery on this tablespace before bringing it back online. This is the default.

TEMPORARY: If you specify TEMPORARY, Oracle performs a checkpoint for all online datafiles in the tablespace but does not ensure that all files can be written. Any offline files may require media recovery before you bring the tablespace back online.

IMMEDIATE: If you specify IMMEDIATE, Oracle does not ensure that tablespace files are available and does not perform a checkpoint. You must perform media recovery on the tablespace before bringing it back online.

NOTE
The FOR RECOVER setting for ALTER TABLESPACE ... OFFLINE has been deprecated. The syntax is supported for backward compatibility. However, users are encouraged to use the transportable tablespaces feature for tablespace recovery.

BEGIN BACKUP   Specify BEGIN BACKUP to indicate that an open backup is to be performed on the datafiles that make up this tablespace. This clause does not prevent users from accessing the tablespace. You must use this clause before beginning an open backup.

Restrictions: You cannot specify this clause for a read-only tablespace or for a temporary locally managed tablespace.

NOTE
While the backup is in progress, you cannot take the tablespace offline normally, shut down the instance, or begin another backup of the tablespace.

END BACKUP   Specify END BACKUP to indicate that an online backup of the tablespace is complete. Use this clause as soon as possible after completing an online backup. Otherwise, if an instance failure or SHUTDOWN ABORT occurs, Oracle assumes that media recovery (possibly requiring archived redo log) is necessary at the next instance start up.

Restriction: You cannot use this clause on a read-only tablespace.

READ ONLY | READ WRITE   Specify READ ONLY to place the tablespace in **transition read-only mode**. In this state, existing transactions can complete (commit or roll back), but no further write operations (DML) are allowed to the tablespace except for rollback of existing transactions that previously modified blocks in the tablespace.

Once a tablespace is read only, you can copy its files to read-only media. You must then rename the datafiles in the control file to point to the new location by using the SQL statement ALTER DATABASE ... RENAME.

Specify READ WRITE to indicate that write operations are allowed on a previously read-only tablespace.

PERMANENT | TEMPORARY   Specify PERMANENT to indicate that the tablespace is to be converted from a temporary to a permanent one. A permanent tablespace is one in which permanent database objects can be stored. This is the default when a tablespace is created.

Specify TEMPORARY to indicate specifies that the tablespace is to be converted from a permanent to a temporary one. A temporary tablespace is one in which no permanent database objects can be stored. Objects in a temporary tablespace persist only for the duration of the session.

Restriction: If tablespace was not created with a standard block size, you cannot change it from permanent to temporary.

COALESCE   For each datafile in the tablespace, this clause combines all contiguous free extents into larger contiguous extents.

LOGGING | NOLOGGING   Specify LOGGING if you want logging of all tables, indexes, and partitions within the tablespace. The tablespace-level logging attribute can be overridden by logging specifications at the table, index, and partition levels.

When an existing tablespace logging attribute is changed by an ALTER TABLESPACE statement, all tables, indexes, and partitions created *after* the statement will have the new default logging attribute (which you can still subsequently override). The logging attributes of existing objects are not changed.

Only the following operations support NOLOGGING mode:

- DML: direct-path INSERT (serial or parallel); Direct Loader (SQL*Loader)
- DDL: CREATE TABLE ... AS SELECT, CREATE INDEX, ALTER INDEX ... REBUILD, ALTER INDEX ... REBUILD PARTITION, ALTER INDEX ... SPLIT PARTITION, ALTER TABLE ... SPLIT PARTITION, ALTER TABLE ... MOVE PARTITION.

In NOLOGGING mode, data is modified with minimal logging (to mark new extents invalid and to record dictionary changes). When applied during media recovery, the extent invalidation records mark a range of blocks as logically corrupt, because the redo data is not logged. Therefore, if you cannot afford to lose the object, it is important to back it up after the NOLOGGING operation.

ALTER TRIGGER

PURPOSE
Use the ALTER TRIGGER statement to enable, disable, or compile a database trigger.

NOTE
This statement does not change the declaration or definition of an existing trigger. To redeclare or redefine a trigger, use the CREATE TRIGGER statement with the OR REPLACE keywords.

PREREQUISITES
The trigger must be in your own schema or you must have ALTER ANY TRIGGER system privilege. In addition, to alter a trigger on DATABASE, you must have the ADMINISTER DATABASE TRIGGER system privilege.

SYNTAX
alter_trigger::=

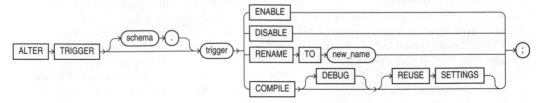

KEYWORDS AND PARAMETERS

schema   Specify the schema containing the trigger. If you omit schema, Oracle assumes the trigger is in your own schema.

trigger   Specify the name of the trigger to be altered.

ENABLE Clause   Specify ENABLE to enable the trigger. You can also use the ENABLE ALL TRIGGERS clause of ALTER TABLE to enable all triggers associated with a table.

DISABLE Clause   Specify DISABLE to disable the trigger. You can also use the DISABLE ALL TRIGGERS clause of ALTER TABLE to disable all triggers associated with a table.

RENAME Clause   Specify RENAME TO *new_name* to rename the trigger. Oracle renames the trigger and leaves it in the same state it was in before being renamed.

COMPILE Clause   Specify COMPILE to explicitly compile the trigger, whether it is valid or invalid. Explicit recompilation eliminates the need for implicit run-time recompilation and prevents associated run-time compilation errors and performance overhead.

Oracle first recompiles objects upon which the trigger depends, if any of these objects are invalid. If Oracle recompiles the trigger successfully, the trigger becomes valid.

During recompilation, Oracle drops all persistent compiler switch settings, retrieves them again from the session, and stores them at the end of compilation. To avoid this process, specify the REUSE SETTINGS clause.

If recompiling the trigger results in compilation errors, then Oracle returns an error and the trigger remains invalid. You can see the associated compiler error messages with the SQL*Plus command SHOW ERRORS.

DEBUG: Specify DEBUG to instruct the PL/SQL compiler to generate and store the code for use by the PL/SQL debugger.

REUSE SETTINGS: Specify REUSE SETTINGS to prevent Oracle from dropping and reacquiring compiler switch settings. With this clause, Oracle preserves the existing settings and uses them for the recompilation.

If you specify both DEBUG and REUSE SETTINGS, Oracle sets the persistently stored value of the PLSQL_COMPILER_FLAGS parameter to INTERPRETED, DEBUG. No other compiler switch values are changed.

ALTER USER

PURPOSE
Use the ALTER USER statement:

■ To change the authentication or database resource characteristics of a database user.

■ To permit a proxy server to connect as a client without authentication.

NOTE

ALTER USER syntax does not accept the old password. Therefore it neither authenticates using the old password nor checks the new password against the old before setting the new password. If these checks against the old password are important, use the OCIPasswordChange() call instead of ALTER USER. For more information, see Oracle Call Interface Programmer's Guide.

PREREQUISITES

You must have the ALTER USER system privilege. However, you can change your own password without this privilege.

SYNTAX

alter_user::=

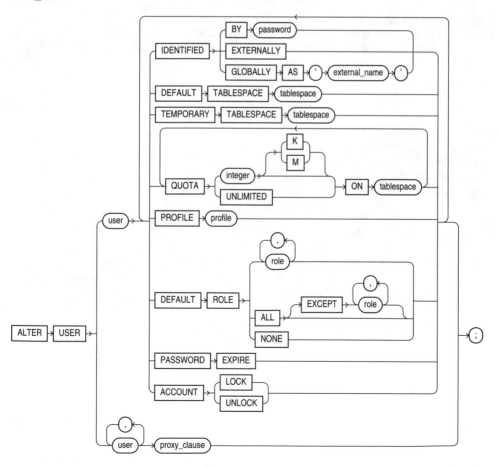

proxy_clause::=

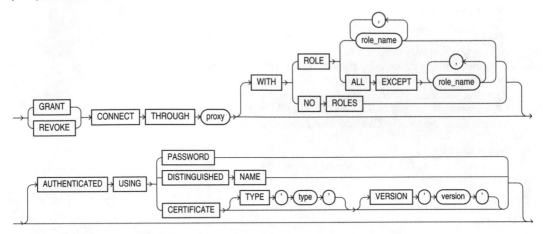

KEYWORDS AND PARAMETERS

The keywords and parameters shown below are unique to ALTER USER or have different semantics than they have in CREATE USER. All the remaining keywords and parameters in the ALTER USER statement have the same meaning as in the CREATE USER statement.

IDENTIFIED Clause

■ Specify BY *password* to specify a new password for the user.

NOTE
Oracle expects a different timestamp for each resetting of a particular password. If you reset one password multiple times within one second (for example, by cycling through a set of passwords using a script), Oracle may return an error message that the password cannot be reused. For this reason, Oracle Corporation recommends that you avoid using scripts to reset passwords.

■ Specify GLOBALLY AS *'external_name'* to indicate that the user must be authenticated by way of an LDAP V3 compliant directory service such as Oracle Internet Directory.

You can change a user's access verification method to IDENTIFIED GLOBALLY AS *'external_name'* only if all external roles granted directly to the user are revoked.

You can change a user created as IDENTIFIED GLOBALLY AS *'external_name'* to IDENTIFIED BY *password* or IDENTIFIED EXTERNALLY.

TEMPORARY TABLESPACE Clause   The tablespace you assign or reassign as the user's temporary tablespace must have a standard block size.

DEFAULT ROLE Clause   Specify the roles granted by default to the user at logon. This clause can contain only roles that have been granted directly to the user with a GRANT statement. You cannot use the DEFAULT ROLE clause to enable:

- Roles not granted to the user
- Roles granted through other roles
- Roles managed by an external service (such as the operating system), or by the Oracle Internet Directory

Oracle enables default roles at logon without requiring the user to specify their passwords.

proxy_clause   The proxy_clause lets you control the ability of a proxy (an application or application server) to connect as the specified database or enterprise user and to activate all, some, or none of the user's roles.

NOTE
The proxy_clause provides several varieties of proxy authentication of database and enterprise users. For information on proxy authentication of application users, see Oracle9i Application Developer's Guide—Fundamentals.

GRANT | REVOKE: Specify GRANT to allow the connection. Specify REVOKE to prohibit the connection.

CONNECT THROUGH Clause: Identify the proxy connecting to Oracle. Oracle expects the proxy to authenticate the user unless you specify the AUTHENTICATED USING clause.

WITH ROLE: WITH ROLE role_name permits the proxy to connect as the specified user and to activate only the roles that are specified by role_name.

WITH ROLE ALL EXCEPT: WITH ROLE ALL EXCEPT role_name permits the proxy to connect as the specified user and to activate all roles associated with that user except those specified by role_name.

WITH NO ROLES: WITH NO ROLES permits the proxy to connect as the specified user, but prohibits the proxy from activating any of that user's roles after connecting.

If you do not specify any of these WITH clauses, Oracle activates all roles granted to the specified user automatically.

AUTHENTICATED USING: Specify the AUTHENTICATED USING clause if you want proxy authentication to be handled by a source other than the proxy. This clause is relevant only as part of a GRANT CONNECT THROUGH proxy clause.

PASSWORD: Specify PASSWORD if you want the proxy to present the database password of the user for authentication. The proxy relies on the database to authenticate the user based on the password.

DISTINGUISHED NAME: Specify DISTINGUISHED NAME to allow the proxy to act as the globally identified user indicated by the distinguished name.

CERTIFICATE: Specify CERTIFICATE to allow the proxy to act as the globally identified user whose distinguished name is contained in the certificate.

In both the DISTINGUISHED NAME and CERTIFICATE cases, the proxy has already authenticated and is acting on behalf of a global database user.

- For type, specify the type of certificate to be presented. If you do not specify type, the default is 'X.509'.

- For version, specify the version of the certificate that is to be presented. If you do not specify version, the default is '3'.

Restriction: You cannot specify this clause as part of a REVOKE CONNECT THROUGH proxy clause.

ASSOCIATE STATISTICS

PURPOSE
Use the ASSOCIATE STATISTICS statement to associate a statistics type (or default statistics) containing functions relevant to statistics collection, selectivity, or cost with one or more columns, standalone functions, packages, types, domain indexes, or indextypes.

For a listing of all current statistics type associations, query the USER_ASSOCIATIONS data dictionary view. If you analyze the object with which you are associating statistics, you can also query the associations in the USER_USTATS view.

PREREQUISITES
To issue this statement, you must have the appropriate privileges to alter the base object (table, function, package, type, domain index, or indextype). In addition, unless you are associating only default statistics, you must have execute privilege on the statistics type. The statistics type must already have been defined.

SYNTAX
associate_statistics::=

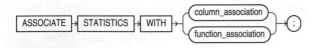

column_association::=

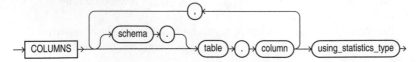

function_association::=

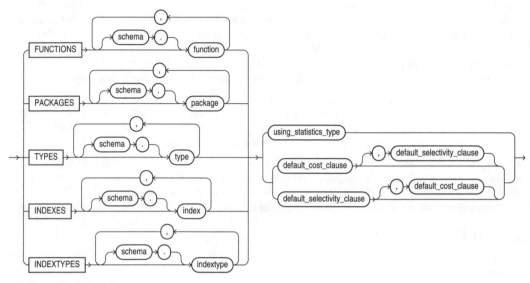

using_statistics_type::=

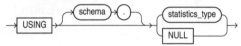

default_cost_clause::=

default_selectivity_clause::=

KEYWORDS AND PARAMETERS

column_association   Specify one or more table columns. If you do not specify schema, Oracle assumes the table is in your own schema.

function_association   Specify one or more standalone functions, packages, user-defined datatypes, domain indexes, or indextypes. If you do not specify schema, Oracle assumes the object is in your own schema.

- ■ FUNCTIONS refers only to standalone functions, not to method types or to built-in functions.
- ■ TYPES refers only to user-defined types, not to built-in SQL datatypes.

   Restriction: You cannot specify an object for which you have already defined an association. You must first disassociate the statistics from this object.

using_statistics_type   Specify the statistics type being associated with column, function, package, type, domain index, or indextype. The statistics_type must already have been created.

The NULL keyword is valid only when you are associating statistics with a column or an index. When you associate a statistics type with an object type, columns of that object type inherit the statistics type. Likewise, when you associate a statistics type with an indextype, index instances of the indextype inherit the statistics type. You can override this inheritance by associating a different statistics type for the column or index. Alternatively, if you do not want to associate any statistics type for the column or index, you can specify NULL in the using_statistics_type clause.

Restriction: You cannot specify NULL for functions, packages, types, or indextypes.

default_cost_clause   Specify default costs for standalone functions, packages, types, domain indexes, or indextypes. If you specify this clause, you must include one number each for CPU cost, I/O cost, and network cost, in that order. Each cost is for a single execution of the function or method or for a single domain index access. Accepted values are integers of zero or greater.

default_selectivity_clause   Specify as a percent the default selectivity for predicates with standalone functions, types, packages, or user-defined operators. The default_selectivity must be a whole number between 0 and 100. Values outside this range are ignored.

Restriction: You cannot specify DEFAULT SELECTIVITY for domain indexes or indextypes.

AUDIT

PURPOSE
Use the AUDIT statement to:

■ Track the occurrence of SQL statements in subsequent user sessions. You can track the occurrence of a specific SQL statement or of all SQL statements authorized by a particular system privilege. Auditing operations on SQL statements apply only to subsequent sessions, not to current sessions.

■ Track operations on a specific schema object. Auditing operations on schema objects apply to current sessions as well as to subsequent sessions.

PREREQUISITES
To audit occurrences of a SQL statement, you must have AUDIT SYSTEM system privilege.

To audit operations on a schema object, the object you choose for auditing must be in your own schema or you must have AUDIT ANY system privilege. In addition, if the object you choose for auditing is a directory object, even if you created it, you must have AUDIT ANY system privilege.

To collect auditing results, you must set the initialization parameter AUDIT_TRAIL to DB. You can specify auditing options regardless of whether auditing is enabled. However, Oracle does not generate audit records until you enable auditing.

SYNTAX
audit::=

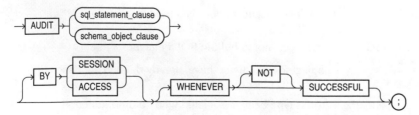

sql_statement_clause::=

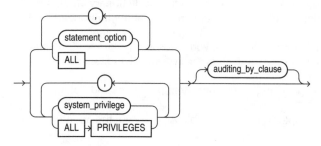

auditing_by_clause::=

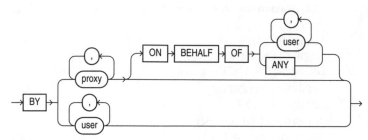

schema_object_clause::=

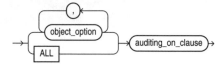

auditing_on_clause::=

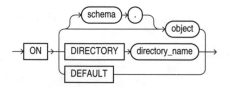

KEYWORDS AND PARAMETERS

sql_statement_clause   Use the sql_statement_clause to audit SQL statements.

  statement_option: Specify a statement option to audit specific SQL statements.

  For each audited operation, Oracle produces an audit record containing this information:

- The user performing the operation
- The type of operation
- The object involved in the operation
- The date and time of the operation

Oracle writes audit records to the audit trail, which is a database table containing audit records. You can review database activity by examining the audit trail through data dictionary views.

system_privilege: Specify a system privilege to audit SQL statements that are authorized by the specified system privilege.

Rather than specifying many individual system privileges, you can specify the roles CONNECT, RESOURCE, and DBA. Doing so is equivalent to auditing all of the system privileges granted to those roles.

Oracle also provides two shortcuts for specifying groups of system privileges and statement options at once:

ALL: Specify ALL to audit all statements options shown in Table A–1 but not the additional statement options shown in Table A–2.

Statement Option	SQL Statements and Operations
CLUSTER	CREATE CLUSTER AUDIT CLUSTER DROP CLUSTER TRUNCATE CLUSTER
CONTEXT	CREATE CONTEXT DROP CONTEXT
DATABASE LINK	CREATE DATABASE LINK DROP DATABASE LINK
DIMENSION	CREATE DIMENSION ALTER DIMENSION DROP DIMENSION
DIRECTORY	CREATE DIRECTORY DROP DIRECTORY
INDEX	CREATE INDEX ALTER INDEX DROP INDEX
NOT EXISTS	All SQL statements that fail because a specified object does not exist.
PROCEDURE[1]	CREATE FUNCTION CREATE LIBRARY CREATE PACKAGE CREATE PACKAGE BODY CREATE PROCEDURE DROP FUNCTION DROP LIBRARY DROP PACKAGE DROP PROCEDURE

[1]Java schema objects (sources, classes, and resources) are considered the same as procedures for purposes of auditing SQL statements.

TABLE A-1. *Statement Auditing Options for Database Objects*

Statement Option	SQL Statements and Operations
PROFILE	CREATE PROFILE ALTER PROFILE DROP PROFILE
PUBLIC DATABASE LINK	CREATE PUBLIC DATABASE LINK DROP PUBLIC DATABASE LINK
PUBLIC SYNONYM	CREATE PUBLIC SYNONYM DROP PUBLIC SYNONYM
ROLE	CREATE ROLE ALTER ROLE DROP ROLE SET ROLE
ROLLBACK SEGMENT	CREATE ROLLBACK SEGMENT ALTER ROLLBACK SEGMENT DROP ROLLBACK SEGMENT
SEQUENCE	CREATE SEQUENCE DROP SEQUENCE
SESSION	Logons
SYNONYM	CREATE SYNONYM DROP SYNONYM
SYSTEM AUDIT	AUDIT *sql_statements* NOAUDIT *sql_statements*
SYSTEM GRANT	GRANT *system_privileges_and_roles* REVOKE *system_privileges_and_roles*
TABLE	CREATE TABLE DROP TABLE TRUNCATE TABLE
TABLESPACE	CREATE TABLESPACE ALTER TABLESPACE DROP TABLESPACE
TRIGGER	CREATE TRIGGER ALTER TRIGGER with ENABLE and DISABLE clauses DROP TRIGGER ALTER TABLE with ENABLE ALL TRIGGERS clause and DISABLE ALL TRIGGERS clause

TABLE A-1. *Statement Auditing Options for Database Objects* (continued)

Statement Option	SQL Statements and Operations
TYPE	CREATE TYPE
	CREATE TYPE BODY
	ALTER TYPE
	DROP TYPE
	DROP TYPE BODY
USER	CREATE USER
	ALTER USER
	DROP USER
VIEW	CREATE VIEW
	DROP VIEW

TABLE A-1.   *Statement Auditing Options for Database Objects* (continued)

Statement Option	SQL Statements and Operations
ALTER SEQUENCE	ALTER SEQUENCE
ALTER TABLE	ALTER TABLE
COMMENT TABLE	COMMENT ON TABLE *table, view, materialized view*
	COMMENT ON COLUMN *table.column, view.column, materialized view.column*
DELETE TABLE	DELETE FROM *table, view*
EXECUTE PROCEDURE	CALL
	Execution of any procedure or function or access to any variable, library, or cursor inside a package.
GRANT DIRECTORY	GRANT privilege ON directory
	REVOKE privilege ON directory
GRANT PROCEDURE	GRANT privilege ON procedure, function, package
	REVOKE privilege ON procedure, function, package
GRANT SEQUENCE	GRANT privilege ON sequence
	REVOKE privilege ON sequence

TABLE A-2.   *Additional Statement Auditing Options for SQL Statements*

Statement Option	SQL Statements and Operations
GRANT TABLE	GRANT privilege ON table, view, materialized view. REVOKE privilege ON table, view, materialized view
GRANT TYPE	GRANT privilege ON TYPE REVOKE privilege ON TYPE
INSERT TABLE	INSERT INTO table, view
LOCK TABLE	LOCK TABLE table, view
SELECT SEQUENCE	Any statement containing sequence.CURRVAL or sequence.NEXTVAL
SELECT TABLE	SELECT FROM table, view, materialized view
UPDATE TABLE	UPDATE table, view

TABLE A-2. *Additional Statement Auditing Options for SQL Statements* (continued)

ALL PRIVILEGES: Specify ALL PRIVILEGES to audit system privileges.

NOTE
Oracle Corporation recommends that you specify individual system privileges and statement options for auditing rather than roles or shortcuts. The specific system privileges and statement options encompassed by roles and shortcuts change from one release to the next and may not be supported in future versions of Oracle.

auditing_by_clause: Specify the auditing_by_clause to audit only those SQL statements issued by particular users. If you omit this clause, Oracle audits all users' statements.

BY user: Use this clause to restrict auditing to only SQL statements issued by the specified users.

BY proxy: Use this clause to restrict auditing to only SQL statements issued by the specified proxies.

ON BEHALF OF: Specify user to indicate auditing of statements executed on behalf of a particular user. ANY indicates auditing of statements executed on behalf of any user.

schema_object_clause   Use the schema_object_clause to audit operations on schema objects.

object_option: Specify the particular operation for auditing. Table A–3 shows each object option and the types of objects to which it applies. The name of each object option specifies a SQL statement to be audited. For example, if you choose to audit a table with the ALTER option, Oracle audits all ALTER TABLE statements issued against the table. If you choose to audit a sequence with the SELECT option, Oracle audits all statements that use any of the sequence's values.

ALL: Specify ALL as a shortcut equivalent to specifying all object options applicable for the type of object.

Object Option	Table	View	Sequence	Procedure Function Package[1]	Materialized View	Directory	Library	Object Type	Context
ALTER	X		X		X			X	
AUDIT	X	X	X	X	X	X		X	X
COMMENT	X	X			X				
DELETE	X	X			X				
EXECUTE				X			X		
GRANT	X	X	X	X		X	X	X	X
INDEX	X				X				
INSERT	X	X			X				
LOCK	X	X			X				
READ						X			
RENAME	X	X		X	X				
SELECT	X	X	X		X				
UPDATE	X	X			X				

[1]Java schema objects (sources, classes, and resources) are considered the same as procedures, functions, and packages for purposes of auditing options.

TABLE A-3. *Object Auditing Options*

auditing_on_clause: The auditing_on_clause lets you specify the particular schema object to be audited.

schema: Specify the schema containing the object chosen for auditing. If you omit schema, Oracle assumes the object is in your own schema.

object: Specify the name of the object to be audited. The object must be a table, view, sequence, stored procedure, function, package, materialized view, or library.

You can also specify a synonym for a table, view, sequence, procedure, stored function, package, or materialized view.

ON DEFAULT: Specify ON DEFAULT to establish the specified object options as default object options for subsequently created objects. Once you have established these default auditing options, any subsequently created object is automatically audited with those options. The default auditing options for a view are always the union of the auditing options for the view's base tables. You can see the current default auditing options by querying the ALL_DEF_AUDIT_OPTS data dictionary view.

If you change the default auditing options, the auditing options for previously created objects remain the same. You can change the auditing options for an existing object only by specifying the object in the ON clause of the AUDIT statement.

ON DIRECTORY directory_name: The ON DIRECTORY clause lets you specify the name of a directory chosen for auditing.

BY SESSION: Specify BY SESSION if you want Oracle to write a single record for all SQL statements of the same type issued and operations of the same type executed on the same schema objects in the same session.

BY ACCESS: Specify BY ACCESS if you want Oracle to write one record for each audited statement and operation.

If you specify statement options or system privileges that audit data definition language (DDL) statements, Oracle automatically audits by access regardless of whether you specify the BY SESSION clause or BY ACCESS clause.

For statement options and system privileges that audit SQL statements other than DDL, you can specify either BY SESSION or BY ACCESS. BY SESSION is the default.

WHENEVER [NOT] SUCCESSFUL: Specify WHENEVER SUCCESSFUL to audit only SQL statements and operations that succeed.

Specify WHENEVER NOT SUCCESSFUL to audit only statements and operations that fail or result in errors.

If you omit this clause, Oracle performs the audit regardless of success or failure.

constraint_clause

PURPOSE

Use the constraint_clause in a CREATE TABLE or ALTER TABLE statement to define an integrity constraint. An integrity constraint is a rule that restricts the values for one or more columns in a table, an index-organized table, or a view.

NOTE
Oracle does not support constraints on columns or attributes whose type is an object, nested table, varray, REF, or LOB. The only exception is that NOT NULL constraints are supported for columns or attributes whose type is object, VARRAY, REF, or LOB.

PREREQUISITES

Constraint clauses can appear in CREATE TABLE, ALTER TABLE, CREATE VIEW, or ALTER VIEW statements. To define an integrity constraint, you must have the privileges necessary to issue one of these statements.

To create a referential integrity constraint, the parent table must be in your own schema, or you must have the REFERENCES privilege on the columns of the referenced key in the parent table.

SYNTAX

table_or_view_constraint::=

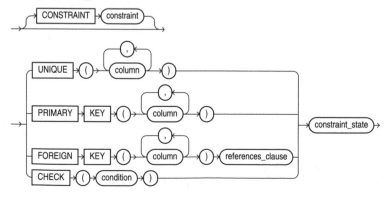

column_constraint::=

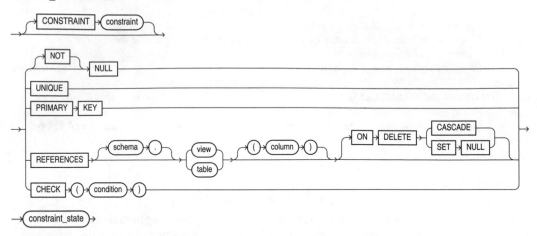

table_ref_constraint::=

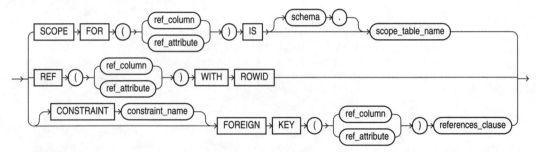

column_ref_constraint::=

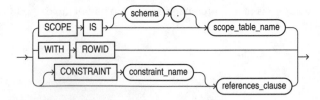

references_clause::=

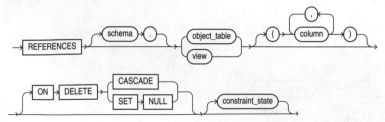

constraint_state::=

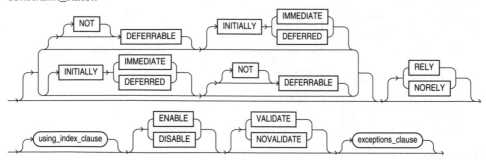

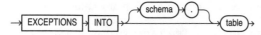

exceptions_clause::=

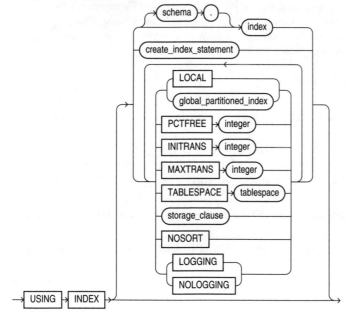

using_index_clause::=

global_partitioned_index::=

global_partitioning_clause::=

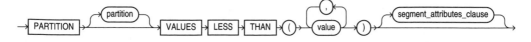

physical_attributes_clause::=

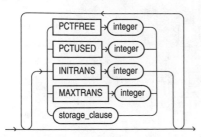

KEYWORDS AND PARAMETERS

table_or_view_constraint   The table_or_view_constraint syntax is part of the table or view definition. An integrity constraint defined with this syntax can impose rules on any columns in the table or view.

Table constraint syntax can appear in a CREATE TABLE or ALTER TABLE statement. This syntax can define any type of integrity constraint except a NOT NULL constraint.

View constraints are a subset of table constraints. View constraint syntax can appear in CREATE VIEW and ALTER VIEW statements. View constraints are declarative only. That is, Oracle does not enforce them. However, operations on views are subject to the integrity constraints defined on the underlying base tables, so you can enforce constraints on views t hrough constraints on base tables.

Restrictions on Table and View Constraints:

For table constraints:

- You cannot define a constraint on an attribute or column whose type is user defined.

In addition, for view constraints:

- You can specify only unique, primary key, and foreign key constraints on views.
- Because view constraints are not enforced directly, you cannot specify any DEFERRED or DEFERRABLE clause.
- View constraints are supported only in DISABLE NOVALIDATE mode. You cannot specify any other mode.
- You cannot specify the using_index_clause, the EXCEPTIONS INTO clause, or the ON DELETE clause in view constraints.
- You cannot define view constraints on attributes of an object column or on attributes of an object attribute.

column_constraint   The column_constraint syntax is part of a column definition. For tables, an integrity constraint defined with this syntax can usually impose rules only on the column in which it is defined. For views, constraints are declarative only. That is, Oracle does not enforce them. However, operations on views are subject to the integrity constraints defined on the underlying base tables, so you can enforce constraints on views through constraints on base tables.

- The column_constraint syntax that appears in a CREATE TABLE or ALTER TABLE ADD statement can define any type of integrity constraint.

- Column_constraint syntax that appears in an ALTER TABLE MODIFY column_options statement can only define or remove a NOT NULL constraint.
- Column_constraint syntax that appears in a CREATE VIEW or ALTER VIEW statement is subject to the same restrictions as view constraints. See "Restrictions on Table and View Constraints".

Restrictions:

- The only column constraint allowed on an XMLType column is NOT NULL.
- The only column constraint allowed on a VARRAY column is NOT NULL. However, you can specify any type of column constraint on the scalar attributes of a NESTED TABLE column.

CONSTRAINT   Specify a name for the constraint. Oracle stores this name in the data dictionary along with the definition of the integrity constraint. If you omit this identifier, Oracle generates a name with the form SYS_Cn.

If you do not specify NULL or NOT NULL in a column definition, NULL is the default.

Restriction: You cannot create a constraint on columns or attributes whose type is user-defined object, LOB, or REF, with the following exceptions:

- You can specify a NOT NULL constraint on columns or attributes of user-defined object type, varray, and LOB.
- You can specify NOT NULL and referential integrity constraints on a column of type REF.

UNIQUE Clause   Specify UNIQUE to designate a column or combination of columns as a unique key. To satisfy a UNIQUE constraint, no two rows in the table can have the same value for the unique key. However, the unique key made up of a single column can contain nulls.

A composite unique key is made up of a combination of columns. To define a composite unique key, you must use table_or_view_constraint syntax rather than column_constraint syntax. Any row that contains nulls in all key columns automatically satisfies the constraint. However, two rows that contain nulls for one or more key columns and the same combination of values for the other key columns violate the constraint.

NOTE
When you specify a UNIQUE constraint on one or more columns, Oracle implicitly creates an index on the unique key. If you are defining uniqueness for purposes of query performance, Oracle Corporation recommends that you instead create the unique index explicitly using a CREATE UNIQUE INDEX statement. See "CREATE INDEX".

Restrictions:

- None of the columns in the unique key can have datatype TIMESTAMP WITH TIME ZONE. However, the unique key can contain a column of TIMESTAMP WITH LOCAL TIME ZONE.
- For a composite unique key, no two rows in the table or view can have the same combination of values in the key columns.

- A composite unique key cannot have more than 32 columns. The overall size of the key (in bytes) should not exceed approximately the width of all indexed columns plus the number of indexed columns.
- A unique key column cannot be of datatype LONG or LONG RAW.
- You cannot designate the same column or combination of columns as both a unique key and a primary key.

PRIMARY KEY Clause   Specify PRIMARY KEY to designate a column or combination of columns as the primary key or the table or view. A composite primary key is made up of a combination of columns. To define a composite primary key, you must use the table_or_view_constraint syntax rather than the column_constraint syntax.

Restrictions:

- A table or view can have only one primary key.
- None of the columns in the primary key can have datatype LONG, LONG RAW, VARRAY, NESTED TABLE, OBJECT, LOB, BFILE, or REF, or TIMESTAMP WITH TIME ZONE.
- No primary key value can appear in more than one row in the table.
- No column that is part of the primary key can contain a null.
- The size of the PRIMARY KEY of an index-organized table cannot exceed one-half of the database block size or 3800 bytes, whichever is less. (PRIMARY KEY is required for an index-organized table.)
- A composite primary key cannot have more than 32 columns. The overall size of the key (in bytes) should not exceed approximately the width of all indexed columns plus the number of indexed columns.
- You cannot designate the same column or combination of columns as both a primary key and a unique key.
- You cannot specify a primary key when creating a subview. The primary key can be specified only for the top-level (root) view.

NULL | NOT NULL   Indicate whether a column can contain nulls. You must specify NULL and NOT NULL with column_constraint syntax, not with table_or_view_constraint syntax.

NULL: Specify NULL if a column can contain null values. The NULL keyword does not actually define an integrity constraint. If you do not specify either NOT NULL or NULL, the column can contain nulls by default.

NOT NULL: Specify NOT NULL if a column cannot contain null values. To satisfy this constraint, every row in the table must contain a value for the column.

Restrictions:

- You cannot specify NULL or NOT NULL for a view.
- You cannot specify NULL or NOT NULL for an attribute of an object. Instead, use a CHECK constraint with the IS [NOT] NULL condition.

Referential Integrity Constraints   Referential integrity constraints designate a column or combination of columns as the foreign key and establish a relationship between that foreign key and a specified primary or unique key, called the referenced key. The table or view containing the foreign key is called the child object, and the table or view containing the referenced key is called the parent object. The foreign key and the referenced key can be in the same table or view. In this case, the parent and child tables are the same.

- From the table or view level, specify referential integrity using the FOREIGN KEY clause with the table_or_view_constraint syntax. This syntax lets you specify a composite foreign key, which is made up of a combination of columns.

- From the column level, use the REFERENCES clause of the column_constraint syntax to specify a referential integrity constraint in which the foreign key is made up of a single column.

You can designate the same column or combination of columns as both a foreign key and a primary or unique key. You can also designate the same column or combination of columns as both a foreign key and a cluster key.

You can define multiple foreign keys in a table or view. Also, a single column can be part of more than one foreign key.

Restrictions on Referential Integrity Constraints:

- A foreign key cannot be of type LONG or LONG RAW.

- The referenced UNIQUE or PRIMARY KEY constraint on the parent table or view must already be defined.

- The child and parent tables must be on the same database. To enable referential integrity constraints across nodes of a distributed database, you must use database triggers.

- If either the child or parent object is a view, then the constraint is subject to all restrictions on view constraints. See "Restrictions on Table and View Constraints".

- You cannot define a referential integrity constraint in a CREATE TABLE statement that contains an AS subquery clause. Instead, you must create the table without the constraint and then add it later with an ALTER TABLE statement.

FOREIGN KEY Clause   The FOREIGN KEY clause lets you designate a column or combination of columns as the foreign key from the table level. You must use this syntax to define a composite foreign key.

To satisfy a referential integrity constraint involving composite keys, either the values of the foreign key columns must match the values of the referenced key columns in a row in the parent table or view, or the value of at least one of the columns of the foreign key must be null.

REFERENCES Clause   The REFERENCES clause lets you designate the current column or attribute as the foreign key and identifies the parent table or view and the column or combination of columns that make up the referenced key. If you identify only the parent table or view and omit the column names, the foreign key automatically references the primary key of the parent table or view. The corresponding columns of the referenced key and the foreign key must match in number and datatypes.

ON DELETE Clause   For table constraints, the ON DELETE clause lets you determine how Oracle automatically maintains referential integrity if you remove a referenced primary or unique key value.

If you omit this clause, Oracle does not allow you to delete referenced key values in the parent table that have dependent rows in the child table. This clause is not valid for view constraints.

- Specify CASCADE if you want Oracle to remove dependent foreign key values.
- Specify SET NULL if you want Oracle to convert dependent foreign key values to NULL.

Restrictions on Foreign Keys:

- A composite foreign key cannot have more than 32 columns. The overall size of the key (in bytes) should not exceed approximately the width of all indexed columns plus the number of indexed columns.
- A composite foreign key must refer to a composite unique key or a composite primary key.

CHECK Constraints   The CHECK clause lets you specify a condition that each row in the table must satisfy. To satisfy the constraint, each row in the table must make the condition either TRUE or unknown (due to a null). When Oracle evaluates a CHECK constraint condition for a particular row, any column names in the condition refer to the column values in that row.

If you create multiple CHECK constraints for a column, design them carefully so their purposes do not conflict, and do not assume any particular order of evaluation of the conditions. Oracle does not verify that CHECK conditions are not mutually exclusive.

Restrictions on CHECK Constraints:

- You cannot specify a CHECK constraint for a view.
- The condition of a CHECK constraint can refer to any column in the table, but it cannot refer to columns of other tables.
- CHECK constraint conditions cannot contain the following constructs:
  - Subqueries
  - Calls to the functions SYSDATE, UID, USER, or USERENV
  - The pseudocolumns CURRVAL, NEXTVAL, LEVEL, or ROWNUM
  - Date constants that are not fully specified

table_ref_constraint and column_ref_constraint   The table_ref and column_ref constraints let you further describe a column of type REF. The only difference between these clauses is that you specify table_ref_constraint from the table level, so you must identify the REF column or attribute you are defining. You specify column_ref_constraint after you have already identified the REF column or attribute. Both types of constraint let you specify a SCOPE constraint, a WITH ROWID constraint, or a referential integrity constraint.

As is the case for regular table and column constraints, you use FOREIGN KEY syntax for a referential integrity constraint at the table level, and REFERENCES syntax for a referential integrity constraint at the column level.

If the REF column's scope table or reference table has a primary-key-based object identifier, then it is a user-defined REF column.

ref_column   Specify the name of a REF column of an object or relational table.

ref_attribute   Specify an embedded REF attribute within an object column of a relational table.

SCOPE Clause   In a table with a REF column, each REF value in the column can conceivably reference a row in a different object table. The SCOPE clause restricts the scope of references to a single table, scope_table_name. The values in the REF column or attribute point to objects in scope_table_name, in which object instances (of the same type as the REF column) are stored. You can specify only one scope table for each REF column.

Restrictions on the SCOPE Clause:

■ You cannot add a SCOPE constraint to an existing column unless the table is empty.

■ You cannot specify SCOPE for the REF elements of a varray column.

■ You must specify this clause if you specify AS subquery and the subquery returns user-defined REFs.

■ The scope_table_name must be in your own schema or you must have SELECT privileges on scope_table_name or SELECT ANY TABLE system privileges.

■ You cannot drop a SCOPE table constraint from a REF column.

WITH ROWID Clause   Specify WITH ROWID to store the rowid along with the REF value in ref_column or ref_attribute. Storing a REF value with a rowid can improve the performance of dereferencing operations, but will also use more space. Default storage of REF values is without rowids.

Restrictions on the WITH ROWID Clause:

■ You cannot specify a WITH ROWID constraint for the REF elements of a varray column.

■ You cannot drop a WITH ROWID constraint from a REF column.

■ If the REF column or attribute is scoped, then this clause is ignored and the rowid is not stored with the REF value.

references_clause   The references_clause lets you specify a referential integrity constraint on the REF column.This clause also implicitly restricts the scope of the REF column or attribute to the reference table.

If you do not specify CONSTRAINT, Oracle generates a system name for the constraint.

Restrictions on the references_clause:

■ If you add a referential integrity constraint to an existing REF column that is scoped, then the referenced table must be the same as the scope table of the REF column.

■ The system adds a scope constraint when you add a referential integrity constraint to an existing unscoped REF column. Therefore, all the restrictions that apply for the SCOPE constraint also apply in this case.

■ If you later drop the referential integrity constraint, the REF column will remain scoped to the referenced table.

constraint_state   Use the constraint_state to specify how and when Oracle should enforce the constraint.

DEFERRABLE I NOT DEFERRABLE: Specify DEFERRABLE to indicate that constraint checking can be deferred until the end of the transaction by using the SET CONSTRAINT(S) statement.

Specify NOT DEFERRABLE to indicate that this constraint is checked at the end of each DML statement. If you do not specify either word, then NOT DEFERRABLE is the default.

INITIALLY IMMEDIATE: Specify INITIALLY IMMEDIATE to indicate that at the start of every transaction, the default is to check this constraint at the end of every DML statement. If you do not specify INITIALLY, INITIALLY IMMEDIATE is the default.

INITIALLY DEFERRED: Specify INITIALLY DEFERRED to indicate that this constraint is DEFERRABLE and that, by default, the constraint is checked only at the end of each transaction.

Restrictions on DEFERRABLE and NOT DEFERRABLE:

■ You cannot defer a NOT DEFERRABLE constraint with the SET CONSTRAINT(S) statement.

■ You cannot specify either DEFERRABLE or NOT DEFERRABLE if you are modifying an existing constraint directly (that is, by specifying the ALTER TABLE ... MODIFY constraint statement).

■ You cannot alter a constraint's deferrability status. You must drop the constraint and re-create it.

■ You cannot specify these clauses for a view constraint.

RELY | NORELY   The RELY and NORELY parameters specify whether a constraint in NOVALIDATE mode is to be taken into account for query rewrite. Specify RELY to activate an existing constraint in NOVALIDATE mode for query rewrite in an unenforced query rewrite integrity mode. The constraint is in NOVALIDATE mode, so Oracle does not enforce it. The default is NORELY.

Unenforced constraints are generally useful only with materialized views and query rewrite. Depending on the QUERY_REWRITE_INTEGRITY, query rewrite can use only constraints that are in VALIDATE mode, or that are in NOVALIDATE mode with the RELY parameter set, to determine join information.

Restrictions on RELY and NORELY:

■ RELY and NORELY are relevant only if you are modifying an existing constraint (that is, you have issued the ALTER TABLE ... MODIFY constraint statement).

■ You cannot set a NOT NULL constraint to RELY.

using_index_clause   The using_index_clause lets you specify an index for Oracle to use to enforce a UNIQUE and PRIMARY KEY constraint, or lets you instruct Oracle to create the index used to enforce the constraint.

■ If you specify schema.index, Oracle will attempt to enforce the constraint using the specified index. If Oracle cannot find the index or cannot use the index to enforce the constraint, Oracle returns an error.

■ If you specify the create_index_statement, Oracle will attempt to create the index and use it to enforce the constraint. If Oracle cannot create the index or cannot use the index to enforce the constraint, Oracle returns an error.

■ If you neither specify an existing index or create a new index, Oracle creates the index. In this case:

  ■ The index receives the same name as the constraint.

  ■ You can choose the values of the INITRANS, MAXTRANS, TABLESPACE, STORAGE, and PCTFREE parameters for the index.

  ■ If table is partitioned, you can specify a locally or globally partitioned index for the unique or primary key constraint.

Restrictions on the using_index_clause:

■ You cannot specify this clause for a view constraint.

- You can specify the using_index_clause only when enabling UNIQUE and PRIMARY KEY constraints.

- You cannot specify an index (schema.index) or create an index (create_index_statement) when enabling the primary key of an index-organized table.

global_partitioned_index   The global_partitioned_index clause lets you specify that the partitioning of the index is user defined and is not equipartitioned with the underlying table. By default, nonpartitioned indexes are global indexes.

PARTITION BY RANGE: Specify PARTITION BY RANGE to indicate that the global index is partitioned on the ranges of values from the columns specified in column_list. You cannot specify this clause for a local index.

column_list: For column_list, specify the name of the column(s) of a table on which the index is partitioned. The column_list must specify a left prefix of the index column list.

You cannot specify more than 32 columns in column_list, and the columns cannot contain the ROWID pseudocolumn or a column of type ROWID.

NOTE
If your enterprise has or will have databases using different character sets, use caution when partitioning on character columns. The sort sequence of characters is not identical in all character sets.

PARTITION: The PARTITION clause lets you describe the individual index partitions. The number of clauses determines the number of partitions. If you omit partition, Oracle generates a name with the form SYS_Pn.

VALUES LESS THAN: For VALUES LESS THAN (value_list), specify the (noninclusive) upper bound for the current partition in a global index. The value_list is a comma-separated, ordered list of literal values corresponding to column_list in the partition_by_range_clause. Always specify MAXVALUE as the value_list of the last partition.

NOTE
If index is partitioned on a DATE column, and if the date format does not specify the first two digits of the year, you must use the TO_DATE function with a 4-character format mask for the year. The date format is determined implicitly by NLS_TERRITORY or explicitly by NLS_DATE_FORMAT.

NOSORT Clause   Specify NOSORT to indicate that the rows are stored in the database in ascending order and therefore Oracle does not have to sort the rows when creating the index.

ENABLE Clause   Specify ENABLE if you want the constraint to be applied to all new data in the table.

- ENABLE VALIDATE specifies that all old data also complies with the constraint. An enabled validated constraint guarantees that all data is and will continue to be valid.

  If any row in the table violates the integrity constraint, the constraint remains disabled and Oracle returns an error. If all rows comply with the constraint, Oracle enables the constraint. Subsequently, if new data violates the constraint, Oracle does not execute the statement and returns an error indicating the integrity constraint violation.

If you place a primary key constraint in ENABLE VALIDATE mode, the validation process will verify that the primary key columns contain no nulls. To avoid this overhead, mark each column in the primary key NOT NULL before enabling the table's primary key constraint. (For optimal results, do this before entering data into the column.)

■ ENABLE NOVALIDATE ensures that all new DML operations on the constrained data comply with the constraint. This clause does not ensure that existing data

■ in the table complies with the constraint and therefore does not require a table lock.

If you specify neither VALIDATE nor NOVALIDATE, the default is VALIDATE.

If you enable a unique or primary key constraint, and if no index exists on the key, Oracle creates a unique index. This index is dropped if the constraint is subsequently disabled, so Oracle rebuilds the index every time the constraint is enabled.

To avoid rebuilding the index and eliminate redundant indexes, create new primary key and unique constraints initially disabled. Then create (or use existing) nonunique indexes to enforce the constraint. Oracle does not drop a nonunique index when the constraint is disabled, so subsequent ENABLE operations are facilitated.

If you change the state of any single constraint from ENABLE NOVALIDATE to ENABLE VALIDATE, the operation can be performed in parallel, and does not block reads, writes, or other DDL operations.

Restriction on ENABLE: You cannot enable a foreign key that references a unique or primary key that is disabled.

DISABLE Clause   Specify DISABLE to disable the integrity constraint. Disabled integrity constraints appear in the data dictionary along with enabled constraints. If you do not specify this clause when creating a constraint, Oracle automatically enables the constraint.

■ DISABLE VALIDATE disables the constraint and drops the index on the constraint, but keeps the constraint valid. This feature is most useful in data warehousing situations, where the need arises to load into a range-partitioned table a quantity of data with a distinct range of values in the unique key. In such situations, the disable validate state enables you to save space by not having an index. You can then load data from a nonpartitioned table into a partitioned table using the exchange_partition_clause of the ALTER TABLE statement or using SQL*Loader. All other modifications to the table (inserts, updates, and deletes) by other SQL statements are disallowed.

If the unique key coincides with the partitioning key of the partitioned table, disabling the constraint saves overhead and has no detrimental effects. If the unique key does not coincide with the partitioning key, Oracle performs automatic table scans during the exchange to validate the constraint, which might offset the benefit of loading without an index.

■ DISABLE NOVALIDATE signifies that Oracle makes no effort to maintain the constraint (because it is disabled) and cannot guarantee that the constraint is true (because it is not being validated).

You cannot drop a table whose primary key is being referenced by a foreign key even if the foreign key constraint is in DISABLE NOVALIDATE state. Further, the optimizer can use constraints in DISABLE NOVALIDATE state.

If you specify neither VALIDATE nor NOVALIDATE, the default is NOVALIDATE.

If you disable a unique or primary key constraint that is using a unique index, Oracle drops the unique index.

exceptions_clause   The EXCEPTIONS INTO clause lets you specify a table into which Oracle places the rowids of all rows violating the constraint. If you omit schema, Oracle assumes the exceptions table is in your own schema. If you omit this clause altogether, Oracle assumes that the table is named EXCEPTIONS. The exceptions table must be on your local database.

The EXCEPTIONS INTO clause is valid only when validating a constraint.

You can create the EXCEPTIONS table using one of these scripts:

- UTLEXCPT.SQL uses physical rowids. Therefore it can accommodate rows from conventional tables but not from index-organized tables. (See the Note that follows.)

- UTLEXPT1.SQL uses universal rowids, so it can accommodate rows from both conventional and index-organized tables.

If you create your own exceptions table, it must follow the format prescribed by one of these two scripts.

Restrictions:

- You cannot specify this clause for a view constraint.

- You cannot specify this clause in a CREATE TABLE statement, because no rowids exist until after the successful completion of the statement.

NOTE
If you are collecting exceptions from index-organized tables based on primary keys (rather than universal rowids), you must create a separate exceptions table for each index-organized table to accommodate its primary-key storage. You create multiple exceptions tables with different names by modifying and resubmitting the script.

CREATE CONTROLFILE

CAUTION
Oracle recommends that you perform a full backup of all files in the database before using this statement. For more information, see Oracle9i User-Managed Backup and Recovery Guide.

PURPOSE
Use the CREATE CONTROLFILE statement to re-create a control file in one of the following cases:

- All copies of your existing control files have been lost through media failure.

- You want to change the name of the database.
- You want to change the maximum number of redo log file groups, redo log file members, archived redo log files, datafiles, or instances that can concurrently have the database mounted and open.

When you issue a CREATE CONTROLFILE statement, Oracle creates a new control file based on the information you specify in the statement. If you omit any clauses, Oracle uses the default values rather than the values for the previous control file. After successfully creating the control file, Oracle mounts the database in the mode specified by the initialization parameter CLUSTER_DATABASE. You then must perform media recovery before opening the database. It is recommended that you then shut down the instance and take a full backup of all files in the database.

PREREQUISITES

To create a control file, you must have the SYSDBA system privilege. The database must not be mounted by any instance.

If the REMOTE_LOGIN_PASSWORDFILE initialization parameter is set to EXCLUSIVE, Oracle returns an error when you attempt to re-create the control file. To avoid this message, either set the parameter to SHARED, or re-create your password file before re-creating the control file.

SYNTAX

create_controlfile::=

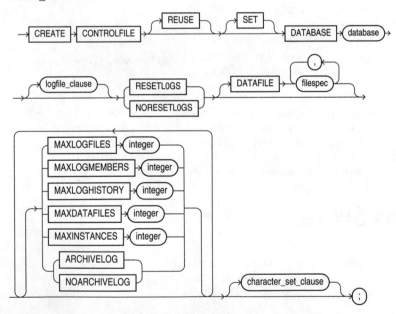

logfile_clause::=

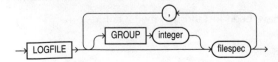

character_set_clause::=

KEYWORDS AND PARAMETERS

REUSE   Specify REUSE to indicate that existing control files identified by the initialization parameter CONTROL_FILES can be reused, thus ignoring and overwriting any information they may currently contain. If you omit this clause and any of these control files already exists, Oracle returns an error.

DATABASE Clause   Specify the name of the database. The value of this parameter must be the existing database name established by the previous CREATE DATABASE statement or CREATE CONTROLFILE statement.

SET DATABASE Clause   Use SET DATABASE to change the name of the database. The name of a database can be as long as eight bytes.

logfile_clause   Use the logfile_clause to specify the redo log files for your database. You must list all members of all redo log file groups.

   GROUP integer: Specify the logfile group number. If you specify GROUP values, Oracle verifies these values with the GROUP values when the database was last open.

   If you omit this clause, Oracle creates logfiles using system default values. In addition, if either the DB_CREATE_ONLINE_LOG_DEST_n or DB_CREATE_FILE_DEST initialization parameter (or both) has been set, and if you have specified RESETLOGS, then Oracle creates two logs in the default logfile destination specified in the DB_CREATE_ONLINE_LOG_DEST_n parameter, and if it is not set, then in the DB_CREATE_FILE_DEST parameter.

   RESETLOGS: Specify RESETLOGS if you want Oracle to ignore the contents of the files listed in the LOGFILE clause. These files do not have to exist. Each filespec in the LOGFILE clause must specify the SIZE parameter. Oracle assigns all online redo log file groups to thread 1 and enables this thread for public use by any instance. After using this clause, you must open the database using the RESETLOGS clause of the ALTER DATABASE statement.

   NORESETLOGS: Specify NORESETLOGS if you want Oracle to use all files in the LOGFILE clause as they were when the database was last open. These files must exist and must be the current online redo log files rather than restored backups. Oracle reassigns the redo log file groups to the threads to which they were previously assigned and reenables the threads as they were previously enabled.

DATAFILE Clause   Specify the datafiles of the database. You must list all datafiles. These files must all exist, although they may be restored backups that require media recovery.

NOTE
You should list only datafiles in this clause, not temporary datafiles (tempfiles). Please refer to Oracle9i User-Managed Backup and Recovery Guide *for more information on handling tempfiles.*

MAXLOGFILES Clause   Specify the maximum number of online redo log file groups that can ever be created for the database. Oracle uses this value to determine how much space in the control file to allocate for the names of redo log files. The default and maximum values depend on your operating system. The value that you specify should not be less than the greatest GROUP value for any redo log file group.

MAXLOGMEMBERS Clause   Specify the maximum number of members, or identical copies, for a redo log file group. Oracle uses this value to determine how much space in the control file to allocate for the names of redo log files. The minimum value is 1. The maximum and default values depend on your operating system.

MAXLOGHISTORY Clause   This parameter is useful only if you are using Oracle in ARCHIVELOG mode with Real Application Clusters. Specify the maximum number of archived redo log file groups for automatic media recovery of Real Application Clusters. Oracle uses this value to determine how much space in the control file to allocate for the names of archived redo log files. The minimum value is 0. The default value is a multiple of the MAXINSTANCES value and depends on your operating system. The maximum value is limited only by the maximum size of the control file.

MAXDATAFILES Clause   Specify the initial sizing of the datafiles section of the control file at CREATE DATABASE or CREATE CONTROLFILE time. An attempt to add a file whose number is greater than MAXDATAFILES, but less than or equal to DB_FILES, causes the control file to expand automatically so that the datafiles section can accommodate more files.

The number of datafiles accessible to your instance is also limited by the initialization parameter DB_FILES.

MAXINSTANCES Clause   Specify the maximum number of instances that can simultaneously have the database mounted and open. This value takes precedence over the value of the initialization parameter INSTANCES. The minimum value is 1. The maximum and default values depend on your operating system.

ARCHIVELOG | NOARCHIVELOG   Specify ARCHIVELOG to archive the contents of redo log files before reusing them. This clause prepares for the possibility of media recovery as well as instance or crash recovery.

If you omit both the ARCHIVELOG clause and NOARCHIVELOG clause, Oracle chooses NOARCHIVELOG mode by default. After creating the control file, you can change between ARCHIVELOG mode and NOARCHIVELOG mode with the ALTER DATABASE statement.

character_set_clause   If you specify a character set, Oracle reconstructs character set information in the control file. In case media recovery of the database is required, this information will be available before the database is open, so that tablespace names can be correctly interpreted during recovery. This clause is useful only if you are using a character set other than the default US7ASCII.

If you are re-creating your control file and you are using Recovery Manager for tablespace recovery, and if you specify a different character set from the one stored in the data dictionary, then tablespace recovery will not succeed. (However, at database open, the control file character set will be updated with the correct character set from the data dictionary.)

NOTE
You cannot modify the character set of the database with this clause.

CREATE DATABASE

CAUTION
This statement prepares a database for initial use and erases any data currently in the specified files. Use this statement only when you understand its ramifications.

In this release of Oracle 9i and in subsequent releases, several enhancements are being made to ensure the security of default database user accounts:

- Beginning with this release, during initial installation with the Oracle Database Configuration Assistant (DCBA), all default database user accounts except SYS, SYSTEM, SCOTT, DBSNMP, OUTLN, AURORAJISUTILITY$, AURORA$ORB$UNAUTHENTICATED and OSE$HTTP$ADMIN will be locked and expired. To activate a locked account, the DBA must manually unlock it and reassign it a new password.

- In the next release of the database server, the DBCA will prompt for passwords for users SYS and SYSTEM during initial installation of the database rather than assigning default passwords to them. In addition, a CREATE DATABASE SQL statement issued manually will require you to specify passwords for these two users.

- Oracle9*i* will be the last major release to support the user SYSTEM as a default database user created during any type of installation or by the CREATE DATABASE SQL statement.

PURPOSE
Use the CREATE DATABASE statement to create a database, making it available for general use. This statement erases all data in any specified datafiles that already exist in order to prepare them for initial database use. If you use the statement on an existing database, all data in the datafiles is lost.

After creating the database, this statement mounts it in either exclusive or parallel mode (depending on the value of the CLUSTER_DATABASE initialization parameter) and opens it, making it available for normal use. You can then create tablespaces and rollback segments for the database.

PREREQUISITES
To create a database, you must have the SYSDBA system privilege.

If the REMOTE_LOGIN_PASSWORDFILE initialization parameter is set to EXCLUSIVE, Oracle returns an error when you attempt to re-create the database. To avoid this message, either set the parameter to SHARED, or re-create your password file before re-creating the database.

SYNTAX

create_database::=

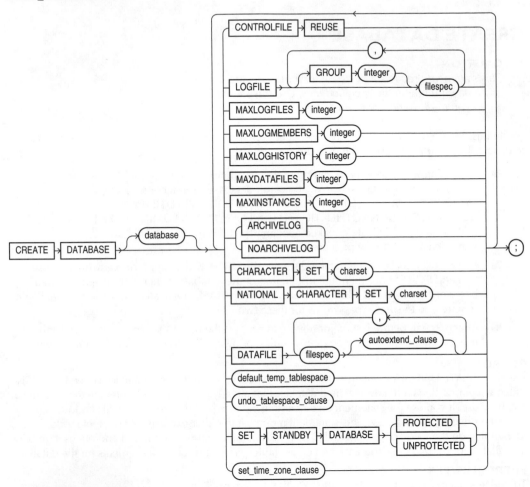

autoextend_clause::=

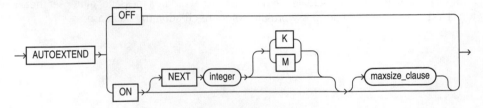

maxsize_clause::=

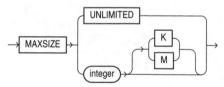

default_temp_tablespace::=

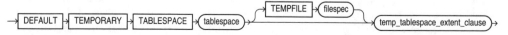

temp_tablespace_extent::=

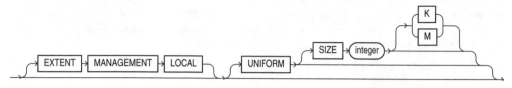

undo_tablespace_clause::=

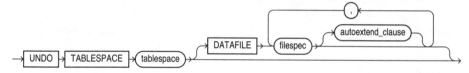

set_time_zone_clause::=

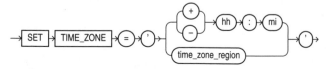

KEYWORD AND PARAMETERS

database   Specify the name of the database to be created. The name can be up to 8 bytes long. The database name can contain only ASCII characters. Oracle writes this name into the control file. If you subsequently issue an ALTER DATABASE statement that explicitly specifies a database name, Oracle verifies that name with the name in the control file.

NOTE
You cannot use special characters from European or Asian character sets in a database name. For example, characters with umlauts are not allowed.

If you omit the database name from a CREATE DATABASE statement, Oracle uses the name specified by the initialization parameter DB_NAME. If the DB_NAME initialization parameter has been set, and you specify a different name from the value of that parameter, Oracle returns an error.

CONTROLFILE REUSE Clause   Specify CONTROLFILE REUSE to reuse existing control files identified by the initialization parameter CONTROL_FILES, thus ignoring and overwriting any information they currently contain. Normally you use this clause only when you are re-creating a database, rather than creating one for the first time. You cannot use this clause if you also specify a parameter value that requires that the control file be larger than the existing files. These parameters are MAXLOGFILES, MAXLOGMEMBERS, MAXLOGHISTORY, MAXDATAFILES, and MAXINSTANCES.

If you omit this clause and any of the files specified by CONTROL_FILES already exist, Oracle returns an error.

LOGFILE Clause   Specify one or more files to be used as redo log files. Each *filespec* specifies a redo log file group containing one or more redo log file members (copies). All redo log files specified in a CREATE DATABASE statement are added to redo log thread number 1.

GROUP *integer:* Specify the number that identifies the redo log file group. The value of *integer* can range from 1 to the value of the MAXLOGFILES parameter. A database must have at least two redo log file groups. You cannot specify multiple redo log file groups having the same GROUP value. If you omit this parameter, Oracle generates its value automatically. You can examine the GROUP value for a redo log file group through the dynamic performance view V$LOG.

If you omit the LOGFILE clause:

- If either the DB_CREATE_ONLINE_LOG_DEST_*n* or DB_CREATE_FILE_DEST initialization parameter (or both) is set, then Oracle creates two Oracle-managed logfiles with system-generated names, 100 MB in size, in the default logfile directory specified in the DB_CREATE_ONLINE_LOG_DEST_*n* parameter, and if it is not set, then in the DB_CREATE_FILE_DEST parameter.

- If neither of these parameters is set, Oracle creates two redo log file groups. The names and sizes of the default files depend on your operating system.

MAXLOGFILES Clause   Specify the maximum number of redo log file groups that can ever be created for the database. Oracle uses this value to determine how much space in the control file to allocate for the names of redo log files. The default, minimum, and maximum values depend on your operating system.

MAXLOGMEMBERS Clause   Specify the maximum number of members, or copies, for a redo log file group. Oracle uses this value to determine how much space in the control file to allocate for the names of redo log files. The minimum value is 1. The maximum and default values depend on your operating system.

MAXLOGHISTORY Clause   This parameter is useful only if you are using Oracle in ARCHIVELOG mode with Real Application Clusters. Specify the maximum number of archived redo log files for automatic media recovery of Real Application Clusters. Oracle uses this value to determine how much space in the control file to allocate for the names of archived redo log files. The minimum value is 0. The default value is a multiple of the MAXINSTANCES value and depends on your operating system. The maximum value is limited only by the maximum size of the control file.

MAXDATAFILES Clause   Specify the initial sizing of the datafiles section of the control file at CREATE DATABASE or CREATE CONTROLFILE time. An attempt to add a file whose number is greater than MAXDATAFILES, but less than or equal to DB_FILES, causes the Oracle control file to expand automatically so that the datafiles section can accommodate more files.

The number of datafiles accessible to your instance is also limited by the initialization parameter DB_FILES.

MAXINSTANCES Clause   Specify the maximum number of instances that can simultaneously have this database mounted and open. This value takes precedence over the value of initialization parameter INSTANCES. The minimum value is 1. The maximum and default values depend on your operating system.

ARCHIVELOG | NOARCHIVELOG   ARCHIVELOG: Specify ARCHIVELOG if you want the contents of a redo log file group to be archived before the group can be reused. This clause prepares for the possibility of media recovery.

NOARCHIVELOG: Specify NOARCHIVELOG if the contents of a redo log file group need not be archived before the group can be reused. This clause does not allow for the possibility of media recovery.

The default is NOARCHIVELOG mode. After creating the database, you can change between ARCHIVELOG mode and NOARCHIVELOG mode with the ALTER DATABASE statement.

CHARACTER SET Clause   Specify the character set the database uses to store data. The supported character sets and default value of this parameter depend on your operating system.

Restriction: You cannot specify the AL16UTF16 character set as the database character set.

NATIONAL CHARACTER SET Clause   Specify the national character set used to store data in columns specifically defined as NCHAR, NCLOB, or NVARCHAR2 (either AF16UTF16 or UTF8). The default is 'AL16UTF16'.

DATAFILE Clause   Specify one or more files to be used as datafiles. All these files become part of the SYSTEM tablespace.

If you omit this clause:

- If the DB_CREATE_FILE_DEST initialization parameter is set, Oracle creates a 100 MB Oracle-managed datafile with a system-generated name in the default file destination specified in the parameter.

- If the DB_CREATE_FILE_DEST initialization parameter is not set, Oracle creates one datafile whose name and size depend on your operating system.

NOTE

Oracle recommends that the total initial space allocated for the SYSTEM tablespace be a minimum of 5 megabytes.

autoextend_clause   Use the autoextend_clause to enable or disable the automatic extension of a new datafile or tempfile. If you do not specify this clause, these files are not automatically extended.

ON: Specify ON to enable autoextend.

OFF: Specify OFF to turn off autoextend if is turned on.

NOTE

When you turn off autoextend, the values of NEXT and MAXSIZE are set to zero. If you turn autoextend back on in a subsequent statement, you must reset these values.

NEXT: Use the NEXT clause to specify the size in bytes of the next increment of disk space to be allocated automatically when more extents are required. Use K or M to specify this size in kilobytes or megabytes. The default is the size of one data block.

MAXSIZE: Use the MAXSIZE clause to specify the maximum disk space allowed for automatic extension of the datafile.

UNLIMITED: Use the UNLIMITED clause if you do not want to limit the disk space that Oracle can allocate to the datafile or tempfile.

default_temp_tablespace   Specify this clause to create a default temporary tablespace for the database. Oracle will assign to this temporary tablespace any users for whom you do not specify a different temporary tablespace. If you do not specify this clause, the SYSTEM tablespace is the default temporary tablespace.

NOTE
On some operating systems, Oracle does not allocate space for the tempfile until the tempfile blocks are actually accessed. This delay in space allocation results in faster creation and resizing of tempfiles, but it requires that sufficient disk space is available when the tempfiles are later used. Please refer to your operating system documentation to determine whether Oracle allocates tempfile space in this way on your system.

Restrictions:

■ You cannot specify the SYSTEM tablespace in this clause.

■ The default temporary tablespace must have a standard block size.

The temp_tablespace_extent clause lets you specify how the tablespace is managed.

EXTENT MANAGEMENT LOCAL: This clause indicates that some part of the tablespace is set aside for a bitmap. All temporary tablespaces have locally managed extents, so this clause is optional.

UNIFORM integer: Specify the size of the extents of the temporary tablespace in bytes. All extents of temporary tablespaces are the same size (uniform). If you do not specify this clause, Oracle uses uniform extents of 1M.

SIZE integer: Specify in bytes the size of the tablespace extents. Use K or M to specify the size in kilobytes or megabytes.

If you do not specify SIZE, Oracle uses the default extent size of 1M.

undo_tablespace_clause   If you have opened the instance in Automatic Undo Management mode, you can specify the undo_tablespace_clause to create a tablespace to be used for undo data. If you want undo space management to be handled by way of rollback segments, omit this clause.

■ If you specify this clause, Oracle creates an undo tablespace named tablespace, creates the specified datafiles as part of the undo tablespace, and assigns this tablespace as the undo tablespace of the instance. Oracle will handle management of undo data using this undo tablespace. The DATAFILE clause of this clause has the same behavior as described in "DATAFILE Clause".

NOTE
If you have specified a value for the UNDO_TABLESPACE initialization parameter in your initialization parameter file before mounting the database, be sure you specify the same name in this clause. If these names differ, Oracle will return an error when you open the database.

■ If you omit this clause, Oracle creates a default database with a default undo tablespace named SYS_UNDOTBS and assigns this default tablespace as the undo tablespace of the instance. This undo tablespace allocates disk space from the default files used by the CREATE DATABASE statement, and has an initial extent of 10M. Oracle handles the system-generated datafile as described in "DATAFILE Clause". If Oracle is unable to create the undo tablespace, the entire CREATE DATABASE operation fails.

SET STANDBY DATABASE Clause   The SET STANDBY DATABASE clause lets you specify whether your database environment is in **no-data-loss mode**. In this mode, Oracle places highest priority on maintaining an absolute match between the primary and standby databases. The standby database must be mounted, and no Real Application Clusters instance can have the primary database open, even in exclusive mode.

PROTECTED: Specify PROTECTED to indicate that the standby instance must contain at least one standby archivelog destination to be archived by the logwriter (LGWR) process in order for the primary database to be opened and to remain open in the event the last connection from primary to standby database is lost. In a Real Application Clusters environment, Oracle will verify that the LGWR processes of all instances that have the primary database open archive to the same standby databases.

If a connection to the last standby database is lost, Oracle will shut down the primary instance. Therefore, you should use this setting only if absolute correspondence between the primary and standby databases is more important than availability of the database.

UNPROTECTED: Specify UNPROTECTED to indicate that the instance does not require any standby databases to be maintained by the logwriter process. This is the default.

Use this setting if the absolute correspondence between the primary and standby databases is not as important as availability of the database.

To determine whether a database is in PROTECTED or UNPROTECTED mode, query the STANDBY_DATABASE column of the V$DATABASE dynamic performance view.

set_time_zone_clause   Use the SET TIME_ZONE clause to set the time zone of the database. You can specify the time zone in two ways:

- By specifying a displacement from UTC (Coordinated Universal Time—formerly Greenwich Mean Time). The valid range of hh:mm is -12:00 to +14:00.

- By specifying a time zone region. To see a listing of valid region names, query the TZNAME column of the V$TIMEZONE_NAMES dynamic performance view.

Oracle normalizes all TIMESTAMP WITH LOCAL TIME ZONE data to the time zone of the database when the data is stored on disk. If you do not specify the SET TIME_ZONE clause, Oracle uses the operating system's time zone of the server. If the operating system time zone is not a valid Oracle time zone, the database time zone defaults to UTC.

CREATE DATABASE LINK

PURPOSE
Use the CREATE DATABASE LINK statement to create a database link. A **database link** is a schema object in the local database that enables you to access objects on a remote database. The remote database need not be an Oracle system.

Once you have created a database link, you can use it to refer to tables and views on the remote database. You can refer to a remote table or view in a SQL statement by appending *@dblink* to the table or view name. You can query a remote table or view with the SELECT statement. If you are using Oracle with the distributed option, you can also access remote tables and views using any INSERT, UPDATE, DELETE, or LOCK TABLE statement.

PREREQUISITES

To create a private database link, you must have CREATE DATABASE LINK system privilege. To create a public database link, you must have CREATE PUBLIC DATABASE LINK system privilege. Also, you must have CREATE SESSION privilege on the remote Oracle database.

Oracle Net must be installed on both the local and remote Oracle databases.

To access non-Oracle systems you must use Oracle Heterogeneous Services.

SYNTAX

create_database_link::=

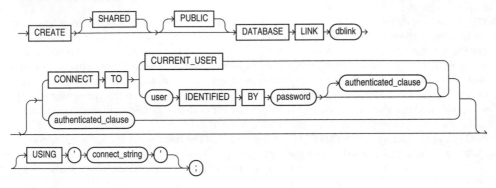

authenticated_clause::=

KEYWORD AND PARAMETERS

SHARED   Specify SHARED to use a single network connection to create a public database link that can be shared between multiple users.

PUBLIC   Specify PUBLIC to create a public database link available to all users. If you omit this clause, the database link is private and is available only to you.

dblink   Specify the complete or partial name of the database link. The value of the GLOBAL_NAMES initialization parameter determines whether the database link must have the same name as the database to which it connects.

The maximum number of database links that can be open in one session or one instance of a Real Application Clusters configuration depends on the value of the OPEN_LINKS and OPEN_LINKS_PER_INSTANCE initialization parameters.

Restriction: You cannot create a database link in another user's schema, and you cannot qualify *dblink* with the name of a schema. (Periods are permitted in names of database links, so Oracle interprets the entire name, such as ralph.linktosales, as the name of a database link in your schema rather than as a database link named linktosales in the schema ralph.)

CONNECT TO Clause   The CONNECT TO clause lets you enable a connection to the remote database.

CURRENT_USER Clause: Specify CURRENT_USER to create a **current user database link**. The current user must be a global user with a valid account on the remote database for the link to succeed.

If the database link is used directly, that is, not from within a stored object, then the current user is the same as the connected user.

When executing a stored object (such as a procedure, view, or trigger) that initiates a database link, CURRENT_USER is the username that owns the stored object, and not the username that called the object. For example, if the database link appears inside procedure scott.p (created by scott), and user jane calls procedure scott.p, the current user is scott.

However, if the stored object is an invoker-rights function, procedure, or package, the invoker's authorization ID is used to connect as a remote user. For example, if the privileged database link appears inside procedure scott.p (an invoker-rights procedure created by scott), and user Jane calls procedure scott.p, then CURRENT_USER is jane and the procedure executes with Jane's privileges.

user IDENTIFIED BY password   Specify the username and password used to connect to the remote database using a fixed user database link. If you omit this clause, the database link uses the username and password of each user who is connected to the database. This is called a connected user database link.

authenticated_clause   Specify the username and password on the target instance. This clause authenticates the user to the remote server and is required for security. The specified username and password must be a valid username and password on the remote instance. The username and password are used only for authentication. No other operations are performed on behalf of this user.

You must specify this clause when using the SHARED clause.

USING 'connect string'   Specify the service name of a remote database.

CREATE DIRECTORY

PURPOSE
Use the CREATE DIRECTORY statement to create a directory object. A directory object specifies an alias for a directory on the server's file system where external binary file LOBs (BFILEs) and external table data are located. You can use directory names when referring to BFILEs in your PL/SQL code and OCI calls, rather than hard coding the operating system path name, thereby providing greater file management flexibility.

All directories are created in a single namespace and are not owned by an individual's schema. You can secure access to the BFILEs stored within the directory structure by granting object privileges on the directories to specific users.

PREREQUISITES
You must have CREATE ANY DIRECTORY system privileges to create directories.

When you create a directory, you are automatically granted the READ and WRITE object privileges on the directory, and you can grant these privileges to other users and roles. The DBA can also grant these privileges to other users and roles.

WRITE privileges on a directory are useful in connection with external tables. They let the grantee determine whether the external table agent can write a log file or a bad file to the directory.

You must also create a corresponding operating system directory for file storage. Your system or database administrator must ensure that the operating system directory has the correct read and write permissions for Oracle processes.

Privileges granted for the directory are created independently of the permissions defined for the operating system directory. Therefore, the two may or may not correspond exactly. For example, an error occurs if demo user hr is granted READ privilege on the directory schema object but the corresponding operating system directory does not have READ permission defined for Oracle processes.

SYNTAX

create_directory::=

KEYWORDS AND PARAMETERS

OR REPLACE   Specify OR REPLACE to re-create the directory database object if it already exists. You can use this clause to change the definition of an existing directory without dropping, re-creating, and regranting database object privileges previously granted on the directory.

Users who had previously been granted privileges on a redefined directory can still access the directory without being regranted the privileges.

directory   Specify the name of the directory object to be created. The maximum length of *directory* is 30 bytes. You cannot qualify a directory object with a schema name.

NOTE
Oracle does not verify that the directory you specify actually exists. Therefore, take care that you specify a valid directory in your operating system. In addition, if your operating system uses case-sensitive path names, be sure you specify the directory in the correct format. (However, you need not include a trailing slash at the end of the path name.)

'path_name'   Specify the full pathname of the operating system directory on the server where the files are located. The single quotes are required, with the result that the path name is case sensitive.

CREATE INDEX

PURPOSE
Use the CREATE INDEX statement to create an index on

- One or more columns of a table, a partitioned table, an index-organized table, or a cluster
- One or more scalar typed object attributes of a table or a cluster
- A nested table storage table for indexing a nested table column

An **index** is a schema object that contains an entry for each value that appears in the indexed column(s) of the table or cluster and provides direct, fast access to rows. Oracle supports several types of index:

- **Normal indexes** (by default, Oracle creates B-tree indexes)
- **Bitmap indexes**, which store rowids associated with a key value as a bitmap
- **Partitioned indexes**, which consist of partitions containing an entry for each value that appears in the indexed column(s) of the table
- **Function-based indexes**, which are based on expressions. They enable you to construct queries that evaluate the value returned by an expression, which in turn may include functions (built-in or user-defined).
- **Domain indexes**, which are instances of an application-specific index of type *indextype*

PREREQUISITES

To create an index in your own schema, one of the following conditions must be true:

- The table or cluster to be indexed must be in your own schema.
- You must have INDEX privilege on the table to be indexed.
- You must have CREATE ANY INDEX system privilege.

To create an index in another schema, you must have CREATE ANY INDEX system privilege. Also, the owner of the schema to contain the index must have either the UNLIMITED TABLESPACE system privilege or space quota on the tablespaces to contain the index or index partitions.

To create a domain index in your own schema, in addition to the prerequisites for creating a conventional index, you must also have EXECUTE privilege on the indextype. If you are creating a domain index in another user's schema, the index owner also must have EXECUTE privilege on the indextype and its underlying implementation type. Before creating a domain index, you should first define the indextype.

To create a function-based index in your own schema on your own table, in addition to the prerequisites for creating a conventional index, you must have the QUERY REWRITE system privilege. To create the index in another schema or on another schema's table, you must have the GLOBAL QUERY REWRITE privilege. In both cases, the table owner must also have the EXECUTE object privilege on the function(s) used in the function-based index. In addition, in order for Oracle to use function-based indexes in queries, the QUERY_REWRITE_ENABLED parameter must be set to TRUE, and the QUERY_REWRITE_INTEGRITY parameter must be set to TRUSTED.

SYNTAX

create_index::=

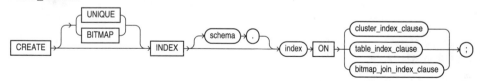

cluster_index_clause::=

table_index_clause::=

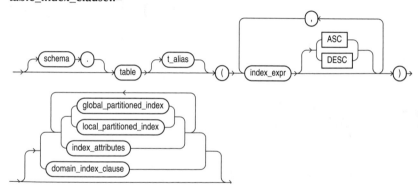

index_expr::=

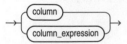

index_attributes::=

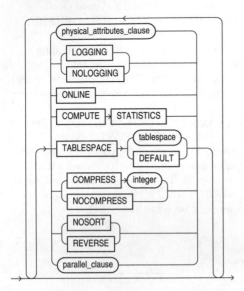

physical_attributes_clause::=

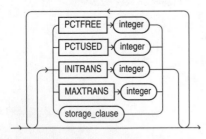

domain_index_clause::=

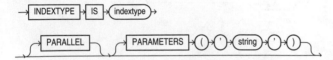

bitmap_join_index_clause::=

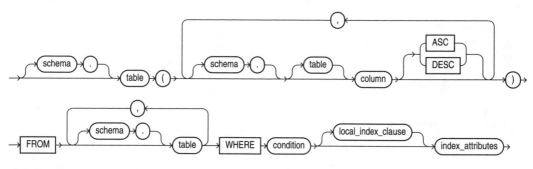

global_partitioned_index::=

global_partitioning_clause::=

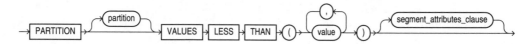

local_partitioned_index::=

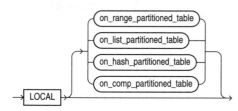

on_range_partitioned_table::=

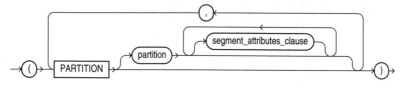

on_list_partitioned_table::=

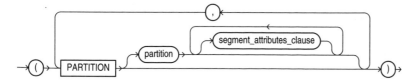

segment_attributes_clause::=

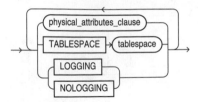

on_hash_partitioned_table::=

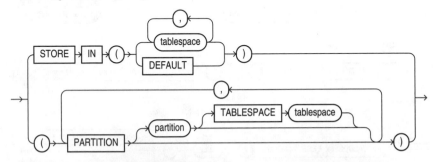

on_comp_partitioned_table::=

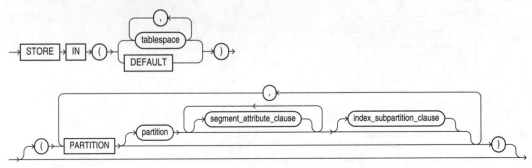

index_subpartition_clause::=

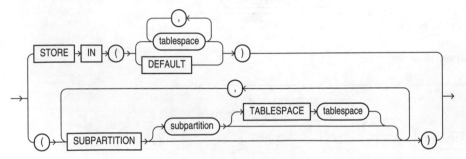

parallel_clause::=

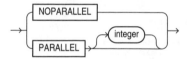

KEYWORDS AND PARAMETERS

UNIQUE   Specify UNIQUE to indicate that the value of the column (or columns) upon which the index is based must be unique. If the index is local nonprefixed, then the index key must contain the partitioning key.

> **Restrictions:**
>
> ■   You cannot specify both UNIQUE and BITMAP.
>
> ■   You cannot specify UNIQUE for a domain index.

BITMAP   Specify BITMAP to indicate that *index* is to be created with a bitmap for each distinct key, rather than indexing each row separately. Bitmap indexes store the rowids associated with a key value as a bitmap. Each bit in the bitmap corresponds to a possible rowid, and if the bit is set, it means that the row with the corresponding rowid contains the key value. The internal representation of bitmaps is best suited for applications with low levels of concurrent transactions, such as data warehousing.

> **Restrictions:**
>
> ■   You cannot specify BITMAP when creating a global partitioned index.
>
> ■   You cannot create a bitmapped secondary index on an index-organized table unless the index-organized table has a mapping table associated with it.
>
> ■   You cannot specify both UNIQUE and BITMAP.
>
> ■   You cannot specify BITMAP for a domain index.

schema   Specify the schema to contain the index. If you omit schema, Oracle creates the index in your own schema.

index   Specify the name of the index to be created.

cluster_index_clause   Use the cluster_index_clause to identify the cluster for which a cluster index is to be created. If you do not qualify cluster with schema, Oracle assumes the cluster is in your current schema. You cannot create a cluster index for a hash cluster.

table_index_clause   Specify the table (and its attributes) on which you are defining the index. If you do not qualify table with schema, Oracle assumes the table is contained in your own schema.

   You create an index on a nested table column by creating the index on the nested table storage table. Include the NESTED_TABLE_ID pseudocolumn of the storage table to create a UNIQUE index, which effectively ensures that the rows of a nested table value are distinct.

> **Restrictions:**
>
> ■   If the index is locally partitioned, then table must be partitioned.
>
> ■   If the table is index-organized, this statement creates a secondary index. You cannot specify REVERSE for this secondary index, and the combined size of the index key and the logical rowid should be less than half the block size.

■ If table is a temporary table, the index will also be temporary with the same scope (session or transaction) as table. The following restrictions apply to indexes on temporary table:

 ■ The index cannot be a partitioned index or a domain index.

 ■ You cannot specify the physical_attributes_clause or the parallel_clause.

 ■ You cannot specify LOGGING, NOLOGGING, or TABLESPACE.

t_alias Specify a correlation name (alias) for the table upon which you are building the index.

NOTE
This alias is required if the index_expr *references any object type attributes or object type methods.*

index_expr For index_expr, specify the column or column expression upon which the index is based.

column: Specify the name of a column in the table. A bitmap index can have a maximum of 30 columns. Other indexes can have as many as 32 columns.

You can create an index on a scalar object attribute column or on the system-defined NESTED_TABLE_ID column of the nested table storage table. If you specify an object attribute column, the column name must be qualified with the table name. If you specify a nested table column attribute, it must be qualified with the outermost table name, the containing column name, and all intermediate attribute names leading to the nested table column attribute.

Restriction: You cannot create an index on columns or attributes whose type is user-defined, LONG, LONG RAW, LOB, or REF, except that Oracle supports an index on REF type columns or attributes that have been defined with a SCOPE clause.

column_expression: Specify an expression built from columns of table, constants, SQL functions, and user-defined functions. When you specify column_expression, you create a function-based index.

Name resolution of the function is based on the schema of the index creator. User-defined functions used in column_expression are fully name resolved during the CREATE INDEX operation.

After creating a function-based index, collect statistics on both the index and its base table using the ANALYZE statement. Oracle cannot use the function-based index until these statistics have been generated.

Notes on Function-Based Indexes:
When you subsequently query a table that uses a function-based index, you must ensure in the query that column_expression is not null. However, Oracle will use a function-based index in a query even if the columns specified in the WHERE clause are in a different order than their order in the column_expression that defined the function-based index.

If the function on which the index is based becomes invalid or is dropped, Oracle marks the index DISABLED. Queries on a DISABLED index fail if the optimizer chooses to use the index. DML operations on a DISABLED index fail unless the index is also marked UNUSABLE and the parameter SKIP_UNUSABLE_INDEXES is set to true.

Oracle's use of function-based indexes is also affected by the setting of the QUERY_REWRITE_ENABLED session parameter.

If a public synonym for a function, package, or type is used in column_expression, and later an actual object with the same name is created in the table owner's schema, then Oracle will disable the function-based index. When you subsequently enable the function-based index using ALTER

INDEX ... ENABLE or ALTER INDEX ... REBUILD, the function, package, or type used in the column_expression will continue to resolve to the function, package, or type to which the public synonym originally pointed. It will not resolve to the new function, package, or type.

If the definition of a function-based index generates internal conversion to character data, use caution when changing NLS parameter settings. Function-based indexes use the current database settings for NLS parameters. If you reset these parameters at the session level, queries using the function-based index may return incorrect results. Two exceptions are the collation parameters (NLS_SORT and NLS_COMP). Oracle handles the conversions correctly even if these have been reset at the session level.

Restrictions on Function-Based Indexes:

■ Any user-defined function referenced in column_expression must be DETERMINISTIC.

■ For a function-based globally partitioned index, the column_expression cannot be the partitioning key.

■ column_expression can be any form of expression except a scalar subquery expression.

■ All functions must be specified with parentheses, even if they have no parameters. Otherwise Oracle interprets them as column names.

■ Any function you specify in column_expression must return a repeatable value. For example, you cannot specify the SYSDATE or USER function or the ROWNUM pseudocolumn.

■ The column_expression cannot contain any aggregate functions.

■ You cannot create a function-based index on a nested table.

ASC | DESC   Use ASC or DESC to indicate whether the index should be created in ascending or descending order. Indexes on character data are created in ascending or descending order of the character values in the database character set.

Oracle treats descending indexes as if they were function-based indexes. You do not need the QUERY REWRITE or GLOBAL QUERY REWRITE privileges to create them, as you do with other function-based indexes. However, as with other function-based indexes, Oracle does not use descending indexes until you first analyze the index and the table on which the index is defined. See the column_expression clause of this statement.

Restriction: You cannot specify either of these clauses for a domain index. You cannot specify DESC for a reverse index. Oracle ignores DESC if index is bitmapped or if the COMPATIBLE initialization parameter is set to a value less than 8.1.0.

index_attributes

physical_attributes_clause: Use the physical_attributes_clause to establish values for physical and storage characteristics for the index. See "CREATE TABLE".

Restriction: You cannot specify the PCTUSED parameter for an index.

■ For PCTFREE, specify the percentage of space to leave free for updates and insertions within each of the index's data blocks.

■ Use the storage_clause to establish the storage characteristics for the index.

TABLESPACE: For tablespace, specify the name of the tablespace to hold the index, index partition, or index subpartition. If you omit this clause, Oracle creates the index in the default tablespace of the owner of the schema containing the index.

For a local index, you can specify the keyword DEFAULT in place of tablespace. New partitions or subpartitions added to the local index will be created in the same tablespace(s) as the corresponding partitions or subpartitions of the underlying table.

COMPRESS: Specify COMPRESS to enable key compression, which eliminates repeated occurrence of key column values and may substantially reduce storage. Use integer to specify the prefix length (number of prefix columns to compress).

- For unique indexes, the valid range of prefix length values is from 1 to the number of key columns minus 1. The default prefix length is the number of key columns minus 1.

- For nonunique indexes, the valid range of prefix length values is from 1 to the number of key columns. The default prefix length is the number of key columns.

- Oracle compresses only nonpartitioned indexes that are nonunique or unique indexes of at least two columns.

Restriction: You cannot specify COMPRESS for a bitmap index.

NOCOMPRESS: Specify NOCOMPRESS to disable key compression. This is the default.

NOSORT: Specify NOSORT to indicate to Oracle that the rows are stored in the database in ascending order, so that Oracle does not have to sort the rows when creating the index. If the rows of the indexed column or columns are not stored in ascending order, Oracle returns an error. For greatest savings of sort time and space, use this clause immediately after the initial load of rows into a table.

Restrictions on NOSORT:

- You cannot specify REVERSE with this clause.

- You cannot use this clause to create a cluster, partitioned, or bitmap index.

- You cannot specify this clause for a secondary index on an index-organized table.

REVERSE: Specify REVERSE to store the bytes of the index block in reverse order, excluding the rowid.

Restrictions on REVERSE:

- You cannot specify NOSORT with this clause.

- You cannot reverse a bitmap index or an index-organized table.

LOGGING | NOLOGGING: Specify whether the creation of the index will be logged (LOGGING) or not logged (NOLOGGING) in the redo log file. This setting also determines whether subsequent Direct Loader (SQL*Loader) and direct-path INSERT operations against the index are logged or not logged. LOGGING is the default.

If index is nonpartitioned, this clause specifies the logging attribute of the index.

If index is partitioned, this clause determines:

- The default value of all partitions specified in the CREATE statement (unless you specify LOGGING|NOLOGGING in the PARTITION description clause)

- The default value for the segments associated with the index partitions

- The default value for local index partitions or subpartitions added implicitly during subsequent ALTER TABLE ... ADD PARTITION operations

In NOLOGGING mode, data is modified with minimal logging (to mark new extents INVALID and to record dictionary changes). When applied during media recovery, the extent invalidation records mark a range of blocks as logically corrupt, since the redo data is not logged. Thus if you cannot afford to lose this index, it is important to take a backup after the NOLOGGING operation.

If the database is run in ARCHIVELOG mode, media recovery from a backup made before the LOGGING operation will re-create the index. However, media recovery from a backup made before the NOLOGGING operation will not re-create the index.

The logging attribute of the index is independent of that of its base table. If you omit this clause, the logging attribute is that of the tablespace in which it resides.

ONLINE: Specify ONLINE to indicate that DML operations on the table will be allowed during creation of the index.

Restrictions:

■ Parallel DML is not supported during online index building. If you specify ONLINE and then issue parallel DML statements, Oracle returns an error.

■ You cannot specify ONLINE for a bitmap index or a cluster index.

■ You cannot specify ONLINE for a conventional index on a UROWID column.

COMPUTE STATISTICS: Specify COMPUTE STATISTICS to collect statistics at relatively little cost during the creation of an index. These statistics are stored in the data dictionary for ongoing use by the optimizer in choosing a plan of execution for SQL statements.

The types of statistics collected depend on the type of index you are creating.

NOTE

If you create an index using another index (instead of a table), the original index might not provide adequate statistical information. Therefore, Oracle generally uses the base table to compute the statistics, which will improve the statistics but may negatively affect performance.

Additional methods of collecting statistics are available in PL/SQL packages and procedures.

parallel_clause   Specify the *parallel_clause* if you want creation of the index to be parallelized.

NOTE

The syntax of the parallel_clause *supersedes syntax appearing in earlier releases of Oracle. Superseded syntax is still supported for backward compatibility, but may result in slightly different behavior than that documented.*

NOPARALLEL: Specify NOPARALLEL for serial execution. This is the default.

PARALLEL: Specify PARALLEL if you want Oracle to select a degree of parallelism equal to the number of CPUs available on all participating instances times the value of the PARALLEL_THREADS_PER_CPU initialization parameter.

PARALLEL *integer*: Specification of integer indicates the degree of parallelism, which is the number of parallel threads used in the parallel operation. Each parallel thread may use one or two parallel execution servers. Normally Oracle calculates the optimum degree of parallelism, so it is not necessary for you to specify *integer*.

Index Partitioning Clauses   Use the *global_partitioned_index* clause and the *local_partitioned_index* clauses to partition *index*.

NOTE
The storage of partitioned database entities in tablespaces of different block sizes is subject to several restrictions. Please refer to Oracle9i Database Administrator's Guide for a discussion of these restrictions.

global_partitioned_index The global_partitioned_index clause lets you specify that the partitioning of the index is user defined and is not equipartitioned with the underlying table. By default, nonpartitioned indexes are global indexes.

PARTITION BY RANGE: Specify PARTITION BY RANGE to indicate that the global index is partitioned on the ranges of values from the columns specified in column_list. You cannot specify this clause for a local index.

column_list: For column_list, specify the name of the column(s) of a table on which the index is partitioned. The column_list must specify a left prefix of the index column list.

You cannot specify more than 32 columns in column_list, and the columns cannot contain the ROWID pseudocolumn or a column of type ROWID.

NOTE
If your enterprise has or will have databases using different character sets, use caution when partitioning on character columns. The sort sequence of characters is not identical in all character sets.

PARTITION: The PARTITION clause lets you describe the individual index partitions. The number of clauses determines the number of partitions. If you omit partition, Oracle generates a name with the form SYS_Pn.

VALUES LESS THAN: For VALUES LESS THAN (value_list), specify the (noninclusive) upper bound for the current partition in a global index. The value_list is a comma-separated, ordered list of literal values corresponding to column_list in the partition_by_range_clause. Always specify MAXVALUE as the value_list of the last partition.

NOTE
If index is partitioned on a DATE column, and if the date format does not specify the first two digits of the year, you must use the TO_DATE function with a 4-character format mask for the year. The date format is determined implicitly by NLS_TERRITORY or explicitly by NLS_DATE_FORMAT.

local_partitioned_index The local_partitioned_index clauses let you specify that the index is partitioned on the same columns, with the same number of partitions and the same partition bounds as table. Oracle automatically maintains LOCAL index partitioning as the underlying table is repartitioned.

on_range_partitioned_table: Specify the name and attributes of an index on a range-partitioned table.

■   For PARTITION, specify the names of the individual partitions. The number of clauses determines the number of partitions. For a local index, the number of index partitions must be equal to the number of the table partitions, and in the same order.

■   If you omit partition, Oracle generates a name that is consistent with the corresponding table partition. If the name conflicts with an existing index partition name, the form SYS_Pn is used.

on_hash_partitioned_table: Specify the name and attributes of an index on a hash-partitioned table. If you do not specify partition, Oracle uses the name of the corresponding base table partition, unless it conflicts with an explicitly specified name of another index partition. In this case, Oracle generates a name of the form SYS_Pnnn.

You can optionally specify TABLESPACE for all index partitions or for one or more individual partitions. If you do not specify TABLESPACE at the index or partition level, Oracle stores each index partition in the same tablespace as the corresponding table partition.

on_comp_partitioned_table: Specify the name and attributes of an index on a composite-partitioned table. The first STORE IN clause specifies the default tablespace for the index subpartitions. You can override this storage by specifying a different tablespace in the index_subpartitioning_clause.

If you do not specify TABLESPACE for subpartitions either in this clause or in the index_subpartitioning_clause, Oracle uses the tablespace specified for index. If you also do not specify TABLESPACE for index, Oracle stores the subpartition in the same tablespace as the corresponding table subpartition.

on_list_partitioned_table: The on_list_partitioned_table clause is identical to on_range_partitioned_table.

STORE IN: The STORE IN clause lets you specify how index hash partitions (for a hash-partitioned index) or index subpartitions (for a composite-partitioned index) are to be distributed across various tablespaces. The number of tablespaces does not have to equal the number of index partitions. If the number of index partitions is greater than the number of tablespaces, Oracle cycles through the names of the tablespaces.

■   The DEFAULT clause is valid only for a local index on a hash or composite-partitioned table. This clause overrides any tablespace specified at the index level for a partition or subpartition, and stores the index partition or subpartition in the same partition as the corresponding table partition or subpartition.

■   The index_subpartition_clause lets you specify one or more tablespaces in which to store all subpartitions in partition or one or more individual subpartitions in partition. The subpartition inherits all other attributes from partition. Attributes not specified for partition are inherited from index.

domain_index_clause   Use the domain_index_clause to indicate that index is a domain index.

column: Specify the table columns or object attributes on which the index is defined. You can define multiple domain indexes on a single column only if the underlying indextypes are different and the indextypes support a disjoint set of user-defined operators.

Restriction: You cannot create a domain index on a column of datatype REF, varray, nested table, LONG, or LONG RAW.

indextype: For indextype, specify the name of the indextype. This name should be a valid schema object that you have already defined.

NOTE
If you have installed Oracle Text, you can use various built-in indextypes to create Oracle Text domain indexes. For more information on Oracle Text and the indexes it uses, please refer to Oracle Text Reference.

PARAMETERS: In the PARAMETERS clause, specify the parameter string that is passed uninterpreted to the appropriate ODCI indextype routine. The maximum length of the parameter string is 1000 characters.

When you specify this clause at the top level of the syntax, the parameters become the default parameters for the index partitions. If you specify this clause as part of the LOCAL [PARTITION] clause, you override any default parameters with parameters for the individual partition.

Once the domain index is created, Oracle invokes the appropriate ODCI routine. If the routine does not return successfully, the domain index is marked FAILED. The only operations supported on an failed domain index are DROP INDEX and (for non-local indexes) REBUILD INDEX.

Restrictions on the domain_index_clause:

- The index_expr can specify only a single column.
- You cannot specify a bitmap or unique domain index.

bitmap_join_index_clause   Use the bitmap_join_index_clause to define a bitmap join index. A bitmap join index is defined on a single table. For an index key made up of dimension table columns, it stores the fact table rowids corresponding to that key. In a data warehousing environment, the table on which the index is defined is commonly referred to as a fact table, and the tables with which this table is joined are commonly referred to as dimension tables. However, a star schema is not a requirement for creating a join index.

ON: In the ON clause, first specify the fact table, and then inside the parentheses specify the columns of the dimension tables on which the index is defined.

FROM: In the FROM clause, specify the joined tables.

WHERE: In the WHERE clause, specify the join condition.

If the underlying fact table is partitioned, you must also specify one of the local_index_clauses.

Restrictions: In addition to the restrictions on bitmap indexes in general, the following restrictions apply to bitmap join indexes:

- You cannot create a bitmap join index on an index-organized table or a temporary table.
- No table may appear twice in the FROM clause.
- You cannot create a function-based join index.
- The dimension table columns must be either primary key columns or have unique constraints.
- If a dimension table has a composite primary key, each column in the primary key must be part of the join.
- You cannot specify the local_index_clauses unless the fact table is partitioned.

CREATE LIBRARY

PURPOSE
Use the CREATE LIBRARY statement to create a schema object associated with an operating-system shared library. The name of this schema object can then be used in the *call_spec* of CREATE FUNCTION or CREATE PROCEDURE statements, or when declaring a function or procedure in a package or type, so that SQL and PL/SQL can call to third-generation-language (3GL) functions and procedures.

PREREQUISITES
To create a library in your own schema, you must have the CREATE LIBRARY system privilege. To create a library in another user's schema, you must have the CREATE ANY LIBRARY system privilege. To use the procedures and functions stored in the library, you must have EXECUTE object privileges on the library.

The CREATE LIBRARY statement is valid only on platforms that support shared libraries and dynamic linking.

SYNTAX
create_library::=

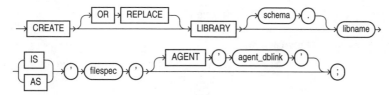

KEYWORDS AND PARAMETERS

OR REPLACE   Specify OR REPLACE to re-create the library if it already exists. Use this clause to change the definition of an existing library without dropping, re-creating, and regranting schema object privileges granted on it.

Users who had previously been granted privileges on a redefined library can still access the library without being regranted the privileges.

libname   Specify the name you wish to represent this library when declaring a function or procedure with a call_spec.

'filespec'   Specify a string literal, enclosed in single quotes. This string should be the path or filename your operating system recognizes as naming the shared library.

The 'filespec' is not interpreted during execution of the CREATE LIBRARY statement. The existence of the library file is not checked until an attempt is made to execute a routine from it.

AGENT Clause   Specify the AGENT clause if you want external procedures to be run from a database link other than the server. Oracle will use the database link specified by *agent_dblink* to run external procedures. If you omit this clause, the default agent on the server (extproc) will run external procedures.

CREATE MATERIALIZED VIEW

PURPOSE
Use the CREATE MATERIALIZED VIEW statement to create a **materialized view**. A materialized view is a database object that contains the results of a query. The FROM clause of the query can

name tables, views, and other materialized views. Collectively these are called **master tables** (a replication term) or **detail tables** (a data warehouse term). This reference uses "master tables" for consistency. The databases containing the master tables are called the **master databases**.

NOTE
The keyword SNAPSHOT is supported in place of MATERIALIZED VIEW for backward compatibility.

For replication purposes, materialized views allow you to maintain copies of remote data on your local node. The copies can be updatable with the Advanced Replication feature and are read-only without this feature. You can select data from a materialized view as you would from a table or view. In replication environments, the materialized views commonly created are primary key, rowid, object, and subquery materialized views.

For data warehousing purposes, the materialized views commonly created are materialized aggregate views, single-table materialized aggregate views, and materialized join views. All three types of materialized views can be used by query rewrite, an optimization technique that transforms a user request written in terms of master tables into a semantically equivalent request that includes one or more materialized views.

PREREQUISITES
The privileges required to create a materialized view should be granted directly rather than through a role.

To create a materialized view **in your own schema:**

- You must have been granted the CREATE MATERIALIZED VIEW system privilege *and* either the CREATE TABLE or CREATE ANY TABLE system privilege.

- You must also have access to any master tables of the materialized view that you do not own, either through a SELECT object privilege on each of the tables or through the SELECT ANY TABLE system privilege.

To create a materialized view **in another user's schema:**

- You must have the CREATE ANY MATERIALIZED VIEW system privilege.

- The owner of the materialized view must have the CREATE TABLE system privilege. The owner must also have access to any master tables of the materialized view that the schema owner does not own (for example, if the master tables are on a remote database), *and* to any materialized view logs defined on those master tables, either through a SELECT object privilege on each of the tables or through the SELECT ANY TABLE system privilege.

To create a refresh-on-commit materialized view (ON COMMIT REFRESH clause), in addition to the preceding privileges, you must have the ON COMMIT REFRESH object privilege on any master tables that you do not own or you must have the ON COMMIT REFRESH system privilege.

To create the materialized view **with query rewrite enabled**, in addition to the preceding privileges:

- The owner of the master tables must have the QUERY REWRITE system privilege.

- If you are not the owner of the master tables, you must have the GLOBAL QUERY REWRITE system privilege or the QUERY REWRITE object privilege on each table outside your schema.

- If the schema owner does not own the master tables, then the schema owner must have the GLOBAL QUERY REWRITE privilege or the QUERY REWRITE object privilege on each table outside the schema.

■ If you are defining the materialized view on a prebuilt container (ON PREBUILD TABLE), you must have the SELECT privilege WITH GRANT OPTION on the container table.

The user whose schema contains the materialized view must have sufficient quota in the target tablespace to store the materialized view's master table and index or must have the UNLIMITED TABLESPACE system privilege.

When you create a materialized view, Oracle creates one internal table and at least one index, and may create one view, all in the schema of the materialized view. Oracle uses these objects to maintain the materialized view's data. You must have the privileges necessary to create these objects.

SYNTAX

create_materialized_view::=

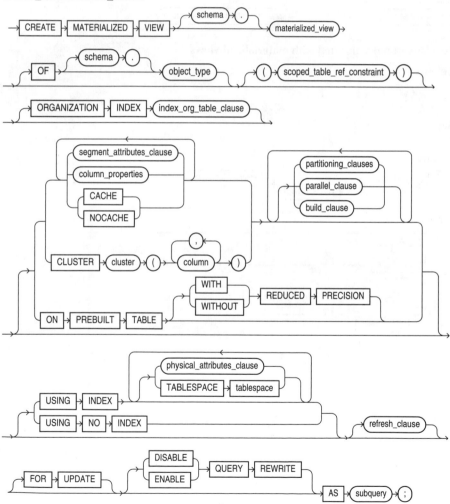

scoped_table_ref_constraint::=

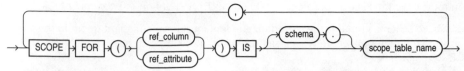

index_org_table_clause::=

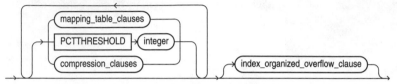

mapping_table_clauses: not supported with materialized views

compression_clauses::=

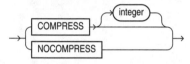

index_org_overflow_clause::=

create_mv_refresh_clause::=

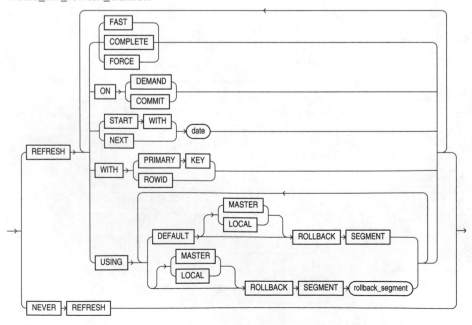

segment_attributes_clause::=

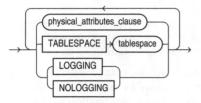

physical_attributes_clause::=

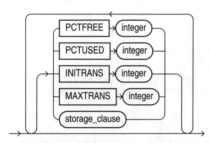

column_properties::=

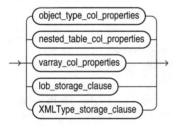

parallel_clause::=

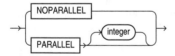

build_clause::=

KEYWORDS AND PARAMETERS

schema   Specify the schema to contain the materialized view. If you omit *schema*, Oracle creates the materialized view in your schema.

materialized_view   Specify the name of the materialized view to be created. Oracle generates names for the table and indexes used to maintain the materialized view by adding a prefix or suffix to the materialized view name.

OF type_name The OF type_name clause lets you explicitly create an object materialized view of type object_type.

scoped_table_ref_constraint Use the SCOPE FOR clause to restrict the scope of references to a single table, scope_table_name. The values in the REF column or attribute point to objects in scope_table_name, in which object instances (of the same type as the REF column) are stored.

ORGANIZATION INDEX Clause The ORGANIZATION INDEX clause lets you create an index-organized materialized view. In such a materialized view, data rows are stored in an index defined on the primary key of the materialized view. You can specify index organization for the following types of materialized views:

- Read-only and updatable object materialized views. You must ensure that the master table has a primary key.
- Read-only and updatable primary key based materialized views.
- Read-only rowid materialized views.

The keywords and parameters of the *index_org_table_clause* have the same semantics as described in CREATE TABLE, with the restrictions that follow.

Restrictions:

- You cannot specify the following CREATE MATERIALIZED VIEW clauses: CACHE or NOCACHE, CLUSTER, or ON PREBUILT TABLE.
- In the *index_org_table_clause*:
  - You cannot specify the *mapping_table_clauses*.
  - You can specify COMPRESS only for a materialized view based on a composite primary key. You can specify NOCOMPRESS for a materialized view based on either a simple or composite primary key.

segment_attributes_clause Use the segment_attributes_clause to establish values for the PCTFREE, PCTUSED, INITRANS, and MAXTRANS parameters (or, when used in the USING INDEX clause, for the INITRANS and MAXTRANS parameters only), the storage characteristics for the materialized view, to assign a tablespace, and to specify whether logging is to occur.

TABLESPACE Clause Specify the tablespace in which the materialized view is to be created. If you omit this clause, Oracle creates the materialized view in the default tablespace of the schema containing the materialized view.

column_properties The *column_properties* clause lets you specify the storage characteristics of a LOB, nested table, varray, or XMLType column.

Restriction: The *object_type_col_properties* are not relevant for a materialized view.

LOGGING | NOLOGGING Specify LOGGING or NOLOGGING to establish the logging characteristics for the materialized view.

CACHE | NOCACHE For data that will be accessed frequently, CACHE specifies that the blocks retrieved for this table are placed at the *most recently used* end of the least recently used (LRU) list in the buffer cache when a full table scan is performed. This attribute is useful for small lookup tables. NOCACHE specifies that the blocks are placed at the *least recently used* end of the LRU list.

NOTE
NOCACHE has no effect on materialized views for which you specify KEEP in the storage_clause.

CLUSTER Clause   Use the CLUSTER clause to create the materialized view as part of the specified cluster. A clustered materialized view uses the cluster's space allocation. Therefore, do not specify the *physical_attributes_clause* or the TABLESPACE clause with the CLUSTER clause.

partitioning_clauses   The partitioning_clauses let you specify that the materialized view is partitioned on specified ranges of values or on a hash function. Partitioning of materialized views is the same as partitioning of tables.

parallel_clause   The parallel_clause lets you indicate whether parallel operations will be supported for the materialized view and sets the default degree of parallelism for queries and DML on the materialized view after creation.

NOTE
The syntax of the parallel_clause supersedes syntax appearing in earlier releases of Oracle. Superseded syntax is still supported for backward compatibility, but may result in slightly different behavior than that documented.

NOPARALLEL: Specify NOPARALLEL for serial execution. This is the default.
PARALLEL: Specify PARALLEL if you want Oracle to select a degree of parallelism equal to the number of CPUs available on all participating instances times the value of the PARALLEL_THREADS_ PER_CPU initialization parameter.
PARALLEL *integer*: Specification of integer indicates the degree of parallelism, which is the number of parallel threads used in the parallel operation. Each parallel thread may use one or two parallel execution servers. Normally Oracle calculates the optimum degree of parallelism, so it is not necessary for you to specify integer.

build_clause   The build_clause lets you specify when to populate the materialized view.
IMMEDIATE: Specify IMMEDIATE to indicate that the materialized view is populated immediately. This is the default.
DEFERRED: Specify DEFERRED to indicate that the materialized view will be populated by the next REFRESH operation. The first (deferred) refresh must always be a complete refresh. Until then, the materialized view has a staleness value of UNUSABLE, so it cannot be used for query rewrite.

ON PREBUILT TABLE Clause   The ON PREBUILT TABLE clause lets you register an existing table as a preinitialized materialized view. This is particularly useful for registering large materialized views in a data warehousing environment. The table must have the same name and be in the same schema as the resulting materialized view.
    If the materialized view is dropped, the preexisting table reverts to its identity as a table.

CAUTION
This clause assumes that the table object reflects the materialization of a subquery. Oracle Corporation strongly recommends that you ensure that this assumption is true in order to ensure that the materialized view correctly reflects the data in its master tables.

WITH REDUCED PRECISION: Specify WITH REDUCED PRECISION to authorize the loss of precision that will result if the precision of the table or materialized view columns do not exactly match the precision returned by *subquery*.

WITHOUT REDUCED PRECISION: Specify WITHOUT REDUCED PRECISION to require that the precision of the table or materialized view columns match exactly the precision returned by *subquery*, or the create operation will fail. This is the default.

Restrictions:

- Each column alias in *subquery* must correspond to a column in *table_name*, and corresponding columns must have matching datatypes.

- If you specify this clause, you cannot specify a NOT NULL constraint for any column that is unmanaged (that is, not referenced in *subquery*) unless you also specify a default value for that column.

USING INDEX Clause   The USING INDEX clause lets you establish the value of INITRANS, MAXTRANS, and STORAGE parameters for the default index Oracle uses to maintain the materialized view's data. If USING INDEX is not specified, then default values are used for the index. Oracle uses the default index to speed up incremental ("fast") refresh of the materialized view.

Restriction: You cannot specify the PCTUSED or PCTFREE parameters in this clause.

USING NO INDEX Clause   Specify USING NO INDEX to suppress the creation of the default index. You can create an alternative index explicitly by using the CREATE INDEX statement. You should create such an index if you specify USING NO INDEX and you are creating the materialized view with the incremental refresh method (REFRESH FAST).

create_mv_refresh_clause   Use the create_mv_refresh_clause to specify the default methods, modes, and times for Oracle to refresh the materialized view. If the master tables of a materialized view are modified, the data in the materialized view must be updated to make the materialized view accurately reflect the data currently in its master tables. This clause lets you schedule the times and specify the method and mode for Oracle to refresh the materialized view.

NOTE

This clause only sets the default refresh options. For instructions on actually implementing the refresh, refer to Oracle9i Replication *and* Oracle9i Data Warehousing Guide.

FAST Clause   Specify FAST to indicate the incremental refresh method, which performs the refresh according to the changes that have occurred to the master tables. The changes are stored either in the materialized view log associated with the master table (for conventional DML changes) or in the direct loader log (for direct-path INSERT operations).

If you specify REFRESH FAST, the CREATE statement will fail unless materialized view logs already exist for the materialized view's master tables. (Oracle creates the direct loader log automatically when a direct-path INSERT takes place. No user intervention is needed.)

For both conventional DML changes and for direct-path INSERT operations, other conditions may restrict the eligibility of a materialized view for fast refresh.

Materialized views are not eligible for fast refresh if the defining subquery contains an analytic function.

COMPLETE Clause   Specify COMPLETE to indicate the complete refresh method, which is implemented by executing the materialized view's defining subquery. If you request a complete refresh, Oracle performs a complete refresh even if a fast refresh is possible.

FORCE Clause   Specify FORCE to indicate that when a refresh occurs, Oracle will perform a fast refresh if one is possible or a complete refresh otherwise. If you do not specify a refresh method (FAST, COMPLETE, or FORCE), FORCE is the default.

ON COMMIT Clause   Specify ON COMMIT to indicate that a fast refresh is to occur whenever Oracle commits a transaction that operates on a master table of the materialized view. This clause may increase the time taken to complete the commit, because Oracle performs the refresh operation as part of the commit process.

Restriction: This clause is not supported for materialized views containing object types.

ON DEMAND Clause   Specify ON DEMAND to indicate that the materialized view will be refreshed on demand by calling one of the three DBMS_MVIEW refresh procedures. If you omit both ON COMMIT and ON DEMAND, ON DEMAND is the default.

If you specify ON COMMIT or ON DEMAND, you cannot also specify START WITH or NEXT.

START WITH Clause   Specify a date expression for the first automatic refresh time.

NEXT Clause   Specify a date expression for calculating the interval between automatic refreshes.

Both the START WITH and NEXT values must evaluate to a time in the future. If you omit the START WITH value, Oracle determines the first automatic refresh time by evaluating the NEXT expression with respect to the creation time of the materialized view. If you specify a START WITH value but omit the NEXT value, Oracle refreshes the materialized view only once. If you omit both the START WITH and NEXT values, or if you omit the *create_mv_refresh_clause* entirely, Oracle does not automatically refresh the materialized view.

WITH PRIMARY KEY Clause   Specify WITH PRIMARY KEY to create a primary key materialized view. This is the default, and should be used in all cases except those described for WITH ROWID. Primary key materialized views allow materialized view master tables to be reorganized without affecting the eligibility of the materialized view for fast refresh. The master table must contain an enabled primary key constraint.

Restriction: You cannot specify this clause for an object materialized view. Oracle implicitly refreshes object materialized WITH OBJECT ID.

WITH ROWID Clause   Specify WITH ROWID to create a rowid materialized view. Rowid materialized views provide compatibility with master tables in releases of Oracle prior to 8.0.

You can also use rowid materialized views if the materialized view does not include all primary key columns of the master tables. Rowid materialized views must be based on a single remote table and cannot contain any of the following:

- Distinct or aggregate functions
- GROUP BY or CONNECT BY clauses
- Subqueries
- Joins
- Set operations

Rowid materialized views are not eligible for fast refreshed after a master table reorganization until a complete refresh has been performed.

Restriction: You cannot specify this clause for an object materialized view. Oracle implicitly refreshes object materialized WITH OBJECT ID.

USING ROLLBACK SEGMENT Clause   Specify the remote rollback segment to be used during materialized view refresh, where *rollback_segment* is the name of the rollback segment to be used.

DEFAULT: DEFAULT specifies that Oracle will choose automatically which rollback segment to use. If you specify DEFAULT, you cannot specify *rollback_segment.*

DEFAULT is most useful when modifying (rather than creating) a materialized view.

MASTER: MASTER specifies the remote rollback segment to be used at the remote master site for the individual materialized view.

LOCAL: LOCAL specifies the remote rollback segment to be used for the local refresh group that contains the materialized view.

If you do not specify MASTER or LOCAL, Oracle uses LOCAL by default. If you do not specify *rollback_segment,* Oracle automatically chooses the rollback segment to be used.

One master rollback segment is stored for each materialized view and is validated during materialized view creation and refresh. If the materialized view is complex, the master rollback segment, if specified, is ignored.

NEVER REFRESH Clause   Specify NEVER REFRESH to prevent the materialized view from being refreshed with any Oracle refresh mechanism or packaged procedure. Oracle will ignore any REFRESH statement on the materialized view issued from such a procedure. To reverse this clause, you must issue an ALTER MATERIALIZED VIEW ... REFRESH statement.

FOR UPDATE Clause   Specify FOR UPDATE to allow a subquery, primary key, object, or rowid materialized view to be updated. When used in conjunction with Advanced Replication, these updates will be propagated to the master.

QUERY REWRITE Clause   The QUERY REWRITE clause lets you specify whether the materialized view is eligible to be used for query rewrite.

ENABLE Clause   Specify ENABLE to enable the materialized view for query rewrite.
Restrictions:

- You can enable query rewrite only if all user-defined functions in the materialized view are DETERMINISTIC.

- You can enable query rewrite only if expressions in the statement are repeatable. For example, you cannot include CURRENT_TIME or USER, sequence values (such as the CURRVAL or NEXTVAL pseudocolumns), or the SAMPLE clause (which may sample different rows as the contents of the materialized view change).

NOTE
Query rewrite is disabled by default, so you must specify this clause to make materialized views eligible for query rewrite.

NOTE
Be sure to analyze the materialized view after you create it. Oracle needs the statistics generated by the ANALYZE operation to optimize query rewrite.

DISABLE Clause   Specify DISABLE to indicate that the materialized view is not eligible for use by query rewrite. However, a disabled materialized view can be refreshed.

AS subquery   Specify the defining subquery of the materialized view. When you create the materialized view, Oracle executes this subquery and places the results in the materialized view.

This subquery is any valid SQL subquery. However, not all queries are fast refreshable, nor are all subqueries eligible for query rewrite.

Notes on the Materialized View's Defining Subquery:

- Oracle does not execute the defining subquery immediately if you specify BUILD DEFERRED.

- Oracle recommends that you qualify each table and view in the FROM clause of the defining subquery of the materialized view with the schema containing it.

Restrictions on the Defining Subquery of a Materialized View:

- The defining subquery of a materialized view can select from tables, views, or materialized views owned by the user SYS, but you cannot enable QUERY REWRITE on such a materialized view.

- Materialized join views and materialized aggregate views with a GROUP BY clause cannot select from an index-organized table.

- Materialized views cannot contain columns of datatype LONG.

- You cannot create a materialized view log on a temporary table. Therefore, if the defining subquery references a temporary table, this materialized view will not be eligible for FAST refresh, nor can you specify the QUERY REWRITE clause in this statement.

- If the FROM clause of the defining subquery references another materialized view, then you must always refresh the materialized view referenced in the defining subquery before refreshing the materialized view you are creating in this statement.

If you are creating a materialized view enabled for query rewrite:

- The defining subquery cannot contain (either directly or through a view) references to ROWNUM, USER, SYSDATE, remote tables, sequences, or PL/SQL functions that write or read database or package state.

- Neither the materialized view nor the master tables of the materialized view can be remote.

If you want the materialized view to be eligible for fast refresh using a materialized view log, some additional restrictions may apply.

CREATE MATERIALIZED VIEW LOG

PURPOSE

Use the CREATE MATERIALIZED VIEW LOG statement to create a materialized view log, which is a table associated with the master table of a materialized view.

NOTE

The keyword SNAPSHOT is supported in place of MATERIALIZED VIEW for backward compatibility.

When DML changes are made to the master table's data, Oracle stores rows describing those changes in the materialized view log and then uses the materialized view log to refresh materialized views based on the master table. This process is called an incremental or **fast refresh**. Without a materialized view log, Oracle must reexecute the materialized view query to refresh the materialized view. This process is called a **complete refresh**. Usually, a fast refresh takes less time than a complete refresh.

A materialized view log is located in the master database in the same schema as the master table. You need only a single materialized view log for a master table. Oracle can use this materialized view log to perform fast refreshes for all fast-refreshable materialized views based on the master table.

To fast refresh a materialized join view (a materialized view containing a join), you must create a materialized view log for each of the tables referenced by the materialized view.

PREREQUISITES

The privileges required to create a materialized view log directly relate to the privileges necessary to create the underlying objects associated with a materialized view log.

- If you own the master table, you can create an associated materialized view log if you have the CREATE TABLE privilege.

- If you are creating a materialized view log for a table in another user's schema, you must have the CREATE ANY TABLE and COMMENT ANY TABLE privileges, as well as either the SELECT privilege for the master table or SELECT ANY TABLE.

In either case, the owner of the materialized view log must have sufficient quota in the tablespace intended to hold the materialized view log or must have the UNLIMITED TABLESPACE system privilege.

SYNTAX

create_materialized_vw_log::=

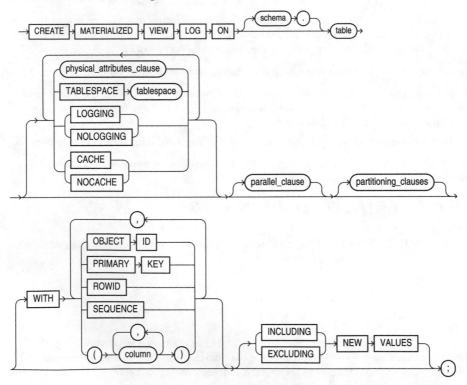

physical_attributes_clause::=

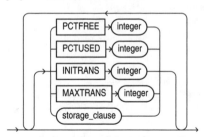

parallel_clause::=

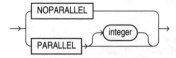

KEYWORDS AND PARAMETERS

schema   Specify the schema containing the materialized view log's master table. If you omit schema, Oracle assumes the master table is contained in your own schema. Oracle creates the materialized view log in the schema of its master table. You cannot create a materialized view log for a table in the schema of the user SYS.

table   Specify the name of the master table for which the materialized view log is to be created.
  Restriction: You cannot create a materialized view log for a temporary table or for a view.

physical_attributes_clause   Use the physical_attributes_clause to establish values for physical and storage characteristics for the materialized view log.

TABLESPACE Clause   Specify the tablespace in which the materialized view log is to be created. If you omit this clause, Oracle creates the materialized view log in the default tablespace of the schema of the materialized view log.

LOGGING | NOLOGGING   Specify either LOGGING or NOLOGGING to establish the logging characteristics for the materialized view log. The default is the logging characteristic of the tablespace in which the materialized view log resides.

CACHE | NOCACHE   For data that will be accessed frequently, CACHE specifies that the blocks retrieved for this log are placed at the *most recently used* end of the least recently used (LRU) list in the buffer cache when a full table scan is performed. This attribute is useful for small lookup tables.
  NOCACHE specifies that the blocks are placed at the *least recently used* end of the LRU list. The default is NOCACHE.

NOTE
*NOCACHE has no effect on materialized view logs for which
you specify KEEP in the* storage_clause.

parallel_clause   The parallel_clause lets you indicate whether parallel operations will be supported for the materialized view log.

NOTE
The syntax of the parallel_clause supersedes syntax appearing in earlier releases of Oracle. Superseded syntax is still supported for backward compatibility, but may result in slightly different behavior than that documented.

NOPARALLEL: Specify NOPARALLEL for serial execution. This is the default.

PARALLEL: Specify PARALLEL if you want Oracle to select a degree of parallelism equal to the number of CPUs available on all participating instances times the value of the PARALLEL_THREADS_PER_CPU initialization parameter.

PARALLEL *integer:* Specification of integer indicates the degree of parallelism, which is the number of parallel threads used in the parallel operation. Each parallel thread may use one or two parallel execution servers. Normally Oracle calculates the optimum degree of parallelism, so it is not necessary for you to specify integer.

partitioning_clauses   Use the partitioning_clauses to indicate that the materialized view log is partitioned on specified ranges of values or on a hash function. Partitioning of materialized view logs is the same as partitioning of tables, as described in "CREATE TABLE".

WITH Clause   Use the WITH clause to indicate whether the materialized view log should record the primary key, the rowid, object ID, or a combination of these row identifiers when rows in the master are changed. You can also use this clause to add a sequence to the materialized view log to provide additional ordering information for its records.

This clause also specifies whether the materialized view log records additional columns that might be referenced as **filter columns** (non-primary-key columns referenced by subquery materialized views) or **join columns** (non-primary-key columns that define a join in the subquery WHERE clause).

If you omit this clause, or if you specify the clause without PRIMARY KEY, ROWID, or OBJECT ID, then Oracle stores primary key values by default. However, Oracle does not store primary key values implicitly if you specify only OBJECT ID or ROWID at create time. A primary key log, created either explicitly or by default, performs additional checking on the primary key constraint.

OBJECT ID: Specify OBJECT ID to indicate that the system-generated or user-defined object identifier of every modified row should be recorded in the materialized view log.

Restriction: You can specify OBJECT ID only when creating a log on an object table, and you cannot specify it for storage tables.

PRIMARY KEY: Specify PRIMARY KEY to indicate that the primary key of all rows changed should be recorded in the materialized view log.

ROWID: Specify ROWID to indicate that the rowid of all rows changed should be recorded in the materialized view log.

SEQUENCE: Specify SEQUENCE to indicate that a sequence value providing additional ordering information should be recorded in the materialized view log. Sequence numbers are necessary to support fast refresh after some update scenarios.

column: Specify the columns whose values you want to be recorded in the materialized view log for all rows that are changed. Typically these columns are filter columns (non-primary-key columns referenced by materialized views) and join columns (non-primary-key columns that define a join in the WHERE clause of the subquery).

Restrictions on the WITH Clause:

- You can specify only one PRIMARY KEY, one ROWID, one OBJECT ID, and one column list for each materialized view log.

- Primary key columns are implicitly recorded in the materialized view log. Therefore, you cannot specify either of the following combinations if *column* contains one of the primary key columns:

```
WITH ... PRIMARY KEY ... (column)
WITH ... (column) ... PRIMARY KEY
WITH (column)
```

NEW VALUES Clause   The NEW VALUES clause lets you indicate whether Oracle saves both old and new values in the materialized view log.

INCLUDING: Specify INCLUDING to save both new and old values in the log. If this log is for a table on which you have a single-table materialized aggregate view, and if you want the materialized view to be eligible for fast refresh, you must specify INCLUDING.

EXCLUDING: Specify EXCLUDING to disable the recording of new values in the log. This is the default. You can use this clause to avoid the overhead of recording new values. However, do not use this clause if you have a fast-refreshable single-table materialized aggregate view defined on this table.

CREATE OUTLINE

PURPOSE

Use the CREATE OUTLINE statement to create a **stored outline**, which is a set of attributes used by the optimizer to generate an execution plan. You can then instruct the optimizer to use a set of outlines to influence the generation of execution plans whenever a particular SQL statement is issued, regardless of changes in factors that can affect optimization. You can also modify an outline so that it takes into account changes in these factors.

NOTE
The SQL statement issued subsequently must be an exact string match of the statement specified when creating the outline.

PREREQUISITES

To create a public or private outline, you must have the CREATE ANY OUTLINE system privilege. If you are creating a clone outline from a source outline, you must also have the SELECT_CATALOG_ROLE role.

To create a private outline, you must provide an outline editing table to hold the outline data in your schema by executing the DBMS_OUTLN_EDIT.CREATE_EDIT_TABLES procedure. You must have the EXECUTE privilege on the DBMS_OUTLN_EDIT package to execute this procedure.

You enable or disable the use of stored outlines dynamically for an individual session or for the system:

- Enable the USE_STORED_OUTLINES parameter to use public outlines
- Enable the USE_PRIVATE_OUTLINES parameter to use private stored outlines.

SYNTAX

create_outline::=

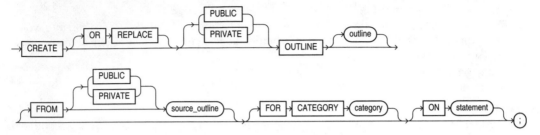

KEYWORDS AND PARAMETERS

OR REPLACE   Specify OR REPLACE to replace an existing outline with a new outline of the same name.

PUBLIC | PRIVATE   Specify PUBLIC if you are creating an outline for use by PUBLIC. This is the default. Specify PRIVATE to create an outline for private use by the current session only. The data of this outline is stored in the current schema.

NOTE
Before first creating a private outline, you must run the OUTLN_PKG.CREATE_EDIT_TABLES procedure to create the required outline tables and indexes in your schema.

outline   Specify the unique name to be assigned to the stored outline. If you do not specify *outline*, the system generates an outline name.

FROM ... source_outline Clause   Use the FROM clause to create a new outline by copying an existing one. By default, Oracle looks for *source_category* in the public area. If you specify PRIVATE, Oracle will look for the outline in the current schema.

   Restriction: If you specify the FROM clause, you cannot specify the ON clause.

FOR CATEGORY Clause   Specify an optional name used to group stored outlines. For example, you could specify a category of outlines for end-of-week use and another for end-of-quarter use. If you do not specify *category*, the outline is stored in the DEFAULT category.

ON Clause   Specify the SQL statement for which Oracle will create an outline when the statement is compiled. This clause is optional only if you are creating a copy of an existing outline using the FROM clause.

   You can specify any one of the following statements:

- SELECT
- DELETE
- UPDATE
- INSERT ... SELECT
- CREATE TABLE ... AS SELECT

Restrictions:

■ If you specify the ON clause, you cannot specify the FROM clause.

■ You cannot create an outline on a multitable INSERT statement.

NOTE
*You can specify multiple outlines for a single statement,
but each outline for the same statement must be in a
different category.*

CREATE PFILE

PURPOSE

Use the CREATE PFILE statement to export a binary server parameter file into a text initialization parameter file. Creating a text parameter file is a convenient way to get a listing of the current parameter settings being used by the database, and it lets you edit the file easily in a text editor and then convert it back into a server parameter file using the CREATE SPFILE statement.

Upon successful execution of this statement, Oracle creates a text parameter file on the server. In a Real Application Clusters environment, it will contain all parameter settings of all instances. It will also contain any comments that appeared on the same line with a parameter setting in the server parameter file.

PREREQUISITES

You must have the SYSDBA or the SYSOPER role to execute this statement. You can execute this statement either before or after instance startup.

SYNTAX

create_pfile::=

KEYWORDS AND PARAMETERS

pfile_name   Specify the name of the text parameter file you want to create. If you do not specify *pfile_name*, Oracle uses the platform-specific default initialization parameter file name.

spfile_name   Specify the name of the binary server parameter from which you want to create a text file.

■ If you specify *spfile_name*, the file must exist on the server. If the file does not reside in the default directory for server parameter files on your operating system, you must specify the full path.

■ If you do not specify *spfile_name*, Oracle looks in the default directory for server parameter files on your operating system, for the platform-specific default server parameter file name, and uses that file. If that file does not exist in the expected directory, Oracle returns an error.

CREATE PROFILE

PURPOSE

Use the CREATE PROFILE statement to create a **profile**, which is a set of limits on database resources. If you assign the profile to a user, that user cannot exceed these limits.

PREREQUISITES

To create a profile, you must have CREATE PROFILE system privilege. To specify resource limits for a user, you must:

- Enable resource limits dynamically with the ALTER SYSTEM statement or with the initialization parameter RESOURCE_LIMIT. (This parameter does not apply to password resources. Password resources are always enabled.)
- Create a profile that defines the limits using the CREATE PROFILE statement
- Assign the profile to the user using the CREATE USER or ALTER USER statement

SYNTAX

create_profile::=

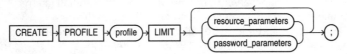

resource_parameters::=

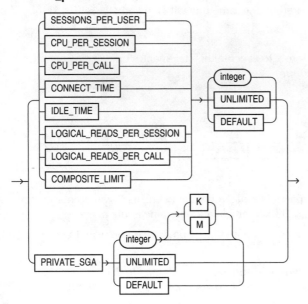

password_parameters::=

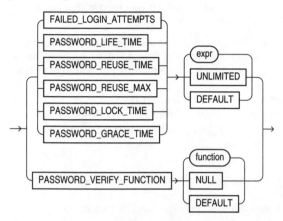

KEYWORDS AND PARAMETERS

profile Specify the name of the profile to be created. Use profiles to limit the database resources available to a user for a single call or a single session.

Oracle enforces resource limits in the following ways:

- If a user exceeds the CONNECT_TIME or IDLE_TIME session resource limit, Oracle rolls back the current transaction and ends the session. When the user process next issues a call, Oracle returns an error.

- If a user attempts to perform an operation that exceeds the limit for other session resources, Oracle aborts the operation, rolls back the current statement, and immediately returns an error. The user can then commit or roll back the current transaction, and must then end the session.

- If a user attempts to perform an operation that exceeds the limit for a single call, Oracle aborts the operation, rolls back the current statement, and returns an error, leaving the current transaction intact.

NOTE
You can use fractions of days for all parameters that limit time, with days as units. For example, 1 hour is 1/24 and 1 minute is 1/1440. You can specify resource limits for users regardless of whether the resource limits are enabled. However, Oracle does not enforce the limits until you enable them.

UNLIMITED   When specified with a resource parameter, UNLIMITED indicates that a user assigned this profile can use an unlimited amount of this resource. When specified with a password parameter, UNLIMITED indicates that no limit has been set for the parameter.

DEFAULT   Specify DEFAULT if you want to omit a limit for this resource in this profile. A user assigned this profile is subject to the limit for this resource specified in the DEFAULT profile. The DEFAULT profile initially defines unlimited resources. You can change those limits with the ALTER PROFILE statement.

Any user who is not explicitly assigned a profile is subject to the limits defined in the DEFAULT profile. Also, if the profile that is explicitly assigned to a user omits limits for some resources or specifies DEFAULT for some limits, the user is subject to the limits on those resources defined by the DEFAULT profile.

resource_parameters
SESSIONS_PER_USER: Specify the number of concurrent sessions to which you want to limit the user.

CPU_PER_SESSION: Specify the CPU time limit for a session, expressed in hundredth of seconds.

CPU_PER_CALL: Specify the CPU time limit for a call (a parse, execute, or fetch), expressed in hundredths of seconds.

CONNECT_TIME: Specify the total elapsed time limit for a session, expressed in minutes.

IDLE_TIME: Specify the permitted periods of continuous inactive time during a session, expressed in minutes. Long-running queries and other operations are not subject to this limit.

LOGICAL_READS_PER_SESSION: Specify the permitted number of data blocks read in a session, including blocks read from memory and disk.

LOGICAL_READS_PER_CALL: Specify the permitted the number of data blocks read for a call to process a SQL statement (a parse, execute, or fetch).

PRIVATE_SGA: Specify the amount of private space a session can allocate in the shared pool of the system global area (SGA), expressed in bytes. Use K or M to specify this limit in kilobytes or megabytes.

NOTE
This limit applies only if you are using Shared Server architecture. The private space for a session in the SGA includes private SQL and PL/SQL areas, but not shared SQL and PL/SQL areas.

COMPOSITE_LIMIT: Specify the total resource cost for a session, expressed in **service units**. Oracle calculates the total service units as a weighted sum of CPU_PER_SESSION, CONNECT_TIME, LOGICAL_READS_PER_SESSION, and PRIVATE_SGA.

If you specify *expr* for any of these parameters, the expression can be of any form except scalar subquery expression.

password_parameters
FAILED_LOGIN_ATTEMPTS: Specify the number of failed attempts to log in to the user account before the account is locked.

PASSWORD_LIFE_TIME: Specify the number of days the same password can be used for authentication. The password expires if it is not changed within this period, and further connections are rejected.

PASSWORD_REUSE_TIME: Specify the number of days before which a password cannot be reused. If you set PASSWORD_REUSE_TIME to an integer value, then you must set PASSWORD_REUSE_MAX to UNLIMITED.

PASSWORD_REUSE_MAX: Specify the number of password changes required before the current password can be reused. If you set PASSWORD_REUSE_MAX to an integer value, then you must set PASSWORD_REUSE_TIME to UNLIMITED.

PASSWORD_LOCK_TIME: Specify the number of days an account will be locked after the specified number of consecutive failed login attempts.

PASSWORD_GRACE_TIME: Specify the number of days after the grace period begins during which a warning is issued and login is allowed. If the password is not changed during the grace period, the password expires.

PASSWORD_VERIFY_FUNCTION: The PASSWORD_VERIFY_FUNCTION clause lets a PL/SQL password complexity verification script be passed as an argument to the CREATE PROFILE statement. Oracle provides a default script, but you can create your own routine or use third-party software instead.

- For *function*, specify the name of the password complexity verification routine.
- Specify NULL to indicate that no password verification is performed.

Restrictions on password parameters:

- If PASSWORD_REUSE_TIME is set to an integer value, PASSWORD_REUSE_MAX must be set to UNLIMITED. If PASSWORD_REUSE_MAX is set to an integer value, PASSWORD_REUSE_TIME must be set to UNLIMITED.

- If both PASSWORD_REUSE_TIME and PASSWORD_REUSE_MAX are set to UNLIMITED, then Oracle uses neither of these password resources.

- If PASSWORD_REUSE_MAX is set to DEFAULT and PASSWORD_REUSE_TIME is set to UNLIMITED, then Oracle uses the PASSWORD_REUSE_MAX value defined in the DEFAULT profile.

- If PASSWORD_REUSE_TIME is set to DEFAULT and PASSWORD_REUSE_MAX is set to UNLIMITED, then Oracle uses the PASSWORD_REUSE_TIME value defined in the DEFAULT profile.

- If both PASSWORD_REUSE_TIME and PASSWORD_REUSE_MAX are set to DEFAULT, then Oracle uses whichever value is defined in the DEFAULT profile.

CREATE ROLE

PURPOSE
Use the CREATE ROLE statement to create a **role**, which is a set of privileges that can be granted to users or to other roles. You can use roles to administer database privileges. You can add privileges to a role and then grant the role to a user. The user can then enable the role and exercise the privileges granted by the role.

A role contains all privileges granted to the role and all privileges of other roles granted to it. A new role is initially empty. You add privileges to a role with the GRANT statement.

When you create a role that is NOT IDENTIFIED or is IDENTIFIED EXTERNALLY or BY *password,* Oracle grants you the role with ADMIN OPTION. However, when you create a role IDENTIFIED GLOBALLY, Oracle does not grant you the role.

PREREQUISITES
You must have CREATE ROLE system privilege.

SYNTAX

create_role::=

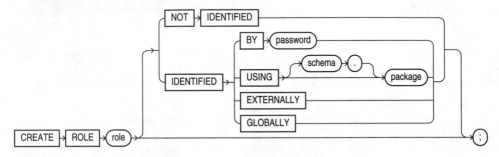

KEYWORDS AND PARAMETERS

role   Specify the name of the role to be created. Oracle recommends that the role contain at least one single-byte character regardless of whether the database character set also contains multibyte characters.

Some roles are defined by SQL scripts provided on your distribution media.

NOT IDENTIFIED Clause   Specify NOT IDENTIFIED to indicate that this role is authorized by the database and that no password is required to enable the role.

IDENTIFIED Clause   Use the IDENTIFIED clause to indicate that a user must be authorized by the specified method before the role is enabled with the SET ROLE statement.

BY password: The BY *password* clause lets you create a **local user** and indicates that the user must specify the password to Oracle when enabling the role. The password can contain only single-byte characters from your database character set regardless of whether this character set also contains multibyte characters.

USING *package*: The USING *package* clause lets you create an **application role**, which is a role that can be enabled only by applications using an authorized package. If you do not specify *schema*, Oracle assumes the package is in your own schema.

EXTERNALLY: Specify EXTERNALLY to create an **external user.** An external user must be authorized by an external service (such as an operating system or third-party service) before enabling the role.

Depending on the operating system, the user may have to specify a password to the operating system before the role is enabled.

GLOBALLY: Specify GLOBALLY to create a **global user.** A global user must be authorized to use the role by the enterprise directory service before the role is enabled with the SET ROLE statement, or at login.

If you omit both the NOT IDENTIFIED clause and the IDENTIFIED clause, the role defaults to NOT IDENTIFIED.

CREATE ROLLBACK SEGMENT

PURPOSE

Use the CREATE ROLLBACK SEGMENT statement to create a **rollback segment**, which is an object that Oracle uses to store data necessary to reverse, or undo, changes made by transactions.

The information in this section assumes that your database is running in rollback undo mode (the UNDO_MANAGEMENT initialization parameter is set to MANUAL or not set at all).

If your database is running in Automatic Undo Management mode (the UNDO_MANAGEMENT initialization parameter is set to AUTO), then user-created rollback segments are irrelevant. In this case, Oracle returns an error in response to any CREATE ROLLBACK SEGMENT or ALTER ROLLBACK SEGMENT statement. To suppress these errors, set the UNDO_SUPPRESS_ERRORS parameter to TRUE.

NOTE

To use objects in a tablespace other than the SYSTEM tablespace: (1) If you are running the database in rollback undo mode, at least one rollback segment (other than the SYSTEM rollback segment) must be online. (2) If you are running the database in Automatic Undo Management mode, at least one UNDO tablespace must be online.

PREREQUISITES

To create a rollback segment, you must have CREATE ROLLBACK SEGMENT system privilege.

SYNTAX

create_rollback_segment::=

KEYWORD AND PARAMETERS

PUBLIC   Specify PUBLIC to indicate that the rollback segment is public and is available to any instance. If you omit this clause, the rollback segment is private and is available only to the instance naming it in its initialization parameter ROLLBACK_SEGMENTS.

rollback_segment   Specify the name of the rollback segment to be created.

TABLESPACE   Use the TABLESPACE clause to identify the tablespace in which the rollback segment is created. If you omit this clause, Oracle creates the rollback segment in the SYSTEM tablespace.

   Restriction: You cannot create a rollback segment in a tablespace that is system managed (that is, during creation you specified EXTENT MANAGEMENT LOCAL AUTOALLOCATE).

NOTE
Tablespace can have multiple rollback segments. Generally, multiple rollback segments improve performance. The tablespace must be online for you to add a rollback segment to it.

NOTE
When you create a rollback segment, it is initially offline. To make it available for transactions by your Oracle instance, bring it online using the ALTER ROLLBACK SEGMENT statement. To bring it online automatically whenever you start up the database, add the segment's name to the value of the ROLLBACK_SEGMENTS initialization parameter.

storage_clause   The storage_clause lets you specify the characteristics for the rollback segment.

NOTE
The OPTIMAL parameter of the storage_clause is of particular interest, because it applies only to rollback segments.

NOTE
You cannot specify the PCTINCREASE parameter of the storage_clause with CREATE ROLLBACK SEGMENT.

CREATE SEQUENCE

PURPOSE
Use the CREATE SEQUENCE statement to create a **sequence**, which is a database object from which multiple users may generate unique integers. You can use sequences to automatically generate primary key values.

When a sequence number is generated, the sequence is incremented, independent of the transaction committing or rolling back. If two users concurrently increment the same sequence, the sequence numbers each user acquires may have gaps because sequence numbers are being generated by the other user. One user can never acquire the sequence number generated by another user. Once a sequence value is generated by one user, that user can continue to access that value regardless of whether the sequence is incremented by another user.

Sequence numbers are generated independently of tables, so the same sequence can be used for one or for multiple tables. It is possible that individual sequence numbers will appear to be skipped, because they were generated and used in a transaction that ultimately rolled back. Additionally, a single user may not realize that other users are drawing from the same sequence.

Once a sequence is created, you can access its values in SQL statements with the CURRVAL pseudocolumn (which returns the current value of the sequence) or the NEXTVAL pseudocolumn (which increments the sequence and returns the new value).

PREREQUISITES
To create a sequence in your own schema, you must have CREATE SEQUENCE privilege. To create a sequence in another user's schema, you must have CREATE ANY SEQUENCE privilege.

SYNTAX

create_sequence::=

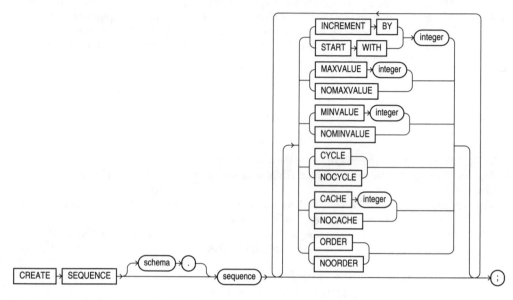

KEYWORDS AND PARAMETERS

schema   Specify the schema to contain the sequence. If you omit schema, Oracle creates the sequence in your own schema.

sequence   Specify the name of the sequence to be created.

If you specify none of the following clauses, you create an ascending sequence that starts with 1 and increases by 1 with no upper limit. Specifying only INCREMENT BY -1 creates a descending sequence that starts with -1 and decreases with no lower limit.

- **To create a sequence that increments without bound**, for ascending sequences, omit the MAXVALUE parameter or specify NOMAXVALUE. For descending sequences, omit the MINVALUE parameter or specify the NOMINVALUE.

- **To create a sequence that stops at a predefined limit**, for an ascending sequence, specify a value for the MAXVALUE parameter. For a descending sequence, specify a value for the MINVALUE parameter. Also specify the NOCYCLE. Any attempt to generate a sequence number once the sequence has reached its limit results in an error.

- **To create a sequence that restarts after reaching a predefined limit**, specify values for both the MAXVALUE and MINVALUE parameters. Also specify the CYCLE. If you do not specify MINVALUE, then it defaults to NOMINVALUE (that is, the value 1).

Sequence Parameters

INCREMENT BY: Specify the interval between sequence numbers. This integer value can be any positive or negative integer, but it cannot be 0. This value can have 28 or fewer digits. The absolute of this value must be less than the difference of MAXVALUE and MINVALUE. If this value is negative, then the sequence descends. If the increment is positive, then the sequence ascends. If you omit this clause, the interval defaults to 1.

START WITH: Specify the first sequence number to be generated. Use this clause to start an ascending sequence at a value greater than its minimum or to start a descending sequence at a value less than its maximum. For ascending sequences, the default value is the minimum value of the sequence. For descending sequences, the default value is the maximum value of the sequence. This integer value can have 28 or fewer digits.

NOTE
This value is not necessarily the value to which an ascending cycling sequence cycles after reaching its maximum or minimum value.

MAXVALUE: Specify the maximum value the sequence can generate. This integer value can have 28 or fewer digits. MAXVALUE must be equal to or greater than START WITH and must be greater than MINVALUE.

NOMAXVALUE: Specify NOMAXVALUE to indicate a maximum value of 10^{27} for an ascending sequence or -1 for a descending sequence. This is the default.

MINVALUE: Specify the minimum value of the sequence. This integer value can have 28 or fewer digits. MINVALUE must be less than or equal to START WITH and must be less than MAXVALUE.

NOMINVALUE: Specify NOMINVALUE to indicate a minimum value of 1 for an ascending sequence or -10^{26} for a descending sequence. This is the default.

CYCLE: Specify CYCLE to indicate that the sequence continues to generate values after reaching either its maximum or minimum value. After an ascending sequence reaches its maximum value, it generates its minimum value. After a descending sequence reaches its minimum, it generates its maximum.

NOCYCLE: Specify NOCYCLE to indicate that the sequence cannot generate more values after reaching its maximum or minimum value. This is the default.

CACHE: Specify how many values of the sequence Oracle preallocates and keeps in memory for faster access. This integer value can have 28 or fewer digits. The minimum value for this parameter is 2. For sequences that cycle, this value must be less than the number of values in the cycle. You cannot cache more values than will fit in a given cycle of sequence numbers. Therefore, the maximum value allowed for CACHE must be less than the value determined by the following formula:

$$(CEIL\ (MAXVALUE - MINVALUE))\ /\ ABS\ (INCREMENT)$$

If a system failure occurs, all cached sequence values that have not been used in committed DML statements are lost. The potential number of lost values is equal to the value of the CACHE parameter.

NOTE
Oracle Corporation recommends using the CACHE setting to enhance performance if you are using sequences in a Real Application Clusters environment.

NOCACHE: Specify NOCACHE to indicate that values of the sequence are not preallocated.

If you omit both CACHE and NOCACHE, Oracle caches 20 sequence numbers by default.

ORDER: Specify ORDER to guarantee that sequence numbers are generated in order of request. You may want to use this clause if you are using the sequence numbers as timestamps. Guaranteeing order is usually not important for sequences used to generate primary keys.

ORDER is necessary only to guarantee ordered generation if you are using Oracle with Real Application Clusters. If you are using exclusive mode, sequence numbers are always generated in order.

NOORDER: Specify NOORDER if you do not want to guarantee sequence numbers are generated in order of request. This is the default.

CREATE SPFILE

PURPOSE

Use the CREATE SPFILE statement to create a **server parameter file** from a client-side initialization parameter file. Server parameter files are binary files that exist only on the server and are called from client locations to start up the database.

Server parameter files let you make persistent changes to individual parameters. When you use a server parameter file, you can specify in an ALTER SYSTEM SET *parameter* statement that the new parameter value should be persistent. This means that the new value applies not only in the current instance, but also to any instances that are started up subsequently. Traditional client-side parameter files do not let you make persistent changes to parameter values.

To use a server parameter file when starting up the database, you must create it from a traditional text initialization parameter file using the CREATE SPFILE statement.

All instances in a Real Application Clusters environment must use the same server parameter file. However, when otherwise permitted, individual instances can have different settings of the same parameter within this one file. Instance-specific parameter definitions are specified as *SID.parameter = value*, where *SID* is the instance identifier.

The method of starting up the database with a server parameter file depends on whether you create a default or nondefault server parameter file.

PREREQUISITES

You must have the SYSDBA or the SYSOPER system privilege to execute this statement. You can execute this statement before or after instance startup. However, if you have already started an instance using *spfile_name*, you cannot specify the same *spfile_name* in this statement.

SYNTAX

create_spfile::=

KEYWORDS AND PARAMETERS

spfile_name   This clause lets you specify a name for the server parameter file you are creating.

■   If you do not specify spfile_name, Oracle uses the platform-specific default server parameter filename. If spfile_name already exists on the server, this statement will overwrite it. When using a default server parameter file, you start up the database without referring to the file by name.

■ If you do specify spfile_name, you are creating a nondefault server parameter file. In this case, to start up the database, you must first create a single-line traditional parameter file that points to the server parameter file, and then name the single-line file in your STARTUP command.

pfile_name   Specify the traditional initialization parameter file from which you want to create a server parameter file.

■ If you specify pfile_name, the parameter file must reside on the server. If it does not reside in the default directory for parameter files on your operating system, you must specify the full path.

■ If you do not specify pfile_name, Oracle looks in the default directory for parameter files on your operating system for the default parameter filename, and uses that file. If that file does not exist in the expected directory, Oracle returns an error.

NOTE
In a environment, you must first combine all instance parameter files into one file before specifying it in this statement to create a server parameter file. For information on accomplishing this step, see Oracle9i Real Application Clusters Installation and Configuration.

CREATE SYNONYM

PURPOSE
Use the CREATE SYNONYM statement to create a **synonym**, which is an alternative name for a table, view, sequence, procedure, stored function, package, materialized view, Java class schema object, or another synonym.

Synonyms provide both data independence and location transparency. Synonyms permit applications to function without modification regardless of which user owns the table or view and regardless of which database holds the table or view.

Table A-4 lists the SQL statements in which you can refer to synonyms.

PREREQUISITES
To create a private synonym in your own schema, you must have CREATE SYNONYM system privilege. To create a private synonym in another user's schema, you must have CREATE ANY SYNONYM system privilege. To create a PUBLIC synonym, you must have CREATE PUBLIC SYNONYM system privilege.

SYNTAX
create_synonym::=

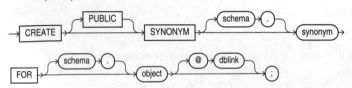

DML Statements	DDL Statements
SELECT	AUDIT
INSERT	NOAUDIT
UPDATE	GRANT
DELETE	REVOKE
EXPLAIN PLAN	COMMENT
LOCK TABLE	

TABLE A-4. *Using Synonyms*

KEYWORDS AND PARAMETERS

PUBLIC   Specify PUBLIC to create a public synonym. Public synonyms are accessible to all users. Oracle uses a public synonym only when resolving references to an object if the object is not prefaced by a schema and the object is not followed by a database link.

If you omit this clause, the synonym is private and is accessible only within its schema. A private synonym name must be unique in its schema.

schema   Specify the schema to contain the synonym. If you omit schema, Oracle creates the synonym in your own schema. You cannot specify a schema for the synonym if you have specified PUBLIC.

synonym   Specify the name of the synonym to be created.

CAUTION
The functional maximum length of the synonym name is 32 bytes. Names longer than 30 bytes are permitted for Java functionality only. If you specify a name longer than 30 bytes, Oracle encrypts the name and places a representation of the encryption in the data dictionary. The actual encryption is not accessible, and you cannot use either your original specification or the data dictionary representation as the synonym name.

FOR Clause   Specify the object for which the synonym is created. If you do not qualify object with *schema*, Oracle assumes that the schema object is in your own schema. The schema object can be of the following types:

- Table or object table
- View or object view
- Sequence
- Stored procedure, function, or package
- Materialized view

- Java class schema object
- Synonym

The schema object need not currently exist and you need not have privileges to access the object.
Restrictions:

- The schema object cannot be contained in a package.
- You cannot create a synonym for an object type.

dblink   You can specify a complete or partial database link to create a synonym for a schema object on a remote database where the object is located. If you specify dblink and omit schema, the synonym refers to an object in the schema specified by the database link. Oracle Corporation recommends that you specify the schema containing the object in the remote database.

If you omit dblink, Oracle assumes the object is located on the local database.

Restriction: You cannot specify dblink for a Java class synonym.

CREATE TABLE

PURPOSE
Use the CREATE TABLE statement to create one of the following types of tables:

- A **relational table** is the basic structure to hold user data.
- An **object table** is a table that uses an object type for a column definition. An object table is a table explicitly defined to hold object instances of a particular type.

You can also create an object type and then use it in a column when creating a relational table.

Tables are created with no data unless a query is specified. You can add rows to a table with the INSERT statement. After creating a table, you can define additional columns, partitions, and integrity constraints with the ADD clause of the ALTER TABLE statement. You can change the definition of an existing column or partition with the MODIFY clause of the ALTER TABLE statement.

PREREQUISITES
To create a **relational table** in your own schema, you must have the CREATE TABLE system privilege. To create a table in another user's schema, you must have CREATE ANY TABLE system privilege. Also, the owner of the schema to contain the table must have either space quota on the tablespace to contain the table or UNLIMITED TABLESPACE system privilege.

In addition to the table privileges above, to create an **object table** (or a relational table with an object type column), the owner of the table must have the EXECUTE object privilege in order to access all types referenced by the table, or you must have the EXECUTE ANY TYPE system privilege. These privileges must be granted explicitly and not acquired through a role.

Additionally, if the table owner intends to grant access to the table to other users, the owner must have been granted the EXECUTE privileges on the referenced types with the GRANT OPTION, or have the EXECUTE ANY TYPE system privilege with the ADMIN OPTION. Without these privileges, the table owner has insufficient privileges to grant access to the table to other users.

To enable a UNIQUE or PRIMARY KEY constraint, you must have the privileges necessary to create an index on the table. You need these privileges because Oracle creates an index on the columns of the unique or primary key in the schema containing the table.

To create an external table, you must have the READ object privilege on the directory in which the external data resides.

SYNTAX

create_table::=

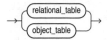

relational_table::=

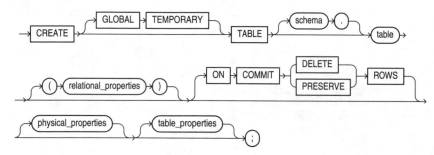

relational_properties::=

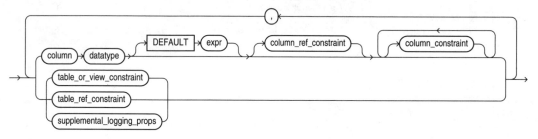

object_table::=

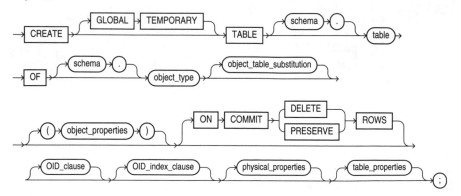

object_table_substitution::=

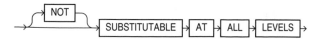

object_properties::=

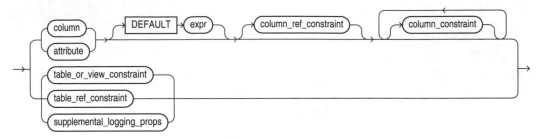

OID_clause::=

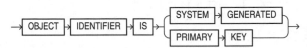

OID_index_clause::=

physical_properties::=

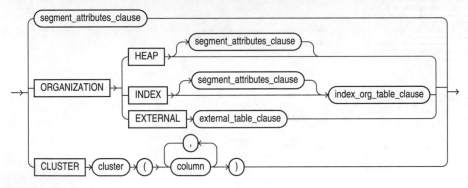

table_properties::=

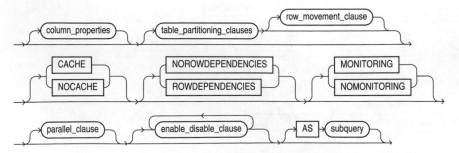

column_properties::=

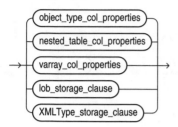

object_type_col_properties::=

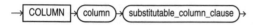

substitutable_column_clause::=

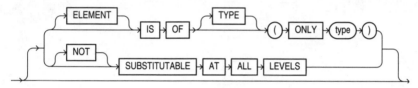

nested_table_col_properties::=

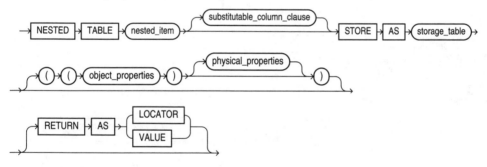

varray_col_properties::=

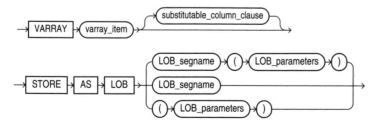

LOB_storage_clause::=

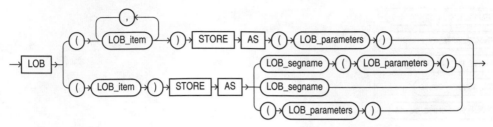

LOB_parameters::=

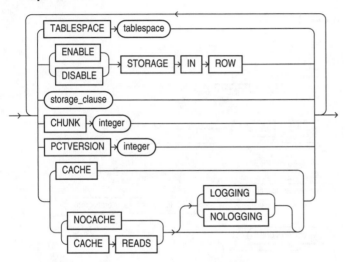

xmltype_storage_clause::=

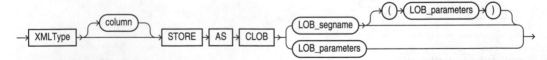

segment_attributes_clause::=

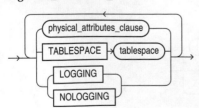

row_movement_clause::=

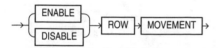

physical_attributes_clause::=

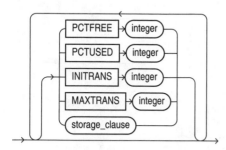

index_org_table_clause::=

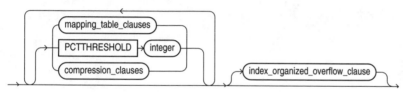

mapping_table_clauses::=

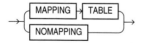

compression_clauses::=

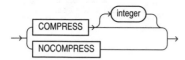

index_org_overflow_clause::=

supplemental_logging_props::=

external_table_clause::=

external_data_properties::=

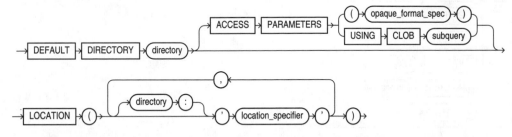

table_partitioning_clauses::=

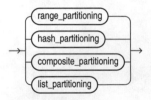

range_partitioning::=

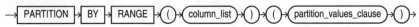

composite_partitioning::=

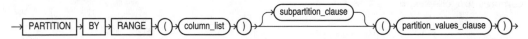

partition_values_clause::=

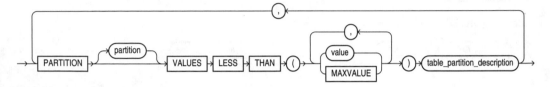

list_partitioning::=

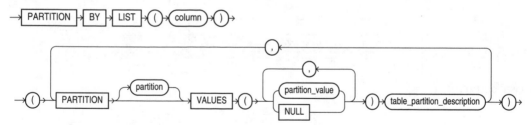

table_partition_description::=

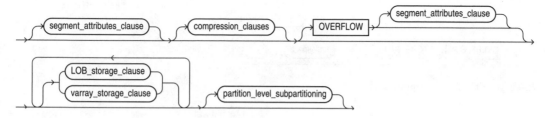

subpartition_clause::=

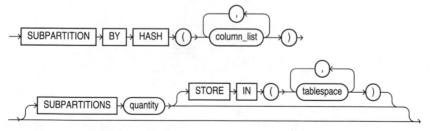

partition_level_subpartition::=

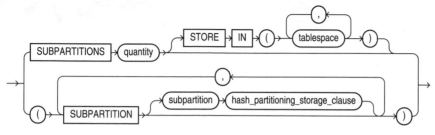

hash_partitioning::=

individual_hash_partitions::=

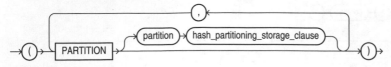

hash_partitions_by_quantity::=

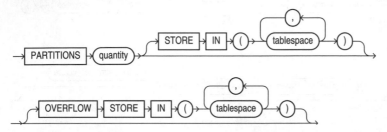

hash_partitioning_storage::=

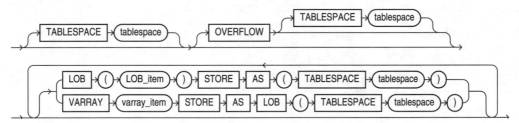

parallel_clause::=

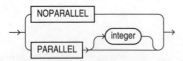

enable_disable_clause::=

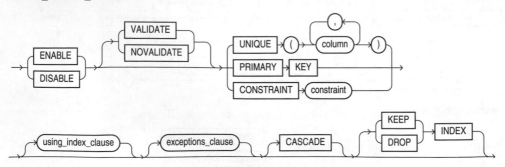

using_index_clause::=

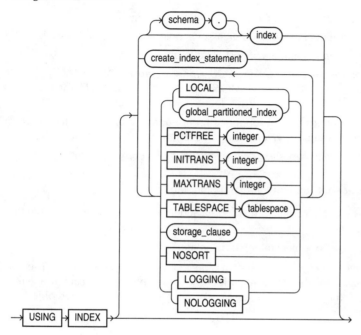

exceptions_clause::=

global_partitioned_index::=

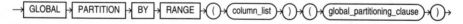

global_partitioning_clause::=

KEYWORDS AND PARAMETERS

GLOBAL TEMPORARY   Specify GLOBAL TEMPORARY to indicate that the table is temporary and that its definition is visible to all sessions. The data in a temporary table is visible only to the session that inserts the data into the table.

A temporary table has a definition that persists the same as the definitions of regular tables, but it contains either **session-specific** or **transaction-specific** data. You specify whether the data is session- or transaction-specific with the ON COMMIT keywords.

Restrictions:

- Temporary tables cannot be partitioned, clustered, or index organized.
- You cannot specify any referential integrity (foreign key) constraints on temporary tables.
- Temporary tables cannot contain columns of nested table or varray type.
- You cannot specify the following clauses of the *LOB_storage_clause*: TABLESPACE, *storage_clause*, LOGGING or NOLOGGING, MONITORING or NOMONITORING, or *LOB_index_clause*.
- Parallel DML and parallel queries are not supported for temporary tables. (Parallel hints are ignored. Specification of the *parallel_clause* returns an error.)
- You cannot specify the *segment_attributes_clause, nested_table_col_properties,* or *parallel_clause.*
- Distributed transactions are not supported for temporary tables.

schema   Specify the schema to contain the table. If you omit schema, Oracle creates the table in your own schema.

table   Specify the name of the table (or object table) to be created.

object_table   The OF clause lets you explicitly create an object table of type object_type. The columns of an object table correspond to the top-level attributes of type object_type. Each row will contain an object instance, and each instance will be assigned a unique, system-generated object identifier (OID) when a row is inserted. If you omit schema, Oracle creates the object table in your own schema.

You can reference objects residing in an object table.

object_table_substitution   Use the object_table_substitution clause to specify whether row objects corresponding to subtypes can be inserted into this object table.

NOT SUBSTITUTABLE AT ALL LEVELS: NOT SUBSTITUTABLE AT ALL LEVELS indicates that the object table being created is not substitutable. In addition, substitution is disabled for all embedded object attributes and elements of embedded nested tables and arrays. The default is SUBSTITUTABLE AT ALL LEVELS.

relational_properties   The relational properties describe the components of a relational table.

column   Specify the name of a column of the table.

If you also specify AS subquery, you can omit column and datatype unless you are creating an index-organized table. If you specify AS subquery when creating an index-organized table, you must specify column, and you must omit datatype.

The absolute maximum number of columns in a table is 1000. However, when you create an object table (or a relational table with columns of object, nested table, varray, or REF type), Oracle maps the columns of the user-defined types to relational columns, creating in effect "hidden columns" that count toward the 1000-column limit.

datatype   Specify the datatype of a column.

NOTE
You can omit datatype under these conditions:
(1) If you also specify AS subquery. (If you are creating an
index-organized table and you specify AS subquery, you
must omit the datatype.) (2) If the statement also designates
the column as part of a foreign key in a referential integrity
constraint. (Oracle automatically assigns to the column
the datatype of the corresponding column of the referenced
key of the referential integrity constraint.)

Restrictions:

■ You cannot specify a LOB column or a column of type VARRAY for a hash-partitioned
index-organized table. The datatypes for nonpartitioned and range-partitioned index-
organized tables are not restricted.

■ You can specify a column of type ROWID, but Oracle does not guarantee that the values
in such columns are valid rowids.

DEFAULT   The DEFAULT clause lets you specify a value to be assigned to the column if a
subsequent INSERT statement omits a value for the column. The datatype of the expression must
match the datatype of the column. The column must also be long enough to hold this expression.

The DEFAULT expression can include any SQL function as long as the function does not return
a literal argument, a column reference, or a nested function invocation.

Restrictions: A DEFAULT expression cannot contain references to PL/SQL functions or to
other columns, the pseudocolumns LEVEL, PRIOR, and ROWNUM, or date constants that are
not fully specified.

table_ref_constraint and column_ref_constraint   These clauses let you further describe a
column of type REF. The only difference between these clauses is that you specify table_ref from
the table level, so you must identify the REF column or attribute you are defining. You specify
column_ref after you have already identified the REF column or attribute.

column_constraint   Use the column_constraint to define an integrity constraint as part of the
column definition.

You can create UNIQUE, PRIMARY KEY, and REFERENCES constraints on scalar attributes of
object type columns. You can also create NOT NULL constraints on object type columns, and
CHECK constraints that reference object type columns or any attribute of an object type column.

table_or_view_constraint   Use the table_or_view_constraint to define an integrity constraint as
part of the table definition.

NOTE
You must specify a PRIMARY KEY constraint for an
index-organized table, and it cannot be DEFERRABLE.

object_properties   The properties of object tables are essentially the same as those of relational
tables. However, instead of specifying columns, you specify attributes of the object.

For attribute, specify the qualified column name of an item in an object.

ON COMMIT   The ON COMMIT clause is relevant only if you are creating a temporary table.
This clause specifies whether the data in the temporary table persists for the duration of a
transaction or a session.

DELETE ROWS: Specify DELETE ROWS for a transaction-specific temporary table (this is the default). Oracle will truncate the table (delete all its rows) after each commit.

PRESERVE ROWS: Specify PRESERVE ROWS for a session-specific temporary table. Oracle will truncate the table (delete all its rows) when you terminate the session.

OID_clause   The OID_clause lets you specify whether the object identifier (OID) of the object table should be system generated or should be based on the primary key of the table. The default is SYSTEM GENERATED.

Restrictions:

- You cannot specify OBJECT IDENTIFIER IS PRIMARY KEY unless you have already specified a PRIMARY KEY constraint for the table.

- You cannot specify this clause for a nested table.

NOTE
A primary key OID is locally (but not necessarily globally) unique. If you require a globally unique identifier, you must ensure that the primary key is globally unique.

OID_index_clause   This clause is relevant only if you have specified the OID_clause as SYSTEM GENERATED. It specifies an index, and optionally its storage characteristics, on the hidden object identifier column.

For index, specify the name of the index on the hidden system-generated object identifier column. If you omit index, Oracle generates a name.

physical_properties   The physical properties relate to the treatment of extents and segments and to the storage characteristics of the table.

segment_attributes_clause

physical_attributes_clause: The physical_attributes_clause lets you specify the value of the PCTFREE, PCTUSED, INITRANS, and MAXTRANS parameters and the storage characteristics of the table.

- For a nonpartitioned table, each parameter and storage characteristic you specify determines the actual physical attribute of the segment associated with the table.

- For partitioned tables, the value you specify for the parameter or storage characteristic is the default physical attribute of the segments associated with all partitions specified in this CREATE statement (and in subsequent ALTER TABLE ... ADD PARTITION statements), unless you explicitly override that value in the PARTITION clause of the statement that creates the partition.

PCTFREE integer: Specify the percentage of space in each data block of the table, object table OID index, or partition reserved for future updates to the table's rows. The value of PCTFREE must be a value from 0 to 99. A value of 0 means that the entire block can be filled by inserts of new rows. The default value is 10. This value reserves 10% of each block for updates to existing rows and allows inserts of new rows to fill a maximum of 90% of each block.

PCTFREE has the same function in the PARTITION description and in the statements that create and alter clusters, indexes, materialized views, and materialized view logs. The combination of PCTFREE and PCTUSED determines whether new rows will be inserted into existing data blocks or into new blocks.

PCTUSED integer: Specify the minimum percentage of used space that Oracle maintains for each data block of the table, object table OID index, or index-organized table overflow data segment. A block becomes a candidate for row insertion when its used space falls below PCTUSED. PCTUSED is specified as a positive integer from 0 to 99 and defaults to 40.

PCTUSED has the same function in the PARTITION description and in the statements that create and alter clusters, materialized views, and materialized view logs.

PCTUSED is not a valid table storage characteristic for an index-organized table (ORGANIZATION INDEX).

The sum of PCTFREE and PCTUSED must be equal to or less than 100. You can use PCTFREE and PCTUSED together to utilize space within a table more efficiently.

INITRANS integer: Specify the initial number of transaction entries allocated within each data block allocated to the table, object table OID index, partition, LOB index segment, or overflow data segment. This value can range from 1 to 255 and defaults to 1. In general, you should not change the INITRANS value from its default.

Each transaction that updates a block requires a transaction entry in the block. The size of a transaction entry depends on your operating system.

This parameter ensures that a minimum number of concurrent transactions can update the block and helps avoid the overhead of dynamically allocating a transaction entry.

The INITRANS parameter serves the same purpose in the PARTITION description, clusters, indexes, materialized views, and materialized view logs as in tables. The minimum and default INITRANS value for a cluster or index is 2, rather than 1.

MAXTRANS integer: Specify the maximum number of concurrent transactions that can update a data block allocated to the table, object table OID index, partition, LOB index segment, or index-organized overflow data segment. This limit does not apply to queries. This value can range from 1 to 255 and the default is a function of the data block size. You should not change the MAXTRANS value from its default.

If the number of concurrent transactions updating a block exceeds the INITRANS value, Oracle dynamically allocates transaction entries in the block until either the MAXTRANS value is exceeded or the block has no more free space.

The MAXTRANS parameter serves the same purpose in the PARTITION description, clusters, materialized views, and materialized view logs as in tables.

storage_clause: The storage_clause lets you specify storage characteristics for the table, object table OID index, partition, LOB data segment, LOB index segment, or index-organized table overflow data segment. This clause has performance ramifications for large tables. Storage should be allocated to minimize dynamic allocation of additional space.

TABLESPACE: Specify the tablespace in which Oracle creates the table, object table OID index, partition, LOB data segment, LOB index segment, or index-organized table overflow data segment. If you omit TABLESPACE, then Oracle creates that item in the default tablespace of the owner of the schema containing the table.

For heap-organized tables with one or more LOB columns, if you omit the TABLESPACE clause for LOB storage, Oracle creates the LOB data and index segments in the tablespace where the table is created.

However, for an index-organized table with one or more LOB columns, if you omit TABLESPACE, the LOB data and index segments are created in the tablespace in which the primary key index segment of the index-organized table is created.

For nonpartitioned tables, the value specified for TABLESPACE is the actual physical attribute of the segment associated with the table. For partitioned tables, the value specified for TABLESPACE is the default physical attribute of the segments associated with all partitions specified in the CREATE statement (and on subsequent ALTER TABLE ... ADD PARTITION statements), unless you specify TABLESPACE in the PARTITION description.

Restrictions: You cannot specify a tablespace with automatic segment-space management if table contains any LOB columns.

LOGGING | NOLOGGING: Specify whether the creation of the table (and any indexes required because of constraints), partition, or LOB storage characteristics will be logged in the redo log file (LOGGING) or not (NOLOGGING).The logging attribute of the table is independent of that of its indexes.

This attribute also specifies whether subsequent Direct Loader (SQL*Loader) and direct-path INSERT operations against the table, partition, or LOB storage are logged (LOGGING) or not logged (NOLOGGING).

For a table or table partition, if you omit this clause, the logging attribute of the table or table partition defaults to the logging attribute of the tablespace in which it resides.

For LOBs, if you omit this clause,

- If you specify CACHE, then LOGGING is used (because you cannot have CACHE NOLOGGING).
- If you specify NOCACHE or CACHE READS, the logging attribute defaults to the logging attribute of the tablespace in which it resides.

NOLOGGING does not apply to LOBs that are stored inline with row data. That is, if you specify NOLOGGING for LOBs with values less than 4000 bytes and you have not disabled STORAGE IN ROW, Oracle ignores the NOLOGGING specification and treats the LOB data the same as other table data.

For nonpartitioned tables, the value specified for LOGGING is the actual physical attribute of the segment associated with the table. For partitioned tables, the logging attribute value specified is the default physical attribute of the segments associated with all partitions specified in the CREATE statement (and in subsequent ALTER TABLE ... ADD PARTITION statements), unless you specify the logging attribute in the PARTITION description.

In NOLOGGING mode, data is modified with minimal logging (to mark new extents INVALID and to record dictionary changes). When applied during media recovery, the extent invalidation records mark a range of blocks as logically corrupt, because the redo data is not fully logged. Therefore, if you cannot afford to lose this table, you should take a backup after the NOLOGGING operation.

The size of a redo log generated for an operation in NOLOGGING mode is significantly smaller than the log generated in LOGGING mode.

If the database is run in ARCHIVELOG mode, media recovery from a backup made before the LOGGING operation restores the table. However, media recovery from a backup made before the NOLOGGING operation does not restore the table.

RECOVERABLE | UNRECOVERABLE: These keywords are deprecated and have been replaced with LOGGING and NOLOGGING, respectively. Although RECOVERABLE and UNRECOVERABLE are supported for backward compatibility, Oracle Corporation strongly recommends that you use the LOGGING and NOLOGGING keywords.

Restrictions:

- You cannot specify RECOVERABLE for partitioned tables or LOB storage characteristics.
- You cannot specify UNRECOVERABLE for a partitioned or index-organized tables.
- You can specify UNRECOVERABLE only with AS subquery.

ORGANIZATION   The ORGANIZATION clause lets you specify the order in which the data rows of the table are stored.

HEAP: HEAP indicates that the data rows of table are stored in no particular order. This is the default.

INDEX: INDEX indicates that table is created as an index-organized table. In an index-organized table, the data rows are held in an index defined on the primary key for the table.

EXTERNAL: EXTERNAL indicates that table is a read-only table located outside the database.

index_org_table_clause   Use the index_org_table_clause to create an index-organized table. Oracle maintains the table rows (both primary key column values and nonkey column values) in an index built on the primary key. Index-organized tables are therefore best suited for primary key-based access and manipulation. An index-organized table is an alternative to:

- A nonclustered table indexed on the primary key by using the CREATE INDEX statement

- A clustered table stored in an indexed cluster that has been created using the CREATE CLUSTER statement that maps the primary key for the table to the cluster key

If an index-organized table is partitioned and contains LOB columns, you should specify the index_org_table_clause first, then the LOB_storage_clause, and then the appropriate table_partitioning_clauses.

Restrictions:

- You cannot specify a column of type ROWID for an index-organized table.

- You cannot specify the composite_partitioning_clause for an index-organized table.

NOTE
You must specify a primary key for an index-organized table, because the primary key uniquely identifies a row. The primary key cannot be DEFERRABLE. Use the primary key instead of the rowid for directly accessing index-organized rows.

PCTTHRESHOLD integer: Specify the percentage of space reserved in the index block for an index-organized table row. PCTTHRESHOLD must be large enough to hold the primary key. All trailing columns of a row, starting with the column that causes the specified threshold to be exceeded, are stored in the overflow segment. PCTTHRESHOLD must be a value from 1 to 50. If you do not specify PCTTHRESHOLD, the default is 50.

Restriction: You cannot specify PCTTHRESHOLD for individual partitions of an index-organized table.

mapping_table_clause: Specify MAPPING TABLE to instruct Oracle to create a mapping of local to physical ROWIDs and store them in a heap-organized table. This mapping is needed in order to create a bitmap index on the index-organized table.

Oracle creates the mapping table in the same tablespace as its parent index-organized table. You cannot query, perform DML operations on, or modify the storage characteristics of the mapping table.

Restriction: You cannot specify this clause for a partitioned index-organized table.

compression_clauses: The compression_clauses lets you enable or disable key compression for index-organized tables.

- Specify COMPRESS to enable key compression, which eliminates repeated occurrence of primary key column values in index-organized tables. Use integer to specify the prefix length (number of prefix columns to compress).

  - The valid range of prefix length values is from 1 to the number of primary key columns minus 1. The default prefix length is the number of primary key columns minus 1.

Restriction: At the partition level, you can specify COMPRESS, but you cannot specify the prefix length with integer.

■ Specify NOCOMPRESS to disable key compression in index-organized tables. This is the default.

index_org_overflow_clause: The index_org_overflow_clause lets you instruct Oracle that index-organized table data rows exceeding the specified threshold are placed in the data segment specified in this clause.

■ When you create an index-organized table, Oracle evaluates the maximum size of each column to estimate the largest possible row. If an overflow segment is needed but you have not specified OVERFLOW, Oracle raises an error and does not execute the CREATE TABLE statement. This checking function guarantees that subsequent DML operations on the index-organized table will not fail because an overflow segment is lacking.

■ All physical attributes and storage characteristics you specify in this clause after the OVERFLOW keyword apply only to the overflow segment of the table. Physical attributes and storage characteristics for the index-organized table itself, default values for all its partitions, and values for individual partitions must be specified before this keyword.

■ If the index-organized table contains one or more LOB columns, the LOBs will be stored out-of-line unless you specify OVERFLOW, even if they would otherwise be small enough be to stored inline.

■ If table is partitioned, Oracle equipartitions the overflow data segments with the primary key index segments.

INCLUDING *column_name:* Specify a column at which to divide an index-organized table row into index and overflow portions. The primary key columns are always stored in the index. column_name can be either the last primary-key column or any non-primary-key column. All non-primary-key columns that follow column_name are stored in the overflow data segment.

Restriction: You cannot specify this clause for individual partitions of an index-organized table.

NOTE

If an attempt to divide a row at column_name causes the size of the index portion of the row to exceed the PCTTHRESHOLD value (either specified or default), Oracle breaks up the row based on the PCTTHRESHOLD value.

supplemental_logging_props   The supplemental_logging_props clause lets you instruct Oracle to put additional data into the log stream to support log-based tools.

external_table_clause   Use the external_table_clause to create an external table, which is a read-only table whose metadata is stored in the database but whose data in stored outside database. External tables let you query data without first loading it into the database, among other capabilities.

Because external tables have no data in the database, you define them with a small subset of the clauses normally available when creating tables.

■ Within the relational_properties clause, you can specify only column, datatype, and column_constraint. Further, the only constraints valid for an external table are NULL, NOT NULL, and CHECK constraints.

- Within the physical_properties_clause, you can specify only the organization of the table (ORGANIZATION EXTERNAL external_table_clause).
- Within the table_properties clause, you can specify only the parallel_clause and the enable_disable clause:
  - The parallel_clause lets you parallelize subsequent queries on the external data.
  - The enable_disable clause lets you either enable or disable a NULL, NOT NULL, or CHECK constraint. You can specify only ENABLE or DISABLE, and CONSTRAINT constraint_name. No other parts of this clause are permitted.

Restrictions on External Tables:

- No other clauses are permitted in the same CREATE TABLE statement if you specify the external_table_clause.
- An external table cannot be a temporary table.

TYPE: TYPE access_driver_type indicates the access driver of the external table. The access driver is the API that interprets the external data for the database. If you do not specify TYPE, Oracle uses the default access driver, ORACLE_LOADER.

DEFAULT DIRECTORY: DEFAULT DIRECTORY lets you specify one or more default directory objects corresponding to directories on the file system where the external data sources may reside. Default directories can also be used by the access driver to store auxiliary files such as error logs. Multiple default directories are permitted to facilitate load balancing on multiple disk drives.

ACCESS PARAMETERS: The optional ACCESS PARAMETERS clause lets you assign values to the parameters of the specific access driver for this external table:

- The opaque_format_spec lets you list the parameters and their values. Please refer to *Oracle9i Database Utilities* for information on how to specify values for the opaque_format_spec.
- USING CLOB subquery lets you derive the parameters and their values through a subquery. The subquery cannot contain any set operators or an ORDER BY clause. It must return one row containing a single item of datatype CLOB.

Whether you specify the parameters in an opaque_format_spec or derive them using a subquery, Oracle does not interpret anything in this clause. It is up to the access driver to interpret this information in the context of the external data.

LOCATION: The LOCATION clause lets you specify one external locator for each external data source. Usually the location_specifier is a file, but it need not be. Oracle does not interpret this clause. It is up to the access driver to interpret this information in the context of the external data.

REJECT LIMIT: The REJECT LIMIT clause lets you specify how many conversion errors can occur during a query of the external data before an Oracle error is returned and the query is aborted. The default value is 0.

CLUSTER Clause   The CLUSTER clause indicates that the table is to be part of *cluster*. The columns listed in this clause are the table columns that correspond to the cluster's columns. Generally, the cluster columns of a table are the column or columns that make up its primary key or a portion of its primary key.

Specify one column from the table for each column in the cluster key. The columns are matched by position, not by name.

A clustered table uses the cluster's space allocation. Therefore, do not use the PCTFREE, PCTUSED, INITRANS, or MAXTRANS parameters, the TABLESPACE clause, or the *storage_clause* with the CLUSTER clause.

Restrictions:

■ Object tables and tables containing LOB columns cannot be part of a cluster.

■ You cannot specify CLUSTER with either ROWDEPENDENCIES or NOROWDEPENDENCIES unless the cluster has been created with the same ROWDEPENDENCIES or NOROWDEPENDENCIES setting.

table_properties

column_properties   Use the column_properties clauses to specify the storage attributes of a column.

object_type_col_properties   The object_type_col_properties determine storage characteristics of an object column or attribute or an element of a collection column or attribute.

    column: For column, specify an object column or attribute.

    substitutable_column_clause: The substitutable_column_clause indicates whether object columns or attributes in the same hierarchy are substitutable for each other. You can specify that a column is of a particular type, or whether it can contain instances of its subtypes, or both.

■ If you specify ELEMENT, you constrain the element type of a collection column or attribute to a subtype of its declared type.

■ The IS OF [TYPE] (ONLY type) clause constrains the type of the object column to a subtype of its declared type.

■ NOT SUBSTITUTABLE AT ALL LEVELS indicates that the object column cannot hold instances corresponding to any of its subtypes. Also, substitution is disabled for any embedded object attributes and elements of embedded nested tables and varrays. The default is SUBSTITUTABLE AT ALL LEVELS.

Restrictions on the substitutable_column_clause:

■ You can specify this clause only for top-level object columns, not for attributes of object columns.

■ For a collection type column, the only part of this clause you can specify is [NOT] SUBSTITUTABLE AT ALL LEVELS.

LOB_storage_clause   The LOB_storage_clause lets you specify the storage attributes of LOB data segments.

■ For a nonpartitioned table (that is, when specified in the physical_properties clause without any of the partitioning clauses), this clause specifies the table's storage attributes of LOB data segments.

■ For a partitioned table specified at the table level (that is, when specified in the physical_properties clause along with one of the partitioning clauses), this clause specifies the default storage attributes for LOB data segments associated with each partition or subpartition. These storage attributes apply to all partitions or subpartitions unless overridden by a LOB_storage_clause at the partition or subpartition level.

- For an individual partition of a partitioned table (that is, when specified as part of a table_partition_description), this clause specifies the storage attributes of the data segments of the partition or the default storage attributes of any subpartitions of the partition. A partition-level LOB_storage_clause overrides a table-level LOB_storage_clause.

- For an individual subpartition of a partitioned table (that is, when specified as part of a subpartition_clause), this clause specifies the storage attributes of the data segments of the subpartition. A subpartition-level LOB_storage_clause overrides both partition-level and table-level LOB_storage_clauses.

Restriction: You cannot specify the LOB_index_clause if table is partitioned.

LOB_item: Specify the LOB column name or LOB object attribute for which you are explicitly defining tablespace and storage characteristics that are different from those of the table. Oracle automatically creates a system-managed index for each LOB_item you create.

LOB_segname: Specify the name of the LOB data segment. You cannot use LOB_segname if you specify more than one LOB_item.

LOB_parameters: The LOB_parameters clause lets you specify various elements of LOB storage.

- ENABLE STORAGE IN ROW: If you enable storage in row, the LOB value is stored in the row (inline) if its length is less than approximately 4000 bytes minus system control information. This is the default.

  Restriction: For an index-organized table, you cannot specify this parameter unless you have specified an OVERFLOW segment in the index_org_table_clause.

- DISABLE STORAGE IN ROW: If you disable storage in row, the LOB value is stored out of line (outside of the row) regardless of the length of the LOB value.

NOTE

The LOB locator is always stored inline (inside the row)
regardless of where the LOB value is stored. You cannot change
the value of STORAGE IN ROW once it is set except by moving
the table. See the move_table_clause of "ALTER TABLE".

- CHUNK integer: Specify the number of bytes to be allocated for LOB manipulation. If integer is not a multiple of the database block size, Oracle rounds up (in bytes) to the next multiple. For example, if the database block size is 2048 and integer is 2050, Oracle allocates 4096 bytes (2 blocks). The maximum value is 32768 (32K), which is the largest Oracle block size allowed. The default CHUNK size is one Oracle database block.

  You cannot change the value of CHUNK once it is set.

NOTE

The value of CHUNK must be less than or equal to the value
of NEXT (either the default value or that specified in the
storage_clause). If CHUNK exceeds the value of NEXT,
Oracle returns an error.

- PCTVERSION integer: Specify the maximum percentage of overall LOB storage space used for creating new versions of the LOB. The default value is 10, meaning that older versions of the LOB data are not overwritten until 10% of the overall LOB storage space is used.

LOB_index_clause: This clause has been deprecated. Oracle automatically generates an index for each LOB column and names and manages the LOB indexes internally.

Although it is still possible for you to specify this clause, Oracle Corporation strongly recommends that you no longer do so. In any event, do not put the LOB index in a different tablespace from the LOB data.

varray_col_properties The varray_col_properties let you specify separate storage characteristics for the LOB in which a varray will be stored. In addition, if you specify this clause, Oracle will always store the varray in a LOB, even if it is small enough to be stored inline.

- For a nonpartitioned table (that is, when specified in the physical_properties clause without any of the partitioning clauses), this clause specifies the storage attributes of the LOB data segments of the varray.

- For a partitioned table specified at the table level (that is, when specified in the physical_properties clause along with one of the partitioning clauses), this clause specifies the default storage attributes for the varray's LOB data segments associated with each partition (or its subpartitions, if any).

- For an individual partition of a partitioned table (that is, when specified as part of a table_partition_description), this clause specifies the storage attributes of the varray's LOB data segments of that partition or the default storage attributes of the varray's LOB data segments of any subpartitions of this partition. A partition-level varray_col_properties overrides a table-level varray_col_properties.

- For an individual subpartition of a partitioned table (that is, when specified as part of a subpartition_clause), this clause specifies the storage attributes of the varray's data segments of this subpartition. A subpartition-level varray_col_properties overrides both partition-level and table-level varray_col_properties.

R striction: You cannot specify the TABLESPACE parameter of LOB_parameters as part of this clause. The LOB tablespace for a varray defaults to the containing table's tablespace.

nested_table_col_properties The nested_table_col_properties let you specify separate storage characteristics for a nested table, which in turn enables you to define the nested table as an index- organized table. The storage table is created in the same tablespace as its parent table (using the default storage characteristics) and stores the nested table values of the column for which it was created.

You must include this clause when creating a table with columns or column attributes whose type is a nested table. Clauses within nested_table_col_properties that function the same way they function for parent object tables are not repeated here.

nested_item: Specify the name of a column (or a top-level attribute of the table's object type) whose type is a nested table.

storage_table: Specify the name of the table where the rows of nested_item reside. For a nonpartitioned table, the storage table is created in the same schema and the same tablespace as the parent table. For a partitioned table, the storage table is created in the default tablespace of the schema.

Restrictions on storage_table:

- You cannot partition the storage table of a nested table.

- You cannot query or perform DML statements on storage_table directly, but you can modify its storage characteristics by specifying its name in an ALTER TABLE statement.

RETURN AS: Specify what Oracle returns as the result of a query.

- VALUE returns a copy of the nested table itself.
- LOCATOR returns a collection locator to the copy of the nested table.

NOTE
The locator is scoped to the session and cannot be used across sessions. Unlike a LOB locator, the collection locator cannot be used to modify the collection instance.

If you do not specify the segment_attributes_clause or the LOB_storage_clause, the nested table is heap organized and is created with default storage characteristics.

Restrictions on nested_table_col_properties:

- You cannot specify this clause for a temporary table.
- You cannot specify the OID_clause.
- You cannot specify TABLESPACE (as part of the segment_attributes_clause) for a nested table. The tablespace is always that of the parent table.
- At create time, you cannot specify (as part of object_properties) a table_ref_constraint, column_ref_constraint, or referential constraint for the attributes of a nested table. However, you can modify a nested table to add such constraints using ALTER TABLE.
- You cannot query or perform DML statements on the storage table directly, but you can modify the nested table column storage characteristics by using the name of storage table in an ALTER TABLE statement.

xmltype_storage_clause   The xmltype_storage_clauses let you specify storage attributes for an XMLType column. XMLType columns are always stored as character LOBs.

table_partitioning_clauses   Use the table_partitioning_clauses to create a partitioned table.
   Restriction: You cannot specify a TIMESTAMP WITH TIME ZONE column as part of the partitioning key.

NOTE
The storage of partitioned database entities in tablespaces of different block sizes is subject to several restrictions. Please refer to Oracle 9i Database Administrator's Guide for a discussion of these restrictions.

range_partitioning   Use the range_partitioning clause to partition the table on ranges of values from column_list. For an index-organized table, column_list must be a subset of the primary key columns of the table.
   column_list: Specify an ordered list of columns used to determine into which partition a row belongs (the partitioning key).
   Restriction: The columns in column_list can be of any built-in datatype except ROWID, LONG, or LOB.
   PARTITION *partition*: Specify the physical partition attributes. If partition is omitted, Oracle generates a name with the form SYS_Pn for the partition. The partition must conform to the rules for naming schema objects and their part.

NOTE
You can specify up to 64K-1 partitions and 64K-1 subpartitions. For a discussion of factors that might impose practical limits less than this number, please refer to Oracle9i Database Administrator's Guide.

NOTE
You can create a partitioned table with just one partition. Note, however, that a partitioned table with one partition is different from a nonpartitioned table. For instance, you cannot add a partition to a nonpartitioned table.

VALUES LESS THAN Clause: Specify the noninclusive upper bound for the current partition. value_list is an ordered list of literal values corresponding to column_list in the partition_by_range_clause. You can substitute the keyword MAXVALUE for any literal in value_list. MAXVALUE specifies a maximum value that will always sort higher than any other value, including NULL.

Specifying a value other than MAXVALUE for the highest partition bound imposes an implicit integrity constraint on the table.

NOTE
If table is partitioned on a DATE column, and if the NLS date format does not specify the first two digits of the year, you must use the TO_DATE function with the YYYY 4-character format mask for the year. (The RRRR format mask is not supported.) The NLS date format is determined implicitly by NLS_TERRITORY or explicitly by NLS_DATE_FORMAT.

list_partitioning   Use the list_partitioning clause to partition the table on lists of literal values from column. List partitioning is useful for controlling how individual rows map to specific partitions.

Each partition_value list must have at least one value. The MAXVALUE keyword is not valid because it is meaningless for list partitions. List partitions are not ordered.

The string comprising the list of values for each partition can be up to 4K bytes. The total number of partition_values for all partitions cannot exceed 64K-1.

NOTE
You can specify the literal NULL for a partition value in the VALUES clause. However, to access data in that partition in subsequent queries, you must use a NOT NULL condition in the WHERE clause, rather than a comparison condition.

Restrictions on List Partitioning:

- ■ You can specify only one partitioning key in column_list, and it cannot be a LOB column.
- ■ If the partitioning key is an object type column, you can partition on only one attribute of the column type.
- ■ You cannot specify MAXVALUE in the VALUES clause.
- ■ Each partition_value in the VALUES clause must be unique among all partitions of table.
- ■ You cannot list partition an index-organized table.

hash_partitioning   Use the hash_partitioning clause to specify that the table is to be partitioned using the hash method. Oracle assigns rows to partitions using a hash function on values found in columns designated as the partitioning key. You can specify hash partitioning in one of two ways:

individual_hash_partitions: You can specify individual partitions by name. The TABLESPACE clause specifies where the partition should be stored.

NOTE

If your enterprise has or will have databases using different character sets, use caution when partitioning on character columns. The sort sequence of characters is not identical in all character sets.

hash_partitions_by_quantity: Alternatively, you can specify the number of partitions. In this case, Oracle assigns partition names of the form SYS_Pnnn. The STORE IN clause specifies one or more tablespaces where the hash partitions are to be stored. The number of tablespaces does not have to equal the number of partitions. If the number of partitions is greater than the number of tablespaces, Oracle cycles through the names of the tablespaces.

For both methods of hash partitioning, the only attribute you can specify for hash partitions (or subpartitions) is TABLESPACE. Hash partitions inherit all other attributes from table-level defaults. Hash subpartitions inherit any attributes specified at the partition level, and inherit all other attributes from the table-level defaults.

Tablespace storage specified at the table level is overridden by tablespace storage specified at the partition level, which in turn is overridden by tablespace storage specified at the subpartition level.

If you specify tablespace storage in both the STORE IN clause of the hash_partitioning clause and the TABLESPACE clause of the hash_partitioning_storage clause, the STORE IN clause determines placement of partitions as the table is being created. The TABLESPACE clause determines the default tablespace at the table level for subsequent operations.

column_list: Specify an ordered list of columns used to determine into which partition a row belongs (the partitioning key).

Restrictions on Hash Partitioning:

- You cannot specify more than 16 columns in column_list.
- The column_list cannot contain the ROWID or UROWID pseudocolumns.
- The columns in column_list can be of any built-in datatype except ROWID, LONG, or LOB.

composite_partitioning   Use the composite_partitioning clause to first partition table by range, and then partition the partitions further into hash subpartitions. This combination of range partitioning and hash subpartitioning is called composite partitioning.

Restriction: You cannot specify composite partitioning for an index-organized table.

subpartition_clause: Use the subpartition_clause to indicate that Oracle should subpartition by hash each partition in table. The subpartitioning column_list is unrelated to the partitioning key, but is subject to the same restrictions.

SUBPARTITIONS *quantity*: Specify the default number of subpartitions in each partition of table, and optionally one or more tablespaces in which they are to be stored.

The default value is 1. If you do not specify the subpartition_clause here, Oracle will create each partition with one hash subpartition unless you subsequently specify the partition_level_subpartition clause.

table_partition_description
LOB_storage_clause: The LOB_storage_clause lets you specify LOB storage characteristics for one or more LOB items in this partition. If you do not specify the LOB_storage_clause for a LOB item, Oracle generates a name for each LOB data partition. The system-generated names for LOB data and LOB index partitions take the form SYS_LOB_Pn and SYS_IL_Pn, respectively, where P stands for "partition" and n is a system-generated number.

varray_col_properties: The varray_col_properties lets you specify storage characteristics for one or more varray items in this partition.

partition_level_subpartition: The partition_level_subpartition clause lets you specify hash subpartitions for partition. This clause overrides the default settings established in the subpartition_clause.

Restriction: You can specify this clause only for a composite-partitioned table.

- You can specify individual subpartitions by name, and optionally the tablespace where each should be stored, or

- You can specify the number of subpartitions (and optionally one or more tablespaces where they are to be stored). In this case, Oracle assigns subpartition names of the form SYS_SUBPnnn. The number of tablespaces does not have to equal the number of subpartitions. If the number of partitions is greater than the number of tablespaces, Oracle cycles through the names of the tablespaces.

row_movement_clause   The row_movement_clause lets you specify whether a row can be moved to a different partition or subpartition because of a change to one or more of its key values during an update operation.

ENABLE: Specify ENABLE to allow Oracle to move a row to a different partition or subpartition as the result of an update to the partitioning or subpartitioning key.

CAUTION
For a normal (heap-organized) table, moving a row in the course of an UPDATE operation changes that row's rowid.

CAUTION
For a moved row in an index-organized table row, the logical rowid remains valid, although the physical guess component of the logical rowid becomes inaccurate.

DISABLE: Specify DISABLE if you want Oracle to return an error if an update to a partitioning or subpartitioning key would result in a row moving to a different partition or subpartition. This is the default.

Restriction: You can specify this clause only for a partitioned table.

CACHE | NOCACHE | CACHE READS
CACHE Clause: For data that is accessed frequently, this clause indicates that the blocks retrieved for this table are placed at the *most recently used* end of the least recently used (LRU) list in the buffer cache when a full table scan is performed. This attribute is useful for small lookup tables.

As a parameter in the *LOB_storage_clause*, CACHE specifies that Oracle places LOB data values in the buffer cache for faster access.

Restriction: You cannot specify CACHE for an index-organized table. However, index-organized tables implicitly provide CACHE behavior.

NOCACHE Clause: For data that is not accessed frequently, this clause indicates that the blocks retrieved for this table are placed at the *least recently used* end of the LRU list in the buffer cache when a full table scan is performed.

As a parameter in the *LOB_storage_clause*, NOCACHE specifies that the LOB value is either not brought into the buffer cache or brought into the buffer cache and placed at the least recently used end of the LRU list. (The latter is the default behavior.) NOCACHE is the default for LOB storage.

Restriction: You cannot specify NOCACHE for index-organized tables.

CACHE READS: CACHE READS applies only to LOB storage. It specifies that LOB values are brought into the buffer cache only during read operations, but not during write operations.

NOROWDEPENDENCIES | ROWDEPENDENCIES   This clause lets you specify whether *table* will use **row-level dependency tracking**. With this feature, each row in the table has a system change number (SCN) that represents a time greater than or equal to the commit time of the last transaction that modified the row. You cannot change this setting after *table* is created.

ROWDEPENDENCIES: Specify ROWDEPENDENCIES if you want to enable row-level dependency tracking. This setting is useful primarily to allow for parallel propagation in replication environments. It increases the size of each row by 6 bytes.

NOROWDEPENDENCIES: Specify NOROWDEPENDENCIES if you do not want table to use the row level dependency tracking feature. This is the default.

MONITORING | NOMONITORING

MONITORING: Specify MONITORING if you want modification statistics to be collected on this table. These statistics are estimates of the number of rows affected by DML statements over a particular period of time. They are available for use by the optimizer or for analysis by the user.

Restriction: You cannot specify MONITORING for a temporary table.

NOMONITORING: Specify NOMONITORING if you do not want Oracle to collect modification statistics on the table. This is the default.

Restriction: You cannot specify NOMONITORING for a temporary table.

parallel_clause   The parallel_clause lets you parallelize creation of the table and set the default degree of parallelism for queries and DML on the table after creation.

NOTE
The syntax of the parallel_clause supersedes syntax appearing in earlier releases of Oracle. Superseded syntax is still supported for backward compatibility, but may result in slightly different behavior than that documented.

NOPARALLEL: Specify NOPARALLEL for serial execution. This is the default.

PARALLEL: Specify PARALLEL if you want Oracle to select a degree of parallelism equal to the number of CPUs available on all participating instances times the value of the PARALLEL_THREADS_PER_CPU initialization parameter.

PARALLEL *integer*: Specification of integer indicates the degree of parallelism, which is the number of parallel threads used in the parallel operation. Each parallel thread may use one or two parallel execution servers. Normally Oracle calculates the optimum degree of parallelism, so it is not necessary for you to specify integer.

Notes on the parallel_clause:

- If table contains any columns of LOB or user-defined object type, this statement as well as subsequent INSERT, UPDATE, or DELETE operations on table are executed serially without notification. Subsequent queries, however, will be executed in parallel.

- A parallel hint overrides the effect of the parallel_clause.

- DML statements and CREATE TABLE ... AS SELECT statements that reference remote objects can run in parallel. However, the "remote object" must really be on a remote database. The reference cannot loop back to an object on the local database (for example, by way of a synonym on the remote database pointing back to an object on the local database).

enable_disable_clause   The enable_disable_clause lets you specify whether Oracle should apply a constraint. By default, constraints are created in ENABLE VALIDATE state.

Restrictions:

- To enable or disable any integrity constraint, you must have defined the constraint in this or a previous statement.

- You cannot enable a referential integrity constraint unless the referenced unique or primary key constraint is already enabled.

ENABLE Clause   Specify ENABLE if you want the constraint to be applied to all new data in the table.

- ENABLE VALIDATE specifies that all old data also complies with the constraint. An enabled validated constraint guarantees that all data is and will continue to be valid.

- If any row in the table violates the integrity constraint, the constraint remains disabled and Oracle returns an error. If all rows comply with the constraint, Oracle enables the constraint. Subsequently, if new data violates the constraint, Oracle does not execute the statement and returns an error indicating the integrity constraint violation.

- If you place a primary key constraint in ENABLE VALIDATE mode, the validation process will verify that the primary key columns contain no nulls. To avoid this overhead, mark each column in the primary key NOT NULL before enabling the table's primary key constraint. (For optimal results, do this before entering data into the column.)

- ENABLE NOVALIDATE ensures that all new DML operations on the constrained data comply with the constraint. This clause does not ensure that existing data in the table complies with the constraint and therefore does not require a table lock.

If you specify neither VALIDATE nor NOVALIDATE, the default is VALIDATE.

If you enable a unique or primary key constraint, and if no index exists on the key, Oracle creates a unique index. This index is dropped if the constraint is subsequently disabled, so Oracle rebuilds the index every time the constraint is enabled.

To avoid rebuilding the index and eliminate redundant indexes, create new primary key and unique constraints initially disabled. Then create (or use existing) nonunique indexes to enforce the constraint. Oracle does not drop a nonunique index when the constraint is disabled, so subsequent ENABLE operations are facilitated.

If you change the state of any single constraint from ENABLE NOVALIDATE to ENABLE VALIDATE, the operation can be performed in parallel, and does not block reads, writes, or other DDL operations.

Restriction on ENABLE: You cannot enable a foreign key that references a unique or primary key that is disabled.

DISABLE Clause   Specify DISABLE to disable the integrity constraint. Disabled integrity constraints appear in the data dictionary along with enabled constraints. If you do not specify this clause when creating a constraint, Oracle automatically enables the constraint.

- DISABLE VALIDATE disables the constraint and drops the index on the constraint, but keeps the constraint valid. This feature is most useful in data warehousing situations, where the need arises to load into a range-partitioned table a quantity of data with a distinct range of values in the unique key. In such situations, the disable validate state enables you to save space by not having an index. You can then load data from a nonpartitioned table into a partitioned table using the *exchange_partition_clause* of the ALTER TABLE statement or using SQL*Loader. All other modifications to the table (inserts, updates, and deletes) by other SQL statements are disallowed.

  If the unique key coincides with the partitioning key of the partitioned table, disabling the constraint saves overhead and has no detrimental effects. If the unique key does not coincide with the partitioning key, Oracle performs automatic table scans during the exchange to validate the constraint, which might offset the benefit of loading without an index.

- DISABLE NOVALIDATE signifies that Oracle makes no effort to maintain the constraint (because it is disabled) and cannot guarantee that the constraint is true (because it is not being validated).

  You cannot drop a table whose primary key is being referenced by a foreign key even if the foreign key constraint is in DISABLE NOVALIDATE state. Further, the optimizer can use constraints in DISABLE NOVALIDATE state.

If you specify neither VALIDATE nor NOVALIDATE, the default is NOVALIDATE.

If you disable a unique or primary key constraint that is using a unique index, Oracle drops the unique index.

UNIQUE   The UNIQUE clause lets you enable or disable the unique constraint defined on the specified column or combination of columns.

PRIMARY KEY: The PRIMARY KEY clause lets you enable or disable the table's primary key constraint.

CONSTRAINT: The CONSTRAINT clause lets you enable or disable the integrity constraint named *constraint*.

KEEP | DROP INDEX: This clause lets you either preserve or drop the index Oracle has been using to enforce a UNIQUE or PRIMARY KEY constraint.

Restriction: You can specify this clause only when disabling a UNIQUE or PRIMARY KEY constraint.

using_index_clause   The using_index_clause lets you specify an index for Oracle to use to enforce a UNIQUE and PRIMARY KEY constraint, or lets you instruct Oracle to create the index used to enforce the constraint.

- If you specify schema.index, Oracle will attempt to enforce the constraint using the specified index. If Oracle cannot find the index or cannot use the index to enforce the constraint, Oracle returns an error.

- If you specify the create_index_statement, Oracle will attempt to create the index and use it to enforce the constraint. If Oracle cannot create the index or cannot use the index to enforce the constraint, Oracle returns an error.

- If you neither specify an existing index or create a new index, Oracle creates the index. In this case:
  - The index receives the same name as the constraint.
  - You can choose the values of the INITRANS, MAXTRANS, TABLESPACE, STORAGE, and PCTFREE parameters for the index.
  - If table is partitioned, you can specify a locally or globally partitioned index for the unique or primary key constraint.

Restrictions on the *using_index_clause*:

- You cannot specify this clause for a view constraint.

- You can specify the using_index_clause only when enabling UNIQUE and PRIMARY KEY constraints.

- You cannot specify an index (schema.index) or create an index (create_index_statement) when enabling the primary key of an index-organized table.

global_partitioned_index   The global_partitioned_index clause lets you specify that the partitioning of the index is user defined and is not equipartitioned with the underlying table. By default, nonpartitioned indexes are global indexes.

PARTITION BY RANGE: Specify PARTITION BY RANGE to indicate that the global index is partitioned on the ranges of values from the columns specified in column_list. You cannot specify this clause for a local index.

column_list: For column_list, specify the name of the column(s) of a table on which the index is partitioned. The column_list must specify a left prefix of the index column list.

You cannot specify more than 32 columns in column_list, and the columns cannot contain the ROWID pseudocolumn or a column of type ROWID.

NOTE
If your enterprise has or will have databases using different character sets, use caution when partitioning on character columns. The sort sequence of characters is not identical in all character sets.

PARTITION: The PARTITION clause lets you describe the individual index partitions. The number of clauses determines the number of partitions. If you omit partition, Oracle generates a name with the form SYS_Pn.

VALUES LESS THAN: For VALUES LESS THAN (value_list), specify the (noninclusive) upper bound for the current partition in a global index. The value_list is a comma-separated, ordered list of literal values corresponding to column_list in the partition_by_range_clause. Always specify MAXVALUE as the value_list of the last partition.

NOTE
If index is partitioned on a DATE column, and if the date format does not specify the first two digits of the year, you must use the TO_DATE function with a 4-character format mask for the year. The date format is determined implicitly by NLS_TERRITORY or explicitly by NLS_DATE_FORMAT.

exceptions_clause   Specify a table into which Oracle places the rowids of all rows violating the constraint. If you omit schema, Oracle assumes the exceptions table is in your own schema. If you omit this clause altogether, Oracle assumes that the table is named EXCEPTIONS. The exceptions table must be on your local database.

You can create the EXCEPTIONS table using one of these scripts:

- UTLEXCPT.SQL uses physical rowids. Therefore it can accommodate rows from conventional tables but not from index-organized tables. (See the Note that follows.)

- UTLEXPT1.SQL uses universal rowids, so it can accommodate rows from both conventional and index-organized tables.

If you create your own exceptions table, it must follow the format prescribed by one of these two scripts.

CASCADE: Specify CASCADE to disable any integrity constraints that depend on the specified integrity constraint. To disable a primary or unique key that is part of a referential integrity constraint, you must specify this clause.

Restriction: You can specify CASCADE only if you have specified DISABLE.

AS subquery   Specify a subquery to determine the contents of the table. The rows returned by the subquery are inserted into the table upon its creation.

parallel_clause: If you specify the parallel_clause in this statement, Oracle will ignore any value you specify for the INITIAL storage parameter, and will instead use the value of the NEXT parameter.

ORDER BY: The ORDER BY clause lets you order rows returned by the statements.

NOTE
When specified with CREATE TABLE, this clause does not necessarily order data cross the entire table. (For example, it does not order across partitions.) Specify this clause if you intend to create an index on the same key as the ORDER BY key column. Oracle will cluster data on the ORDER BY key so that it corresponds to the index key.

For object tables, subquery can contain either one expression corresponding to the table type, or the number of top-level attributes of the table type.

If subquery returns (in part or totally) the equivalent of an existing materialized view, Oracle may use the materialized view (for query rewrite) in place of one or more tables specified in subquery.

Oracle derives datatypes and lengths from the subquery. Oracle also follows the following rules for integrity constraints:

- Oracle automatically defines any NOT NULL constraints on columns in the new table that existed on the corresponding columns of the selected table if the subquery selects the column rather than an expression containing the column.

- If a CREATE TABLE statement contains both AS subquery and a CONSTRAINT clause or an ENABLE clause with the EXCEPTIONS INTO clause, Oracle ignores AS subquery. If any rows violate the constraint, Oracle does not create the table and returns an error.

If all expressions in subquery are columns, rather than expressions, you can omit the columns from the table definition entirely. In this case, the names of the columns of table are the same as the columns in subquery.

You can use subquery in combination with the TO_LOB function to convert the values in a LONG column in another table to LOB values in a column of the table you are creating.

Restrictions:

- The number of columns in the table must equal the number of expressions in the subquery.

- The column definitions can specify only column names, default values, and integrity constraints, not datatypes.

- You cannot define a referential integrity constraint in a CREATE TABLE statement that contains AS subquery. Instead, you must create the table without the constraint and then add it later with an ALTER TABLE statement.

CREATE TABLESPACE

PURPOSE
Use the CREATE TABLESPACE statement to create a **tablespace**, which is an allocation of space in the database that can contain persistent schema objects.

When you create a tablespace, it is initially a read/write tablespace. You can subsequently use the ALTER TABLESPACE statement to take the tablespace offline or online, add datafiles to it, or make it a read-only tablespace. You can also drop a tablespace from the database with the DROP TABLESPACE statement.

You can use the CREATE TEMPORARY TABLESPACE statement to create tablespaces that contain schema objects only for the duration of a session.

NOTE
To use objects in a tablespace other than the SYSTEM tablespace: (1) If you are running the database in rollback undo mode, at least one rollback segment (other than the SYSTEM rollback segment) must be online. (2) If you are running the database in Automatic Undo Management mode, at least one UNDO tablespace must be online.

PREREQUISITES
You must have CREATE TABLESPACE system privilege. Before you can create a tablespace, you must create a database to contain it, and the database must be open.

SYNTAX

create_tablespace::=

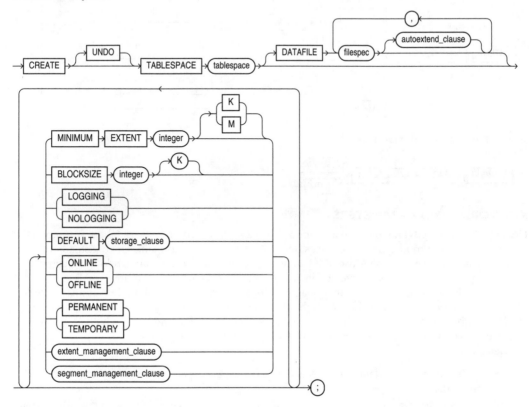

autoextend_clause::=

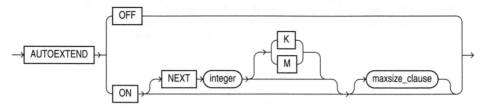

maxsize_clause::=

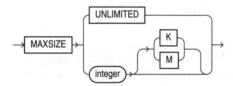

extent_management_clause::=

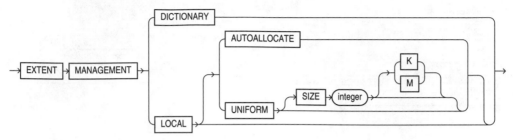

segment_management_clause::=

KEYWORDS AND PARAMETERS

UNDO   Specify UNDO to create an undo tablespace. When you run the database in Automatic Undo Management mode, Oracle manages undo space using the undo tablespace instead of rollback segments. This clause is useful if you are now running in Automatic Undo Management mode but your database was not created in Automatic Undo Management mode.

   Oracle always assigns an undo tablespace when you start up the database in Automatic Undo Management mode. If no undo tablespace has been assigned to this instance, Oracle will use the SYSTEM rollback segment. You can avoid this by creating an undo tablespace, which Oracle will implicitly assign to the instance if no other undo tablespace is currently assigned.

   Restrictions:

- You cannot create database objects in this tablespace. It is reserved for system-managed undo data.

- The only clauses you can specify for an undo tablespace are the DATAFILE clause and the *extent_management_clause* to specify local extent management. (You cannot specify dictionary extent management using the *extent_management_clause*.) All undo tablespaces are created permanent, read/write, and in logging mode. Values for MINIMUM EXTENT and DEFAULT STORAGE are system generated.

tablespace   Specify the name of the tablespace to be created.

DATAFILE filespec   Specify the datafile or files to make up the tablespace.

> **NOTE**
> *For operating systems that support raw devices, the REUSE keyword of filespec has no meaning when specifying a raw device as a datafile. Such a CREATE TABLESPACE statement will succeed whether or not you specify REUSE.*

   The DATAFILE clause is optional only if the DB_CREATE_FILE_DEST initialization parameter is set. In this case, Oracle creates a system-named 100MB file in the default file destination specified in the parameter.

autoextend_clause   Use the autoextend_clause to enable or disable the automatic extension of a new datafile or tempfile. If you do not specify this clause, these files are not automatically extended.

ON: Specify ON to enable autoextend.

OFF: Specify OFF to turn off autoextend if is turned on.

NOTE
When you turn off autoextend, the values of NEXT and MAXSIZE are set to zero. If you turn autoextend back on in a subsequent statement, you must reset these values.

NEXT: Use the NEXT clause to specify the size in bytes of the next increment of disk space to be allocated automatically when more extents are required. Use K or M to specify this size in kilobytes or megabytes. The default is the size of one data block.

MAXSIZE: Use the MAXSIZE clause to specify the maximum disk space allowed for automatic extension of the datafile.

UNLIMITED: Use the UNLIMITED clause if you do not want to limit the disk space that Oracle can allocate to the datafile or tempfile.

MINIMUM EXTENT Clause   Specify the minimum size of an extent in the tablespace. This clause lets you control free space fragmentation in the tablespace by ensuring that every used or free extent size in a tablespace is at least as large as, and is a multiple of, *integer*.

NOTE
This clause is not relevant for a dictionary-managed temporary tablespace.

BLOCKSIZE Clause   Use the BLOCKSIZE clause to specify a nonstandard block size for the tablespace. In order to specify this clause, you must have the DB_CACHE_SIZE and at least one DB_*n*K_CACHE_SIZE parameter set, and the integer you specify in this clause must correspond with the setting of one DB_*n*K_CACHE_SIZE parameter setting.

Restriction: You cannot specify nonstandard block sizes for a temporary tablespace (that is, if you also specify TEMPORARY) or if you intend to assign this tablespace as the temporary tablespace for any users.

LOGGING | NOLOGGING   Specify the default logging attributes of all tables, indexes, and partitions within the tablespace. LOGGING is the default.

The tablespace-level logging attribute can be overridden by logging specifications at the table, index, and partition levels.

Only the following operations support the NOLOGGING mode:

- **DML:** direct-path INSERT (serial or parallel), Direct Loader (SQL*Loader)
- **DDL:** CREATE TABLE ... AS SELECT, CREATE INDEX, ALTER INDEX ... REBUILD, ALTER INDEX ... REBUILD PARTITION, ALTER INDEX ... SPLIT PARTITION, ALTER TABLE ... SPLIT PARTITION, and ALTER TABLE ... MOVE PARTITION

In NOLOGGING mode, data is modified with minimal logging (to mark new extents INVALID and to record dictionary changes). When applied during media recovery, the extent invalidation records mark a range of blocks as logically corrupt, because the redo data is not logged. Therefore, if you cannot afford to lose the object, you should take a backup after the NOLOGGING operation.

DEFAULT storage_clause   Specify the default storage parameters for all objects created in the tablespace.

For a dictionary-managed temporary tablespace, Oracle considers only the NEXT parameter of the *storage_clause*.

ONLINE | OFFLINE Clauses

ONLINE: Specify ONLINE to make the tablespace available immediately after creation to users who have been granted access to the tablespace. This is the default.

OFFLINE: Specify OFFLINE to make the tablespace unavailable immediately after creation.

The data dictionary view DBA_TABLESPACES indicates whether each tablespace is online or offline.

PERMANENT | TEMPORARY Clauses

PERMANENT: Specify PERMANENT if the tablespace will be used to hold permanent objects. This is the default.

TEMPORARY: Specify TEMPORARY if the tablespace will be used only to hold temporary objects, for example, segments used by implicit sorts to handle ORDER BY clauses.

Restriction: If you specify TEMPORARY, you cannot specify EXTENT MANAGEMENT LOCAL or the BLOCKSIZE clause.

extent_management_clause   The extent_management_clause lets you specify how the extents of the tablespace will be managed.

NOTE
Once you have specified extent management with this clause, you can change extent management only by migrating the tablespace.

- Specify LOCAL if you want the tablespace to be locally managed. Locally managed tablespaces have some part of the tablespace set aside for a bitmap. This is the default.
    - AUTOALLOCATE specifies that the tablespace is system managed. Users cannot specify an extent size. This is the default if the COMPATIBLE initialization parameter is set to 9.0.0 or higher.
    - UNIFORM specifies that the tablespace is managed with uniform extents of SIZE bytes. Use K or M to specify the extent size in kilobytes or megabytes. The default SIZE is 1 megabyte.
- Specify DICTIONARY if you want the tablespace to be managed using dictionary tables. This is the default if the COMPATIBLE initialization parameter is set less than 9.0.0.

If you do not specify the extent_management_clause, Oracle interprets the COMPATIBLE setting, the MINIMUM EXTENT clause and the DEFAULT storage_clause to determine extent management:

- If the COMPATIBLE initialization parameter is less than 9.0.0, Oracle creates a dictionary managed tablespace. If COMPATIBLE = 9.0.0 or higher:
- If you do not specify the DEFAULT storage_clause at all, Oracle creates a locally managed autoallocated tablespace.
- If you did specify the DEFAULT storage_clause:
    - If you specified the MINIMUM EXTENT clause, Oracle evaluates whether the values of MINIMUM EXTENT, INITIAL, and NEXT are equal and the value of PCT_INCREASE is

0. If so, Oracle creates a locally managed uniform tablespace with extent size = INITIAL. If the MINIMUM EXTENT, INITIAL, and NEXT parameters are not equal, or if PCT_INCREASE is not 0, Oracle ignores any extent storage parameters you may specify and creates a locally managed, autoallocated tablespace.

■ If you did not specify MINIMUM EXTENT clause, Oracle evaluates only whether the storage values of INITIAL and NEXT are equal and PCT_INCREASE is 0. If so, the tablespace is locally managed and uniform. Otherwise, the tablespace is locally managed and autoallocated.

Restrictions:

■ A permanent locally managed tablespace can contain only permanent objects. If you need a locally managed tablespace to store temporary objects (for example, if you will assign it as a user's temporary tablespace, use the CREATE TEMPORARY TABLESPACE statement.

■ If you specify LOCAL, you cannot specify DEFAULT storage_clause, MINIMUM EXTENT, or TEMPORARY.

segment_management_clause   The segment_management_clause is relevant only for permanent, locally managed tablespaces. It lets you specify whether Oracle should track the used and free space in the segments in the tablespace using free lists or bitmaps.

MANUAL: Specify MANUAL if you want Oracle to manage the free space of segments in the tablespace using free lists.

AUTO: Specify AUTO if you want Oracle to manage the free space of segments in the tablespace using a bitmap. If you specify AUTO, Oracle ignores any specification for FREELIST and FREELIST GROUPS in subsequent storage specifications for objects in this tablespace. This setting is called automatic segment-space management.

To determine the segment management of an existing tablespace, query the SEGMENT_SPACE_MANAGEMENT column of the DBA_TABLESPACES or USER_TABLESPACES data dictionary view.

NOTES
If you specify AUTO, then: (1) If you set extent management to LOCAL UNIFORM, you must ensure that each extent contains at least 5 database blocks, given the database block size. (2) If you set extent management to LOCAL AUTOALLOCATE, and if the database block size is 16K or greater, Oracle manages segment space management by creating extents with a minimum size of 1M.

Restrictions on AUTO:

■ You can specify this clause only for permanent, locally managed tablespace.

■ You cannot specify this clause for the SYSTEM tablespace.

■ You cannot store LOBs in AUTO segment-managed tablespaces.

CREATE TEMPORARY TABLESPACE

PURPOSE
Use the CREATE TEMPORARY TABLESPACE statement to create a **temporary tablespace**, which is an allocation of space in the database that can contain schema objects for the duration of a session.

If you subsequently assign this temporary tablespace to a particular user, then Oracle will also use this tablespace for sorting operations in transactions initiated by that user.

To create a tablespace to contain persistent schema objects, use the CREATE TABLESPACE statement.

NOTE
Media recovery does not recognize tempfiles.

PREREQUISITES
You must have the CREATE TABLESPACE system privilege.

SYNTAX

create_temporary_tablespace::=

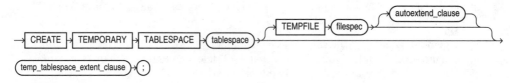

autoextend_clause::=

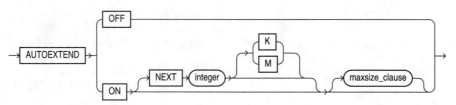

maxsize_clause::=

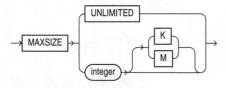

temp_tablespace_extent::=

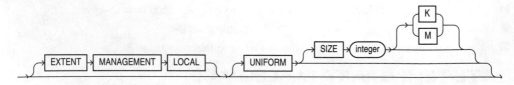

KEYWORDS AND PARAMETERS

tablespace   Specify the name of the temporary tablespace.

TEMPFILE filespec   Specify the tempfiles that make up the tablespace.
You can omit the TEMPFILE clause only if the DB_CREATE_FILE_DEST initialization parameter has been set. In this case, Oracle creates a 100 MB Oracle-managed tempfile in the default file destination specified in the parameter. If this parameter is not set, you must specify the TEMPFILE clause.

NOTE

On some operating systems, Oracle does not allocate space for the tempfile until the tempfile blocks are actually accessed. This delay in space allocation results in faster creation and resizing of tempfiles, but it requires that sufficient disk space is available when the tempfiles are later used. Please refer to your operating system documentation to determine whether Oracle allocates tempfile space in this way on your system.

autoextend_clause   Use the autoextend_clause to enable or disable the automatic extension of a new datafile or tempfile. If you do not specify this clause, these files are not automatically extended.
ON: Specify ON to enable autoextend.
OFF: Specify OFF to turn off autoextend if is turned on.

NOTE

When you turn off autoextend, the values of NEXT and MAXSIZE are set to zero. If you turn autoextend back on in a subsequent statement, you must reset these values.

NEXT: Use the NEXT clause to specify the size in bytes of the next increment of disk space to be allocated automatically when more extents are required. Use K or M to specify this size in kilobytes or megabytes. The default is the size of one data block.
MAXSIZE: Use the MAXSIZE clause to specify the maximum disk space allowed for automatic extension of the datafile.
UNLIMITED: Use the UNLIMITED clause if you do not want to limit the disk space that Oracle can allocate to the datafile or tempfile.

temp_tablespace_extent   The temp_tablespace_extent clause lets you specify how the tablespace is managed.
EXTENT MANAGEMENT LOCAL: This clause indicates that some part of the tablespace is set aside for a bitmap. All temporary tablespaces have locally managed extents, so this clause is optional.
UNIFORM: All extents of temporary tablespaces are the same size (uniform), so this keyword is optional. However, you must specify UNIFORM in order to specify SIZE.
SIZE integer: Specify in bytes the size of the tablespace extents. Use K or M to specify the size in kilobytes or megabytes.
If you do not specify SIZE, Oracle uses the default extent size of 1M.

CREATE TRIGGER

PURPOSE

Use the CREATE TRIGGER statement to create and enable a **database trigger**, which is

- A stored PL/SQL block associated with a table, a schema, or the database or
- An anonymous PL/SQL block or a call to a procedure implemented in PL/SQL or Java

Oracle automatically executes a trigger when specified conditions occur.

When you create a trigger, Oracle enables it automatically. You can subsequently disable and enable a trigger with the DISABLE and ENABLE clause of the ALTER TRIGGER or ALTER TABLE statement.

PREREQUISITES

Before a trigger can be created, the user SYS must run a SQL script commonly called DBMSSTDX.SQL. The exact name and location of this script depend on your operating system.

- To create a trigger in your own schema on a table in your own schema or on your own schema (SCHEMA), you must have the CREATE TRIGGER privilege.
- To create a trigger in any schema on a table in any schema, or on another user's schema (*schema*.SCHEMA), you must have the CREATE ANY TRIGGER privilege.
- In addition to the preceding privileges, to create a trigger on DATABASE, you must have the ADMINISTER DATABASE TRIGGER system privilege.

If the trigger issues SQL statements or calls procedures or functions, then the owner of the trigger must have the privileges necessary to perform these operations. These privileges must be granted directly to the owner rather than acquired through roles.

SYNTAX

create_trigger::=

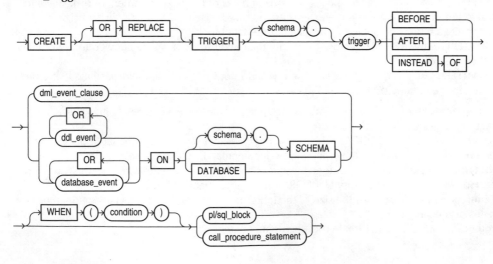

dml_event_clause::=

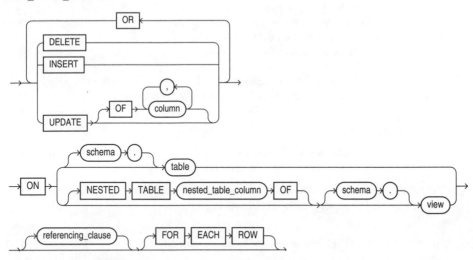

referencing_clause::=

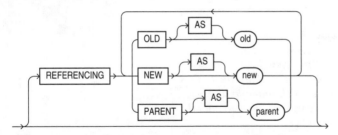

KEYWORDS AND PARAMETERS

OR REPLACE   Specify OR REPLACE to re-create the trigger if it already exists. Use this clause to change the definition of an existing trigger without first dropping it.

schema   Specify the schema to contain the trigger. If you omit schema, Oracle creates the trigger in your own schema.

trigger   Specify the name of the trigger to be created.

If a trigger produces compilation errors, it is still created, but it fails on execution. This means it effectively blocks all triggering DML statements until it is disabled, replaced by a version without compilation errors, or dropped. You can see the associated compiler error messages with the SQL*Plus command SHOW ERRORS.

NOTE
*If you create a trigger on a base table of a materialized view,
you must ensure that the trigger does not fire during a refresh of
the materialized view. (During refresh, the DBMS_MVIEW
procedure I_AM_A_REFRESH returns TRUE.)*

BEFORE   Specify BEFORE to cause Oracle to fire the trigger before executing the triggering
event. For row triggers, the trigger is fired before each affected row is changed.
Restrictions:

- You cannot specify a BEFORE trigger on a view or an object view.
- When defining a BEFORE trigger for LOB columns, you can read the :OLD value but not
  the :NEW value. You cannot write either the :OLD or the :NEW value.

AFTER   Specify AFTER to cause Oracle to fire the trigger after executing the triggering event.
For row triggers, the trigger is fired after each affected row is changed.
Restrictions:

- You cannot specify an AFTER trigger on a view or an object view.
- When defining an AFTER trigger for LOB columns, you can read the :OLD value but not
  the :NEW value. You cannot write either the :OLD or the :NEW value.

NOTE
*When you create a materialized view log for a table, Oracle
implicitly creates an AFTER ROW trigger on the table. This
trigger inserts a row into the materialized view log whenever
an INSERT, UPDATE, or DELETE statement modifies the table's
data. You cannot control the order in which multiple row
triggers fire. Therefore, you should not write triggers intended
to affect the content of the materialized view.*

INSTEAD OF   Specify INSTEAD OF to cause Oracle to fire the trigger instead of executing the
triggering event. INSTEAD OF triggers are valid for DML events on views. They are not valid for
DDL or database events.
      If a view is inherently updatable and has INSTEAD OF triggers, the triggers take preference. In
other words, Oracle fires the triggers instead of performing DML on the view. If the view belongs to
a hierarchy, the trigger is not inherited by subviews.
Restrictions:

- INSTEAD OF triggers are valid only for views. You cannot specify an INSTEAD OF trigger
  on a table.
- If a view has INSTEAD OF triggers, any views created on it must have INSTEAD OF
  triggers, even if the views are inherently updatable.
- When defining INSTEAD OF triggers for LOB columns, you can read both the :OLD and
  the :NEW value, but you cannot write either the :OLD or the :NEW values.

NOTE
You can create multiple triggers of the same type (BEFORE, AFTER, or INSTEAD OF) that fire for the same statement on the same table. The order in which Oracle fires these triggers is indeterminate. If your application requires that one trigger be fired before another of the same type for the same statement, combine these triggers into a single trigger whose trigger action performs the trigger actions of the original triggers in the appropriate order.

dml_event_clause   The dml_event_clause lets you specify one of three DML statements that can cause the trigger to fire. Oracle fires the trigger in the existing user transaction.

DELETE   Specify DELETE if you want Oracle to fire the trigger whenever a DELETE statement removes a row from the table or removes an element from a nested table.

INSERT   Specify INSERT if you want Oracle to fire the trigger whenever an INSERT statement adds a row to table or adds an element to a nested table.

UPDATE   Specify UPDATE if you want Oracle to fire the trigger whenever an UPDATE statement changes a value in one of the columns specified after OF. If you omit OF, Oracle fires the trigger whenever an UPDATE statement changes a value in any column of the table or nested table.

For an UPDATE trigger, you can specify object type, varray, and REF columns after OF to indicate that the trigger should be fired whenever an UPDATE statement changes a value in one of the columns. However, you cannot change the values of these columns in the body of the trigger itself.

NOTE
Using OCI functions or the DBMS_LOB package to update LOB values or LOB attributes of object columns does not cause Oracle to fire triggers defined on the table containing the columns or the attributes.

Restrictions:

- You cannot specify UPDATE OF for an INSTEAD OF trigger. Oracle fires INSTEAD OF triggers whenever an UPDATE changes a value in any column of the view.
- You cannot specify nested table or LOB columns with UPDATE OF.

Performing DML operations directly on nested table columns does not cause Oracle to fire triggers defined on the table containing the nested table column.

ddl_event   Specify one or more types of DDL statements that can cause the trigger to fire. You can create triggers for these events on DATABASE or SCHEMA unless otherwise noted. You can create BEFORE and AFTER triggers for these events. Oracle fires the trigger in the existing user transaction.

Restriction: You cannot specify as a triggering event any DDL operation performed through a PL/SQL procedure.

The following ddl_event values are valid:

ALTER: Specify ALTER to fire the trigger whenever an ALTER statement modifies a database object in the data dictionary.

Restriction: The trigger will not be fired by an ALTER DATABASE statement.

ANALYZE: Specify ANALYZE to fire the trigger whenever Oracle collects or deletes statistics or validates the structure of a database object.

ASSOCIATE STATISTICS: Specify ASSOCIATE STATISTICS to fire the trigger whenever Oracle associates a statistics type with a database object.

AUDIT: Specify AUDIT to fire the trigger whenever Oracle tracks the occurrence of a SQL statement or tracks operations on a schema object.

COMMENT: Specify COMMENT to fire the trigger whenever a comment on a database object is added to the data dictionary.

CREATE: Specify CREATE to fire the trigger whenever a CREATE statement adds a new database object to the data dictionary.

Restriction: The trigger will not be fired by a CREATE DATABASE or CREATE CONTROLFILE statement.

DISASSOCIATE STATISTICS: Specify DISASSOCIATE STATISTICS to fire the trigger whenever Oracle disassociates a statistics type from a database object.

DROP: Specify DROP to fire the trigger whenever a DROP statement removes a database object from the data dictionary.

GRANT: Specify GRANT to fire the trigger whenever a user grants system privileges or roles or object privileges to another user or to a role.

NOAUDIT: Specify NOAUDIT to fire the trigger whenever a NOAUDIT statement instructs Oracle to stop tracking a SQL statement or operations on a schema object.

RENAME: Specify RENAME to fire the trigger whenever a RENAME statement changes the name of a database object.

REVOKE: Specify REVOKE to fire the trigger whenever a REVOKE statement removes system privileges or roles or object privileges from a user or role.

TRUNCATE: Specify TRUNCATE to fire the trigger whenever a TRUNCATE statement removes the rows from a table or cluster and resets its storage characteristics.

DDL: Specify DDL to fire the trigger whenever any of the preceding DDL statements is issued.

database_event   Specify one or more particular states of the database that can cause the trigger to fire. You can create triggers for these events on DATABASE or SCHEMA unless otherwise noted. For each of these triggering events, Oracle opens an autonomous transaction scope, fires the trigger, and commits any separate transaction (regardless of any existing user transaction).

SERVERERROR: Specify SERVERERROR to fire the trigger whenever a server error message is logged. The following errors do not cause a SERVERERROR trigger to fire:

- ORA-01403: data not found

- ORA-01422: exact fetch returns more than requested number of rows

- ORA-01423: error encountered while checking for extra rows in exact fetch

- ORA-01034: ORACLE not available

- ORA-04030: out of process memory

LOGON: Specify LOGON to fire the trigger whenever a client application logs onto the database.

LOGOFF: Specify LOGOFF to fire the trigger whenever a client applications logs off the database.

STARTUP: Specify STARTUP to fire the trigger whenever the database is opened.

SHUTDOWN: Specify SHUTDOWN to fire the trigger whenever an instance of the database is shut down.

SUSPEND: Specify SUSPEND to fire the trigger whenever a server error causes a transaction to be suspended.

NOTE

Only AFTER triggers are relevant for LOGON, STARTUP, SERVERERROR, and SUSPEND. Only BEFORE triggers are relevant for LOGOFF and SHUTDOWN. AFTER STARTUP and BEFORE SHUTDOWN triggers apply only to DATABASE.

ON table | view The ON clause lets you determine the database object on which the trigger is to be created.

table | view Specify the schema and table or view name of one of the following on which the trigger is to be created:

- Table or view
- Object table or object view
- A column of nested-table type

If you omit schema, Oracle assumes the table is in your own schema. You can create triggers on index-organized tables.

Restriction: You cannot create a trigger on a table in the schema SYS.

NESTED TABLE Clause Specify the *nested_table_column* of a view upon which the trigger is being defined. Such a trigger will fire only if the DML operates on the elements of the nested table.

Restriction: You can specify NESTED TABLE only for INSTEAD OF triggers.

DATABASE Specify DATABASE to define the trigger on the entire database.

SCHEMA Specify SCHEMA to define the trigger on the current schema.

referencing_clause The referencing_clause lets you specify correlation names. You can use correlation names in the PL/SQL block and WHEN condition of a row trigger to refer specifically to old and new values of the current row. The default correlation names are OLD and NEW. If your row trigger is associated with a table named OLD or NEW, use this clause to specify different correlation names to avoid confusion between the table name and the correlation name.

- If the trigger is defined on a nested table, OLD and NEW refer to the row of the nested table, and PARENT refers to the current row of the parent table.
- If the trigger is defined on an object table or view, OLD and NEW refer to object instances.

Restriction: The referencing_clause is not valid with INSTEAD OF triggers on CREATE DDL events.

FOR EACH ROW Specify FOR EACH ROW to designate the trigger as a row trigger. Oracle fires a row trigger once for each row that is affected by the triggering statement and meets the optional trigger constraint defined in the WHEN condition.

Except for INSTEAD OF triggers, if you omit this clause, the trigger is a statement trigger. Oracle fires a statement trigger only once when the triggering statement is issued if the optional trigger constraint is met.

INSTEAD OF trigger statements are implicitly activated for each row.
Restriction: This clause is valid only for DML event triggers (not DDL or database event triggers).

WHEN Clause   Specify the trigger restriction, which is a SQL condition that must be satisfied for Oracle to fire the trigger. This condition must contain correlation names and cannot contain a query.
   Restrictions:

- If you specify this clause for a DML event trigger, you must also specify FOR EACH ROW. Oracle evaluates this condition for each row affected by the triggering statement.

- You cannot specify trigger restrictions for INSTEAD OF trigger statements.

- You can reference object columns or their attributes, or varray, nested table, or LOB columns. You cannot invoke PL/SQL functions or methods in the trigger restriction.

pl/sql_block   Specify the PL/SQL block that Oracle executes to fire the trigger.
   The PL/SQL block of a database trigger can contain one of a series of built-in functions in the SYS schema designed solely to extract system event attributes. These functions can be used only in the PL/SQL block of a database trigger.
   Restrictions:

- The PL/SQL block of a trigger cannot contain transaction control SQL statements (COMMIT, ROLLBACK, SAVEPOINT, and SET CONSTRAINT) if the block is executed within the same transaction.

- You can reference and use LOB columns in the trigger action inside the PL/SQL block, but you cannot modify the values of LOB columns within the trigger action.

call_procedure_statement   The call_procedure_statement lets you call a stored procedure, rather than specifying the trigger code inline as a PL/SQL block.

CREATE USER

PURPOSE
Use the CREATE USER statement to create and configure a database **user**, or an account through which you can log in to the database and establish the means by which Oracle permits access by the user.

NOTE
You can enable a user to connect to Oracle through a proxy (that is, an application or application server). For syntax and discussion, refer to "ALTER USER".

PREREQUISITES
You must have CREATE USER system privilege. When you create a user with the CREATE USER statement, the user's privilege domain is empty. To log on to Oracle, a user must have CREATE SESSION system privilege. Therefore, after creating a user, you should grant the user at least the CREATE SESSION privilege.

SYNTAX

create_user::=

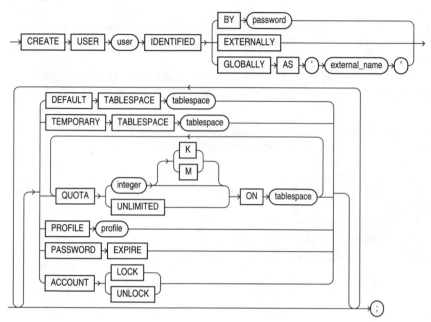

KEYWORDS AND PARAMETERS

user   Specify the name of the user to be created. This name can contain only characters from your database character set. Oracle recommends that the user name contain at least one single-byte character regardless of whether the database character set also contains multibyte characters.

IDENTIFIED Clause   The IDENTIFIED clause lets you indicate how Oracle authenticates the user.

BY password   The BY *password* clause lets you creates a **local user** and indicates that the user must specify *password* to log on. Passwords can contain only single-byte characters from your database character set regardless of whether this character set also contains multibyte characters.

EXTERNALLY Clause   Specify EXTERNALLY to create an **external user.** Such a user must be authenticated by an external service (such as an operating system or a third-party service). In this case, Oracle to relies on the login authentication of the operating system to ensure that a specific operating system user has access to a specific database user.

CAUTION
It's strongly recommended that you do not use IDENTIFIED EXTERNALLY with operating systems that have inherently weak login security. For more information, see Oracle9i Database Administrator's Guide.

GLOBALLY Clause   The GLOBALLY clause lets you create a **global user**. Such a user must be authenticated by the enterprise directory service. The '*external_name*' string can take one of two forms:

- The X.509 name at the enterprise directory service that identifies this user. It should be of the form 'CN=*username,other_attributes*', where *other_attributes* is the rest of the user's distinguished name (DN) in the directory.

- A null string (' ') indicating that the enterprise directory service will map authenticated global users to the appropriate database schema with the appropriate roles.

NOTE
You can control the ability of an application server to connect as the specified user and to activate that user's roles using the ALTER USER statement.

DEFAULT TABLESPACE Clause   Specify the default tablespace for objects that the user creates. If you omit this clause, objects default to the SYSTEM tablespace.
   Restriction: You cannot specify an undo tablespace as the default tablespace.

TEMPORARY TABLESPACE Clause   Specify the tablespace for the user's temporary segments. If you omit this clause, temporary segments default to the SYSTEM tablespace.
   Restrictions:

- The tablespace must have a standard block size.
- If you specify a locally managed tablespace, it must be a temporary tablespace.
- The temporary tablespace cannot be an undo tablespace or a tablespace with automatic segment-space management.

QUOTA Clause   Use the QUOTA clause to allow the user to allocate up to *integer* bytes of space in the tablespace. Use K or M to specify the quota in kilobytes or megabytes. This quota is the maximum space in the tablespace the user can allocate.
   A CREATE USER statement can have multiple QUOTA clauses for multiple tablespaces.
   UNLIMITED lets the user allocate space in the tablespace without bound.

PROFILE Clause   Specify the the profile you want to reassign to the user. The profile limits the amount of database resources the user can use. If you omit this clause, Oracle assigns the DEFAULT profile to the user.

PASSWORD EXPIRE Clause   Specify PASSWORD EXPIRE if you want the user's password to expire. This setting forces the user (or the DBA) to change the password before the user can log in to the database.

ACCOUNT Clause   Specify ACCOUNT LOCK to lock the user's account and disable access. Specify ACCOUNT UNLOCK to unlock the user's account and enable access to the account.

CREATE VIEW

PURPOSE
Use the CREATE VIEW statement to define a **view**, which is a logical table based on one or more tables or views. A view contains no data itself. The tables upon which a view is based are called **base tables**.

You can also create an **object view** or a relational view that supports LOB and object datatypes (object types, REFs, nested table, or varray types) on top of the existing view mechanism. An object view is a view of a user-defined type, where each row contains objects, each object with a unique object identifier.

PREREQUISITES

To create a view in your own schema, you must have CREATE VIEW system privilege. To create a view in another user's schema, you must have CREATE ANY VIEW system privilege.

To create a subview, you must have UNDER ANY VIEW system privilege or the UNDER object privilege on the superview.

The owner of the schema containing the view must have the privileges necessary to either select, insert, update, or delete rows from all the tables or views on which the view is based. The owner must be granted these privileges directly, rather than through a role.

To use the basic constructor method of an object type when creating an object view, one of the following must be true:

- The object type must belong to the same schema as the view to be created.
- You must have EXECUTE ANY TYPE system privileges.
- You must have the EXECUTE object privilege on that object type.

PARTITION VIEWS

Partition views were introduced in Oracle Release 7.3 to provide partitioning capabilities for applications requiring them. Partition views are supported in Oracle 9*i* so that you can upgrade applications from Release 7.3 without any modification. In most cases, subsequent to migration to Oracle 9*i* you will want to migrate partition views into partitions.

In Oracle 9*i*, you can use the CREATE TABLE statement to create partitioned tables easily. Partitioned tables offer the same advantages as partition views, while also addressing their shortcomings. Oracle recommends that you use partitioned tables rather than partition views in most operational environments.

SYNTAX

create_view::=

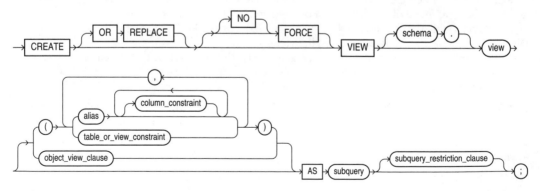

object_view_clause::=

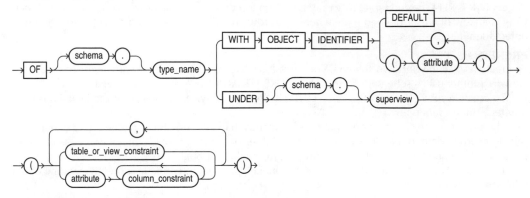

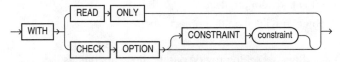

subquery_restriction_clause::=

KEYWORDS AND PARAMETERS

OR REPLACE   Specify OR REPLACE to re-create the view if it already exists. You can use this clause to change the definition of an existing view without dropping, re-creating, and regranting object privileges previously granted on it.

INSTEAD OF triggers defined in the view are dropped when a view is re-created.

If any materialized views are dependent on *view*, those materialized views will be marked UNUSABLE and will require a full refresh to restore them to a usable state. Invalid materialized views cannot be used by query rewrite and cannot be refreshed until they are recompiled.

FORCE   Specify FORCE if you want to create the view regardless of whether the view's base tables or the referenced object types exist or the owner of the schema containing the view has privileges on them. These conditions must be true before any SELECT, INSERT, UPDATE, or DELETE statements can be issued against the view.

If the view definition contains any constraints, CREATE VIEW ... FORCE will fail if the base table does not exist or the referenced object type does not exist. CREATE VIEW ... FORCE will also fail if the view definition references a constraint that does not exist.

NO FORCE   Specify NOFORCE if you want to create the view only if the base tables exist and the owner of the schema containing the view has privileges on them. This is the default.

schema   Specify the schema to contain the view. If you omit schema, Oracle creates the view in your own schema.

view   Specify the name of the view or the object view.

Restriction: If a view has INSTEAD OF triggers, any views created on it must have INSTEAD OF triggers, even if the views are inherently updatable.

alias Specify names for the expressions selected by the view's query. The number of aliases must match the number of expressions selected by the view. Aliases must follow the rules for naming Oracle schema objects. Aliases must be unique within the view.

If you omit the aliases, Oracle derives them from the columns or column aliases in the view's query. For this reason, you must use aliases if the view's query contains expressions rather than only column names. Also, you must specify aliases if the view definition includes constraints.

Restriction: You cannot specify an alias when creating an object view.

table_or_view_constraint and column_constraint You can specify constraints on views and object views. You define the constraint at the view level using the table_or_view_constraint clause. You define the constraint at the column or attribute level using the column_constraint clause after the appropriate alias.

View constraints (at the view and at the column or attribute level) are declarative only. That is, Oracle does not enforce them. However, operations on views are subject to the integrity constraints defined on the underlying base tables, so you can enforce constraints on views through constraints on base tables.

View constraints are a subset of table constraints and are subject to a number of restrictions.

object_view_clause The object_view_clause lets you define a view on an object type.

OF type_name Clause Use this clause to explicitly create an object view of type type_name. The columns of an object view correspond to the top-level attributes of type type_name. Each row will contain an object instance and each instance will be associated with an object identifier (OID) as specified in the WITH OBJECT IDENTIFIER clause. If you omit schema, Oracle creates the object view in your own schema.

WITH OBJECT IDENTIFIER Clause Use the WITH OBJECT IDENTIFIER clause to specify a top-level (root) object view. This clause lets you specify the attributes of the object type that will be used as a key to identify each row in the object view. In most cases these attributes correspond to the primary key columns of the base table. You must ensure that the attribute list is unique and identifies exactly one row in the view.

Restrictions:

- If you try to dereference or pin a primary key REF that resolves to more than one instance in the object view, Oracle returns an error.

- You cannot specify this clause if you are creating a subview, because subviews inherit object identifiers from superviews.

NOTE
The Oracle8i, Release 8.0 syntax WITH OBJECT OID is replaced with this syntax for clarity. The keywords WITH OBJECT OID are supported for backward compatibility, but Oracle Corporation recommends that you use the new syntax WITH OBJECT IDENTIFIER.

If the object view is defined on an object table or an object view, you can omit this clause or specify DEFAULT.

DEFAULT: Specify DEFAULT if you want Oracle to use the intrinsic object identifier of the underlying object table or object view to uniquely identify each row.

attribute: For *attribute*, specify an attribute of the object type from which Oracle should create the object identifier for the object view.

UNDER Clause   Use the UNDER clause to specify a subview based on an object superview.

To learn whether a view is a superview or a subview, query the SUPERVIEW_NAME column of the USER_, ALL_, or DBA_VIEWS data dictionary views.

Restrictions:

- You must create a subview in the same schema as the superview.

- The object type *type_name* must be the immediate subtype of *superview*.

- You can create only one subview of a particular type under the same superview.

AS subquery   Specify a subquery that identifies columns and rows of the table(s) that the view is based on. The select list of the subquery can contain up to 1000 expressions.

If you create views that refer to remote tables and views, the database links you specify must have been created using the CONNECT TO clause of the CREATE DATABASE LINK statement, and you must qualify them with schema name in the view subquery.

Restrictions on the view subquery:

- The view subquery cannot select the CURRVAL or NEXTVAL pseudocolumns.

- If the view subquery selects the ROWID, ROWNUM, or LEVEL pseudocolumns, those columns must have aliases in the view subquery.

- If the view subquery uses an asterisk (*) to select all columns of a table, and you later add new columns to the table, the view will not contain those columns until you re-create the view by issuing a CREATE OR REPLACE VIEW statement.

- For object views, the number of elements in the view subquery select list must be the same as the number of top-level attributes for the object type. The datatype of each of the selecting elements must be the same as the corresponding top-level attribute.

- You cannot specify the SAMPLE clause.

The preceding restrictions apply to materialized views as well.

Notes on Creating Updatable Views:

An updatable view is one you can use to insert, update, or delete base table rows. You can create a view to be inherently updatable, or you can create an INSTEAD OF trigger on any view to make it updatable.

To learn whether and in what ways the columns of an inherently updatable view can be modified, query the USER_UPDATABLE_COLUMNS data dictionary view. (The information displayed by this view is meaningful only for inherently updatable views.)

- If you want the view to be inherently updatable, it must not contain any of the following constructs:
  - A set operator
  - A DISTINCT operator
  - An aggregate or analytic function
  - A GROUP BY, ORDER BY, CONNECT BY, or START WITH clause
  - A collection expression in a SELECT list

- A subquery in a SELECT list
- Joins (with some exceptions—see below).

- In addition, if an inherently updatable view contains pseudocolumns or expressions, you cannot update base table rows with an UPDATE statement that refers to any of these pseudocolumns or expressions.

- If you want a join view to be updatable, all of the following conditions must be true:

  - The DML statement must affect only one table underlying the join.

  - For an INSERT statement, the view must not be created WITH CHECK OPTION, and all columns into which values are inserted must come from a key-preserved table. A key-preserved table in one for which every primary key or unique key value in the base table is also unique in the join view.

  - For an UPDATE statement, all columns updated must be extracted from a key-preserved table. If the view was created WITH CHECK OPTION, join columns and columns taken from tables that are referenced more than once in the view must be shielded from UPDATE.

  - For a DELETE statement, the join can have one and only one key-preserved table. That table can appear more than once in the join, unless the view was created WITH CHECK OPTION.

subquery_restriction_clause   Use the subquery_restriction_clause to restrict the subquery in one of the following ways:

   WITH READ ONLY: Specify WITH READ ONLY if you want no deletes, inserts, or updates to be performed through the view.

   WITH CHECK OPTION: Specify WITH CHECK OPTION to guarantee that inserts and updates performed through the view will result in rows that the view subquery can select. The CHECK OPTION cannot make this guarantee if:

- There is a subquery within the subquery of this view or any view on which this view is based or

- INSERT, UPDATE, or DELETE operations are performed using INSTEAD OF triggers.

   CONSTRAINT *constraint*: Specify the name of the CHECK OPTION constraint. If you omit this identifier, Oracle automatically assigns the constraint a name of the form SYS_Cn, where n is an integer that makes the constraint name unique within the database.

EXPLAIN PLAN

PURPOSE
Use the EXPLAIN PLAN statement to determine the execution plan Oracle follows to execute a specified SQL statement. This statement inserts a row describing each step of the execution plan into a specified table. If you are using cost-based optimization, this statement also determines the cost of executing the statement. If any domain indexes are defined on the table, user-defined CPU and I/O costs will also be inserted.

   The definition of a sample output table PLAN_TABLE is available in a SQL script on your distribution media. Your output table must have the same column names and datatypes as this table.

The common name of this script is UTLXPLAN.SQL. The exact name and location depend on your operating system. You can also issue the EXPLAIN PLAN statement as part of the SQL trace facility.

For information on the execution plan for a cached cursor, query the V$SQL_PLAN dynamic performance view.

PREREQUISITES

To issue an EXPLAIN PLAN statement, you must have the privileges necessary to insert rows into an existing output table that you specify to hold the execution plan.

You must also have the privileges necessary to execute the SQL statement for which you are determining the execution plan. If the SQL statement accesses a view, you must have privileges to access any tables and views on which the view is based. If the view is based on another view that is based on a table, you must have privileges to access both the other view and its underlying table.

To examine the execution plan produced by an EXPLAIN PLAN statement, you must have the privileges necessary to query the output table.

The EXPLAIN PLAN statement is a data manipulation language (DML) statement, rather than a data definition language (DDL) statement. Therefore, Oracle does not implicitly commit the changes made by an EXPLAIN PLAN statement. If you want to keep the rows generated by an EXPLAIN PLAN statement in the output table, you must commit the transaction containing the statement.

SYNTAX

explain_plan::=

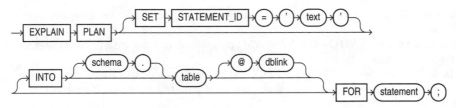

KEYWORDS AND PARAMETERS

SET STATEMENT_ID Clause   Specify the value of the STATEMENT_ID column for the rows of the execution plan in the output table. You can then use this value to identify these rows among others in the output table. Be sure to specify a STATEMENT_ID value if your output table contains rows from many execution plans. If you omit this clause, the STATEMENT_ID value defaults to null.

INTO table Clause   Specify the name of the output table, and optionally its schema and database. This table must exist before you use the EXPLAIN PLAN statement. If you omit *schema*, Oracle assumes the table is in your own schema.

The *dblink* can be a complete or partial name of a database link to a remote Oracle database where the output table is located. You can specify a remote output table only if you are using Oracle's distributed functionality. If you omit *dblink*, Oracle assumes the table is on your local database.

If you omit INTO altogether, Oracle assumes an output table named PLAN_TABLE in your own schema on your local database.

FOR statement Clause   Specify a SELECT, INSERT, UPDATE, DELETE, CREATE TABLE, CREATE INDEX, or ALTER INDEX ... REBUILD statement for which the execution plan is generated.

NOTE
If statement includes the parallel_clause, the resulting execution plan will indicate parallel execution. However, EXPLAIN PLAN actually inserts the statement into the plan table, so that the parallel DML statement you submit is no longer the first DML statement in the transaction. This violates the Oracle restriction of one parallel DML statement in a single transaction, and the statement will be executed serially. To maintain parallel execution of the statements, you must commit or roll back the EXPLAIN PLAN statement, and then submit the parallel DML statement.

NOTE
To determine the execution plan for an operation on a temporary table, EXPLAIN PLAN must be run from the same session, because the data in temporary tables is session specific.

filespec

PURPOSE
Use the filespec syntax to specify a file as a datafile or tempfile, or to specify a group of one or more files as a redo log file group.

PREREQUISITES
A filespec can appear in the statements CREATE DATABASE, ALTER DATABASE, CREATE TABLESPACE, ALTER TABLESPACE, CREATE CONTROLFILE, CREATE LIBRARY, and CREATE TEMPORARY TABLESPACE. You must have the privileges necessary to issue one of these statements.

SYNTAX
filespec::=

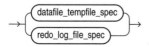

datafile_tempfile_spec::=

redo_log_file_spec::=

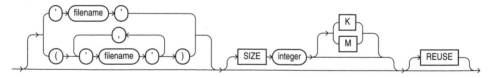

KEYWORDS AND PARAMETERS

'filename'   If filespec refers to a new file:

■ For a datafile or tempfile, if the DB_CREATE_FILE_DEST initialization parameter is set, then filename is optional, as are the remaining clauses of filespec.

■ For a logfile, if the DB_CREATE_ONLINE_LOG_DEST_n or DB_CREATE_FILE_DEST parameter is set, then filename is optional, as are the remaining clauses of filespec.

In either case, Oracle creates an Oracle-managed file in the default file system location for the type of file being created and generates a unique filename. If you omit the SIZE clause, Oracle creates a 100 MB autoextensible file with no maximum size. If the operation containing this filespec fails, any partially created Oracle-managed files are deleted. If neither parameter is set and you omit filename, the operation fails.

If filespec refers to an existing file, you must specify a filename. Specify the name of either a datafile, tempfile, or a redo log file member. The filename can contain only single-byte characters from 7-bit ASCII or EBCDIC character sets. Multibyte characters are not valid.

A redo log file group can have one or more members (copies). Each filename must be fully specified according to the conventions for your operating system.

SIZE Clause   Specify the size of the file in bytes. Use K or M to specify the size in kilobytes or megabytes.

■ For undo tablespaces, you must specify the SIZE clause for each datafile. For other tablespaces, you can omit this parameter if the file already exists, or if you are creating an Oracle-managed file.

■ The size of a tablespace must be one block greater than the sum of the sizes of the objects contained in it.

REUSE   Specify REUSE to allow Oracle to reuse an existing file. You must specify REUSE if you specify a filename that already exists.

■ If the file already exists, Oracle reuses the filename and applies the new size (if you specify SIZE) or retains the original size.

■ If the file does not exist, Oracle ignores this clause and creates the file.

Restriction: You cannot specify REUSE unless you have specified filename.

NOTE
*Whenever Oracle uses an existing file, the file's previous
contents are lost.*

GRANT

PURPOSE
Use the GRANT statement to grant:

■ System privileges to users and roles

- Roles to users and roles. Both privileges and roles are either local, global, or external. Table A-5 lists the system privileges (organized by the database object operated upon). Table A-6 lists Oracle predefined roles.

- Object privileges for a particular object to users, roles, and PUBLIC. Table A-7 summarizes the object privileges that you can grant on each type of object. Table A-8 lists object privileges and the operations that they authorize.

NOTE
You can authorize database users to use roles through means other than the database and the GRANT statement. For example, some operating systems have facilities that let you grant roles to Oracle users with the initialization parameter OS_ROLES. If you choose to grant roles to users through operating system facilities, you cannot also grant roles to users with the GRANT statement, although you can use the GRANT statement to grant system privileges to users and system privileges and roles to other roles.

PREREQUISITES
To grant a system privilege, you must either have been granted the system privilege with the ADMIN OPTION or have been granted the GRANT ANY PRIVILEGE system privilege.

To grant a role, you must either have been granted the role with the ADMIN OPTION or have been granted the GRANT ANY ROLE system privilege, or you must have created the role.

To grant an object privilege, you must own the object or the owner of the object must have granted you the object privileges with the GRANT OPTION. This rule applies to users with the DBA role.

SYNTAX
grant::=

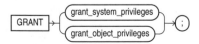

grant_system_privileges::=

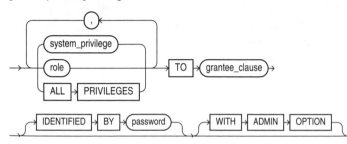

grant_object_privileges::=

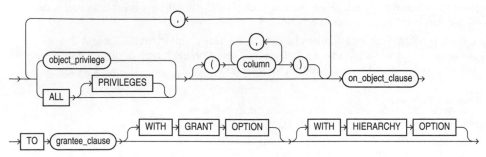

on_object_clause::=

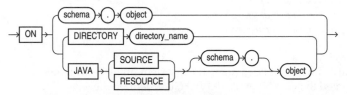

grantee_clause::=

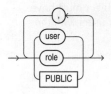

KEYWORDS AND PARAMETERS

grant_system_privileges

system_privilege Specify the system privilege you want to grant. Table A-5 lists the system privileges (organized by the database object operated upon).

- If you grant a privilege to a user, Oracle adds the privilege to the user's privilege domain. The user can immediately exercise the privilege.

- If you grant a privilege to a role, Oracle adds the privilege to the role's privilege domain. Users who have been granted and have enabled the role can immediately exercise the privilege. Other users who have been granted the role can enable the role and exercise the privilege.

- If you grant a privilege to PUBLIC, Oracle adds the privilege to the privilege domains of each user. All users can immediately perform operations authorized by the privilege.

  Oracle provides a shortcut for specifying all system privileges at once:

- ALL PRIVILEGES: Specify ALL PRIVILEGES to grant all the system privileges listed in Table A–5 except the SELECT ANY DICTIONARY privilege.

System Privilege Name	Operations Authorized
CLUSTERS	

Note: When you grant a privilege on "ANY" object (for example, CREATE ANY CLUSTER), you give the user access to that type of object in all schemas, including the SYS schema. If you want to prohibit access to objects in the SYS schema, set the initialization parameter O7_DICTIONARY_ACCESSIBILITY to FALSE. Then privileges granted on "ANY" object will allow access to any schema except SYS.

System Privilege Name	Operations Authorized
CREATE CLUSTER	Create clusters in grantee's schema
CREATE ANY CLUSTER	Create a cluster in any schema. Behaves similarly to CREATE ANY TABLE.
ALTER ANY CLUSTER	Alter clusters in any schema
DROP ANY CLUSTER	Drop clusters in any schema
CONTEXTS	
CREATE ANY CONTEXT	Create any context namespace
DROP ANY CONTEXT	Drop any context namespace
DATABASE	
ALTER DATABASE	Alter the database
ALTER SYSTEM	Issue ALTER SYSTEM statements
AUDIT SYSTEM	Issue AUDIT *sql_statements* statements
DATABASE LINKS	
CREATE DATABASE LINK	Create private database links in grantee's schema
CREATE PUBLIC DATABASE LINK	Create public database links
DROP PUBLIC DATABASE LINK	Drop public database links
DIMENSIONS	
CREATE DIMENSION	Create dimensions in the grantee's schema
CREATE ANY DIMENSION	Create dimensions in any schema
ALTER ANY DIMENSION	Alter dimensions in any schema
DROP ANY DIMENSION	Drop dimensions in any schema
DIRECTORIES	
CREATE ANY DIRECTORY	Create directory database objects
DROP ANY DIRECTORY	Drop directory database objects
INDEXTYPES	
CREATE INDEXTYPE	Create an indextype in the grantee's schema
CREATE ANY INDEXTYPE	Create an indextype in any schema
ALTER ANY INDEXTYPE	Modify indextypes in any schema
DROP ANY INDEXTYPE	Drop an indextype in any schema
EXECUTE ANY INDEXTYPE	Reference an indextype in any schema

TABLE A-5. *System Privileges*

System Privilege Name	Operations Authorized
INDEXES	
CREATE ANY INDEX	Create in any schema a domain index or an index on any table in any schema
ALTER ANY INDEX	Alter indexes in any schema
DROP ANY INDEX	Drop indexes in any schema
QUERY REWRITE	Enable rewrite using a materialized view, or create a function-based index, when that materialized view or index references tables and views that are in the grantee's own schema
GLOBAL QUERY REWRITE	Enable rewrite using a materialized view, or create a function-based index, when that materialized view or index references tables or views in any schema
LIBRARIES	
CREATE LIBRARY	Create external procedure/function libraries in grantee's schema
CREATE ANY LIBRARY	Create external procedure/function libraries in any schema
DROP LIBRARY	Drop external procedure/function libraries in the grantee's schema
DROP ANY LIBRARY	Drop external procedure/function libraries in any schema
MATERIALIZED VIEWS	
CREATE MATERIALIZED VIEW	Create a materialized view in the grantee's schema
CREATE ANY MATERIALIZED VIEW	Create materialized views in any schema
ALTER ANY MATERIALIZED VIEW	Alter materialized views in any schema
DROP ANY MATERIALIZED VIEW	Drop materialized views in any schema
QUERY REWRITE	Enable rewrite using a materialized view, or create a function-based index, when that materialized view or index references tables and views that are in the grantee's own schema
GLOBAL QUERY REWRITE	Enable rewrite using a materialized view, or create a function-based index, when that materialized view or index references tables or views in any schema
ON COMMIT REFRESH	Create a refresh-on-commit materialized view on any table in the database. Alter a refresh-on-demand materialized on any table in the database to refresh-on-commit

TABLE A-5. *System Privileges* (continued)

System Privilege Name	Operations Authorized
OPERATORS	
CREATE OPERATOR	Create an operator and its bindings in the grantee's schema
CREATE ANY OPERATOR	Create an operator and its bindings in any schema
DROP ANY OPERATOR	Drop an operator in any schema
EXECUTE ANY OPERATOR	Reference an operator in any schema
OUTLINES	
CREATE ANY OUTLINE	Create public outlines that can be used in any schema that uses outlines
ALTER ANY OUTLINE	Modify outlines
DROP ANY OUTLINE	Drop outlines
SELECT ANY OUTLINE	Create a clone private outline from a public outline
PROCEDURES	
CREATE PROCEDURE	Create stored procedures, functions, and packages in grantee's schema
CREATE ANY PROCEDURE	Create stored procedures, functions, and packages in any schema
ALTER ANY PROCEDURE	Alter stored procedures, functions, or packages in any schema
DROP ANY PROCEDURE	Drop stored procedures, functions, or packages in any schema
EXECUTE ANY PROCEDURE	Execute procedures or functions (standalone or packaged). Reference public package variables in any schema
PROFILES	
CREATE PROFILE	Create profiles
ALTER PROFILE	Alter profiles
DROP PROFILE	Drop profiles
ROLES	
CREATE ROLE	Create roles
ALTER ANY ROLE	Alter any role in the database
DROP ANY ROLE	Drop roles
GRANT ANY ROLE	Grant any role in the database
ROLLBACK SEGMENTS	
CREATE ROLLBACK SEGMENT	Create rollback segments
ALTER ROLLBACK SEGMENT	Alter rollback segments
DROP ROLLBACK SEGMENT	Drop rollback segments

TABLE A-5. *System Privileges* (continued)

System Privilege Name	Operations Authorized
SEQUENCES	
CREATE SEQUENCE	Create sequences in grantee's schema
CREATE ANY SEQUENCE	Create sequences in any schema
ALTER ANY SEQUENCE	Alter any sequence in the database
DROP ANY SEQUENCE	Drop sequences in any schema
SELECT ANY SEQUENCE	Reference sequences in any schema
SESSIONS	
CREATE SESSION	Connect to the database
ALTER RESOURCE COST	Set costs for session resources
ALTER SESSION	Issue ALTER SESSION statements
RESTRICTED SESSION	Logon after the instance is started using the SQL*Plus STARTUP RESTRICT statement
SNAPSHOTS. See **MATERIALIZED VIEWS**	
SYNONYMS	
CREATE SYNONYM	Create synonyms in grantee's schema
CREATE ANY SYNONYM	Create private synonyms in any schema
CREATE PUBLIC SYNONYM	Create public synonyms
DROP ANY SYNONYM	Drop private synonyms in any schema
DROP PUBLIC SYNONYM	Drop public synonyms
TABLES	

Note: For external tables, the only valid privileges are CREATE ANY TABLE, ALTER ANY TABLE, DROP ANY TABLE, and SELECT ANY TABLE.

CREATE TABLE	Create tables in grantee's schema
CREATE ANY TABLE	Create tables in any schema. The owner of the schema containing the table must have space quota on the tablespace to contain the table.
ALTER ANY TABLE	Alter any table or view in any schema
BACKUP ANY TABLE	Use the Export utility to incrementally export objects from the schema of other users
DELETE ANY TABLE	Delete rows from tables, table partitions, or views in any schema
DROP ANY TABLE	Drop or truncate tables or table partitions in any schema
INSERT ANY TABLE	Insert rows into tables and views in any schema
LOCK ANY TABLE	Lock tables and views in any schema

TABLE A-5. *System Privileges* (continued)

System Privilege Name	Operations Authorized
SELECT ANY TABLE	Query tables, views, or materialized views in any schema
UNDER ANY TABLE	Create subtables under any object tables
UPDATE ANY TABLE	Update rows in tables and views in any schema
TABLESPACES	
CREATE TABLESPACE	Create tablespaces
ALTER TABLESPACE	Alter tablespaces
DROP TABLESPACE	Drop tablespaces
MANAGE TABLESPACE	Take tablespaces offline and online and begin and end tablespace backups
UNLIMITED TABLESPACE	Use an unlimited amount of any tablespace. This privilege overrides any specific quotas assigned. If you revoke this privilege from a user, the user's schema objects remain but further tablespace allocation is denied unless authorized by specific tablespace quotas. You cannot grant this system privilege to roles.
TRIGGERS	
CREATE TRIGGER	Create a database trigger in grantee's schema
CREATE ANY TRIGGER	Create database triggers in any schema
ALTER ANY TRIGGER	Enable, disable, or compile database triggers in any schema
DROP ANY TRIGGER	Drop database triggers in any schema
ADMINISTER DATABASE TRIGGER	Create a trigger on DATABASE. (You must also have the CREATE TRIGGER or CREATE ANY TRIGGER privilege.)
TYPES	
CREATE TYPE	Create object types and object type bodies in grantee's schema
CREATE ANY TYPE	Create object types and object type bodies in any schema
ALTER ANY TYPE	Alter object types in any schema
DROP ANY TYPE	Drop object types and object type bodies in any schema
EXECUTE ANY TYPE	Use and reference object types and collection types in any schema, and invoke methods of an object type in any schema if you make the grant to a specific user. If you grant EXECUTE ANY TYPE to a role, users holding the enabled role will not be able to invoke methods of an object type in any schema.
UNDER ANY TYPE	Create subtypes under any nonfinal object types.

TABLE A-5. *System Privileges* (continued)

System Privilege Name	Operations Authorized
USERS	

CREATE USER	Create users. This privilege also allows the creator to:
	    Assign quotas on any tablespace
	    Set default and temporary tablespaces
	    Assign a profile as part of a CREATE USER statement

ALTER USER	Alter any user. This privilege authorizes the grantee to:
	    Change another user's password or authentication method
	    Assign quotas on any tablespace
	    Set default and temporary tablespaces
	    Assign a profile and default roles

BECOME USER	Become another user. (Required by any user performing a full database import.)
DROP USER	Drop users
VIEWS	
CREATE VIEW	Create views in grantee's schema
CREATE ANY VIEW	Create views in any schema
DROP ANY VIEW	Drop views in any schema
UNDER ANY VIEW	Create subviews under any object views
MISCELLANEOUS	
ANALYZE ANY	Analyze any table, cluster, or index in any schema
AUDIT ANY	Audit any object in any schema using AUDIT *schema_objects* statements
COMMENT ANY TABLE	Comment on any table, view, or column in any schema
EXEMPT ACCESS POLICY	Bypass fine-grained access control

Caution: This is a very powerful system privilege, as it lets the grantee bypass application-driven security policies. Database administrators should use caution when granting this privilege.

FORCE ANY TRANSACTION	Force the commit or rollback of any in-doubt distributed transaction in the local database. Induce the failure of a distributed transaction
FORCE TRANSACTION	Force the commit or rollback of grantee's in-doubt distributed transactions in the local database
GRANT ANY PRIVILEGE	Grant any system privilege
RESUMABLE	Enable resumable space allocation

TABLE A-5. *System Privileges* (continued)

System Privilege Name	Operations Authorized
SELECT ANY DICTIONARY	Query any data dictionary object in the SYS schema. This privilege lets you selectively override the default FALSE setting of the O7_DICTIONARY_ACCESSIBILITY initialization parameter.

Note: This privilege must be granted individually. It is not included in GRANT ALL PRIVILEGES, nor can it be granted through a role.

SYSDBA	Perform STARTUP and SHUTDOWN operations ALTER DATABASE: open, mount, back up, or change character set CREATE DATABASE ARCHIVELOG and RECOVERY CREATE SPFILE Includes the RESTRICTED SESSION privilege
SYSOPER	Perform STARTUP and SHUTDOWN operations ALTER DATABASE OPEN | MOUNT | BACKUP ARCHIVELOG and RECOVERY CREATE SPFILE Includes the RESTRICTED SESSION privilege

TABLE A-5. *System Privileges* (continued)

role   Specify the role you want to grant. You can grant an Oracle predefined role or a user-defined role. Table A–6 lists the predefined roles.

- If you grant a role to a user, Oracle makes the role available to the user. The user can immediately enable the role and exercise the privileges in the role's privilege domain.

- If you grant a role to another role, Oracle adds the granted role's privilege domain to the grantee role's privilege domain. Users who have been granted the grantee role can enable it and exercise the privileges in the granted role's privilege domain.

- If you grant a role to PUBLIC, Oracle makes the role available to all users. All users can immediately enable the role and exercise the privileges in the roles privilege domain.

IDENTIFIED BY Clause   Use the IDENTIFIED BY clause to specifically identify an existing user by password or to create a nonexistent user. This clause is not valid if the grantee is a role or PUBLIC. If the user specified in the *grantee_clause* does not exist, Oracle creates the user with the password and with the privileges and roles specified in this clause.

WITH ADMIN OPTION   Specify WITH ADMIN OPTION to enable the grantee to:

- Grant the role to another user or role, unless the role is a GLOBAL role

- Revoke the role from another user or role

- Alter the role to change the authorization needed to access it

- Drop the role

Predefined Role	Purpose
CONNECT, RESOURCE, and DBA	These roles are provided for compatibility with previous versions of Oracle. You can determine the privileges encompassed by these roles by querying the DBA_SYS_PRIVS data dictionary view.

Note: Oracle Corporation recommends that you design your own roles for database security rather than relying on these roles. These roles may not be created automatically by future versions of Oracle.

Predefined Role	Purpose
DELETE_CATALOG_ROLE EXECUTE_CATALOG_ROLE SELECT_CATALOG_ROLE	These roles are provided for accessing data dictionary views and packages.
EXP_FULL_DATABASE IMP_FULL_DATABASE	These roles are provided for convenience in using the Import and Export utilities.
AQ_USER_ROLE AQ_ADMINISTRATOR_ROLE	You need these roles to use Oracle's Advanced Queuing functionality.
SNMPAGENT	This role is used by Enterprise Manager/Intelligent Agent.
RECOVERY_CATALOG_OWNER	You need this role to create a user who owns a recovery catalog.
HS_ADMIN_ROLE	A DBA using Oracle's heterogeneous services feature needs this role to access appropriate tables in the data dictionary and to manipulate them with the DBMS_HS package.

TABLE A-6. *Oracle Predefined Roles*

If you grant a system privilege or role to a user without specifying WITH ADMIN OPTION, and then subsequently grant the privilege or role to the user WITH ADMIN OPTION, the user has the ADMIN OPTION on the privilege or role.

To revoke the ADMIN OPTION on a system privilege or role from a user, you must revoke the privilege or role from the user altogether and then grant the privilege or role to the user without the ADMIN OPTION.

grantee_clause   TO grantee_clause identifies users or roles to which the system privilege, role, or object privilege is granted.

Restriction: A user, role, or PUBLIC cannot appear more than once in TO grantee_clause.

PUBLIC: Specify PUBLIC to grant the privileges to all users.

Restrictions on granting system privileges and roles:

- A privilege or role cannot appear more than once in the list of privileges and roles to be granted.
- You cannot grant a role to itself.
- You cannot grant a role IDENTIFIED GLOBALLY to anything.
- You cannot grant a role IDENTIFIED EXTERNALLY to a global user or global role.
- You cannot grant roles circularly. For example, if you grant the role banker to the role teller, you cannot subsequently grant teller to banker.

grant_object_privileges

object_privilege   Specify the object privilege you want to grant. You can specify any of the values shown in Table A-7. See also Table A-8.

   Restriction: A privilege cannot appear more than once in the list of privileges to be granted.

ALL [PRIVILEGES]   Specify ALL to grant all the privileges for the object that you have been granted with the GRANT OPTION. The user who owns the schema containing an object automatically has all privileges on the object with the GRANT OPTION. (The keyword PRIVILEGES is provided for semantic clarity and is optional.)

column   Specify the table or view column on which privileges are to be granted. You can specify columns only when granting the INSERT, REFERENCES, or UPDATE privilege. If you do not list columns, the grantee has the specified privilege on all columns in the table or view.

   For information on existing column object grants, query the USER_,ALL_, and DBA_COL_PRIVS data dictionary view.

on_object_clause   The on_object_clause identifies the object on which the privileges are granted. Directory schema objects and Java source and resource schema objects are identified separately because they reside in separate namespaces.

WITH GRANT OPTION   Specify WITH GRANT OPTION to enable the grantee to grant the object privileges to other users and roles.

Object Privilege	Table	View	Sequence	Procedures, Functions, Packages[a]	Materialized View	Directory	Library	User-defined Type	Operator	Indextype
ALTER	X		X							
DELETE	X	X			X[b]					
EXECUTE				X			X	X	X	X
INDEX	X									
INSERT	X	X			X[b]					
ON COMMIT REFRESH	X									
QUERY REWRITE	X									
READ						X				
REFERENCES	X	X								
SELECT	X	X	X		X					
UNDER		X						X		
UPDATE	X	X			X[b]					
WRITE						X				

[a]Oracle treats a Java class, source, or resource as if it were a procedure for purposes of granting object privileges.
[b]The DELETE, INSERT, and UPDATE privileges can be granted only to updatable materialized views.

TABLE A-7.   *Object Privileges Available for Particular Objects*

Object Privilege   Operations Authorized

The following **table privileges** authorize operations on a table. Any one of following object privileges allows the grantee to lock the table in any lock mode with the LOCK TABLE statement.

Note: For external tables, the only valid object privileges are ALTER and SELECT.

ALTER	Change the table definition with the ALTER TABLE statement.
DELETE	Remove rows from the table with the DELETE statement.

Note: You must grant the SELECT privilege on the table along with the DELETE privilege.

INDEX	Create an index on the table with the CREATE INDEX statement.
INSERT	Add new rows to the table with the INSERT statement.
REFERENCES	Create a constraint that refers to the table. You cannot grant this privilege to a role.
SELECT	Query the table with the SELECT statement.
UNDER	Create a subtable under this table. You can grant this object privilege only if you have the UNDER ANY TABLE privilege WITH GRANT OPTION on the immediate supertable of this table.
UPDATE	Change data in the table with the UPDATE statement.

Note: You must grant the SELECT privilege on the table along with the UPDATE privilege.

The following **view privileges** authorize operations on a view. Any one of the following object privileges allows the grantee to lock the view in any lock mode with the LOCK TABLE statement. To grant a privilege on a view, you must have that privilege with the GRANT OPTION on all of the view's base tables.

DELETE	Remove rows from the view with the DELETE statement.
INSERT	Add new rows to the view with the INSERT statement.
REFERENCES	Define foreign key constraints on the view.
SELECT	Query the view with the SELECT statement.
UNDER	Create a subview under this view. You can grant this object privilege only if you have the UNDER ANY VIEW privilege WITH GRANT OPTION on the immediate superview of this view.
UPDATE	Change data in the view with the UPDATE statement.

The following **sequence privileges** authorize operations on a sequence.

ALTER	Change the sequence definition with the ALTER SEQUENCE statement.
SELECT	Examine and increment values of the sequence with the CURRVAL and NEXTVAL pseudocolumns.

The following **procedure, function, and package privilege** authorizes operations on procedures, functions, and packages. This privilege also applies to **Java sources, classes, and resources**, which Oracle treats as though they were procedures for purposes of granting object privileges.

EXECUTE	Compile the procedure or function or execute it directly, or access any program object declared in the specification of a package.

Note: Users do not need this privilege to execute a procedure, function, or package indirectly.

TABLE A-8.   *Object Privileges and the Operations They Authorize*

Object Privilege   Operations Authorized

The following **materialized view privilege** authorizes operations on a materialized view.

ON COMMIT REFRESH	Create a refresh-on-commit materialized on the specified table.
QUERY REWRITE	Create a materialized view for query rewrite using the specified table.
SELECT	Query the materialized view with the SELECT statement.

Synonym privileges are the same as the privileges for the base object. Granting a privilege on a synonym is equivalent to granting the privilege on the base object. Similarly, granting a privilege on a base object is equivalent to granting the privilege on all synonyms for the object. If you grant to a user a privilege on a synonym, the user can use either the synonym name or the base object name in the SQL statement that exercises the privilege.

The following **directory privileges** provide secured access to the files stored in the operating system directory to which the directory object serves as a pointer. The directory object contains the full path name of the operating system directory where the files reside. Because the files are actually stored outside the database, Oracle server processes also need to have appropriate file permissions on the file system server. Granting object privileges on the directory database object to individual database users, rather than on the operating system, allows Oracle to enforce security during file operations.

READ	Read files in the directory.
WRITE	Write files in the directory. This privilege is useful only in connection with external tables. It allows the grantee to determine whether the external table agent can write a log file, or a bad file to the directory. **Restriction:** This privilege does not allow the grantee to write to a BFILE.

The following **object type privilege** authorizes operations on an object type

EXECUTE	Use and reference the specified object and to invoke its methods.
UNDER	Create a subtype under this type. You can grant this object privilege only if you have the UNDER ANY TYPE privilege WITH GRANT OPTION on the immediate supertype of this type.

The following **indextype privilege** authorizes operations on indextypes.

EXECUTE	Reference an indextype.

The following **operator privilege** authorizes operations on user-defined operators.

EXECUTE	Reference an operator.

TABLE A-8. *Object Privileges and the Operations They Authorize* (continued)

Restriction: You can specify WITH GRANT OPTION only when granting to a user or to PUBLIC, not when granting to a role.

WITH HIERARCHY OPTION   Specify WITH HIERARCHY OPTION to grant the specified object privilege on all subobjects of *object*, including subobjects created subsequent to this statement (such as subviews created under a view).

NOTE
This clause is meaningful only in combination with the SELECT object privilege.

object: Specify the schema object on which the privileges are to be granted. If you do not qualify *object* with *schema*, Oracle assumes the object is in your own schema. The object can be one of the following types:

- Table, view, or materialized view
- Sequence
- Procedure, function, or package
- User-defined type
- Synonym for any of the above items
- Directory, library, operator, or indextype
- Java source, class, or resource

NOTE
You cannot grant privileges directly to a single partition of a partitioned table. For information on how to grant privileges to a single partition indirectly, refer to Oracle9i Database Concepts.

DIRECTORY *directory_name:* Specify a directory schema object on which privileges are to be granted. You cannot qualify *directory_name* with a schema name.

JAVA SOURCE | RESOURCE: The JAVA clause lets you specify a Java source or resource schema object on which privileges are to be granted.

NOAUDIT

PURPOSE
Use the NOAUDIT statement to stop auditing previously enabled by the AUDIT statement.

The NOAUDIT statement must have the same syntax as the previous AUDIT statement. Further, it reverses the effects only of that particular statement. For example, suppose one AUDIT statement (statement A) enables auditing for a specific user. A second (statement B) enables auditing for all users. A NOAUDIT statement to disable auditing for all users (statement C) reverses statement B. However, statement C leaves statement A in effect and continues to audit the user that statement A specified.

PREREQUISITES
To stop auditing of SQL statements, you must have the AUDIT SYSTEM system privilege.

To stop auditing of schema objects, you must be the owner of the object on which you stop auditing or you must have the AUDIT ANY system privilege. In addition, if the object you chose for auditing is a directory, even if you created it, you must have the AUDIT ANY system privilege.

SYNTAX
noaudit::=

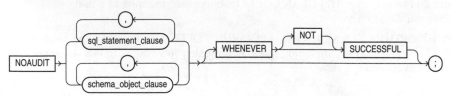

sql_statement_clause::=

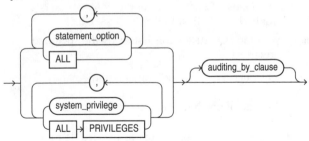

auditing_by_clause::=

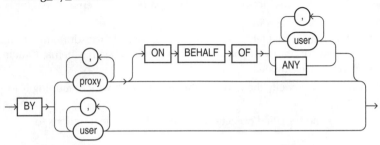

schema_object_clause::=

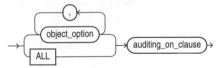

auditing_on_clause::=

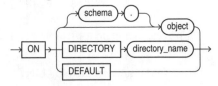

KEYWORDS AND PARAMETERS

sql_statement_clause   Use the sql_statement_clause to stop auditing of a particular SQL statement.

statement_option: For statement_option, specify the statement option for which auditing is to be stopped.

ALL: Specify ALL to stop auditing of all statement options currently being audited.

system_privilege: For system_privilege, specify the system privilege for which auditing is to be stopped.

ALL PRIVILEGES: Specify ALL PRIVILEGES to stop auditing of all system privileges currently being audited.

auditing_by_clause: Use the auditing_by_clause to stop auditing only those SQL statements issued by particular users. If you omit this clause, Oracle stops auditing all users' statements.

- Specify BY user to stop auditing only for SQL statements issued by the specified users in their subsequent sessions. If you omit this clause, Oracle stops auditing for all users' statements, except for the situation described for WHENEVER SUCCESSFUL.

- Specify BY proxy to stop auditing only for the SQL statements issued by the specified proxy, on behalf of a specific user or any user.

schema_object_clause   Use the schema_object_clause to stop auditing of a particular database object.

object_option: For object_option, specify the type of operation for which auditing is to be stopped on the object specified in the ON clause.

ALL: Specify ALL as a shortcut equivalent to specifying all object options applicable for the type of object.

auditing_on_clause: The auditing_on_clause lets you specify the particular schema object for which auditing is to be stopped.

- For object, specify the object name of a table, view, sequence, stored procedure, function, or package, materialized view, or library. If you do not qualify object with schema, Oracle assumes the object is in your own schema.

- The DIRECTORY clause lets you specify the name of the directory on which auditing is to be stopped.

- Specify DEFAULT to remove the specified object options as default object options for subsequently created objects.

WHENEVER [NOT] SUCCESSFUL: Specify WHENEVER SUCCESSFUL to stop auditing only for SQL statements and operations on schema objects that complete successfully.

Specify WHENEVER NOT SUCCESSFUL to stop auditing only for statements and operations that result in Oracle errors.

If you omit this clause, Oracle stops auditing for all statements or operations, regardless of success or failure.

RENAME

PURPOSE
Use the RENAME statement to rename a table, view, sequence, or private synonym for a table, view, or sequence.

- Oracle automatically transfers integrity constraints, indexes, and grants on the old object to the new object.

- Oracle invalidates all objects that depend on the renamed object, such as views, synonyms, and stored procedures and functions that refer to a renamed table.

Do not use this statement to rename public synonyms. Instead, drop the public synonym and then create another public synonym with the new name.

PREREQUISITES
The object must be in your own schema.

SYNTAX

rename::=

KEYWORDS AND PARAMETERS

old   Specify the name of an existing table, view, sequence, or private synonym.

new   Specify the new name to be given to the existing object. The new name must not already be used by another schema object in the same namespace and must follow the rules for naming schema objects.

REVOKE

PURPOSE

Use the REVOKE statement to:

- Revoke system privileges from users and roles
- Revoke roles from users and roles
- Revoke object privileges for a particular object from users and roles

PREREQUISITES

To revoke a **system privilege or role,** you must have been granted the privilege with the ADMIN OPTION.

To revoke a **role**, you must have been granted the role with the ADMIN OPTION. You can revoke any role if you have the GRANT ANY ROLE system privilege.

To revoke an **object privilege**, you must have previously granted the object privileges to each user and role.

The REVOKE statement can revoke only privileges and roles that were previously granted directly with a GRANT statement. You cannot use this statement to revoke:

- Privileges or roles not granted to the revokee
- Roles or object privileges granted through the operating system
- Privileges or roles granted to the revokee through roles

SYNTAX

revoke::=

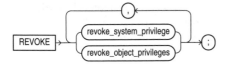

revoke_system_privileges::=

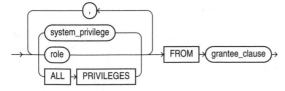

revoke_object_privileges::=

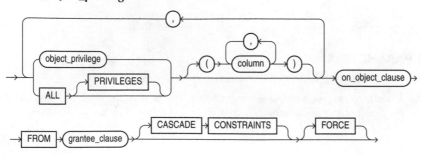

grantee_clause::=

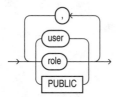

on_object_clause::=

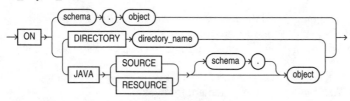

KEYWORDS AND PARAMETERS

revoke_system_privileges

system_privilege   Specify the system privilege to be revoked.

- If you revoke a privilege from a user, Oracle removes the privilege from the user's privilege domain. Effective immediately, the user cannot exercise the privilege.

- If you revoke a privilege from a role, Oracle removes the privilege from the role's privilege domain. Effective immediately, users with the role enabled cannot exercise the privilege. Also, other users who have been granted the role and subsequently enable the role cannot exercise the privilege.

- If you revoke a privilege from PUBLIC, Oracle removes the privilege from the privilege domain of each user who has been granted the privilege through PUBLIC. Effective immediately, such users can no longer exercise the privilege. However, the privilege is not revoked from users who have been granted the privilege directly or through roles.

Restriction: A system privilege cannot appear more than once in the list of privileges to be revoked.

Oracle provides a shortcut for specifying all system privileges at once:

- ALL PRIVILEGES: Specify ALL PRIVILEGES to revoke all the system privileges listed in Table A–5.

role   Specify the role to be revoked.

- If you revoke a role from a user, Oracle makes the role unavailable to the user. If the role is currently enabled for the user, the user can continue to exercise the privileges in the role's privilege domain as long as it remains enabled. However, the user cannot subsequently enable the role.

- If you revoke a role from another role, Oracle removes the revoked role's privilege domain from the revokee role's privilege domain. Users who have been granted and have enabled the revokee role can continue to exercise the privileges in the revoked role's privilege domain as long as the revokee role remains enabled. However, other users who have been granted the revokee role and subsequently enable it cannot exercise the privileges in the privilege domain of the revoked role.

- If you revoke a role from PUBLIC, Oracle makes the role unavailable to all users who have been granted the role through PUBLIC. Any user who has enabled the role can continue to exercise the privileges in its privilege domain as long as it remains enabled. However, users cannot subsequently enable the role. The role is not revoked from users who have been granted the role directly or through other roles.

Restriction: A system role cannot appear more than once in the list of roles to be revoked.

grantee_clause   FROM grantee_clause identifies users or roles from which the system privilege, role, or object privilege is to be revoked.

PUBLIC: Specify PUBLIC to revoke the privileges or roles from all users.

revoke_object_privileges

object_privilege   Specify the object privilege to be revoked. You can substitute any of the following values: ALTER, DELETE, EXECUTE, INDEX, INSERT, READ, REFERENCES, SELECT, UPDATE.

NOTE
Each privilege authorizes some operation. By revoking a privilege, you prevent the revokee from performing that operation. However, multiple users may grant the same privilege to the same user, role, or PUBLIC. To remove the privilege from the grantee's privilege domain, all grantors must revoke the privilege. If even one grantor does not revoke the privilege, the grantee can still exercise the privilege by virtue of that grant.

If you revoke a privilege from a user, Oracle removes the privilege from the user's privilege domain. Effective immediately, the user cannot exercise the privilege.

- If that user has granted that privilege to other users or roles, Oracle also revokes the privilege from those other users or roles.

- If that user's schema contains a procedure, function, or package that contains SQL statements that exercise the privilege, the procedure, function, or package can no longer be executed.

- If that user's schema contains a view on that object, Oracle invalidates the view.
- If you revoke the REFERENCES privilege from a user who has exercised the privilege to define referential integrity constraints, you must specify the CASCADE CONSTRAINTS clause.

If you revoke a privilege from a role, Oracle removes the privilege from the role's privilege domain. Effective immediately, users with the role enabled cannot exercise the privilege. Other users who have been granted the role cannot exercise the privilege after enabling the role.

If you revoke a privilege from PUBLIC, Oracle removes the privilege from the privilege domain of each user who has been granted the privilege through PUBLIC. Effective immediately, all such users are restricted from exercising the privilege. However, the privilege is not revoked from users who have been granted the privilege directly or through roles.

Restriction: A privilege cannot appear more than once in the list of privileges to be revoked. A user, a role, or PUBLIC cannot appear more than once in the FROM clause.

ALL [PRIVILEGES]   Specify ALL to revoke all object privileges that you have granted to the revokee. (The keyword PRIVILEGES is provided for semantic clarity and is optional.)

NOTE
If no privileges have been granted on the object, Oracle takes no action and does not return an error.

CASCADE CONSTRAINTS   This clause is relevant only if you revoke the REFERENCES privilege or ALL [PRIVILEGES]. It drops any referential integrity constraints that the revokee has defined using the REFERENCES privilege (which might have been granted either explicitly or implicitly through a grant of ALL [PRIVILEGES]).

FORCE   Specify FORCE to revoke the EXECUTE object privilege on user-defined type objects with table or type dependencies. You must use FORCE to revoke the EXECUTE object privilege on user-defined type objects with table dependencies.

If you specify FORCE, all privileges will be revoked, but all dependent objects are marked INVALID, data in dependent tables becomes inaccessible, and all dependent function-based indexes are marked UNUSABLE. (Regranting the necessary type privilege will revalidate the table.)

on_object_clause   The on_object_clause identifies the objects on which privileges are to be revoked.

object: Specify the object on which the object privileges are to be revoked. This object can be:

- A table, view, sequence, procedure, stored function, or package, materialized view
- A synonym for a table, view, sequence, procedure, stored function, package, or materialized view
- A library, indextype, or user-defined operator

If you do not qualify object with schema, Oracle assumes the object is in your own schema.

If you revoke the SELECT object privilege (with or without the GRANT OPTION) on the containing table or materialized view of a materialized view, Oracle invalidates the materialized view.

If you revoke the SELECT object privilege (with or without the GRANT OPTION) on any of the master tables of a materialized view, Oracle invalidates both the materialized view and its containing table or materialized view.

DIRECTORY directory_name: Specify the directory object on which privileges are to be revoked. You cannot qualify directory_name with schema. The object must be a directory.

JAVA SOURCE | RESOURCE: The JAVA clause lets you specify a Java source or resource schema object on which privileges are to be revoked.

SET CONSTRAINT[S]

PURPOSE
Use the SET CONSTRAINTS statement to specify, for a particular transaction, whether a deferrable constraint is checked following each DML statement or when the transaction is committed.

PREREQUISITES
To specify when a deferrable constraint is checked, you must have SELECT privilege on the table to which the constraint is applied unless the table is in your schema.

SYNTAX
set_constraints::=

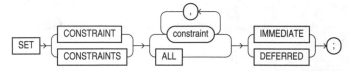

KEYWORDS AND PARAMETERS

constraint   Specify the name of one or more integrity constraints.

ALL   Specify ALL to set all deferrable constraints for this transaction.

IMMEDIATE   Specify IMMEDIATE to indicate that the conditions specified by the deferrable constraint are checked immediately after each DML statement.

DEFERRED   Specify DEFERRED to indicate that the conditions specified by the deferrable constraint are checked when the transaction is committed.

NOTE
You can verify the success of deferrable constraints prior to committing them by issuing a SET CONSTRAINTS ALL IMMEDIATE statement.

SET ROLE

PURPOSE
Use the SET ROLE statement to enable and disable roles for your current session.

When a user logs on, Oracle enables all privileges granted explicitly to the user and all privileges in the user's default roles. During the session, the user or an application can use the SET ROLE statement any number of times to change the roles currently enabled for the session. The number of roles that can be concurrently enabled is limited by the initialization parameter MAX_ENABLED_ROLES.

You can see which roles are currently enabled by examining the SESSION_ROLES data dictionary view.

PREREQUISITES

You must already have been granted the roles that you name in the SET ROLE statement.

SYNTAX

set_role::=

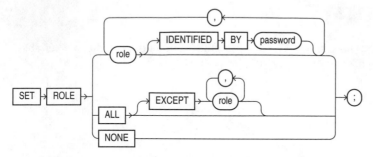

KEYWORDS AND PARAMETERS

role   Specify a role to be enabled for the current session. Any roles not listed and not already enabled are disabled for the current session.

In the IDENTIFIED BY *password* clause, specify the password for a role. If the role has a password, you must specify the password to enable the role.

Restriction: You cannot specify a role unless it was granted to you either directly or through other roles.

ALL   Specify ALL to enable all roles granted to you for the current session except those optionally listed in the EXCEPT clause.

Roles listed in the EXCEPT clause must be roles granted directly to you. They cannot be roles granted to you through other roles.

If you list a role in the EXCEPT clause that has been granted to you both directly and through another role, the role remains enabled by virtue of the role to which it has been granted.

Restriction: You cannot use this clause to enable roles with passwords that have been granted directly to you.

NONE   Specify NONE to disable all roles for the current session, including the DEFAULT role.

SET TRANSACTION

PURPOSE

Use the SET TRANSACTION statement to establish the current transaction as read only or read write, establish its isolation level, or assign it to a specified rollback segment.

The operations performed by a SET TRANSACTION statement affect only your current transaction, not other users or other transactions. Your transaction ends whenever you issue a COMMIT or ROLLBACK statement. Oracle implicitly commits the current transaction before and after executing a data definition language (DDL) statement.

PREREQUISITES

If you use a SET TRANSACTION statement, it must be the first statement in your transaction. However, a transaction need not have a SET TRANSACTION statement.

SYNTAX

set_transaction::=

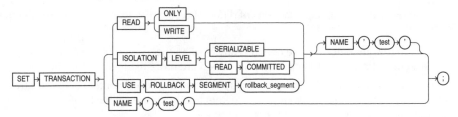

KEYWORDS AND PARAMETERS

READ ONLY   The READ ONLY clause establishes the current transaction as a read-only transaction. This clause established **transaction-level read consistency**.

All subsequent queries in that transaction only see changes committed before the transaction began. Read-only transactions are useful for reports that run multiple queries against one or more tables while other users update these same tables.

NOTE

This clause is not supported for the user SYS. That is, queries by SYS will return changes made during the transaction even if SYS has set the transaction to be READ ONLY.

Restriction: Only the following statements are permitted in a read-only transaction:

- Subqueries (that is, SELECT statements without the *for_update_clause*)
- LOCK TABLE
- SET ROLE
- ALTER SESSION
- ALTER SYSTEM

READ WRITE   Specify READ WRITE to establish the current transaction as a read/write transaction. This clause establishes **statement-level read consistency**, which is the default.

Restriction: You cannot toggle between transaction-level and statement-level read consistency in the same transaction.

ISOLATION LEVEL Clause   Use the ISOLATION LEVEL clause to specify how transactions containing database modifications are handled.

- The SERIALIZABLE setting specifies serializable transaction isolation mode as defined in the SQL92 standard. If a serializable transaction contains data manipulation language (DML) that attempts to update any resource that may have been updated in a transaction uncommitted at the start of the serializable transaction, then the DML statement fails.

NOTE

The COMPATIBLE initialization parameter must be set to 7.3.0 or higher for SERIALIZABLE mode to work.

- The READ COMMITTED setting is the default Oracle transaction behavior. If the transaction contains DML that requires row locks held by another transaction, then the DML statement waits until the row locks are released.

USE ROLLBACK SEGMENT Clause　Specify USE ROLLBACK SEGMENT to assign the current transaction to the specified rollback segment. This clause also implicitly establishes the transaction as a read/write transaction.

This clause lets you to assign transactions of different types to rollback segments of different sizes. For example:

- If no long-running queries are concurrently reading the same tables, you can assign small transactions to small rollback segments, which are more likely to remain in memory.

- You can assign transactions that modify tables that are concurrently being read by long-running queries to large rollback segments, so that the rollback information needed for the read-consistent queries is not overwritten.

- You can assign transactions that insert, update, or delete large amounts of data to rollback segments large enough to hold the rollback information for the transaction.

You cannot use the READ ONLY clause and the USE ROLLBACK SEGMENT clause in a single SET TRANSACTION statement or in different statements in the same transaction. Read-only transactions do not generate rollback information and therefore are not assigned rollback segments.

NAME Clause　Use the NAME clause to assign a name to the current transaction. This clause is especially useful in distributed database environments when you must identify and resolve in-doubt transactions. The *text* string is limited to 255 bytes.

If you specify a name for a distributed transaction, when the transaction commits, the name becomes the commit comment, overriding any comment specified explicitly in the COMMIT statement.

storage_clause

PURPOSE
Use the storage_clause to specify storage characteristics for any of the following schema objects:

- clusters
- indexes
- rollback segments
- materialized views
- materialized view logs
- tables
- tablespaces
- partitions

Storage parameters affect both how long it takes to access data stored in the database and how efficiently space in the database is used. For a discussion of the effects of these parameters, see *Oracle9i Database Performance Guide and Reference*.

When you create a tablespace, you can specify values for the storage parameters. These values serve as default values for segments allocated in the tablespace.

When you alter a tablespace, you can change the values of storage parameters. The new values serve as default values only for subsequently allocated segments (or subsequently created objects).

NOTE

The storage_clause is interpreted differently for locally managed tablespaces. At creation, Oracle ignores MAXEXTENTS and uses the remaining parameter values to calculate the initial size of the segment. For more information, see "CREATE TABLESPACE".

When you create a cluster, index, rollback segment, materialized view, materialized view log, table, or partition, you can specify values for the storage parameters for the segments allocated to these objects. If you omit any storage parameter, Oracle uses the value of that parameter specified for the tablespace.

When you alter a cluster, index, rollback segment, materialized view, materialized view log, table, or partition, you can change the values of storage parameters. The new values affect only future extent allocations.

PREREQUISITES

To change the value of a STORAGE parameter, you must have the privileges necessary to use the appropriate CREATE or ALTER statement.

SYNTAX

storage_clause::=

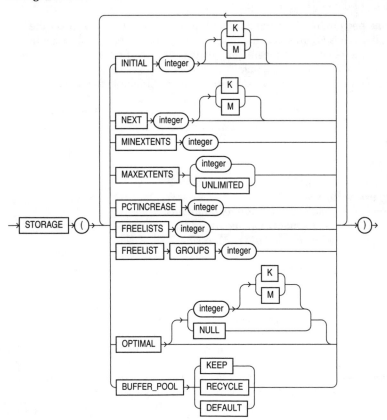

KEYWORDS AND PARAMETERS

INITIAL   Specify in bytes the size of the object's first extent. Oracle allocates space for this extent when you create the schema object. Use K or M to specify this size in kilobytes or megabytes.

The default value is the size of 5 data blocks. For segments with manual space management, the minimum value is the size of 2 data blocks plus one data block for each free list group you specify. For segments with automatic space management, the minimum value is 3 data blocks. The maximum value depends on your operating system. Oracle rounds values up to the next multiple of the data block size for values less than 5 data blocks, and rounds up to the next multiple of 5 data blocks for values greater than 5 data blocks.

Restriction: You cannot specify INITIAL in an ALTER statement.

NEXT   Specify in bytes the size of the next extent to be allocated to the object. Use K or M to specify the size in kilobytes or megabytes. The default value is the size of 5 data blocks. The minimum value is the size of 1 data block. The maximum value depends on your operating system. Oracle rounds values up to the next multiple of the data block size for values less than 5 data blocks. For values greater than 5 data blocks, Oracle rounds up to a value that minimizes fragmentation, as described in *Oracle9i Database Administrator's Guide.*

If you change the value of the NEXT parameter (that is, if you specify it in an ALTER statement), the next allocated extent will have the specified size, regardless of the size of the most recently allocated extent and the value of the PCTINCREASE parameter.

PCTINCREASE   Specify the percent by which the third and subsequent extents grow over the preceding extent. The default value is 50, meaning that each subsequent extent is 50% larger than the preceding extent. The minimum value is 0, meaning all extents after the first are the same size. The maximum value depends on your operating system.

Oracle rounds the calculated size of each new extent to the nearest multiple of the data block size.

If you change the value of the PCTINCREASE parameter (that is, if you specify it in an ALTER statement), Oracle calculates the size of the next extent using this new value and the size of the most recently allocated extent.

TIP

If you wish to keep all extents the same size, you can prevent SMON from coalescing extents by setting the value of PCTINCREASE to 0. In general, Oracle Corporation recommends a setting of 0 as a way to minimize fragmentation and avoid the possibility of very large temporary segments during processing.

Restriction: You cannot specify PCTINCREASE for rollback segments. Rollback segments always have a PCTINCREASE value of 0.

MINEXTENTS   Specify the total number of extents to allocate when the object is created. This parameter lets you allocate a large amount of space when you create an object, even if the space available is not contiguous. The default and minimum value is 1, meaning that Oracle allocates only the initial extent, except for rollback segments, for which the default and minimum value is 2. The maximum value depends on your operating system.

If the MINEXTENTS value is greater than 1, then Oracle calculates the size of subsequent extents based on the values of the INITIAL, NEXT, and PCTINCREASE storage parameters.

When changing the value of MINEXTENTS (that is, in an ALTER statement), you can reduce the value from its current value, but you cannot increase it. Resetting MINEXTENTS to a smaller value might be useful, for example, before a TRUNCATE ... DROP STORAGE statement, if you want to ensure that the segment will maintain a minimum number of extents after the TRUNCATE operation.

Restriction: You cannot change the value of MINEXTENTS for an object that resides in a locally managed tablespace.

MAXEXTENTS   Specify the total number of extents, including the first, that Oracle can allocate for the object. The minimum value is 1 (except for rollback segments, which always have a minimum value of 2). The default value depends on your data block size.

Restriction: You cannot change the value of MAXEXTENTS for an object that resides in a locally managed tablespace.

UNLIMITED: Specify UNLIMITED if you want extents to be allocated automatically as needed. Oracle Corporation recommends this setting as a way to minimize fragmentation.

However, do not use this clause for rollback segments. Rogue transactions containing inserts, updates, or deletes that continue for a long time will continue to create new extents until a disk is full.

CAUTION
A rollback segment that you create without specifying the storage_clause has the same storage parameters as the tablespace in which the rollback segment is created. Thus, if you create the tablespace with MAXEXTENTS UNLIMITED, then the rollback segment will also have the same default.

FREELIST GROUPS   Specify the number of groups of free lists for the database object you are creating. The default and minimum value for this parameter is 1. Oracle uses the instance number of FREELIST GROUPS instances to map each instance to one free list group.

Each free list group uses one database block. Therefore:

- If you do not specify a large enough value for INITIAL to cover the minimum value plus one data block for each free list group, Oracle increases the value of INITIAL the necessary amount.

- If you are creating an object in a uniform locally managed tablespace, and the extent size is not large enough to accommodate the number of freelist groups, the create operation will fail.

NOTE
Oracle ignores a setting of FREELIST GROUPS if the tablespace in which the object resides is in automatic segment-space management mode.

Restriction: You can specify the FREELIST GROUPS parameter only in CREATE TABLE, CREATE CLUSTER, CREATE MATERIALIZED VIEW, CREATE MATERIALIZED VIEW LOG, and CREATE INDEX statements.

FREELISTS   For objects other than tablespaces, specify the number of free lists for each of the free list groups for the table, partition, cluster, or index. The default and minimum value for this parameter is 1, meaning that each free list group contains one free list. The maximum value of this parameter depends on the data block size. If you specify a FREELISTS value that is too large, Oracle returns an error indicating the maximum value.

NOTE
Oracle ignores a setting of FREELISTS if the tablespace in which the object resides is in automatic segment-space management mode.

Restriction: You can specify FREELISTS in the storage_clause of any statement except when creating or altering a tablespace or rollback segment.

OPTIMAL   The OPTIMAL keyword is relevant only to rollback segments. It specifies an optimal size in bytes for a rollback segment. Use K or M to specify this size in kilobytes or megabytes. Oracle tries to maintain this size for the rollback segment by dynamically deallocating extents when their data is no longer needed for active transactions. Oracle deallocates as many extents as possible without reducing the total size of the rollback segment below the OPTIMAL value.

The value of OPTIMAL cannot be less than the space initially allocated by the MINEXTENTS, INITIAL, NEXT, and PCTINCREASE parameters. The maximum value depends on your operating system. Oracle rounds values up to the next multiple of the data block size.

NULL: Specify NULL for no optimal size for the rollback segment, meaning that Oracle never deallocates the rollback segment's extents. This is the default behavior.

BUFFER_POOL   The BUFFER_POOL clause lets you specify a default buffer pool (cache) for a schema object. All blocks for the object are stored in the specified cache.

- If you define a buffer pool for a partitioned table or index, then the partitions inherit the buffer pool from the table or index definition, unless overridden by a partition-level definition.

- For an index-organized table, you can specify a buffer pool separately for the index segment and the overflow segment.

Restrictions:

- You cannot specify this clause for a cluster table. However, you can specify it for a cluster.

- You cannot specify this clause for a tablespace or for a rollback segment.

KEEP: Specify KEEP to put blocks from the segment into the KEEP buffer pool. Maintaining an appropriately sized KEEP buffer pool lets Oracle retain the schema object in memory to avoid I/O operations. KEEP takes precedence over any NOCACHE clause you specify for a table, cluster, materialized view, or materialized view log.

RECYCLE: Specify RECYCLE to put blocks from the segment into the RECYCLE pool. An appropriately sized RECYCLE pool reduces the number of objects whose default pool is the RECYCLE pool from taking up unnecessary cache space.

DEFAULT: Specify DEFAULT to indicate the default buffer pool. This is the default for objects not assigned to KEEP or RECYCLE.

TRUNCATE

CAUTION
You cannot roll back a TRUNCATE statement.

PURPOSE

Use the TRUNCATE statement to remove all rows from a table or cluster and reset the STORAGE parameters to the values when the table or cluster was created.

Removing rows with the TRUNCATE statement can be more efficient than dropping and re-creating a table. Dropping and re-creating a table invalidates the table's dependent objects, requires you to regrant object privileges on the table, and requires you to re-create the table's indexes, integrity constraints, and triggers and respecify its storage parameters. Truncating has none of these effects.

PREREQUISITES

To truncate a table or cluster, the table or cluster must be in your schema or you must have DROP ANY TABLE system privilege.

SYNTAX

truncate::=

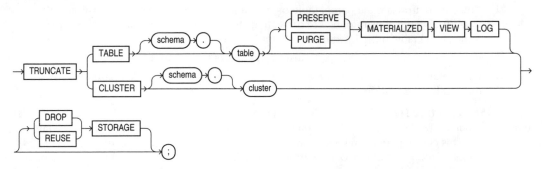

KEYWORDS AND PARAMETERS

TABLE Clause   Specify the schema and name of the table to be truncated. This table cannot be part of a cluster. If you omit *schema*, Oracle assumes the table is in your own cluster.

- You can truncate index-organized tables and temporary tables. When you truncate a temporary table, only the rows created during the current session are removed.

- Oracle changes the NEXT storage parameter of *table* to be the size of the last extent deleted from the segment in the process of truncation.

- Oracle also automatically truncates and resets any existing UNUSABLE indicators for the following indexes on *table*: range and hash partitions of local indexes and subpartitions of local indexes.

- If *table* is not empty, Oracle marks UNUSABLE all nonpartitioned indexes and all partitions of global partitioned indexes on the table.

■ For a domain index, this statement invokes the appropriate truncate routine to truncate the domain index data.

■ If *table* (whether it is a regular or index-organized table) contains LOB columns, all LOB data and LOB index segments are truncated.

■ If *table* is partitioned, all partitions or subpartitions, as well as the LOB data and LOB index segments for each partition or subpartition, are truncated.

NOTE
When you truncate a table, Oracle automatically removes all data in the table's indexes and any materialized view direct-path INSERT information held in association with the table. (This information is independent of any materialized view log.) If this direct-path INSERT information is removed, an incremental refresh of the materialized view may lose data.

Restrictions:

■ You cannot individually truncate a table that is part of a cluster. You must either truncate the cluster, delete all rows from the table, or drop and re-create the table.

■ You cannot truncate the parent table of an enabled referential integrity constraint. You must disable the constraint before truncating the table. (An exception is that you may truncate the table if the integrity constraint is self-referential.)

■ If *table* belongs to a hierarchy, it must be the root of the hierarchy.

■ If a domain index is defined on *table*, neither the index nor any index partitions can be marked IN_PROGRESS.

MATERIALIZED VIEW LOG Clause   The MATERIALIZED VIEW LOG clause lets you specify whether a materialized view log defined on the table is to be preserved or purged when the table is truncated. This clause permits materialized view master tables to be reorganized through export/import without affecting the ability of primary-key materialized views defined on the master to be fast refreshed. To support continued fast refresh of primary-key materialized views, the materialized view log must record primary-key information.

NOTE
The keyword SNAPSHOT is supported in place of MATERIALIZED VIEW for backward compatibility.

PRESERVE: Specify PRESERVE if any materialized view log should be preserved when the master table is truncated. This is the default.
PURGE: Specify PURGE if any materialized view log should be purged when the master table is truncated.

CLUSTER Clause   Specify the schema and name of the cluster to be truncated. You can truncate only an indexed cluster, not a hash cluster. If you omit *schema*, Oracle assumes the cluster is in your own schema.

When you truncate a cluster, Oracle also automatically deletes all data in the indexes of the cluster tables.

STORAGE Clauses   The STORAGE clauses let you determine what happens to the space freed by the truncated rows. The DROP STORAGE clause and REUSE STORAGE clause also apply to the space freed by the data deleted from associated indexes.

DROP STORAGE: Specify DROP STORAGE to deallocate all space from the deleted rows from the table or cluster except the space allocated by the MINEXTENTS parameter of the table or cluster. This space can subsequently be used by other objects in the tablespace. This is the default.

REUSE STORAGE: Specify REUSE STORAGE to retain the space from the deleted rows allocated to the table or cluster. Storage values are not reset to the values when the table or cluster was created. This space can subsequently be used only by new data in the table or cluster resulting from insert or update operations.

NOTE

If you have specified more than one free list for the object you are truncating, the REUSE STORAGE clause also removes any mapping of free lists to instances and resets the high-water mark to the beginning of the first extent.

Index

P

INTERNATIONAL CONTACT INFORMATION

AUSTRALIA
McGraw-Hill Book Company Australia Pty. Ltd.
TEL +61-2-9900-1800
FAX +61-2-9878-8881
http://www.mcgraw-hill.com.au
books-it_sydney@mcgraw-hill.com

CANADA
McGraw-Hill Ryerson Ltd.
TEL +905-430-5000
FAX +905-430-5020
http://www.mcgraw-hill.ca

GREECE, MIDDLE EAST, & AFRICA
(Excluding South Africa)
McGraw-Hill Hellas
TEL +30-210-6560-990
TEL +30-210-6560-993
TEL +30-210-6560-994
FAX +30-210-6545-525

MEXICO (Also serving Latin America)
McGraw-Hill Interamericana Editores S.A. de C.V.
TEL +525-117-1583
FAX +525-117-1589
http://www.mcgraw-hill.com.mx
fernando_castellanos@mcgraw-hill.com

SINGAPORE (Serving Asia)
McGraw-Hill Book Company
TEL +65-6863-1580
FAX +65-6862-3354
http://www.mcgraw-hill.com.sg
mghasia@mcgraw-hill.com

SOUTH AFRICA
McGraw-Hill South Africa
TEL +27-11-622-7512
FAX +27-11-622-9045
robyn_swanepoel@mcgraw-hill.com

SPAIN
McGraw-Hill/Interamericana de España, S.A.U.
TEL +34-91-180-3000
FAX +34-91-372-8513
http://www.mcgraw-hill.es
professional@mcgraw-hill.es

UNITED KINGDOM, NORTHERN,
EASTERN, & CENTRAL EUROPE
McGraw-Hill Education Europe
TEL +44-1-628-502500
FAX +44-1-628-770224
http://www.mcgraw-hill.co.uk
computing_europe@mcgraw-hill.com

ALL OTHER INQUIRIES Contact:
McGraw-Hill/Osborne
TEL +1-510-420-7700
FAX +1-510-420-7703
http://www.osborne.com
omg_international@mcgraw-hill.com

GET FREE SUBSCRIPTION
OUR
TO ORACLE MAGAZINE

Oracle Magazine is essential gear for today's information technology professionals. Stay informed and increase your productivity with every issue of *Oracle Magazine*. Inside each free bimonthly issue you'll get:

- Up-to-date information on Oracle Database, E-Business Suite applications, Web development, and database technology and business trends
- Third-party news and announcements
- Technical articles on Oracle Products and operating environments
- Development and administration tips
- Real-world customer stories

IF THERE ARE OTHER ORACLE USERS AT YOUR LOCATION WHO WOULD LIKE TO RECEIVE THEIR OWN SUBSCRIPTION TO ORACLE MAGAZINE, PLEASE PHOTOCOPY THIS FORM AND PASS IT ALONG.

Three easy ways to subscribe:

① Web
Visit our Web site at www.oracle.com/oraclemagazine. You'll find a subscription form there, plus much more!

② Fax
Complete the questionnaire on the back of this card and fax the questionnaire side only to +1.847.647.9735.

③ Mail
Complete the questionnaire on the back of this card and mail it to P.O. Box 1263, Skokie, IL 60076-8263

Oracle Publishing

FREE SUBSCRIPTION

O Yes, please send me a FREE subscription *Oracle Magazine*.   O **NO**
To receive a free subscription to *Oracle Magazine*, you must fill out the entire card, sign it, and date it (incomplete cards cannot be processed or acknowledged). You can also fax your application to +1.847.647.9735.
Or subscribe at our Web site at www.oracle.com/oraclemagazine/

O From time to time, Oracle Publishing allows our partners exclusive access to our e-mail addresses for special promotions and announcements. To be included in this program, please check this box.

O Oracle Publishing allows sharing of our mailing list with selected third parties. If you prefer your mailing address not to be included in this program, please check here. If at any time you would like to be removed from this mailing list, please contact Customer Service at +1.847.647.9630 or send an e-mail to oracle@halldata.com.

signature (required)   date

X

name   title

company   e-mail address

street/p.o. box

city/state/zip or postal code   telephone

country   fax

YOU MUST ANSWER ALL NINE QUESTIONS BELOW.

① WHAT IS THE PRIMARY BUSINESS ACTIVITY OF YOUR FIRM AT THIS LOCATION?
(check one only)

- N 01 Application Service Provider
- N 02 Communications
- N 03 Consulting, Training
- N 04 Data Processing
- N 05 Education
- N 06 Engineering
- N 07 Financial Services
- N 08 Government (federal, local, state, other)
- N 09 Government (military)
- N 10 Health Care
- N 11 Manufacturing (aerospace, defense)
- N 12 Manufacturing (computer hardware)
- N 13 Manufacturing (noncomputer)
- N 14 Research & Development
- N 15 Retailing, Wholesaling, Distribution
- N 16 Software Development
- N 17 Systems Integration, VAR, VAD, OEM
- N 18 Transportation
- N 19 Utilities (electric, gas, sanitation)
- N 98 Other Business and Services

② WHICH OF THE FOLLOWING BEST DESCRIBES YOUR PRIMARY JOB FUNCTION?
(check one only)

Corporate Management/Staff
- N 01 Executive Management (President, Chair, CEO, CFO, Owner, Partner, Principal)
- N 02 Finance/Administrative Management (VP/Director/ Manager/Controller, Purchasing, Administration)
- N 03 Sales/Marketing Management (VP/Director/Manager)
- N 04 Computer Systems/Operations Management (CIO/VP/Director/ Manager MIS, Operations)

IS/IT Staff
- N 05 Systems Development/ Programming Management
- N 06 Systems Development/ Programming Staff
- N 07 Consulting
- N 08 DBA/Systems Administrator
- N 09 Education/Training
- N 10 Technical Support Director/Manager
- N 11 Other Technical Management/Staff
- N 98 Other

③ WHAT IS YOUR CURRENT PRIMARY OPERATING PLATFORM? (select all that apply)

- N 01 Digital Equipment UNIX
- N 02 Digital Equipment VAX VMS
- N 03 HP UNIX
- N 04 IBM AIX
- N 05 IBM UNIX
- N 06 Java
- N 07 Linux
- N 08 Macintosh
- N 09 MS-DOS
- N 10 MVS
- N 11 NetWare
- N 12 Network Computing
- N 13 OpenVMS
- N 14 SCO UNIX
- N 15 Sequent DYNIX/ptx
- N 16 Sun Solaris/SunOS
- N 17 SVR4
- N 18 UnixWare
- N 19 Windows
- N 20 Windows NT
- N 21 Other UNIX
- N 98 Other
- 99 N None of the above

④ DO YOU EVALUATE, SPECIFY, RECOMMEND, OR AUTHORIZE THE PURCHASE OF ANY OF THE FOLLOWING? (check all that apply)

- N 01 Hardware
- N 02 Software
- N 03 Application Development Tools
- N 04 Database Products
- N 05 Internet or Intranet Products
- 99 N None of the above

⑤ IN YOUR JOB, DO YOU USE OR PLAN TO PURCHASE ANY OF THE FOLLOWING PRODUCTS? (check all that apply)

Software
- N 01 Business Graphics
- N 02 CAD/CAE/CAM
- N 03 CASE
- N 04 Communications
- N 05 Database Management
- N 06 File Management
- N 07 Finance
- N 08 Java
- N 09 Materials Resource Planning
- N 10 Multimedia Authoring
- N 11 Networking
- N 12 Office Automation
- N 13 Order Entry/Inventory Control
- N 14 Programming
- N 15 Project Management
- N 16 Scientific and Engineering
- N 17 Spreadsheets
- N 18 Systems Management
- N 19 Workflow

Hardware
- N 20 Macintosh
- N 21 Mainframe
- N 22 Massively Parallel Processing
- N 23 Minicomputer
- N 24 PC
- N 25 Network Computer
- N 26 Symmetric Multiprocessing
- N 27 Workstation

Peripherals
- N 28 Bridges/Routers/Hubs/Gateways
- N 29 CD-ROM Drives
- N 30 Disk Drives/Subsystems
- N 31 Modems
- N 32 Tape Drives/Subsystems
- N 33 Video Boards/Multimedia

Services
- N 34 Application Service Provider
- N 35 Consulting
- N 36 Education/Training
- N 37 Maintenance
- N 38 Online Database Services
- N 39 Support
- N 40 Technology-Based Training
- N 98 Other
- 99 N None of the above

⑥ WHAT ORACLE PRODUCTS ARE IN USE AT YOUR SITE? (check all that apply)

Software
- N 01 Oracle9i
- N 02 Oracle9i Lite
- N 03 Oracle8
- N 04 Oracle8i
- N 05 Oracle8i Lite
- N 06 Oracle7
- N 07 Oracle9i Application Server
- N 08 Oracle9i Application Server Wireless
- N 09 Oracle Data Mart Suites
- N 10 Oracle Internet Commerce Server
- N 11 Oracle inter Media
- N 12 Oracle Lite
- N 13 Oracle Payment Server
- N 14 Oracle Video Server
- N 15 Oracle Rdb

Tools
- N 16 Oracle Darwin
- N 17 Oracle Designer
- N 18 Oracle Developer
- N 19 Oracle Discoverer
- N 20 Oracle Express
- N 21 Oracle JDeveloper
- N 22 Oracle Reports
- N 23 Oracle Portal
- N 24 Oracle Warehouse Builder
- N 25 Oracle Workflow

Oracle E-Business Suite
- N 26 Oracle Advanced Planning/Scheduling
- N 27 Oracle Business Intelligence
- N 28 Oracle E-Commerce
- N 29 Oracle Exchange
- N 30 Oracle Financials
- N 31 Oracle Human Resources
- N 32 Oracle Interaction Center
- N 33 Oracle Internet Procurement
- N 34 Oracle Manufacturing
- N 35 Oracle Marketing
- N 36 Oracle Order Management
- N 37 Oracle Professional Services Automation
- N 38 Oracle Projects
- N 39 Oracle Sales
- N 40 Oracle Service
- N 41 Oracle Small Business Suite
- N 42 Oracle Supply Chain Management
- N 43 Oracle Travel Management
- N 44 Oracle Treasury

Oracle Services
- N 45 Oracle.com Online Services
- N 46 Oracle Consulting
- N 47 Oracle Education
- N 48 Oracle Support
- N 98 Other
- 99 N None of the above

⑦ WHAT OTHER DATABASE PRODUCTS ARE IN USE AT YOUR SITE? (check all that apply)

- N 01 Access
- N 02 Baan
- N 03 dbase
- N 04 Gupta
- N 05 IBM DB2
- N 06 Informix
- N 07 Ingres
- N 98 Other
- N 08 Microsoft Access
- N 09 Microsoft SQL Server
- N 10 PeopleSoft
- N 11 Progress
- N 12 SAP
- N 13 Sybase
- N 14 VSAM
- 99 N None of the above

⑧ DURING THE NEXT 12 MONTHS, HOW MUCH DO YOU ANTICIPATE YOUR ORGANIZATION WILL SPEND ON COMPUTER HARDWARE, SOFTWARE, PERIPHERALS, AND SERVICES FOR YOUR LOCATION? (check one only)

- N 01 Less than $10,000
- N 02 $10,000 to $49,999
- N 03 $50,000 to $99,999
- N 04 $100,000 to $499,999
- N 05 $500,000 to $999,999
- N 06 $1,000,000 and over

⑨ WHAT IS YOUR COMPANY'S YEARLY SALES REVENUE? (please choose one)

- N 01 $500,000,000 and above
- N 02 $100,000,000 to $500,000,000
- N 03 $50,000,000 to $100,000,000
- N 04 $5,000,000 to $50,000,000
- N 05 $1,000,000 to $5,000,000

123101